Moral Capital

D1089511

Moral

Capital

FOUNDATIONS *of* BRITISH ABOLITIONISM

Christopher Leslie Brown

*Published for the
Omohundro Institute of
Early American History
and Culture, Williamsburg,
Virginia, by the University of
North Carolina Press,
Chapel Hill*

The Omohundro Institute of Early American History and Culture is sponsored jointly by the College of William and Mary and the Colonial Williamsburg Foundation. On November 15, 1996, the Institute adopted the present name in honor of a bequest from Malvern H. Omohundro, Jr.

© 2006 THE UNIVERSITY OF NORTH CAROLINA PRESS
All rights reserved
Manufactured in the United States of America

Library of Congress Cataloging-in-Publication Data
Brown, Christopher Leslie.
Moral capital : foundations of British abolitionism / Christopher Leslie Brown.
p. cm.
Includes bibliographical references and index.
ISBN-13: 978-0-8078-3034-5 (cloth: alk. paper)
ISBN-10: 0-8078-3034-8 (cloth: alk. paper)
ISBN-13: 978-0-8078-5698-7 (pbk.: alk. paper)
ISBN-10: 0-8078-5698-3 (pbk.: alk. paper)
1. Slavery—Great Britain—History. 2. Abolitionists—Great Britain—History. 3. Liberty—Great Britain—History. 4. Great Britain—Race relations. 5. Great Britain—Foreign relations. 6. Great Britain—Politics and government. I. Omohundro Institute of Early American History & Culture. II. Title.
HT1163.B76 2006
306.3'620941—dc22
2005031387

The paper in this book meets the guidelines for permanence and durability of the Committee on Production Guidelines for Book Longevity of the Council on Library Resources.

This volume received indirect support from an unrestricted book publication grant awarded to the Institute by the L. J. Skaggs and Mary C. Skaggs Foundation of Oakland, California.

cloth   10 09 08 07 06   5 4 3 2 1
paper   10 09 08 07 06   5 4 3 2 1

*For my
mother and father,
Michael and Hilary,
with love*

ACKNOWLEDGMENTS

I have had the good fortune to work at five wonderful institutions during the last decade—the departments of history at Vanderbilt University, the College of William and Mary, New York University, The Johns Hopkins University, and Rutgers, The State University of New Jersey. Each afforded me the privilege (and it is a privilege) to practice the historical craft—to research, to write, and to teach. So I am pleased to acknowledge first this most basic of debts to my current and former colleagues and students. More than a few of the ideas, arguments, and claims that appear in this volume developed directly from classroom conversations about "the problem of slavery" with the many outstanding students I have instructed at these schools. And more than a few of the insights arose unexpectedly from stray conversations with colleagues working on other places, other eras, and other problems. Without steady employment, without the intellectual stimulation provided by these fine institutions, Rutgers in particular, there would have been no book.

In preparing this study, I pursued traces of the abolitionist impulse through a variety of archives and record offices. For their assistance in assembling materials crucial to this book, and for calling my attention to materials I might otherwise have overlooked, I extend my thanks to the archivists at the Bedfordshire Record Office, the Bodleian Library (Oxford University), the Bristol Record Office, the British Library, the Center for Kentish Studies, the Durham Record Office, the Gloucestershire Record Office, the Historical Society of Pennsylvania, the Huntington Library, the Leicestershire Record Office, the Lambeth Palace Library, Library of the Society of Friends, the Manchester Central Library, the Public Record Office (London), Rhodes House Library, the Staffordshire Record Office, the William Andrews Clark Library, the William L. Clements Library, and the York Minster Library.

I first worked through the essentials of this subject while fulfilling the requirements for a D. Phil. at Balliol College, Oxford. After a brief period in government service, I returned to the project full time through the assistance of a two-year postdoctoral fellowship at the Omohundro Institute of Early American History and Culture, a fellowship funded by the National Endowment for the Humanities, the Colonial Williamsburg Foundation, and the College of William and Mary. Ronald Hoffman, and the rest of the Institute staff, have my enduring thanks for allowing me the time and the space to restructure the original study, extend its reach, and substantially deepen the research. A short-term fellowship at the Huntington Library in Pasadena, California, funded by the W. M. Keck Foundation allowed for an intensive study of the British pamphlets of the American Revolution, research that turned out to be essential. Most of the book was written between the summer of 1998 and the summer of 1999, during the year that I held the Raoul Wallenberg Fellowship at the Rutgers Center for Historical Analysis. A senior fellowship at the Gilder Lehrman Center for the Study of Slavery, Resistance, and Abolition two years later permitted a tying up of loose ends and a final round of revisions. I am pleased to offer my delayed thanks to the selection committees for these fellowships, who saw with me the need for a further look at Anglo-American antislavery in the eighteenth century.

Along the way, I have been fortunate to have wonderful teachers and mentors. At a formative stage, and in very different ways, David Brion Davis, Melvin Ely, Gary Nash, David Spadafora, and the late Robin W. Winks showed me why history matters and what good history looks like. I have tried to learn from their example, if I have not always matched it. At Oxford University, Joanna Innes helped me figure out what I was trying to do as I struggled through my first encounter with the archives. It is because of her that I did not give up on this endeavor long ago. At the Omohundro Institute, and then at The Johns Hopkins University, Philip Morgan demonstrated how to work with precision, discipline, and generosity, a model easier to admire than to emulate. Most of all, I owe a special debt to David Brion Davis and Seymour Drescher, both of whom have supported this project and its author from the very beginning, even as I have reached conclusions rather different from their magisterial works on the history of antislavery.

I have presented portions of the book in a variety of public symposia, colloquia, and seminars at the College of William and Mary, Columbia University, The Johns Hopkins University, New York University, Northwestern University, the University of Pittsburgh, Syracuse University, Vanderbilt University, and the University of Washington as well as at meetings of the American Society for Eighteenth Century Studies, the American Studies Association, the North American Conference on British Studies, the International Seminar on the History of the Atlantic World, the American Historical Association, and the Institute of United States Studies in England. I thank the audiences at these gatherings for their helpful observations and suggestions, very many of which have influenced the final product. A preliminary version of Chapter 4, "Empire without Slaves: British Concepts of Emancipation in the Age of the American Revolution," first appeared in 1999 as an article under the same title in the *William and Mary Quarterly* (3d Ser., LXI, 273–306). The remaining portions of this book appear now in print for the first time.

The path to publication took more turns than I could have imagined, although I know the book is better for the journey. At the Omohundro Institute, editor of publications Fredrika J. Teute found promise in the original project and helped crystallize its message, particularly in the early stages, as I worked to understand what this book was about. I am pleased to have the book appear under the Institute's imprint. My copy editor Laura Jones Dooley patiently and painstakingly helped finalize the manuscript for the press, no small task when working with an author who likes to change his mind. Ginny Montijo orchestrated the very last stages of the process with characteristic professionalism and good cheer. Robert Whelan, my research assistant, tracked down key references as the manuscript approached completion. Caleb McDaniel of The Johns Hopkins University offered typically meticulous and efficient help in compiling the bibliography.

Although the gift of friendship can be repaid only in kind, I wish to acknowledge here the encouragement of several friends who, though not historians, understood and valued what I was trying to do during the occasionally difficult transition back to academia. My thanks in particular to Tonya Canada, Court Golumbic, Olivia Judson, Sarah Laughton, Dahlia Lithwick, Maia Mulligan, Ronald Noble, Delida Sanchez, Mark Suzman, Keith Walton, Michael Warren, Sascha Whitehurst, and Douglas Whitney. More than a few colleagues and friends read portions of this manuscript as it took shape. My thanks to David Armitage, James Basker, Sharon Block, Joyce Chaplin, Paul Clemens, Linda Colley, Toby Ditz, Timothy Eastman, James Epstein, John Gillis, Eliga Gould, Jack Greene, Michael Guasco, Evan Haefeli, Hilary-Anne Hallett, Ken Himmelman, Ronald Hoffman, James Horn, Walter Johnson, Sarah Knott, Kay Dian Kriz, Phyllis Mack,

P. J. Marshall, Sally Mason, Michael McGiffert, Philip Morgan, Anthony Page, Carla Pestana, Cassandra Pybus, Marcus Rediker, Tom Slaughter, David Steinberg, Jennifer Tucker, David Waldstreicher, Ronald Walters, James Walvin, and Roxann Wheeler, for their generous and penetrating comments. Their observations improved the work, although each will see, no doubt, that I have stubbornly, and perhaps unwisely, resisted at least some of their suggestions. I owe particular thanks to my cohort at the Black Atlantic Project—Mia Bay, Herman Bennett, Carolyn Brown, Kim Butler, Brent Edwards, Al Howard, Daphne Lamothe, Jennifer Morgan, and Deborah Gray White—who together have made Rutgers University a superb place to explore the history and culture of the African Diaspora and the Atlantic world.

My friends and family stopped asking when this book would be published some time ago. And yet they never lost faith in either it or its author. For hanging in there with me, from beginning to end, I thank Tim Allison, Tony Bardonille, Ken Himmelman, David Milner, Marisa Nightingale as well as my grandmother Julia Brown, Marcie Thompson, and the entire Hamer clan. I have dedicated this book to my immediate family, who will be as happy to see this book published as I am to complete it. My parents, Carolyn Brown and Tyrone Brown, read much of the manuscript at an early stage and heard perhaps too much from me about the rest. Long ago, they told me to do my best and, from the first, provided all I would need to see that I could. I thank them for their confidence, for their example, and for their unwavering support. My brother Michael, an accomplished scholar in a very different field, has provided a consistent supply of clarity, honesty, and good sense. His sage advice, at crucial moments, helped me keep my bearings. I met Hilary-Anne Hallet shortly before I finished the first draft of this manuscript, a chance encounter that changed my life entirely for the better. I am happy to send this book into the world and out of our lives so that the conclusion of one story might allow for the beginning of another. Thank you, Hilary, my partner, my love, my friend, for taking this journey with me.

CONTENTS

Acknowledgments vii

List of Illustrations xiii

Introduction 1

PART I: Values and Practice in Conflict

CHAPTER 1. Antislavery without Abolitionism 33

PART II: The Conflict Realized

CHAPTER 2. The Politics of Slavery in the
    Years of Crisis 105

CHAPTER 3. Granville Sharp and the
    Obligations of Empire 155

PART III: The Search for Solutions

CHAPTER 4. British Concepts of Emancipation
    in the Age of the American Revolution 209

CHAPTER 5. Africa, Africans, and the
    Idea of Abolition 259

PART IV: The Conflict Resolved

CHAPTER 6. British Evangelicals and
    Caribbean Slavery after the American War 333

CHAPTER 7. The Society of Friends and the
    Antislavery Identity 391

EPILOGUE: Moral Capital 451

Index 463

ILLUSTRATIONS

1 The "Abolition Map," from Thomas
   Clarkson, *The History of the Rise, Progress,
   and Accomplishment of the Abolition of the
   African Slave-Trade by the British
   Parliament* (1808) 6

2 *The Gaols Committee of the
   House of Commons* 80

3 Granville Sharp 163

4 *Reception of the American Loyalists
   by Great Britain, in the Year 1783* 313

5 The Reverend James Ramsay 374

6 David Barclay 403

7 *Gracechurch Street Meeting* 421

8 Thomas Clarkson 440

Moral Capital

NOTHING IS MORE DIFFICULT

perhaps than to explain how and why, or why not, a new moral perception becomes effective in action. Yet nothing is more urgent if an academical historical exercise is to become a significant investigation of human behavior with direct relevance to the world we now live in.

M. I. Finley, 1967

The story often has been told but never well explained. In June 1783, just months after the conclusion of the American War of Independence, the Religious Society of Friends, then ending its annual summer gathering in London, presented a petition to the House of Commons. Signed by 273 Quakers, this petition called for abolition of the British traffic in African men, women, and children. In the months that followed, a much smaller group of Friends gathered to compose and publish abolitionist texts and distribute those pamphlets across the nation. James Ramsay, an aging Anglican clergyman, seized on the opportunity in 1784 to describe in print what he had learned about colonial slavery during his twenty-five years on the British Caribbean island of Saint Kitts. Inspired by these examples, twenty-five-year-old Thomas Clarkson, then completing his studies at Saint John's, Cambridge, came forward just two years later with a book that presented the British slave trade as a tragedy and a crime. The evident interest of William Wilberforce, the young member of Parliament for Yorkshire and a recent convert to Evangelicalism, encouraged these and other like-minded enthusiasts to launch a national campaign that would force a discussion in the House of Commons and galvanize antislavery sentiment that had circulated through British culture in recent years. This campaign, organized in the summer of 1787 under the stewardship of Granville Sharp (long a public opponent of human bondage), quickly caught fire—the preferred metaphor for observers in these months—so that by the spring of 1788 it seemed that the British public had declared, nearly in unison, that a pillar that long had sustained British wealth and power now must fall. Although the story is well known, it remains poorly understood.

The inspiration for this book lay in my confusion and frustration with this deceptively simple tale of origins. It grows out of a desire to explain the decisions to act, to make sense of the relation between cultural prescription and individual action. The British abolition movement that began in the 1780s did not follow inevitably from enlightened sensibilities, social change, or a shift in economic interests. Nor did it spring forth spontaneously, as an uncaused cause free from circumstance or context. Deeply contingent, the campaign had its roots in a distinct and distinctive moment in British imperial history, a moment that presented both unfamiliar challenges and novel possibilities to those preoccupied with the character and consequences of overseas enterprise. Yet, even then, fortunate circumstances alone did not lead inexorably to a coherent, organized attack on the slave trade, perhaps the most vulnerable link in the plantation complex. Initially the concerned pursued disparate objectives and launched uncoordinated initiatives, each of which reflected ambitions that extended beyond the problem of slavery and often originated in more parochial agendas. Each had as good a chance to fail as to succeed.

Moral Capital is a study of those tentative beginnings, an exploration of the period when antislavery efforts developed cautiously and haphazardly, without unifying purpose or preset goals, before individual initiatives coalesced into a movement. It treats the emergence in Britain of shifting definitions of imperial purpose, of new ways to conceive relations among subjects of the crown, and between overseas colonies and the imperial state. It opens for discussion the vital story of how the American Revolution reshaped British responses to colonial slavery, transformations rich with consequence for slave societies throughout the Atlantic world. And it explores the moment when various individuals and groups found through their challenge to the Atlantic slave trade an opportunity to establish new identities, new self-conceptions, to create for themselves a new place within society and a new role in public life. But most of all, this book is a meditation on the chasm that distinguishes moral opinion from moral action, the wide gulf that divides the mere perception of a moral wrong from decisions to seek a remedy. And it is a rumination on what happens in the space that lies between moral opinion and political action, what happens when moral purposes figure in political choices and when political actors, in turn, make use of moral causes.

It is one thing to notice an injustice and something else to act. For too long, the antislavery movement in Britain has been described as the consequence of shifts in moral perception, as if the mere recognition of a moral duty must have led men and women to act. It can be easy to forget what most of us know from our own lives: that professed values do not always determine the choices we make, that sometimes we decide against what we believe to be right, that we often accept questionable practices because they seem necessary to the world we know or because they enjoy the sanction of age, however troubling they may seem on careful reflection. Antislavery values were not enough in the eighteenth century, or after. The decision to act involved more than thinking of slavery as abhorrent, although clearly this was crucial. Somehow this particular moral wrong had to become important and urgent enough to drive individuals and groups to confront entrenched institutions. Because we have inherited the world that the abolitionists and their allies helped to make, we can overlook far too easily how unpromising antislavery projects looked on first contemplation, before the antislavery campaigns took shape. Appropriately, some commentators have placed great emphasis on the limits of the British antislavery movement: its selectivity, its shortcomings, what it failed to achieve. In appreciating this, though, we need also attend to the unlikely nature of the project, to the ironic fact that a movement of this kind could and did develop at the heart of what was, at the time, the largest slaving empire in the world.

The attempt to explain the history of antislavery has a history of its own. These stories, those accounts that others have told before, shape the character of mine. The first chroniclers found it difficult to think of the antislavery movement, the subsequent success of which later became essential to British national identity, as the result of mundane "causes." Instead, they saw in it the hand of divine providence or the verification of a nobility ostensibly essential to the British character. Thomas Clarkson, an early organizer of the movement and its first historian, devoted himself in 1786 to urging the sympathetic but ambivalent to commit. He dedicated countless hours to gathering information and devising strategies that would give the concerned reason to act. Twenty years later, though, when the time came to tell the movement's history, Clarkson avoided questions relating to motivation and purpose. He preferred instead to treat the "progress" of antislavery as a transcendental force that operated over the heads of the participants and drove them to a predestined end. Indeed, Clarkson explicitly ruled out the possibility that banal aims and motives could have been at work, that self-interest or self-concern could have helped give the movement life. Christian altruism, for him, provided a sufficient explanation. "The abolition of the Slave-trade," he declared, "took its rise, not from persons, who set up a cry for liberty, when they were oppressors themselves, nor from persons who were led to it by ambition, or a love of reputation among men, but where it was most desirable, namely, from the teachers of Christianity in those times."[1]

The originators, Clarkson explained, had been impelled by the spirit of gospel love. Their teachings operated as a slow and subtle influence on subsequent generations until the trickle of antislavery sentiment expanded into a torrent of antislavery opinion. In a graphic rendering of the process, Clarkson placed these early opponents at the headwaters, where their testimony fortified the shallow brooks of early antislavery witness. After 1750, the deepening tributaries of antislavery thought, swelled by the con- tributions of activists like Anthony Benezet and Granville Sharp, spilled into the narrow streams of moral commitment, giving them greater breadth and force. By 1787, the convergence of antislavery "coadjutors"—Quakers, theologians, philosophers, Evangelicals, even Thomas Clarkson himself— stretched the banks into rivers bloated by antislavery fervor that, finally, merged and emptied onto the political landscape, which Clarkson con- ceived as a flooded alluvial plain, swamped by the deluge of popular sup- port for abolitionism.

From this parable about the inexorable growth of righteousness, Clar- kson hoped readers would draw two morals. "The greatest works must have a beginning," the veteran campaigner observed. "However small the beginning and slow the progress may appear in any good work which we may undertake, we need not be discouraged as to the ultimate result of our labours." Second, and most important, "no virtuous effort is ever ultimately lost." Clarkson described the process this way.

> An individual, for example, begins; he communicates his sentiments to others. Thus, while alive, he enlightens; when dead, he leaves his works behind him. Thus, though departed, he yet speaks, and his influence is not lost. Of those enlightened by him, some become authors, and others actors in their turn. While living, they instruct, like their predecessors; when dead they speak also. Thus a number of dead persons are encour- aging us in libraries, and a number of living are conversing and diffusing zeal among us at the same time.[2]

1. Thomas Clarkson, *The History of the Rise, Progress, and Accomplishment of the Abolition of the African Slave-Trade by the British Parliament,* 2 vols. (London, 1808), I, 262.

2. Ibid., 27, 28, 263, 264–265.

For those still engaged in the antislavery campaign when Clarkson published in 1807, his lesson was a counsel of hope, his invention of an Anglo-American antislavery tradition cause for solace. It taught that the individual act, however small, mattered, that choices ramify long after the moment of decision. It told canvassers to think of themselves as part of a lineage that stretched back generations and could extend forward for many decades to come. And it persuaded participants of the purity of their cause and, by extension, the purity of their participation in it.

Clarkson's *History* would provide the framework in which, for more than a century, the origins of the British antislavery movement would be understood. Clarkson was the first to characterize the campaign as the working out of impulses deeply embedded in the society from which it emerged, as the elaboration of principles essential to British Protestantism, as the expression of a distinctively British devotion to liberty and the rule of law. Because the fundamental elements of an antislavery ideology, Clarkson implied, rested latent in Anglo-American culture, its evolution was predictable because it was inevitable, explicable because it was natural, much like rivers running to the sea. The campaign for the abolition of the slave trade demonstrated and proved that civilized peoples, like the British, could achieve moral progress. British primacy in the war against barbarism reaffirmed the nation's place at the apex of refinement and virtue. The campaign represented a moment of transcendence, a heroic triumph superior to the petty, self-interested squabbles typical of conflicts between rival states. "No evil more monstrous has existed upon earth," Clarkson's friend

---

Overleaf: FIGURE 1. The "Abolition Map." From Thomas Clarkson, *The History of the Rise, Progress, and Accomplishment of the Abolition of the African Slave-Trade by the British Parliament,* 2 vols. (London, 1808), which depicts the growth of antislavery opinion in Britain and British North America during the eighteenth century. Courtesy, Alexander Library, Special Collections, Rutgers University, New Brunswick, N.J.

The left branch identifies theologians, philosophers, poets, dramatists, historians, and other intellectuals in Britain who raised questions about the Atlantic slave trade or colonial slavery. The middle branch marks key moments in the evolution of Quaker antislavery in the British Isles. A third branch, on the right, indicates the progress of antislavery organizing among Quakers in North America. A fourth branch, at the bottom and center, running from right to left, presents building antislavery opposition among Anglican Evangelicals.

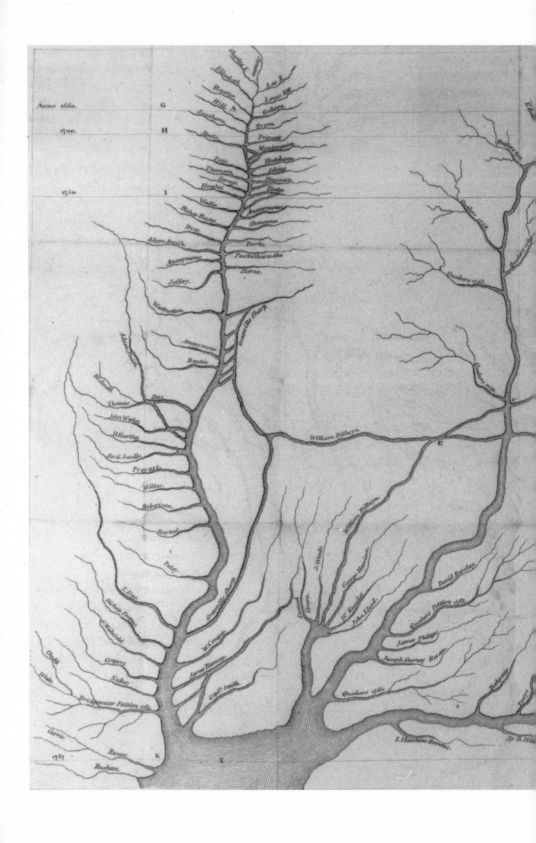

Anno 1650.

1700.

1750.

G

H

I

Charles I.
Elizabeth
Baxter
Hill, A.
Southern
Steele

Leo X.
Louis XIII
Godwyn
Tryon
Primatt
Montesquieu
Hutcheson
Atkins
Rousseau
Foster
Anonymous
Shenstone
Burke
Postlethwayte
Sterne

Pope
Thomson
Savage
Hughes
Wallis
Bishop Hayter
Dyer
Adam Smith
Anonymous
Jeffery
Warburton

Adam Smith

Richard
Thomas
John Wesley
D. Hartley
Sir G. Saville
Provart
Millar
Robertson
Raynal

Anonymous
Beattie

Granville Sharp

Day

William Dilwyn.

J. Woods
William Dilwyn.
George Harrison.
D'. Knowles
John Lloyd.

C

E

David Barclay

Quakers Petition 1783.

James Phillips

Joseph Gurney Bevan.

Quakers 1782.

Paley

T. Day
Bishop Porteus
C. Wakefield
Gregory
Baker
Bridgewater Petition 1783.

1783

Chubb
White
Currie

Rotzce
Rushton.

Granville Sharp

W. Cowper.

James Ramsay.

Cock. Smith.

Samuel Hoare.

L. Hartans Browne.

Sir R. Hill

Ladymin.

Erskine

Quakers 1771.

Quakers 1763.

Quakers 1772.

Quakers 1781.

K

X

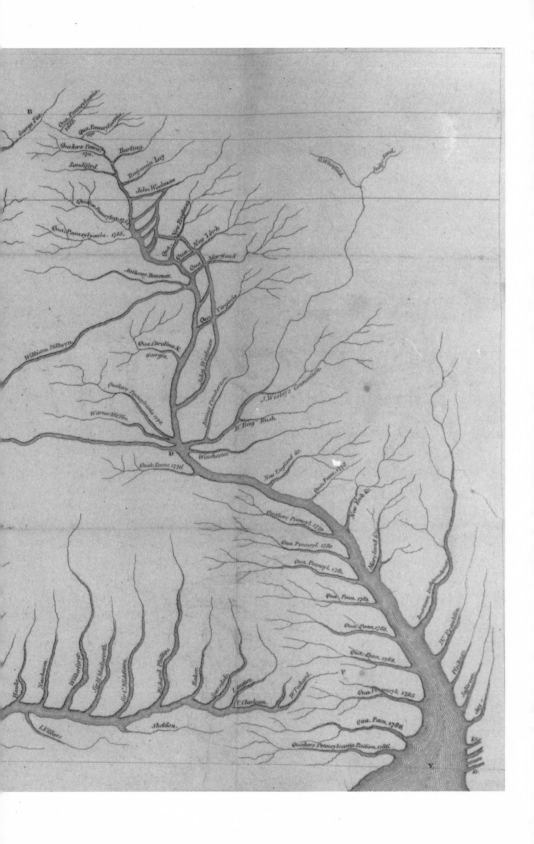

Samuel Taylor Coleridge explained. The "conquests of Napoleon and Alexander" looked "mean" compared to the "Immortal War" against the slave trade.[3] For Clarkson and his contemporaries, the origins of the antislavery movement needed no explanation because, to them, the campaign explained itself. Awakened, during the late eighteenth century, to the presence of a horrific injustice, a nation devoted to Christianity and liberty nobly united to rectify a great wrong.

This interpretive framework, what might be thought of as the Clarkson thesis, with its reliance on narration rather than explanation, with its emphasis on providential mission rather than human calculation, comported nicely with how most in Britain, deep into the twentieth century, preferred to reflect on the nation's slave trading and slaveholding past. To late Victorian and Edwardian historians especially, what mattered about the antislavery movement were, not the origins, but its character and results. The regrettable years of avarice and exploitation, "the old commercialism," thankfully lay in the past. Britain shared in the guilt with the other colonizing nations, the influential John Seeley acknowledged in his widely read *Expansion of England* of 1883. But Britain, unlike the others, acted nobly. "We published our own guilt, repented of it, and did at last renounce it." That view, that insistence on the selfless quality of British actions, that record of redemption for past wrongs, took on special importance in the first half of the twentieth century, when anti-imperialists in Britain and nationalists in the colonies began to question the ends and means of empire. In this environment, the history of antislavery provided a compelling origin story for the modern empire as well as its ideological defense. It displayed Britain as the purveyor of civilization, justice, and order. It established the British state as concerned historically with the welfare of African peoples, even, it was noted, at a cost to itself. Even a casual consideration of this history, declared one account published in 1900, should give "most Englishmen" "a patriotic thrill."[4]

---

3. Samuel Taylor Coleridge to Robert Southey, [February 1808], in Earl Leslie Griggs, ed., *Unpublished Letters of Samuel Taylor Coleridge*, 2 vols. (London, 1932), I, 395. See also Richard Holmes, *Coleridge: Darker Reflections, 1804–1834* (London, 1998), 141–143, and Marcus Wood, *Slavery, Empathy, and Pornography* (Oxford, 2002), 222–228.

4. John R. Seeley, *The Expansion of England* (1883), ed. John Gross (London, 1971), 109; British and Foreign Anti-Slavery Society, *Sixty Years against Slavery: A Brief Record*

For these reasons, a sustained probe into the origins of the antislavery movement could serve little purpose to the first generation of imperial historians. Reginald Coupland, Beit Professor of Colonial History and Fellow of All Souls College at Oxford, participated actively in the promotion and defense of "imperial trusteeship" in India, Africa, and the Middle East on the eve of decolonization. His influential volumes treating British service to "backward peoples" aimed to honor "the great tradition," not interrogate it. To the British celebrants in 1933 at the centennials commemorating emancipation, what mattered was eradicating the remnants of human bondage around the globe—"this country's greatest contribution to mankind"—not the origins of the impulse to export antislavery values. To ask too deeply about beginnings was to ask about motives. And a question about motives might suggest that the motives, themselves, had been questionable. As a consequence, no alternative to Clarkson's narrative emerged

<hr>

of the Work and Aims of the British and Foreign Anti-Slavery Society, 1839–1899; with an Article on the Abolition of the Legal Status of Slavery by Joseph F. Alexander (London, 1900), 3. For Seeley and the development of imperial history as a subdiscipline in the early twentieth century, see Peter Burroughs, "John Robert Seeley and British Imperial History," *Journal of Imperial and Commonwealth History,* I, no. 2 (1973), 191–211; J. G. Greenlee, " 'A Succession of Seeleys': The 'Old School' Re-examined," ibid., IV, no. 3 (1976), 266–282; John L. Herkless, "Seeley and Ranke," *Historian,* XLIII (1980), 1–22; Deborah Wormell, *Sir John Seeley and the Uses of History* (Cambridge, 1980), 154–180; and Robin A. Butlin, "Historical Geographies of the British Empire, c. 1887–1925," in Morag Bell, Robin Butlin, and Michael Heffernan, eds., *Geography and Imperialism, 1820–1940* (Manchester, Eng., 1995), 151–188. James Walvin captures British complacency and self-satisfaction with respect to slavery in the mid-nineteenth century in "Freedom and Slavery and the Shaping of Victorian Britain," *Slavery and Abolition,* XV, no. 2 (August 1994), 246–259; see also P. J. Marshall, "Imperial Britain," *Jour. Imperial and Commonwealth Hist.,* XXIII, no. 3 (1995), 389–392. For scholarly accounts published in the first half of the twentieth century that were inclined to celebrate the British achievement, see Frank J. Klingberg, *The Anti-Slavery Movement in England: A Study in English Humanitarianism* (New Haven, Conn., 1926); Reginald Coupland, *The British Anti-Slavery Movement* (1933; rpt. New York, 1964); Reginald Coupland, "The Abolition of the Slave Trade," in J. Holland Rose, A. P. Newton, and E. A. Benians, eds., *The Cambridge History of the British Empire,* 8 vols. (Cambridge, 1929–1959; rpt. Cambridge, 1961), II, 188–216, 188 ("the old commercialism"); and George Radcliffe Mellor, *British Imperial Trusteeship, 1783–1850* (London, 1951).

from British historians for more than a century. In tone and substance the governing interpretation of the antislavery movement changed little from the end of the Napoleonic wars to the beginning of World War II.[5]

To be sure, in the intervening years, the suspicious detected less honorable agendas. Advocates for the working classes in England in the early nineteenth century, William Cobbett most prominently, sometimes described the antislavery movement as a plot to distract attention from the "enslavement" of nominally free wage labor at home.[6] On the other side of the political spectrum, skeptics and reactionaries rendered unsympathetic assessments of emancipation and emancipationists. The abolitionist leadership they denounced as quixotic knights-errant, as pious charlatans all too happy to ruin the empire with costly and disastrous experiments in social engineering for the good of an inferior race, critics like Thomas Carlyle wrote, unable to benefit from freedom. The heirs to the "West

5. For Coupland's career in politics as well as in history, see J. D. Fage, "Introduction to the Second Edition," in Coupland, *The British Anti-Slavery Movement,* ix–xvii; Richard Symonds, *Oxford and Empire: The Last Lost Cause?* (New York, 1986), 53–55; Ronald Edward Robinson, "Oxford in Imperial Historiography," in Frederick Madden and D. K. Fieldhouse, eds., *Oxford and the Idea of Commonwealth: Essays Presented to Sir Edgar Williams* (London, 1982), 36–38; and W[illia]m Roger Louis, "Introduction," in Robin W. Winks, ed., *The Oxford History of the British Empire,* V, *Historiography* (Oxford, 1999), 23–24. The celebrations of 1933 marking the one-hundred-year anniversary of emancipation have yet to receive extended study. They are described in brief by David Brion Davis, *Slavery and Human Progress* (Oxford, 1984), 279–281, and by Seymour Drescher, "The Historical Context of British Abolition," in David Richardson, ed., *Abolition and Its Aftermath: The Historical Context, 1790–1916* (London, 1985), 3–4. The centenary publications include Coupland, *The British Anti-Slavery Movement;* John Harris, *A Century of Emancipation* (London, 1933); Sir Maurice Watts, *Liberty to the Captives: A Short Account of the Movement to Abolish Slavery* (London, 1933); and C. M. MacInnes, *England and Slavery* (Bristol, 1934), citation on 211.

6. Patricia Hollis, "Anti-Slavery and British Working-Class Radicalism in the Years of Reform," in Christine Bolt and Seymour Drescher, eds., *Anti-Slavery, Religion, and Reform: Essays in Memory of Roger Anstey* (Folkestone, Kent, Eng., 1980), 294–315; Douglas A. Lorimer, *Color, Class, and the Victorians: English Attitudes to the Negro in the Mid-Nineteenth Century* (Leicester, 1978), 94–95; Catherine Gallagher, *The Industrial Reformation of English Fiction: Social Discourse and Narrative Form, 1832–1867* (Chicago, 1985), 3–10; Wood, *Slavery, Empathy, and Pornography,* 151–169, 178–180.

Indian interest" in the nineteenth century liked to accuse the Evangelicals of narcissism, of a fanatic infatuation with their own piety or, alternatively, of serving as a front for commercial interests hoping to promote sugar production in Cuba, Brazil, or India.[7]

Outside the British Isles, rivals often interpreted "humanitarianism" as statecraft in disguise. British attempts to suppress the slave trade looked like a conspiracy to destroy the plantations of European rivals or to shift world sugar production to British India or to violate national sovereignty. The Paris press read British-sponsored right-to-search treaties as pretexts to intercept French ships engaged in legitimate trade. Similar opinions prevailed among ardent nationalists in the United States inclined to view the British government as a self-righteous bully. In Cuba, planters regarded attempts to block the transport of slaves to the island as a stratagem designed to throw the sugar trade to Brazil, where British capital was heavily invested. Brazilians, in turn, suspected that slave trade abolition aimed not only to make the British Caribbean plantations more competitive but also to reduce the Lusophone presence in West and East African markets.[8] A Machiavellian

7. Thomas Carlyle, "Occasional Discourse on the Negro Question," *Fraser's Magazine for Town and Country,* XL (December 1849), 670–679; Anthony Trollope, *The West Indies and the Spanish Main* (London, 1859); James Anthony Froude, *The English in the West Indies; or, The Bow of Ulysses* (London, 1888); Elsa V. Goveia, *A Study on the Historiography of the British West Indies to the Nineteenth Century* (Mexico City, 1956), 102–107, 110–113, 127–134, 152–156; Eric Williams, *British Historians and the West Indies* (1964; rpt. New York, 1994), 38–52, 64–94; Lorimer, *Color, Class, and the Victorians,* 113–114, 116, 119–124; Gordon K. Lewis, *Main Currents in Caribbean Thought: The Historical Evolution of Caribbean Society in Its Ideological Aspects, 1492–1900* (Baltimore, 1983), 119–122; Howard Temperley, *White Dreams, Black Africa: The Antislavery Expedition to the River Niger, 1841–1842* (New Haven, Conn., 1991), 60–62, 161–162, 166; Seymour Drescher, *The Mighty Experiment: Free Labor versus Slavery in British Emancipation* (Oxford, 2002), 161, 167, 176–177, 180–182, 190–191, 210, 217–222; Catherine Hall, *Civilising Subjects: Colony and Metropole in the English Imagination, 1830–1867* (Chicago, 2002), 209, 212, 214–217, 222–223, 347–352, 358–360; Wood, *Slavery, Empathy, and Pornography,* 346–397.

8. Lawrence C. Jennings, *French Reaction to British Slave Emancipation* (Baton Rouge, La., 1988), 85–87, 148–167; Paul Michael Kielstra, *The Politics of Slave Trade Suppression in Britain and France, 1818–48: Diplomacy, Morality, and Economics* (New York, 2000); Don E. Fehrenbacher, *The Slaveholding Republic: An Account of the United*

government, it seemed to very many, intended to achieve world supremacy under the cover of universal philanthropy. The self-congratulatory narrative, therefore, had its doubters. Critics across Europe and the Americas questioned Britons' tendency to parade their purported humanitarianism.

The descendants of British Caribbean slaves, however, first made the "perfidious Albion" theme essential to how the British antislavery movement would be understood in the second half of the twentieth century. A resentment of economic dependency and an emerging fight for political independence, between World War I and World War II, led an emerging class of West Indian intellectuals to denounce constructions of the past that helped legitimate colonial rule. A pointed reevaluation of the "humanitarian tradition" followed as a consequence. Trinidad journalist C. L. R. James, then living in London, peppered his account of the 1938 Haitian Revolution with contemptuous asides on British duplicity during the Napoleonic wars. Eric Williams, who had studied with James as a schoolboy in Trinidad, enlarged on these themes in his classic *Capitalism and Slavery* (1944). The doctoral dissertation of 1938 on which *Capitalism and Slavery* was based had described economic change as a factor in the abolitionist victory of 1807. By 1944, though, Williams had decided that a proper history of British antislavery would emphasize the hypocrisy he thought pervasive in that campaign and by extension pervasive among its latter-day celebrants. In 1942 he had condemned the impact of colonial rule on the British West Indies in his first book, *The Negro in the Caribbean*. With *Capitalism and Slavery*, the future prime minister of Trinidad and Tobago hoped to demystify British humanitarianism by redescribing its founding era.[9]

States Government's Relations to Slavery* (Oxford, 2001), 163–169; Arthur F. Corwin, *Spain and the Abolition of Slavery in Cuba, 1817–1886* (Austin, Tex., 1967), 28; David R. Murray, *Odious Commerce: Britain, Spain, and the Abolition of the Cuban Slave Trade* (Cambridge, 1980), 147–148; Leslie Bethell, *The Abolition of the Brazilian Slave Trade: Britain, Brazil, and the Slave Trade Question, 1807–1869* (Cambridge, 1970), 65; Robert Edgar Conrad, "Economics and Ideals: The British Antislavery Crusade Reconsidered," *Indian Historical Review*, XV (1988–1989), 214–216. The international controversy produced by slave trade suppression policies is documented helpfully in Peter C. Hogg, ed., *The African Slave Trade and Its Suppression: A Classified and Annotated Bibliography of Books, Pamphlets, and Periodical Articles* (London, 1973), 200–244.

9. The outlines of this story have now been told several times. Seymour Drescher, "Eric Williams: British Capitalism and British Slavery," *History and Theory*, XXVI

Eric Williams offered two substantial revisions to the traditional account. First, he put "the developing economic forces" at the center of the story, reducing in importance the skirmishes in Parliament that traditionally received greatest attention from British and imperial historians. The abolitionists campaigned against the slave trade and slavery, Williams insisted, when it became economically convenient to do so. The value of the British sugar colonies, he argued, declined appreciably after the American Revolution. French, Cuban, and Brazilian plantations, increasingly, could produce sugar at a lower cost. As a matter of policy, abolition and emancipation presented less of a threat to the imperial economy in the early nineteenth century, Williams contended, than in the decades before. Ideologically, the abolitionist attack on the slave system was, at heart, an attack on monopoly, on the exclusive right of British Caribbean sugar producers to meet the demand of British consumers. The gospel of free trade, Williams suggested, mattered as much to the abolitionists as the gospel of Christ. Merchants and manufacturers in industrializing Britain increasingly sought

---

(1987), 180–196; Howard Temperley, "Eric Williams and Abolition: The Birth of a New Orthodoxy," and Richard B. Sheridan, "Eric Williams and Capitalism and Slavery: A Biographical and Historiographical Essay," both in Barbara L. Solow and Stanley L. Engerman, eds., *British Capitalism and Caribbean Slavery: The Legacy of Eric Williams* (Cambridge, 1987), 229–257, 317–345; Paul Sutton, "The Historian as Politician: Eric Williams and Walter Rodney," in Alistair Hennessy, ed., *Intellectuals in the Twentieth Century Caribbean, I, Spectre of the New Class: The Commonwealth Caribbean* (London, 1992), 98–105; Colin Palmer, introduction to Eric Williams, *Capitalism and Slavery* (1944; rpt. Chapel Hill, N.C., 1994), xi–xxi; Palmer, "Eric Williams and His Intellectual Legacy," in Heather Cateau and S. H. H. Carrington, eds., *Capitalism and Slavery Fifty Years Later: Eric Eustace Williams—A Reassessment of the Man and His Work* (New York, 2000), 38–41; B. W. Higman, *Writing West Indian Histories* (London, 1999), 90–97. Williams himself writes movingly and informatively about his years in Oxford, where his ideas took shape. Williams, *Inward Hunger: The Education of a Prime Minister* (London, 1969), 43–53. For Williams's acknowledgment of James's influence, see Williams, *Capitalism and Slavery*, 268. Their relationship and divergent careers are treated suggestively in Ivar Oxaal, *Black Intellectuals and the Dilemmas of Race and Class in Trinidad* (Cambridge, Mass., 1982), 72–79, and by Hilary McD. Beckles, "Capitalism, Slavery, and Caribbean Modernity," and William Darity, Jr., "Eric Williams and Slavery: A West Indian Viewpoint?" both in "Eric Williams and the Postcolonial Carribean," *Callaloo*, XX (1997), 777–789, 801–816.

access to the cheapest source of raw commodities, even if those sources lay outside the British Empire. "The whole world now became a British colony," Williams wrote, "and the West Indies were doomed." These transformations in economics and ideology proved decisive, Williams maintained. Parliament abolished the slave trade in 1807 to discourage the expansion of sugar cultivation. Emancipation in 1834 served as a kind of mercy killing for a dying colonial economy. The changing economic circumstances, in short, helped explain the otherwise inexplicable success of the British antislavery movement.[10]

Therefore, those historians infatuated with the heroism of the abolitionists, Williams declared, had substituted romance for facts. Although he accepted the importance of the antislavery movement, Williams questioned the integrity of prominent politicians traditionally associated with the cause. The younger William Pitt, prime minister from 1783 to 1801 and 1804 to 1806, was a particularly easy target. A professed opponent of the slave trade in the 1780s, he spent the nation's wealth and blood in the 1790s on a fruitless mission to suppress the slave insurrection in Saint Domingue and to restore plantation slavery in the crumbling French colony under British control. Outside the halls of power, Williams continued, economic interests clothed in the garb of disinterested philanthropy predominated in the campaign for emancipation. Key figures in the movement, like James Cropper, who had invested heavily in East Indian sugar, needed the Caribbean plantations to fail. Moral inconsistencies abounded in British humanitarianism, according to Williams. The abolitionists encouraged the expansion of slavery outside the British Empire by promoting sugar, coffee, and cotton imports from plantations in Cuba, Brazil, and the United States. At the same time, they neglected inhumanities closer to home, as radicals like Cobbett had argued a century before. "Wilberforce was familiar with all that went on in the hold of a slave ship," Williams observed of the parliamentary leader of the antislavery campaign, "but ignored what went on at the bottom of a mineshaft."[11] Here was the second revision to the humanitarian narrative. Not only did economics matter more than morals. The moralists were themselves often cynics or hypocrites.

These two claims, one about economics, the other about the abolition-

10. Williams, *Capitalism and Slavery*, 142, 210.
11. Ibid., 182, 211.

ists, touched off a prolonged controversy, perhaps one of the most complex in modern historical scholarship. At stake in this debate not only has been the character of the British antislavery movement. The controversy reflected deeper divisions regarding the role of capitalist interests in British imperial history, the relationship between the British and peoples of African descent, and the very possibility of humanitarian action in colonial societies. Initially, scholarly interest centered on the economic question, perhaps because this aspect of the problem seemed most susceptible to empirical analysis. What had become known as the "decline thesis" came under sustained attack during the 1960s and 1970s. This new generation of research made a powerful case for the recovery of the Caribbean economy after the American Revolution. Increasingly, it seemed unlikely that slave trade abolition in 1807 could be attributed primarily to the diminished value of the West Indian colonies as Eric Williams and many others had supposed.[12] But these findings only deepened the paradox that the aboli-

12. For critiques of the decline thesis, see Roger T. Anstey, "Capitalism and Slavery: A Critique," *Economic History Review*, 2d Ser., XXI (1968), 307–320; Anstey, "A Reinterpretation of the Abolition of the British Slave Trade, 1806–1807," *English Historical Review*, LXXXVII (April 1972), 304–322; Seymour Drescher, *Econocide: British Slavery in the Era of Abolition* (Pittsburgh, Pa., 1977); J. R. Ward, "The Profitability of Sugar Planting in the British West Indies, 1650–1834," *Econ. Hist. Rev.*, 2d Ser., XXXI (1978), 197–213; Seymour Drescher, "The Decline Thesis of British Slavery since *Econocide*," *Slavery and Abolition*, VII, no. 1 (May 1986), 3–24; Temperley, "Eric Williams and Abolition," in Solow and Engerman, eds., *British Capitalism and Caribbean Slavery*, 229–257; and John J. McCusker, "The Economy of the British West Indies, 1763–1790: Growth, Stagnation, or Decline?" in John J. McCusker, *Essays in the Economic History of the Atlantic World* (London, 1997), 310–331. The case for the decline thesis is argued thoroughly in several studies by Selwyn H. H. Carrington: "The American Revolution and the British West Indies' Economy," *Journal of Interdisciplinary History*, XVII (1987), 823–850; "British West Indian Economic Decline and Abolition, 1775–1807: Revisiting *Econocide*," *Canadian Journal of Latin American and Caribbean Studies*, XIV, no. 27 (1989), 33–59; "The State of the Debate on the Role of Capitalism in the Ending of the Slave System," *Journal of Caribbean History*, XXII (1990), 20–41; "The American Revolution, British Policy, and the West Indian Economy, 1775–1808," *Revista Interamericana*, XXII (1992), 72–108; "The United States and the British West Indies Trade," in Roderick A. McDonald, ed., *West Indies Accounts: Essays on the History of the British Caribbean and the Atlantic Economy in Honour of Richard Sheridan* (Kingston,

tionists seemed to present. *Capitalism and Slavery* had forever stigmatized the humanitarian narrative. By the 1970s, few academic historians cared to write about "selfless" men engaged in a "virtuous crusade." In the aftermath of decolonization, as the morality of empire became discredited, not many wished to revive an interpretive tradition associated with and implicated in colonial rule. Therefore, instead of returning to the humanitarian narrative, they sought new ways to relate the history of abolition to the dynamics of economic change. In this way, *Capitalism and Slavery* continued to influence the way investigators framed questions about the antislavery movement, even as the decline thesis fell from favor. How did the choices of the abolitionists reflect the interests of their class?[13]

Jamaica, 1996), 149–168; and, most recently, *The Sugar Industry and the Abolition of the Slave Trade, 1775–1810* (Gainesville, Fla., 2002). On behalf of decline, see also David Ryden, "Planters, Slaves, and Decline," in Heather Cateau and S. H. H. Carrington, eds., *Capitalism and Slavery Fifty Years Later: Eric Eustace Williams—A Reassessment of the Man and His Work* (New York, 2000), 155–169, and Ryden, "Does Decline Make Sense? The West Indian Economy and the Abolition of the Slave Trade," *Jour. Interdisciplinary Hist.*, XXXI (2000), 347–374. For commentary on this dispute, see Walter Minchinton, "Williams and Drescher: Abolition and Emancipation," *Slavery and Abolition*, IV, no. 2 (September 1983), 81–105; Hilary McD. Beckles, "Capitalism and Slavery: The Debate over Eric Williams," *Social and Economic Studies* (Jamaica), XXXIII, no. 4 (December 1984), 171–189; Selwyn H. H. Carrington and Seymour Drescher, "Debate: Econocide and West Indian Decline, 1783–1806," *Boletin de Estudios Latinoamericanos y del Caribe*, XXXVI (1984), 13–67; William Darity, Jr., "The Williams Abolition Thesis before Williams," *Slavery and Abolition*, IX, no. 1 (May 1988), 29–41; Minchinton, "Abolition and Emancipation: Williams, Drescher, and the Continuing Debate," in McDonald, ed., *West Indies Accounts*, 253–273; and Drescher, "*Capitalism and Slavery* after Fifty Years," *Slavery and Abolition*, XVIII, no. 3 (December 1997), 212–227. This debate is likely to continue and may be incapable of resolution. As B. W. Higman has noted, decline is as much an ideological as a technical concept and thus depends heavily on the argumentative context in which it is deployed. Higman, *Writing West Indian Histories*, 164. The case I make here for a new approach to the study of British abolitionism depends not at all on the existence of decline or what "decline" means. With or without decline, abolitionism in Britain still needs to be explained.

13. David Brion Davis, *The Problem of Slavery in the Age of Revolution, 1770–1823* (Ithaca, N.Y., 1975), 242–254, 343–468; Howard Temperley, "Capitalism, Slavery, and Ideology," *Past and Present*, no. 75 (May 1977), 94–118; Temperley, "Antislavery as a Form of Cultural Imperialism," in Bolt and Drescher, eds., *Anti-Slavery, Religion, and*

This was an important question insofar as the *character* of the British antislavery movement was at issue. But to comprehend how abolitionism first took shape it has proved to be an unhelpful place from which to begin research. The history of the British antislavery campaign presents three related but distinct subjects: (1) the development of ideas and values hostile to slavery and the slave trade; (2) the crystallization of programs to reform or transform imperial and colonial policy; and (3) the achievement of abolition and emancipation. Each topic, it should be evident, presents a different set of interpretive problems. The first requires an exploration of changing values, perceptions, and beliefs. It recommends attention primarily to intellectual and cultural history. This I will refer to as the history of antislavery ideology. The second calls for an explanation of how those ideas translated into effective action as well as how and why those strategies took the character and shape they did. This topic, the subject of this book, is the history of abolitionism. The third demands an analysis of the political process. It requires an analysis of the forces and interests that led to political change. This is the history of abolition and emancipation.[14] Each one of

---

Reform, 335–350; Temperley, "The Ideology of Antislavery," in David Eltis and James Walvin, eds., *The Abolition of the Atlantic Slave Trade: Origins and Effects in Europe, Africa, and the Americas* (Madison, Wis., 1981), 21–35; Seymour Drescher, "Cart Whip and Billy Roller: Antislavery and Reform Symbolism in Industrializing Britain," *Journal of Social History,* XV (1981–1982), 3–24; Betty Fladeland, "Our Cause Being One and the Same: Abolitionists and Chartism," in James Walvin, ed., *Slavery and British Society, 1776–1846* (London, 1982), 69–99; Fladeland, *Abolitionists and Working-Class Problems in the Age of Industrialization* (Baton Rouge, La., 1984); David Eltis, *Economic Growth and the Ending of the Transatlantic Slave Trade* (Oxford, 1987), 19–23; Seymour Drescher, *Capitalism and Antislavery: British Mobilization in Comparative Perspective* (London, 1987). See also the important collection of essays by David Brion Davis, Thomas Haskell, and John Ashworth published in Thomas Bender, ed., *The Antislavery Debate: Capitalism and Abolitionism as a Problem in Historical Interpretation* (Berkeley, Calif., 1992).

14. My discussion here is indebted to Thomas Holt, "Capitalism and Antislavery: British Mobilization in Comparative Perspective," *Jour. Soc. Hist.,* XXIV (1990–1991), 371–378. Throughout this book, the reader should keep in mind the distinction I draw here between antislavery and abolitionism, terms that had not yet become part of common parlance in the years under consideration. By "antislavery" I mean that complex of values, sentiments, opinions, beliefs, and assumptions critical of some or all aspects of

these subjects, of course, entails the others. The history of abolition and emancipation makes no sense without reference to the history of abolitionism. And abolitionism can be assessed properly only in the context of antislavery ideology. Nonetheless, as distinct topics they require distinct approaches. Too often the history of abolitionism has been presented either as a prologue to the history of abolition and emancipation or in terms more appropriate to the study of antislavery thought.

In the typical survey, for example, the early abolitionist stirrings represent a short chapter in a longer story. Brief descriptions of the first antislavery societies and capsule profiles of the initial activists introduce detailed explanations of how and why abolition and emancipation occurred.[15] Those assessments less sympathetic to the abolitionists often start from a similar place. If Eric Williams took an interest in the character and the consequences of the antislavery movements, he wrote nothing at all about its origins. *Capitalism and Slavery,* in this respect, left the Clarkson thesis unrevised, a choice characteristic, too, in subsequent research emphasizing the importance of economic decline. In this way, the abolitionists have prevailed in more than one sense. Their story—the achievement of abolition and emancipation—has remained the subject of discussion and analysis. Most assessments, both sympathetic and critical, *describe* the efforts that turned the slave trade into a political issue in order to *explain* the process that led to abolition and emancipation. These brief descriptions, however, are not explanations. And it is the premise of this book that abolitionism, no less than abolition, requires an explanation. For this rea-

---

the Atlantic slave system. Active attempts to translate antislavery sentiments and opinions into an active program of reform are designated as "antislavery initiatives." "Abolitionism," therefore, represents one type of antislavery initiative, those efforts that aimed to accomplish the abolition of the slave trade. The reader will notice, however, that in this book I give some attention as well to "antislavery initiatives" of varying types, some of which provided important precursors or alternatives to "abolitionism."

15. For modern accounts of the British antislavery movement that either fail to analyze or severely condense the problem of beginnings, see Klingberg, *The Anti-Slavery Movement;* Coupland, *The British Anti-Slavery Movement;* Dale H. Porter, *The Abolition of the Slave Trade in England, 1784–1807* ([Hamden, Conn.], 1970); Roger Anstey, *The Atlantic Slave Trade and British Abolition, 1760–1810* (London, 1975); C. Duncan Rice, *The Rise and Fall of Black Slavery* (New York, 1975); and James Walvin, *England, Slaves, and Freedom, 1776–1838* (London, 1986).

son, it ends where most begin, with the founding of the Society for Effecting the Abolition of the Slave Trade in 1787.

The scholarship on antislavery ideology encounters a different set of problems. Instead of making a long story too short, it often makes a complicated problem too simple. Most have been careful to acknowledge that "climates of opinion do not give virgin birth to social movements."[16] But the inclination remains to treat the antislavery campaigns as arising from climates of opinion. That tendency has been most prevalent in the study of Quakers and Anglican Evangelicals, the two groups most responsible for organizing the national campaign. The fit between antislavery values and their religious principles is well established. But why these groups waited to act until the 1780s or, alternatively, did not wait longer remains unexplained. The arguments tend to take the form of a tautology: Quakers became abolitionists because traditionally Quakers had religious objections to slaveholding; Evangelicals opposed slavery because of the imperatives arising from the Evangelical worldview.[17]

Comparable problems appear in less obvious ways in the work on antislavery and the culture of capitalism. An emerging faith in the virtue and

16. Davis, *The Problem of Slavery in the Age of Revolution*, 215.

17. This is the tendency of the last extended assessment of early Quaker and Evangelical organizing; Anstey, *The Atlantic Slave Trade and British Abolition*, 157–235. For the beginnings of Evangelical antislavery, in addition to the studies by Klingberg and Coupland referenced above, see Anstey, "Slavery and the Protestant Ethic," in Michael D. Craton, ed., "Roots and Branches: Current Directions in Slave Studies," *Historical Reflections/Reflexions historiques*, VI, no. 1 (Summer 1979), 157–181, and Ernest Marshall Howse, *Saints in Politics: The "Clapham Sect" and the Growth of Freedom* (Toronto, 1952). In most instances, Quaker abolitionism in England is explained as the result of Quaker abolitionism in North America, as the consequence of transatlantic influence. See especially Betty Fladeland, *Men and Brothers: Anglo-American Antislavery Cooperation* (Urbana, Ill., 1972), 16–33, and Davis, *The Problem of Slavery in the Age of Revolution*, 218–226. This, of course, begs the question of why American influence was influential. In this respect, little progress has been made since 1978, when J. William Frost bemoaned "the lacunae in our knowledge of English Friends." Frost, "The Origins of the Quaker Crusade against Slavery: A Review of Recent Literature," *Quaker History*, LXVII (1978), 48. Judith Jennings provides a superbly detailed account of the first Quaker organizers but sidesteps questions pertaining to motivation and purpose. Jennings, *The Business of Abolishing the British Slave Trade, 1783–1807* (London, 1997).

efficiency of free labor helped the first abolitionists conceive alternatives to slavery, as David Eltis and Howard Temperley have proposed. The expansion of overseas trade may have helped the concerned recognize their connection to colonial slavery and, thereby, an obligation to intervene, as Thomas Haskell has suggested. But these ideological frameworks were conditions, not causes. If they predisposed, they did not dispose. The study of antislavery ideas is indispensable to understanding abolitionism. The research on the subject has illuminated key aspects of the abolitionists' worldview. However, when the changes described are too broad, as in the "rise of capitalism" or the "ascent of free labor ideology," we are left with answers that are subject to the same shortcomings as "the Enlightenment" or "Evangelicalism," though less obviously idealist. We learn that certain individuals had certain ideas and that these ideas circulated extensively in the late eighteenth century but not what moved people to take specific initiatives at particular moments.

Understanding the foundations of abolitionism, then, means understanding human choices. And to understand human choices, the now conventional focus on the dynamics of economic change may, in fact, produce more problems than it solves. Almost thirty years ago, historian Howard Temperley expressed well the assumptions that have continued to recommend this route.

> Here we have a system—a highly successful system—of large-scale capitalist agriculture, mass producing raw materials for sale in distant markets, growing up at a time when most production was still small-scale and designed to meet the needs of local consumers. But precisely at a time when capitalist ideas were in the ascendant, and large-scale production of all kinds of goods was beginning, we find this system being dismantled. How could this happen unless "capitalism" has something to do with it? If our reasoning leads to the conclusion that "capitalism" had nothing to do with it the chances are that there is something wrong with our reasoning.[18]

Temperley surely is correct. Capitalism undoubtedly had "something to do with" the antislavery movement in Britain. In practice, however, as a meth-

18. Temperley, "Capitalism, Slavery, and Ideology," *Past and Present*, no. 75 (May 1977), 105.

odological imperative, this starting point has had the unfortunate effect of discouraging investigation into the other agendas and contexts that also had "something to do with" the emergence of abolitionism. Instead of asking how abolitionism began, most of these studies have asked how the history of antislavery movements related to the history of capitalism. As should be apparent, an answer to the second question does not, necessarily, offer a solution to the first. It took a "peculiar historical conjuncture," as the historian Seymour Drescher once wrote, to push slave trade abolition to the top of the public agenda. But we still need a study of that "peculiar historical conjuncture" that does not assume, from the outset, that an explanation *must* begin with the rise of capitalism.[19]

In the most recent generation of research, the attention to class interest and class conflicts in the British antislavery movement served as a talisman to ward off "the ghost of Coupland's past," as one scholar has put it, as a kind of intellectual prophylactic designed to prevent future outbreaks of a romance with empire. It reflected a commendable desire to develop a less credulous assessment of abolitionist motives and aims. And that reluctance to emphasize the familiar heroes, and their heroism, has encouraged a broader understanding of what abolitionism entailed. The antislavery movement, we now know, involved far more than the small circle of propagandists and elite politicians whom the first chroniclers tended to lionize. Resistance by the enslaved, themselves, helped put the legality of slaveholding in Britain on trial in the English and Scottish courts in the 1760s and 1770s and helped diminish sympathy for Caribbean slaveowners, thereafter, especially following slave trade abolition in 1807.[20] A mobilized abolitionist

19. Drescher, *Capitalism and Antislavery,* 22. In reflecting on this last generation of scholarship, Drescher himself has begun to doubt the value of framing the problem in this way. "The capitalism and antislavery debate alerts us to the problematic nature of the original historiographic point of departure. One may tirelessly reiterate that 'it is no accident that' the industrial revolution and antislavery reached critical mass together, or that the early British abolitionist victories coincided with one or another industrial crisis. But temporal coincidence is the weakest form of causal inference. *It may tempt us down a long blind alley"* (emphasis in original). See Drescher, "The Antislavery Debate: Capitalism and Abolitionism as a Problem in Historical Interpretation," *History and Theory,* XXXII (1993), 311–329, citation on 329.

20. For the critical importance of black initiative to the end of slaveholding in England, see especially Douglas A. Lorimer, "Black Slaves and English Liberty: A Re-

public, moreover, helped ensure that the slave trade and slavery remained a political issue during the fifty-year campaign for their eradication.[21] The success of the British antislavery movement depended on a wider variety of actors than the older studies tended to allow.

[II]   This is how things stood when I first became intrigued and then perplexed by the sudden emergence and public success of the British campaign to abolish the slave trade. The facts, as I understood them, made little sense. The British antislavery movement seemed to emerge from

---

examination of Racial Slavery in England," *Immigrants and Minorities,* III (1984), 121–150. In a similar vein, slave insurrections in the colonies are now recognized as having a crucial role in the progress and timing of the antislavery movement after the abolition of the slave trade, a suggestion Eric Williams first made in 1944. See especially Mary Turner, "The Baptist War and Abolition," *Jamaican Historical Review,* XIII (1982), 31–41; Michael Craton, *Testing the Chains: Resistance to Slavery in the British West Indies* (Ithaca, N.Y., 1982), 254–321; Craton, "Slave Culture, Resistance, and the Achievement of Emancipation in the British West Indies, 1783–1838," in Walvin, ed., *Slavery and British Society,* 100–122; Craton, "Emancipation from Below? The Role of the British West Indian Slaves in the Emancipation Movement, 1816–34," in Jack Hayward, ed., *Out of Slavery: Abolition and After* (London, 1985), 110–131; Craton, "What and Who to Whom and What: The Significance of Slave Resistance," in Solow and Engerman, eds., *British Capitalism and Caribbean Slavery,* 259–282; Emilia Viotti da Costa, *Crowns of Glory, Tears of Blood: The Demerara Slave Rebellion of 1823* (Oxford, 1994); and Hilary McD. Beckles, *Bussa: The 1816 Revolution in Barbados* (Barbados, 1998).

21. The scholarship on the public campaign has grown immensely in recent years. The best of these is Drescher, *Capitalism and Antislavery,* and his subsequent "Whose Abolition? Popular Pressure and the Ending of the British Slave Trade," *Past and Present,* no. 143 (May 1994), 136–166. See also the pioneering work of James Walvin: "The Rise of British Popular Sentiment for Abolition, 1787–1832," in Bolt and Drescher, eds., *Antislavery, Religion, and Reform,* 149–162; "The Public Campaign in England against Slavery," in Eltis and Walvin, eds., *The Abolition of the Atlantic Slave Trade,* 63–79; and *England, Slaves, and Freedom,* 123–143. Clare Midgley has brought to the fore the significance and distinctiveness of women's activism in Midgley, *Women against Slavery: The British Campaigns, 1780–1870* (London, 1992), and "Slave Sugar Boycotts, Female Activism and the Domestic Base of British Anti-Slavery Culture," *Slavery and Abolition,* XVII, no. 3 (December 1996), 137–162. See also Iain McCalman, "Anti-Slavery and Ultra-Radicalism in Early Nineteenth-Century England: The Case of Robert Wedderburn," *Slavery and Abolition,* VII, no. 2 (September 1986), 99–117; J. R. Old-

nowhere in 1787–1788. The breadth of its public support in those first heady months had few precedents in late-eighteenth-century British political history. Public opposition to the abolitionists was negligible.[22] If the question could have been decided by public opinion, the slave trade would have been abolished at once. This is what happened, there seemed to be no question about that, but how could that have been? Antislavery movements do not just spontaneously appear, not previously, and not in this way. And even once Britain set the precedent, enthusiastic and unanimous support for antislavery action elsewhere in Europe and the Americas would be exceedingly rare. Moreover, for reasons that now should be clear, it was hard to see how the familiar explanatory categories—"Enlightenment," "Evangelicalism," "Quakerism," "capitalism," "humanitarianism," and the like—could make sense of the sudden rise in political activism.

So I spent many, many months dissecting the first year of the campaign against the British slave trade. The logic that informed my approach was simple (if not simplistic). If I could chart the movement's development month by month, even week by week, it might be possible to understand how the campaign emerged. If I could determine *who* participated in the

---

field, *Popular Politics and British Anti-Slavery: The Mobilization of Public Opinion against the Slave Trade, 1787–1807* (Manchester, Eng., 1995); Charlotte Sussman, *Consuming Anxieties: Consumer Protest, Gender, and British Slavery, 1713–1833* (Stanford, Calif., 2000). The cultural history of the British antislavery movement at its apex now is best approached through the bibliographies and republished primary sources printed in the outstanding collection compiled by Peter J. Kitson and Debbie Lee, gen. eds., *Slavery, Abolition, and Emancipation: Writings in the British Romantic Period,* 8 vols. (London, 1999), and by James G. Basker, ed., *Amazing Grace: An Anthology of Poems about Slavery, 1660–1810* (New Haven, Conn., 2002).

22. This is a central theme in Drescher's work. "It was the revelation of humanitarian priorities within public opinion that first dislodged the economic rationale from its hegemonic political position in the Parliamentary discourse about slavery. In this sense, the overwhelming majority of articulate Britons were abolitionists as soon as they gathered together to discuss the slave trade." Drescher, "People and Parliament: The Rhetoric of the British Slave Trade," *Jour. Interdisciplinary Hist.*, XX (1989–1990), 561–580, citation on 580. In addition to the work cited above, see Drescher, "The Slaving Capital of the World: Liverpool and National Opinion in the Age of Abolition," *Slavery and Abolition*, IX, no. 2 (September 1988), 128–143.

movement, if I could characterize the hundreds of subscribers to the Society for Effecting the Abolition of the Slave Trade and the thousands who signed antislavery petitions sent to the House of Commons in 1788, it might be possible to discern patterns in the public support for abolitionism. This research had its value. It established, among other things, the critical importance of Quaker networks and Quaker money during the first crucial months of the national campaign.[23] Yet the more material I gathered about the campaign in 1787 and 1788 the less satisfied I became with what I had uncovered. I understood, belatedly, that I had the stick by the wrong end. The interesting questions, and the truly difficult questions, were less about "who" and more about "why." It might be possible, with enough patience, to determine with some precision *who* supported the campaign against the slave trade. Yet I would still not understand *why,* in the first place, there was an antislavery organization in the 1780s for those people to support.

Neither public opinion nor slave resistance, together or alone, originated the British antislavery movement, though both contributed decisively to its success. For more than a century, antislavery values in Britain and slave resistance in the colonies had proved unable, separately and together, to push the slave trade or colonial slavery to the top of the political agenda. The popular campaign of the 1780s was the product of conscious effort, not simply the efflorescence of antislavery sentiment. British mobilization would never have developed if particular individuals and groups had not conspired to create it. But why them? Why then? And why in this way? The morality of the slave system had troubled men and women for decades, but no one in Britain had attempted to overthrow it. Necessarily, then, and somewhat reluctantly at first, as this project developed, I found myself taking yet another look at the initial activists and organizers, the now familiar protagonists of the increasingly neglected and long-discredited humanitarian narrative, particularly Anthony Benezet, Thomas Clarkson, William Dillwyn, Olaudah Equiano, Hannah More, Margaret Middleton, John Pemberton, Beilby Porteus, James Ramsay, Granville Sharp, Phillis Wheatley, and William Wilberforce. An explanation of abolitionism, I decided, would have to begin with them. I would have to make sense of their concerns, their purposes, their choices, but, this time, in order to understand the abolitionists rather than to praise them.

23. I report the key conclusions in the final chapter of the present study.

The obvious point has to be made first, since its significance is sometimes overlooked. These men and women did not begin life as abolitionists.
They could not assume, when they began their efforts, that abolishing any
aspect of the slave system could be regarded as a plausible project. They
were not abolitionists by nature, in essence, ontologically (though one may
be forgiven for drawing that conclusion from several of their biographers).
Instead, over the course of their lives they *became* abolitionists. Something
in their experience of the world led them into active opposition to slavery.
Much of this book is concerned with those moments of decision, with the
fissures in experience that moved people troubled by slavery to act on their
concerns. Throughout, I have tried to indicate how the decision to challenge slavery related to the broader needs and aims of particular actors, to
the cultural, political, and even personal agendas that previous studies
centered exclusively on their antislavery activities have tended to underplay
or overlook. I have assumed that hostility to slavery reflected, arose from,
and addressed matters of concern that, in key respects, had little to do with
the problem of slavery. And I have tried to detail those situations that
allowed antislavery to occupy a prominent place within this complex of
aspirations and concerns. For this reason, I have read broadly if necessarily
selectively on issues that, on their face, have limited relevance to slavery
itself but that mattered a great deal to the particular opponents of slavery at
the time. Simultaneously I have tried to locate the activities and publications
of those who did attack human bondage in the context of their related
interests and initiatives. It may seem as if the last thing needed is additional
work on the first abolitionists. But the problem, I have come to realize, is
less that they have received too much attention than that they have received
too much of the wrong kind of attention. In writing this book, when dealing
with the founding generation, one question has been paramount: when men
and women in late-eighteenth-century Britain tried to organize opposition
to some aspect of the Atlantic slave system, what were they trying to do?

As my various answers to this question will make clear, helping enslaved
Africans often mattered far less to the opponents of slavery than more
proximate and sometimes very different goals. Conventionally, self-interest
has been defined in economic terms: the abolitionists were self-interested,
the argument goes, because abolition and emancipation stood to advance
the values and interests of their class. But not all interests are economic
interests. "Interest" can take any number of guises. Men and women often

fought slavery because they disliked what slavery wrought, because it affected colonial or metropolitan society in undesirable ways, or because it threatened cherished values. Often activists took up the issue of slavery less because they cared about Africans than because they regretted its impact on society, on the empire, on public morals, or on the collective sense of self. A few, to varying degrees, did take a genuine interest in the welfare of the enslaved. But many more wanted, above all, to be free of slavery, and thus free from danger or free from corruption or free from guilt. The self-concerned, self-regarding, even self-validating impulse in early British abolitionism represents a key theme in this book.

A second theme concerns the relevance of imperial contexts. No one in Britain could campaign against colonial slavery or the Atlantic slave trade without also confronting fundamental questions about the structure, character, and purpose of empire. How should the empire be governed? When and how should the imperial state intervene in colonial affairs? What responsibility does the British government have to captive and conquered peoples living in British territories? How do the interests of the individual colonies relate to the interests of the empire as a whole? Where does sovereignty lie? Where should it lie? In what ways should power be exercised? These vital questions, which most research on British antislavery has neglected or overlooked, went to the heart of the challenge facing the first abolitionists. Those questions perhaps were easy for historians to overlook in the 1970s, during the years when scholarly interest in the abolitionists revived, since, by then, research on the eighteenth-century empire had fallen into disrepair; by that time, the study of slavery had become a matter for colonial rather than British history. At the time, perhaps, it seemed more promising to regard antislavery in terms of Britain's domestic history, as one result of the Evangelical revival or as an instance in the history of political reform or in the campaign's relationship to industrialization, rather than as a problem in imperial relations. But, for the origins of abolitionism, what mattered more than these domestic contexts, what accounts for the timing of the movement, the urgency the subject acquired, as well as its initial public success were the conflicts between colonial and metropolitan elites that commenced with the Seven Years' War and ended with American independence, the conflicts that forced the British to make sense of their increasingly global empire.

Eric Williams may have been wrong on some points. But he was right to describe the American Revolution as a pivotal event in the history of British slavery. The conflict of the 1760s and 1770s directed unprecedented attention to the moral character of colonial institutions and imperial practices. In North America, the rebellion against imperial authority fostered new interest in dramatic displays of individual and collective virtue. In Britain, it generated attempts to enhance, and justify the enhancement of, authority over the American colonies. Much of this book is concerned with how early abolitionist and emancipationist programs served broader efforts to validate (or question) the moral authority of elites in both British America and the British Isles. The British would discover in the course of this conflict what in the nineteenth century they came to recognize as a truism. Support for slavery could become an embarrassment if and when the virtue of imperial rule became a public question. At the same time, moral capital might be accrued by framing antislavery initiatives as an emblem of the national character. The American Revolution did not cause abolitionism in Britain. It neither moved men and women to act nor indicated what, specifically, they should do. The crisis in imperial authority did, however, make the institution of slavery matter politically in ways it had never mattered before. It turned the slave system into a symbol, not just an institution, the source of self-examination as well as a fount of wealth. Scholars inclined to emphasize British humanitarianism early in the twentieth century tended to present the emergence of abolitionism as a vindication of British liberty. In the process, they obscured the crisis in British liberty that made its vindication necessary.

That crisis in Anglo-American relations, however, suggested a number of possible responses. The path to abolitionism was less linear, more crooked, than has been supposed. It was marked by false starts, routes not taken, initiatives that petered out. A third purpose of this book is to suggest the complexity of this history and to elucidate the process that made slave trade abolition, above all others, the preeminent goal. In Thomas Clarkson's graphic depiction, antislavery opinion flows in one direction, without eddies or crosscurrents, without a diversity in aim, agenda, or interest. In this interpretation, the opponents of slavery all wanted the same thing, and for the same reasons. The agenda was foreordained. The strategy was clear. The attack on the slave trade would come first. In time, when the time was ripe, the challenge to slavery itself would follow. Every work published since, in one form or another, has implicitly accepted this model. In the process, these works have quietly discarded a problem essential to understanding the foundations of the antislavery movements in Britain. Before the late 1780s, there was no consensus on how best to proceed. No one, at first, knew exactly what to do. The eventual focus on the slave trade, like the movement itself, was an artifact of history. It matters a great deal, then, that the first impulses toward reform were ameliorationist rather than abolitionist or emancipationist, that activists often aimed to make slavery more humane or more Christian, not to liberate the enslaved. And it matters a great deal that early antislavery schemes tried to discourage the expansion of slavery within the empire rather than to eradicate slavery throughout it. To write of a singular "antislavery movement" is, for these early years, to obscure the great variety of ambitions and programs that took shape in the era of the American Revolution.

A final theme of this book relates to the sources and character of personal commitment, to the peculiar features of the few in Britain who allowed antislavery to become, during the 1780s, essential to their sense of self. To an extent, the explanations must be as individual as the individuals themselves. And it is true, as well, that the singularly committed took on the antislavery cause for several of the reasons others did, because they disliked what slavery did to colonial societies or to national honor. But for some of the organizers, abolitionism represented more than this. For some it allowed for the creation and elaboration of an innovative Christian politics, for which, at the time, they could find few other outlets. It offered an opportunity to make piety relevant in an age that seemed to some devout men and women too respectful of the secular, too enamored with the joys of polite diversions. It has become customary to characterize British antislavery opinion in the late eighteenth century as an amalgam of secular principles and religious doctrine. If this description suits the public culture of antislavery as a whole, it is off the mark for the few who made antislavery a substantive political question. The British antislavery movement emerged from a religious reaction against what its Evangelical and Quaker founders derided as nominal Christianity. The initiators of the campaign, in most instances, came to the cause from a more general dedication to making religion figure more prominently in private and public life, although they were influenced by the eighteenth-century intellectual and cultural trends that questioned the ethics of slaving, although they quickly won support from men and women hostile to Evangelicalism and dubious about the defense of the established order. If the British antislavery movement, by the 1790s, became associated with political and religious radicalism, it emerged from a concerted attempt to restore the moral authority of Church and State or, more broadly, to rehabilitate the reputation of piety and the personal commitment to faith. Scholars have long understood that the antislavery movement provided moral capital for the expansion of the British Empire in the nineteenth century, but they have not always appreciated how changing perceptions of what antislavery organizing could mean would prove crucial to the prospects for the antislavery movement itself.

For an antislavery movement to develop in Britain, then, four things had to happen. In the first place, the enslavement of Africans had to be considered, in the abstract, a moral wrong. Second, that moral wrong had to attain political significance; it had to attract sustained interest and become a cause for concern. Third, those concerned needed a way to act, a way to address the concerns that had emerged. And, fourth, specific individuals and groups had to make a confrontation with the slave system a personal and collective mission, a priority that lasted beyond initial protests and could sustain itself with coherent organization and institutional commitment. The four parts of this study treat each of these developments in turn. The first is concerned with "antislavery without abolitionism," the ways antislavery ideas could and did exist without generating comprehensive antislavery initiatives. The second part of the book then tracks the circumstances that made the British slave system the subject of political controversy. Here my discussion centers on the politics of the American Revolution and how the experience of that conflict reshaped perceptions of the slave trade, slavery, empire, and antislavery opinion on both sides of the Atlantic, but especially in the British Isles. Part 3 of the book turns to the search for solutions, to early attempts to solve the problem of slavery, and the obstacles that prevented those solutions from generating a sustained campaign for reform. The book then closes, in its fourth part, with a sustained consideration of the Quaker and Evangelical organizers and how abolitionism came to serve the more specific concerns of these groups in the years after the American war.

As should be apparent from this brief outline, readers may expect to find little here regarding the social history of colonial slavery or its economic progress during the eighteenth century. My concern in this volume is less with these social and economic "facts" than with how colonial slavery and the Atlantic slave trade were experienced, perceived, understood, and discussed by those who attacked it. For related reasons, I have devoted relatively little space to slave resistance in the plantation colonies, except as it pertains to its frequently substantial influence on British antislavery opinion and initiative. This is not because the topic is unimportant. To the contrary, the subject of slave resistance is essential and fundamental to the broader history of slavery, abolition, and emancipation. But the causes of slave resistance do not seem particularly mysterious; at least they do not to me. I have not thought it necessary to elaborate at length on why enslaved Africans opposed slavery. By contrast, attacks on human bondage by British men and women, who were not slaves and who benefited from slavery either directly or indirectly, present problems of a rather different order. They raise complicated questions about motivation and aim, timing and purpose. And yet it is just this aspect of these choices—unexpected, unlikely, and historically specific—that has either eluded or been neglected by too many historians of British antislavery. So I have concentrated my energies on those activists whom I found difficult to understand not only to make sense of their particular choices but also to emphasize their peculiar character. For too long, since Thomas Clarkson's time, the antislavery movement in Britain has been treated as a natural consequence of late-eighteenth-century trends, as if, in this era, organizing against the slave trade was an obvious and logical thing to do. This book proceeds from a different set of assumptions. It proposes that, viewed historically, antislavery organizing was odd rather than inevitable, a peculiar institution rather than the inevitable outcome of moral and cultural progress. It will become clear, I hope, that in key respects the British antislavery movement was a historical accident, a contingent event that just as easily might never have occurred. In any case, my aim here is to make better sense of the first abolitionists, to understand more clearly why particular individuals and groups in Britain thought an attack on slavery not only the right thing to do but something that they could choose to do.

PART I

Values and Practice in Conflict

CHAPTER 1

Antislavery without Abolitionism

To appreciate the tenor of British attitudes toward slavery before antislavery movements crystallized, it helps to notice the observations of those slaveholders in the British colonies attuned to metropolitan opinion. On the subject of slavery, few were more sensitive than Nevis clergyman Robert Robertson, who published three apologies for the British Caribbean elite between 1730 and 1740. Certain officials within the Church of England had begun to censure American slaveholders by the 1720s for neglecting the spiritual welfare of the enslaved, for failing to instruct them in the tenets of the national church. Robertson responded in 1730 with a lengthy, rambling tract that defended the efforts of the colonial clergy and insisted on the difficulty of converting heathen Africans to Christianity. In 1735, an anonymous essayist expressed sympathy for maroons in the mountains of Jamaica, then fighting for independence from colonial authority. Robertson answered with a text that, at once, justified the institution of slavery and relieved planters of responsibility for its existence. A letter to the *Gentleman's Magazine* in 1740 stigmatized slaveholders, in Robertson's words, as *"Enemies to the Negroes, Oppressors, ungrateful and merciless Masters, insolent Enslavers, imperious Torturers,* Insulters of the *Negro Colour, and proud Spoilers of the work of* God, *who dare make Beasts of human Forms."* In reply, Robertson explained that each European state with American territories found a need for slavery and agreed on its legality. Only in England, he complained, was there "the current and long Standing Humour" of judging planters "with the most rigorous Severity." Among the English critics, he observed, were "many Gentlemen of Figure" who insist "that to have any Hand in bringing any of the Human Species into *Bondage,* is justly execrable, and that all who partake in the Sweets of *Liberty,* shou'd spare for no Cost to procure the same, as far as possible, for the rest of Mankind every where."[1]

1. [Robert Robertson], *A Letter to the Right Reverend the Lord Bishop of London* (London, 1730); [Robertson], *The Speech of Mr. John Talbot Campo-bell . . .* (London, 1736); *Gentleman's Magazine, and Historical Chronicle,* XI (1741), 145–147, 186. For

Robert Robertson resented the arrogance of those in Britain who judged from afar, on "Surmise or bare Hear-say." So he made it his mission to explain the true situation of colonial slaveholders, to render the Englishman in the Caribbean worthy of sympathy and esteem. Planters in the West Indies keep slaves because they have to, Robertson explained. If the matter lay in their control, they would have procured workers from somewhere else and on different terms. Indeed, he added, they had for a time. During the first decades of colonial settlement, he recalled, English and Irish servants rather than slaves had worked the tobacco and sugar plantations. But the government of Charles II put a stop to that practice in the 1670s and 1680s by discouraging the emigration of white workers to the Americas and licensing, in its place, an English slave trade in African captives. If there were slaves in the British colonies, then, it was because English merchants carried them there and because the state encouraged them to do so. The colonists, themselves, did not organize the slave trade and, even more, did not like owning slaves, Robertson insisted. They continued to purchase African captives because slave labor produced the cheapest sugar, because, without slave labor, French and Dutch planters would undersell English colonists in European markets. The fact was, he concluded, the much-derided Caribbean planter lay at the mercy of forces beyond his control. He endured slave revolts, hurricanes and droughts, competition with French rivals, impositions from the state in the form of duties and taxes, and substantial debts to English merchants. Critics might think of planters as tyrants and plutocrats, but in truth they were, themselves, a kind of "Slaves . . . to their Creditors." "The Masters of the Slaves," he added, "neither are nor can be rich." They deserved pity more than contempt.[2]

---

commentary, Thomas W. Krise, "True Novel, False History: Robert Robertson's Ventriloquized Ex-Slave in 'the Speech of Mr. John Talbot Campo-Bell,'" *Early American Literature*, XXX (1995), 152–164; Krise, *Caribbeana: An Anthology of English Literature of the West Indies, 1657–1777* (Chicago, 1999), 108–109. Jack P. Greene has surveyed the problem of colonial identity in the political literature produced by the West Indian elite but, oddly, omits mention of Robertson. See Greene, "Liberty, Slavery, and the Transformation of British Identity in the Eighteenth-Century West Indies," *Slavery and Abolition*, XXI, no. 1 (April 2000), 1–31.

2. [Robertson], *A Letter to the Right Reverend the Lord Bishop of London*, 55, 127; [Robertson], *The Speech of Mr. John Talbot Campo-bell*, 127–133.

In any case, those in England had no right to judge. They, too, should bear responsibility for colonial slavery, since most of the profits, Robertson asserted, went to the crown, the traders, and "the nation." If slavery was wrong, he reasoned, then so was the slave trade. Yet British slave traders, he asserted, had escaped the condemnation of metropolitan critics. The complaint against human bondage, oddly, was "struck dumb" when the behavior of British merchants rather than American colonists was in question. Addressing the editors of the *Gentleman's Magazine,* Robertson posed the problem directly: "Can you or any Body for you, name any Man in *England* . . . among the boldest Assertors of *Natural Rights,* among the many mighty Partisans of the Cause of *Liberty,* who hath once publickly opened his Mouth, before the Court or any where else, on the Subject of the *Slave*-Trade on the Coast of *Guinea?* or so much attempted in any printed Sermon, Speech, or Pamphlet, to consider the Justice or Legality of it?" Such a selective application of moral principle struck Robertson as suspiciously self-interested. "To Fall into Error is consistent enough with humanity," he acknowledged. The initial involvement in the slave trade could be excused as a lapse. But to persist in the error "for above Seventy years," long after the horrors of the slave trade were known, displayed willful denial, bad faith, an ethics of convenience. The result was not only hypocrisy but a missed opportunity. Rather than insulting helpless colonists in the West Indies, British friends of liberty might instead have proposed alternatives to the slave trade and slave labor. There, the national interest truly lay. For "the happy (unincumber'd) nation," Robertson predicted, that pursued "the Path to true Glory" by putting "an effectual Stop to the horrid Slavery of its Fellow-Creatures, would become Arbiter of the Affairs (not of one Quarter only, but) of the greater Part of our Habitable World."[3]

No one in the early-eighteenth-century British Empire devoted more energy than Robert Robertson to defending the reputation of American slaveholders. A proslavery tradition scarcely existed when he published in the 1730s. Few thought to justify colonial slavery since the institution rarely came under sustained attack. Indeed, in some respects, the preoccupations

3. *Gentleman's Mag.,* XI (1741), 186–187; [Robertson], *The Speech of Mr. John Talbot Campo-bell,* 120; [Robertson], *A Letter to the Right Reverend the Lord Bishop of London,* 70.

that produced these pamphlets were deeply personal. Robertson's defensiveness is telling. The reverend sugar planter justified colonial slavery with a persistence that, in fact, betrayed nagging doubts about the moral character of his own choices. His ambivalence accounts, in part, for his occasional incoherence, for his bewildering tendency to excuse slaveholding on one page and decry it on the next. Like later apologists throughout the Anglo-American world, Robertson tried to have it both ways when confronted by antislavery opinion. He tried to excuse human bondage and, at the same time, to present himself as enlightened and humane. This need for absolution sometimes propelled him into extravagant claims. Robertson was wrong to suggest, as he probably knew, that British slave traders had escaped censure, that only colonial slaveholders had been charged with inhumanity.[4] Robertson, however, needed to think of men like himself as victims and scapegoats, as the sacrificial lambs that purified the national pursuit of wealth and power. To exonerate himself and others like him, he tried to spread the blame, particularly to those who would judge but escaped judgment. Robertson therefore had cause to dwell on the tension between the metropolitan investment in the idea of English liberty and the extensive material investment in the institution of slavery, a conflict that looks crystal clear in hindsight but at the time went largely ignored and often unnoticed.

The writings of Robert Robertson neatly introduce two of the defining features of British antislavery sentiment before the American Revolution. In the British Isles, there was a predisposition among some to judge slaveholding critically, but that impulse was tempered by an almost complete acceptance of the value of slavery to the colonies and to the empire. Antislavery sentiment did circulate in the early eighteenth century, as Robert Robertson's apologia suggests. He would have had no reason to publish these pamphlets otherwise. Yet organized efforts to abolish the slave system would not develop until much later, until the era of the Revolution. Instead

---

4. See most notably *A Letter from a Merchant at Jamaica to a Member of Parliament in London, Touching the African Trade; to Which Is Added, a Speech Made by a Black of Gardaloupe, at the Funeral of a Fellow-Negro* (London, 1709). This pamphlet is republished and discussed in Jack P. Greene, "'A plain and natural Right to Life and Liberty': An Early Natural Rights Attack on the Excesses of the Slave System in Colonial British America," *William and Mary Quarterly,* 3d Ser., VII (2000), 793–808.

(and this is a second defining feature of British attitudes in this period) critics tended to judge American slaveholders and Atlantic slave traders rather than British institutions and British policies. The physical distance between the American plantations and the British Isles, and the very different institutions that took root there, helped many in Britain to think of the slave system as a peculiarly colonial custom tenuously related to the values and needs of the nation and the state. A distasteful practice, some could agree, had emerged in the Americas. However, responsibility for the institution seemed to lie with those directly engaged in it, critics tended to assume, rather than with the British nation or the British government as a whole. In this way, a moral verdict in the British Isles against colonial slavery could coexist with the expansion of the slaving economy. Reservations about this compromise between expressed values and emerging colonial institutions did surface between 1660 and 1760, during the first century of plantation development. Some missionaries tried to "humanize" slavery during the first half of the eighteenth century by making human bondage a vehicle for Christian conversions and moral improvement. Certain social reformers and dissenting sects attempted to discourage the growth of slavery in particular American settlements. In England, enslaved Africans and their allies petitioned the courts to invalidate the practice of slaveholding on English soil. In each instance, these more localized conflicts had the potential to extend into more comprehensive challenges to the slave system itself. Nevertheless, for many decades, discomfort with slavery and slaveholders would have little impact on British politics or imperial governance. Until the American Revolution, there would be antislavery sentiment without abolitionism.

If antislavery sentiment, alone, could have caused an anti- [I]
slavery movement, the campaign against the British slave trade should have commenced at least fifty years before it did. Slave traders in Britain encountered public disapproval early in the eighteenth century, decades before the emergence of those cultural movements often credited for engendering antislavery sentiment, decades before the height of the Evangelical revival, or the apex of the European Enlightenment, or the emergence of a cult of sensibility. William Snelgrave noted in 1734 that "Several Objections have often been raised against the Lawfulness of this Trade." It "hath been charged with *Inhumanity,* and a Contradiction to *good morals,*" com-

plained another writer in the *London Magazine* in 1740. Six years later, a propagandist for the Royal Africa Company observed that "many are pre-possessed against the Trade, thinking it *a barbarous, unhuman, and unlawful traffic for a Christian Country to Trade in Blacks*." Discomfort with the slave system did not surprise its promoters. Indeed, they took such reservations for granted. They knew of men like the Reverend Thomas Rundle, who in 1734 made casual reference to the "honest reluctance in humanity against buying and selling, and regarding those of our own species as our wealth and possessions." If browsing through a copy of the *Old Whig* in 1737, they would have found "A.R." declaring that Africans had a natural right to liberty. An exhaustive troll through the printed record of the early eighteenth century would show that remarks like these were rare. More significant than their number, though, are the offhand manner in which they were expressed and the breadth of antislavery sentiment they assumed decades before antislavery movements developed.[5] The authors of these statements did not regard their opinions as controversial. Moral opposition to the enslavement of Africans required neither justification nor elaboration. It spoke for itself.

The antislavery values of the abolitionist era had distant antecedents, and not only in the British Isles. Certain Spanish and Portuguese commentators had bemoaned the horrors of the African slave trade and the enslave-

---

5. Citations from Snelgrave and the *London Magazine* appear in Wylie Sypher, *Guinea's Captive Kings: British Anti-Slavery Literature of the Eighteenth Century* (Chapel Hill, N.C., 1942), 13; Malachy Postlethwayt, *The National and Private Advantages Considered: Being an Enquiry, How Far It Concerns the Trading Interest of Great Britain, Effectively to Support and Maintain the Forts and Settlements in Africa; Belonging to the Royal African Company of England* (London, 1746), 4; Thomas Rundle cited in Betty Wood, *Slavery in Colonial Georgia, 1730–1775* (Athens, Ga., 1984), 211n; Michael Kraus, "Slavery Reform in the Eighteenth Century: An Aspect of Transatlantic Intellectual Cooperation," *Pennsylvania Magazine of History and Biography*, LX (1936), 57. I would concur, then, with the judgment of the literary critic John Richardson. "What marks attitudes, as far as printed materials show . . . is a kind of managed discomfort. Rather than being truly indifferent to slavery, many eighteenth century Englishmen seem to have found ways of circumventing their sense of its atrociousness. There is evidence that many people felt some revulsion towards slavery, but that they evaded the feeling and its implications for themselves by various mental maneuvers." Richardson, *Slavery and Augustan Literature: Swift, Pope, Gay* (London, 2004), 30.

ment of Africans long before the eighteenth century, indeed many decades before the establishment of the British colonies. Some stunned witnesses had wept in 1444 when a shipload of enslaved Africans was deposited in the Portuguese town of Lagos. A Spanish theologian, Tomas de Mercado, condemned the brutality of the Middle Passage in 1569 more than two centuries before the better-known and more consequential writings of Anthony Benezet. Jurist Bartolome de Albornoz asserted the natural right of enslaved Africans to liberty as early as 1573. Slaveholders in colonial Latin America faced adverse moral judgment more than a century before Robert Robertson tried to defend their Anglophone rivals in the Caribbean islands. A Jesuit priest in Brazil declared all slaveholders sinners in the 1580s. Another, Alonso de Sandoval, devoted more than forty years of his life to ministering among the black captives disembarked from slave ships in Cartagena. His 1627 exposé of the horrid conditions endured by slaves arriving in the West Indies predated the similar but better-known work of the Reverend James Ramsay of Saint Kitts by more than a century and a half. Cuban authorities felt obliged in the early 1680s to silence two Capuchin missionaries who insisted that planters had no legitimate claim to slave labor and that the captives had a right to wages for unpaid work.[6] These hostile assessments of slavery arose more from the particular personalities and needs of the individual critics than from the teachings of the Catholic Church, which, like all organized churches in the early modern era, accommodated itself to human bondage.[7] The complaints of these

6. David Brion Davis, *The Problem of Slavery in Western Culture,* 2d ed., rev. (Oxford, 1988), 181–196; Robin Blackburn, *The Making of New World Slavery: From the Baroque to the Modern, 1492–1800* (London, 1997), 103–105, 150–156, 177–178, 207–210, 287–289, 329–330; John M. Lenhart, "Capuchin Champions of Negro Emancipation in Cuba, 1681–1685," *Franciscan Studies,* VI (1946), 195–217; David G. Sweet, "Black Robes and Black Destiny: Jesuit Views of African Slavery in Seventeenth Century Latin America," *Revista de Historia de America,* LXXXVI (1978), 91–98; A. J. R. Russell-Wood, "Iberian Expansion and the Issue of Black Slavery: Changing Portuguese Attitudes, 1440–1770," *American Historical Review,* LXXXIII (1978), 35–37.

7. In 1686 the Holy Office did back a series of propositions drafted by the ostracized Capuchin missionaries in Cuba that condemned the enslavement and sale of Africans unjustly deprived of liberty. The Catholic Church, in this instance, took action at the behest of the Christian Afro-Brazilian leader Lourenco da Savila de Mendouca, who presented the Propagande de Fide (the missionary arm of the Catholic Church) with a

early protesters represented exclamations of moral sentiment as much as studied ruminations or reasoned deductions on human equality.

The history of antislavery thought, therefore, must be approached with care. We should resist the inclination to view the antislavery movements of the late eighteenth century as the working out of cultural trends or as the consequence of a series of intellectual steps that ascended to a break-through in moral perception. The long history of sincere but inconsequential protest belies such narratives of cultural progress. Antislavery thought in the eighteenth century did not build cumulatively, block by block, to a higher stage of moral consciousness. The essentials of the case against the enslavement of Africans had been articulated long before the antislavery movements began. Nor did the intensity of antislavery sentiment swell to a breaking point in the late eighteenth century from which it loosed abolitionist fervor across the cultural landscape. Politics, as we will see, more than public opinion, placed slave trade abolition on the public agenda. Instead, for many decades, antislavery sentiment lay dormant, inert, and ineffective in the Anglo-American world, sufficient to raise moral doubts but unable to stimulate political action. Intellectual and cultural legacies informed and prepared, but they did not prescribe.[8] Several of the key activists in the late eighteenth century did read the works of their predecessors and self-consciously expanded on their insights. This would be true of the Quaker activist Anthony Benezet in particular.[9] More often, though, the history of antislavery sentiment before the 1760s is the history of isolated moralists, often clergy from the various Protestant denomina-

petition in 1684 detailing the cruelties and injustices of the slave trade. The governments of Spain and Portugal, however, took no notice of the resulting antislavery resolutions issued from Rome. Richard Gray, "The Papacy and the Atlantic Slave Trade: Lourenco da Silva, the Capuchins, and the Decisions of the Holy Office," *Past and Present*, no. 115 (May 1987), 52–68. For a sketch of the tangled history of Catholic doctrine with respect to colonial slavery, see John F. Maxwell, *Slavery and the Catholic Church: The History of Catholic Teaching concerning the Moral Legitimacy of the Institution of Slavery* (Chichester, Eng., 1975).

8. Davis, *The Problem of Slavery in Western Culture*.

9. Maurice Jackson, "The Social and Intellectual Origins of Anthony Benezet's Antislavery Radicalism," supplemental issue to *Pennsylvania History*, LXVI (1999), 86–112.

tions, first reacting to the inhumanities they witnessed, and then laboring (often unassisted) to denounce institutions in which the vast majority of their contemporaries had acquiesced.[10]

Intellectual traditions constitute just one part of the story. In important ways, the origin of antislavery was slavery itself. A first encounter with the Atlantic slave trade sometimes made the squeamish uneasy. In the early seventeenth century, it took a decade for the directors of the Dutch West India Company to overcome the objections of its theological advisers, who opposed an entry into the Atlantic slave trade on moral grounds. An English merchant traveling up the Gambia River in 1618 famously refused to purchase slaves because, he explained, "we were a people who did not deale in any such commodities, neither did wee buy or sell one another, or any that had our owne shapes." Naval surgeon John Atkins declared the slave trade an "extensive Evil" on returning in the early 1730s to England from his first visit to the coast of Africa and the West Indies. Instances of

10. These points seem worth emphasizing, given the deservedly influential account Davis presents in *The Problem of Slavery in Western Culture*. There Davis demonstrates that human bondage long had been a source of tension in Western European thought. However, cultural shifts that took place during the eighteenth century helped make slavery, for the first time, appear barbaric, unjust, counterproductive, and sinful. The new value that the polite assigned to benevolence and sympathy for the downtrodden, the enlightened skepticism toward prescriptive authority, the growing confidence in the capacity to improve both individuals and institutions, the Evangelical belief in the possibility of redemption from original sin, and the increasingly sympathetic image of the African in arts and literature—these developments reinforced doubts about the justice and morality of slavery. Consequently, "by the early 1770s," Davis wrote, "a large number of moralists, poets, intellectuals, and reformers had come to regard American slavery as an unmitigated evil" (488). See also the restatement of the argument in Davis, *The Problem of Slavery in the Age of Revolution*, 39–49. If the conclusion is incontestable, its implications may mislead by seeming to render the emergence of abolitionism, thereafter, as a foregone conclusion. Davis does summon considerable evidence of suppressed impulses, false starts, and haphazard development in his account. The organization of the book, however, with its progression through ancient, medieval, early modern, and Enlightenment responses to slavery, can tend to suggest a linear unfolding of antislavery ideas and values. That interpretive tradition, I suggest, overemphasizes the march of ideas and wrongly minimizes the social and political contexts that allowed ideas to matter.

moral doubt pepper the early history of slaveholding in the British Atlantic. The founders of Rhode Island and Pennsylvania showed reluctance, initially, to permit servitude for life: the Rhode Island General Court in 1652 established a ten-year ceiling on terms of service for all men and women, African and European, brought to the colony; years later, William Penn proposed fourteen-year indentures for slaves imported to Pennsylvania. Sometimes slavery took shape in the British colonies in the face of local opposition. Samuel Rishworth caused a furor in the short-lived Caribbean colony of Providence Island by encouraging newly imported slaves to liberate themselves. Quaker visitors to Bermuda urged the enslaved to petition the governor for their freedom. In Pennsylvania, the importation and use of slaves remained a subject of periodic controversy across the first three decades of settlement.[11]

The great majority of British settlers adapted to slaveholding with little difficulty. Predictably, those expecting to profit from slave labor adapted the quickest; those less likely to benefit from the enslavement of Africans sometimes adjusted more slowly. In the seventeenth century especially, indentured servants occasionally found common cause with the enslaved, particularly when both suffered from exploitation by plantation owners. Historian Hilary Beckles has described how Irish servants and African

---

11. Cornelius Ch. Goslinga, *The Dutch in the Caribbean and on the Wild Coast, 1580–1680* (Gainesville, Fla., 1971), 146; Maarten Kuitenbrouwer, "The Dutch Case of Antislavery: Late Abolitions and Élitist Abolitionism," in Gert Oostindie, ed., *Fifty Years Later: Antislavery, Capitalism, and Modernity in the Dutch Orbit* (Pittsburgh, Pa., 1996), 68; Richard Jobson, *The Golden Trade; or, A Discovery of the River Gambra, and the Golden Trade of the Aethiopians . . .* (1623; rpt. London, 1968), 112; John Atkins, *A Voyage to Guinea, Brasil, and the West-Indies in His Majesty's Ships, the "Swallow" and "Weymouth"* (1735; rpt. London, 1970), 149, also see 176–179; Elizabeth Donnan, ed., *Documents Illustrative of the History of the Slave Trade to America*, III, *New England and the Middle Colonies* (Washington, D.C., 1932), 4, 108; Thomas E. Drake, *Quakers and Slavery in America* (New Haven, Conn., 1950), 10–16, 18–22; Karen Ordahl Kupperman, *Providence Island, 1630–1641* (Cambridge, 1993), 168–169, 177, 243–244; Michael Jarvis, review of Virginia Bernhard, *Slaves and Slaveholders in Bermuda, 1616–1782, WMQ*, 3d Ser., LVII (2000), 686. For a forceful statement about the significance of antislavery thought in the late seventeenth century, see Philippe Rosenberg, "Thomas Tryon and the Seventeenth-Century Dimensions of Antislavery," *WMQ*, 3d Ser., LXI (2004), 609–642.

slaves together formed refugee maroon settlements in the Barbados hinterland during the 1650s. The rebellion in 1676 of the disaffected led by Virginia settler Nathaniel Bacon drew strength from an alliance among dozens of slaves and servants. The Montserrat legislature in the late seventeenth century thought white aid to black freedom struggles sufficiently frequent to merit a raft of disciplinary codes against interracial fraternizing. It took a concerted effort by colonial lawmakers throughout British America to distinguish chattel slavery from indentured servitude and, thereby, to discourage poor whites from identifying with or assisting the enslaved.[12]

Still, no law could prohibit sensitive souls from being affected by the scenes they witnessed. The most pointed denunciations before the late eighteenth century often came from those with direct experience of colonial slavery. The first antislavery pamphleteers, writers like Thomas Tryon, Morgan Godwin, and William Edmundson, composed their pioneering antislavery tracts soon after their first exposure to human bondage.[13] Until the 1760s in the British Atlantic world, antislavery publications—pamphlets concerned solely with the immorality or injustice of slavery—came exclusively from men and women who had seen slavery for themselves.[14] Early antislavery sentiment, then, had emotional as well as intellectual founda-

12. Hilary McD. Beckles, "Rebels and Reactionaries: The Political Responses of White Labourers to Planter-Class Hegemony in Seventeenth Century Barbados," *Journal of Caribbean History*, XV (1981), 9–10, 15, 17; T. H. Breen, *Puritans and Adventurers: Change and Persistence in Early America* (Oxford, 1980), 127–147; Riva Berleant-Schiller, "Free Labor and the Economy in Seventeenth-Century Montserrat," *WMQ*, 3d Ser., XLVI (1989), 560–561; Philip D. Morgan, *Slave Counterpoint: Black Culture in the Eighteenth-Century Chesapeake and Lowcountry* (Chapel Hill, N.C., 1998), 8–18. For an overview of the early slave laws in the Caribbean colonies, see Richard S. Dunn, *Sugar and Slaves: The Rise of the Planter Class in the English West Indies, 1624–1713* (Chapel Hill, N.C., 1972), 238–246; Warren M. Billings, "The Law of Servants and Slaves in Seventeenth-Century Virginia," *Virginia Magazine of History and Biography*, XCIX (1991), 45–62; and Anthony S. Parent, Jr., *Foul Means: The Formation of a Slave Society in Virginia, 1660–1740* (Chapel Hill, N.C., 2003), 105–134.

13. Davis, *The Problem of Slavery in Western Culture*, 204–206, 307, 339–341; Alden T. Vaughan, *Roots of American Racism: Essays on the Colonial Experience* (Oxford, 1995), 55–81.

14. I do not include, of course, the countless instances in which antislavery sentiments appeared in publications primarily concerned with other subjects.

tions. It sometimes represented more (or perhaps less) than the working out of abstract ideas. Antislavery sentiment often flowed as much from the commands of the heart as from the exercise of the intellect. Extemporaneous declamations supplemented reasoned denunciations. Moral outrage occurred at least as frequently as studied argument. "It chills one's blood," Horace Walpole famously exclaimed in 1750 when reflecting to a friend on the forty-six thousand "wretches" carried by British ships to the Americas the previous year.[15]

Colonial slavery would have been less troubling if human bondage had been more familiar. Villeinage, the only legal form of human bondage in England, had fallen into disuse by the early sixteenth century. Subsequent attempts in the Tudor era to enslave vagrants and criminals failed from want of official and public support.[16] In the British Isles, there was nothing remotely like chattel slavery, although in the eighteenth century certain aspects of the institution had domestic analogues. Severe restraints on their autonomy and mobility left most apprentices, servants, and day laborers in England a species of unfree labor. Involuntary service in parish workhouses increasingly was the prescribed fate for the orphaned and impoverished. Routinely and legally in time of war, the admiralty forcibly impressed sailors into the Royal Navy, a practice that its opponents sometimes derided as a form of slavery. Like slaveholders, ship captains enforced discipline with the whip. Scottish coal miners were tied for life to the mines they worked. More generally, in England, property in persons was common. Under the common law, the head of a household held property in his dependents—in his wife, their children, the resident servants. Still, the authority exercised by slaveholders in the Americas was something new in

15. Horace Walpole to Horace Mann, Feb. 25, 1750, cited in Davis, *The Problem of Slavery in Western Culture*, 150n.

16. C. S. L. Davies, "Slavery and Protector Somerset: The Vagrancy Act of 1547," *Economic History Review*, 2d Ser., XIX (1966), 533–549; J. H. Baker, "Personal Liberty under the Common Law of England, 1200–1600," in R. W. Davis, ed., *The Origins of Modern Freedom in the West* (Palo Alto, Calif., 1995), 178–202; Michael J. Guasco, "Encounters, Identities, and Human Bondage: The Foundations of Racial Slavery in the Anglo-Atlantic World" (Ph.D. diss., College of William and Mary, 2000), 24–44; Guasco, "Settling with Slavery: Human Bondage in the Early Anglo-Atlantic World," in Robert Applebaum and John Wood Sweet, eds., *Envisioning an English Empire: Jamestown and the Making of the North Atlantic World* (Philadelphia, 2005), 241–244.

both scope and kind. In England, poor men sometimes sold their wives on the open market, and, in the Americas, employers routinely sold and purchased the contracts of convicts and indentured servants. Yet neither traffic occurred on a scale approaching the trade in African labor.[17] Moreover, enslaved Africans suffered a degree of powerlessness in the colonies wholly without equal elsewhere in British dominions. The potentially interminable length of service, the transmission of unfree status from parent to child, and

17. Robert J. Steinfeld, *The Invention of Free Labor: The Employment Relation in English and American Law, 1350–1870* (Chapel Hill, N.C., 1991), 1–120; David Eltis, "Labour and Coercion in the English Atlantic World from the Seventeenth to the Early Twentieth Century," *Slavery and Abolition*, XIV, no. 1 (April 1993), 207–226; Nicholas Rogers, "Vagrancy, Impressment, and the Regulation of Labour in Eighteenth-Century Britain," *Slavery and Abolition*, XV, no. 2 (August 1994), 102–113; Tim Hitchcock, "Paupers and Preachers: The SPCK and the Parochial Workhouse Movement," in Lee Davison et al., *Stilling the Grumbling Hive: The Response to Social and Economic Problems in England, 1689–1750* (New York, 1992), 145–166; Marcus Rediker, *Between the Devil and the Deep Blue Sea: Merchant Seamen, Pirates, and the Anglo-American Maritime World, 1700–1750* (Cambridge, 1987), 212–222; Peter Earle, *Sailors: English Merchant Seamen, 1650–1775* (London, 1998), 145–158, 189–194, 199–202; Daniel James Ennis, *Enter the Press-Gang: Naval Impressment in Eighteenth-Century British Literature* (Newark, Del., 2002), 125–126; Baron F. Duckham, "Serfdom in Eighteenth Century Scotland," *History*, LIV (1969), 178–197; P. E. H. Hair, "Slavery and Liberty: The Case of the Scottish Colliers," *Slavery and Abolition*, XXI, no. 3 (December 2000), 136–151; Teresa Michals, " 'That Sole and Despotic Dominion': Slaves, Wives, and Game in Blackstone's *Commentaries,*" *Eighteenth Century Studies*, XXVII (1993–1994), 195–216; E. P. Thompson, *Customs in Common* (London, 1991), 404–462; A. Roger Ekirch, *Bound for America: The Transportation of British Convicts to the Colonies, 1718–1775* (Oxford, 1987); Alan Atkinson, "The Free-Born Englishman Transported: Convict Rights as a Measure of Eighteenth-Century Empire," *Past and Present*, no. 144 (August 1994), 88–108; David W. Galenson, *Traders, Planters, and Slaves: Market Behavior in Early English America* (Cambridge, 1986); Christopher Tomlins, "Early British America, 1585–1830: Freedom Bound," in Douglas Hay and Paul Craven, eds., *Masters, Servants, and Magistrates in Britain and the Empire, 1562–1955* (Chapel Hill, N.C., 2004), 117–152; David Eltis, *The Rise of African Slavery in the Americas* (Cambridge, 2000), 5–7. For a particularly effective delineation of the different experiences of enslaved men and women and poor whites in the colonies, see Philip D. Morgan, "The Poor: Slaves in Early America," in David Eltis, Frank D. Lewis, and Kenneth L. Sokoloff, *Slavery in the Development of the Americas* (Cambridge, 2004), 288–323.

the lack of access to legal protection (particularly in the plantation colonies) distinguished the servitude of slaves from the servitude of English laborers. Dishonor, distinctions in rank, physical abuse, and a varying claim to rights and privileges were familiar to the British and regarded as unremarkable. The legal apparatus constructed to define the place of African slaves, however, was an innovation, a deviation from customary English practice.

In the long run, the novelty of chattel slavery in the colonies and the uncertain legality of human bondage in the British Isles would prove critical to the rise of abolitionism. The conflict between the opponents and defenders of slavery would emerge out of the tensions between metropolitan and colonial norms. The turn against colonial slavery in late-eighteenth-century Britain would represent less a sudden revolution in moral consciousness than the imposition of existing metropolitan customs on the dependent plantation societies of the Americas.[18] Historians of antislavery thought, it now seems, have given too little attention to the way institutional bulwarks against arbitrary power in England became entwined with a precocious sense of English national identity. In the late sixteenth and early seventeenth centuries, just as they began to establish American colonies, the English started to think of themselves as unusually and distinctively free. In the protection of personal liberty, the common law was fundamental. By 1600, it was taken to either have delimited or eliminated private jurisdiction in England, subjecting everyone, regardless of status, to

18. Seymour Drescher, *Capitalism and Antislavery: British Mobilization in Comparative Perspective* (London, 1987), 12–24; Drescher, "The Antislavery Debate: Capitalism and Abolitionism as a Problem in Historical Interpretation," *History and Theory,* XXXII (1993), 328–329; Eltis, *The Rise of African Slavery in the Americas,* 7, 281–283. In an important essay, Michal Rozbicki has drawn attention to early eighteenth-century schemes to enslave the poor in England. In each instance, these schemes were conceived to transform the idle into laborers for the public good. Bondage remained an imaginable option for the poor at least until 1750. But it matters that, in each instance, this bondage was to be regulated by the state and by the church rather than by individual owners. As I intend to make clear, in chapter 4 particularly, antislavery thought in England tended to concentrate on the abuses arising from the absolute jurisdiction of individual masters rather than enslavement as such. The aim would be to establish well-ordered societies in the Americas, not to defend "natural rights." See Michal J. Rozbicki, "To Save Them from Themselves: Proposals to Enslave the British Poor, 1698–1755," *Slavery and Abolition,* XXII, no. 2 (August 2001), 29–50.

the rule of law. The most immediate benefit was due process, which, in practical terms, meant trial by jury, an independent judiciary, protection against arbitrary imprisonment, procedural remedies for unlawful detentions, and safeguards for the protection of property. Of equal importance to the emerging idea of liberty was constitutional government. Parliament emerged from a turbulent era of revolution, restoration, and dynastic rivalry by the early eighteenth century as the guarantor of public liberty, as the principal restraint on royal absolutism, and as the champion of Protestantism in a Europe dominated by Catholic rulers. The conjoined sovereign of king-in-parliament, it was understood, ensured that the monarch ruled responsibly, that the liberties of the subject were secure. This arrangement, it was believed, had put an end to the internecine conflicts of the seventeenth century and made possible the growth of commerce and national power, which also, increasingly, were identified as cornerstones of English liberty and, after the union of Scotland and England in 1707, British liberty.[19]

The British were immensely proud of this history. It taught them to see themselves as uniquely favored, to see their freedom as part of a distinctive national inheritance. This self-conscious devotion to liberty helped keep the British from lavishing praise on colonial slaveholding, even as the nation and state profited from the colonial trade in the staples that slaves produced. More important, this history instilled certain assumptions about power that, in the end, would prove threatening to the practice of human bondage in the colonies. The British tended to believe that political authority was legitimate when it was limited and constitutional rather than arbitrary and absolute. Where there was no law, many assumed, there was tyranny. Moreover, the purpose of government, most accepted, was to serve the public good rather than its own purposes. There was in some circles a growing confidence in the power of human reason and an accompanying skepticism toward prescriptive authority. The moral and political philosophy of the era tended to take for granted the possibility of human progress.

19. Helpful introductions to this rich and complex history may be gleaned from Baker, "Personal Liberty," in Davis, ed., *Origins of Modern Freedom,* 178–202, and the essays collected in J. H. Hexter, ed., *Parliament and Liberty: From the Reign of Elizabeth to the Civil War* (Stanford, Calif., 1992), and in J. R. Jones, ed., *Liberty Secured? Britain before and after 1688* (Palo Alto, Calif., 1992).

The countless public projects that the upper and middling classes promoted to better the commonweal reflected the prevailing ethos of improvement.[20] This reverence for liberty, progress, and improvement, of course,
failed to inspire political opposition to slavery during the first century and a
half of colonial settlement. All understood the ways that overseas slavery
enhanced British freedom and happiness. What matters, however, is that
the British thought of themselves as champions of liberty and accepted that
gradual and incremental changes to public institutions sometimes best
advanced national interests. In the last quarter of the eighteenth century,
under a peculiar set of circumstances, Britons' abiding need to think of
themselves as a people uniquely dedicated to liberty would make it difficult
for them to regard overseas slavery with complacency.

An antislavery prejudice, then, did percolate below the surface of Anglo-
American culture between 1660 and 1760, even as the plantation economy
expanded and the wealth and power that it generated grew. To the uniniti-
ated, the brutalities of colonial slavery could seem inhumanely cruel. In
England, there was a reflexive unease with institutions that allowed for
arbitrary, extralegal authority. The institution of slavery, moreover, seemed
to transgress traditional notions of Christian propriety and stewardship. It
made a mockery of the mission to spread the gospel of Christ. No business
could be good, it seemed to some, if it led masters to treat men and women
like brutes. A culture of sympathy made it increasingly fashionable by the
middle of the eighteenth century to romanticize enslaved Africans as exemplars of wounded innocence. The moral philosophy of sentiment encouraged the conscientious to imagine their way into unfamiliar experiences,
to judge from feeling and not merely from rules. And as David Brion Davis
has emphasized, the luminaries of the Enlightenment increasingly subjected human bondage to a sustained critique. It would have been difficult,
as Robert Robertson knew, to find many in the British Isles willing to
describe colonial slavery and the Atlantic trade as an emblem of social,
cultural, or moral progress during the mid-eighteenth century, however
important these institutions were to both collective and individual wealth
and power. These reservations were real and substantial, but, on balance,

20. Paul Langford, *A Polite and Commercial People: England, 1727–1783* (Oxford,
1989), 389–459; Roy Porter, *The Creation of the Modern World: The Untold Story of the
British Enlightenment* (London, 2000).

they presented no real threat to the several interests aligned behind the slave system.

The enslavement of Africans in the Americas appeared to the first English sojourners as a necessary fact of colonial settlement. Like the distinctive topography, flora, fauna, and peoples, the institutions of human bondage made the New World new. They helped define the differences between the Americas and Europe. When the first English settlers established colonies during the reign of James I, enslaved Africans had been laboring in the Americas for more than a century. English colonists hoping to make their fortunes had in front of them the example of the Spanish tobacco fields on the Venezuelan coast and the Portuguese sugar plantations of Brazil. Matching their success seemed to mean tapping into the Spanish and Portuguese supplies of African labor. African slaves first entered the English colonies as booty seized from Spanish settlements or as captives sold off of Dutch ships. By employing slaves in the new settlements of Virginia, Barbados, Bermuda, and Providence Island during the early seventeenth century, the English were not so much innovating as catching up. A vast body of scholarship has treated the origins of slavery in the English settlements as a historical problem. Yet, given the precedents set elsewhere in the Americas before the English arrived, a refusal to acquire and employ slaves would have been the truly surprising choice. In the Americas, those who had access to slave labor, and could afford the price, bought slaves. If a similar practice might have been thought of as repugnant in Britain, it seemed permissible to tolerate in the colonies customs undesirable in the metropole. When English courts wished to sentence men and women to involuntary labor during the eighteenth century, they shipped them to America, where the slaves were.[21]

21. On the importance of the Spanish and Portuguese precedents for slavery in seventeenth-century English colonies, see April Lee Hatfield, "A 'Very Wary People in Their Bargaining' or 'Very Good Marchandise': English Traders' Views of Free and Enslaved Africans, 1550–1650," *Slavery and Abolition*, XXV, no. 3 (December 2004), 1–17, and Guasco, "Encounters, Identities, and Human Bondage," 350–405, 465–468, 478–482, although note that his "Settling with Slavery," in Applebaum and Sweet, eds., *Envisioning an English Empire*, offers a somewhat different view (see 250). For recent overviews of the "origins debate," see Alden T. Vaughan, "The Origins Debate: Slavery and Racism in Seventeenth-Century Virginia," in Vaughan, *Roots of American Racism*, 136–174. For the Dutch provenance of the first slaves in British North America, see Engel

It helped, of course, that the African men and women purchased by American colonists and their suppliers were already slaves, from a European point of view. European traders on the African coast raided for captives on occasion. In most instances, though, ship captains did not have to enslave anyone. They had only to purchase from local merchants and rulers captives enslaved by others. If the enslaved had been Christians, European traders might have arranged for their rescue rather than their transportation and resale in the colonies. The English spent a tidy sum in the sixteenth and seventeenth century ransoming English sailors captured by Muslims in North Africa and the Levant.[22] But for those Europeans who visited the West African coast, the dark-skinned captives available for sale seemed sufficiently different, physically as well as culturally, to perpetuate their enslavement. That sense of racial difference would help quell potential doubts in both the Americas and Europe about the legitimacy of slavery. It now seems certain that coherent theories of biological difference did not take concrete shape until the early nineteenth century. What matters more, though, as David Eltis has stressed, were the prevailing assumptions among Europeans, including Britons, about who deserved enslavement. In the end, the English, like other Europeans, declined the opportunity to systematically enslave men and women of their own nation or from elsewhere in the British Isles, although only after a brief period in the mid-seventeenth century when authorities experimented with spiriting political prisoners, Irish rebels, children, and the luckless poor into West Indian servitude. The cosmopolitan and the intensely pious might think of Africans, in theory, as human beings and fellow creatures. Yet, in practice, Europeans

---

Sluiter, "New Light on the '20. and Odd Negroes,' Arriving in Virginia, August 1619," *WMQ*, 3d Ser., LIV (1997), 395–398, and John Thornton, "The African Experience of the '20. and Odd Negroes' Arriving in Virginia in 1619," ibid., LV (1998), 421–434. For the convict trade, see Ekirch, *Bound for America*.

22. Ellen G. Friedman, "Christian Captives at 'Hard Labor' in Algiers, Sixteenth–Eighteenth Centuries," *International Journal of African Historical Studies*, XIII (1980), 616–632; Roslyn L. Knutson, "Elizabethan Documents, Captivity Narratives, and the Market for Foreign History Plays," *English Literary Renaissance*, XXVI (1996), 75–110; G. E. Aylmer, "Slavery under Charles II: The Mediterranean and Tangier," *English Historical Review*, CXIV (1999), 378–388; Linda Colley, *Captives* (New York, 2002), 48–56, 75–81; Guasco, "Settling with Slavery," in Applebaum and Sweet, eds., *Envisioning an English Empire*, 244–250.

both at home and in the colonies learned to associate slavery with black skin and, of equal importance, found it difficult to imagine Africans as the equal of Europeans. Few in England thought of Africans as natural slaves, in an Aristotelian sense. At the same time, many did seem to assume that, in some way, the African captives, as heathens, savages, and inferiors, had deserved their fate. Assumptions about racial difference would limit the development of a sincere concern for unfree Africans throughout the eighteenth century, even as antislavery campaigns first took shape.[23]

Physical distance compounded the obstacles presented by racial difference. Slavery often was out of mind because it was very much out of sight. The British enjoyed the fruits of slavery while incurring few of its social or cultural costs. Not faced daily with the dangers of living in a slave society, the residents of the British Isles had no immediate reason to dwell on the customs taking shape several thousands of miles away. The anxieties that gave urgency to colonial debates about controlling the growth of slavery meant little to those safe from the prospect of insurrection or revolution. Through novels, poetry, plays, works of moral philosophy, charity sermons, ethnologies, and economic treatises many in Britain learned to see Africans as exemplars of primitive and uncorrupted human nature, unfortunates deserving sympathy, and possessors of redeemable souls as well as

23. Eltis, *The Rise of African Slavery in the Americas*. Seymour Drescher correctly observes that Eltis unduly minimizes the political and institutional barriers to producing English captives for the new colonies on a systematic basis. See Drescher, "White Atlantic? The Choice for African Slave Labor in the Plantation Americas," in Eltis, Lewis, and Sokoloff, eds., *Slavery in the Development of the Americas*, 31–69. The transportation of children to the colonies is treated in John Wareing, "Preventive and Punitive Regulation in Seventeenth-Century Social Policy: Conflicts of Interest and the Failure to Make 'Stealing and Transporting Children, and Other Persons,' a Felony, 1645–73," *Social History*, XXVII (2002), 296–299. The large literature on English attitudes toward Africans in the era of the Atlantic slave trade continues to swell. From a very large literature, my brief comments here draw particularly on Winthrop D. Jordan, *White over Black: American Attitudes toward the Negro, 1550–1812* (Chapel Hill, N.C., 1968); Anthony J. Barker, *The African Link: British Attitudes to the Negro in the Era of the Atlantic Slave Trade, 1550–1807* (London, 1978); Vaughan, *Roots of American Racism;* Kim F. Hall, *Things of Darkness: Economies of Race and Gender in Early Modern England* (Ithaca, N.Y., 1995); and Roxann Wheeler, *The Complexion of Race: Categories of Difference in Eighteenth-Century British Culture* (Philadelphia, 2000).

unfree laborers. Yet this exposure was too abstract and remote to be of compelling interest when in competition with workaday concerns.

A profound ambivalence, in fact, nested in the antislavery prejudices extant in the colonial era. If few would offer a moral defense of slavery, not everyone believed that English customs and conventions required extra-territorial application. The professors of the new science of human society, moreover, conveyed a mixed message. By affirming the sanctity of the individual and by describing society as the product of evolutionary growth through successive stages, they provided a defense to property rights on one hand and justification for resisting radical change on the other. The sympathy of the man of feeling could just as easily express itself in empty moralizing as in concerted political action, since the "delectable tear" often mattered most.[24] If the English in the eighteenth century made a fetish of liberty, they tended to consider it a national possession peculiar to English soil and inappropriate for less civilized people and to define it in a way that reinforced social hierarchies rather than undermined them. Metropolitan doubts about human bondage in the colonies, moreover, tended to shrink before more powerful opinions about the nature of the empire taking shape in the Americas. As David Armitage and Kathleen Wilson have shown, the empire had become a source of public pride by the mid-eighteenth century, a pride that derived in part from the belief that it differed qualitatively from its forerunners and contemporaries. The British knew their overseas empire as Protestant, commercial, maritime, and free, and that self-conception helped quiet suggestions that exploitative, territorially aggressive, and tyrannical regimes were developing in their colonies.[25] These more positive

24. For the limits of early antislavery thought, see particularly Davis, *The Problem of Slavery in Western Culture,* and Sypher, *Guinea's Captive Kings.* The mixed legacy of the Enlightenment for American attitudes toward slavery receives thoughtful treatment in Nancy V. Morrow, "The Problem of Slavery in the Polemic Literature of the American Enlightenment," *Early Am. Lit.,* XX (1985), 236–255. For the initial reluctance to bring overseas colonies into conformity with metropolitan legal norms, see Eliga H. Gould, "Zones of Law, Zones of Violence: The Legal Geography of the British Atlantic, circa 1772," *WMQ,* 3d Ser., LX (2003), 471–510.

25. Kathleen Wilson, *The Sense of the People: Politics, Culture, and Imperialism in England, 1715–1785* (Cambridge, 1995); David Armitage, *The Ideological Origins of the British Empire* (Cambridge, 2000); Suvir Kaul, *Poems of Nation, Anthems of Empire: English Verse in the Long Eighteenth Century* (Charlottesville, Va., 2000). See also Pat-

ideas of empire could, then, "contextualize" the more upsetting reports about British societies overseas. The worst abuses might be excused as a lapse and unrepresentative of a nation devoted to the expansion of liberty. Behind such apologies lay a more pragmatic mindset. One might indeed wish that the pursuit of wealth would remain in ethical bounds. But, at a time when the expansion of commerce stirred patriotic hearts, too much sensitivity to the less savory consequences of overseas expansion could look like unsophisticated carping against the public good.

Above all, the British slave system operated nearly unopposed for more than a century because it produced spectacular results for a variety of commercial, public, and official interests. Owning an American plantation gave entrepreneurs the chance to make substantial fortunes. For British manufacturers, the slave trade and colonial slavery enlarged the market for their exports in both America and Europe. For British merchants, slave-produced commodities helped expand domestic markets and facilitate access to European ports. For British consumers, the slave plantations in the British Empire made exotic luxuries like sugar and tobacco affordable. British slave traders purchased African captives predominantly with the textiles imported by the East India Company, which benefited also from the new market in England for tea encouraged by greater imports of sugar. Colonial trade expanded the demand for ships, thereby fostering the growth of the shipping industry. The North Atlantic ports constructed or enlarged during the eighteenth century in Bristol, Liverpool, Cork, Boston, Newport, New York, and Philadelphia all depended heavily on trade with the plantation colonies. Increased overseas trade added to the supply of trained sailors available to the Royal Navy. Atlantic commerce provided a key source of revenue for the state. For the nation, it promoted a sense of national greatness and independence from European rivals. With the crucial exception of the slaves themselves, everyone seemed to benefit.[26] Only

---

rick K. O'Brien, "Inseparable Connections: Trade, Economy, Fiscal State, and the Expansion of Empire, 1688–1815," in P. J. Marshall, ed., *The Oxford History of the British Empire*, II, *The Eighteenth Century* (Oxford, 1998), 70–74.

26. The vast and growing scholarship on the contribution of slavery and the slave trade to the British economy is nicely synthesized and assessed in Kenneth Morgan, *Slavery, Atlantic Trade, and the British Economy, 1660–1800* (Cambridge, 2000), although see also David Eltis and Stanley L. Engerman, "The Importance of Slavery and

in the nineteenth century, several years after the antislavery movement began and the slave trade had been abolished, did this coalition of interests begin to diverge.

The slave system, then, enjoyed what looked like insurmountable political support before the Revolutionary era. Both the plantation colonies and the network of Atlantic slave traders sustained lobbies to see that Parliament and the crown honored their needs and interests.[27] Those who disliked the slave system, by contrast, represented an ungathered constituency without an advocate. As a result, the many who expressed unhappiness

---

the Slave Trade to Industrializing Britain," *Journal of Economic History*, LX (2000), 123–144, and Joseph E. Inikori, *Africans and the Industrial Revolution in England: A Study in International Trade and Economic Development* (Cambridge, 2002). The place of slavery in the growing English taste for exotic goods is treated in Sidney W. Mintz, *Sweetness and Power: The Place of Sugar in Modern History* (New York, 1985), 74–150, and James Walvin, *Fruits of Empire: Exotic Produce and British Taste* (New York, 1997). For a compelling sketch of the centrality of slavery and the slave trade to the British Atlantic economy at the microeconomic level, see David Hancock, *Citizens of the World: London Merchants and the Integration of the British Atlantic Community, 1735–1785* (Cambridge, 1995). Madge Dresser provides a detailed account of the ways slavery influenced social and economic development in an important British city, in Dresser, *Slavery Obscured: The Social History of the Slave Trade in an English Provincial Port* (London, 2001), esp. chaps. 1–3. See also David Richardson, "Slavery and Bristol's 'Golden Age,'" *Slavery and Abolition*, XXVI, no. 1 (April 2005), 47–49. Richardson concludes that "up to 40 per cent or more of Bristol's income in 1790 . . . derived from slave-related trades" (49).

27. See Lillian M. Penson, *The Colonial Agents of the British West Indies: A Study in Colonial Administration, Mainly in the Eighteenth Century* (London, 1924); Andrew Jackson O'Shaughnessy, *An Empire Divided: The American Revolution and the British Caribbean* (Philadelphia, 2000), 15–17; Eveline Christiana Martin, *The British West African Settlements, 1750–1821: A Study in Local Administration* (London, 1927), 15–28; James A. Rawley, "Richard Harris, Slave Trader Spokesmen," in Rawley, *London, Metropolis of the Slave Trade* (London, 2003), 57–81; and, more generally, Frank Wesley Pitman, *The Development of the British West Indies, 1700–1763* (New Haven, Conn., 1917); Richard B. Sheridan, *Sugar and Slavery: An Economic History of the British West Indies, 1623–1775* (Baltimore, 1974); Rebecca Starr, *A School for Politics: Commercial Lobbying and Political Culture in Early South Carolina* (Baltimore, 1998); and Alison Gilbert Olson, *Making the Empire Work: London and American Interest Groups, 1690–1790* (Cambridge, Mass., 1992).

with human bondage, in public or in private, thought it futile to pursue political change. No one before 1760 believed that the British government could be persuaded to adjust its priorities. And the decentralized structure of the British Empire made the prospect of imperial regulation almost impossible to imagine. The colonial legislatures constructed slave codes through the freedom they enjoyed to govern their own affairs. If the crown had the authority to veto these laws, it rarely chose to do so. Thus, the early opponents of slavery were confronted with, not one slave system, but rather a patchwork of privileges and practices that varied from place to place. The plethora of jurisdictions enabled attempts at the provincial level for improvement and reform but seemed to rule out the possibility of coordinated change across the empire. These were the reasons why so many of the first initiatives focused on changing private behavior, why the inspired tended to concentrate on local improvements. Comprehensive reform appeared politically improbable and constitutionally impossible.

No amount of moralizing was going to change these economic, political, and institutional facts. Antislavery sentiment circulated in the first century of imperial expansion to an extent too often underestimated. Yet, however common, these early reservations made no practical difference when set against the far more powerful forces of inertia and interest that conspired to keep the slave system secure. As a consequence antislavery impulses would be channeled into more modest projects that looked to make slavery gentler or limit its expansion. That orientation would remain until the American Revolution shifted the terms of debate.

[II] When those troubled by colonial slavery looked for a remedy early in the eighteenth century, they typically turned to religion rather than to law. This was in part because clergymen preoccupied with the state of piety in the colonies numbered disproportionately among the concerned. Predictably, they regarded the gospel as the appropriate source for moral instruction. The law, moreover, looked like an unpromising instrument for change. Slaveholders and their allies controlled the legislatures dispersed across the British Empire: the colonial assemblies had defined enslaved men and women as chattels; in licensing the slave trade, Parliament had recognized its victims as commodities. The countervailing tendencies perhaps implicit in the common law seemed not to apply overseas, as the common law courts at Westminster, at best, had uncertain authority in the Americas. The colonies seemed to lie outside their jurisdiction. American settlers felt certain that they had brought with them the ancient rights and liberties that protected English men and women from arbitrary authority. Yet because they regarded these freedoms as part of their national inheritance, it would prove difficult (even for the most sympathetic) to imagine slaves enjoying an English birthright, to conceive of Africans possessing English liberty.[28]

To Christianity, by contrast, British settlers would find it difficult to assert an exclusive claim. No true Christian could deny that Christ had offered salvation to all, that the gospel was intended for all lands and all peoples, including those who had abandoned God or who had never known him. If it had not occurred to English adventurers to describe colonization as an opportunity to bring foreigners within the compass of English law, evangelizing among the heathens had been an avowed if largely ignored aim from the beginning. For these reasons, those looking for ways to "help" the enslaved were inclined to choose religious rather than legal solutions. They endorsed measures that would bring slavery in line with concepts of Christian servitude: ideally, slaves would honor their masters as earthly representatives of divine authority; masters, in turn, would tend to

28. For the law of slavery in British North America generally, see William M. Wiecek, "The Statutory Law of Slavery and Race in the Thirteen Mainland Colonies of British America," *WMQ*, 3d Ser., XXXIV (1977), 58–80; A. Leon Higginbotham, Jr., *In the Matter of Color: Race and the American Legal Process: The Colonial Period* (New York, 1978); Thomas D. Morris, *Southern Slavery and the Law, 1619–1860* (Chapel Hill, N.C., 1996), 37–56; and Jonathan A. Bush, "The British Constitution and the Creation of American Slavery," in Paul Finkelman, ed., *Slavery and the Law* (Madison, Wis., 1996), 379–418. Note also Andrew Fede, *People without Rights: An Interpretation of the Fundamentals of the Law of Slavery in the U.S. South* (New York, 1992), 29–44. There is no work of comparable breadth and scope for the British West Indies generally, although see Dunn, *Sugar and Slaves*, 238–246, and David Barry Gaspar, " 'Rigid and Inclement': Origins of the Jamaica Slave Laws of the Seventeenth Century," in Christopher L. Tomlins and Bruce H. Mann, eds., *The Many Legalities of Early America* (Chapel Hill, N.C., 2001), 78–96. For the common law as an aspect of English identity outside the British Isles, see Jack P. Greene, "Empire and Identity from the Glorious Revolution to the American Revolution," in Marshall, ed., *The Oxford History of the British Empire,* II, 221–223, and Greene, " 'By Their Laws Shall Ye Know Them': Law and Identity in British Colonial America," *Journal of Interdisciplinary History,* XXXIII (2002–2003), 252–256.

the spiritual welfare of the enslaved because God had tended to them, because the enslaved also were children of God. In this way, the authority of God would sanctify and circumscribe the authority of the master, putting an end to the cycle of intimidation and violence endemic to colonial slavery.

This is what the first "humanitarians," those British men and women who took an interest in the welfare of the enslaved, hoped to achieve in the late seventeenth and early eighteenth centuries. Stunned by the savagery of slavery, they recommended, not liberation of enslaved bodies, but the redemption of souls enslaved to sin. For the ills of colonial society, they prescribed a Christian moral economy centered on reciprocal duties and obligations rather than on a liberal political economy organized around individual rights and liberties. The dissenting divine Richard Baxter declared slaveholders in "rebellion against God" and described the slave trade "as one of the worst kinds of Thievery in the world." Even with this rebuke, though, he asked slaveholders only to show mercy to their slaves, to value their "salvation" more "than their service." In an early diatribe against Virginia slaveholders, Anglican minister Morgan Godwin named "the restraining of ordinary Necessaries," like food, "an unmerciful *Cruelty* and Injustice," but even more *"Barbarous* and *Inhumane,"* he continued, was "to withhold from [slaves] the exercise of *Religion,* and the knowledg of *God."* Quaker William Edmundson asked whether a genuine Christian would keep slaves at all, heathen or otherwise. Yet, when it came to considering solutions, he went no further than admonishing Friends to refrain from slaveholding, so that both they and their slaves could find liberty to do God's will. Baxter, Godwin, and Edmundson, like several other clergymen in the colonies (Cotton Mather and George Fox most notably), could see that slavery facilitated sinful behavior among both masters and slaves. They regarded enslaved men and women as equal before God, not simply as beasts of burden. A few even thought slavery itself sinful. Yet, rather than abolishing slavery, they hoped above all to baptize the infant children of the unfree and convert adult Africans to Christianity.[29]

29. Richard Baxter, *A Christian Directory; or, A Summ of Practical Theologie and Cases of Conscience* . . . (London, 1673), 557, 559, 560; Morgan Godwyn *[sic], The Negro's and Indians Advocate, Suing for Their Admission into the Church; or, A Persuasive to the Instructing and Baptizing of the Negro's and Indians in Our Plantations; Shewing, That as the Compliance Therewith Can Prejudice No Mans Just Interest; So the*

Today, the offer of salvation in the place of liberty is sometimes hard to regard as an act of kindness. The efforts to convert slaves to Christianity in retrospect tend to look more like an attack on the Africans' cultural inheritance, like an "invasion within," in the words of historian James Axtell, like an attempt to colonize the spirit to better exploit the body. Predictably, enslaved Africans often held Protestant Christianity, as well as Protestant Christians, in open contempt, particularly before the Evangelical revivals in North America that commenced in the 1740s. The doctrine of obedience and nonresistance held limited appeal to the enslaved. The Protestant clergy of every denomination offered converts no more than a lifetime of service, with the possibility of redemption reserved for the hereafter. Echoing the apostle Paul, they taught that baptism left the unfree in the same condition as before, that the embrace of Christianity did not set the enslaved convert free. Ministers could urge nothing more, it must be stressed, if they were to attain permission from slaveholders to work among the captives. They had little room for independent action. Nonetheless, the consequence was a severely compromised "humanitarianism." Men like George Fox, Cotton Mather, and their many successors believed that they worked in the interest of the enslaved when they advocated Christian instruction and, thereby, recognized the humanity of African men and women. Yet the Christian paternalism that they espoused ultimately would provide slaveholders throughout the southern colonies in North America with a way to cast slavery as morally acceptable. Since slavery civilized "savages" and converted heathens to Christianity, slavery could be understood as a positive good.[30]

Wilful Neglecting and Opposing of It, Is No Less Than a Manifest Apostacy from the Christian Faith; To Which Is Added, a Brief Account of Religion in Virginia (London, 1680), 78–79. The work of William Edmundson is discussed in Sydney V. James, *A People among Peoples: Quaker Benevolence in Eighteenth-Century America* (Cambridge, Mass., 1963), 105–107. See also Davis, *The Problem of Slavery in Western Culture*, 204–205, 307–309, 338–341. For Fox and Mather as proponents of Christianization, see Kenneth L. Carroll, "George Fox and Slavery," *Quaker History*, LXXXII, no. 2 (Fall 1997), 16–25; Lawrence W. Towner, "The Sewell-Saffin Dialogue on Slavery," *WMQ*, 3d Ser., XXI (1964), 51–52; and Mark A. Peterson, "The Selling of Joseph: Bostonians, Antislavery, and the Protestant International, 1689–1733," *Massachusetts Historical Review*, IV (2002), 1–22.

30. James Axtell, *The Invasion Within: The Contest of Cultures in Colonial North*

The benefits that slaveholders stood to draw from promoting Christianity may seem obvious now. At the time, though, few slaveholders thought that Christian preaching would make slavery more secure. Like the clergy, most slaveholders in the plantation colonies regarded the offer of baptism as an act of kindness. They feared less a dramatic overthrow of colonial slavery than the slow erosion of their authority. The conversion of the proportionally small number of domestic slaves some slaveholders could approve, if only to bind trusted men and women more closely to the household. Converting fieldworkers en masse, however, threatened a dangerous restructuring of social relations. To uphold slavery, it helped to regard Africans as a radically different and inferior people. Converting heathens into Christians risked removing a fundamental marker of difference. The enslaved would begin to worship with and among the free. Under such circumstances, it would be difficult to think of the enslaved as brutes and thus to treat them brutally. As fellow parishioners, the enslaved might find reason to hope that spiritual liberties would anticipate civil liberties. Although those zealous for Christian conversion promised to defend the social order, slaveholders knew that such men tended to hold different values and priorities. Plantation owners purchased slaves to generate wealth. Christian missionaries, by contrast, tended to worship God more than profit. They tended to value the souls of the enslaved more than their labor. Even worse, their claim to sovereignty in spiritual matters threatened to intrude on the authority of planters in temporal affairs. Would the will of the master remain supreme if subject continually to the higher

---

America (New York, 1985). On contempt for Christianity among Africans in British America, see particularly Sylvia R. Frey and Betty Wood, *Come Shouting to Zion: African American Protestantism in the American South and British Caribbean to 1830* (Chapel Hill, N.C., 1998), 35–62, 74–79. For the argument that missionaries prepared the way for the ethos of paternalism in the southern United States after the American Revolution, see especially Jon Butler, "Enlarging the Bonds of Christ: Slavery, Evangelism, and the Christianization of the White South, 1690–1710," in Leonard I. Sweet, ed., *The Evangelical Tradition in America* (Macon, Ga., 1984), 98–112; Butler, *Awash in a Sea of Faith: Christianizing the American People* (Cambridge, Mass., 1990), 132–151; Larry Tise, *Proslavery: A History of the Defense of Slavery in America, 1701–1840* (Athens, Ga., 1987), 19–21; Alan Gallay, *The Formation of a Planter Elite: Jonathan Bryan and the South Carolina Frontier* (Athens, Ga., 1989), 30–54; and Sylvia Frey, *Water from the Rock: Black Resistance in a Revolutionary Age* (Princeton, N.J., 1991), 243–283.

standard of divine law? Could a slaveholder govern as he wished if mission-aries intervened routinely in the management of his slaves?[31]

These were not theoretical questions. During the first three decades of the eighteenth century, officials within the Church of England pushed repeatedly for the conversion of enslaved Africans in the colonies to Chris-tianity. Historians often compare the missionary work of the Anglican Church unfavorably with the missions sponsored by the Catholic orders in French, Spanish, and Portuguese colonies. In the late seventeenth and early eighteenth century, several powerful Anglican churchmen in England did, too. As a consequence, to enhance the standing of the Church of England overseas and to counter the influence of Protestant Dissenters in the colo-nies, the episcopacy attempted to include the American provinces within its growing movement in England, after the Restoration, to deepen commit-ment to the Anglican faith. Henry Compton, bishop of London for nearly four decades (1675–1713), initiated this intensified concern with the colo-nies by uniting Anglican clergy in America under his patronage and super-vision. But the impetus for the missionary movement would originate with Thomas Bray, who served as Bishop Compton's commissary (or chief deputy) in Maryland from 1696 to 1700 before returning to England as an ardent and unusually energetic advocate for the assertion of Anglican supremacy in the British colonies. Bray's initiative eventually led to the

31. The story of slaveholder opposition to Christian instruction of the slaves has been told many times. See particularly Marcus W. Jernegan, "Slavery and Conversion in the American Colonies," *AHR,* XXI (1916), 504–527; Frank J. Klingberg, *Anglican Human-itarianism in Colonial New York* (Philadelphia, 1940), 157–186; Davis, *The Problem of Slavery in Western Culture,* 215–216; Jordan, *White over Black,* 180–187; Lester B. Scherer, *Slavery and the Churches in Early America, 1619–1819* (Grand Rapids, Mich., 1975), 89–91; and John C. Van Horne, "Impediments to the Christianization and Educa-tion of Blacks in Colonial America: The Case of the Associates of Dr. Bray," *Historical Magazine of the Protestant Episcopal Church,* L (1981), 243–269. In this period, the threat of dissolving social barriers seems to have mattered more than concerns about specific doctrine. What the Bible taught about exodus, divine retribution, and the exalta-tion of the meek certainly looked subversive, too. But as anthropologist Andrew Beahrs has put it, I think correctly, Christian knowledge to planters "was less 'knowledge of Christ' than 'knowledge possessed by Christians.' " Beahrs, " 'Ours Alone Must Needs Be Christians': The Production of Enslaved Souls on the Codrington Estates," *Planta-tion Society in the Americas,* IV (1997), 279–310.

formation of the three institutions that, together, accounted for almost every formal effort by the Church of England to convert enslaved Africans in the colonies to Christianity during the eighteenth century. The declared mission of the standard-bearer, the Society for the Propagation of the Gospel (SPG), founded in 1701, included the religious instruction of heathens throughout British dominions. A bequest of 1706 from Christopher Codrington, planter and former governor-general of the Leeward Islands, enabled the SPG to establish a college for colonial clergy in Barbados, which Codrington envisioned as a preparatory school for Anglican missionaries and as a site on which to experiment with Christian instruction of the enslaved. Finally, in 1723, shortly before his death, Bray secured a gift from a Dutch donor to institute a trust, subsequently established as the Associates of Dr. Bray, to fund schools in the colonies for the education of black children, free and slave.[32]

32. The role of the bishop of London in encouraging this process is considered in Arthur Lyon Cross, *The Anglican Episcopate and the American Colonies* (New York, 1902), 25–51; Edward Carpenter, *The Protestant Bishop: Being the Life of Henry Compton, 1632–1713: Bishop of London* (London, 1956); J. H. Bennett, "English Bishops and Imperial Jurisdiction, 1660–1725," *Hist. Mag. Prot. Epis. Church*, XXXII (1963), 175– 188; G. Yeo, "A Case without Parallel: The Bishops of London and the Anglican Church Overseas, 1660–1748," *Journal of Ecclesiastical History*, XLIV (1993), 450–475; and, in superb detail, James B. Bell, *The Imperial Origins of the King's Church in Early America, 1607–1783* (Basingstoke, Eng., 2004), 10–73. The beginnings of the Anglican missionary movement itself are discussed in Hans Cnattingius, *Bishops and Societies: A Study of Anglican Colonial Missionary Expansion, 1698–1850* (London, 1952), 11–12; John Frederick Woolverton, *Colonial Anglicanism in North America* (Detroit, Mich., 1984), 82–98; Butler, "Enlarging the Bonds of Christ," in Sweet, ed., *The Evangelical Tradition in America*, 93–97; and Butler, *Awash in a Sea of Faith*, 98–111. The standard history of the SPG is H. P. Thompson, *Into All Lands: The History of the Society for the Propagation of the Gospel in Foreign Parts* (London, 1951). Andrew Porter provides a brief but effective overview in Porter, *Religion versus Empire? British Protestant Missionaries and Overseas Expansion, 1700–1914* (Manchester, Eng., 2004), 16–28. Laura M. Stevens offers a thoughtful and thought-provoking assessment of the society and its labors in Stevens, *The Poor Indians: British Missionaries, Native Americans, and Colonial Sensibility* (Philadelphia, 2004), 84–110. Of the many brief biographies of Thomas Bray, the best is Edgar L. Pennington, *Thomas Bray's Associates and Their Work among the Negroes* (Worcester, Mass., 1939). For a brief, authoritative overview of Bray's career, see John C. Van Horne, ed., *Religious Philanthropy and Colonial Slavery: The American*

Historians of antislavery frequently dismiss these initiatives since they fell short of an attack on slavery and, with respect to Christian conversions, produced meager results. After more than a half century of work, Anglican ministers would convert perhaps a thousand black men and women by the American Revolution, and primarily in North America. From this perspective, the outcome of the Codrington experiment becomes emblematic. Rather than making slaves Christians on their Barbados plantations, the SPG had slaves make sugar, and in sufficient quantities to yield a substantial profit. Yet, as is often the case in the history of antislavery, understanding failures is as important as recounting instances of progress. The Anglican campaign to Christianize slavery in the British Americas during the eighteenth century provides an initial indication of diverging values between the plantation colonies and the metropolis. The missionary program marks out a key difference in priorities between certain English authorities and the majority of slaveholding elites. And the failure of that campaign hints at the limits on the power of the Church of England in the overseas empire, limits that those dedicated to evangelizing would decide, later, required a remedy of its own. If the navigation laws represented an attempt by secular authorities to make the colonial economies serve the needs of the state, the missionary program represented an effort by religious authorities to make colonial elites internalize the cultural priorities of the church. Just as evasion of the navigation laws would ultimately lead to more rigorous enforcement by the state, thwarted attempts to convert the enslaved would

---

Correspondence of the Associates of Dr. Bray (Urbana, Ill., 1985), 2–9. The beginnings of the Codrington experiment are presented in Samuel Clyde McCulloch and John A. Schutz, "Of the Noble and Generous Benefaction of General Christopher Codrington; of the Society 'Composed of Wise and Good Men'; the Unhappy Disputes with the Late General's Executor; and the Society's Concern to Promote the Good Design," in Frank J. Klingberg, *Codrington Chronicle: An Experiment in Anglican Altruism on a Barbados Plantation, 1710–1834,* University of California Publications in History, XXXVII (Berkeley, Calif., 1949), 15–24. A more extensive study appears in J. Harry Bennett, *Bondsmen and Bishops: Slavery and Apprenticeship on the Codrington Plantations of Barbados, 1710–1838* (Berkeley, Calif., 1958). See also Noel Titus, "Concurrence without Compliance: SPG and the Barbadian Plantations, 1710–1834," in Daniel O'Connor, ed., *Three Centuries of Mission: The United Society for the Propagation of the Gospel, 1701–2000* (London, 2000), 249–261.

encourage, by the end of the eighteenth century, greater scrutiny of the freedom allowed to colonial planters.

Church officials in England did fail, in the end, to Christianize American slavery, but not from a want of interest, at least at first. As early as 1682, the Board of Trade had instructed royal governors to "find out the best means to facilitate and encourage the conversion of Negroes AND INDIANS to the Christian religion." The SPG tried to reinforce these orders by securing from Parliament a law that required the baptism of all black children born in the colonies. No one thought to propose slave trade abolition in the early eighteenth century, even during the prolonged and public dispute on the future of the Royal Africa Company, a debate that turned instead on how best to organize and orchestrate the traffic in human bodies. Three times, however, in 1703, 1710, and 1714, the SPG attempted (and failed) to introduce legislation that would have made Christian instruction of slaves imperial law. When that approach failed, the SPG redirected its efforts into mobilizing public support for its agenda, into presenting missionary work as a national cause in the national interest. In well-circulated annual sermons, Church of England bishops called on American colonists to admit enslaved men and women to the privileges of religious fellowship. If these sermons grew formulaic and uninspired in the 1730s, 1740s, and 1750s, increasingly placing the expression of pity and feeling above action, in the years before they had helped generate some enthusiasm for overseas missions in some quarters. Bishop William Fleetwood of Saint Asaph had written searchingly in 1705 of the duties that masters owed to both servants and slaves. In the SPG sermon of 1711, he told slaveholders that they put their own salvation at stake by denying the unfree access to the gospel. He described the SPG's work as of national importance, as a debt owed to the colonies and the slaves for the wealth they produced for England. Shortly after ascending to the see of London, Edmund Gibson in 1727 took the unusual step of issuing an open letter to the colonists, "exhorting them to encourage and promote the Instruction of their Negroes in the Christian Faith." He followed with an equally novel request to Anglican ministers abroad for detailed reports on the progress made toward Christianizing slavery.[33]

33. Leonard Woods Labaree, ed., *Royal Instructions to British Colonial Governors, 1670–1776*, 2 vols. (1935; rpt. New York, 1967), II, 505–506. On the SPG's attempt to secure favorable legislation in Parliament, see [Faith W. Vibert], "The Society for the

The SPG funded a variety of initiatives designed to extend the reach of colonial Anglicanism. Between 1701 and 1785 it sent out more than three hundred clergymen to North America, supplemented their incomes, and gave them tens of thousands of books to establish parochial libraries. Some of the colonial missionaries, particularly in North America, took to heart the charge to catechize the enslaved. Indeed, as historian Faith Vibert reported many years ago, persons not affiliated with the society sometimes emphasized their work among the slaves to ingratiate themselves with the SPG and draw on its largesse. This institutional backing reinforced dozens of individual efforts by ministers across North America to bring enslaved Africans within the Anglican communion. Church patronage sustained a school for black children in New York City from 1712 to the American Revolution. South Carolina commissary Alexander Garden established in 1743 an academy in Charleston dedicated to training black catechists. Joseph Ottolenghe taught black and white children together in Georgia. By the early 1770s, the Associates of Dr. Bray had established schools in Newport, New York, and Philadelphia, as well as in Fredericksburg, Norfolk, and Williamsburg, Virginia. Elsewhere, energetic ministers prepared instructional materials designed specifically to promote the conversion of

---

Propagation of the Gospel in Foreign Parts: Its Work for the Negroes in North America before 1783," *Journal of Negro History*, XVIII (1933), 186–187; J. Harry Bennett, Jr., "Of the Negroes Thereon," in Klingberg, ed., *Codrington Chronicle*, 85–103, citation on 88; and Van Horne, *Religious Philanthropy and Colonial Slavery*, 28–29. According to Tim Keirn, the debate on the future of the Royal Africa Company in the early eighteenth century generated only one pamphlet that referenced the moral aspects of the slave trade. See Keirn, "Monopoly, Economic Thought, and the Royal African Company," in John Brewer and Susan Staves, eds., *Early Modern Conceptions of Property* (London, 1996), 443. For a description of the SPG sermons and for a reprint of Fleetwood's sermon of 1711, see Klingberg, *Anglican Humanitarianism in Colonial New York*, 19–26, 195–212. Laura M. Stevens recovers the domestic religious politics at work in these sermons in *The Poor Indians*, 117–137. See also Scherer, *Slavery and the Churches in Early America*, 87–89. On Fleetwood's tract, *The Relative Duties of Parents and Children, Husbands and Wives, Masters and Servants, Consider'd in Sixteen Sermons; with Three More upon the Case of Self-Murther* (London, 1705), see Butler, *Awash in a Sea of Faith*, 135–142. The initiatives of Bishop Gibson are described in Norman Sykes, *Edmund Gibson, Bishop of London, 1669–1748: A Study in Politics and Religion in the Eighteenth Century* (London, 1926), 363–378, citation on 363n.

Africans. The sermons for slaves composed by Thomas Bacon of Maryland in 1749 and 1750 received wide distribution throughout North America (with assistance from the Associates of Dr. Bray) in the quarter century before the American Revolution.[34]

The energy that Anglican clerics invested in these projects after 1740 owed much to competition from the Evangelical revival.[35] All Protestant

34. See Klingberg, *Codrington Chronicle*, 7; John Calam, *Parsons and Pedagogues: The S. P. G. Adventure in American Education* (New York, 1971) 8; [Vibert], "Society for the Propagation of the Gospel in Foreign Parts," *Jour. Negro Hist.*, XVIII (1933), 171–212; Scherer, *Slavery and the Churches in Early America*, 91–100; Van Horne, *Religious Philanthropy and Colonial Slavery*, 16–25; Frey and Wood, *Come Shouting to Zion*, 64–75; Thomas Bacon, *Two Sermons, Preached to a Congregation of Black Slaves* (London, 1749); and Bacon, *Four Sermons, upon the Great and Indispensible Duty of All Christian Masters and Mistresses to Bring up Their Negro Slaves in the Knowledge and Fear of God . . .* (London, 1750). For New York, see William Webb Kemp, *The Support of Schools in Colonial New York by the Society for the Propagation of the Gospel* (New York, 1913); Klingberg, *Anglican Humanitarianism in Colonial New York*, 121–154; and Graham Russell Hodges, *Root and Branch: African Americans in New York and East Jersey, 1613–1863* (Chapel Hill, N.C., 1999), 54–64, 84–85, 119–121. For South Carolina, see Edgar Legare Pennington, "The Reverend Le Jau's Work among Indians and Negro Slaves," *Journal of Southern History*, I (1935), 453–458; Frank J. Klingberg, ed., *The Carolina Chronicle of Dr. Francis Le Jau, 1706–1717* (Berkeley, Calif., 1956); Klingberg, *An Appraisal of the Negro in Colonial South Carolina: A Study in Americanization* (Washington, D.C., 1941); Charles S. Bolton, *Southern Anglicanism: The Church of England in Colonial South Carolina* (Westport, Conn., 1982), 108–119; and Jeffrey Robert Young, *Domesticating Slavery: The Master Class in Georgia and South Carolina, 1670–1837* (Chapel Hill, N.C., 1999), 23–35. For Virginia, see Thad W. Tate, *The Negro in Eighteenth-Century Williamsburg* (Charlottesville, Va., 1965), 134–152, and Joan R. Gundersen, *The Anglican Ministry in Virginia, 1723–1766: A Study of a Social Class* (New York, 1989), 112–116. For Maryland, see Beatriz Betancourt Hardy, " 'The Papists . . . Have Shewn a Laudable Care and Concern': Catholicism, Anglicism, and Slave Religion in Colonial Maryland," *Maryland Historical Magazine*, CXLIII (2003), 15–19. For Georgia, see Timothy James Lockley, *Lines in the Sand: Race and Class in Lowcountry Georgia, 1750–1860* (Athens, Ga., 2001), 131.

35. Anglican schools for black children appeared in Philadelphia and Charleston within a year after the arrival of Methodist ministers. Gary B. Nash, *Forging Freedom: The Formation of Philadelphia's Black Community, 1720–1840* (Cambridge, Mass., 1988), 19–23; Young, *Domesticating Slavery*, 32.

missionaries in the American colonies faced barriers imposed by language and culture. Many of the enslaved had been born in West Africa and so possessed a limited command of English. Few had the leisure or the language skills to participate in Bible study. And most of the enslaved remained faithful to their own conceptions of the sacred. Anglican ministers had the additional disadvantage of needing to insist on the exegetical skills demanded by catechetical study. Evangelicals, by contrast, offered a less formal Christianity that stressed the ecstatic experience of repentance, commitment, and conversion and that more closely matched notions of piety among some of the enslaved. The Evangelical revivalists, in addition, sometimes overlooked racial and ethnic difference more readily. There were important differences in theology and in practice among the Evangelical sects. Yet they possessed a shared tendency to assume the spiritual equality of black men and women. Methodist converts in Georgia, South Carolina, and Antigua welcomed the enslaved, including their own slaves, into the religious fellowship, then drew in more through itinerant preaching in the Chesapeake on the eve of the American war. The Moravians invited black men and women to share with them in the kiss of peace and the ritual washing of feet at their missions in Antigua, Jamaica, Barbados, and South Carolina. Samuel Davies opened the doors of Presbyterian churches to the enslaved residing throughout the Virginia backcountry. The emotive, charismatic style of Evangelical preachers attracted hundreds of slaves to Baptist meetinghouses throughout the southern colonies in the 1760s and 1770s.[36]

Predictably, these initiatives caused friction with slaveholders. In several instances, planters took aggressive steps to obstruct Christian missionaries. The Barbados assembly in 1676, for example, prohibited Quakers from bringing their slaves to meetings for worship and fined them severely for disobedience. Virginia planters blamed intensified missionary work for the social unrest that culminated in a scotched insurrection among the slaves in 1730. In 1743, a South Carolina grand jury indicted Hugh Bryan and three others, all followers of Methodist preacher George Whitefield, for endan-

36. Frey and Wood, *Come Shouting to Zion*, 80–117. Beatriz Betancourt Hardy observes that in Maryland Catholics also achieved more success in bringing enslaved Africans to Christianity. Hardy, " 'The Papists . . . Have Shewn a Laudable Care and Concern,' " *Md. Hist. Mag.*, CXLIII (2003), 4–33.

gering the community by gathering the enslaved at camp meetings to receive the gospel.[37] More frequently, planters simply harassed subversive or disruptive ministers into silence. Anglican clergy proved especially vulnerable since slaveholders dominated the lay vestries that often controlled the hire and pay of ministers.[38] Aspiring missionaries often complained privately about the restrictions slaveholders placed on their work among the enslaved. A few expressed these grievances in print—most notably George Whitefield, who attracted considerable attention when he publicly condemned "heathen" American slaveholders for preventing the spread of Christianity in the colonies.[39]

Yet, for individuals working at cross-purposes, the relative infrequency of public dispute stands out even more. Struggles between planters and missionaries rarely erupted into open conflict. Some clergy thought that slaveholders should honor their Christian duties with more consistency. Most slaveholders wanted the clergy to leave slaves alone. Between them, though, with respect to slavery, there prevailed a settled (if sometimes uneasy) peace. The combatants, of course, were unevenly matched. Frustrated missionaries acceded to the interests of slaveholders because they

37. Drake, *Quakers and Slavery in America*, 7–9; Dunn, *Sugar and Slaves*, 103–106; John K. Nelson, *A Blessed Company: Parishes, Parsons, and Parishioners in Anglican Virginia, 1690–1776* (Chapel Hill, N.C., 2001), 263–264; Harvey H. Jackson, "Hugh Bryan and the Evangelical Movement in Colonial South Carolina," *WMQ*, 3d Ser., XLIII (1986), 594–614; Gallay, *The Formation of a Planter Elite*, 30–54.

38. Robert Olwell, *Masters, Slaves, and Subjects: The Culture of Power in the South Carolina Low Country, 1740–1790* (Ithaca, N.Y., 1998), 110–116; Herbert S. Klein, "Anglicanism, Catholicism, and the Negro Slave," *Comparative Studies in Society and History*, VIII (1966), 310–327; Michael Anesko, "So Discreet a Zeal: Slavery and the Anglican Church in Virginia, 1680–1730," *VMHB*, XCIII (1985), 247–278; Patricia U. Bonomi, *Under the Cope of Heaven: Religion, Society, and Politics in Colonial America* (Oxford, 1986), 39–50; Keith Hunte, "Protestantism and Slavery in the British Caribbean," in Armando Lampe, ed., *Christianity in the Caribbean: Essays on Church History* (Kingston, 2001), 92–95; Bell, *The Imperial Origins of the King's Church*, 90–104, 125–141; Parent, *Foul Means*, 238–249.

39. William A. Sloat, "George Whitefield, African-Americans, and Slavery," *Methodist History*, XXXIII (1994), 3–13; Alan Gallay, "The Great Sellout: George Whitefield on Slavery," in Winifred B. Moore, Jr., and Joseph F. Tripp, eds., *Looking South: Chapters in the Story of an American Region* (Westport, Conn., 1989), 21–23.

had little choice. Unable to marshal substantial resources of their own, all clergy (Anglican or otherwise) depended on the tolerance if not the patronage of colonial authorities to continue their work. Colonial slaveholders may have decided, for this reason, that even when the zealous irritated they typically did not represent a sustained threat to unfree labor. The Anglican clergy in particular did not need constant harassment from the authorities to know their place. It helped, too, that all Protestant ministers avowed support for slavery in practice. Those hoping to proselytize on the plantations explained to both slaves and slaveholders that baptism would not liberate, as the colonial legislatures had affirmed as well through statute. The sermons and instructional materials that the SPG distributed to its agents reinforced this position in every instance. If slaveholders remained skeptical and suspicious of those committed to propagating the gospel, they understood that, with respect to slavery, missionaries thought of themselves as defenders of the social order. Indeed, among Anglican ministers, particularly, slaveholding was common.[40] The low incidence of open conflict, therefore, probably indicates the achievement of an unbalanced compromise. In addition, what looks like a failure in retrospect may have looked to many churchmen at the time like a justifiable degree of success. Modest accomplishments perhaps satisfied equally modest ambitions. Just a small percentage of the clergy in America took the conversion of slaves to heart, despite the urging of church officials in England. Those efforts compare poorly, of course, with the more comprehensive work of the Catholic Church elsewhere in the Americas (although there, too, the impact of Christianity varied from place to place and over time). Given the size of the task, however, those few who worked tirelessly among the enslaved may have been more impressed with how much they had achieved than discouraged by the work that remained, particularly in the Chesapeake, where greater ardor among missionaries and less opposition among

40. Carson I. A. Ritchie, *An Account of the Society for the Propagation of the Gospel and the Anglican Church in America: Drawn from the Records of the Bishop of London* (Rutherford, N.J., 1976), 50; Calaam, *Parsons and Pedagogues,* 50; Olwell, *Masters, Slaves, and Subjects,* 113; Anesko, "So Discreet a Zeal," *VMHB,* XCIII (1985), 278; Gallay, "The Great Sellout," in Moore and Tripp, eds., *Looking South,* 25–27; Nelson, *A Blessed Company,* 262; J. C. S. Mason, *The Moravian Church and the Missionary Awakening in England, 1760–1800* (Woodbridge, Suffolk, Eng., 2001), 102–103.

planters helped produce by the American Revolution several thousand converts among the various Protestant denominations.[41]

Adamant resistance from the planters could produce, by contrast, discontent and resentment among the more willful clergy, as developments in the British Caribbean had shown. The publications of the Reverend Morgan Godwin draw frequent notice from historians because early in the colonial period he protested the oppression of Africans and Indians within the empire.[42] But the frustrations that inspired these publications, however, need further emphasis if we are to understand how the missionary impulse could become a first step toward a more active challenge to slavery itself. Godwin went to Virginia in 1667 expecting to bring pagans and infidels to a knowledge of Christ. He quickly ran afoul of colonial settlers who informed him that Christianity was inappropriate for the enslaved Africans, whom they regarded as beasts of burden. Bullied into exile by the tobacco lords, he shifted his mission to Barbados, where he found even more dreadful conditions. The *"Soul-Murthering and Brutifying state of Bondage"* on the sugar colony appalled him. He had not been prepared for the almost routine resort to castration, amputation, maiming, and decapitation. Nor could he approve of laws that prohibited Quakers from converting their slaves to Christianity. Shocked by the behavior of professed Christians in the plantations, offended by rough treatment from planters in both Virginia and Barbados, ashamed that Quakers and Puritans surpassed Anglicans in ministering to the heathen, Godwin returned to England enraged against a colonial ethos that had made profit the "chief Deity." Posing as the "Negro's and Indians Advocate," he explained that Africans had a right to learn of God's saving grace, that Christians had an obligation to teach the gospel

41. For Le Jau's comments in the early eighteenth century comparing the potential for missionary work in North America and the Caribbean, see [Vibert], "The Society for the Propagation of the Gospel in Foreign Parts," *Jour. Negro Hist.*, XVIII (1933), 177. See also Ritchie, *An Account of the Society for the Propagation of the Gospel*, 83–84. On the relative frequency of baptisms in the Chesapeake, see Morgan, *Slave Counterpoint*, 421–422; Nelson, *A Blessed Company*, 264–272; and Parent, *Foul Means*, 249–264.

42. The best essay is Alden T. Vaughan, "Slaveholders' 'Hellish Principles': A Seventeenth-Century Critique," in Vaughan, *Roots of American Racism*, 55–81. For samples of further comment, note especially Woolverton, *Colonial Anglicanism in North America*, 71–73. Larry E. Tise casts Godwin, wrongly in my view, as a defender of slavery in *Proslavery*, 19–20, 77.

to all, that "no Interest how great or (otherwise) just soever, may be admitted to stand in Competition with *Christianity*."[43]

Richard Baxter and George Fox had said as much before. Many others in the eighteenth century would do so after. Before the era of the American Revolution, though, perhaps only George Whitefield and the Quaker hermit Benjamin Lay would write in the same white hot rage against the "Gentilism" of colonial slaveholders. And no one outside the Society of Friends was devoted with more single-minded fervor to exposing the sins of the planters. Years later, Godwin would not forget the almost sadistic cruelty of American slaveholders. A century before Thomas Clarkson made his famous tour of the slave ports to gather information for the Committee for Effecting the Abolition of the Slave Trade in 1787, Godwin spent months perambulating London and its vicinity to preach on England's obligation to convert Africans to Christianity and treat them with humanity.

In the course of this campaign, Godwin conceived what may have been the first moral reform scheme for the plantation colonies, a scheme not unlike the amelioration plans that became far more prominent in the 1770s, nearly a century later. The clergy stood no chance of improving the mores of colonial society while they remained dependent on the vestries for their positions and income. So Godwin called for independent funding for American curates and more consistent protection for the clergy from royal governors. He knew that ambitious clergymen would avoid service in the colonies because those postings would harm their chances for preferment at home. So he proposed that those who had served in the Americas for a designated time receive special consideration for advancement on returning to England. These suggestions to improve the stature and image of the Church of England overseas agreed with priorities already beginning to take shape among church officials, priorities that would culminate in the formation of the SPG. In his concern with raising the profile of the church, Godwin differed little from Thomas Bray, his savvier and better-connected

43. Godwyn, *The Negro's and Indians Advocate*, 2, 13, 29; G[odwin], *A Supplement to the Negro's and Indian's Advocate; or, Some Further Considerations and Proposals for the Effectual and Speedy Carrying on of the Negro's Christianity in Our Plantations (Notwithstanding the Late Pretended Impossibilities) without Any Prejudice to Their Owners* (London, 1681), 5.

successor. Godwin, however, had in mind a far grander plan than Bray or any other cleric had or would have for some time.

More than a century before the formation of the Society for Effecting the Abolition of the Slave Trade, Godwin hoped to make the amelioration of slavery a political issue and popular cause in England. He called for the English clergy to speak regularly to their congregations on the crucial importance of preaching the gospel overseas. He wanted to establish a body of lecturers, "Persons of *Esteem* and *Repute*," to travel the colonies and instruct slaveholders on the substance of their moral duties. He proposed frequent "inveighing against this *impietie*" in the "chief Cities and Sea-port *Towns*," where merchants from the colonies "do most resort." He called for the declaration of a general fast to direct attention to the iniquitous practices prevailing in the American colonies. And he tried to commission a public sculpture that would depict the suffering of Indians and Africans in the British Empire. In short, as early as the 1680s, Godwin hoped to turn public opinion against colonial slaveholders. In England, he knew, "*planters* have an extraordinary *Ambition* to be *thought well of*." Metropolitan opponents of colonial slavery thus had the chance to "shame them into better principles." For "when in the *Plantations* it should come to be understood that their *impiety* was so *decryed* and *odious* here, it would go near to fall even of itself."[44] Half a century before Robert Robertson published his apologies for the West Indian planter class, Morgan Godwin understood the slaveholders' sensitivity to public opinion in the British Isles.

Slaveholders risked making enemies and, worse, inspiring intrusive plans for reform when they ridiculed and obstructed attempts to make slaves Christians. North American missionaries achieved just enough success to prevent them from developing severe resentments. In most of the Spanish and Portuguese colonies, even more, the social and political influence of the church prevented its isolation and discouraged alienation among the clergy. In the British Caribbean, by contrast, the commitment to religion among planters was so low that the clergy could not imagine getting *white* men and women to attend church services, even less establishing a modest program of Christian instruction for the slaves. To recommend the most basic attention to morals, the Barbados commissary re-

44. G[odwin], *A Supplement to the Negro's and Indians Advocate*, 3–9, citations on 8.

ported, made him "the object of fierce hostility" in the colony. In Jamaica, another clergyman reported to London, ministers have "very little, if any, power." This was not a situation amenable to reform or innovation. As a consequence, far more than the clergy in North America, Caribbean ministers chose to ignore calls from the SPG to further missionary work in the colonies. Twenty-eight clergymen in the West Indies answered Edmund Gibson's questionnaire of 1727 regarding religious life in the colonies. Only three could claim to have done anything to promote conversion of the slaves.[45]

The Anglican clergy represented just a fraction of the tiny white minority in the West Indian islands. Predictably, they took their values and priorities from the planters, their neighbors and kinsmen, far more than from distant administrators in London. Indeed, this had been the concern that led Christopher Codrington to leave his initial bequest. Perhaps representative of opinion among Caribbean ministers was the response of Robert Robertson, who reacted to the bishop of London's injunctions by defending colonial slavery and opposing metropolitan interference. The SPG would have preferred to duplicate in the Caribbean the modest gains it achieved in North America. However, its agents in the West Indies were no match for local planters. Between 1713 and 1768, the SPG sent thirteen missionaries to Barbados with the specific assignment of educating the slaves on its Codrington estates. But these efforts were hindered by the competing demands of the managers responsible for sugar cultivation and the uncertain commitment and abilities of the men they sent. In 1730, in writing a history of British overseas missions, the secretary to the SPG produced evidence of progress in North America yet omitted all mention of the Codrington estate since the experiment was regarded as an embarrassing failure. Five years later, Bishop Gibson advised the Associates of Dr. Bray that planter opposition had made missionary work impossible in the Caribbean.[46]

45. Sykes, *Gibson, Bishop of London*, 360, 361.

46. Ibid., 360–367. For the impoverished Anglican Church in the eighteenth-century Caribbean, see A. Caldecott, *The Church in the West Indies* (London, 1898), 47–70; Bennett, *Bondsmen and Bishops*, 87–93; R. A. Minter, *Episcopacy without Episcopate: The Church of England in Jamaica before 1824* (Upton-upon-Severn, Worcs., 1990), 140–147, 150–152, 156; Arthur Charles Dayfoot, *The Shaping of the West Indian Church,*

Slaveholders in the British West Indies won decisively the contest with Protestant missionaries in the eighteenth century. Methodist and Moravian ministers established successful missions on several plantations in Jamaica and Antigua after 1750, but only because the owners of those plantations had themselves experienced a spiritual awakening.[47] Otherwise, the sugar planters remained entirely hostile to religious reforms. By 1760, Codrington officials had given up any attempt to make the Codrington estate an exemplar of Christian servitude, although the SPG continued to urge the work on while promising little that would ensure its success. As the frustrated Codrington chaplain, John Hodgson, explained in the late 1750s, a renewed effort to convert the slaves would require far more than a dedicated agent and instructional books. In fact, little could be done for the slaves until there had been "a general Change of their Condition, by introducing among them the Regulations, and Advantages of civil Life," until something was done to ameliorate slavery. Hodgson's successor, Thomas Wharton, reached a similar conclusion ten years later. "In vain will it be to attempt inculcating the purest and most perfect System of Religion," Wharton declared in his sermon to the SPG, "without first implanting amongst them the Principles of civil Government and social Life," adding, "and such a Government, I may venture to affirm, the Policy of this Colony will never admit of." Church ministers had long taught that Christianity would improve slavery. However, some were beginning to think, as Godwin had argued many years before, that the rule of law would have to precede Christian instruction if the enslaved were to become converts in substantial numbers.[48]

1492–1962 (Gainesville, Fla., 1999), 89–109; Hunte, "Protestantism and Slavery in the British Caribbean," in Lampe, ed., *Christianity in the Caribbean,* 96–99; and David Humphreys, *An Historical Account of the Incorporated Society for the Propagation of the Gospel in Foreign Parts* (London, 1730). The pessimistic conclusion reached by Bishop Gibson is noticed in Mason, *The Moravian Church and the Missionary Awakening in England,* 91.

47. Frey and Wood, *Come Shouting to Zion,* 86–87, 104–106; Edgar N. Thompson, *Nathaniel Gilbert: Lawyer and Evangelist* (London, 1960); Richard S. Dunn, *Moravian Missionaries at Work in a Jamaican Slave Community, 1754–1835* (Minneapolis, Minn., 1994).

48. Hodgson and Wharton cited in Bennett, *Bondsmen and Bishops,* 85, 86.

This emerging view, that only civil reform in the West Indies could enable religious reform, would have far-reaching consequences. It would encourage frustrated churchmen to take an interest in colonial law. The Reverend James Ramsay, like Morgan Godwin before him, settled in British America intending to minister to African slaves. As a naval surgeon in the late 1750s, he had come to the aid of a distressed slave ship wracked by dysentery. The human suffering he saw there gave him his life's mission. In his parishes of Saint Johns and Cappesterre, Ramsay devoted himself to preaching among the enslaved. Like those who had gone before him, he quickly encountered staunch opposition. If slaveholders in Saint Kitts had permitted Ramsay to instruct some of the enslaved men and women in his parish, his appetite for reform might have been satisfied. Perhaps, like Alonso de Sandoval of Cartagena 150 years before, he would have labored for the conversion of Africans without subjecting slavery to further scrutiny. But neighboring planters made his work impossible and so forced him to dwell more broadly, as Morgan Godwin had, on the sins of West Indian society.

James Ramsay already knew that he did not like much about life in the Caribbean. Local grandees manipulated interest rates in the island to defraud their creditors in the British Isles. The planters displayed contempt for Christianity purely to irritate him. "It was a kind of fashion," he wrote in 1771, "which prevails almost universally among all our ranks of people to refrain from coming to church." Although Ramsay had married into a prominent Saint Kitts family, he refused to identify with an aristocracy that, as he saw it, lacked manners, honor, or humanity. In 1768 he began to write an essay that detailed ways to facilitate the religious instruction of enslaved Africans in the sugar colonies. By the time he had completed a draft in 1771, he had decided that only intervention by the state, legal protection for the slaves, and provisions for limited civil rights would facilitate the spread of Christianity in the slave quarters.[49] That text, inspired by years of frustration with the impiety of sugar planters, would figure importantly in the development of abolitionism when revised and published in 1784 shortly after the American War of Independence.

49. James Ramsay to Margaret Middleton, Mar. 20, 1771, Noel Papers, DE 32124/ 322/1, fol. 19, Leicestershire Record Office. For Ramsay in Saint Kitts, see Folarin Shyllon, *James Ramsay: The Unknown Abolitionist* (Edinburgh, 1977), 2–13, and O'Shaughnessy, *An Empire Divided*, 123–124.

In the long run, as historian Jon Butler has emphasized, the North American clergy helped protect slavery in the southern districts of the new United States from abolitionist attack. The paternalist ethos they instilled among American slaveholders helped neutralize the antislavery movement by enabling masters to cast themselves as stewards and patrons and slavery as a civilizing institution. Planters in the southern colonies of North America had not always approved of those who would proselytize among the enslaved, but as events in the Caribbean would show, the early if modest gains that Protestant ministers made in Virginia and South Carolina turned out to be a blessing in disguise. West Indian planters succeeded almost completely at keeping the missionary movement at bay during the first century and a half of settlement, from the mid-seventeenth century until the last decades of the eighteenth century. Few ministers attended to enslaved Africans. No church official in England meddled in the day-to-day affairs of the sugar plantations. But Caribbean slaveholders purchased this independence at a high price. By failing to permit even modest missionary efforts, they convinced an impassioned few in the colonies and in Britain that only comprehensive reforms to West Indian society could make the promotion of Christianity possible. By rejecting the idea of Christian stewardship, they forfeited the chance to present themselves as benign paternalists in the late eighteenth century when slavery came under attack. If officials in Britain and in the West Indies had assisted the labors of Protestant missionaries, concluded one knowledgeable proslavery writer in 1789, at the height of the first public campaign for abolition, "much of the present outcry against the slave trade would have been prevented."[50]

Few planters detected any harm in alienating the colonial [III] clergy. The danger in converting the enslaved to Christianity seemed much more apparent. If there was a genuine threat to slaveholders before the American Revolution, it came from the slaves themselves far more than from moralists like Morgan Godwin. Public criticism most slaveholders took far less seriously, overall, than the more immediate risk of revolt. Now and again, during the colonial era, slaves plotted to massacre slaveholders and seize their freedom. Occasionally these plots climaxed in violent insur-

50. William Knox to Lord Chancellor Edward Thurlow, May 29, 1789, cited in Mason, *The Moravian Church and the Missionary Awakening in England,* 134.

rections, particularly in the seventeenth-century Caribbean but also in eighteenth-century South Carolina (1739) and Jamaica (1760). At other times, planters uncovered conspiracies before they took effect, most notably in Barbados (1692), Virginia (1729), Antigua (1739), New York (1741), and Jamaica (1776). These plots, as well as innumerable additional instances of smaller-scale collective action, left slaveholders throughout British America in a state of perpetual unease.[51]

New attempts at social engineering usually followed in the aftermath. Legislatures tried to rectify demographic imbalances in the plantation colo-

51. For a comprehensive survey of plots and rebellions in the British West Indies through 1776 and beyond, see Michael Craton, *Testing the Chains: Resistance to Slavery in the British West Indies* (Ithaca, N.Y., 1982). The best book-length study is David Barry Gaspar, *Bondsmen and Rebels: A Study of Master-Slave Relations in Antigua, with Implications for Colonial British America* (Baltimore, 1985). There is no comparable overview for British North America, though see Merton L. Dillon, *Slavery Attacked: Southern Slaves and Their Allies, 1619–1865* (Baton Rouge, La., 1990), 1–18, 21–27. The major incidents still must be approached on a colony-by-colony basis. From a large literature, see Gerald W. Mullin, *Flight and Rebellion: Slave Resistance in Eighteenth-Century Virginia* (New York, 1972); Parent, *Foul Means,* 135–172; Peter H. Wood, *Black Majority: Negroes in Colonial South Carolina from 1670 through the Stono Rebellion* (New York, 1974); Thomas J. Davis, *A Rumor of Revolt: The "Great Negro Plot" in Colonial New York* (New York, 1985); and Serena Zabin, ed., *The New York Conspiracy Trials of 1741: Daniel Horsmanden's Journal of the Proceedings, with Related Documents* (Boston, 2004). The Atlantic context is well sketched in Peter Linebaugh and Marcus Rediker, *The Many-Headed Hydra: Sailors, Slaves, Commoners, and the Hidden History of the Revolutionary Atlantic* (Boston, 2000), esp. 193–198. For resistance and fears of slave resistance in New England, see Robert Desrochers, Jr., " 'Surprizing Deliverance'? Slavery and Freedom, Language, and Identity in the Narrative of Briton Hammon, 'A Negro Man,' " in Vincent Carretta and Philip Gould, eds., *Genius in Bondage: Literature of the Early Black Atlantic* (Lexington, Ky., 2001), 161–163, and Patricia Bradley, *Slavery, Propaganda, and the American Revolution* (Jackson, Miss., 1998), 8–13. For metropolitan awareness of this cycle of rebellion in the mid-eighteenth-century press and in early antislavery literature, see James G. Basker, " 'The Next Insurrection': Johnson, Race, and Rebellion," *Age of Johnson: A Scholarly Annual,* XI (2000), 37–43, and Jackson, "Social and Intellectual Origins of Anthony Benezet's Antislavery Radicalism," Suppl. ed. to *Pa. Hist.,* LXVI (1999), 100–103. As Madge Dresser has concluded from a careful reading of the Bristol press, "The overwhelming image of the slave abroad was of a violent, treacherous, and dangerous being." Dresser, *Slavery Obscured,* 59.

nies either by promoting the migration of white servants and their families or by temporarily restricting slave imports. Authorities tried to control the slaves' behavior through law by regulating their movements, labor, and social life. After 1750, several prominent slaveholders experimented with what they regarded as ameliorative measures, in the hopes that a kinder, gentler slavery would quell rebellious impulses. Most commonly, though, officials tried to terrorize the rebellious into submission through orgies of vicious retribution, by maiming, torturing, and executing conspirators or, in some instances, by transporting them far away from the colony. Possible and actual armed resistance by the enslaved made violence and the anticipation of violence a defining fact of life in the southern and Caribbean colonies.[52]

52. For the violent aftermath to slave rebellions, see the discussion scattered in the studies of insurrection listed above as well as in Sally E. Hadden, *Slave Patrols: Law and Violence in Colonial Virginia and the Carolinas* (Cambridge, Mass., 2001), 6–40, 136–144. For additional work on plantation violence in the British West Indies, see Diana Paton, "Punishment, Crime, and the Bodies of Slaves in Eighteenth-Century Jamaica," *Journal of Social History,* XXXIV (2000–2001), 923–954, and Vincent Brown, "Spiritual Terror and Sacred Authority in Jamaican Slave Society," *Slavery and Abolition,* XXIV, no. 1 (April 2003), 24–53. The attempt by British colonies to regulate slave imports draws most extended analysis in several studies by Darold D. Wax. See especially "Negro Import Duties in Colonial Virginia," *VMHB,* LXXIX (1971), 29–44, and " 'The Great Risque We Run': The Aftermath of Slave Rebellion at Stono, South Carolina, 1739–1745," *Jour. Negro Hist.*, LXVII (1982), 136–147. For the middle and northern colonies, see Oscar Williams, *African Americans and Colonial Legislation in the Middle Colonies* (New York, 1998), 55–82, and James J. Allegro, " 'Increasing and Strengthening the Country': Law, Politics, and the Antislavery Movement in Early-Eighteenth-Century Massachusetts Bay," *New England Quarterly,* LXXV (2002), 15–23. For a helpful overview, see Marilyn C. Baseler, *"Asylum for Mankind": America, 1607–1800* (Ithaca, N.Y., 1998), 77–88. Nicholas Rogers reports that West Indian officials often opposed the impressments of sailors resident in the Caribbean because, in the words of Governor Edward Trelawney of Jamaica in 1743, the planters needed those men "to quell any rebellions that may suddenly arise among their Slaves." Rogers, "Archipelagic Encounters: War, Race, and Labor in American-Caribbean Waters," in Felicity A. Nussbaum, ed., *The Global Eighteenth Century* (Baltimore, 2003), 216. On the emerging ethos of "improvement" in the British plantation colonies, see Richard B. Sheridan, "Samuel Martin, Innovating Sugar Planter of Antigua, 1750–1776," *Agricultural History,* XXXIV, no. 3 (July 1960), 126–139; David S. Shields, *Oracles of Empire: Poetry, Politics, and*

The expense of slaves, for this reason, went beyond the price of purchase. The social costs also could be steep. Most colonists able to purchase slaves bore the dangers and the risks of slaveholding with equanimity because they wanted the labor. Not everyone in Britain and North America, however, thought slaveholding worth the trouble. Some feared the impact of slavery on the security of colonial settlements, or on the moral character of their communities, or on the integrity of revered institutions like their churches or the law. Such anxieties animated the early published antislavery protests of Thomas Tryon (1684), formerly of Barbados, and Samuel Sewall of Massachusetts (1704), both of whom despaired at the ways slaveholding disrupted the harmony of colonial society.[53] A few regretted what slavery did to the enslaved. Typically, they offered the solace of redemption in Christ, as should now be clear. Perhaps more, however, worried about what slavery did to those who owned slaves or lived in slaveholding societies. To them, the solution seemed to lie in discouraging the expansion of slavery, in expelling it from particular jurisdictions, or in establishing a quarantine around specific communities. If the slave system itself could not be abolished, the concerned still might prevent it from infecting those societies where it had yet to take deep root.

In at least three instances before the American Revolution, individuals and groups troubled by slavery sought ways to curtail the liberties of colonial slaveholders. English authorities prohibited slavery in the new colony of Georgia during the 1730s and 1740s. In the 1760s and 1770s, Quakers expelled slaveholders from the religious fellowship. And in 1772 the case of *Somerset v. Steuart* severely curtailed the powers of slaveowners who brought enslaved men and women to England. Each of these attempts at moral and social improvement differed from the others in origins, character, and outcome. For this reason, they are not usually considered as as-

---

Commerce in British America, 1690–1750 (Chicago, 1990), 71–82; Joyce E. Chaplin, *An Anxious Pursuit: Agricultural Innovation and Modernity in the Lower South, 1730–1815* (Chapel Hill, N.C., 1993); and Young, *Domesticating Slavery,* 40–48.

53. Rosenberg, "Thomas Tryon and the Seventeenth-Century Dimensions of Antislavery," *WMQ,* 3d Ser., LXI (2004), 628–640; Peterson, "The Selling of Joseph," *Mass. Hist. Rev.*, IV (2002), 2–8. See also Kim F. Hall, " 'Extravagant Viciousness': Slavery and Gluttony in the Works of Thomas Tryon," in Philip D. Beidler and Gary Taylor, eds., *Writing Race across the Atlantic World, Medieval to Modern* (New York, 2005), 93–111.

pects of a single process. All three, however, reflect a common impulse among those unhappy with human bondage to establish communities or societies where slaveholders and their slaves would be unwelcome. Such schemes to debar slavery implied and often propounded genuine concerns about the morality of human bondage. They fostered and nurtured antislavery opinion in each instance. But these were local renunciations of slavery rather than comprehensive challenges to the institution itself. They share far more with later attempts by Free Soilers in the United States to prevent the expansion of slavery into the American West than with the Garrisonian commitment to immediate emancipation. Defensive in spirit, these attempts to expel slavery from a particular community arose from doubts about the benefits of slavery while accepting that elsewhere, among others, the institution would continue.

By the late 1720s, some in England had grown troubled by English expansion in the Americas and the social consequences that attended rapid commercial growth. In England, unbridled speculation had precipitated a massive collapse in the value of South Sea Company stock and the loss of substantial fortunes. Increasingly punitive attitudes toward the poor helped intensify the use of workhouses to discipline the "idle." Such reservations about the social consequences of the expanding commercial economy suffused the climate from which the Georgia plan emerged. When James Oglethorpe joined with the earl of Egmont in 1730 to establish the Georgia Trust, he had just completed an investigation into the state of English jails for Parliament. Together, Oglethorpe and Egmont built on a developing interest among improving patricians to make American settlements promote the rehabilitation of the poor and relief of the persecuted. Certain aspects of the Georgia scheme seem to have originated with shipwright Thomas Coram, subsequently creator of the London Foundling Hospital. Twice in the early eighteenth century Coram tried to institute a charitable colony in North America, first in the Maine district of Massachusetts for discharged sailors, and later in Nova Scotia for unemployed tradesmen—in both instances as an alternative to the rapacious landgrabbing he thought rampant in the existing British colonies. Disturbed by the "corrupt and degenerate age we live in," the Irish Protestant divine George Berkeley sought support for a new college in Bermuda between 1722 and 1728 to promote the "reformation of manners among the English in our western plantations and the propagation of the Gospel among the American savages."

FIGURE 2. *The Gaols Committee of the House of Commons.* By William Hogarth. Circa 1729. Courtesy, National Portrait Gallery, London.

James Oglethorpe is seated farthest to the left. Sir John Perceval (later first earl of Egmont), seated two chairs to the right of Oglethorpe, served as president of the Georgia Trustees. The founders of Georgia hoped the new colony would promote the moral redemption of the English poor, not the extension of African slavery.

Berkeley's plan never came to fruition in part because Oglethorpe persuaded the like-minded to back a similar scheme for the southern frontier of North America. Oglethorpe, in turn, owed much of his success to financial support from the Associates of Dr. Bray, just then looking for new ways to pursue its charge to Christianize British America. The interests united behind the Georgia plan shared a general ambition to better the character of the empire and redeem the English poor.[54]

54. The quotation from George Berkeley appears in Amon E. Ettinger, *James Edward Oglethorpe: Imperial Idealist* (Oxford, 1936), 119. For Berkeley, see Edwin S. Gaustad, *George Berkeley in America* (New Haven, Conn., 1979), 25–50; A. A. Luce, *The Life of George Berkeley, Bishop of Cloyne* (London, 1949), 94–114; and Carole Fabricant,

The Georgia experiment represented an explicit repudiation of customs prevailing throughout the British Americas, and the plantation societies in particular. The Georgia trustees regarded the southern and Caribbean colonies as exemplars of profiteering run amok. The unregulated pursuit of private gain, they concluded, created unstable, dissolute societies in which a few colonists engrossed the wealth while the rest wallowed in vice and misery. A refusal to consider the common good of the empire left the colonists at once avaricious and insecure, eager to seize new lands from American Indians while perpetually exposed to devastating attacks. The history of South Carolina provided the Georgia trustees with an object example of what to avoid. A society dominated by plutocrats and slaves, they could see, demoralized white yeomen and artisans incapable of competing for wealth and standing. South Carolina enriched a few, but for too many settlers it failed to provide an adequate living. Nor did it give the empire secure dominion. The exploitation of Indian slaves and the unregulated rum trade with Indian neighbors had led to a debilitating war in 1715 that nearly extinguished the Carolina settlements. The trustees established Georgia just three years after the proprietors of South Carolina surrendered the colony to the crown because of an inability to provide for the settlers' safety.[55]

"George Berkeley the Islander: Some Reflections on Utopia, Race, and Tar-Water," in Nussbaum, ed., *The Global Eighteenth Century*, 263–278. For Thomas Coram, consult Ruth K. McClure, *Coram's Children: The London Foundling Hospital in the Eighteenth Century* (New Haven, Conn., 1981), 18–19, 25, and H. F. B. Compston, *Thomas Coram: Churchman, Empire Builder, and Philanthropist* (London, 1918). For ties between the Associates of Dr. Bray and the Georgia trustees, see particularly Van Horne, *Religious Philanthropy and Colonial Slavery*, 4–16. The social vision of the trustees is sketched brilliantly by John B. Crowley in *This Sheba, Self: The Conceptualization of Economic Life in Eighteenth-Century America* (Baltimore, 1974), 16–34. This theme emerges also in Paul S. Taylor, *Georgia Plan, 1732–1752* (Berkeley, Calif., 1972), 10, 12; Milton L. Ready, "Philanthropy and the Origins of Georgia," Phinizy Spalding, "James Edward Oglethorpe's Quest for an American Zion," and Betty Wood, "The Earl of Egmont and the Georgia Colony," all in Harvey H. Jackson and Phinizy Spalding, eds., *Forty Years of Diversity: Essays on Colonial Georgia* (Athens, Ga., 1984), 52, 55, 63–70, 83–86.

55. Taylor, *Georgia Plan*, 3, 10–11, 22–23, 43; Wood, *Slavery in Colonial Georgia*, 6–8; Jack P. Greene, "Travails of an Infant Colony: The Search for Viability, Coherence, and Identity in Colonial Georgia," in Jackson and Spalding, eds., *Forty Years of Diversity*, 282–283; Rodney M. Baine and Phinizy Spalding, eds., *Some Account of the Design*

George II awarded the Georgia trustees a charter in 1732 to fortify and expand the southern border of British North America, not to expose it to greater danger. The location on the southern frontier, near Spanish rivals to the south and French antagonists to the west, made wide-scale slaveholding risky. In addition to these strategic considerations, the Georgia trustees had further reasons to have doubts about instituting human bondage. They intended the settlement to be for white men and women in need of reform or refuge. They hoped to send felons, vagrants, and unemployed persons as well as Protestant refugees from continental Europe. Slavery, they feared, would depress settlers' wages, stigmatize manual labor, and therefore promote idleness among those they hoped to improve. The colonists would not need slaves, the trustees explained, because the colony would produce wines and silk, which, they expected, would not require the backbreaking labor that made slaves an apparent necessity elsewhere. To prevent the colonists from establishing plantations, they restricted each household to fifty acres of land and prohibited its sale or transfer. And to ensure enforcement of these regulations, the trustees reserved authority over the colony to themselves, denying the colonists a representative, governor, or local seat of power.[56]

The trustees thought of the Georgia settlers as wards and of themselves

---

of the Trustees for Establishing Colonys in America, by James Edward Oglethorpe (Athens, Ga., 1990), xii–xvii. Claudio Saunt has suggested that Creek hostility to English settlement followed in part from the development of plantation slavery in the colony and the resulting transformation to the regional economy. See Saunt, " 'The English Has Now a Mind to Make Slaves of Them All': Creeks, Seminoles, and the Problem of Slavery," *American Indian Quarterly,* XXII (1998), 159–164. For a detailed account of the proprietary period, see L. H. Roper, *Conceiving Carolina: Proprietors, Planters, and Plots, 1662–1729* (New York, 2004).

56. The story of the Georgia experiment has been told many times. The best overviews appear in Trevor R. Reese, *Colonial Georgia: A Study in British Imperial Policy in the Eighteenth Century* (Athens, Ga., 1963); Taylor, *Georgia Plan;* and Wood, *Slavery in Colonial Georgia.* See also the essays in Jackson and Spalding, eds., *Forty Years of Diversity.* On James Edward Oglethorpe, the primary promoter, see Leslie F. Church, *Oglethorpe: A Study of Philanthropy in England and Georgia* (London, 1932); Ettinger, *James Edward Oglethorpe;* and Phinizy Spalding, *Oglethorpe in America* (Chicago, 1977). Note also Phinizy Spalding and Harvey H. Jackson, eds., *Oglethorpe in Perspective: Georgia's Founder after Two Hundred Years* (Tuscaloosa, Ala., 1989).

as patrons. Concerned for their charges, the trustees regarded enslaved men and women as potential corrupters of virtue rather than as unfortunate objects of charity. Most of the Georgia colonists, by contrast, saw themselves and, by extension, the enslaved very differently. They wanted to become planters and merchants, like other American colonists. Slave labor represented to them the means for self-advancement rather than invitations to idleness and sin. The conflict in priorities between settlers and patrons surfaced almost immediately. The Georgia trustees seem to have expected that the strictures on economic production and land ownership would make an explicit policy on slavery unnecessary. Indeed, James Oglethorpe permitted the temporary employment of South Carolina slaves in the construction of Savannah when he arrived with the first settlers in 1733. He came to regret this decision only after visiting South Carolina, where the arrogance of slaveholders crystallized for Oglethorpe the troubles that the Georgia experiment would face. The avarice of the South Carolina rice planters—who tried unsuccessfully to bribe Oglethorpe into relaxing the Georgia land policy—left him with a lasting contempt for slaveholders. Then, on returning to Savannah, Oglethorpe found that the industry of the colonists had flagged and that the South Carolina slaves were performing, in his view, too much of the work. Oglethorpe reacted like an angry parent. He scolded the settlers, insisted that he knew their interests best, and robbed them of the opportunity for further self-indulgence. After returning to England in 1734, he persuaded the trustees to secure from Parliament a ban on the transportation of slaves to the new colony.[57]

The first British challenge to colonial slavery, then, arose from a dedication among certain elites in London—themselves troubled by the moral character of the plantation colonies—to molding an overseas society in the shape of their ideals and preventing those societies from evolving in a way that the majority of settlers preferred. The fight to control the direction of the Georgia experiment anticipated the conflicts between metropolitan authoritarianism and colonial autonomy that would resurface repeatedly in struggles over British slavery for a century to come.

57. Spalding, "American Zion," in Jackson and Spalding, eds., *Forty Years of Diversity*, 70–76; Betty Wood, "James Oglethorpe, Race, and Slavery: A Reassessment," in Spalding and Jackson, eds., *Oglethorpe in Perspective*, 66–79; Lockley, *Lines in the Sand*, 2–4.

In defending this policy during the years that followed, the Georgia trustees made British colonial slavery for the first time the subject of prolonged controversy. Settlers in Savannah hoping to become planters insisted that Africans worked in subtropical climates more effectively than the English, that slave labor was more efficient and less expensive, that only slave labor (and a liberalized land policy) could make the colony an economic success. Spokesmen for the trustees explained that slavery would increase the risk of invasion and insurrection, discourage the immigration of white laborers, and corrupt the virtue of those already there. Moreover, the trustees warned, slavery would promote both aristocracy and debt by mortgaging the wealth of the community to local grandees, absentee landlords, or overseas merchants. An invocation to broad moral principles occasionally emerged in the dispute. For example, one proslavery petition from the colony explained that enslaved Africans would find greater happiness in America than in their native lands. From the other side, an impassioned scribe among the Highland Scots of Darien in 1739 famously described slaveholding as "shocking to human Nature." To another Scot, Isaac Gibbs, it was "Inhumane and Abominable." James Oglethorpe, himself, thought permitting slave importation in Georgia would "occasion the misery of thousands in Africa." On balance, though, statements of this kind were rare. In the 1730s and 1740s, few participants in the Georgia experiment cared much about injustices to the enslaved. At the time, there were no abolition societies, no antislavery petitions, and no dedicated propagandists prepared to campaign against slavery in the Americas. Those who participated in the debate on the Georgia plan had a direct interest in the outcome. The Georgia trustees believed slaveholding a danger to the community they wished to create. Yet they would not go so far as to describe slavery as morally wrong, in Georgia or anywhere else. They would lift the ban in the late 1740s once the Spanish threat from the south seemed less acute, once they decided that their social goals could be achieved through less stringent measures, once it became clear that both the colonists and Parliament had lost patience with the experiment.[58]

58. For a thorough account of the dispute on the Georgia ban on slavery including Oglethorpe's comments, see Wood, *Slavery in Colonial Georgia,* 1–89, citation on 31, and Wood, "James Oglethorpe, Race, and Slavery," in Spalding and Jackson, eds., *Oglethorpe in Perspective,* 66–79. Note also Davis, *The Problem of Slavery in Western*

If the debate on Georgia was not specifically about ethics, it was, however, a contest over values. Although the ambitions that shaped the Georgia experiment reflected the priorities of patrician philanthropists in England, they found favor with a small but significant minority in the colony. German-speaking migrants especially continued to back the essentials of the Georgia plan, even as the cause was lost. Generous gifts from Parliament and from private charities had enabled the Georgia trustees to supply several hundred Protestant exiles from Salzburg (in present-day Austria) with passage to the new colony. Once there, they established a settlement of their own in Ebeneezer, twenty-four miles north and west from the Anglo-Scot settlement of Savannah. It took only a brief experience with enslaved men and women on the South Carolina side of the Santee River for the Salzburgers to draw conclusions about the nature of colonial slavery. Enslaved men and women, they decided, caused endless trouble. They stole. They refused to work. They ran away. They were, generally, a menace to the community. These inconveniences would have been overlooked if the Salzburgers, like other settlers, had hoped to set up plantations. However, they brought from Austria a commitment to working their own farms, to producing to meet their own needs rather than to supply transatlantic markets. This preference for industry and self-sufficiency exemplified the ethos the trustees hoped to encourage. The Salzburgers held themselves apart from the capitalist economy in part to escape the social consequences that often followed.[59]

Few in British North America opposed slavery with more ardor during the first half of the eighteenth century than Johann Martin Bolzius, the religious leader of the Salzburg settlers. He stood almost alone during the last

---

Culture, 144–150, and Ruth Scarborough, Opposition to Slavery in Georgia prior to 1860 (Nashville, Tenn., 1933), 1–75. Several of the pertinent documents generated by this conflict are republished in Trevor R. Reese, The Clamarous Malcontents: Criticisms and Defenses of the Colony of Georgia, 1741–1743 (Savannah, Ga., 1973). The political context behind the timing of the famous Darien petition is discussed in Harvey H. Jackson, "The Darien Antislavery Petition of 1739 and the Georgia Plan," WMQ, 3d Ser., XXXIV (1977), 618–631. For Isaac Gibbs, see Taylor, Georgia Plan, 133.

59. George Fenwick Jones, The Salzburger Saga: Religious Exiles and Other Germans along the Savannah (Athens, Ga., 1984); Jones, The Georgia Dutch: From the Rhine and Danube to the Savannah, 1733–1783 (Athens, Ga., 1992), 1–138; Taylor, Georgia Plan, 109–110, 229, 234, 238.

years of the Georgia experiment in lobbying for the ban on slavery to continue. His brief time in Georgia convinced him that slavery was sinful, a "frightful wickedness," "a most abominable thing" destined to bring divine punishment. He doubted that a true Christian could purchase a slave "in good conscience." He thought the slave trade unjust. Privately and publicly, Bolzius worried about the possibility of an insurrection by oppressed slaves. He insisted, moreover, that slavery was unnecessary to the American colonies. He challenged the view that only blacks could work in tropical climates, that white settlers could never answer the labor shortage. The Georgia plan still had promise, he insisted in the late 1740s, when nearly every settler and informed observer in England had come to regard the project as a disappointment. The scheme had not been given sufficient time to succeed. And too many colonists, he added, were unwilling to labor as the Salzburgers did.[60]

Bolzius readily acknowledged the profitability of slavery. Indeed, its economic benefits gave him particular concern. He dreaded what slavery would do to settlers without slaves, to those laborers, like many in his congregation, rich only in their willingness to work. Everywhere, he attested, "the introduction of Negroes means smaller earnings for poor white people." Those who tried to work land with indentured servants would not find a market for their goods because slaveholders would produce the same goods more cheaply. Those unable to secure land of their own would then be left with several unattractive options: purchase slaves on credit and thus submit to the inescapable downward spiral of debt, work for wages depressed by the ubiquity of slave labor, or serve plantation owners as an overseer and thereby risk an endangered body and a corrupted soul. Unlike

60. Remarkably, the antislavery labors of Johann Martin Bolzius seem to have escaped sustained attention from researchers. Most of his commentary on slavery resides in his private correspondence with neighbors and the Georgia trustees in England. My account in this paragraph and the next draws principally on Taylor, *Georgia Plan*, 132, 230, 240–256, 264–269, and Jones, *The Georgia Dutch*, 266–274, 324n54. See also Scarborough, *Opposition to Slavery in Georgia*, 28, 37; Davis, *The Problem of Slavery in Western Culture*, 64–67; Lockley, *Lines in the Sand*, 4–10; and Renate Wilson, "Land, Population, and Labor: Lutheran Immigrants in Colonial Georgia," in Hartmut Lehmann, Hermann Wellenreuther, and Renate Wilson, eds., *In Search of Peace and Prosperity: New German Settlements in Eighteenth-Century Europe and America* (University Park, Pa., 2000), 230–235, 237–239.

most involved in this controversy, Bolzius also expressed concern for enslaved Africans. In later years he would defend the intellectual capacities of
black people at a time when few others would. Still, he devoted his energy
to lobbying on behalf of the "white industrious people" the Georgia experiment promised to benefit. There were other colonies in the Americas
where settlers could "keep as many Negroes as their ability will allow."
Georgia, he insisted, should remain an "Asylum." Several Salzburgers confided, he reported, that they would never have come to Georgia if they had
known that slavery would be permitted. Now they wanted to settle somewhere else in the British Empire where slavery and slaveholders would not
be welcome. They would not, if it was in their power, reconcile themselves
to the plantation complex.[61]

Some colonists in British North America wanted nothing to do with
slaves or slavery. Slaveholding conflicted with who they thought they were
and why they had chosen to settle in the colonies. Religious pilgrims from
German-speaking Europe, for example, seem to have taken to slavery especially slowly. A communal ethos discouraged the individual pursuits of
wealth more common among English-speaking colonists in British America. An inclination toward insularity led them to keep outsiders, including
enslaved Africans, at a distance. The Salzburgers were more unusual in
their persistence against slaveholding than in their reluctance. Almost fifty
years earlier, in 1688, German-speaking converts to Quakerism residing
along the Delaware River wrote the well-known Germantown protest, a
pioneering statement that declared slavery to be an injustice and an embarrassment to the Quaker faith. It emphasized the troubles that followed from
"bringing negroes in." Ten years would pass before the Moravian brethren
at Wachovia acceded to the purchase of slaves for their first settlements in
the North Carolina backcountry. Philip Baron Von Reck, who had escorted
Salzburgers to Georgia, expressed relief when he reached Boston after his
travels through Jamaica, South Carolina, and New York, places he recalled
that "swarm with Negroes." Calvinist settlers in Northfield, Massachusetts,
inspired by the Evangelical revivals in the Connecticut River valley, disparaged the religious authority of their Old Light minister by declaring that
his ownership of a slave offered sufficient proof of his greed. Similar discomfort with slaveholding appeared in the early eighteenth century among

61. Taylor, *Georgia Plan*, 290; Jones, *The Georgia Dutch*, 267, 268.

members of the Society of Friends, who decided that the practice upset the peace. Although he needed the extra labor, Robert Pyle of Chester County, Pennsylvania, manumitted his only slave in 1698 because he thought that slaveholding brought sin into his home. Cadwalader Morgan of Radnor County the same year set free a recently purchased bondman in part because he worried that the enslaved man would terrorize his family if not disciplined constantly. Tom Hazard of South County, Rhode Island, re-fused to receive slaves as part of a marriage dowry because he thought that slaveholding would call his faith into question. For those protective of their way of life, the need for slaves did not always lead to the holding of slaves.[62]

Unlike the Georgia trustees, Quakers' hostility to slavery in the early eighteenth century was often grounded in explicitly moral concerns. For certain Friends opposing slavery represented more than an attempt to insulate the community from the sins and dangers of slaveholding. The problem of slavery went beyond questions of utility. Quaker moralists from William Edmundson to John Woolman insisted on a conflict between slav-ery and the fundamental principles of justice, morality, and righteousness. This attitude reflected, in part, the peculiar cast of the Quaker faith. More than other sects, Quakers attempted to realize in practice the egalitar-ian principles implicit in the radical wing of the Protestant Reformation. Friends knew that Christ had enjoined compassion for the weak. And they knew that the violence required to institute and sustain slavery conflicted with their unique commitment to pacifism; Friends in Barbados in 1675 and in Virginia in 1740, for example, resolved not to participate in the slave patrols that protected the colonists from escapes and insurrections. More-over, Friends could identify more readily with the enslaved since they, too, in both England and North America, had known persecution. Quakers, moreover, regarded themselves as a people apart, committed distinctively to sustaining distance from a sinful world. They placed particular emphasis

---

62. Jones, *The Georgia Dutch*, 269; Jon F. Sensbach, *A Separate Canaan: The Making of an Afro-Moravian World in North Carolina, 1763–1840* (Chapel Hill, N.C., 1998), 49–50, 54–66; Drake, *Quakers and American Slavery*, 19–21, 50, citation on 20; Peterson, "The Selling of Joseph," *Mass. Hist. Rev.*, IV (2002), 16; Kenneth P. Minkema, "Jonathan Edwards's Defense of Slavery," ibid., 31–32; Barry Levy, *Quakers and the American Family: British Settlement in the Delaware Valley* (Oxford, 1988), 138–139.

on renouncing worldly luxuries, on demonstrating through everyday life the disavowal of greed and self-interest. To expropriate the labor of others without compensation, and for an unlimited term, was not only an injustice but also a renunciation of Christian humility. Ethical injunctions basic to the Christian tradition took on for these moral perfectionists an unusual importance. The most strident, particularly Ralph Sandiford and Benjamin Lay, described slaveholding as a sin and manumission a sacred obligation. No rationalization, no pretense of necessity, could change what these early campaigners knew as "Truth." Slavery violated the Golden Rule, brought misery on men and women, and inhibited the spread of divine love and Christian fellowship.[63]

These doctrines did not prevent the vast majority of Quakers from investing in the slave trade or holding slaves. Most did who could. Instead, they provided the basis for a dissenting tradition within the Society of Friends that helped the exceptionally pious expose the infidelity of their less strict brethren. Those who considered themselves faithful to the Quaker tradition of self-mortification found the self-indulgence of slaveholding Friends offensive. Quaker minister Elizabeth Hooton thought that the English poor in Barbados suffered from recurring depredations by "Rich mens Negroes." Faction leader George Keith in the 1690s challenged the spiritual authority of Quaker elders in Philadelphia by directing attention to their investment in slaves. Two decades later, a recent Quaker immigrant from England, John Farmer, took on the slave trading Friends of Newport, Rhode Island, while John Hepburn of East Jersey begged the "weighty" Friends of Pennsylvania to liberate Quakerdom from slavery. Elihu Coleman of Nantucket told rich Friends in 1729 that a lust for wealth had blinded them to their religious duty. To impress the point, several protestors made a show of their contempt for affluence. Ralph Sandiford

---

63. Davis, *The Problem of Slavery in Western Culture*, 291–307; J. William Frost, *The Quaker Origins of Antislavery* (Norwood, Pa., 1980), 2–22; Jean R. Soderlund, *Quakers and Slavery: A Divided Spirit* (Princeton, N.J., 1985), 17–18; Moira Ferguson, *Subject to Others: British Women Writers and Colonial Slavery, 1670–1834* (New York, 1992), 56–64; David L. Crosby, "Anthony Benezet's Transformation of Anti-Slavery Rhetoric," *Slavery and Abolition*, XXIII, no. 3 (December 2002), 45–46; Maurice Jackson, " 'Ethiopia Shall Soon Stretch Her Hands unto God': Anthony Benezet and the Atlantic Antislavery Revolution" (Ph.D. diss., Georgetown University, 2001), 261, 312.

avoided the sins of a South Carolina employer by refusing to share in the profits. The notorious eccentric Benjamin Lay smashed his teacups in the streets of Philadelphia to discourage the use of sugar. "The love of ease and gain are the motives in general of keeping slaves," John Woolman observed. When he accepted the hospitality of slaveholders in his travels through the southern colonies, he made a point of giving money directly to the slaves who served him.[64] No religious community in the Americas struggled more persistently than the Society of Friends with the tension between wealth and virtue.

Yet slaveholding became the subject of sustained debate among Quakers in the colonies only in the late 1750s, when the Society of Friends as a whole found new reasons to examine the relationship between their principles and their practice. The crisis that occurred during and after the Seven Years' War, which culminated in a reformation of American Quakerism, has been well described.[65] Moral reformers concerned with decline of piety within the religious society made use of the war's strain on Quaker politicians to promote a renunciation of worldliness and a new fidelity to sectarian principles. Quaker elders agreed to disown slave traders and dis-

64. Elizabeth Hooton, quote in Moira Ferguson, "Seventeenth-Century Quaker Women: Displacement, Colonialism, and Anti-Slavery Discourse," in Gerald MacLean, ed., *Culture and Society in the Stuart Restoration: Literature, Drama, History* (Cambridge, 1995), 235; Drake, *Quakers and Slavery in America*, 14–15, 29–37; Davis, *The Problem of Slavery in Western Culture*, 309–332; Soderlund, *Quakers and Slavery*, 15–17, 22–26; Andreas Mielke, "'What's Here to Do?': An Inquiry concerning Sarah and Benjamin Lay, Abolitionists," *Quaker Hist.*, LXXXI (1997), 22–44; Frederick B. Tolles, ed., *The Journal of John Woolman, and a Plea for the Poor* (Gloucester, Mass., 1971), 56.

65. The standard works are James, *A People among Peoples;* Richard Bauman, *For the Reputation of Truth: Politics, Religion, and Conflict among the Pennsylvania Quakers, 1750–1800* (Baltimore, 1971); and Jack D. Marietta, *The Reformation of American Quakerism, 1748–1783* (Philadelphia, 1984). See also the superbly detailed chronology compiled by Jackson in "'Ethiopia Shall Soon Stretch Her Hands unto God,'" 312–334. The Quaker withdrawal from slavery is discussed authoritatively in Soderlund, *Quakers and Slavery*, although see also Darold D. Wax, "Reform and Revolution: The Movement against Slavery and the Slave Trade in Revolutionary Pennsylvania," *Western Pennsylvania Historical Magazine*, LVII (1974), 403–416. The immediate aftermath is treated in depth in Gary B. Nash and Jean R. Soderlund, *Freedom by Degrees: Emancipation in Pennsylvania and Its Aftermath* (New York, 1991).

courage slaveholding within the sect as part of a more general campaign to purify the religious society. As with the Georgia experiment, the Quaker turn against slavery represented the triumph of an alternative conception of social and economic life. In attempting to prevent further corruption of their community, Friends articulated a powerful case against an institution fundamental to the world in which they lived. By deciding to manumit slaves rather than buy them, they confronted their neighbors with a rival system of justice and virtue.

In practice, though, the Quaker antislavery ethic of the 1750s and 1760s aimed at separatism rather than abolitionism. Friends showed more interest, initially, in removing themselves from slavery than pushing for wholesale challenges to the slave system in the colonies or throughout the empire. They tried primarily to cleanse the religious society of sin. The welfare of enslaved men and women generally mattered less to them. Thus, with the important exception of Anthony Benezet, Quaker antislavery initially did not lead to organized humanitarianism within the Society of Friends. Its more immediate effect was to help Friends further differentiate themselves from the society in which they lived. Opposition to slavery became a key part of the Salzburger mentalité in Georgia because, in a colony growing to revere the pursuit of profit, the stance helped the German migrants reaffirm their distinctive values. In a similar way, the Quaker turn against slavery represented an assertion of collective identity, a refinement of what it meant to be a member of the Society of Friends. Quakers believed, in principle, that their witness against slavery should have universal application. Yet they also took pride in their willingness to do what others would not. A few within the society hoped perhaps that the reformation of Quakerism would also inspire attempts to reform colonial society or, perhaps, the empire as a whole. But in its origins and its character the drive for purity directed Quakers inward, away from the world, rather than outward and into public canvassing for abolition and emancipation.

A similar dynamic was at work when the legality of slave- [IV] holding on English soil became in the 1760s and 1770s the subject of public controversy in London. There, blacks made slavery an issue by making themselves a nuisance. In the "land of liberty," many refused to continue as slaves. Some sought baptism, since they continued to believe that a conversion to Christianity, in principle, should liberate men and women from bondage. Many of the enslaved petitioned for wages so that they could work and live as free servants, so that they could "certify a free status," in the words of Douglas Lorimer, with an implicit contract. A few hoped that through marriage to a free person they would gain property in themselves. Others exploited the absence of a fugitive slave law and simply ran away.[66]

Because the legality of slaveholding in England was uncertain, slaveholders there found it difficult to sustain control over human property. In the Americas, they could assume that their local governments would permit the private exercise of absolute authority. In the British Isles, by contrast, slaveholders not only lacked support from the state. They also encountered the skepticism of an unsympathetic public often willing to shelter runaway slaves. Many British men and women believed, as Robert Robertson had, that slaveholding was illegal in England, even in the face of evidence to the contrary. They were less likely than American colonists to assume that black servants had also to be slaves, that blacks lacked claims to rights possessed by white workers. Recovery of runaways thus depended on the extralegal work of hired thugs or the occasional cooperation of well-inclined magistrates.[67] When enslaved men and women escaped, they

66. For attempts at liberty among enslaved blacks in London, see Douglas A. Lorimer, "Black Resistance to Slavery and Racism in Eighteenth-Century England," in Jagdish S. Gundara and Ian Duffield, eds., *Essays on the History of Blacks in Britain: From Roman Times to the Mid-Twentieth Century* (Brookfield, Vt., 1992), 59–65, 69–70; Lorimer, "Black Slaves and English Liberty: A Re-examination of Racial Slavery in England," *Immigrants and Minorities*, III (1984), 122–134, citation on 130.

67. For public reservations about slaveholding in England, see Sir John Fielding, *Extracts from Such of the Penal Laws, as Particularly Relate to the Peace and Good Order of the Metropolis with Observations for the Better Execution of Some and on the Defects of Others to Which Are Added the Felonies Made So by Statute, Some General Cautions to Shop-Keepers and a Short Treatise on the Office of Constable . . .* (London, 1768), cited in Shyllon, *Black People in Britain*, 97; Edward Long, *Candid Reflections upon the Judgment Lately Awarded by the Court of King's Bench in Westminster-Hall, on What Is Commonly Called the Negro Cause, by a Planter* (London, 1772); K[enneth] Little, *Negroes in Britain: A Study of Racial Relations in English Society,* rev. ed. (London, 1972), 193–195; J. Jean Hecht, *Continental and Colonial Servants in Eighteenth-Century England* (Northampton, Mass., 1954), 46; and David Dabydeen, *Hogarth's Blacks: Images of Blacks in Eighteenth Century English Art* (Mundelstrap, Denmark, 1985). The social context at midcentury is sketched in detail by Shyllon, *Black People in Britain*, 75–

forced slaveholders to behave like autocratic tyrants. And when slave-holders in England tried to assert their authority, they risked alienating a public that tended to revere the rule of law.

Granville Sharp did not begin life as a humanitarian. The antics of slaveholders made him one. Because he worked closely with the enslaved on freedom suits in the 1760s and 1770s, his first encounter with a black bondsman may look, in retrospect, like the inspiration for his later work. Sharp became an abolitionist, it may appear, from the moment in 1765 when he discovered a gravely injured young black man, Jonathan Strong, at the doorstep of his brother William's medical practice. Yet two more years passed before Sharp became a champion of abolition. He found physical cruelty despicable but unsurprising. He must have known of other in-stances in which *white* servants had been beaten by their employers. What surprised Sharp more was the attempt in 1767 by David Lisle, the erstwhile owner, to reclaim property rights in Strong, once the former slave had recovered from his injuries and had begun to live as a free man. Sharp was shocked that Lisle thought himself authorized to ship a free man to the Caribbean against his will. Nor could Sharp believe that Strong's new owner, James Kerr, had the audacity to sue Granville and his brother James for theft because they had helped Strong escape from Lisle's control. Even more upsetting was the opinion of several lawyers who informed them that, even in England, colonial slaveholders had a right to retrieve their human property. Servitude in itself did not anger Sharp. The apparently unre-stricted power of slaveholders residing in England did.[68]

If Sharp knew little about the law in 1767, he felt certain that it pro-hibited the kind of power men like Lisle claimed for themselves. Over the next two years Sharp mastered the law of personal liberty in England, giving particular attention to the decline of villeinage and subsequent pre-cedents delimiting unlawful imprisonment. From this research, Sharp con-

---

113; James Walvin, *England, Slaves, and Freedom, 1776–1838* (London, 1986), 26–41, 46–57; Seymour Drescher, "Manumission in a Society without Slave Law: Eigh-teenth Century England," *Slavery and Abolition*, X, no. 3 (December 1989), 86–96; and Gretchen Gerzina, *Black London: Life before Emancipation* (New Brunswick, N.J., 1995), 1–89.

68. F. O. Shyllon, *Black Slaves in Britain* (Oxford, 1974), 17–23; Gerzina, *Black London*, 97–101.

cluded that slaveholding in England was an unconstitutional innovation, a violation of foundational rights pregnant with vast and dangerous consequences for English liberties. On the off chance a right to slavery had become a recognized custom in England, Sharp felt sure that, if left unopposed, the outrages would multiply and England would become a new home to the horrors of plantation justice. It was a "growing evil," he told the absentee planter and London politician William Beckford. There was a "dangerous increase of slaves in this Kingdom," he wrote to the archbishop of Canterbury. The number of slaves is "already much too numerous," he stated in his first antislavery treatise; "the public good seems to require some restraints on the unnatural increase of black subjects." To one lawyer's estimation that there were twenty thousand blacks in England, Sharp predicted that soon, without a ruling against slavery, there would be twenty thousand more. Only a determination in the courts against the legality of slavery would prevent "West Indian masters" from bringing them.[69]

Researchers may never know with certainty if the number of blacks in England increased in the 1760s, as Granville Sharp believed. But others at the time also thought slaveholding in England, and in London particularly, to be a deepening problem. Contributors to the *Gentleman's Magazine* and the *London Chronicle* in 1764 described the importation of black servants to England as "a growing piece of ill policy." "The great numbers of Negro slaves . . . brought into this Kingdom," London magistrate John Fielding echoed in 1768, "deserves the most serious attention."[70] The conclusion of the Seven Years' War seems to have deposited a number of black sailors and servants in the British Isles, many of whom found themselves casting about

69. Granville Sharp to William Beckford, May 17, 1768, in Prince Hoare, *Memoirs of Granville Sharp . . .* (London, 1820), 48; Sharp to archbishop of Canterbury, May 15, 1769, G. Sharp MSS, D3549 13/1/C3, Gloucestershire Record Office (GRO); Sharp, *A Representation of the Injustice and Dangerous Tendency of Tolerating Slavery, or of Admitting the Least Claim of Private Property in the Persons of Men, in England . . .* (London, 1769), 75; "Some Remarks on the Case of John Hylas and His Wife Mary," Granville Sharp MS Letterbook, fols. 19–20, York Minster Library (YML). On Sharp's labors in this period more generally, see Shyllon, *Black Slaves in Britain*, 28–54, and Gerzina, *Black London*, 101–115.

70. *London Chronicle*, XVI (Sept. 29–Oct. 20, 1764), 317, *Gentleman's Mag.*, XXXIV (1764), 495, Sir John Fielding, *Extracts from Such of the Penal Laws . . .*, 143–145, all cited in Shyllon, *Black People in Britain*, 94, 97.

for work. At least that was the experience of one black man, Ukawsaw Gronniosaw (James Albert), who served the British army in Cuba and Martinique before receiving his discharge and settling in England. Thereafter, he struggled fitfully to provide for his family at a time when work was scarce. Fear about competition for jobs contributed directly to the new public reaction against slaveholding in England during the 1760s. Not only were black servants "sullen, spiteful, treacherous, and revengeful," as "Anglicanus" explained in the *Gentleman's Magazine,* they also displaced white workers. In the *London Chronicle,* "F. Freeman" a year later called for a head tax on each slave, "who of late years are becoming too abundant in this kingdom," to reduce the debt and save jobs for English men and women.[71]

The importation of slaves and slavery looked to some like an emerging threat to English society. It seemed to license arbitrary authority on English soil, the impoverishment of white servants, and the corruption of English blood. Increasing numbers of blacks in England, both opponents and defenders of slavery feared, would mongrelize the English nation. Granville Sharp himself struck a xenophobic note when in 1769 he declared blacks in England "much too numerous." In a passage more remarkable for its venom than its prejudice, Jamaican planter Edward Long warned that soon the English would resemble "the Portuguese and Moriscos in complexion of skin and baseness of mind." Miscegenation he described as a "dangerous ulcer that threatens to disperse its malignancy far and wide, until every family catches infection from it."[72] An anxiety about a colonial contami-

---

71. "Anglicanus," *Gentleman's Mag.,* XXXIV (1764), 495, *London Chron.,* XVIII (Oct. 19–22, 1765), 387, both cited in Shyllon, *Black People in Britain,* 94–95; James Albert Ukawsaw Gronniosaw, *A Narrative of the Most Remarkable Particulars in the Life of James Albert Ukawsaw Gronniosaw, an African Prince, as Related by Himself* (Bath, 1772). Like Gronniosaw, both Jupiter Hammon and Olaudah Equiano, two other black writers well known to scholars of this period, found themselves discharged in London at the end of the Seven Years' War. The anecdotal evidence presented here does not prove the case. There is, as yet, no firm estimate for the number of blacks who served in the Royal Navy during this conflict. Drawing upon data culled from the records from preceding conflicts in the Caribbean, Nicholas Rogers proposes that black participation had been limited. See Rogers, "Archipelagic Encounters," in Nussbaum, ed., *The Global Eighteenth Century,* 217–219.

72. Sharp, *A Representation of the Injustice and Dangerous Tendency,* 75; Long,

nation of metropolitan culture suffused the public discussion about the right of Africans in England. English institutions as well as English people seemed to need protection from the scourge of the Americas. The lawyers in the decisive Somerset case of 1772 gave particular attention to the social consequences of slavery, to the need for a *cordon sanitaire* around the British Isles. To permit slavery was to make colonial laws the law of England, to allow the incivilities of the unrefined provincial world to become customary at home, and to make England, as Sharp put it, "as base, wicked and Tyrannical as our colonies." "The horrid cruelties . . . perpetuated in America," one attorney predicted, would "be introduced here," unless Somerset was set free. England, the land of liberty, would soon become the home of tyranny, explained Francis Hargrave, if the courts permitted "domestic slavery, with its horrid train of evils." About these evils, Granville Sharp was specific:

Candid Reflections, 49. As Granville Sharp explained privately after the Somerset case, "I am far from having an particular Esteem for the Negroes; but as I think myself—*obliged* to consider them as *men,* I am certainly *obliged,* also, to use my best endeavours to prevent their being treated *as beasts* by our unchristian Countrymen, who deny them the privledges of *human nature.*" Sharp to Jacob Bryant, Oct. 19, 1772, G. Sharp MSS. To shock his readers, Long suggested that a black lottery winner might not only purchase land in England but secure a seat in Parliament. Another proslavery writer defending the right to property in slaves in England also hoped that planters would desist bringing them from the colonies. He urged Parliament to make a law prohibiting the importation of slaves to England. Samuel Estwick, *Considerations on the Negro Cause Commonly So Called: Addressed to the Right Honourable Lord Mansfield, Lord Chief Justice of the Court of King's Bench, by a West Indian* (London, 1772), 41–43. For the significance of fears among the propertied of miscegenation among the rabble, see Lorimer, "Black Slaves and English Liberty," *Immigrants and Minorities,* III (1984), 136–139; Shyllon, *Black People in Britain,* 102–106; Walvin, *England, Slaves, and Freedom,* 48–51; and Gerzina, *Black London,* 103. The twin fears of miscegenation and a loss of English jobs to African servants informed the Reverend Henry Bates's comic opera *The Blackamoor Wash'd White* in 1776. See Felicity A. Nussbaum, "The Theatre of Empire: Racial Counterfeit, Racial Realism," in Kathleen Wilson, ed., *A New Imperial History: Culture, Identity, and Modernity in Britain and the Empire, 1660–1840* (Cambridge, 2004), 74, 78–83. Some years ago, David Brion Davis observed that anxieties regarding future imports of slaves in Scotland helped animate an unusually pointed protest against slavery jurist George Wallace in 1760. See Davis, "New Sidelights on Early Antislavery Radicalism," *WMQ,* 3d Ser., XXVIII (1971), 588.

We should not only be over run with a vast multitude of poor wretched Slaves from the East or West Indies to engross the employment and subsistence of the free labourer and industrious poor, but the latter (and indeed the lower Class in general even of our own Countrymen) would be inevitably involved by degrees in the same horrid Slavery and oppression; for that *is always the case wherever Slavery is tolerated.*

For those who supported James Somerset, the question at hand was not only whether Africans in England could be slaves but also whether England would remain English and free. Fourteen years later Granville Sharp would describe the Somerset case as deterring West Indian slaveholders from "bringing with them swarms of Negro attendants into this island."[73]

In a Delphic verdict laced with ambiguities, Mansfield preserved the slaveholders' right to the service of their slaves but not the right to enforce it. The decision left the legality of slavery in England as ill defined as before.[74] Yet the impulse to think of England as a land of liberty gave the public interpretation of Mansfield's words a clarity the verdict itself lacked. The ambiguities in the decision mattered little to those looking for confirmation of what they already knew to be true, for proof that freedom, "the Idol of Britons" as one poet expressed it, had prevailed, that English law guaranteed liberty, that English soil was and would remain free soil. Newspapers ignored the nuances of the judgment to report that Mansfield had struck down slavery. Even Edward Long and Samuel Estwick, the leading

73. Sharp to Bryant, Oct. 19, 1772, and Sharp to archbishop of Canterbury, Aug. 1, 1786, both in G. Sharp MSS, GRO; Sharp to Mr. Lloyd, June 30, 1772, Granville Sharp MS Letterbook, fol. 110, YML. An especially detailed discussion of the arguments made in the Somerset case and the nature of public opinion appears in Shyllon, *Black Slaves in Britain,* 82–164 (quotations from Hargrave and Alleyne on 96 and 100).

74. Scholarly interpretations of Mansfield's judgment abound. For recent careful but slightly different views, see James Oldham, "New Light on Mansfield and Slavery," *Journal of British Studies,* XXVII (1988), 45–68, and William R. Cotter, "The Somerset Case and the Abolition of Slavery in England," *History,* LXXIX, no. 255 (February 1994), 31–56. Note also Shyllon, *Black Slaves in Britain,* 165–176. The personal histories of Somerset and Steuart are detailed in Mark S. Wiener, "New Biographical Evidence on Somerset's Case," *Slavery and Abolition,* XXIII, no. 1 (April 2002), 121–136. For a recent book-length account, see Steven M. Wise, *Though the Heavens May Fall: The Landmark Trial That Led to the End of Human Slavery* (Cambridge, Mass., 2005).

apologists for British Caribbean slaveholders, conceded in the following months that slavery was, in Long's words, "repugnant to the spirit of the English laws." After the Somerset case, blacks and whites in England behaved as though the institution had been outlawed. Portsmouth customs officers, for example, appealed in 1776 on behalf of a black sailor imprisoned aboard a New York sloop because they thought him "emancipated from his Slavery now he in this Country."[75]

The values that lay behind the antislavery movement had long been in place by the 1770s. A range of cultural shifts had helped crystallize those abstract English prejudices against slavery fostered by the customs enshrined in the common law. It had become easier, at midcentury, for British men and women to perceive the enslaved African as the victim of injustice. Over time the British knew more about the nature of life in the colonies and how the slave system operated. It became more common to doubt the morality of the slave system because certain intellectuals did too, because prominent theologians, philosophers, and historians raised troubling questions about the moral and legal foundations on which the system stood.

The Somerset case, moreover, made these somewhat abstract issues matter in England in a concrete way. It promoted an intensive public discussion of the rights of slaves and slaveholders and called attention to the peculiar character of the colonial labor system. In his decision, Lord Mansfield went as far as to label the institution "odious." The verdict inspired the publication of the first comprehensive emancipation scheme for the British Empire and the first sustained defenses in print of colonial slavery and the Atlantic slave trade since the 1730s.[76] Poets and playwrights

75. Shyllon, *Black Slaves in Britain,* 133, 165; Edward Long, *The History of Jamaica; or, General Survey of the Antient and Modern State of That Island . . . ,* 3 vols. (London, 1774), II, 323; Estwick, *Considerations on the Negro Cause,* 5, 9; W. Cooley and W. Stiles to the Commissioners of Customs, May 17, 1776, PRO CO 5/148, fol. 71. For the difficulty of holding blacks as slaves after the Somerset case, see particularly Cotter, "The Somerset Case," *History,* LXXIX, no. 255 (February 1994), 40–56, and Wiener, "New Biographical Evidence," *Slavery and Abolition,* XXIII, no. 1 (April 2002), 125.

76. [Maurice Morgann], *Plan for the Abolition of Slavery in the West Indies* (London, 1772). In addition to the works by Edward Long and Samuel Estwick cited above, see John Peter Demarin, *A Treatise upon the Trade from Great-Britain to Africa: Humbly Recommended to the Attention of Government* (London, 1772), and Tho[mas] Thomp-

ANTISLAVERY WITHOUT ABOLITIONISM 99

took advantage of the increasingly fashionable sympathy for the African by provoking tears among their audiences on behalf of wounded innocence. Ukawsaw Gronniosaw's narrative went to press less than six months after the conclusion of the Somerset case. Boston poet Phillis Wheatley found in London a publisher and an appreciative public who welcomed her during a celebrity tour of the city one year after Mansfield's judgment. The Somerset case led directly to a series of court cases in Scotland, which concluded in 1778 in a ban on slaveholding in North Briton. It inspired freedom suits in Massachusetts in the years before the American war and provided an incentive for fugitives across the empire to seek passage to English soil. The five-year fight for the rights of blacks in England transformed Granville Sharp into a lifelong champion of abolition in all British territories. His landmark pamphlet of 1769 challenging slaveholding in England brought Sharp to the attention of Anthony Benezet and several other Quakers along the Delaware River just becoming interested in recasting their drive for sectarian purity into a broad public movement for a more general reformation. That correspondence established the transatlantic networks critical to the success of the subsequent campaigns in both Britain and British America.[77] In all these ways, the Somerset case seemed to produce a decisive

---

son, *The African Trade for Negro Slaves, Shewn to Be Consistent with Principles of Humanity, and with the Laws of Revealed Religion* (Canterbury, [1772]).

77. For the publication date of Gronniosaw's text, see Vincent Carretta, ed., *Unchained Voices: An Anthology of Black Authors in the English-Speaking World of the Eighteenth Century* (Lexington, Ky., 1996), 53–54. On Wheatley in London, see particularly Julian D. Mason, Jr., ed., *The Poems of Phillis Wheatley* (Chapel Hill, N.C., 1989), 188–208; Keith A. Sandiford, *Measuring the Moment: Strategies of Protest in Eighteenth-Century Afro-English Writing* (London, 1988); Mukhtar Ali Isani, "The British Reception of Wheatley's *Poems on Various Subjects,*" *Jour. Negro Hist.*, LXVI (1981), 144–149; Kristin Wilcox, "The Body into Print: Marketing Phillis Wheatley," *American Literature*, LXXI (1999), 1–29; Frank Shuffleton, "On Her Own Footing: Phillis Wheatley in Freedom," in Vincent Carretta and Philip Gould, eds., *Genius in Bondage: Literature of the Early Black Atlantic* (Lexington, Ky., 2001), 175–176, 180–182; and Carretta, "Phillis Wheatley, the Mansfield Decision of 1772, and the Choice of Identity," in Klaus H. Schmidt and Fritz Fleischmann, eds., *Early America Re-Explored: New Readings in Colonial, Early National, and Antebellum Culture* (New York, 2000), 210–223. On early transatlantic networks, see Betty Fladeland, *Men and Brothers: Anglo-American Antislavery Cooperation* (Urbana, Ill., 1982). Much of the pertinent correspon-

change in public responses toward slavery, to mark the moment when an international movement against slavery took definitive shape.

Yet for all the importance of the Somerset case, formidable obstacles to a full-scale attack on the slave system remained. Outside the British Isles, where their political power mattered most, slaveholders remained nearly unopposed. Almost no one in England, moreover, had thought to challenge the practices of slave traders operating from Liverpool, Bristol, and London. Granville Sharp worked tirelessly against the institution of slavery everywhere within the British Empire after 1772, but for many years in England he would stand nearly alone. The man was not a movement, and the Somerset case failed to produce one. Ten more years would pass before an organized antislavery lobby would coalesce, in part because those who cared knew neither how to proceed nor what end to seek. If the slave system seemed ethically suspect to some, few had concrete ideas about what to do. Slavery might be contemptible, but who should be held in contempt? Should British men and women regard themselves as responsible for British slavery when the bulk of the injustices occurred overseas?

The Somerset case left an ambiguous legacy. In one respect, it gave the moral case against slavery a full and public hearing. At the same time, most involved continued to take the legality of slavery in the colonies for granted. In limiting the rights of slaveholders in England, the counsel for Somerset seemed to acknowledge the rights of slaveholders in British America. The case left colonial slaveholders with a tarnished reputation but neither a public indictment nor a command to reform. The champions of English liberty displayed little interest in the slave system as a whole. Like the Quakers, they sought first to expel slavery from their midst, to reaffirm the purity of their institutions, to prevent corrupt, alien practices from endangering honored customs. Like the Georgia trustees, the great majority accepted that slavery would continue elsewhere, as long as England would remain free, as long as slavery in the land of liberty would never exist again. In the end, such compromises presented two possibilities: a local contest over slaveholding could embolden reformers to pursue an expanded cam-

---

dence is published in George S. Brookes, *Friend Anthony Benezet* (Philadelphia, 1937). See also John A. Woods, ed., "The Correspondence of Benjamin Rush and Granville Sharp, 1773–1809," *Journal of American Studies*, I (1969), 1–38.

paign for universal liberty, or a freedom from slaveholding would satisfy the inclination to mark a difference between England and the less civilized world. The Somerset case helped establish the British Isles, in the minds of the British, as a unique asylum for liberty. It might only have reinforced their toleration of *colonial* slavery and the Atlantic slave trade if the American Revolution had not intervened.

PART II

The Conflict Realized

CHAPTER 2

The Politics of Slavery in the Years of Crisis

Resolution of the Somerset case in 1772 coincided with the first abolitionist stirrings in North America, where the colonial revolt against British rule touched off a revolution in the public conversation about human bondage. Few British settlers had given much thought to the ethics of slavery before the Revolutionary era. And only members of the Religious Society of Friends had conceived the liberation of slaves as a moral obligation and a religious duty. The propriety of enslaving Africans began to matter to the colonists only in the 1760s and 1770s, as patriots articulated their reasons for resisting British authority, when Revolutionary ideology gave the institution of chattel slavery an unexpected and unintended pertinence. If American colonists had presented their case in more parochial and exclusively constitutional terms, if they had argued only for the customary rights and liberties of Englishmen, perhaps, as before, few settlers in British North America would have thought about the rights of Africans. But by invoking purportedly universal principles rather than established law or custom, by describing liberty as a natural right, and by defining their political crusade as a campaign against slavery, North American colonists inadvertently alerted themselves to the dubious justice of holding African men and women, girls and boys, in lifelong bondage. The colonists' own words invited them to see chattel slavery anew. And in those parts of America where slave labor seemed less than critical to the economy, some colonists increasingly disliked what they saw. Few Europeans in North America had considered their commitment to slaveholding or slave trading worthy of extended ethical reflection as late as 1763, at the end of the Seven Years' War. By 1775, though, in the last months of imperial rule, the sale, purchase, and ownership of slaves had become for several communities what these practices had been for some time within the Society of Friends: customs that troubled the conscience.[1]

1. Mary S. Locke, *Anti-Slavery in America from the Introduction of African Slaves to the Prohibition of the Slave Trade (1619–1808)* (Boston, 1910); Bernard Bailyn, *The Ideological Origins of the American Revolution* (Cambridge, Mass., 1967), 232–246;

More than a decade before the development of abolitionism in Britain, the middle and northern colonies in North America presented the unusual spectacle of societies with slaves turning against the practice of human bondage, in part, to abide by the dictates of professed values, or to liberate themselves from moral corruption. A substantial minority in Revolutionary America came to think of slavery not only as a moral wrong but also of antislavery as a moral good, perhaps even a moral duty. Evangelical clergy warned that the fate of the Revolution turned upon the renunciation of collective sins like slavery. When listing the vices threatening the American people in 1774, the Reverend Ebenezer Baldwin of Connecticut placed the enslavement of Africans at the top of his "dreadful catalogue." "Would we enjoy liberty?" asked the Reverend Nathaniel Niles. "Then we must grant it to others," he pronounced in 1774. "For shame, let us either cease to enslave our fellow-men, or else let us cease to complain of those who would enslave us." This was a time "when we solemnly engaged against further importations under a pretence of working by gradual steps a total abolition," recalled South Carolina planter, merchant, and politician Henry Laurens. "We were then indeed in a religious mood and—had appealed to God." The impulse to legitimate rebellion through scrupulous adherence to public virtue placed a premium on exhibitions of moral sincerity. A Massachusetts writer argued in 1773 that patriots had an obligation to assist

Arthur Zilversmit, *The First Emancipation: The Abolition of Slavery in the North* (Chicago, 1967), 93–108; Winthrop D. Jordan, *White over Black: American Attitudes toward the Negro, 1550–1812* (Chapel Hill, N.C., 1968), 276–304, 308–311; Duncan J. Macleod, *Slavery, Race, and the American Revolution* (London, 1974), 14–31; James D. Essig, *The Bonds of Wickedness: American Evangelicals against Slavery, 1770–1808* (Philadelphia, 1982), 3–114; David Grimsted, "Anglo-American Racism and Phillis Wheatley's 'Sable Veil,' 'Length'ned Chain,' and 'Knitted Heart,'" in Ronald Hoffman and Peter J. Albert, eds., *Women in the Age of the American Revolution* (Charlottesville, Va., 1989), 394–414; Gary B. Nash, *Race and Revolution* (Madison, Wis., 1990), 3–24; Patricia Bradley, *Slavery, Propaganda, and the American Revolution* (Jackson, Miss., 1998), 81–131; John Saillant, *Black Puritan, Black Republican: The Life and Thought of Lemuel Haynes, 1753–1833* (Oxford, 2003), 53–60; Peter A. Dorsey, "To 'Corroborate Our Own Claims': Public Positioning and the Slavery Metaphor in Revolutionary America," *American Quarterly*, LV (2003), 353–386. An extensive collection of representative documents appears in Roger Bruns, *Am I Not a Man and a Brother: The Antislavery Crusade of Revolutionary America, 1688–1788* (New York, 1977), 103–391.

those enslaved men and women seeking their freedom, since this would show that instead of "being *pretended* Friends to *Liberty,* we are *really hearty* for the general and unalienable Rights of Mankind." Rhode Island legislators instituted a ban on slave imports because, they declared in their abolition law of 1774, "those who are desirous of enjoying all the advantages of liberty themselves, should be willing to extend personal liberty to others." A committee of Georgia patriots thought it necessary in January 1775 "to show that we are not influenced by any contracted or interested motives, but a general philanthropy for all mankind." For this reason, they declared their "disapprobation and abhorrence of the unnatural practice of slavery in America" and pledged themselves "to use our utmost endeavors for the manumission of our Slaves in this Colony." "Few resistance movements," David Brion Davis has observed, "have been so psychologically dependent on a consistent defense of abstract principles."[2]

What followed was less a coherent antislavery movement than a haphazard, uneven, loosely connected, though mutually reinforcing efflorescence of antislavery impulses and gestures. From Philadelphia to Boston, between 1767 and 1775, there issued a parade of antislavery resolutions, petitions, sermons, pamphlets, and legislation aimed principally at halting the slave trade to the American colonies. Across New England—in Providence, Rhode Island, in Danbury, Enfield, and Norwich, Connecticut, in Boston, Leicester, Medford, Salem, Sandwich, and Worcester, Massachusetts—colonists instructed their representatives to bring antislavery measures before the colonial legislatures. New York City distillers in 1774

2. The Reverend Ebenezer Baldwin cited in Essig, *The Bonds of Wickedness,* 22; Henry Laurens to John Faucheraud Grimké, Jan. 31, 1785, in Philip M. Hamer et al., *The Papers of Henry Laurens,* 16 vols. (Columbia, S.C., [1968]–2003), XVI, 531; *The Appendix; or, Some Observations on the Expediency of the Petition of the Africans Living in Boston, etc., Lately Presented to the General Assembly of This Province; to Which Is Annexed, the Petition Referred to; Likewise, Thoughts on Slavery; with a Useful Extract from the Massachusetts Spy, of January 28, 1773, by Way of an Address to the Members of the Assembly; by a Lover of Constitutional Liberty* (Boston, [1773]), 6; Elizabeth Donnan, ed., *Documents Illustrative of the History of the Slave Trade to America,* 4 vols. (Washington, D.C., 1930–1935), III, 289; Nathaniel Niles and the Darien Resolutions cited in Dorsey, " 'To Corroborate Our Own Claims,' " *Am. Qtly.,* LV (2003), 363, 369; David Brion Davis, *The Problem of Slavery in the Age of Revolution, 1770–1823* (Ithaca, N.Y., 1975), 281 (see also his discussion therein on 273–299).

refused to supply African merchants with molasses for the slave trade. At its constitutional convention in 1777, the New York legislature resolved that, in principle, "every human being who breathes the air of the state shall enjoy the privileges of a freeman" and urged future legislators "to take the most effective measures consistent with public safety for abolishing domestic slavery." Emancipation proposals circulated publicly and privately. John Adams received from Fredericksburg, Virginia, in 1775 a draft plan for arming slaves to fight the British and for establishing a settlement in Canada for the liberated after the achievement of American independence. Less than two months after the bloodshed at Lexington and Concord, a gathering of town leaders in Worcester, Massachusetts, pledged themselves to the abolition of slavery. The same year, Philadelphia Quakers established the Society for the Relief of Free Negroes Unlawfully Held in Bondage, the first association in the British Atlantic world dedicated to the promotion of antislavery principles.[3]

In practice, the Revolutionary generation set in motion only a gradual and "grudging emancipation," in the historian Alfred Young's apt words, and only in those regions where slavery was of limited and declining importance.[4] There, north of the Chesapeake, the pace of change displayed a persistent willingness to honor propertied interests. In most instances northern governments liberated only the unborn children of the enslaved, and only once those children reached adulthood. The decline of slavery also reflected a capitulation to heightened expectations among the enslaved who during the Revolutionary era petitioned for freedom, negotiated for shorter terms of service, and, in growing numbers, deserted slaveowners.[5]

3. Zilversmit, *The First Emancipation*, 100, 106, 108; Jordan, *White over Black,* 299; Gwendolyn Evans Logan, "The Slave in Connecticut during the American Revolution," *Connecticut Historical Society Bulletin,* XXX (1965), 74; Edgar J. McManus, *A History of Negro Slavery in New York* (Syracuse, N.Y., 1966), 152, 161; John P. Kaminski, *A Necessary Evil? Slavery and the Debate over the Constitution* (Madison, Wis., 1995), 4: Lee Nathaniel Newcomer, *The Embattled Farmers: A Massachusetts Countryside in the American Revolution* (New York, 1953), 161. For further examples of emancipation proposals in North America in the years of crisis, see chapter 4.

4. Alfred F. Young, "Afterword: How Radical Was the American Revolution," in Young, ed., *Beyond the American Revolution: Explorations in the History of American Radicalism* (Dekalb, Ill., 1993), 339.

5. On these points, see particularly Gary B. Nash and Jean R. Soderlund, *Freedom by*

But if the governing elite typically possessed only an uncertain commitment to slave trade abolition and serious doubts about slave emancipation, they often clung to the pose of moral sincerity with telling ferocity. Even once accommodations and compromises secured slaveholding in a way that allowed for its expansion in the United States deep into the nineteenth

---

Degrees: Emancipation in Pennsylvania and Its Aftermath (New York, 1991); Nash, *Race and Revolution;* Shane White, *Somewhat More Independent: The End of Slavery in New York City, 1770–1810* (Athens, Ga., 1991); Joanne Pope Melish, *Disowning Slavery: Gradual Emancipation and "Race" in New England, 1780–1830* (Ithaca, N.Y., 1998); Ira Berlin, *Many Thousands Gone: The First Two Centuries of Slavery in North America* (Cambridge, Mass., 1998), 228–255; and Graham Russell Hodges, *Root and Branch: African Americans in New York and East Jersey, 1613–1863* (Chapel Hill, N.C., 1999), 144–146, 150–153, 158–186. Note also Frances D. Pingeon, "Slavery in New Jersey on the Eve of the Revolution," in William C. Wright, ed., *New Jersey in the American Revolution: Political and Social Conflict: Papers Presented at the First Annual New Jersey History Symposium, December 6, 1969, Held by the New Jersey Historical Commission,* rev. ed. (Trenton, N.J., 1975), 48–64; and William H. Williams, *Slavery and Freedom in Delaware, 1639–1865* (Wilmington, Del., 1996), 141–146. For careful studies of the freedom struggles of enslaved men and women in New England in particular, see also Thomas J. Davis, "Emancipation Rhetoric, Natural Rights, and Revolutionary New England: A Note on Four Black Petitions in Massachusetts, 1773–1777," *New England Quarterly,* LXII (1989), 248–263; T. H. Breen, "Making History: The Force of Public Opinion and the Last Years of Slavery in Revolutionary Massachusetts," in Ronald Hoffman, Michal Sobel, and Fredrika J. Teute, eds., *Through a Glass Darkly: Reflections on Personal Identity in Early America* (Chapel Hill, N.C., 1997), 67–95; Emily Blanck, "Seventeen Eighty-Three: The Turning Point in the Law of Slavery and Freedom in Massachusetts," *NEQ,* LXXV (2002), 24–51; John Wood Sweet, *Bodies Politic: Negotiating Race in the American North, 1730–1830* (Baltimore, 2003); and Blanck, "Revolutionizing Slavery: The Legal Culture of Slavery in Revolutionary Massachusetts and South Carolina" (Ph.D. diss., Emory University, 2003). Much of this scholarship receives thoughtful review in Douglas R. Egerton, "Black Independence Struggles and the Tale of Two Revolutions: A Review Essay," *Journal of Southern History,* LXIV (1998), 95–116. There is no reason to believe that antislavery opinion necessarily would have developed when or as it did in the absence of the conflict with the British government. William Freehling has described the Revolutionary era as causing simultaneous "advances" and "retreats" on the slavery issue. In his words, the Revolutionaries launched both an "antislavery process and a proslavery counteroffensive." Independence left the slave system "stronger in the South, where it was already strongest, and weaker in the

century, the moral and ethical injunctions that took shape in the years of rebellion remained a factor in American politics and culture. The American Revolution occasioned in the former colonies a permanent reorientation in assumptions about slavery as an institution. It transformed the persistence of human bondage into a political and moral issue. Thereafter, chattel slavery would require an active defense.

The British antislavery movement that began in the late 1780s was, therefore, a late-born sibling in the family of Anglo-American antislavery campaigns. It took shape after the individual initiatives that first arose during the 1760s and 1770s in New England, the Delaware Valley, and, with much more ambivalence, in the northern reaches of the Chesapeake Bay. As will happen to younger siblings, the nascent British movement felt the influence of its predecessors. Campaigners in Pennsylvania and New Jersey, in particular, sent east across the Atlantic correspondence and tracts that inspired and encouraged the first antislavery spokesmen in Britain.[6] So any explanation of British abolitionism must assess carefully the impact and character of American precursors. "Transatlantic influence," however, does not tell the whole story. Attempts to influence did not always prove influential. Repudiation of the American example mattered as much as imitation to the history of the British campaigns. Moreover, the campaigns emerged from a shared set of conditions—a dynamic interplay of politics, ideology, and values—that belie reductive attempts to mark out linear influences. Viewed in comparative perspective, as Seymour Drescher has emphasized, British and American abolitionism reveal a broad kinship. They were organized through ad hoc associations for reform, often mobilized through tight-knit religious communities, and oriented toward legislative action. They emerged as social movements that drew on and in turn generated

---

North, where it was weakest." See William W. Freehling, "The Founding Fathers, Conditional Antislavery, and the Nonradicalism of the American Revolution," in Freehling, *The Reintegration of American History: Slavery and the Civil War* (New York, 1994), 12–33, citations on 14, 30–31.

6. This theme is explored most lucidly in Betty Fladeland, *Men and Brothers: Anglo-American Antislavery Cooperation* (Urbana, Ill., 1972), 16–33, and Davis, *The Problem of Slavery in the Age of Revolution*, 213–232. See also Michael Kraus, "Slavery Reform in the Eighteenth Century: An Aspect of Transatlantic Intellectual Cooperation," *Pennsylvania Magazine of History and Biography*, LX (1936), 53–66.

public debate and popular participation. These features distinguished the British and American campaigns from subsequent initiatives in continental Europe, which absorbed the Enlightenment critique of slavery but not the urgency of reform or the ethos of collective action.[7] This familial resemblance between the British and American movements presents the possibility that they not only exchanged influences but also shared a common descent. If the American Revolution stirred self-scrutiny in North America, what impact did the conflict have on British responses to slavery in the years before and during the American war?

This question has been approached in at least four ways. Some interpreters have treated the conflict within the empire as irrelevant to the British campaigns of the succeeding decades.[8] Others have emphasized

7. Seymour Drescher, "Two Variants of Anti-Slavery: Religious Organization and Social Mobilization in Britain and France, 1780–1870," in Christine Bolt and Seymour Drescher, eds., *Anti-Slavery, Religion, and Reform: Essays in Memory of Roger Anstey* (Folkestone, Kent, Eng., 1980), 43–63; Drescher, *Capitalism and Antislavery: British Mobilization in Comparative Perspective* (Oxford, 1986), 50–58; Drescher, "Brazilian Abolition in Comparative Perspective," *Hispanic American Historical Review*, LXVIII (1988), 429–460; Drescher, "British Way, French Way: Opinion Building and Revolution in the Second French Slave Emancipation," *American Historical Review*, XCI (1991), 709–735; Drescher, "The Long Goodbye: Dutch Capitalism and Antislavery in Comparative Perspective," in Gert Oostindie, ed., *Fifty Years Later: Antislavery, Capitalism, and Modernity in the Dutch Orbit* (Pittsburgh, Pa., 1996), 25–66. On the affinities between early American and early British abolitionism, one may still benefit from passages in Howard R. Temperley, "The British and American Abolitionists Compared," in Martin Duberman, ed., *The Antislavery Vanguard: New Essays on the Abolitionists* (Princeton, N.J., 1965), 343–361. Throughout *The Problem of Slavery in the Age of Revolution,* Davis presents detailed comparisons of the first British and American movements and, as a consequence, gives particular attention to contrasts.

8. The major studies of the past forty years make only the most minimal references to the American war. The term *American Revolution* does not appear in the indexes to Dale H. Porter, *The Abolition of the Slave Trade in England, 1784–1807* ([Hamden, Conn.], 1970), Roger Anstey, *The Atlantic Slave Trade and British Abolition, 1760–1810* (London, 1975), and James Walvin, *England, Slaves, and Freedom, 1776–1838* (London, 1986), although each of these works describes the imperial conflict as interrupting nascent Anglo-American abolitionism. Nor has the conflict typically figured in the several works on early British abolitionism by Seymour Drescher, although in a more recent essay he suggests that "the American Revolution of 1776 accelerated political actions

that the American Revolution interrupted and postponed the work of nascent transatlantic reform networks.[9] Several have proposed that the loss of the North American empire enabled emancipation in the long run by confining slavery in the British Empire to the West Indies, colonies incapable of seeking political independence. More recently, a few have observed that abolitionism helped restore national honor in the wake of humiliating defeat. In every instance, in each of these interpretations, the American Revolution mattered (if it mattered) because of how the British reacted to the experience of defeat.[10] The war years themselves, and the political crises that *preceded* the war—both recognized as central to the

---

against the transatlantic slave trade" and adds that "antislavery was one of the ideological movements that survived and counteracted the political rupture of Anglo-America." See Drescher, "The Long Goodbye," in Oostindie, ed., *Fifty Years Later,* 48, 49.

9. Fladeland, *Men and Brothers,* 27–30; Paul Thomas, "Changing Attitudes in an Expanding Empire: The Anti-Slavery Movement, 1760–1783," *Slavery and Abolition,* V, no. 1 (May 1984), 50–72.

10. For the Revolution as confining British slavery to the far more dependent British West Indies and thereby making possible the emancipation of 1833, see Reginald Coupland, *The British Anti-Slavery Movement,* 2d ed. (London, 1964), 60–66; Eric Williams, *Capitalism and Slavery* (1944; rpt. Chapel Hill, N.C., 1994), 123–124; George R. Mellor, *British Imperial Trusteeship, 1783–1850* (London, 1951), 25; Porter, *The Abolition of the Slave Trade in England,* 32; Fladeland, *Men and Brothers,* 29–30; C. Duncan Rice, *The Rise and Fall of Black Slavery* (New York, 1975), 216; and Robert Edgar Conrad, "Economics and Ideals: The British Anti-Slavery Crusade Reconsidered," *Indian Historical Review,* XV (1988–1989), 217–218. It is impossible, David Brion Davis has written, to imagine Parliament passing the celebrated Emancipation Act of 1833 had the United States remained part of the empire. Davis, "American Slavery and the American Revolution," in Ira Berlin and Ronald Hoffman, eds., *Slavery and Freedom in the Age of the American Revolution* (Charlottesville, Va., 1980), 279. For the suggestion that, with regard to abolitionism, the American Revolution converted "existing qualms into positive action," see the incisive analysis by Linda Colley in *Britons: Forging the Nation, 1707–1837* (New Haven, Conn., 1992), 352–360, citation on 352. Her thesis has been echoed in J. R. Oldfield, *Popular Politics and British Anti-Slavery: The Mobilization of Public Opinion against the Slave Trade, 1787–1807* (Manchester, Eng., 1995), 32–33, and in Stephen Conway, *The British Isles and the War of American Independence* (Oxford, 2000), 117–118. Robin Blackburn also situates British abolitionism in the context of postwar reform. See Blackburn, *The Overthrow of Colonial Slavery, 1776–1848* (London, 1988), 133–137.

history of American abolitionism—scarcely figure in accounts of the anti-slavery movement in Britain. The history of British antislavery, to be sure, differs from the history of American antislavery in crucial ways. The American Revolution did not engender in Britain comparable concerns with how the moral character of the nation looked on the world stage. Nor did the British nation and the British government, at first, develop a similar need to legitimate political ambitions through dramatic demonstrations of collective virtue. The British army offered freedom to the slaves owned by colonial rebels, but to win a war, not to establish moral authority for the right to rule. An antislavery movement failed to develop in Britain *during* the American Revolution. A hopeful few lobbied discreetly for antislavery legislation, but these tentative, isolated appeals did not coalesce during the 1770s into organized protest.[11]

Nonetheless, the American Revolution did mark a turning point in British as well as American responses to colonial slavery. The affinities, however, reside as much with the political uses of antislavery values as with the circulation of antislavery arguments. Too often a focus on the libertarian ideals set loose by Revolutionary ideology obscures the more narrow political goals that antislavery rhetoric came to serve in these years. The expression of antislavery opinion in the Revolutionary era did not always represent the effusions of sentiment. Nor should it be conflated, in every instance, with humanitarianism. A committed circle of moral idealists did take a genuine interest in the welfare of Africans during the Revolutionary War. For some, particularly in North America, the language of natural rights helped crystallize the iniquities. On both sides of the Atlantic, however, political conflict gave new meaning to antislavery opinion. Antislavery statements and gestures emerged as frequently to meet tactical needs, to answer immediate ideological objectives, or to erase doubts about individual and collective self-worth. In the Revolutionary era, expressing opposition to chattel slavery was a means to other ends as often as an end in itself. Understanding what the American Revolution meant to the British antislavery movement means, first, understanding the novel purposes to which antislavery opinion was put before and during the American war.

The expression of antislavery sentiment before the achievement of American independence had a variety of political uses, as an examination of

---

11. These initiatives and schemes and their significance are treated in chapters 3 and 4.

the British pamphlet literature concerned with the emerging North American rebellion will show. The problem of slavery, by any measure, was of marginal concern to those who wrote about the deepening crisis between the thirteen colonies and the British government. The vast majority of the texts do not refer to colonial slavery or the Atlantic slave trade. Those that do mention the subject treat it in passing. The problem of slavery surfaced in the years of crisis as a talking point in the transatlantic debate, as a way to make the case for or against American independence. Propagandists on both sides of the Atlantic took the abstract injustice of the slave system for granted. They did not attempt to argue the point—further evidence of the diffuse if inert antislavery consensus prevailing among certain Anglo-American intellectuals in the later eighteenth century. Instead, they exploited that unspoken consensus on the abstract injustice to scrutinize and condemn the politics of those they opposed. British and American pamphleteers competed to assign or escape blame for the existence of slavery in the British Empire, casting slavery in the process, though with little reflection, as an archetype of injustice. This cycle of "reciprocal rebuke, retaliation, and reproach," as historian Brian Harrison once characterized such dynamics, had profound and lasting consequences.[12] This debate politicized the institution of slavery for the first time, in Britain as well as in North America. It made the very existence of slavery not merely a moral problem but a political problem, leaving the question as not only a subject for ethical rumination and reflection but also a target for political action.

[I]   Certain habits had prevailed when British men and women discussed the horrors of colonial slavery before the era of the American Revolution. Almost without exception they assigned responsibility for slavery to British colonials, to the North American and Caribbean owners of human chattel. Without reflection, they distanced the British state and the residents of the British Isles from reproach. Rarely was mention made of the British merchants who shipped slaves from the African coast or the role of the state in subsidizing the Atlantic trade. Even less frequently was attention drawn to the profits earned by British merchants who sold goods to the slave colonies or to the hundreds of thousands of men and women in

12. Brian Harrison, "A Genealogy of Reform in Modern Britain," in Bolt and Drescher, eds., *Anti-Slavery, Religion, and Reform*, 122.

Britain who consumed slave-produced sugar and tobacco. This inclination to single out slaveholders for censure reflected a long-standing tendency among some in Britain to cast the enslavement of Africans as a colonial innovation wholly unrelated to the needs and values of the more civilized metropolis, as a consequence, instead, of choices made by degenerate Britons. Adam Smith, for example, famously tarred colonial slaveholders in 1759 as "the refuse of the jails of Europe," who through their deeds and manners had forfeited a place in polite society. These "wretches," wrote Smith, "possess the virtues neither of the countries which they come from, nor of those which they go to." "Fortune never exerted more cruelly her empire over mankind, than when she subjected those nations of heroes," the peoples of Africa, "to the levity, brutality, and baseness" of British Americans.[13] Insulting as these views were to colonists, British condescension historically bore few consequences for colonial interests or planters' day-to-day affairs. Their public image in England began to matter rather more to North Americans during the 1760s, when a reputation for oppressing Africans began to damage metropolitan opinion of colonial rights.

A response published in 1764 challenging Adam Smith's unflattering assessment of British settlers signaled the conflicts to come. The author, twenty-four-year-old Arthur Lee, was the youngest son of a prominent Virginia patriarch, at the time a medical student at the University of Edinburgh, and soon to be a leading spokesman in England for the rights of the North American colonies. Lee had spent much of his youth in British schools and, perhaps for this reason, possessed (for a Virginian) an unusual contempt for the institution of slavery. His *Essay in Vindication of the Continental Colonies in America* (1764), in which he declared slavery to be

13. D. D. Raphael and A. L. Macfie, eds., *Adam Smith, The Theory of Moral Sentiments* (Oxford, 1976), 206–207. The metropolitan image of the colonial planter is treated in Wylie Sypher, "The West-Indian as a 'Character' in the Eighteenth Century," *Studies in Philology*, XXXVI (1939), 503–520; James Raven, *Judging New Wealth: Popular Publishing and Responses to Commerce in England, 1750–1800* (Oxford, 1992), 231, 245–246; Maaja A. Stewart, "Inexhaustible Generosity: The Fictions of Eighteenth-Century British Imperialism in Richard Cumberland's *The West Indian*," *Eighteenth Century Studies*, XXXVII (1996), 42–55; Michal J. Rozbicki, "The Curse of Provincialism: Negative Perceptions of Colonial American Plantation Gentry," *Jour. So. Hist.*, LXIII (1987), 727–752; and Andrew Jackson O'Shaughnessy, *An Empire Divided: The American Revolution and the British Caribbean* (Philadelphia, 2000), 12–14.

"absolutely repugnant to justice," may have been the first antislavery pamphlet ever written by a slaveholder. But Arthur Lee, in this instance, took
up his pen, not because he objected to slavery, but because he despised
black people and disliked seeing them described as "heroes" by Adam
Smith. Even more, he could not tolerate Smith's slanderous characteriza-
tions of his family in Virginia and fellow colonials in North America. Lee
agreed that slavery was "shocking to humanity, violative of every generous
sentiment, abhorrent utterly from the Christian religion." Yet he committed
the bulk of his text to portraying the African race as "the most detestable
and vile that the earth produced" and to characterizing English colonists as
"descended from worthy ancestors," as "a humane, hospitable, and polished people." Driving this atypical (for the time) mélange of antislavery
and racism was Lee's overriding anxiety about the standing of British
Americans within the empire. Arthur Lee believed that metropolitan contempt for American slaveholders helped justify imperial policies that de-
valued American interests and denied colonists the liberty to establish
manufactures or sell their crops to foreign traders, policies that treated
British colonials, "not as fellow subjects, but as the servants of Britain."[14]

Benjamin Franklin also came to resent British chauvinism, particularly
in the decade following the Stamp Act crisis, during his tenure as London
agent for Pennsylvania, Georgia, New Jersey, and Massachusetts. Like Lee,
Franklin feared that polite distaste for slaveholding would harm the colonists' reputation in the British Isles. In 1770, he composed for a London
newspaper the substance of a conversation he claimed to have overheard

14. Arthur Lee, *An Essay in Vindication of the Continental Colonies in America, from
a Censure of Mr. Adam Smith, in His Theory of Moral Sentiments* (London, 1764), 20,
30, 42, 43; Richard K. MacMaster, "Arthur Lee's 'Address on Slavery': An Aspect of
Virginia's Struggle to End the Slave Trade, 1765–1775," *Virginia Magazine of History
and Biography,* LXXX (1972), 141–157; Louis W. Potts, *Arthur Lee: A Virtuous Revolutionary* (Baton Rouge, La., 1981), 23–37. John Laurens of South Carolina experienced a
similar, if more lasting, conversion to polite antislavery opinion during his years of
schooling in London at the Inns of Court. Gregory D. Massey, *John Laurens and the
American Revolution* (Columbia, S.C., 2000), 62–64. For the trials that colonial youth
like Arthur Lee and John Laurens experienced in the British Isles during their apprenticeship for a career in public life, see Julie M. Flavell, "The 'School for Modesty and
Humility': Colonial American Youth in London and Their Parents, 1755–75," *Historical
Journal,* XL (1999), 377–403.

"between an ENGLISHMAN, a SCOTCHMAN, and an AMERICAN, on the subject of slavery." Not all colonists hold slaves, nor are all slaveholders tyrants, argued "the American," Franklin's surrogate. Besides, there were slaves in the colonies because British merchants shipped them there. And, further, he asked, what was the state of Scottish colliers or impressed English sailors if not also a species of slavery?[15] Well into the next century, pro-slavery writers would offer comparisons of this kind to divert attention from American slavery in the colonies. But Benjamin Franklin, like Arthur Lee, had no particular interest in defending human bondage. What enraged them both (and Eric Williams more than two hundred years later, although for very different reasons) was British moral arrogance. They deplored the sense of superiority and presumption of innocence that allowed the British to stand in judgment of Americans while blithely ignoring the ways the nation benefited from the labor of nearly a million enslaved Africans in the British Americas and from the annual shipment of approximately forty thousand slaves to the colonies.

On the rare occasions they thought about the subject, the British did consider the exploitation of slave labor to be a peculiarly American vice, an inclination the outcome of the Somerset case simply reinforced. Lord Mansfield's decision of 1772 merely prohibited slaveholders living in England from forcibly expelling their human property from the British Isles. However, it was "generally felt," Arthur Lee reported from London, "as

15. "A Conversation between an Englishman, a Scotchman, and an American, on the Subject of Slavery," *Public Advertiser* (London), Jan. 30, 1770, in Verner W. Crane, "Benjamin Franklin on Slavery and American Liberties," *PMHB*, LXII (1938), 1–11. David Waldstreicher attends to the political work embedded in Franklin's antislavery writings with nuance and insight in Waldstreicher, *Runaway America: Benjamin Franklin, Slavery, and the American Revolution* (New York, 2004), 192–204. On the colonists' fear of being relegated to second-class status within the empire, more generally, see Jack P. Greene, "Pride, Prejudice, and Jealousy: Benjamin Franklin's Explanation for the American Revolution," in J. A. Leo Lemay, *Reappraising Benjamin Franklin: A Bicentennial Perspective* (Newark, Del., 1993), 133–136; Greene, "Empire and Identity from the Glorious Revolution to the American Revolution," in P. J. Marshall, ed., *The Oxford History of the British Empire*, II, *The Eighteenth Century* (Oxford, 1998), 208–230; and T. H. Breen, "Ideology and Nationalism on the Eve of the American Revolution: Revisions *Once More* in Need of Revising," *Journal of American History*, LXXXIV (1997), 28–34.

putting a negative on the existence of slavery in this country."[16] To deflate this self-congratulatory mood, Benjamin Franklin wrote for the *Gazetteer* one week later what he after described to Quaker abolitionist Anthony Benezet as "Remarks on the Hypocrisy of this Country . . . for promoting the [slave] Trade, while it piqu'd itself on its Virtue[,] Love of Liberty, and the Equity in its Courts in setting free a single Negro." For Franklin more was at stake than putting the Somerset verdict in proper perspective, than drawing attention to the Atlantic slave trade. He understood correctly, as early as 1770, that the British tendency to think of Americans as boorish despots would compromise respect for colonists' political rights and "encourage those who would oppress us, by representing us as unworthy of the Liberty we are now contending for."[17] London moralist Thomas Day would prove to be sympathetic to the American Revolution. Yet even he thought that colonial slavery discredited the patriot cause, that the apparent abolition of slavery in England established the metropolis as the standard-bearer for liberty. "Let the wild, inconsistent claims of America prevail, when they shall be unmixed with the clank of chains, and the groans of anguish," he wrote in 1774. "Let her aim a dagger at the breast of her Milder parent, if she can advance a step without trampling on the dead and dying carcasses of her slaves:—But let her remember that it is in Britain alone . . . the most sacred rights of nature have received their most awful ratification."[18] By validating the virtue of English law, by bolstering an already

16. Arthur Lee to Joseph Reed, Feb. 18, 1773, in William B. Reed, ed., *Life and Correspondence of Joseph Reed . . .*, 2 vols. (Philadelphia, 1847), I, 48.

17. Benjamin Franklin to Anthony Benezet, Aug. 22, 1772, in Leonard W. Labaree et al., eds., *The Papers of Benjamin Franklin,* 37 vols. to date (New Haven, Conn., 1959–), XIX, 269; Crane, "Benjamin Franklin on Slavery and American Liberties," *PMHB,* LXII (1938), 5. As Patricia Bradley has shown, the patriot press in the thirteen colonies opted to suppress information about the Somerset case in its pages. See Bradley, *Slavery, Propaganda, and the American Revolution,* 66–80.

18. Thomas Day, *The Dying Negro, a Poetical Epistle from a Black, Who Shot Himself on Board a Vessel in the River Thames, to His Intended Wife,* 2d ed. (London, 1774), viii. Day continued at some length questioning the virtue of British Americans: "Let us remember, there is a people who share the government and name of Britons; among whom the cruelty of Sparta is renewed without its virtue. It was some excuse for the disciples of Lycurgus, that if one man had been created by Heaven to obey another, the citizens he had formed best deserved the empire of the world. But what has *America* to

well-developed sense of cultural superiority, the Somerset case offered an ideological prop to imperial rule. Lord Mansfield's decision reassured the English that they lived in a land of liberty. And it conveyed this comforting message just when certain colonists in North America had started to insist that colonial subordination to a British parliament, almost by definition, meant enslavement to tyrannical authority.

Ambrose Serle worked as a senior clerk in the American department for Secretaries of State Wills Hill, first earl of Hillsborough, and William Legge, Lord Dartmouth, from 1768 to 1776, in the years when British ministers struggled to maintain their authority over the thirteen colonies. Not surprisingly, Serle took a special interest in praising the moral excellence of British institutions. "Slavery is no part of our Constitution," the government aide boasted in 1775. "We have no idea of it in our law. It is not to be found in our country. Negroes here, wherever they have been slaves before are emancipated in a moment by setting foot upon our liberating shores." These words appeared in a tract Serle titled *Americans against Liberty,* where he argued, co-opting a phrase from the colonial patriots' favorite John Locke, "where there is no law, there is no freedom." In England, in contrast to America, the law respected neither persons nor races, Serle pontificated. Proof resided near the London hamlet of Blackwall, where a Virginia ship captain named Ferguson hung in chains for murdering while at sea his fourteen-year-old black servant. English law assured justice as well as liberty, Serle declared, even when justice required stringing up British Americans who committed felonies that would have gone unpunished in the colonies.[19]

Ambrose Serle had no particular interest in Africans or their enslave-

---

boast? What are the graces or the virtues which distinguish its inhabitants? What are *their* triumphs in war, or their inventions in peace? Inglorious soldiers, yet seditious citizens; sordid merchants, and indolent usurpers; behold the men, who avarice has been more fatal to the interests of humanity, and has more desolated the world than the ambition of its ancient Conquerers!" (16). On Day, see Paul Langford, "Thomas Day and the Politics of Sentiment," *Journal of Imperial and Commonwealth History,* XII, no. 2 (1983-1984), 57-79.

19. [Ambrose Serle], *Americans against Liberty; or, An Essay on the Nature and Principles of True Freedom Shewing That the Designs and Conduct of the Americans Tend Only to Tyranny and Slavery . . .* (London, 1775), 33. For reference to Ambrose Serle as an imperial bureaucrat, see Margaret Marion Spector, *The American Department of the British Government, 1768-1782* (New York, 1940), 34, 35.

ment. Rather he made a (false) claim about the laws of slavery in England to bolster the argument on behalf of British governance in America. Serle needed English law to surpass colonial laws on the scale of virtue, if only to support related assertions regarding the virtues of imperial authority. The conjoined sovereign of king-in-parliament guaranteed liberty to British subjects throughout the empire, Serle insisted. The Somerset case proved that the courts rescued even "helpless foreigners" from "oppression." Colonists, then, had no reason to suspect a conspiracy to "enslave" America. The very idea conflicted with "all fact and experience"; it was "directly opposite to common sense." By rejecting the authority of Parliament, by inching toward republicanism, designing factions in the colonies threatened to exchange mild and just government for the insecurity of mob rule. In truth, Serle stated, the "Rebel Americans" were "THE OPEN ENEMIES TO THE PUBLIC AND GENERAL LIBERTY OF THE BRITISH EMPIRE."[20]

In the service of Admiral Richard Howe, Ambrose Serle reached New York's Staten Island in July 1776, less than a week after the Continental Congress issued the Declaration of Independence, which he denounced as an "impudent, false and atrocious Proclamation." In North America, Serle found, "there is nothing to be heard but the Sound of Liberty, and nothing to be felt but the most detestable Slavery." Witness the immoderate abuses inflicted on innocent loyalists; witness the oaths of fidelity to the Republic that the self-professed Sons of Liberty extracted from wavering neighbors. "Such men," Serle concluded, "are no Enemies to absolute Rule: they only hate it in others, but ardently pursue it for themselves." While sailing with Lord Howe's fleet down the Chesapeake Bay in September 1777, several days after the Battle of Brandywine, Serle reflected on the "Huts" and "Hovels" that housed the enslaved residing along Maryland's Eastern Shore. The slaves, he had observed during his fourteen months in North America, "are treated as a better kind of Cattle, being bought or sold, according to Fancy or Interest." "Such is the Practice or Sentiment of Americans," he mused, "while they are bawling about the Rights of *human Nature,* and oppose the freest Govt. and most liberal System of Polity known upon the Face of the Earth."[21]

20. [Serle], *Americans against Liberty,* 28, 33.

21. Edward H. Tatum, Jr., *The American Journal of Ambrose Serle* (San Marino, Calif., 1940), 31, 46, 98, 249.

The American rebellion forced the British government and its supporters to defend on principle a constitutional order that derived its authority from precedent, from prescription, and, above all, from its success in promoting political stability and economic prosperity far more than from abstract doctrine.[22] Typically, proponents of parliamentary supremacy turned to law in reply: supreme legislative authority must lie somewhere within the empire; and the conjoined sovereign of king-in-parliament rightfully possessed the power to legislate for the realm. To complement these constitutional claims, however, writers like Ambrose Serle sometimes seized on the horrors of American slavery to emphasize the vices characteristic of colonial society and mark, by contrast, the virtues of metropolitan customs, manners, and laws. Every major writer in the pay of the government interest at some point took up this theme. The exiled Boston printer John Mein in the London *Public Ledger* savaged his erstwhile countrymen for their treason to principle.[23] English pamphleteers John Lind, John Shebbeare, and Samuel Johnson, with the Methodist leaders John Wesley and John William Fletcher, decried colonial slavery in tracts otherwise concerned with imperial politics.

22. L. F. S. Upton, "The Dilemma of the Loyalist Pamphleteers," *Studies in Burke and His Time,* XVIII (1977), 71–84; Paul Langford, "Old Whigs, Old Tories, and the American Revolution," *Jour. Imperial and Commonwealth Hist.*, VIII, no. 2 (1980), 106–130; H. T. Dickinson, "Britain's Imperial Sovereignty," in Dickinson, *Britain and the American Revolution* (London, 1998), 81–96; P. J. Marshall, "The Case for Coercing America before the Revolution," in Fred M. Leventhal and Ronald Quinault, eds., *Anglo-American Attitudes: From Revolution to Partnership* (Aldershot, Eng., 2000), 9–22; Eliga Gould, "American Independence and Britain's Counter-Revolution," *Past and Present,* no. 154 (February 1997), 107–146; Gould, *The Persistence of Empire: Political Culture in the Age of the American Revolution* (Chapel Hill, N.C., 2000), 136–147.

23. [John Mein], *Sagittarius's Letters and Political Speculations* (Boston, 1775); John E. Alden, "John Mein: Scourge of Patriots," Colonial Society of Massachusetts, *Publications,* XXVI, *Transactions* (Boston, 1937–1942), 571–599. These letters were first published in the London newspaper *Public Ledger*. For further instances of antislavery views of loyalist elites, see Dorsey, " 'To Corroborate Our Own Claims,' " *Am. Qtly.*, LV (2003), 362–364, and Blanck, "Revolutionizing Slavery," 133–136, 230–231. For additional discussion of the government press and its treatment of colonial slavery, see James J. Sack, *From Jacobite to Conservative: Reaction and Orthodoxy in Britain, c. 1760–1832* (Cambridge, 1993), 165, and Benjamin Labaree, "The Idea of American Independence: The British View, 1774–1776," Massachusetts Historical Society, *Proceedings,* LXXXII (1970), 11.

Rarely did these British defenders of the established order linger on the subject. The facts about American slavery always were of limited importance to pro-government propaganda. Ministerial writers were far more anxious about slaveholders' politics than about slavery itself. Instead, expressions of shock and disgust at American hypocrisy performed a vital rhetorical function. They accentuated broader claims about the legitimacy of British rule and the illegitimacy of rebellion. Samuel Johnson saved his now famous query regarding the "drivers of Negroes" and their "yelps for liberty" for the final passage of *Taxation No Tyranny* to ensure its dramatic effect. Taking note of colonial slavery also helped British opponents of the American Revolution establish certain "facts" about the American character and unmask the "true" principles animating colonial rebellion. Through the issue of slavery, in part, they cast Americans as uncouth, insolent, hypocritical petty tyrants whose politics, if honored, would compromise liberty, law, and government throughout the British Empire.

[II]   By the time of the Stamp Act crisis, Britons had grown accustomed to thinking of the slave colonies as providing a specific shape and disposition to the American character. It surprised no one to learn from Matthew Wheelock in 1770 that slaveholding gave the Virginia and Maryland gentry "a certain haughtiness." "Their authority over their slaves," wrote the Reverend Andrew Burnaby after several years of travel in the American colonies, "renders [Virginians] vain and imperious, and intire strangers to that elegance of sentiment, which is so peculiarly characteristic of refined and polished nations." For this reason, William Russell wrote in his *History of America* (1778), the company of slaveholders was "little relished in Europe." Weaned "from their earliest infancy" on the enslavement of Africans, "they insensibly imbibe the most extravagant opinion of their own consequence." West Indian slaveholders possessed neither discipline nor manners. "Seldom meeting with any opposition to their will . . . they assume a domineering air, and look down with disdain on the bulk of mankind." This, Russell concluded ruefully, is "what must masters become, who have never obeyed."[24]

24. [Matthew Wheelock], *Reflections Moral and Political on Great Britain and Her Colonies* (London, 1770), 38; Andrew Burnaby, *Travels through the Middle Settlements in North-America; in the Years 1759 and 1760; With Observations upon the State of the*

The delusions of grandeur slaveholding instilled helped British commentators explain colonial intransigence. The arrogance bred by unrestricted authority over their slaves led Virginians, Wheelock wrote, "to forget their state as British subjects and colonists" and encouraged them to "talk of Great Britain as their *sister state*." The private character of the Virginians, Andrew Burnaby observed, shaped their political temper: "They are haughty and jealous of their liberties, impatient of restraint, and can scarcely bear the thought of being controuled by any superior power." Securing submission in the slave colonies would be difficult, Edmund Burke warned, because, there, a love of freedom arose from "the vast multitude of slaves." "Where this is the case in any part of the world," Burke declared, "those who are free, are by far the most proud and jealous of their freedom. Freedom to them is not only an enjoyment, but a kind of rank and privilege." "In such a people," he concluded, "the haughtiness of domination combines with the spirit of freedom, fortifies it, and renders it invincible."[25]

Because the prevalence of slave ownership distinguished the American colonies from the British Isles and because slave ownership seemed to explain why some North American colonists were inclined to reject imperial authority, slaveowners received particular abuse from those British commentators unhappy about the emerging divide between American rebels and the British government. Indeed, slaveholding helped them cast colonists as "American," rather than "British," and thus less worthy of respect. It figured in the crucial process of fixing new definitions of difference and national identity.[26] The metropolitan opponents of colonial re-

---

Colonies (London, 1775), 18; William Russell, *The History of America, from Its Discovery by Columbus to the Conclusion of the Late War; With an Appendix, Containing an Account of the Rise and Progress of the Present Unhappy Contest between Great Britain and Her Colonies,* 2 vols. (London, 1778), I, 594. See also Rozbicki, "The Curse of Provincialism," *Jour. So. Hist.*, LXIII, no. 4 (1987), 743–746.

25. [Wheelock], *Reflections Moral and Political*, 38; Burnaby, *Travels through the Middle Settlements in North-America*, 20; Edmund Burke, "Speech on Conciliation with America," in Paul Langford, ed., *The Writings and Speeches of Edmund Burke* (Oxford, 1981–), III, 122–123.

26. This process of differentiation has become a subject of interest in recent scholarship. In addition to the works by Breen, Greene, and Rozbicki cited above, see P. J. Marshall, "Britain and the World in the Eighteenth Century, II, Britons and Americans," *Transactions of the Royal Historical Society*, 6th Ser., IX (1999), 9–13; Gould, "The

sistance found it simple to distinguish American degenerates from the more civilized British. "I take your word for it," wrote a defender of the Stamp Act, "and believe you are as sober, temperate, upright, humane, and virtuous, as the posterity of independents and anabaptists, presbyterians and quakers, convicts and felons, savages and negro-whippers, can be." "That people should be enslaved because of their complexion is an American logic," another observer commented, "unknown to the generous Briton who detests the idea and execrates the practice." Even Horace Walpole, who avowed sympathy for the American cause, scarcely could "wish perfect freedom to merchants," he confessed to William Mason, "who are the bloodiest of all tyrants." Contrasts in practice and manners inevitably drew notice from those in Britain looking for ways to demean colonial pretensions to political equality. Such pretensions could never be taken seriously, exponents of parliamentary supremacy insisted, because moral inferiors could never be admitted as political equals.[27]

No one stated this case more boldly than William Innes, member of

---

American Revolution in Britain's Imperial Identity," in Leventhal and Quinault, eds., *Anglo-American Attitudes*, 26–31; Gould, *Persistence of Empire*, 187–192; Dror Wahrman, "The English Problem of Identity in the American Revolution," *AHR*, CVI (2001), 1236–1262; Stephen Conway, "From Fellow-Nationals to Foreigners: British Perceptions of the Americans, circa 1739–1785," *William and Mary Quarterly*, 3d Ser., LIX (2002), 65–100; and Glynis Ridley, "National Identity and Empire: Britain and the American Colonies, 1763–1787," in Bob Moore and Henk Van Nierop, eds., *Colonial Empires Compared: Britain and the Netherlands, 1750–1850: Papers Delivered to the Fourteenth Anglo-Dutch Historical Conference, 2000* (Aldershot, Eng., 2003), 47–75. Northern colonists, like southern colonists, received unflattering portrayals in the British press in these years, although these commentators, necessarily, emphasized different traits. See Julie Flavell, "British Perceptions of New England and the Decision for a Coercive Colonial Policy, 1774–1775," in Flavell and Stephen Conway, eds., *Britain and America Go to War: The Impact of War and Warfare in Anglo-America, 1754–1815* (Gainesville, Fla., 2004), 95–115.

27. *The Justice and Necessity of Taxing the American Colonies, Demonstrated; Together with a Vindication of the Authority of Parliament* (London, 1766), 23; William Allen, *The American Crisis: A Letter, Addressed by Permission to the Earl of Gower . . . on the Present Alarming Disturbances in the Colonies . . .* (London, 1774), 14; Horace Walpole to William Mason, Feb. 14, 1774, in W. S. Lewis, ed., *The Yale Edition of Horace Walpole's Correspondence*, XXVIII, *Horace Walpole's Correspondence with William Mason* (New Haven, Conn., 1955).

Parliament for Ilchester and outspoken opponent of the American rebellion. Late in the fall of 1775, in the same months that Thomas Paine prepared *Common Sense* for publication, the House of Commons debated, among other topics pertaining to the thirteen colonies, the budget estimates for His Majesty's army in North America. Several members of Parliament held out hope that a war might still be averted, that terms of peace might be found, that an accommodation could be reached that would allow to each side a dignified retreat. Innes, however, would have none of it; he had no interest in conciliation. Innes regarded the Stamp Act as a wise measure that, regrettably, had been poorly enforced and prematurely abandoned. He believed that the American rebellion owed its strength to what he thought of as seditious factions in England who had encouraged American pretensions. He was certain, as he put it, "that a well regulated government maintains its authority by a proper force." Innes hoped that the North ministry would cease wrangling with "mad men," as he called the New England patriots, and instead send soldiers and money to the colonies south of the Delaware River. There, he said, imperial authorities could reinforce the king's government, open trade with friends of the crown, and wait for those who persisted in the rebellion to come to their senses.[28]

Innes had only contempt for the American rebels. "It has been asserted that the colonists are offspring of Englishmen, and as such, entitled to the privileges of Britons." These were his words on the floor of the House of Commons. "Sir, I am bold to deny it, for it is well known that they not only consist of English, Scots, and Irish, but also of French, Dutch, Germans innumerable, Indians, Africans, and a multitude of felons from this country. Is it possible to tell which are the most turbulent among such a mixture of people? To which of them is England to give up her original right over an estate belonging to herself?" The American colonists had no claims to the rights of Englishmen because too many of them, in fact, were not Englishmen at all. And they did not deserve the liberties enjoyed by British subjects, Innes insisted, because they did not honor what he considered to be British customs of honor and justice. "The North American spirit and practice," he told the House of Commons, have "nothing in them similar to what prevails in Great Britain." It would be "absurd," Innes declared, that "a people who import slaves, and are despotic over them," should "have a

28. John Almon, *The Political Register,* III (London, 1780), 136, 139.

right to the freedom which the inhabitants of this country enjoy." Political liberty, therefore, was not a birthright, according to Innes. It was earned, in part, through a demonstrated capacity for just dealings with fellow subjects. In his view, the colonists' exploitation of slave labor helped justify their subordination to imperial authorities.[29]

The rebels in America claimed to want the rights of British subjects. Yet they demanded from the state, their critics observed, privileges no other subjects enjoyed—exemption from the sovereign authority of king-in-parliament. Moreover, they sometimes demanded those rights in a language that reflected poorly on their own sincerity. With respect to slavery, two claims stood out: the suggestion that Parliament was scheming to enslave America, and the idea that all men, as some put it, possessed a natural right to liberty. Slaveholding in North America, as many British commentators stressed repeatedly, exposed the first claim as ludicrous and the second as hypocritical. Describing subordination to Parliament as slavery seemed especially ill considered, given the ubiquity of chattel slavery in the colonies. If rights and liberties were natural, then colonial institutions honored those rights and liberties with inexcusable selectivity.

The self-evident hypocrisy of American slaveholders allowed British exponents of parliamentary supremacy to make more general and, for them, more critical points about the rebellion and the views of its English fellow travelers. In particular, drawing attention to colonial slavery helped them fix the meaning of such contested terms as *slavery* and *liberty* in ways that validated British rule and invalidated colonial resistance. These efforts figured particularly in the voluminous response to the pro-American and highly controversial tract English philosopher Richard Price published in February 1776, *Observations on Civil Liberty, the Principles of Government, and the Justice and Policy of War in America*. Several scholars have described how his opponents invoked the security of the community and the interests of the state to counter Price's definition of liberty as self-government and slavery as restraint of its exercise.[30] For present purposes, what matters most is how government pamphleteers used chattel slavery in the colonies to discredit the way Richard Price defined political slavery.

29. Ibid., 137–138.

30. See most recently Peter N. Miller, *Defining the Common Good: Empire, Religion and Philosophy in Eighteenth-Century Britain* (Cambridge, 1994), 373–399.

The defenders of imperial authority understood that when Americans and their British allies like Richard Price complained of being enslaved by Parliament they were deploying a traditional idiom in English political discourse typically deployed to describe subjection to arbitrary power. But the opponents of the Revolution had no interest in being understanding. Therefore, they took advantage of the colonists' distinct social arrangements to scoff at their choice of words. "On what just foundation," asked John Shebbeare, "is this external monotony of *slave, slavery, enslavement* of the colonists, *tyrants,* and *tyranny* by the supreme legislature?" "Does he reflect on what he writes?" Shebbeare asked of Richard Price. "Are *lives* of *ease* and *freedom* from *care,* the markers of slavery? Flagrant self-contradiction! Preposterous defense of unprovoked rebellion! Flagitious exercise of Presbyterian falsehood!" John Wesley strengthened this position by invoking the concrete experiences of the oppressed and dispossessed. First Wesley cited words that Price himself had published: "I have no other notion of slavery, but being bound by a law, to which I do not consent." To this, Wesley replied with incredulity: "If you have not, look at that man chained to the oar: He is a *slave:* He cannot, at all, dispose of his own person. Look at that negro sweating beneath his load: He is a *slave:* He has neither goods nor Liberty left. Look at that wretch in the inquisition: Then you will have a far other notion of *slavery.*" The colonists' subordination to Parliament scarcely ranked in the hierarchy of genuine injustices, Wesley insisted. To him, plantation slavery set the standard for human degradation. As Richard Hey explained more dispassionately in another response to Price, "it might be of use, in considering the nature of Slavery, to distinguish carefully between the *proper* sense of the word" *slavery* and the "*figurative* senses," which tended to confuse subjection with oppression. "Perhaps, the original and only proper meaning of it is, Domestic Slavery; including what Montesquieu speaks of under the names of Domestic and Civil Slavery, but not what he calls Political Slavery."[31] British pamphleteers characterized the

---

31. J[ohn] Shebbeare, *An Essay on the Origin, Progress, and Establishment of National Society; in Which the Principles of Government . . . Contained in Dr. Price's Observations, etc. Are Fairly Examined and Fully Refuted: Together with a Justification of the Legislature, in Reducing America to Obedience by Force; to Which Is Added an Appendix on . . . Mr. Burke's Speech of the 22d of March, 1775* (London, 1776), 108, 156; John Wesley, *Some Observations on Liberty: Occasioned by a Late Tract* (London, 1776),

bondage Americans claimed to suffer as nominal if not purely imaginary, particularly when set against the experience of enslaved Africans.

If Americans misconstrued the true condition of slavery, they were equally confused, these propagandists insisted, about the proper definition of liberty. Natural rights and natural liberties, government writers acknowledged, were attractive notions. But in practice, only government under the rule of law made the possession and enjoyment of rights and liberties possible. "If dependence in politicks is slavery," wrote Matthew Wheelock, "there can hardly be any liberty in the world." By defining slavery as any restraint on self-government, agreed Henry Goodricke, Richard Price "will be found to introduce *slavery* almost every where, and to make it absolutely necessary to the happiness of mankind." For, added another, to be governed only by one's own will "is, in fact *not to be governed at all*." Even "in the freest government," stated John Roebuck, "every man is a slave to the laws; and must either submit to such slavery, or forfeit the benefits of public order." These defenders of king-in-parliament had no doubt that they lived under the freest of governments because the British were "slaves to the law, but free in every thing else," as Sir John Dalrymple put it. Just as law made true liberty possible, law rather than nature enabled the British to enjoy rights. "Natural rights" had no practical meaning, insisted Anthony Bacon, since "men are born members of society, and consequently can have no rights, but such as are given by the laws of that society to which they belong." Richard Price, then, erred terribly when he invoked a natural right to representation. It was "impossible," explained an anonymous pamphleteer, "for representation to be a natural right because representative government itself" was "a distinctive British institution." As William Innes expressed it, "liberty, genuine liberty, if it exist at all, is confined to this and our sister kingdom."[32] In addition, then, to defining liberty as the product

---

34; [Richard Hey], *Observations on the Nature of Civil Liberty, and the Principles of Government* (London, 1776), 24; G. I. Molivas, "A Right, Utility, and the Definition of Liberty as a Negative Idea: Richard Hey and the Benthamite Conception of Liberty," *History of European Ideas*, XXV (1999), 85.

32. [Wheelock], *Reflections Moral and Political*, 29; [Henry Goodricke], *Observations on Dr. Price's Theory and Principles of Civil Liberty and Government, Preceded by a Letter to a Friend, on the Pretensions of the American Colonies, in Respect of Right and Equity* (York, 1776), 81; *An Essay on Civil Government; in Which the Right of Chusing*

of well-constituted authority, the propagandists stressed the conventional view that liberty was peculiar to the national heritage and made possible only by Britain's singular customs. In England, freedom reached as close to a state of perfection as was practically attainable. Africans in England, as nowhere else, Ambrose Serle reiterated, enjoyed the best any society could offer: "something like natural rights."[33]

Slaveholding in North America proved useful in yet another way to British defenders of imperial authority. It also helped them describe what Americans were doing when they invoked concepts like natural rights and natural liberties. Samuel Johnson, John Wesley, Josiah Tucker, and John William Fletcher genuinely detested the enslavement of Africans. But when these and other pro-government writers denounced Americans for crying out for liberty while holding Africans in slavery, they were not always arguing that the rights of Africans ought also to be acknowledged. Instead, they were calling on American patriots to abandon the pretense that *any society* could be organized and governed on the kind of principles the Revolutionaries professed to embrace. There were no such things, in practical terms, as "natural rights" or "natural liberties." If there were, Josiah Tucker wrote in 1775, "permit me therefore to ask, Why are not the poor

---

Officers and Members of Parliam[e]nt, for the City and Corporation of London, Is Shewn to Be Anciently and Unalienably Vested in the Freemen at Large . . . Inscribed to Sir William Withers, the Lord Mayor of London: by Dr. William King, . . . to Which Is Added, a Remonstrance with the Court of Common-Council, on Their Presenting the Freedom of the City to Dr. Price, for His Observations on Civil Liberty; Setting Forth the Inconsistency of Their Concern for the Liberties of Americans While They Trample on the Rights and Privileges of Their Fellow Citizens (London, 1776), 19; [John Roebuck], *An Enquiry Whether the Guilt of the Present Civil War in America, Ought to Be Imputed to Great Britain or America* (London, 1776), 21; [Sir John Dalrymple], *The Address of the People of Great-Britain to the Inhabitants of America* (London, 1775), 24; Anthony Bacon, *A Short Address to the Government, the Merchants, Manufacturers, and the Colonists in America, and the Sugar Islands, on the Present State of Affairs* (London, 1775), 5; *The Present Crisis, with Respect to America, Considered* (London, 1775), 17; R. C. Simmons and P. D. G. Thomas, eds., *Proceedings and Debates of the British Parliaments respecting North America, 1754–1783*, 6 vols. (Millwood, N.Y., 1982), VI, 203.

33. [Ambrose Serle], *Americans against Liberty; or, An Essay on the Nature and Principles of True Freedom, Shewing That the Designs and Conduct of the Americans Tend Only to Tyranny and Slavery . . .* , 3d ed. (London, 1776), 25.

Negroes, and the poor *Indians,* entitled to the like Rights and Benefits? And how comes it to pass, that these *immutable Laws* of Nature are become so very mutable, and so very insignificant in respect to them?" John Lind confronted Richard Price with a similar question. "How came there to be slaves in your land of liberty?" "Are rights, which can never be forfeited by conquest, nor ceded by compact, nor purchased by obligation, alienable by a change in the colour of the skin? Why did not these sons of liberty restore their slaves to rights, which the one could not acquire, nor the other alienate?"[34] Tucker and Lind implied answers through the questions. All orderly societies require social hierarchies and inequalities in rank. The institution of slavery represented one less-than-admirable way of securing them. Colonists knew that liberty without authority was impractical; this was one reason why they refused to liberate their slaves. The "outcry" in America over "Liberty and Slavery," then, decided John Wesley, was "mere rant" and "playing upon words."[35] The patriots' aims were parochial and self-serving, not disinterested and principled. The apparent embrace of natural rights was purely instrumental. The rebels did not genuinely believe in their own words. They wished to seize power from the British government, not enlarge the dominion of liberty.

This improvised political philosophy, the British defenders of the established order insisted, represented post-hoc justifications for a long-established conspiracy to overthrow parliamentary rule. Parliamentary legislation had not pushèd or provoked the colonies into rebellion. From the beginning, they said, Americans had schemed to seize independence. Here, too, in portraying the "revolted Americans" as deceitful and duplicitous, the institution of colonial slavery proved useful yet again, in this case as a way to evaluate the integrity of the patriots. The apparent embrace of universal liberty disguised a continuing commitment to exploit slave

34. Josiah Tucker, *The Respective Pleas and Arguments of the Mother Country and of the Colonies, Distinctly Set Forth . . .* (London, 1775), v; John Lind, *Three Letters to Dr. Price Containing Remarks on His Observations on the Nature of Civil Liberty, the Principles of Government, and the Justice and Policy of War with America; by a Member of Lincoln's Inn, F.R.S., F.S.A.* (London, 1776), 157.

35. John Wesley cited in John Derry, *English Politics and the American Revolution* (London, 1976), 164.

labor, just as false avowals of fidelity to George III had disguised the agitators' long-standing plan to cast off British authority. The colonists in revolt lacked honor. Their words meant nothing.

> *In principle* they pretend to be the most zealous champions of freedom; in practise they are the severest of tyrants. "The rights of life, liberty, and the pursuit of happiness, they hold to be unalienable;" yet they have, in various instances, *violated these unalienable rights* without even a pretence to urge in excuse for their unjust and despotic conduct. They assert that "all men are created equal," yet they shamefully make a property of their fellow creatures, whom they purchase for gold, condemn to the most servile and laborious employments, and render completely miserable by inflicting on them the most unjust and severe torments that ingenious cruelty can invent, or unrelenting tyranny can practise.[36]

The rhetoric of liberty entangled the patriots, British commentators noted, in countless contradictions. Consider, for example, the question of arming slaves to preserve imperial authority. John Shebbeare found it curious that a self-professed "friend of liberty and the rights of humankind" could inveigh against the offer of freedom to slaves by Virginia governor John Murray, earl of Dunmore, "because they are to suppress rebellion in Presbyterians." This was, Shebbeare exclaimed, "abominable hypocrisy! Ignominious desertion of principle to support iniquity."[37] Who "speaks the

36. [William Pulteney], *An Appeal to Reason and Justice, in Behalf of the British Constitution, and the Subjects of the British Empire; in Which the Present Important Contest with the Revolted Colonies Is Impartially Considered, the Inconsistency of Modern Patriotism Is Demonstrated, the Supremacy of Parliament Is Asserted on Revolution Principles and American Independence Is Proved to Be a Manifest Violation of the Rights of British Subjects; to Which Is Added, an Appendix, Containing Remarks on a Pamphlet Intitled, "Thoughts on the Present State of Affairs with America"* (London, 1778), 76; Ira D. Gruber, "The American Revolution as a Conspiracy: The British View," *WMQ,* 3d Ser., XXVI (1969), 368–372; Wahrman, "The English Problem of Identity in the American Revolution," *AHR,* CVI (2001), 1236–1237.

37. Shebbeare, *An Essay on the Origin, Progress, and Establishment of National Society,* 178. On Nov. 14, 1775, Dunmore offered freedom to slaves and indentured servants willing to desert rebel masters. See Benjamin Quarles, *The Negro in the American Revolution* (Chapel Hill, N.C., 1961), 19–32.

language of liberty," John Lind asked rhetorically, the Virginia planter who exploits slave labor or Governor Dunmore, who would set slaves free? The planter informs his slaves:

> You are my property; I bought you; stay with me; be faithful to me; fight for the honour of being my beast of burthen? What says the Governor? See, my brethren, see your masters under arms against the authority of the state.—For what? Because they are not exempted from the power to which their ancestors, as well as their fellow-subjects in Great Britain have submitted; because they are not indulged in privileges to which neither their ancestors, nor their fellow-subjects in Great Britain, had ever before pretended.

Like John Wesley, Lind then turned to the experience of enslaved Africans to establish the "true" meaning of slavery. The Virginia governor, he concluded, might answer this way:

> But in you, my friends, no disputed privilege is attacked; neither distant nor doubtful are the dangers with which you are threatened; the loads which crush your limbs, the whip which harrows your back, are present, real evils. Rise then, assist us to reduce your tyrants to a due obedience to the laws, and raise yourselves to an equality with them.

"To my understanding," Lind concluded, to make the point explicit for Richard Price and other British sympathizers, "there would be more of the general spirit of freedom in this address, than is to be found in all your observations."[38]

No one in England defended Dunmore's actions in Virginia with greater clarity or force than John Lind, an early exponent and popularizer of the utilitarian philosophy of Jeremy Bentham. Lind possessed a particular appreciation for the value of strong central authority. As chaplain to the British embassy in Constantinople and later as tutor to the son of the Polish monarch Stanislaw Poniatowski, Lind had witnessed the corruption and inefficiencies of the Ottoman Empire and the partition of Poland in 1772 by Prussia, Russia, and Austria. To Lind, the threatened dissolution of the British Empire reinforced the lesson he learned during his years on the Continent: only an omnicompetent sovereign legislature could successfully

38. Lind, *Three Letters to Dr. Price*, 158, 159.

mediate among competing interests and thereby preserve the integrity of the state. Liberating slaves was defensible, Lind stated, because Lord Dunmore aimed to stabilize His Majesty's government, because there were "men who had excited, and were continuing to excite, one set of citizens to pillage the effects, burn the houses, torture the persons, cut the throats of another set of citizens." No action taken by Parliament justified rebellion against legitimate, properly constituted authority, Lind asserted in August 1776 in his *Answer to the Declaration of the American Congress,* the lone reply to the Declaration of Independence commissioned by the ministry of Frederick, Lord North. On what grounds, he asked, could slaveholding insurrectionists justly object to Dunmore's instigation of "domestic insurrections"? Who were these Americans?

> Is it for *them* to say, that it is tyranny to bid a slave to be free? to bid him take courage, to rise and assist in reducing his tyrants to a due obedience to *law?* to hold out as a motive to him, that the load which crushed his limbs shall be lightened; that the whip which harrowed up his back shall be broken, that he shall be raised to the rank of a freeman and a citizen? It is their boast that they have taken up arms in support of these their own *self-evident truths*—"that all men are *equal*"—"that all men are endowed with the *unalienable* rights of life, *liberty,* and the *pursuit of happiness.*" Is it for *them* to complain *of the offer of freedom* held out to these wretched beings? of the offer of reinstating them in that *equality,* which, in this very paper, is declared to be the *gift of God to all;* in those *unalienable rights,* with which, in this very paper, God is declared to have *endowed all* mankind?[39]

In this way, the injustice of colonial slavery became the subject of comment in British political discourse, for the first time, during the 1770s—

---

39. John Lind, *An Answer to the Declaration of the American Congress,* 5th ed. (London, 1776), 106–107. For a superb sketch of this important but neglected writer, see Margaret E. Avery, "Toryism in the Age of the American Revolution: John Lind and John Shebbeare," *Historical Studies* (Melbourne, Australia), XVIII, no. 70 (April 1978), 24–36. For Lind's relationship with Bentham, see David Armitage, "The Declaration of Independence and International Law," *WMQ,* 3d Ser., LIX (2002), 52–54. His service to the Polish court is treated in Richard Butterwick, *Poland's Last King and English Culture: Stanislaw August Poniatowski, 1732–1798* (Oxford, 1998), 130, 132, 234, 239–240.

through the much wider debate on the rights of the thirteen colonies. When slavery figured in public discourse before the Revolutionary era, it typically arose in treatments of mercantile policy or the promotion of overseas trade and settlement. In the middle decades of the eighteenth century it also became a routine subject for abuse in sentimental and polite literature. The years between 1763 and 1776 witnessed the publication of a small number of antislavery tracts in England, tracts that are analyzed in detail later in this book. But, even more, these years brought dozens of off-handed exclamations against British colonials and their apparent hypocrisy. The polemics attending the years of crisis deepened perennial questions about the morality of slavery, extending them from the more abstract realms of sentiment and moral judgment to the politically charged arena of ideological dispute, in the process vesting the long-evaded ethical questions with a new salience and immediacy.

When the British opponents of the American Revolution accused slaveholders of hypocrisy, they were offering more than a critique of American morals. They were characterizing the rebels as unworthy of liberty, as possessing wrongheaded notions of freedom and slavery, as lacking adequate grounds for rebellion, as misrepresenting their true ambitions, as clothing selfish ends in the dress of universal philanthropy. With these statements, British defenders of the established order said far more than they appreciated or intended. The unrecognized premises nesting in the attack on American slaveholders bore potent messages with far-reaching implications. How individuals, communities, even nations conducted themselves with regard to human bondage could provide a legitimate standard for evaluating their politics. And only those who divested themselves from chattel slavery could rightfully campaign for political liberty.

[III]   British critics of North American slaveholders would have been taken more seriously, perhaps, if they had been more sincere. Even as they condemned hypocrisy, even as they described the ownership of slaves as unbecoming a free people, the government writers treated the slave trade from Africa with almost willful indifference. Samuel Johnson and like-minded scribes sniffed at "drivers of negroes" in the colonies and their "yelps for liberty" but gave decidedly little thought to the role of the state and British merchants in ferrying slave labor to the colonies. If Adam Smith cared about the abuse of Africans, wrote Arthur Lee, "instead of listening to the gratification of a slanderous prejudice," he should have "exerted his abilities in dissuading Europeans from a barbarous trade." It was absurd for the British to congratulate themselves for "setting free a *single Slave*," observed Benjamin Franklin days after the Somerset case, when British merchants were "encouraged by thy laws to continue a commerce whereby so many *hundreds of thousands*" were "dragged into a slavery."[40]

Lee and Franklin had an agenda, but they also had a point. British attacks on colonial slavery intensified just as the North American colonial assemblies began to prohibit the importation of slaves to North American shores. If genuinely outraged, then, about the exploitation of Africans, those in Britain inclined to disparage North American slaveowners should have endorsed the burgeoning abolitionist movement in the North American colonies. There, a small circle of moralists, chiefly Quakers, began in the 1760s to lobby for legislative action and question the wisdom of allowing a continued influx of slave labor. In the colonies, the principal weapon against the slave trade was the power to tax. Maryland, New Jersey, Pennsylvania, Connecticut, and Rhode Island imposed bans or severely restrictive duties on slave imports between 1769 and 1774. Other colonies would have enacted similar laws if imperial administrators had allowed. Abolition-

---

40. Lee, *An Essay in Vindication of the Continental Colonies in America,* 46; "The Somersett Case and the Slave Trade," *London Chronicle,* June 18–20, 1772, cited in Labaree et al., eds., *Papers of Benjamin Franklin,* XIX, 188. It might be noted, as well, that West Indian slaveholders received much less attention in these years than North American slaveholders, a fact rarely commented on at the time, though indicative of the limits of antislavery thought among these British defenders of the established order. The West Indian elite escaped metropolitan criticism during the American war while they remained loyal to the state. The Caribbean planters would come under sustained attack only after the American war. See chapter 6. North American commentators did, however, single out West Indian slaveholders for denunciation, in part to distinguish evolving North American sensibilities from West Indian practices. See the discussion of the pertinent tracts by writers such as James Otis and Benjamin Rush in Nancy V. Morrow, "The Problem of Slavery in the Polemic Literature of the American Enlightenment," *Early American Literature,* XX (1985–1986), 240–241, 244–247, and in Waldstreicher, *Runaway America,* 175–178. Christopher Iannini calls attention to adverse assessments of Caribbean life in the work of J. Hector St. John de Crèvecoeur in " 'The Itinerant Man': Crèvecoeur's Caribbean, Raynal's Revolution, and the Fate of Atlantic Cosmopolitanism," *WMQ,* 3d Ser., LXI (2004), 201–234.

ist measures failed in the early 1770s to win the assent of royal governors in Delaware, New York, and Massachusetts. In executing its powers of legislative review, George III's Privy Council also vetoed duties passed by the Virginia General Assembly in 1767, 1769, and 1772.[41] Eventually, the colonies accomplished by compact what they could not achieve by statute. The nonimportation movements of 1769 and 1770 had a limited effect on the slave trade to North America, except in South Carolina, where a thriving trade came to a brief but nearly total halt. However, the more vigorously enforced resolves instituted by the Continental Congress in 1774 and 1776 brought the slave trade to a standstill until the end of the Revolutionary War.[42]

British conservatives preferred to overlook these initiatives since, taken together, they seemed to reflect well on American patriots and poorly on the imperial state. Historians of antislavery in Britain unwittingly have

41. For an overview of these efforts, see W. E. B. Dubois, *The Suppression of the African Slave Trade to the United States of America, 1638–1870,* ed. A. Norman Klein (1896; rpt. New York, 1969), 7–37. Further details on measures adopted in specific regions appear in George H. Moore, *Notes on the History of Slavery in Massachusetts* (New York, 1866); Mack Thompson, *Moses Brown: Reluctant Reformer* (Chapel Hill, N.C., 1962); Zilversmit, *The First Emancipation,* 91; Darold D. Wax, "Negro Import Duties in Colonial Pennsylvania," *PMHB,* XCVII (1973), 43–44; Nash and Soderlund, *Freedom by Degrees,* 71–72; Donnan, ed., *Documents Illustrative of the Slave Trade to America,* III, 72–73, 76–77, 289–290; Darold D. Wax, "Negro Import Duties in Colonial Virginia: A Study of British Commercial Policy and Local Public Policy," *VMHB,* LXXXIX (1971), 29–44; MacMaster, "Arthur Lee's 'Address on Slavery,' " ibid., LXXX (1972), 41–53; and Bruce A. Ragsdale, *A Planters' Republic: The Search for Economic Independence in Revolutionary Virginia* (Madison, Wis., 1996), 111–122, 128–135.

42. Only Georgia continued to import slaves and outfit slavers into the summer of 1775. See Dubois, *The Suppression of the African Slave-Trade to the United States of America,* 45–46; and Darold D. Wax, "New Negroes Are Always in Demand': The Slave Trade in Eighteenth-Century Georgia," *Georgia Historical Quarterly,* LXVIII (1984), 212–214. For the enforcement of slave trade prohibitions in other crucial locales, see Jay Coughtry, *The Notorious Triangle: Rhode Island and the African Slave Trade, 1700–1807* (Philadelphia, 1981), 205, 333; Ragsdale, *A Planter's Republic,* 231–232; David Richardson, "The British Slave Trade to Colonial South Carolina," *Slavery and Abolition,* XII, no. 3 (December 1991), 131. Walter Minchinton reports less consistent enforcement in North Carolina. See Minchinton, "The Seaborne Slave Trade of North Carolina," *North Carolina Historical Review,* LXXI, no. 1 (1994), 14–15.

followed their example by minimizing or neglecting the British campaign's North American precedents. The reading public in England learned of the miseries of the slave trade from American publications, among other sources, particularly from the pamphlets Anthony Benezet published in the 1760s and 1770s. The first British writings to condemn the slave trade at length relied heavily on the information Benezet compiled and the generic conventions he pioneered.[43] In a sense, colonial activists like Benezet exported the idea of slave trade abolition to the British Isles. But, to reiterate, the history of Anglo-American antislavery in this period is as often the history of politics as the history of ideas. Even once printed and distributed, books do not always reshape the course of public debate instantly or directly. As it happens, few in Britain took notice of Benezet's pamphlets until they were republished in 1784, several years after the war. At the time, in the 1770s, what often mattered more to British observers were the agendas that seemed to lie behind antislavery legislation, what colonists seemed to be up to when they stood against the slave trade. The interpretation of these measures frequently depended on how commentators understood the provenance of American abolitionism, how they regarded its proponents, their agendas, the timing.

From recent research, the tangle of pragmatic and principled motives that animated abolitionism in Revolutionary America has become clearer. In Virginia, the turn against the slave trade arose with unease over a continued dependence on tobacco cultivation and unfree labor and with an emerging ambition to diversify the economy, principally through an establishment of manufactures. If farther north, Revolutionary principles stirred closer scrutiny of human bondage, attempts to end the slave trade gained momentum only where the need for bound labor had stagnated or de-

---

43. The antislavery tract circulated most widely in Britain before the 1780s, John Wesley's *Thoughts upon Slavery* (London, 1774), borrowed liberally from Benezet's *Some Historical Account of Guinea*. See the discussion by Warren Thomas Smith in *John Wesley and Slavery* (Nashville, Tenn., 1986), 90–97. Other British pamphlets exhibiting Benezet's influence include Thomas Clarkson, *An Essay on the Slavery and Commerce of the Human Species* (London, 1786); Peter Peckard, *Am I Not a Man and a Brother? With All Humility Addressed to the British Legislature* (London, 1788); and William Leigh, *Remarks on the Slave Trade, and the Slavery of the Negroes, in a Series of Letters* (London, 1788).

clined, where the further import of black labor conflicted with conceptions of the public good and where slave resistance or the threat of slave resistance heightened fears of insurrection, disorder, or mass desertion.[44] All of this is clear in hindsight. At the time, though, the British knew and could know little about why Americans acted as they did. So they focused instead on how the Americans explained their initiatives, on the priorities and purposes that seemed to guide colonial actors.

American patriots presented their embrace of abolitionism as an expression of their political principles, as proof of their commitment to freedom. Simultaneously, they used their stand against the Atlantic slave trade to justify the struggle for political liberty, to sanctify their rejection of imperial authority, to render the Revolutionary movement worthy of esteem. Quakers in North America had rendered devotion to antislavery principles a measure of commitment to sectarian discipline when threatened in the 1760s by internal dissension and a loss of political power. A similar ethos was at work a decade later when rural Massachusetts towns, in the midst of imperial restrictions on colonial liberties, resolved no longer to have slaves among them. The crusade against British tyranny provided the infrastructure for antislavery organization and the occasions for disseminating antislavery principles. Protests against the slave trade traveled along those intracolonial networks of correspondence established to mobilize political resistance. This is who we are! proclaimed Leicester residents in 1773—"as we have the highest regard for (so as to revere the name of) liberty, we cannot but behold with the greatest abhorrence any of our fellow creatures in a state of slavery." When the Leicester petitioners instructed their representative Thomas Denny to back emerging proposals for a union among the colonies, they directed him, as well, to push for an end to the slave trade. At the same time, patriots used antislavery initiatives to inflict political damage on the crown's colonial agents. A lobbying campaign against

44. The best overviews appear in Ragsdale, *A Planters' Republic;* Nash and Soderlund, *Freedom by Degrees;* and White, *Somewhat More Independent.* See also Woody Holton, *Forced Founders: Indians, Debtors, Slaves, and the Making of the American Revolution in Virginia* (Chapel Hill, N.C., 1999), 67–71; James J. Allegro, " 'Increasing and Strengthening the Country': Law, Politics, and the Antislavery Movement in Early-Eighteenth-Century Massachusetts Bay," *NEQ,* LXXV (2002), 19–21; and Blanck, "Seventeen Eighty-Three," *NEQ,* LXXV (2002), 48–49.

slave imports in 1773 aimed to embarrass Massachusetts governor Thomas Hutchinson, far more than to change the laws of the colony. Legislators knew Hutchinson would block the proposed abolition bill. He had royal instructions to do so and had vetoed a similar bill three years earlier. No matter. The abolition bill placed colonists on record as champions of liberty, positioned Hutchinson as a defender of the slave trade, and cast an unflattering light on the royal prerogative.[45]

If antislavery in Massachusetts served as an instrument of political resistance, opposition to the British slave trade in Virginia was resistance itself, an explicit rejection of second-class status within the empire. The Privy Council's refusal to permit restrictive taxes on slave imports exampled what irritated Virginians most: their vulnerability to the interests of merchants and politicians residing several thousands of miles away. "This is one instance," Arthur Lee wrote of the unwanted slave imports in 1773, "in which we feel the galling yoke of dependence." In an earlier era, Virginians might have argued against the slave trade solely on political or economic grounds. They might have stressed the need for revenue or the benefits of controlling the size of the slave population. The growing respect accorded to antislavery gestures in the 1770s, however, encouraged them to ennoble their more parochial interests with the language of moral indignation. "They wished a stop to the slave trade," the House of Burgesses explained in a petition to the crown in 1772, in part because the commerce was "an inhumanity." The slave trade, stated the Fairfax County gentry in 1774, was "wicked cruel and unnatural."[46]

45. *The Appendix: or, Some Observations on the Expediency of the Petition of the Africans Living in Boston,* 6; Emory Washburn, *Historical Sketches of the Town of Leicester, Massachusetts, during the First Century of Its Settlement* (Boston, 1860), 442; Bernard Bailyn, *The Ordeal of Thomas Hutchinson* (Cambridge, Mass., 1974), 378. There was clearly some coordination at work. Salem instructed its representative to back slave trade abolition on May 18. Sandwich and Leicester did the same on the following day. Moore, *Notes on the History of Slavery in Massachusetts,* 133. It seems to me that Patricia Bradley, in her valuable work *Slavery, Propaganda, and the American Revolution,* overstates the hostility of Massachusetts patriots to antislavery gestures.

46. Lee to Reed, Feb. 18, 1773, in Reed, ed., *Life and Correspondence of Joseph Reed,* I, 48; D(w) 1778/II/534, Dartmouth Papers, Staffordshire Record Office (SRO); "Fairfax County Resolves," July 18, 1774, in Robert A. Rutland, ed., *The Papers of George Mason,* 3 vols. (Chapel Hill, N.C., 1970), I, 207; Holton, *Forced Founders,* 71–73.

Because of Quaker leadership, the antislavery movement in the Delaware Valley drew its energy from sources that lay outside the mainstream of Revolutionary politics. The Society of Friends, led by Anthony Benezet, directed attention to the cruelties of the slave trade, not only the danger of adding new slaves to Pennsylvania. With several committed colleagues, Benezet turned Philadelphia opinion against the traffic on principle. A well-signed petition presented to the Pennsylvania Assembly in 1773 called for a ban on the entire British slave trade, not merely on imports to Pennsylvania or North America.[47] The petitioners chose not to describe abolition as sanctifying the patriot cause or as a challenge to the authority of the British state. There was a short distance, though, between thinking of abolitionism as a moral duty and thinking of British support for the slave trade as evidence of imperial tyranny. Benjamin Rush the abolitionist thought Pennsylvanians should set all slaves free. Benjamin Rush the politician took pleasure in heaping responsibility for colonial slavery on British slave traders and the British government. He described England's Company of Merchants Trading to Africa as an "incorporated band of robbers." Closing the slave trade, Rush explained to a correspondent in England, was part of America's offensive against "the monster of British tyranny."[48] Quaker efforts notwithstanding, Philadelphia patriots presented their antislavery gestures as proof of their political virtue during the course of the American war, after the evacuation of the British army from the Delaware River valley in the spring of 1778. "Honored will that state be in the Annals of History which shall first abolish this violation of the rights of mankind," Pennsylvania's Executive Council had declared in 1779. So, a year later, the ruling

47. Wax, "Negro Import Duties in Colonial Pennsylvania," *PMHB,* XCVII, no. 1 (1973), 38–43. The Quaker influence on the antislavery movement in Pennsylvania is surveyed effectively in Wax, "Reform and Revolution: The Movement against Slavery and the Slave Trade in Revolutionary Pennsylvania," *Western Pennsylvania Historical Magazine,* LVII (1974), 416–429.

48. [Benjamin Rush], *An Address to the Inhabitants of the British Settlements in America upon Slave-Keeping* (Philadelphia, 1773), in Bruns, *Am I Not a Man and a Brother,* 229; Benjamin Rush to Granville Sharp, Oct. 29, 1773, in John A. Woods, ed., "The Correspondence of Benjamin Rush and Granville Sharp, 1773–1809," *Journal of American Studies,* I (1967), 3. For more on Rush's tendency to exaggerate progress in America, see David Brion Davis, *The Problem of Slavery in Western Culture,* 2d ed., rev. (Oxford, 1988), 443.

radicals of the newly independent state described their gradual emancipation law of 1780 as the fulfillment of the Revolutionary movement, as an instance in which they could "extend a portion of that freedom to others, which has been extended to us . . . and release them from a state of thraldom, to which we ourselves were tyrannically doomed, and from which we have now every prospect of being delivered." In the preamble to the legislation, they made a point to add that "no effectual relief" had been allowed for slaves before 1776 because of "the assumed authority of Great Britain."[49]

Those American patriots deeply involved but increasingly ill at ease with the slave system welcomed the ways that guilt for their increasingly embarrassing sins could be pushed off on a government whose authority they now renounced. South Carolina merchant Henry Laurens spent much of his adult life bringing enslaved Africans to North America and from the trade made something of a fortune. No one in North America during the half century before the American Revolution imported more slaves than Laurens—perhaps as many as sixty-nine hundred individuals according to one recent estimate. By 1774, though, he found commerce in slaves "So repugnant" that only "dire necessity could drive me to it." In an impressive feat of selective recall, he chose to forget his lifelong investment in purchasing and selling men and women from Africa. "I abhor Slavery," he told his son in 1776. "I was born in a Country where Slavery had been established by British Kings and Parliaments as well as by the Laws of that Country. . . . Ages before my existence, I found the Christian Religion and Slavery growing under the same authority and cultivation." If he had profited from the practice, he now confessed that "I nevertheless disliked it." "In former days," he continued, "there was no combatting the prejudices of Men supported by Interest"; "the day I hope is approaching when from principles of gratitude as well as justice every Man will strive to be foremost in shewing his readiness to comply with the Golden Rule." If the conversion was sincere—there is evidence that he remained discomfited by American slavery and the importation of slaves until his death in 1792—Laurens could not resist harping on British sins. "I am not the Man who enslaved them,

---

49. Nash and Soderlund, *Freedom by Degrees,* 101; Preamble to Pennsylvania's "Act for the Gradual Abolition of Slavery," quoted in Bruns, *Am I Not a Man and a Brother,* 446; Wax, "Reform and Revolution," *W. Pa. Hist. Mag.,* LVII (1974), 420.

they are indebted to English Men for that favour." Even after American independence, he never lost interest in drawing attention to British hypocrisy. Three years after the conclusion of the American war, Laurens compared the English "to a pious, externally pious, Man's prohibiting fornication under his roof and keeping a dozen Mistresses abroad."[50]

It was a relief to find a scapegoat. Virginians once had complained that they could not get enough slaves from Africa. Now, in the decade after the Stamp Act, some colonists began to describe the slave trade as the epitome of open seas piracy, conducted as it was, Thomas Jefferson wrote, by "a few British corsairs." If Congress had let Jefferson have his way, the Declaration of Independence would have closed with a ringing indictment of George III for permitting the British Atlantic slave trade, which Jefferson described as "a cruel war against human nature itself." The boldness of the rhetoric, the audacity of the claim hinted at the importance that planter patriots, like Jefferson, assigned to exculpating themselves from the charge of hypocrisy. "The abolition of domestic slavery," Jefferson had written either disingenuously or mendaciously in 1774, "is the great object of desire in those colonies, where it was unhappily introduced." "Long have the Americans, moved by compassion, and actuated by sound policy," declared the *Virginia Gazette* a year later, "endeavoured to stop the progress of slavery." But "humane intentions" were "frustrated by the cruelty and covetousness of a

50. Henry Laurens to John Lewis Gervais, Feb. 5, 1774, Henry Laurens to John Laurens, Aug. 14, 1776, and Henry Laurens to Edward Bridgen, Feb. 13, 1786, all in Hamer et al., eds., *The Papers of Henry Laurens*, IX, 264, X, 224, XVI, 534n7. The views of Henry Laurens are placed in context in Gregory D. Massey, "The Limits of Antislavery Thought in the Revolutionary Lower South: John Laurens and Henry Laurens," *Jour. So. Hist.*, LXIII (1997), 495–530; James A. Rawley, "Henry Laurens and the Atlantic Slave Trade," in Rawley, *London, Metropolis of the Slave Trade* (Columbia, Mo., 2003), 82–97; and Dorsey, " 'To Corroborate Our Own Claims,' " *Am. Qtly.*, LV (2003), 355–357. For his career in the slave trade, see W. Robert Higgins, "Charles Town Merchants and Factors Dealing in the External Negro Trade, 1735–1775," *South Carolina Historical Magazine*, LXV (1964), 206; Daniel J. McDonough, *Christopher Gadsden and Henry Laurens: The Parallel Lives of Two American Patriots* (Sellingsgrove, Pa., 2000), 21–25; and Massey, *John Laurens and the American Revolution*, 14–16, 66–67. As McDonough notes, Laurens was responsible after the American war for insisting that the Treaty of Peace provide for the return of slaves that had deserted North American plantations. McDonough, *Christopher Gadsden and Henry Laurens*, 263.

set of English merchants." This grasp for innocence became a kind of cliché in Virginia political rhetoric for many years after. It resurfaced in Jefferson's well-known *Notes on the State of Virginia* of 1785, where the United States minister to France described an end to slavery in the new nation as imminent. In 1796, two decades after the Declaration of Independence, jurist St. George Tucker was still characterizing the institution of slavery as the product of a British plot to undermine American liberty. As late as 1819, nearly forty years after the end of British authority in the thirteen colonies, American defenders of the national reputation such as Robert Walsh of Philadelphia continued to insist that American slavery was Britain's fault.[51]

[IV] If such arguments presented an incomplete, if not misleading, account of colonial motives and intentions, they were accurate depictions of how American patriots wished to think of themselves and how they wished others to think of them. By pairing antislavery initiatives with challenges to imperial sovereignty, American patriots encouraged British observers to think of abolitionism as an aspect of patriot politics, to conceive those gestures not only as moral action but also as a grasp for self-governance. Behind the contest over setting duties on the slave trade, then, appeared to lie the more basic conflict regarding where legislative authority in the British Empire should reside. Therefore, how the British reacted to American abolitionism often depended on what they thought of American resistance.

Consider the administrators of empire and their customary response to

51. [Thomas Jefferson], *A Summary View of the Rights of British America* (Williamsburg, Va., [1774]), 15; *Virginia Gazette,* Nov. 25, 1775, in Wax, "Negro Import Duties in Colonial Virginia," *VMHB,* LXXXIX (1971), 29; St. George Tucker, *A Dissertation on Slavery: With a Proposal for the Gradual Abolition of It, in the State of Virginia* (Philadelphia, 1796), in Nash, *Race and Revolution,* 154; Matthew Mason, "The Battle of the Slaveholding Liberators: Great Britain, the United States, and Slavery in the Early Nineteenth Century," *WMQ,* 3d Ser., LIX (2002), 683–688. From a very large literature on Jefferson and slavery, see in particular Peter A. Dorsey's penetrating commentary on Jefferson's writings on slavery during the Revolutionary crisis in " 'To Corroborate Our Own Claims,' " *Am. Qtly.,* LV (2003), 371–378. I would endorse his conclusion that "the pressure of debate—rather than deeply felt conviction—persuaded many patriots to speak as they did" (377).

colonial duties on the British slave trade. In principle, before the Revolutionary era, the Privy Council permitted those taxes on the slave trade intended to generate income for local government while rejecting duties designed to inhibit or prohibit the sale of newly imported slaves. This had been the convention, but the lords of trade failed to apply it with rigorous consistency. North American assemblies, acting on their own, severely restricted slave imports successfully in several instances during the first half of the eighteenth century. As late as 1764, to ease indebtedness following a flurry of slave purchases after the Seven Years' War, the South Carolina Assembly, for example, enacted a three-year ban on the slave trade (1766–1768) without drawing metropolitan opposition. In practice, flexibility prevailed in the enforcement of mercantile policy before the Stamp Act. It often required lobbying by British merchants engaged in the African trade to secure disallowance of prohibitive duties.[52]

The political conflicts of the late 1760s and early 1770s inspired greater vigilance. It appeared to London officials that the North American colonies aimed to regulate British commerce, to usurp parliamentary authority, to take on themselves powers that, rightfully, they did not possess. Matthew Lamb, legal counsel for the Board of Trade, found the Virginia duties of 1767 unobjectionable as a matter of law. He recommended disallowance because, in the midst of the Townshend duties crisis, ministers could not concede the principle articulated in the preamble to the Virginia bill, that only the colonial assembly and not Parliament could tax Virginia residents. A similar Virginia bill prepared in 1769 removed the offending clause. But by this time British officials were inclined to judge slave trade abolition as a

52. One hopes that this subject will soon receive systematic research. For the temporary ban on the South Carolina slave trade in 1764, see Henry Laurens to John Knight, Aug. 24, 1764, in Hamer et al., eds., *The Papers of Henry Laurens,* IV, 379–381. Walter Minchinton reports that Bristol slave merchants, for reasons that remain unclear, chose not to lobby against the temporary South Carolina slave trade ban. Walter E. Minchinton, "The Political Activities of Bristol Merchants with Respect to the Southern Colonies before the Revolution," *VMHB,* LXXIX (1971), 177. For merchant lobbying on behalf of the slave traders, see James A. Rawley, "Richard Harris, Slave Trader Spokesman," in Rawley, *London, Metropolis of the Slave Trade,* 70–75. For reference to the customary privilege allowed to colonial legislatures wishing to establish moderate duties on the slave trade for the sake of revenue, see Board of Trade to George III, Nov. 23, 1770, Dartmouth Papers.

species of nonimportation, as an invasion of the property rights of British merchants, not simply as a disagreement over policy or an instance of moral zeal. "We cannot allow the colonies to check or discourage, in any manner, a traffic so beneficial to the nation," wrote the earl of Dartmouth about similar duties enacted in Jamaica in 1774.[53]

English slave trade apologist John Peter Demarin worked upon these fears by describing the American antislavery movement as a colonial plot to destroy British commerce and overthrow the empire, a view embraced by hireling scribe John Lind weeks after the Declaration of Independence. Lind claimed to be appalled by slaveholder hypocrisy. At the same time, he had no qualms about defending the interests of British slave traders. Colonists had condemned George III, Lind noted, for forbidding governors to pass laws of pressing importance. Lind understood, as his answer revealed, that this was a reference to the slave trade: "To what bills do these instructions apply? To such only as are of an extraordinary nature, affecting the trade and shipping of Great Britain; the prerogatives of the Crown, and the property of the subjects of the empire in general." Like those he criticized, Lind had no interest in establishing a coherent moral stance. Rather, he took the position that, in the moment, seemed best to serve the cause of parliamentary sovereignty. If we may judge by their silence, most ministerial writers preferred not to acknowledge colonial antislavery initiatives at all. That was the path taken by the Reverend James Ramsay of Saint Kitts, who promoted comprehensive slavery reform in the British Empire but would not mention in any of his publications the antislavery initiatives already under way in the North American colonies. When British defenders of parliamentary supremacy acknowledged American antislavery initiatives, they tended to impugn the colonists' motives. They dismissed the various abolition bills as disingenuous, as mere propaganda.[54]

The British intelligentsia sympathetic to the American rebellion, however, interpreted colonial actions differently. Colonial resistance appealed

53. Ragsdale, *A Planters' Republic,* 129–130; Moore, *Notes on the History of the Slave Trade in Massachusetts,* 142; Selwyn H. H. Carrington, *The Sugar Industry and the Abolition of the Slave Trade, 1775–1810* (Gainesville, Fla., 2002), 189.

54. John Peter Demarin, *A Treatise upon the Trade from Great-Britain to Africa: Humbly Recommended to the Attention of Government* (London, 1772); Lind, *An Answer to the Declaration of the American Congress,* 17.

to those radical political theorists, dissenting clergy, and latitudinarian Anglicans whom, during his years at the center of these circles, Benjamin Franklin dubbed "Honest Whigs." Among these self-described "friends of America" numbered several influential pamphleteers, including John Cartwright, John Jebb, Granville Sharp, Thomas Hollis, Jonathan Shipley, James Burgh, Richard Price, Catherine Macaulay, and Caleb Evans. Increasingly ill at ease, in these years, with what they regarded as a conspiracy among the "king's friends" to corrupt the House of Commons, in some cases opposed to the hegemony of the Church of England, they conducted, during the 1770s, an ardent defense of the American right to self-governance. The "Honest Whigs" tended to think of American resistance as a blow against the encroachments of tyranny rather than as treason against constitutional authority.[55] So colonial opposition to the slave trade, to several in this group, seemed in line with Americans' intensifying commitment to universal liberty. "Liberty has an asylum on that continent," wrote the latitudinarian divine John Jebb in 1775; "the abominable slave trade will I trust be abolished." In America, Richard Price asserted optimistically, slaves "will soon become extinct, or have their condition changed into that of Freemen."[56]

Confidence in America and Americans led David Hartley, the high-minded member of Parliament for Kingston-upon-Hull, to make an anti-slavery initiative the centerpiece of an eleventh-hour effort to prevent a war.

55. Caroline Robbins, *The Eighteenth-Century Commonwealthman: Studies in the Transmission, Development, and Circumstances of English Liberal Thought from the Restoration of Charles II until the War with the Thirteen Colonies* (Cambridge, Mass., 1959), 320–377; Verner W. Crane, "The Club of Honest Whigs: Friends of Science and Liberty," *WMQ,* 3d Ser., XXIII (1966), 210–233; Colin Bonwick, *English Radicals and the American Revolution* (Chapel Hill, N.C., 1977); Bonwick, "English Radicals and American Resistance to British Authority," in Walter H. Conser et al., eds., *Resistance, Politics, and the American Struggle for Independence, 1765–1775* (Boulder, Colo., 1986), 403–415. See also Jerome R. Reich, *British Friends of the American Revolution* (Armonk, N.Y., 1998), and Anthony Page, " 'Liberty Has an Asylum': John Jebb, British Radicalism, and the American Revolution," *History,* LXXXVII (2002), 204–226.

56. John Disney, ed., *The Works Theological, Medical, Political, and Miscellaneous of John Jebb, M.D., F.R.S. with Memoirs of the Life of the Author* (London, 1787), I, 94–96; Richard Price, *Observations on the Nature of Civil Liberty, the Principles of Government, and the Justice and Policy of War with America . . . ,* 3d ed. (London, 1776), 41n.

In December 1775, when the prospects for reconciliation looked increasingly dim, Hartley proposed a repeal of all acts of Parliament passed after 1763 that impinged on the jurisdiction of colonial legislatures. In exchange, he would have had the colonies honor the principle of imperial sovereignty by submitting to a benign, token act of Parliament. A law that "no American could hesitate an instant to comply with," Hartley suggested, would lay "the first stone of universal liberty to mankind." He acknowledged that it would be "infinitely absurd to send over to America an act to abolish slavery at one word" since "an evil which has spread so far" would require "information of facts and circumstances . . . to root it out." So, instead, he moved that Parliament require that "every slave in North America should be entitled to his trial by jury in all criminal cases," which, Hartley hoped, would be the first step to effecting a gradual abolition of slavery, an institution, he said, "contrary to the laws of God and man, and to the fundamental principles of the British constitution."[57]

As a peace initiative, the proposal was astonishingly ill conceived. Hartley failed to appreciate that American patriots would reject the principle of imperial sovereignty, however couched. Indeed, meddling with slave property, a step for which there was no precedent, promised only to alienate British Americans further. Few moments better illustrate how inadequately the self-professed "friends of America" understood the nature of the developing revolution in North America or the place of slavery in colonial society. Hartley assumed, wrongly, that the patriots' campaign against the Atlantic slave trade indicated an intention to liberate American slaves. He not only expected colonists to embrace a comprehensive scheme for state-sponsored emancipation. Incredibly, he thought it *the best* way to retrieve colonial affections.

Honest Whigs like David Hartley made such mistakes, in part, because the Americans they knew best, colonials residing in London like Benjamin

---

57. Simmons and Thomas, eds., *Proceedings and Debates of the British Parliaments respecting North America*, VI, 335, 336. See also George Herbert Guttridge, *David Hartley, M.P., an Advocate of Conciliation, 1774–1783* (Berkeley, Calif., 1926), 327–328. Attempts at conciliation in 1775 may be traced, on the American side, through Julie M. Flavell, "American Patriots and the Quest for Talks, 1773–1775," *Jour. Imperial and Commonwealth Hist.*, XX (1992), 335–369, and Flavell, "Lord North's Conciliatory Proposal and the Patriots in London," *English Historical Review*, CVII (1992), 302–322.

Franklin and Arthur Lee, made a show of their opposition to slavery. The antislavery statements sprinkled throughout patriot propaganda in the colonies reached British allies along the conduits supplied by friendship, correspondence, and ideological sympathy. Hartley seems to have picked up the idea of allowing jury trials for slaves from Benjamin Rush's *Address to the Inhabitants of the British Settlements in America upon Slave-Keeping* (1773), which, though never published in London, circulated privately among English radicals. Two London reprintings of the *Summary View of the Rights of British America* publicized Thomas Jefferson's expostulations against the British slave trade. Even a casual reader of the British press might gather from the "American News" that colonial resistance had spawned widespread rejection of the slave system. In the *Gentleman's Magazine* antislavery resolutions passed by the town of Salem, Massachusetts, in 1773 appeared at the foot of an extended report on New England corresponding committees.[58]

If patriot propaganda presented a misleading picture of American attitudes toward slavery, British sympathizers also wanted to be misled. The "friends of America" tended to believe the best about colonial resistance because the American cause echoed their aspirations, because the patriots' complaints resonated with their grievances. The British defenders of the established order thought of Americans as vulgar cousins. The "friends of

---

58. C. C. Bonwick, "An English Audience for American Revolutionary Pamphlets," *Historical Journal*, XIX (1976), 355–374; L. H. Butterfield, "The American Interests of the Firm of E. and C. Dilly, with Their Letters to Benjamin Rush, 1770–1795," *Papers of the Bibliographical Society of America*, XLV (1951), 283–322; [Rush], *An Address to the Inhabitants of the British Settlements in America upon Slave-Keeping;* Rush to Sharp, Oct. 29, 1773, in Woods, ed., "The Correspondence of Rush and Sharp," *JAS*, I (1969), 3; *Gentleman's Magazine, and Historical Chronicle*, XLIII (1773), 358. For notes on editions of British reprints of the proceedings of the Continental Congress, see Thomas R. Adams, ed., *The American Controversy: A Bibliographical Study of the British Pamphlets about the American Disputes, 1764–1783*, 2 vols. (Providence, R.I., 1980), I, 243–247. As David Waldstreicher has shown, Benjamin Franklin promoted the image of an antislavery America in France as well. "In Franklin's French period, as in his years in England, this kind of appropriation of antislavery for the purpose of justifying America trumped antislavery itself"; "whether he believed that North American slavery was being eliminated or not . . . it was extremely useful to say it was." Waldstreicher, *Runaway America*, 219, 221.

America," by contrast, regarded the colonists as exemplars of rustic virtue. The Honest Whigs thought of the North American colonies as, in Jebb's words, "an asylum for liberty," where freedom could thrive unburdened by the yoke of monarchy, aristocracy, or an established church. Moreover, Parliament's violation of American liberties seemed suspiciously similar to what several British radicals had begun to regard as a conspiracy to restrict constitutional freedoms in England. British sympathizers, then, understood the repression of American liberties as a challenge, more broadly, to values they held dear.[59] Advocating the right of Americans to self-governance, for them, was partially an exercise in self-defense and self-justification. By exonerating colonists from the charge of hypocrisy, they could help clear the reputation of all who professed a devotion to their more expansive concepts of liberty.

This decision to side with colonial patriots helped commit British radicals to an embrace of American antislavery politics. The pamphlets that advocated the rights of Americans sometimes made pointed critiques of the British slave trade, but rarely of colonial slavery. "Where did this infamous commerce originate," asked the Reverend John Erskine, a Scottish Evangelical opponent of the war. "Where is it still carried on with all the eagerness which avarice can inspire? Where, but in England?" Americans have tried to prohibit the slave trade but faced each time the objections of the "parent state." The official support given to the British Africa traders should free the colonists from criticism, agreed Richard Price. "It is not the fault of the Colonies" that they have among them so many of those unhappy people. The "torchbearer of freedom," as biographer Carl Cone labeled Richard Price, possessed only a limited interest in the liberation of Africans in 1776. Price once called political slavery (government without representation and consent) "much worse" than chattel slavery.[60] He drew attention to the British slave trade, not to argue for its abolition, but instead to quiet accusations that Americans behaved with remarkable inconsistency. Ameri-

59. Bonwick, *English Radicals and the American Revolution,* 114–128.

60. John Erskine, *Reflections on the Rise, Progress, and Probable Consequences, of the Present Contentions with the Colonies* . . . (Edinburgh, 1776), 27; Price, *Observations on the Nature of Civil Liberty,* 41n. For Erskine's political opinions, see Dalphy I. Fagerstorm, "Scottish Opinion and the American Revolution," *WMQ,* 3d Ser., XII (1954), 265.

cans might be inconsistent, Price conceded, but this inconsistency was unremarkable when set against the official sanction given by British ministers to the Company of Merchants Trading to Africa. The point, literally, was a footnote to *The Observations on Civil Liberty*. Price wanted primarily to argue against war in America and to develop a definition of liberty that privileged private judgment and self-governance. Introducing the slave trade into this discussion was expeditious. It bolstered the more critical claims. Yet by echoing American complaints about the negation of slave trade duties, Richard Price brought home to the British Isles the colonial challenge to metropolitan arrogance. Responsibility for American slavery rested with the British state, he asserted in passing. And if responsibility lay with the state, he implied but did not insist, then it was incumbent on the state, not just the colonies, to change its policies.

Outside Parliament, especially, sympathy for American politics sometimes evolved into hostility toward the British slave trade. One of the many contemporary histories of the American war provides a telling example. During the conflict, the iconoclastic author the Reverend James Murray of Newcastle waged a war of words against every species of power and authority in England. Relentlessly, Murray savaged the Church of England, the law courts, the aristocracy, the propertied—each of which he denounced as "usurpers" that had robbed the English people of liberty and their passion for freedom. If he could have had his way, the courts would have outlawed private ownership of land. Not surprisingly, Murray lauded the colonists' rejection of parliamentary authority and zeal for independence, which he witnessed firsthand during a brief tour of North America in 1776.[61] Like most English defenders of the American Revolution, Murray found slavery embarrassing to the patriot cause and, like others who shared his politics, emphasized the ways that the British, too, were complicit in the exploitation of Africans. A publication of 1776 in Britain had argued that North American slaveholders must never be permitted to make laws for free subjects. Murray conceded, in his inaptly titled *An Impartial History of the Present War in America*, that slaveholders had a questionable claim to

<hr/>

61. James E. Bradley, *Religion, Revolution, and English Radicalism: Nonconformity in Eighteenth-Century Politics and Society* (Cambridge, 1990), 128–185; Kathleen Wilson, *The Sense of the People: Politics, Culture, and Imperialism in England, 1715–1785* (Cambridge, 1995), 348–350, 354, 359.

political rights. But "if this argument were fairly analyzed," Murray added, "it would be bound to go a great length, and much farther than the writer seems to intend." Specifically, disenfranchising the owners of slaves "will exclude a great number in England from being represented in the British parliament," since "if there is any truth at all in the stories of the slave trade, there are not a few in Britain that are concerned in it, to their disgrace." But Americans do not want representation in Parliament, he noted. They only want to govern themselves. Too many in Britain, though, seemed to think that holding slaves should not only disqualify colonists from representation in Parliament but also qualify them for oppression by Parliament.

The closer one studied the question the more perplexing the views of writers like John Shebbeare, John Lind, and Samuel Johnson became. Why, Murray asked, should American slaveholders be held to a higher standard than slaveholders and slave traders living in Britain? If American slaveholders came to England, "they could not be denied a share in the government of this country"; "and suppose they employed in the thousands in the slave trade, it would be no objection to their sitting in parliament." Indeed, "it is no uncommon thing," he added, "to see a British member of parliament have his *Negro slave* following him, which plainly shows that the practice is not peculiar to America." Perhaps, then, this was where the wrongs originated, Murray concluded, almost stumbling into the idea: "It is a point to be soberly considered whether Great Britain is not as guilty as Virginia in this particular; for amongst all the laws for regulating the trade of the colonies, the British parliament has not yet made a law against this most infamous traffic."[62]

At some point, perhaps, the British public would have begun to debate the ethics of trading in slaves without prompting from North American propagandists. It may be that a concern with the morals of the slave trade could have arisen, eventually, by some other means. But that is not what happened. The American attempt to ban slave imports originated the first sustained attention in the British Isles to the problem of the Atlantic slave trade. Through their attempts to curtail the arrival of enslaved men and women, the colonial assemblies placed the British slave trade on the politi-

62. James Murray, *An Impartial History of the Present War in America; Containing an Account of Its Rise and Progress, the Political Springs Thereof, with Its Various Successes and Disappointments, on Both Sides* (London, [1778]), I, 26–28.

cal agenda. In arguing for the colonists' right to self-governance, British radicals like the Reverend James Murray circulated the patriot view. They noted that the British government had a share in the crime of American slavery.[63] Murray wrote as if Parliament should have acted many years before—the legislature had "not yet" passed an abolition law. More commonly, American sympathizers implied that no one in Britain should judge American slaveholders while Parliament continued to license slave shipments to the colonies.

These claims about moral authority and the right to judge others reordered the norms of political debate, although this was hardly their primary intent. North American colonists found that their campaign for independence, in ways increasingly impossible to ignore, made the institution of chattel slavery a moral issue and, as a consequence, a political liability. In wrestling with this discovery, they forced the British to notice that they, too, lived with a conflict between conduct and professed values. American abolitionism undermined British innocence on the question of slavery. It became increasingly difficult in Britain during the imperial conflict to maintain the fiction that the slave system existed to serve only degenerate American colonists, that, as Adam Smith had supposed, moral responsibility lay only on the western side of the Atlantic. Revolutionary era polemic intensified metropolitan awareness of the slave system. It exposed the gulf between a national ideology premised on a distinctively British devotion to liberty and British institutions that depended on the ownership and sale of slaves. Growing awareness of this divide had almost no immediate impact on British behavior. However, it made the tension between values and practices tangible and, ultimately, some form of resolution necessary.

Together, British and American propagandists during the era of the American Revolution politicized involvement in the slave system. Indeed, with respect to Atlantic slavery, they invented the notion of complicity. The years of crisis produced a preoccupation with affixing blame. And the consequence was a profound shift in what the historian Thomas Haskell once called the conventions governing the attribution of moral responsibility.[64]

63. The next chapter, through a discussion of Granville Sharp, develops this point at length.

64. See Thomas L. Haskell, "Capitalism and the Origins of the Humanitarian Sensibility, Part 1," Haskell, "Capitalism and the Origins of the Humanitarian Sensibility,

No longer was disapproval directed vaguely against the slave system as a whole or against archetypal slaveholders. The American conflict offered up identifiable villains: colonials who cried out for liberty but denied freedom to their slaves, British statesmen who honored the interests of African traders and prevented colonials from curtailing slave imports. Most in Britain had tended to think of colonial slavery and the Atlantic slave trade as unfortunate and distasteful but beyond the power of anyone to address effectively. Now, with greater frequency in the Revolutionary era, the slave system was characterized as someone's fault, as the consequence of greedy planters or callous slave traders, as a consequence of laws and policies instituted by particular British officials or specific colonial governments. This sharpened sense of the slave system as a product of human choice and preference enabled radically different descriptions of moral duty. If particular individuals and groups could be held responsible for slavery, then they also could be held responsible for correcting the wrongs they had created. By describing complicity in slavery as proof of collective vice, disputants in the Revolutionary era helped define opposition to slavery as proof of collective virtue.

Part 2," Haskell, "Convention and Hegemonic Interest in the Debate over Antislavery: A Reply to Davis and Ashworth," all in Thomas Bender, ed., *The Antislavery Debate: Capitalism and Abolitionism as a Problem in Historical Interpretation* (Berkeley, Calif., 1992), 107–135, 136–160, 200–259. My view is that Haskell was correct to call attention to changing trends in the attribution of moral responsibility but misunderstood the sources for that shift and its character.

CHAPTER 3

Granville Sharp and the
Obligations of Empire

If conflict with the American patriots helped some in
Britain reflect on the problem of slavery, most resisted, for a time, thinking
of the slave trade as a national crime. The very idea conflicted with what the
British knew, or thought they knew, about the character of their overseas
enterprise. In the public imagination, the British Empire was defined by its
commitment to liberty, a view reinforced by the habit of comparing the
British American settlements with Spain's Kingdom of the Indies. In every
respect, it was presumed, the British brought freedom to the Americas
while the Spanish brought only despotism. Spain had destroyed ancient
civilizations in Mexico and Peru in pursuit of universal monarchy, whereas
Britain had nurtured peace and tranquillity in the Americas by promoting
agriculture and commerce. Where Spain imposed the hegemony of the
Catholic Church, Britain had tolerated in its colonies a free exercise of
religion. Where Spain ruled its American territories on absolutist principles, Britain had allowed its settlers substantial political autonomy. And
where the Spanish had annihilated or enslaved the native population, the
English had settled peacefully with the Indians and, sometimes it was said,
liberated them from Spanish rule. It did not matter that these contrasts
rendered inaccurate portraits of both empires. Nor did it matter that England had entered the Atlantic, initially, to emulate Spanish achievements.
By the mid-eighteenth century, what mattered to the British was that theirs
could and was seen to be an empire of trade rather than an empire of
dominion.[1]

1. Anthony C. Pagden, "The Struggle for Legitimacy and the Image of Empire in the
Atlantic to c. 1700," in Nicholas Canny, ed., *The Oxford History of the British Empire*, I,
*The Origins of Empire: British Overseas Enterprise to the Close of the Seventeenth Cen-
tury* (Oxford, 1998), 36–38, 51–55; Pagden, *Lords of All the World: Ideologies of Empire
in Spain, Britain, and France, c.1500–c.1800* (New Haven, Conn., 1995), 66–70, 86–
88, 128–129; Kathleen Wilson, *The Sense of the People: Politics, Culture, and Imperialism in England, 1715–1785* (Cambridge, 1995), 155, 157, 194–195, 201–202; David Armi-

The results of the Seven Years' War began to unsettle this satisfied self-image in the late 1760s and the early 1770s, as British speculators raced to claim captured territories in the Americas, and as East India Company agents took authority over vast regions of the subcontinent. The attempt in 1772–1773 to oust Caribs from the newly conquered isle of Saint Vincent stirred protest in Parliament and derisive commentary in the press. It generated in Britain one of the earliest sustained critiques of the empire on humanitarian grounds. Butchering "a parcel of innocent savages in cold blood," one military officer wrote to the *London Evening Post,* brought "infamy" upon "the national character." Barlow Trecothick, member of Parliament for the City of London, told the House of Commons that the attacks on a "defenceless, innocent, and inoffensive people" embarrassed the nation, dishonored "the British flag," and, worst of all, mimicked "the barbarities of the Spaniards against the Mexicans." Depredations by British nationals in one part of the empire began to call attention to abuses elsewhere. To several commentators in the London press, the war against the Caribs bore an uncomfortable resemblance to the new spirit of conquest in India.[2] The most vociferous critics of the Saint Vincent expedition—

tage, *The Ideological Origins of the British Empire* (Cambridge, 2000). Early English critiques of Spanish colonialism may be traced in William S. Maltby, *The Black Legend in England: The Development of Anti-Spanish Sentiment, 1558–1660* (Durham, N.C., 1931), and Jonathan Hart, *Representing the New World: The English and French Uses of the Example of Spain* (New York, 2001). For the emphasis placed on these perceived contrasts and their ideological importance, see John Robertson, "Universal Monarchy and the Liberties of Europe: David Hume's Critique of an English Whig Doctrine," in Nicholas Phillipson and Quentin Skinner, eds., *Political Discourse and Early Modern Britain* (Cambridge, 1993), 349–373. Gabriel B. Paquette presents these perceptions of Spain as increasingly complex and varied with the onset of reforms within the Spanish Empire after the Seven Years' War. See Paquette, "The Image of Imperial Spain in British Political Thought, 1750–1800," *Bulletin of Spanish Studies,* LXXXI (2004), 187–214.

2. Paul Thomas, "The Caribs of St. Vincent: A Study in Imperial Maladministration," *Journal of Caribbean History,* XVIII (1983), 61, 68; William Cobbett and T. C. Hansard, *The Parliamentary History of England from the Earliest Period to the Year 1803, from Which Last-Mentioned Epoch It Is Continued Downwards in the Work Entitled "Hansard's Parliamentary Debates"* . . . , 36 vols. (London, 1806–1820), XVII, 568–569. See also Michael Craton, "Planters, British Imperial Policy, and the Black Caribs of St. Vincent," in Craton, *Empire, Enslavement, and Freedom in the Caribbean*

Trecothick, Issac Barre, Viscount Folkestone, George Germain, and Hans Stanley—each served, at that time, on one of the two committees established by Parliament to investigate the plunder of Bengal.[3] These early investigations into the East India Company arose as much from political opportunism as outrage at specific actions in India. The professed concern for the welfare of Bengal in official quarters was not always sincerely meant. However, the evidence of profiteering and corruption that these investigations produced did stir genuine concern and protest. Sir George Savile, member of Parliament for Yorkshire and a member of the Commons select committee, described the "territorial acquisitions" in India as "public robberies." "Having heretofore censured the extravagant claims of empire made by the *Spaniards* in *America*," one pamphleteer wrote, "it certainly behoved those who were concerned in the late acquest of large dominions in *Asia* to avoid their resemblance." Richard Price, too, in his tract on civil liberty in 1776 derided the ways Englishmen had "depopulated whole kingdoms and ruined millions of innocent peoples by the most infamous oppression and rapacity."[4]

It became difficult after the Seven Years' War to think of the British Empire as merely an empire of trade. Yet the consequence, at first, was less a concern with what the British were doing within the empire than

---

(Kingston, Jamaica, 1997), 125–129, and Robin F. A. Fabel, *Colonial Challenges: Britons, Native Americans, and Caribs, 1759–1775* (Gainesville, Fla., 2000), 187–193.

3. Barre, Folkestone, Germain, and Trecothick numbered among the thirty-one appointed to John Burgoyne's Select Committee instituted on Apr. 15, 1772. Hans Stanley was one of thirteen named to the North ministry's Secret Committee designated six months later to investigate the East India Company's finances. See H. V. Bowen, *Revenue and Reform: The Indian Problem in British Politics, 1757–1773* (Cambridge, 1991), 133–150. Of the seven who spoke in Parliament against the Saint Vincent expedition, only Thomas Townshend and Richard Whitworth did not have formal roles in the East India Company inquiry.

4. Sir George Savile cited in P. J. Marshall, *The Making and Unmaking of Empires: Britain, India, and America, c. 1750–1783* (Oxford, 2005), 198; [William Bollan], *Britannia Librera; or, A Defence of the Free State of Man in England, against the Claims of Any Man There as a Slave; Inscribed and Submitted to the Jurisconsulti, and the Free People of England* (London, 1772), 42; Price cited in Pagden, *Lords of All the World*, 185. On public concern with India in 1773, see P. J. Marshall, *Problems of Empire: Britain and India, 1757–1813* (London, 1968), 53–63, and Bowen, *Revenue and Reform*, 95–97, 134–135.

what the empire was doing to Britain. These anxieties fixed particularly on "Nabobs" and absentee planters, British men who returned from India and from the Caribbean with outsized wealth and who threatened not only to exceed their place in society but also, more dangerously, to exercise a disproportionate influence in local and national politics.[5] Some suspected that the expanded empire would encourage the state to adopt, as William Pitt, earl of Chatham, put it, "Asiatic principles of government" that would endanger freedom in the British Isles as well as overseas. With this in mind a contributor to a London newspaper linked crimes in India with "The St. Vincent's exterminating scheme" and compared both to the massacre of Wilkesite protesters at Saint George's Fields in 1768.[6] Some commentators anticipated a march of tyranny from the colonies to the metropole: an extended empire meant an empowered state; an empowered state compromised the liberty of the subject; an extended empire, therefore, threatened to destroy the balanced constitution. An important minority among the intelligentsia, for these reasons, dissented from the popular embrace of the recent conquests. To them, the fate of Rome and the more recent experience of Spain showed abrupt expansion to bring debt, depopulation, tyranny, and cultural decline. In striking reevaluations, Josiah Tucker and David Hume proposed casting off the colonies to ensure institutional stability and the integrity of British liberty. Adam Smith weighed in with the stunning suggestion, in *The Wealth of Nations* (1776), that

5. James M. Holzman, *The Nabobs in England: A Study of the Returned Anglo-Indian, 1760–1785* (New York, 1926); Wylie Sypher, "The West-Indian as a 'Character' in the Eighteenth Century," *Studies in Philology*, XXXVI (1939), 503–520; Philip Lawson and Jim Philips, " 'Our Execrable Banditti': Perceptions of Nabobs in Mid-Eighteenth-Century Britain," *Albion*, XVI (1984), 225–241; James Raven, *Judging New Wealth: Popular Publishing and Responses to Commerce in England, 1750–1800* (Oxford, 1992), 221–248.

6. William Pitt, earl of Chatham, cited in Lawson and Phillips, " 'Our Execrable Banditti,' " 238; Thomas, "The Caribs of St. Vincent," *Jour. Caribbean Hist.*, XVIII (1983), 61. References to the Asiatic principles purportedly taking hold within the British government appear as well in American patriot propaganda published in this period. See H. V. Bowen, "Perceptions from the Periphery: Colonial American Views of Britain's Asiatic Empire, 1756–1783," in Christine Daniels and Michael V. Kennedy, *Negotiated Empires: Center and Peripheries in the Americas, 1500–1820* (New York, 2002), 292–296.

empire was an economic burden to the nation rather than a boon as widely was supposed.[7]

Those who doubted the benefits of imperial expansion asked questions about administration and governance, direction and purpose, extent and expense, but rarely justice, ethics, or morals. The political economists who interrogated mercantilist assumptions, David Hume and Adam Smith most notably, sometimes described the slave system as cruel, wasteful, and emblematic of the unwise principles guiding Atlantic enterprise. But this was rather different from insisting, as some American patriots claimed, that the slave trade showed Britain to be carrying on an empire of tyranny. Colonial slavery and the Atlantic slave trade mattered little to those British writers who questioned the wisdom of imperial expansion. Few in this period went as far as the Abbé Raynal and his collaborators in France, who used the injustice of slavery to challenge the legitimacy of empire itself. Even those like Josiah Tucker, who consistently cast aspersions on the slave system during the 1760s and 1770s, never allowed human bondage in the colonies to become for them a primary concern. Few condemned slavery more consistently or forcefully than Samuel Johnson during the third quarter of the eighteenth century. And yet Johnson, like many others, chose not to make his antislavery opinions the starting point for a public crusade.[8]

7. J. G. A. Pocock, *Virtue, Commerce, and History: Essays on Political Thought and History, Chiefly in the Eighteenth Century* (Cambridge, 1985), 125–141, 157–191; Robertson, "Universal Monarchy and the Liberties of Europe," in Phillipson and Skinner, eds., *Political Discourse and Early Modern Britain*, 368–373; Norman Vance, "Imperial Rome and Britain's Language of Empire, 1600–1837," *History of European Ideas*, XXVI (2000), 211–224. On a less elevated level, as well, an undercurrent of anxiety accompanied the more apparent enthusiasm for national aggrandizement. References to public reservations about the expansion of empire dot the secondary literature on this period, but they have yet to receive systematic discussion or analysis. The most extensive treatment appears in Nancy F. Koehn, *The Power of Commerce: Economy and Governance in the First British Empire* (Ithaca, N.Y., 1994), 149–184. For the broader intellectual background on the perceived dangers attending imperial expansion, see Pagden, *Lords of All the World*, 103–125, 161–163.

8. Pagden, *Lords of All the World*, 165–176. For reference to Tucker's antislavery views, see Pocock, *Virtue, Commerce, and History*, 178n; James G. Basker, " 'The Next Insurrection': Johnson, Race, and Rebellion," *The Age of Johnson: A Scholarly Annual,*

There was some discomfort with an empire of conquest after the Seven Years' War. However, that discomfort did not lead, necessarily, to the promotion of an empire of virtue. The British came to see more clearly during the 1770s how the nation benefited from the exploitation of Africans. The American Revolution put the ethos of the slave system on the political agenda. Yet this growing awareness did not mean that anyone in Britain would think these facts especially important. It was one thing to recognize that the nation encouraged and perpetuated injustices overseas. It was something else to believe that those practices, when compared with other issues of the moment, deserved particular attention or official action.

The dissolution of the North American empire, however, would intensify the impulse in Britain toward collective self-scrutiny, an inclination that originated shortly after the Seven Years' War but would become influential only with the loss of the thirteen colonies. The outcome of the American war inspired the first sustained doubts about the moral character of British overseas enterprise. In these years, as many began to question the ends of state and the virtue of its rulers, as some began to explore and promote strategies for institutional reform at home and abroad, several in Britain would propose that the nation, not merely individuals, bore responsibility for colonial slavery and the Atlantic slave trade. No one espoused this view during the American war with more vigor than Granville Sharp. His personal campaign for government action against slavery and the slave trade between 1772 and 1781 represented, in a proper sense, the beginnings of British abolitionism. That campaign often gets ignored or overlooked in the stories told about this period because in key respects it failed. Granville Sharp, it must be emphasized, did not originate and did not lead the abolitionist movement that emerged in Britain at the end of the 1780s. That effort took shape, as will become apparent, primarily because of Evangelical and Quaker initiatives and agendas. Yet his frustrated efforts help specify both the limits of individual commitment and the obstacles that aspiring abolitionists faced. To understand the deficiencies of this first campaign is to understand the strengths of the programs that followed.

The Granville Sharp campaign matters in a second way, too. It docu-

---

XI (2000), 43–49; John Ingledew, "Samuel Johnson's Jamaican Connection," *Caribbean Quarterly*, XXX (1984), 1–17.

ments what is otherwise an elusive shift in British self-perception during the American war, a shift crucial to the emergence of organized abolitionism in the decade that followed. Sharp shared with many others the fear that war in America foreshadowed national decline. Like several of his peers, he looked to diverse schemes of institutional and moral reform to right the listing ship of state. By the early 1780s, some in Britain had begun to select new criteria when evaluating overseas enterprise. The moral character of imperial authority, the ethics of British conduct outside the British Isles, started to figure in public discussions of empire with increasing frequency. With this growing concern with British behavior outside the British Isles came new ideas, still notional and half-formed, about the obligations of empire—new ideas that aimed to bring imperial practices in line with older assumptions about the British commitment to liberty.

Granville Sharp had much in common with the "friends [I] of America" considered at the close of the previous chapter. Like John Cartwright and Richard Price, he wanted the imperial union preserved, but he denounced attempts to impose parliamentary authority on British America. Unlike them, he held an office in government, as a clerk at the Board of Ordnance, and, perhaps for this reason, he developed an unusually sustained interest in the role of the state in overseas enterprise. Sharp regarded the American colonies as separate communities under the crown and, therefore, entitled to their own independent legislatures. He distrusted the principles enunciated in the Declaratory Act of 1766, which struck him as a recrudescence of absolutism, a kind of "popery in politics." Sharp thought the custom of allowing American assemblies to govern their own affairs sufficiently established to invalidate interference by a British legislature. His *Declaration of the People's Natural Right to a Share in the Legislature* (1774) represented one of the first attempts in England to make a case for colonial legislative autonomy. As the title of this tract indicated, Sharp believed the right to representation fundamental to the British constitution and regarded its denial to Americans as evidence of a creeping invasion everywhere within the empire into political liberties that "British Subjects in general are commonly supposed to inherit by *Birth-right*." Only the formal procedure of representation and assent, Sharp held, could make law valid: for "law to bind all, it must be assented to by all." This was, he insisted, "a principle of *natural equity*," owed to every community within the empire. On similar grounds, Sharp lamented the supremacy claimed by Parliament over the Irish legislature. Several years later, he made the highly original suggestion to establish representative government in India.[9] To him, only representation (only the possession of a voice in the legislature) could render government legitimate.

Granville Sharp arrived at this defense of colonial rights by an unusual route. His support for colonial autonomy represented an extension of his crusade against slaveholding on English soil, a working out of his inquiries on the common law and the "ancient" constitution. Like the English right to personal liberty, Sharp conceived "a share in the legislature" to be a question of justice, a fundamental right guaranteed under English law. Like the practice of slaveholding, Sharp considered the concept of parliamentary supremacy over American affairs to be an unconstitutional innovation. Most English radicals, by contrast, described the conflict with America as a consequence of political corruption at home, as evidence of the tyrannical principles favored by successive administrations after the accession of George III. In addition to advocating peace with America, they wanted to reform the political order by promoting shorter parliaments and more equitable representation, by reducing the influence of the crown on the legislature. Sharp sometimes wrote in this idiom and would lobby for parliamentary reform, too, during the American war. However, his original concern with problems of law and justice led him to question specific imperial practices, not merely the structure of metropolitan institutions. Unlike other radicals, Sharp took an interest in the concrete experience of colonial workers, both white and black, and in the rights of the Irish, and in violence against American Indians. At a time when the other "friends of

9. Granville Sharp, *A Declaration of the People's Natural Right to a Share in the Legislature* (London, 1774), ii, iv. The first edition of this tract appeared as a pamphlet in Boston, Philadelphia, and New York and as an essay in Virginia and New York newspapers. Through the assistance of Benjamin Franklin, two hundred copies were sent to the Continental Congress in July 1774. Benjamin Rush to Granville Sharp, Sept. 20, 1774, in John A. Woods, ed., "The Correspondence of Benjamin Rush and Granville Sharp, 1773–1809," *Journal of American Studies,* I (1967), 11–12; Colin Bonwick, *English Radicals and the American Revolution* (Chapel Hill, N.C., 1977), 73–75; Robert E. Toohey, *Liberty and Empire: British Radical Solutions to the American Problem, 1774–1776* (Louisville, Ky., 1978), 53–63.

FIGURE 3. Granville Sharp. By George Dance. 1794.
Courtesy, National Portrait Gallery, London.

As the American crisis turned toward war, Granville Sharp's fight against the keeping of slaves in England widened into a broader campaign against the practice of slavery and the traffic in slaves throughout the British Empire.

America" concerned themselves with the political rights of British colonists, Sharp gave equal attention to what he would later describe as "the natural rights of mankind."[10]

Each crisis in British liberty led him to ruminate on the next. His inquiries progressed from slavery in England to the coercion of America and then to the moral character of the empire as a whole. He concluded, as his interrogations widened in scope, that each injustice entailed the others and that together they indicated a waning commitment to liberty. Sharp found it impossible to write about one injustice without referencing another. He first wrote sympathetically about American resistance in a private letter addressed to the first minister, Lord North, in 1772, in the months when the case of James Somerset lay before the Court of King's Bench. No issue, Sharp explained, required more immediate attention than "the present miserable and *deplorable slavery of* Negroes and Indians, as well as white English servants, in our colonies." But colonial slavery, he emphasized, was not an issue on which Parliament could legislate, since "no Parliament," he maintained, "can have a just right to enact laws for places which it does not *represent*." Therefore the king acting through the Privy Council should only *recommend* to the American assemblies the repeal of colonial slave codes. Sharp's purpose here was to denounce slaveholding in the colonies. He set out to "oppose domestic Tyranny and Slavery without any other view." Yet, in the process, he wanted to draw attention to the legitimacy of American opposition to parliamentary supremacy. It pleased him to learn from Quaker abolitionist Benezet, who circulated the letter in North America, that defending the rights of slaves "should be a means of warning the Americans of the natural independence of their several assemblies with respect to the British Parliament." The apparent complement between African and colonial rights satisfied Sharp's belief that all liberties stood on the single foundation of "*natural Equity*." When he framed the rights of colonists as inviolable as the rights of slaves, he drew himself into defending American resistance. In later letters to Benezet and Pennsylvania statesman Benjamin Rush, Sharp insisted that colonists address abolition

10. Sharp to Henry Seymour Conway, Sept. 30, 1768, Sharp to James Sharp, Sept. 12, 1769, Sharp to Rev. Robert Findlay, July 21, 1772, and Sharp to Anthony Benezet, Sept. 23, 1772, all in Granville Sharp Letterbook, fols. 4–10, 28–30, 82–87, 70–72, York Minister Library (YML).

petitions to the king, as a petition to king and Parliament would seem to legitimate unconstitutional authority and compromise the dignity of their legislatures.[11]

Granville Sharp assumed the role of London agent for American abolitionists in the years before the American war. He publicized North American antislavery initiatives and, in the process, cast Americans as the emerging champions of African liberty. From colonial correspondents, Benezet in particular, Sharp learned of the developing interest in slave trade abolition. The Quaker activist described attempts in New England to abolish the slave trade and promote gradual emancipation. He recounted debates in Pennsylvania on the best means of approaching the king's ministers with appeals for slave trade abolition. Between ten and twenty thousand signatures, the Quaker activist assured Sharp, could be gathered for petitions against the slave trade in Virginia and Maryland alone. In turn, Sharp disseminated this information among his friends in England. He reprinted for an English audience in 1776 a transcript of antislavery petitions drafted in Virginia, Pennsylvania, and New Jersey. He distributed colonial antislavery resolutions to those "whose interest," he said, "I thought of sufficient consequence to have weight in promoting a Reformation." He told Secretary of State for the American Colonies Lord Dartmouth, and likely many others, that the people of New York and Boston were inclined to implement emancipations.[12] English "friends of America" like David Hartley believed

11. Sharp to Lord North, Feb. 18, 1772, and Anthony Benezet to Sharp, Nov. 8, 1772, Feb. 18, 1773, all in Prince Hoare, *Memoirs of Granville Sharp* . . . (London, 1820), 78–80, 112; Benezet to Sharp, May 14, 1772, in George S. Brookes, *Friend Anthony Benezet* (Philadelphia, 1937), 290–293; Sharp to Benezet, Aug. 21, 1772, Granville Sharp MSS Letterbook, fols. 62–65, YML; Sharp to Benezet, Jan. 7, 1774, Granville Sharp Papers, D3549 13/1/B19, Gloucestershire Record Office (GRO); Diary G, fols. 17–18, Granville Sharp Papers, D3549 13/4/2; Sharp to Rush, Feb. 21, 1774, in Woods, ed., "The Correspondence of Rush and Sharp," *JAS*, I (1969), 4.

12. Benezet to Sharp, May 14, 1772, in Brookes, *Friend Anthony Benezet*, 290–293; Benezet to Sharp, Nov. 8, 1772, Feb. 18, 1773, both in Granville Sharp Received Letterbook, Historical Society of Pennsylvania (HSP), Philadelphia; Benezet to Sharp, May 25, June 7, 1773, both in Hoare, *Memoirs*, 112, 113; Sharp to Lord Dartmouth, Jan. 16, 1773, Dartmouth Papers, D(w)1778/II/534, Staffordshire Record Office (SRO); Sharp to Benezet, Aug. 21, 1772, July 7, 1773, and Sharp to the earl of Macclesfield, Feb. 20, 1773, all in Granville Sharp Letterbook, fols. 63, 74–75, 174–175, YML; Diary G, fols. 44–46,

that American patriots intended to abolish slavery in the colonies in part because of Sharp's canvassing and publishing in the years before the war.

Yet, perhaps because Sharp had tangled with slaveholders before the Court of King's Bench, he knew well the challenges that American abolitionists faced and the extent of colonial resistance to emancipation. Indeed, for this reason, he initially had regarded with skepticism American protests against parliamentary interference. As late as 1769, his description of American patriots reads more like the subsequent writings of conservatives like John Lind and John Shebbeare than the sympathetic texts later produced by the "friends of America." His first antislavery tract treated the injustice of slaveholding on English soil, not slaveholding in the British Americas. But in several lengthy asides Sharp denounced as well those colonial laws that allowed American patriarchs unqualified dominion over their dependents. In the colonies, Sharp asserted, employers *grind the face of the poor,* they treat laborers "as if they were merely wild beasts." In New York, for example, "this infringement on civil and domestic liberty is become notorious and scandalous, notwithstanding that the political controversies of the inhabitants are stuffed with theatrical bombast and ranting expressions in praise of liberty." The British colony along the Hudson River deserved the name of "New Barbary" rather than New York. Thus, the colonists' complaints against tyranny and oppression were unworthy of attention, he wrote in 1769, since those "who do not scruple to detain others in Slavery, have but a very partial and unjust claim to the protection of the laws of liberty." In a passage that would have pleased Samuel Johnson, Sharp concluded that American liberty "has so little right to that sacred name, that it seems to differ from the arbitrary power of despotic monarchies only in one circumstance; viz. that it is a *many-headed monster of tyranny,* which entirely subverts our excellent constitution."[13]

At some point, in the three years that followed, Sharp became less criti-

---

Granville Sharp Papers, D3549 13/4/2; Sharp to Benezet, Jan. 7, 1774, ibid., D3549 13/1/B19; Sharp, *The Law of Retribution; or, A Serious Warning to Great Britain and Her Colonies, Founded on Unquestionable Examples of God's Temporal Vengeance against Tyrants, Slave-Holders, and Oppressors* (London, 1776), 308n–313n.

13. Granville Sharp, *A Representation of the Injustice and Dangerous Tendency of Tolerating Slavery, or of Admitting the Least Claims of Private Property in the Persons of Men, in England . . .* (London, 1769), 57, 66, 81, 82.

cal of American patriots. His voluminous correspondence, manuscripts, and publications, unfortunately, do not establish exactly when or why. The energy that he later gave to defending American rights to self-governance hints that study of the constitutional problem led him to reject parliamentary supremacy in colonial affairs on principle by 1772. The government crackdown on the Massachusetts Bay Colony in 1774 likely enlarged his sympathy for the colonial struggle and seems to have inspired the publication of *A Declaration of a Natural Right of the People to a Share in the Legislature*. Perhaps, too, the development of an antislavery movement in North America facilitated his support for the Revolutionary cause. With Granville Sharp, at least, American patriots may have succeeded in legitimating rebellion by promoting antislavery initiatives. Because their rights had been violated, because they had expressed a discomfort with the Atlantic slave trade, their resistance to British rule perhaps had justice on its side, it might have seemed to Granville Sharp. This possibility meant, however, that the outcome of the patriot struggle depended considerably on their commitment to antislavery principles. Here he espoused a view increasingly common among the Evangelical clergy throughout North America. Colonial resistance could only succeed, according to Sharp, if the patriots collectively renounced their supposed right to purchase and possess enslaved men and women, if they heeded the warning their own troubles revealed.

"American liberty cannot be firmly established," Sharp told Benjamin Rush, without "some scheme of general Enfranchisment," since "the toleration of domestic slavery in the colonies greatly weakens the claim or *natural Right* of our American Brethren to Liberty." "Let them put away *the accursed thing* (that horrid *Oppression*) from among them, before they presume to implore the imposition of *divine Justice;* for while they retain their *brethren of the world* in the most shameful involuntary servitude, it is profane in them to look up to the *merciful* Lord of all, and call him *Father!"* A "tremendous Cloud of Trouble" hovered over North America, Sharp warned four months after the passage of the Coercive Acts, which "seems ready to burst with destructive Vengeance." "Reformation must begin! or vain will be our Endeavours," he continued, invoking an alliance of Anglo-American patriots, "to preserve the British constitution." Always, *"National Injustice,* (such as the public Toleration of Slavery) must be punished even in this World and it is remarkable," he added, alluding to the

colonists' troubles, "that the most general punishment of Tyranny and Oppression is *political slavery*."[14]

Granville Sharp found in the North American campaign for political liberty a new way to promote emancipation and abolition. He regarded the regrettable crisis in Anglo-American relations as an opportunity to share a lesson about the consequences of collective vice. It offered as well, he decided, an advantageous moment for action. If colonial abolitionists could gather petitions against the slave trade from across British North America, as Benezet claimed, this would "retrieve, in some respects, the Honor of the Colonies, and be a glorious Proof that they are not Destitute of Christian and Social Principles." The colonial assemblies, Sharp advised, should repeal laws that prohibit voluntary manumissions and send additional abolition bills to the king. They must not allow the veto of the Virginia duties to discourage them. First attempts must not be the last: "The said petition is but one, whereas the Evil to be remedied is *general*, and therefore requires a *more general* Testimony . . . in order to balance the Misrepresentation and unaccountable influence of the African Traders and the West India Merchants." For his part, he pledged to harass defenders of slavery with "severe remarks" that "will make their *Ears* Tingle" and promised to prepare for the British press a series of pamphlets against slavery and, characteristically, "*oppression in general*."[15]

The North American campaign against the British slave trade helped Granville Sharp understand colonial slavery as a British institution. The antislavery petitions from the colonies, Sharp recalled two decades later, moved him to trace "*the evil to its source*." Confidently, in 1772, Sharp had called on colonial legislatures to ban slave imports, certain that such measures would win "the King's Concurrence" if it was "asked by a Majority" of the public. Two years later, after the dismissal of the Virginia address, after inaction on the Pennsylvania petition, Sharp understood better that ministerial intransigence prevented abolition of the slave trade to North

14. Sharp to Rush, July 18, 1775, in Woods, ed., "The Correspondence of Rush and Sharp," *JAS*, I (1969), 16; Granville Sharp, *A Declaration of the People's Natural Right to a Share in the Legislature; Which Is the Fundamental Principle of the British Constitution of State,* 2d ed. (London, 1775), 28n; Sharp to Samuel Allinson, July 28, 1774, Granville Sharp Papers, D3549 13/1/A8.

15. Sharp to Benezet, Jan. 7, 1774, Granville Sharp Papers, D3549 13/1/B19.

America and undermined colonial self-governance. Veto of these bills manifested in concrete terms the unjust limits Britain imposed on American legislatures. Now, Sharp decided, by inhibiting American abolitionists, "the *horrid* Guilt of persisting in that *monstrous Wickedness* must reside on this side of the Atlantic!" No wonder Americans had lost faith in British rule. In December 1774, just months before war commenced, Sharp told Lord Dartmouth, the government secretary responsible for American policy, that ministers should allow the colonists direct representation in Parliament. He added that if the danger of tolerating slavery had been acknowledged when he first brought the issue to Lord North's attention in 1772, the entire crisis could have been avoided.[16] For anyone else this would have been a non sequitur. But Granville Sharp came to defend the rights of the colonies through his campaign against slavery. And by 1776 he had concluded that the developing civil war within the empire in part originated in and represented divine punishment for public toleration of the slave trade and chattel slavery.

Understanding the dynamics at work here is essential. Most "friends of America" became opponents of the British slave trade because they wished to exonerate the American patriots. They emphasized the role of the state so that the colonists would not bear sole responsibility for the horrors of slavery. By arguing their case this way, they directed attention to the problem of slavery more generally and thereby obliged themselves to condemn human bondage. But there is a difference in kind, not merely in degree, between seeing a problem and feeling the compulsion to act. When English "friends of America" characterized the British slave trade as an emblem of imperial tyranny, they wrote to embarrass the government rather than force action on the slavery question. Nor did they take responsibility themselves for initiating change. Indeed, they wrote as if their alienation from the Church of England and their limited influence on the legislature could distance them from abuses sanctioned by the state and conducted by British traders. They wrote as if they had neither an interest in slavery nor the capacity to affect its fate. To an important extent, this detachment among "friends of America" mirrored the complacency of their domestic

16. Hoare, *Memoirs*, 118; Sharp to Benezet, Aug. 21, 1772, Granville Sharp Letterbook, fol. 63; Sharp, *The Law of Retribution*, 314; Sharp to Lord Dartmouth, Dec. 4, 1774, Granville Sharp Papers, D3549 13/1/D4.

antagonists—writers like Ambrose Serle or John Shebbeare who chastised Americans for hypocrisy but made no effort to seek a remedy. Characterizing the oppression of Africans as the fault of others allowed them to parade their allegiance to moral principle while fixing the burden of reform on someone else.

Granville Sharp had no patience with such moral posturing. He, too, had a point to make about the American Revolution, like many who judged slavery or the slave trade critically in these years. But unlike the others, he did not condemn the slave system instrumentally. He did not make a case against slavery because doing so would assist arguments for or against colonial independence. Just the opposite. Sharp, at first, used the imperial crisis instrumentally. He used the building conflict to reshape how the British thought about the oppression of Africans, to reorient British antislavery sentiment in a way increasingly common in Revolutionary America. What Granville Sharp saw in the first colonial antislavery measures—in the town and county petitions against the slave trade, in the numerous antislavery publications, in the legislation written by colonial assemblies—was not only resistance to British rule but also a willingness in the colonies to inspect their own institutions, to conceive the guilt of slavery as a common possession of the American people. Sharp hoped to inspire similar self-recognition in Britain, an awareness of the ways that a nation bore responsibility for the exploitation of Africans, the self-scrutiny that would generate a sustained commitment to change.

In the last years of imperial rule over the thirteen colonies, Granville Sharp launched a crusade against injustices within the empire and the moral complacency in Britain that allowed them to flourish. At a time when most critics focused on how empire corrupted the nation, Sharp called attention, instead, to how the empire spread violence and destruction. The problems, in his view, went far beyond the building rebellion in America or the corrupt politicians who orchestrated an unconstitutional program of oppression. British settlers in West Florida fomented war between Choctaws and Creeks. British speculators invaded Carib lands in Saint Vincent. These actions, as well as the coercion of the American colonies, as well as the British slave trade and colonial slavery, brought on Britain "indelible disgrace." They "must be esteemed," he said, "a *National* undertaking, which may occasion the imputation of a *National* Guilt!" "A Guilt, including the horrid crime of *Robbery* and *Willful* Murder, deliberately and openly perpetuated by *national* Authority." The "Age of National Retribution" was at hand, Sharp cautioned. Notice, he insisted, the variety of instances in which the oppressed now rose against their abusers. Witness the revolt in Chile against the Spaniards, or the revolts in Surinam against the Dutch, or the revolts in Brazil against the Portuguese, or the long and bloody war the French waged against the Corsicans: "Have we not reason to dread the same Divine Vengeance, since it is notorious that the English exceed all other Nations in the multitude of these slaves, and in the iniquitous Traffic by which the same are supplied?"[17]

This was very different from charging the Americans with inconsistency or suggesting that the British state bore some responsibility for colonial slavery. It differed, too, from the view that the empire had expanded too far and too fast or that empire would corrupt British morals or subvert the ancient constitution. On the eve of the American war, Granville Sharp introduced in Britain the seminal idea that the fate of the nation depended on its liberation from the sins of slaving.

In the absence of an adequate biography, the origins of [II] Granville Sharp's religious views must remain somewhat uncertain.[18] Sharp sometimes has been identified as a member of the Clapham Sect, the circle of Evangelical politicians and reformers who led the antislavery crusade in Parliament and the public movement for a reformation of manners from the

17. Sharp to Henry Seymour Conway, May 17, 1768, Sharp to John Fothergill, Oct. 27, 1772, and Sharp to Dartmouth, Jan. 16, 1773, all in Granville Sharp Letterbook, fols. 4–10, 55, 143–145.

18. Remarkably, the best published work remains Prince Hoare's documentary history commissioned by the Sharp family in the early nineteenth century, although see also E. C. P. Lascelles, *Granville Sharp and the Freedom of Slaves in England* (London, 1928). David Brion Davis provides the most insightful assessment of Sharp to date in *The Problem of Slavery in the Age of Revolution, 1770–1823* (Ithaca, N.Y., 1975), 386–398. See also F. O. Shyllon, *Black Slaves in Britain* (London, 1974), 25–40; Steven M. Wise, *Though the Heavens May Fall: The Landmark Trial That Led to the End of Human Slavery* (Cambridge, Mass., 2005), 31–33; and Adam Hochschild, *Bury the Chains: Prophets and Rebels in the Fight to Free an Empire's Slaves* (New York, 2005), 41–46. A fine survey of Sharp's various reforming interests appears in Betty Fladeland, *Abolitionists and Working-Class Problems in the Age of Industrialization* (Baton Rouge, La., 1984), 1–16.

1790s into the nineteenth century.[19] Yet Sharp never had more than a tenuous relation with this or any other Evangelical group. And his rigorous parsing of scripture differed substantially from the more emotive spirituality typical of those gathered around William Wilberforce and Henry Thornton or around John Wesley's Methodists. One should resist too the temptation to associate Granville Sharp with what Jack Fruchtman has called the "republican millennialism" of Richard Price and Joseph Priestley, since Sharp neither looked expectantly to the realization of an earthly paradise nor shared their embrace of republicanism or, more precisely, their discomfort with monarchy.[20] If modern scholars have not known what to make of Sharp's religious beliefs, the odd mixture of radical politics and High Church prejudices confused contemporaries, too. John Adams, who met Granville Sharp in the last years of the American war when serving as ambassador to the Court of Saint James's, later remarked that "the grandson of the famous Archbishop [of York]" was "as Zealously attached to Episcopacy and the Athanasian Creed as he is to civil and religious Liberty—a mixture which in this Country is not common."[21]

What is clear is that Britain's first abolitionist inhabited one corner of England's counter-Enlightenment. Granville Sharp numbered among the Anglican devout critical of the confidence some dissenters placed in human reason and contemptuous of Arian skepticism toward doctrinal authority and the divinity of Christ. From his grandfather John Sharp, archbishop of York during the reign of Queen Anne, and his father Thomas Sharp, archdeacon of Northumberland, Granville Sharp inherited a fidelity to High Church orthodoxies. He shared their reverence of apostolic suc-

19. See, for example, Roger T. Anstey, *The Atlantic Slave Trade and British Abolition, 1760–1810* (London, 1975), 157–158. Clapham Park Church in 1919 claimed Sharp as one of its own in a tablet commemorating the work of the Clapham Sect. Lascelles, *Granville Sharp and the Freedom of Slaves in England*, 133–134.

20. Jack Fruchtman, Jr., *The Apocalyptic Politics of Richard Price and Joseph Priestley: A Study in Late Eighteenth-Century English Republican Millennialism* (Philadelphia, 1983).

21. John Adams cited in Bonwick, *English Radicals and the American Revolution*, 7. One may note, in this vein, that the leading modern study on the integration of High Church religion and politics finds no place for a discussion of Granville Sharp. See J. C. D. Clark, *English Society, 1660–1832: Religion, Ideology, and Politics during the Ancien Regime*, 2d ed. (Cambridge, 2000).

cession, mysticism, and veneration of the Hebrew scriptures.[22] Granville Sharp's first published work challenged the writings of a prominent biblical scholar who, in his view, distorted scripture from its original rendering.[23] It may be that Sharp experienced an awakening or a deepening of his religious commitment in the late 1760s. In this period, Granville Wheeler, an

22. Anglican High Churchmanship has received extensive study in recent years. The most careful definition of *High Church* that manages to embrace its diversity without compromising specificity is provided by Peter Benedict Nockles in *The Oxford Movement in Context: Anglican High Churchmanship, 1760–1857* (Oxford, 1994), 25–26. The initial focus on the political dimensions of orthodox Anglicanism in the works of J. C. D. Clark, James Bradley, J. A. W. Dunn, and Robert Hole has now been complemented appropriately by studies of orthodox theology, although in this respect, attention tends to center on the first half of the eighteenth century rather than the second. See particularly Robert D. Cornwall, *Visible and Apostolic: The Constitution of the Church in High Church Anglican and Non-Juror Thought* (Newark, Del., 1993), and B. W. Young, *Religion and Enlightenment in Eighteenth-Century England: Theological Debate from Locke to Burke* (Oxford, 1998). A recent essay cast to treat politics but that has much of value on theology is offered by A. M. C. Waterman, "The Nexus between Theology and Political Doctrine in Church and Dissent," in Knud Haakonssen, ed., *Enlightenment and Religion: Rational Dissent in Eighteenth-Century Britain* (Cambridge, 1996), 193–218. See also Nigel Aston, "Horne and Heterodoxy: The Defence of Anglican Beliefs in the Late Enlightenment," *English Historical Review,* CVIII (1993), 895–919. A less recent but very useful article by Richard Sharp provides an overview of several prominent High Churchmen in the middle decades of the eighteenth century, with particular reference to John and Thomas Sharp, Granville Sharp's grandfather and father, respectively: "New Perspectives on the High Church Tradition: Historical Background, 1730–1780," in Geoffrey Rowell, ed., *Tradition Renewed: The Oxford Movement Conference Papers* (Allison Park, Pa., 1976), 4–34. Also See Nicholas Hudson, " 'Britons Will Never Be Slaves': National Myth, Conservatism, and the Beginnings of British Antislavery," *Eighteenth Century Studies,* XXXIV (2001), 559–560.

23. [Granville Sharp], *Remarks on a Printed Paper Lately Handed about, Intituled, "A Catalogue of the Sacred Vessels Restored by Cyrus; and of the Chief Jews, Who Returned at First from the Captivity . . ." Addressed to All Such Gentlemen as Have Received or Read the Same* (London, 1765). The author of this "catalogue" was Benjamin Kennicott, an Oxford theologian. Sharp's work in defense of the patristic tradition awaits assessment. For context, see Eamon Duffy, "Primitive Christianity Revived: Religious Renewal in Augustan England," in Derek Baker, ed., *Renaissance and Renewal in Christian History: Papers Read at the Fifteenth Summer Meeting and the Sixteenth Winter Meeting of the*

uncle, encouraged Sharp to take orders and offered him the living in the parish of Great Lake, Nottinghamshire. However the provenance of his faith is explained, the centrality of scripture to his daily life and worldview is indisputable. Granville Sharp lived with an acute fear of eternal damnation. He filled his commonplace books, which date from the late 1760s, with such headings as "Retribution," "Demons and Devils," "Presages," "Right and Righteousness," and "Hell," under the last of which he scribbled "the torments are *everlasting*."[24]

The luminaries of the European Enlightenment, in Britain and elsewhere, helped define the institution of slavery as inefficient, anachronistic, and inimical to the promotion of human happiness during the last half of the eighteenth century. Yet their preference for gradual, orderly reform tended to postpone the moment for concrete change to an unspecified

---

Ecclesiastical History Society, Studies in Church History 14 (Oxford, 1977), 287–300, and Robert D. Cornwall, "The Search for the Primitive Church: The Use of the Early Church Fathers in the High Church Anglican Tradition, 1680–1745," *Anglican and Episcopal History,* LIX (1990), 303–329. On Kennicott, see William McKane, "Benjamin Kennicott: An Eighteenth-Century Researcher," *Journal of Theological Studies,* XXVIII, pt. 2 (1977), 445–464.

24. Hoare, *Memoirs,* 45; Commonplace Book A, 100, 101, and Commonplace Book B, 6–8, 31–33, 120, both in Granville Sharp Papers, D3549 13/4/1. A recent study of ideas of heaven and hell in the early eighteenth century hints that such views at the time were unusual. See Philip C. Almond, *Heaven and Hell in Enlightenment England* (Cambridge, 1994), 87. A similar suggestion appears in Geoffrey Rowell, *Hell and the Victorians: A Study of the Nineteenth-Century Theological Controversies concerning Eternal Punishment and the Future Life* (Oxford, 1974), 28–30. The shift in emphasis from secular to religious arguments was dramatic in Sharp's work. His *Representation of the Injustice and Dangerous Tendency of Slavery* (1769) lacks a single religious argument against slavery. Undoubtedly this was because the manuscript was prepared to assist lawyers hoping to establish the rights of blacks in England. However, his private correspondence in the 1760s contains no hint of the distinctively prophetic voice that suffused his works in subsequent years. In 1772 Sharp added a new reason for outlawing slavery in England. Failure to do so would "draw down upon us some dreadful and speedy *national* calamity." Sharp, *Appendix to the Representation (Printed in the Year 1769) of the Injustice and Dangerous Tendency of Tolerating Slavery* (London, 1772), 27–28. After reading a biblical defense of slavery in 1772, Sharp informed Benezet that his subsequent antislavery publications would be grounded in scripture. Sharp to Benezet, Aug. 21, 1772, Sharp MS Letterbook, fol. 58.

future date. Granville Sharp's preoccupation with Judgment Day, by contrast, gave his antislavery appeals a distinctive urgency. For all that had been said against the slave system, Sharp was one of the very few in England to insist, at length, on viewing the purchase, sale, or ownership of slaves as a sin. He loaded his texts with dark warnings of divine retribution to underscore for wrongdoers that, at each moment, their "everlasting welfare" hung in the balance. In his letter to Lord North of 1772, he reminded the king's first minister that "*to be in power* and to neglect (as life is very uncertain) even a day in endeavouring to put a stop to such monstrous injustice and abandoned wickedness, must necessarily endanger a man's *eternal* welfare, be he ever so great in *temporal* dignity or office." Although concerned that the Saint Vincent campaign would prove fatal to British troops, although troubled by "*unjust oppression, Robbery,* and *premeditated Murder,*" Sharp worried, above all, that the expedition would involve such "complicated guilt," he told the earl of Dartmouth, that it would "occasion the withdrawing of God's blessing from the King's family, and the Kingdom." This fear led him to articulate what he called the "*first and most fundamental principles of Government,*" principles to which he would advert repeatedly throughout the American war: "Open and avowed injustice; and willful Murder cannot be vindicated before God by any deceitful sophistry about the necessity of such measures to produce the Nation's Good . . . because Good and Evil can never change Places, and because we must *not do evil that good may come.*"[25] Sharp derided an exclusive attention to the temporal consequences of individual and collective action. He held no stock in the customary ways of evaluating government decisions. Sharp assigned little value to the standards of utility, the common good, or reasons of state. The maxim "Fiat Justitia, Ruat Coelum" provided the

---

25. Sharp, *A Representation of the Injustice,* 72n; Sharp to North, Feb. 18, 1772, in Hoare, *Memoirs,* 79; Sharp to Dartmouth, Oct. 10, 1772, Granville Sharp Papers, D3549 13/1/D4. There were precedents for this emphasis on the slave trade as a sin, particularly among Quaker antislavery writers resident in the North American colonies. When Sharp wrote, this point of view was still rare in England, although see the even more uncompromising statements of J. Philmore in *Two Dialogues on the Man-Trade* (London, 1760), and the assessment of this remarkable text in David Brion Davis, "New Sidelights on Early Antislavery Radicalism," *William and Mary Quarterly,* 3d Ser., XXVIII (1971), 585–594.

foundation for his approach to politics: Let justice be done, even if the heavens should fall.

In this effort to undercut rationalizations for injustice and violence, to discourage the instinct to avoid and delay, Lord Dartmouth presented a particularly inviting target. The deeply pious secretary of state for the American colonies was an intimate friend of Evangelical leaders John Wesley and Selina, countess of Huntingdon, and regularly opened the doors of his country seat at Blackheath to their followers. At least once, George Whitefield preached to a throng of listeners from the steps of Dartmouth's estate. And over the course of many years, Dartmouth carried on a warm, familiar correspondence with the Reverend John Newton, the Evangelical former slave ship captain of Olney, whom Dartmouth served as a patron. Sharp knew Dartmouth to be "a humane" and "religious man" and on several occasions attempted to mobilize his piety in the service of policy, in the first instance on the case of the Caribs in Saint Vincent. In a sense, Sharp invited Dartmouth to take on the role William Wilberforce would assume a dozen years later, to serve as the patron and chief mover of antislavery measures among the governing elite. This was neither the last time a devout opponent of slavery turned to Dartmouth for assistance nor the last time that Dartmouth would disappoint. In 1777, Methodist minister Thomas Vivian of Cornwood would seek, with no success, to persuade Dartmouth to endorse the emancipation of American slaves.[26] Sharp left a visit to Blackheath in January 1774 confident that Dartmouth "detests the traffic as much as I do," but the very cautious secretary of state was not the type to challenge established institutions or pick a fight with the Africa traders, even if he thought it the right thing to do. And he insisted to Sharp that even his lukewarm embrace of antislavery principles should remain a secret. Indeed, Sharp had more confidence in the Evangelical politician than Dartmouth

26. B. D. Bargar, *Lord Dartmouth and the American Revolution* (Columbia, S.C., 1965), 9–15; D. Bruce Hindmarsh, *John Newton and the English Evangelical Tradition: Between the Conversions of Wesley and Wilberforce* (Oxford, 1996), 47, 103–105, 109–110, 118, 185–186, 200, 233, 259, 293, 298; Fabel, *Colonial Challenges*, 194–195; Great Britain, Royal Commission on Historical Manuscripts, *The Manuscripts of the Earl of Dartmouth*, 3 vols. (1887–1896; Boston, 1972), III, 171, 180–192, 196, 199–203, 207–212, 216–220, 234, 237, 245, 248, 256, 268, 270; Sharp to Benezet, Aug. 21, 1772, Granville Sharp Letterbook, fol. 69; Thomas Vivian to Dartmouth, Jan. 16, 1777, Dartmouth Papers, D(W)1778/II/1773.

deserved. In these same months, Dartmouth was acting aggressively to disallow a prohibitive ban on slave imports recently enacted by the Assembly of Jamaica.[27] Lord Dartmouth willingly endured polite contempt for the intensity of his piety. But piety, alone, could not move him to align his politics with professed values or prevent him from separating his private convictions from his public responsibilities as a servant of the crown.

This kind of temporizing, this expedient retreat from principle even by the most pious, enraged Sharp in the months when animosity turned to war in North America. At bottom, the conflict with the colonies, the enslavement of Africans, the oppression of subject peoples throughout the British Empire issued from the same source, Sharp believed—a failure to regard the pursuit of justice a moral obligation and, for those in power, the preeminent duty. He thought the prevailing belief that right and righteousness could be subordinated to interest, power, and national pride responsible for the rift between the peoples of Britain and North America. After witnessing the frustrated attempt by the colonies to halt the British slave trade, growing disconsolate with the impending dissolution of the western empire, Sharp resolved to devote his energies to establishing the necessity of a reformation in public affairs. In July 1775, three months after the first bloodshed in Massachusetts, less than a year after his disappointing conference with Dartmouth, Sharp took a two-month leave from his post at the Board of Ordnance to complete four antislavery tracts.[28]

These pamphlets, David Brion Davis has observed, resembled in impor-

27. Sharp to Benezet, Jan. 7, 1774, Granville Sharp Papers, D3549 13/1/B19.

28. Diary G (July 26, 1775), 50, ibid., D3549 13/4/2. Granville Sharp, *The Just Limitation of Slavery in the Laws of God, Compared with the Unbounded Claims of the African Traders and British American Slaveholders; by Granville Sharp; with a Copious Appendix: Containing, An Answer to the Rev. Mr. Thompson's Tract in Favor of the Slave Trade . . . a Proposal on the Same Principle for the Gradual Enfranchisement of Slaves in America* . . . (London, 1776); Sharp, *The Law of Liberty; or, Royal Law, by Which All Mankind Will Certainly Be Judged! Earnestly Recommended to the Serious Consideration of All Slave Holders and Slave Dealers* (London, 1776); Sharp, *The Law of Passive Obedience; or, Christian Submission to Personal Injuries; Wherein Is Shewn, That the Several Texts of Scripture, Which Command the Entire Submission of Servants and Slaves to Their Masters, Cannot Authorise the Latter to Exact an Involuntary Servitude, nor, in the Least Degree, Justify the Claims of Modern SlaveHolders* (London, 1776); Sharp, *The Law of Retribution.*

tant ways the writings of Jonathan Edwards's disciples in late-eighteenth-century New England, who, at the time of the American Revolution, began to cast an antislavery commitment as necessary for collective salvation.[29] Granville Sharp does not seem to have read the works of Joseph Bellamy, Samuel Hopkins, the younger Jonathan Edwards, Levi Hart, or Nathaniel Niles; he did not correspond with the exponents of the "New Divinity" and, indeed, probably did not know of them. But Sharp shared with the self-described "consistent Calvinists" of New England the conviction that only scripture could provide a proper foundation for ethics.[30] With them, he rejected the prevailing view that a philosophy of morals could be grounded in observation and experience or could be rooted in sensibility and a putatively innate moral instinct to seek virtue and avoid vice.[31] Sharp, like

29. Davis, *The Problem of Slavery in the Age of Revolution*, 393.

30. Joseph A. Conforti, *Samuel Hopkins and the New Divinity Movement: Calvinism, the Congregational Ministry, and Reform in New England between the Great Awakenings* (Grand Rapids, Mich., 1981); William Breitenbach, "The Consistent Calvinism of the New Divinity Movement," *WMQ*, 3d Ser., XLI (1984), 241–264; Mark Valeri, "The New Divinity and the American Revolution," ibid., XLVI (1989), 741–769; Valeri, *Law and Providence in Joseph Bellamy's New England: The Origins of the New Divinity in Revolutionary America* (New York, 1994). The antislavery writings of the New England Calvinists are treated at length in David S. Lovejoy, "Samuel Hopkins: Religion, Slavery, and the Revolution," *New England Quarterly*, XL (1967), 227–243; David E. Swift, "Samuel Hopkins: Calvinist Social Concern in Eighteenth Century New England," *Journal of Presbyterian History*, XLVII (1969), 31–54; Davis, *The Problem of Slavery in the Age of Revolution*, 290–299; Joseph Conforti, "Samuel Hopkins and the Revolutionary Antislavery Movement," *Rhode Island History*, XXXVIII (1979), 39–49; James D. Essig, *The Bonds of Wickedness: American Evangelicals against Slavery, 1770–1808* (Philadelphia, 1982); Patricia Bradley, *Slavery, Propaganda, and the American Revolution* (Jackson, Miss., 1998), 87–97; Joanne Pope Melish, *Disowning Slavery: Gradual Emancipation and "Race" in New England, 1780–1830* (Ithaca, N.Y., 1998), 54–64; John Saillant, "Slavery and Divine Providence in New England Calvinism: The New Divinity and a Black Protest," *NEQ*, LXVIII (1995), 584–608; and Saillant, ed., " 'Some Thoughts on the Subject of Freeing the Negro Slaves in the Colony of Connecticut, Humbly Offered to the Consideration of All Friends to Liberty and Justice,' by Levi Hart; with a Response from Samuel Hopkins," *NEQ*, LXXV (2002), 107–128.

31. The scholarship on this subject is extensive. For present purposes, I have relied heavily on Knud Haakonssen, *Natural Law and Moral Philosophy: From Grotius to the Scottish Enlightenment* (Cambridge, 1994).

the Edwardseans, placed no faith in unassisted human judgment on moral questions. He believed too deeply in original sin to think mortals capable of evaluating right and wrong without divine guidance. This skepticism about the human capacity for benevolence helps explain the otherwise curious absence of social description or sociology in his antislavery tracts. Granville Sharp made no attempt to publicize the horrors of slavery, to stir the emotions or touch sensibilities. Such an approach might be appropriate for charities, he believed. Sharp, however, could not think of antislavery as a philanthropic cause. Philanthropies turned on the voluntary participation of donors. They needed the benevolence and generosity of the giver. For Sharp, the institution of slavery presented problems of a different order. Slavery was a sin of the enslavers, not simply a misfortune for the enslaved. Its very existence defied scriptural injunctions. Sharp, then, felt no need to *explain* why slavery was wrong or to *prove* that it was abhorrent. For him, it was enough to know that slavery violated the laws of God.

Granville Sharp considered the abolition of slavery a moral duty far more than an act of kindness, and here, too, comparison with the disciples of Jonathan Edwards proves instructive. As William Breitenbach and Mark Valeri have explained, the "consistent Calvinists" looked to negotiate a course between the antinomian image of God as a mysterious, arbitrary redeemer and the Arminian belief that God saved all who labored for their salvation. The theologians of the "New Divinity" preserved the Calvinist principle of divine sovereignty, of God as the legislator of the moral law but chose to discard the accompanying view of God as a capricious sovereign. God ruled, they insisted, instead, through transcendent moral principles, on the basis of a universal standard of right and wrong, on the basis of laws manifest, and thus accessible, in the infallible revealed word of scripture. For these latter-day Puritans, piety alone, reverence for the divine, did not constitute true faith. Genuine faith could be achieved only through fidelity to the moral law, through the daily practice of those social duties commanded by the Lord. Morality they conceived as obedience.[32] Granville Sharp's exact relationship to Calvinism remains elusive. Nonetheless, it is

32. William K. Breitenbach, "Unregenerate Doings: Selflessness and Selfishness in New Divinity Theology," *American Quarterly*, XXXIV (1982), 479–502; Breitenbach, "The Consistent Calvinism of the New Divinity Movement," *WMQ*, 3d Ser., XLI (1984), 241–264; Valeri, *Law and Providence in Joseph Bellamy's New England*, 47–67.

clear that he shared with the New England Calvinists an equally legalistic conception of morality. Sharp regarded a decision to ignore or violate scriptural injunctions as treason against the kingdom of God. The moral law, the eternal, universal, knowable commands of the Lord, conveyed not simply what individuals and nations *should* do. It prescribed, as well, what they *must* do.

By 1775, Sharp no longer considered the problem of slavery as merely one consequence of a corrupted English common law. Now, as well, he wished to prove, as the title of the first of his four tracts of 1776 stated, "the just limitation of slavery in the laws of God," to establish that the principles enjoined by the scriptures "are entirely opposite to the selfish and uncharitable pretensions of our American slaveholders and African Traders."[33] He worked out this view in the second tract that explained that the "Royal Law" of Liberty—that Christians love their neighbors—superseded positive law or custom. "Slavery is absolutely inconsistent with Christianity, because we cannot say of any *Slaveholder,* that he *doth not* to another, what he would not have done to himself!" The Golden Rule was God's command. Opposing injustices such as slavery was more than virtuous. It was a moral imperative, an ethical obligation, a mark of fidelity to the divine will—custom, statute, or kingly authority notwithstanding.[34] As Sharp explained in his third tract, *The Law of Passive Obedience,* the duty to obey temporal laws applied only to just authority. Rightfully, no Christian ought ever to accede to tyranny. Further, the duty of "*absolute submission* required of Christian servants, by no means implies the *legality* of slaveholding ON THE PART OF THE MASTERS."[35] In the fourth book, which extended to 340 pages, Sharp detailed the likely consequences of neglecting to honor the commands of the Lord. Sharp's *Law of Retribution* predicted the destruction of the British Empire, a fate augured by the bloodshed in Massachusetts: "A speedy Reformation is absolutely necessary (as well with respect to the *African Slave-trade,* encouraged in this Kingdom, as the *Toleration of*

33. Sharp, *The Just Limitation of Slavery in the Laws of God,* 2–3.

34. Sharp, *The Law of Liberty,* 33.

35. Sharp, *The Law of Passive Obedience,* 11. Sharp hedged on whether the right and duty to oppose tyranny justified slave revolts. "The gospel of peace cannot authorise the oppression of these lawless men, though it clearly enjoins patience, submission, and acquiesence, to the individuals that are injured, whether freemen or slaves"; ibid., 40.

Slavery in the British American Dominions) if we mean to entertain the least hope of escaping a severe *National Retribution,* which (if we may judge by our present Civil Dissentions and horrid *mutual* Slaughters of *National Brethren*) seem ready to burst upon us!"[36]

Unlike his contemporaries, Granville Sharp took no interest in apportioning blame. He had no desire to judge some for their involvement with slavery and, implicitly, to exculpate others. In his *Thoughts upon Slavery* of 1774, John Wesley admonished slaveholders and slave traders, those directly engaged in the exploitation of Africans. A dozen years of combat with the slaving interest convinced Sharp that, to these people, nothing effectual could be said.[37] What needed to be stressed now was that "the whole Community," the entire empire, "every individual (without even excepting those who never had the least concern in promoting *Slavery*) is personally interested in the Consideration of the Subject!" Such a *"public* Infringement of his ROYAL LAW, THE PERFECT LAW OF LIBERTY, by *national* Authority" must be "hateful in the sight of God."[38] Sin lay on both sides of the Atlantic, with everyone. "The AFRICAN SLAVE TRADE, which includes the most contemptuous Violations of *Brotherly Love* and *Charity,* that men can be guilty of, is openly encouraged and promoted by the British Parliament." At the same time, "the most detestable and oppressive *Slavery* that ever disgraced even the unenlightened Heathens is notoriously *tolerated* in the British Colonies by the *public Acts* of their respective Assemblies—by Acts that have been ratified with the Assent and Concurrence of BRITISH KINGS!" It was absurd, then, to assign responsibility to one portion of the empire. "The colonies PROTEST against the Iniquity of the SLAVE-TRADE; but, nevertheless, continue to hold the poor wretched *Slaves* in a most detestable bondage! GREAT BRITAIN, indeed, keeps *no Slaves,* but publicly encourages the *Slave-trade,* and contemptuously neglects every petition or attempt of the *Colonists* against that notorious wickedness!" The fact was, Sharp pronounced, "The Inhabitants of *Great Britain* and the Inhabitants

36. Sharp, *The Law of Retribution,* 3.

37. "To *worldly* minded Men the Judgments of *another World* seem too far distant to awaken their Attention, though they are liable to be called away," he noted, "in the very next Hour, to a State of Existence, wherein the most pungent Remorse will still Avail them nothing!" Sharp, *The Law of Liberty,* 46.

38. Ibid., 46, 47.

of *the Colonies* seem to be almost equally guilty of *Oppression!*" And from these facts only one conclusion could be drawn. "The horrible guilt . . . which is incurred by Slave-dealing and Slave-holding, is no longer confined to a few hardened *Individuals,* that are immediately concerned in those baneful practices, but alas! the whole BRITISH EMPIRE is involved!"[39]

[III]   The final years of the American war represented an ideal moment to launch an antislavery movement, *if* such a movement required a loss of confidence in the established order. The years 1778 to 1781 would seem to have been an opportune time to make a case for an atonement for national sins. Few in Britain could deny that colonial affairs had taken a grave turn, that matters of state had acquired an unfortunate cast. The regretted war against the North American colonists led to close scrutiny of the ruling elite and sustained reflections on the national character. Increasingly, the war provoked throughout the nation a vague fear of impending doom. The informed public divided sharply on the merits of the American war during its initial stages, although the great majority wished to see the thirteen colonies retained. Victory in North America looked rather less essential, however, by 1779, when the empire itself appeared to be on the brink of collapse. French offensives put the Caribbean colonies at risk. British men and women looked anxiously across the English Channel in the summer of 1779, expecting an imminent invasion from their ancient enemy. In Ireland, the mobilization of Protestant volunteers to fend off the feared French attack threatened to spin off into a second revolt against Parliament. At home, the repercussions of the Atlantic war were almost equally severe. Merchants and creditors lost tens of thousands of pounds in assets, capital, and colonial debts. Overseas trade experienced sharp declines. Unemployment soared in some parts of the country. Everywhere, bankruptcies multiplied. If some profited handsomely from privateering, contracting, and provisioning, many others suffered from the wartime drain on cash and capital and from the increased costs of shipping and insurance.[40]

39. Ibid., 48, 49; Sharp, *The Law of Retribution,* 301, 305.

40. The best survey of the ways the American war affected British society and economy is now provided by Stephen Conway, *The British Isles and the War of American Independence* (Oxford, 2000), key aspects of which are briefly anticipated in Conway, *The War of American Independence, 1775–1783* (London, 1995), 187–211. I draw on

A fragmented and fractious governing elite contributed to the sense of crisis. The government of Lord North steadily lost domestic support during the American war. North's lieutenants, Lord Sandwich of the Admiralty and Lord Germain in the Office of the Secretary of State, were widely reviled for their management of the effort and its execution. The Bedford faction, an important part of Lord North's governing coalition, abandoned the administration in 1779 in protest over the uncertain direction of imperial affairs. Even George III, who kept North in office until the bitter end, regarded the first minister as a listless and indecisive leader. "Lord North has a sad time of it," member of Parliament John Thornton reported in 1779, "and has been twice brot. to tears in the House." To the parliamentary opposition, and to those with genuine doubts about government policy, the absence of effective leadership established the need for a change in men as well as measures. In the last years of the war the followers of the marquis of Rockingham and the followers of the earl of Shelburne jockeyed to succeed the crumbling ministry. Outside Parliament came renewed demands for constitutional reform. The Reverend Christopher Wyvill led the

---

these works for the discussion in this paragraph and the four that follow. The devastating impact of the war on British Caribbean society and economy is treated in Richard B. Sheridan, "The Crisis of Slave Subsistence in the British West Indies during and after the American Revolution," *WMQ*, 3d Ser., XXX (1976), 615–641; Andrew Jackson O'Shaughnessy, *An Empire Divided: The American Revolution and the British Caribbean* (Philadelphia, 2000), 160–174; and Selwyn H. H. Carrington, *The Sugar Industry and the Abolition of the Slave Trade, 1775–1810* (Gainesville, Fla., 2002), 38–62. For divisions within Britain over the American war, see especially John Sainsbury, *Disaffected Patriots: London Supporters of Revolutionary America, 1769–1782* (Montreal, 1987); James E. Bradley, *Popular Politics and the American Revolution in England: Petitions, the Crown, and Public Opinion* (Macon, Ga., 1986); Bradley, *Religion, Revolution, and English Radicalism: Nonconformity in Eighteenth-Century Politics and Society* (Cambridge, 1990); Wilson, *The Sense of the People*, 237–284; and Margaret Stead, "Contemporary Responses in Print to the American Campaigns of the Howe Brothers," in Julie Flavell and Stephen Conway, eds., *Britain and America Go to War: The Impact of War and Warfare in Anglo-America, 1755–1815* (Gainesville, Fla., 2004), 116–142. Note also the several essays by Bradley, Conway, Frank O' Gorman, and Neil York in H. T. Dickinson, ed., *Britain and the American Revolution* (London, 1998). British management of the war effort itself receives most considered assessment in Piers Mackesy, *The War for America, 1775–1783* (Cambridge, Mass., 1964).

Yorkshire gentry (including a young William Wilberforce) in a national campaign to rein in public spending, reduce the crown's influence on the legislature, add seats in the House of Commons, and substitute triennial elections for the customary septennial polls. London radicals put forward an even more ambitious agenda that included annual elections, an extension of the franchise, secret ballots, and the abolition of property requirements for members of Parliament.[41]

The disaffection and anxieties that these campaigns expressed only hint at the breadth of discontent. The fast-day sermons delivered by the Anglican clergy had displayed few reservations about crushing the colonial rebellion in the first years of the American war. By 1780, however, the routine appeals for loyalty and piety began to show greater doubt about the direction of imperial affairs. The colossal failures of the American war, the clergy increasingly preached, proved that only a national reformation could retrieve Britain from further shame.[42] The Reverend David Grant captured the prevailing mood: "Trusting too much in the arm of flesh; loaded with national guilt; scarce ever considering the superintendency of heaven, we have met alas! disappointment, where we expected success; loss, where we expected gain; shame where we expected honour. Anxiety in every breast at

41. John Thornton to John Newton, June 24, 1779, Bull Papers, MS 3096, fol. 159, Lambeth Palace Library, London. British politics in the last years of the American war are surveyed in Ian R. Christie, *Wars and Revolutions: 1760–1815* (Cambridge, Mass., 1982), 129–157, and covered in greater detail in H. Butterfield's classic study, *George III, Lord North, and the People, 1779–1780* (London, 1949). The best treatments of the Revolutionary era campaign for parliamentary reform remain Ian R. Christie, *Wilkes, Wyvill, and Reform: The Parliamentary Reform Movement in British Politics, 1760–1785* (London, 1962), and Eugene Charlton Black, *The Association: British Extraparliamentary Political Organization, 1769–1793* (Cambridge, Mass., 1963). On economical reform more specifically, see Philip Harling, *The Waning of "Old Corruption": The Politics of Economical Reform in Britain, 1779–1846* (Oxford, 1996), 31–38.

42. Henry P. Ippel, "Blow the Trumpet, Sanctify the Fast," *Huntington Library Quarterly*, XLIV (1980), 43–60; Paul Langford, "The English Clergy and the American Revolution," in Eckhart Hellmuth, ed., *The Transformation of Political Culture: England and Germany in the Late Eighteenth Century* (Oxford, 1990), 275–307; James E. Bradley, "The Anglican Pulpit, Social Order, and the Resurgence of Toryism during the American Revolution," *Albion*, XXI (1989), 361–388. For the dissenting clergy, see Bradley, *Religion, Revolution, and English Radicalism.*

home; rage and resentment abroad; poverty and decline of trade; property in a sinking, staggering and fluctuating condition, all proclaim aloud the judgments of heaven."[43]

These years of anxiety, division, and introspection presented a fortuitous moment, it may appear, for Sharp to have described slavery and the slave trade as national sins. He would seem to have offered those intent on defending the established order one way to restore credit to institutions increasingly under severe domestic criticism. This was the possibility suggested by Methodist leader John William Fletcher in his panegyric of 1777 against American patriotism. Rather than fighting to possess North America, Britons should "contend with our American Colonies for *supremacy* in VIRTUE and DEVOTION." In such a contest, "how noble would be the strife! How worthy of a protestant kingdom, and a mother-country!" More to the point, a renunciation of the slave trade might provide a sop to those in North America who complained of British tyranny. Surely, "political wisdom, as well as brotherly love, require us to do something in order to root up the inveterate prejudices against us and our church?" "Timely reformation" might return Dissenters and rebels to the fold, "convince Dr. Price and all the Americans, that in submitting to the British legislature, they will not submit to *libertinism* and *atheism*" but will instead follow "virtuous and godly senators" who made their "principal study" "setting a good example before the people" and "steadily enforcing the observance of the moral law." A commitment to antislavery reform, in this point of view, could make British rule seem benevolent. Another Methodist preacher, Thomas Vivian of Cornwood, had a more positive, less defensive take on the ways the mantle of godliness could give a beneficent veneer to the preservation of imperial rule. Emancipating slaves in North America would "reflect an honour on Great Britain (as the parent of Liberty and Vindicator of the Natural Rights of Mankind) Supreme to that gained by all her Victories. The persons that shall be instrumental in effecting such a measure will justly be styled the Friends of Mankind."[44] For these Methodist ministers,

---

43. David Grant, *The Living Manners of the Times, and Their Consequences; Together with the Motives to Reformation; a Sermon Preached in the Tolbooth Church of Edinburgh, on Tuesday the 9th of February 1779; Being the Day Appointed for a General Fast, and Printed at the Desire of Several Who Heard It* (Edinburgh, 1779), 19.

44. [John William] Fletcher, *American Patriotism Farther Confronted with Reason,*

national redemption lay in a demonstrable commitment to the pursuit of national virtue. An attack on slavery, David Hartley agreed, could provide a divided empire with a collective identity in a time of strife. "Let us all be re-united in this," he said on the floor of the House of Commons. "Let the only contention henceforward between Great Britain and America be, which shall exceed the other in zeal for the establishing the fundamental rights of liberty to all mankind."[45]

Granville Sharp's crusade could have served as a response to national troubles in a second, less reactionary way. Savvy, enterprising advocates had the opportunity to link antislavery with the extraparliamentary campaign for political reform, with efforts to restore the purity of the ancient constitution, with patriotic defenses of liberty against the encroachments of the crown and special interests. The last years of the American war proved themselves amenable to fundamental reform. The conflict led to substantial legislative independence for Ireland, the reduction of corruption and patronage in state offices, the dismantling of penal laws against Catholics, and a relaxation of restrictions on Protestant Dissenters. The communication networks that an antislavery movement would require were already in place. Wyvill's Associated Counties, particularly, provided an infrastructure through which abolitionists could have propagated the antislavery

---

Scripture, and the Constitution: Being Observations on the Dangerous Politics Taught by the Rev. Mr. Evans, M.A. and the Rev. Dr. Price; with a Scriptural Plea for the Revolted Colonies, 2d ed. (London, 1777), 110, 111, 112; Vivian to Dartmouth, Jan. 16, 1777, Dartmouth Papers, D(W) 1778/II/1733. Like Granville Sharp, Fletcher found no virtue with respect to slavery on either side of the Atlantic. "By fomenting contentions and wars among the natives of Africa, in order to buy the prisoners whom they take from each other; have not some of our countrymen turned Africa into a field of blood? Do not the sighs of myriads of innocent negroes unjustly transported from their native country to the British dominions, call night and day for vengeance upon us; whilst their groans upbraid the hypocritical friends of liberty, who buy and sell, and whip their fellow men as if they were brutes; and absurdly complain that *they* are enslaved, when it is they themselves, who deal in the liberties and bodies of men, as graziers do in the liberties and bodies of oxen?" Fletcher, *American Patriotism,* 109.

45. R. C. Simmons and P. D. G. Thomas, eds., *Proceedings and Debates of the British Parliaments respecting North America, 1754–1783,* 6 vols. (Millwood, N.Y., 1982), VI, 336.

gospel.[46] Such a campaign, moreover, almost certainly would have received a sympathetic hearing. Polite opinion, encouraged by the culture of sensibility, had long since turned against the morality of slaveholding in principle. American slaveholders had received a torrent of abuse in the British press during the American war. The informed public would seem to have been ready for a sustained consideration of the problem of slavery. In October 1779, a debating society at London's Coachmaker's Hall drew more than a thousand women and men to moot the question, "Is the slave trade justifiable?" Six months later the attendees of a similar gathering decided against this proposition: "Are there sufficient reasons to justify Englishmen in continuing the Slave Trade?"[47] As is now well known, the abolition campaign launched in 1787 proved immensely popular with the public, then and for many years after. A social movement promoting "liberty, justice, and humanity" should have been no less compelling one decade before, had a campaign taken shape to advance it.

Granville Sharp's challenge to the slave system, for these reasons, should have had great promise: he could cast antislavery as one of several reforms required to address past abuses; at the same time, he could argue that state action could help replenish the moral capital of the governing elite. Initially, the first of these two approaches brought the best results. His antislavery tracts appealed most to those uneasy with ministerial efforts to subdue America and concerned, more generally, with the prospects for the British Empire. One advocate of conciliation, Staffordshire entrepreneur Josiah Wedgwood, welcomed Sharp's "disinterested love of mankind" at a moment when "universal benevolence seems to be discouraged." Similarly, an aged, alienated James Oglethorpe lauded Sharp's *Law of Retribution*, not least for its denunciations of the North ministry, which he faulted for driving the colonists into rebellion. General Oglethorpe retained in his last years the opinions that led him in his youth to secure a ban on human bondage in the Georgia settlement. History as well as scripture established that peoples who "fat their luxuries on the labour of wretched slaves"

46. Conway, *The British Isles and the War of American Independence,* 203–238.

47. Donna T. Andrew, comp., *London Debating Societies, 1776–1799,* London Record Society, *Publications,* XXX (London, 1994), 59, 93; Merle M. Bevington, ed., *The Memoirs of James Stephen, Written by Himself for the Use of His Children* (London, 1954), 275–277.

invited divine retribution. In this regard, "the ruins of Babylon, Memphis, and Tyre" should serve as an omen, to Paris, London, and Lisbon: the initial European traffickers in African slaves, the Portuguese, suffered the devastation of the Lisbon earthquake as "the *first* example"; the "unnatural war" with America, said Oglethorpe, "seems to give the *second*" (the Haitian Revolution perhaps marked the third, observed Granville Sharp's first biographer several decades later). Oglethorpe agreed that it was "the proper time to bring those abominable abuses" of trading and owning slaves "under consideration." Perhaps, Oglethorpe added, "if those who have the power of legislation will be admonished, and correct them, it may save them and us from the justly-menaced destruction."[48]

Sharp stood at the center of a network of reform-minded activists during the American conflict. His persistent defense of personal liberties and his principled advocacy of constitutional reform linked him to those "friends of America" in London who opposed the war, its cost, and the dislocations it produced. Sharp revived his role as public advocate for the liberties of the subject during the American war and, with James Oglethorpe, fought the impressment of London seamen in the months following the publication of his antislavery tracts. With the earl of Effingham and John Cartwright, military officers who refused to fight in the American conflict, Sharp publicly opposed the wartime suspension of habeas corpus rights.[49] Simultaneously, beginning in 1777, Sharp began to work closely with Cartwright,

48. Josiah Wedgwood to Sharp, Mar. 10, 1777, Granville Sharp Papers, D3549 13/1/W13; James Oglethorpe to Sharp, [received] Sept. 26, 1776, and [sent] Oct. 13, 1776, in Hoare, *Memoirs,* 156, 159. For the evolution of Wedgwood and Oglethorpe's views of the American conflict, see J. H. Plumb, "British Attitudes to the American Revolution," in Plumb, *In the Light of History* (London, 1972), 75–83, and Phinizy Spalding, "James Oglethorpe and the American Revolution," *Journal of Imperial and Commonwealth History,* III, no. 3 (1975), 396–407.

49. Hoare, *Memoirs,* 161–171; Diary G (Jan. 29, 1777), 56, Granville Sharp Papers, D3549 13/4/2; [Sharp], *An Address to the People of England: Being the Protest of a Private Person against Every Suspension of Law . . . and Also Stating the Illegality of Impressing Seamen* (London, 1778); John A. Woods, "The City of London and Impressment, 1776–1777," Leeds Philosophical Society, *Proceedings,* VIII, no. 2 (1956), 111–127; Paul Conner, " 'Maynard' Unmasked: Oglethorpe and Sharp versus the Press Gangs," American Philosophical Society, *Proceedings,* CXI (1967), 199–211; Sainsbury, *Disaffected Patriots,* 134–139.

John Jebb, Capel Lofft, and the duke of Richmond, the nucleus of the group that in 1780 coalesced as the Society for Constitutional Information, the intellectual wing of London political dissent.[50] Sharp lobbied Dartmouth again in March 1777, this time for a "reduction of the enormous inequality of Parliamentary Representation at present enjoyed by the petty venal boroughs to the manifest injury of the counties and great cities, and, indeed, to the extreme danger of the whole state." A corrupted legislature, Sharp elaborated, deprives "the king of the faithful disinterested councils and genuine sentiments of the nation." Further, there was reason to believe, Sharp wrote with typical misplaced optimism, that political reformation in England would lead to a reconciliation with America, a *"recovery of a great and extensive empire"*: "No ground of accommodation," he wrote in an echo of Hartley and Fletcher, "will be so effectual and certain as such 'a proof of sincerity' in the sovereign, that he desires to rule his subjects at *home* according to the strictest rule of *legal* and *constitutional* principles."[51] Sharp

50. David Drinkwater-Lunn, "John Cartwright: Political Education and English Radicalism, 1774–1794" (D.Phil. thesis, Oxford University, 1971), 45–68; Diary G (Feb. 11, 1777), 56, Granville Sharp Papers, D3549 13/4/2; Sharp to Capel Lofft, July 15, 1777, ibid., D3549 13/1/L14; Hoare, *Memoirs,* 180. For the work of the Society for Constitutional Information, see Caroline Robbins, *The Eighteenth-Century Commonwealthman: Studies in the Transmission, Development, and Circumstances of English Liberal Thought from the Restoration of Charles II until the War with the Thirteen Colonies* (Cambridge, Mass., 1959), 369–377; Black, *The Association,* 174–205; Kenneth S. Pearl, "The Society for Constitutional Information and the Publication of the Radical Agenda," in Bernard Cook, ed., *The Consortium on Revolutionary Europe, 1750–1850: Selected Papers* (Tallahassee, Fla., 1995), 77–85; and Anthony Page, *John Jebb and the Enlightenment Origins of British Radicalism* (Westport, Conn., 2003), 180–189.

51. Sharp to Dartmouth, Mar. 22, 1777, Dartmouth Papers, D(W) 1778/III/357; Diary G (Mar. 14, 22, 1777), 56–58, Granville Sharp Papers, D3549 13/4/2; [Granville Sharp], *Equitable Representation Necessary to the Establishment of Law, Peace, and Good Government: Shewn in Some Extracts from Mr. Prynne's Brevia Parliamentaria Rediviva (Printed in 1662, and Dedicated to K. Charles II.) relative to Examples of Joint Elections for Knights, Citizens, and Burgesses, for Whole Counties, by the Same Electors, at One Time and Place; with Some Occasional Remarks Thereupon, concerning the Necessity as Well as the Means of Reforming the Enormous Inequality of Representatives Which the Borough-Voters Enjoy to the Prejudice of the Counties and Great Cities* (London, 1780), 19 (written in March 1777). A manuscript copy of this essay was attached to Sharp's letter of

was an early and influential mover in the extra-parliamentary campaigns for reform that crested in 1780. In December 1777, two years before Wyvill organized the first meeting of Yorkshire freeholders, Sharp met with John Cartwright at Capel Lofft's rooms in Lincoln's Inn to refine John Wilkes's "scheme for an association of parliamentary reform." When the London Common Council met in 1780 to consider the Yorkshire plan of association, it was Granville Sharp who pushed the council to call for annual, not triennial, parliaments. And it was Sharp who sent to the petitioning counties, cities, and towns a circular stating the case for yearly elections.[52]

Because of his standing among metropolitan radicals, Granville Sharp helped ensure that the opposition intelligentsia perceived antislavery as consistent with their agenda. John Cartwright held Sharp in especially high regard, not least for resigning from the Board of Ordnance at the start of the American war, "rather than be concerned in carrying into execution orders which he esteems iniquitous." In *The Legislative Rights of the Commonalty Vindicated* (1777), Cartwright referenced Sharp's writings extensively, directing readers to the *Representation against Slavery, The Law of Retribution,* and *The Law of Liberty,* the last for the affinities between "the characters of the *patriot,* the *citizen of the world,* and the *Christian.*" In a tract

---

Mar. 22, 1777. In the printed text of 1780, Sharp explained that "the desire of pointing out such a *plan of reformation,* as might be suitable to the proposed *reunion,* occasioned these remarks." At the time, in March 1777, he claimed to have specific intelligence from Americans in London that constitutional reform "would certainly be accepted" by the colonies as a mark of conciliation "if tendered within two or three months; but that no terms short of independency would or could be accepted after the expiration of six months after that time" (19n). Because he had earned the trust of Americans by defending their liberties and supporting their abolition petitions, he was ideally placed, Sharp told the duke of Richmond, to negotiate a peace with America. Through Oglethorpe, Sharp offered himself and his plan to William Pitt, Lord Chatham, in the spring of 1778, in the months when the former first minister was negotiating with the king on terms that would return him to office. Sharp's text recommending parliamentary reform was received and ignored by the ministry. Hoare, *Memoirs,* 175–181.

52. Diary G (Dec. 3, 1777), fol. 68, Granville Sharp Papers, D3549 13/4/2; Hoare, *Memoirs,* 193–194, 194n; Sainsbury, *Disaffected Patriots,* 154–155; Granville Sharp, *A Circular Letter to the Several Petitioning Counties, Cities, and Towns, Addressed to Their Respective General Meetings, against the Late Proposition for a Triennial Election of Representatives* (London, 1780); Christie, *Wilkes, Wyvill, and Reform,* 109–110.

that espoused annual elections and universal male suffrage, Cartwright followed Sharp in excoriating "national criminality in Europe, Africa, Asia, and America." He explained these national crimes as originating in political corruption. "Unpolluted Parliaments," Cartwright maintained, would never have sanctioned such "ravages," "inhumanities," and "murders." Instead, ministers would have done *those things which were right,* in order to have obtained the support and aid of an unbribed, unplaced, unpensioned House of Commons, watching over the morals, studying the interest, and speaking the real sense of *the whole nation.*"[53] If an abolition bill should ever reach the floor of the Commons, John Jebb stated several years later, a truly independent Parliament would honor public sentiment, not the needs of self-serving, parochial "interests." The Reverend Richard Watson attributed the war to corruption of the legislature in a fast-day sermon distinguished by dark warnings about the overgrown influence of the crown. To Watson, evidence of Parliament's lost "dignity" lay in its refusal to scrutinize slave trading "because of the interests aligned against it."[54]

Scholars may never know if Cartwright, Jebb, and Watson intended to echo arguments first expressed by the Virginia House of Burgesses in 1772. But, like the Virginians, these London opponents of the American war had decided that parliamentary support for the slave trade showed that the legislature too readily ignored or discounted the desires of those it ruled. A

53. John Cartwright to unidentified recipient, [1775], in F. D. Cartwright, *The Life and Correspondence of Major Cartwright,* 2 vols. (London, 1826), I, 59; John Cartwright, *The Legislative Rights of the Commonalty Vindicated; or, Take Your Choice!* 2d ed. (London, 1777), 23, 24, 25n, 166n–167n, 212, 212n. Sharp resigned permanently from the Board of Ordnance on Apr. 10, 1777. Diary G (Apr. 10, 1777), 60, Granville Sharp Papers, D3549 13/4/2.

54. John Jebb, *An Address to the Freeholders of Middlesex, Assembled at Free Masons Tavern, in Great Queen Street, upon Monday the 20th of December, 1779, Being the Day Appointed for a Meeting of the Freeholders, for the Purpose of Establishing Meetings to Maintain and Support the Freedom of Election,* 2d ed. (London, 1779), 5n; Page, *John Jebb and the Enlightenment Origins of British Radicalism,* 225–226; Richard Watson, *A Sermon Preached before the University of Cambridge on Friday, February 4th, 1780, Being the Day Appointed for a General Fast* (Cambridge, 1780), 6–7. Sharp made a point of praising Watson for the performance. Sharp to Richard Watson, Feb. 17, 1780, Granville Sharp Papers, D3549 13/1/L2. For Watson, see Henry P. Ippel, "British Sermons and the American Revolution," *Journal of Religious History,* XII (1982), 197n.

government that could authorize a trade in human bodies, they observed, would also, in time, disregard the rights and liberties of British subjects. Liberating the House of Commons from the overreaching authority of the executive, then, would enable representatives to subject the ethics of the slave system to official inquiry. John Cartwright appropriated Granville Sharp's language—only "national amendment" could provide an escape from national punishment.[55] For Cartwright, as for other London reformers, amendment entailed concrete constitutional reforms in addition to a collective renunciation of national sins. The slave trade represented one of several grievances more easily addressed after the restoration of Parliament's independence.

In the same years that he tried to link the antislavery cause to the movement for parliamentary reform, Granville Sharp also commenced a methodical antislavery campaign within the Church of England. The spiritual leaders of the nation he considered an important target and, potentially, powerful allies. As early as 1772, he had hoped that the bishops would "unite their influence and authority as a body," expecting that, once prelates understood the moral questions at stake, they would work to "prevent so dangerous an accession of licentiousness and hardness of heart." Not only were the clergy particularly suited to promote antislavery, Sharp believed, but they also had a special interest in speaking out for justice and humanity. Like John William Fletcher, "he thought the honour of our Episcopal Church is not a little concerned in the present question." To acknowledge the injustice of slavery and the slave trade and yet leave it unchallenged in the corridors of power would disgrace the Church of England. By contrast, to stand forward, to champion the rights of enslaved Africans would, as Fletcher had also stressed, attract to the church all men and women of virtue and perhaps, too, have a "very conciliating and cordial effect upon the Dissenters from the Church."[56] Antislavery, according to Granville Sharp, would do more than restore harmony between Britain and the North American rebels. It could also heal the fissures within British Protestantism.

Granville Sharp invited the episcopacy to enhance the prestige of the national church through a dramatic display of moral leadership. In 1777,

55. Cartwright, *The Legislative Rights of the Commonalty Vindicated*, 213.

56. Sharp to Benezet, Aug. 21, 1772, and Sharp to Lloyd of Gray's Inn, July 30, 1772, both in Granville Sharp Letterbook, fols. 64, 184.

Sharp gave each bishop several copies of the fourth of his four tracts, *The Law of Retribution,* a text that closed with perhaps the most pointed antislavery appeal directed to the British ruling elite during the Revolutionary War. There he insisted that the bench of bishops, as the spiritual leaders of the nation, had a special obligation to *"Stand in the Gap,"* to prepare the nation for divine retribution if they did not soon renounce the enslavement of Africans.

Great Britain . . . has not produced, out of her numerous *Peerage,* ONE SINGLE CHIEF to stand up *"for the Land,"* and remove her burthen! Mark this, ye Right Reverend Fathers of our Church, who sit with the PRINCES *of the Realm* to consult the welfare of the State! Think not that I am inclined, through any misguided prejudice, to charge *your Order,* in particular, with the omission. The *crying sin* has hitherto been far distant from your *sight,* and perhaps was never fully represented to you, or, like *faithful Watchmen of Israel,* you would long ago have warned our Nation of the Danger: but I now call upon you IN THE NAME of GOD, for assistance! *Ye Know the Scriptures,* and therefore to you, my Lords, in particular I appeal! If I have misrepresented *the Word of God,* on which my *Opposition to* SLAVERY is founded, point out my errors, and I submit: but if, on the other hand, you should perceive that the Texts here quoted are really applicable to the question before us, that my conclusions from thence are fairly drawn, and the Examples of God's VENGEANCE against TYRANTS and SLAVE-HOLDERS ought strictly to warn us against *similar Oppressions* and *similar Vengeance,* you will not then, I trust, be backward *in this Cause of* GOD *and* MAN. *Stand up* (let me intreat you) *"for the Land;* MAKE UP THE HEDGE," to save your Country; perhaps it is not yet too late! Enter a solemn protest, my Lords, against those who *"have oppressed the Stranger wrongfully."* Ye know that the Testimonies I have quoted are of God! Warn therefore the Nobles and Senators of these Kingdoms, that they incur not a double load of Guilt! as the burthen, not only of the *much-injured African Strangers,* but also of *our Country's Ruin,* must rest on the heads of those who withhold their Testimony against the CRYING SIN OF TOLERATED SLAVERY! For "I know *that the* LORD *will maintain the* CAUSE *of the Afflicted, and the* RIGHT *of the Poor.*"[57]

57. Sharp, *The Law of Retribution,* 328, 331–340.

Sharp lobbied the bishops to introduce an abolition bill two years later, in 1779, when the House of Commons established a committee to investigate the administration of the African trade. Of the twenty-two prelates he visited that spring, he claimed to have spoken "with none that did not concur with my sentiments on the subject," while "a great majority . . . expressed abhorrence of that Trade and a desire to suppress it." James Yorke, bishop of Saint Davids, "was particularly polite, as well as earnest in the business." John Hinchliffe, bishop of Peterborough, "exerted himself in an extraordinary manner, in calling upon a variety of people that have knowledge of the trade and reading all the books that he can find upon the subject, in order that he may be enabled to answer the pleas of interested people who endeavour to promote the trade."[58]

Several promising partnerships resulted from these meetings. Briefly in 1781 Sharp served as a kind of éminence grise to the bishop of Peterborough. Through him Sharp initiated a series of conversations within the episcopacy regarding the problem of slavery within the British Empire. Sharp presented Hinchliffe with specific strategies for encouraging emancipation, particularly the Spanish practice of *coartación* that enabled slaves to repurchase their freedom. With this model at hand, Sharp helped Hinchliffe develop a plan of reform for the West Indian colonies, a plan that received the tentative endorsement in March 1781 of Thomas Robinson, second Baron Grantham, recent British ambassador to Spain, the newly appointed president of the Board of Trade, and subsequently foreign secretary for the Shelburne ministry at the end of the American war. After learning of the proposed scheme for gradual emancipation, James Yorke offered to join Hinchliffe in presenting the plan to the archbishop of Canterbury, whom they hoped to persuade into gathering an informal convocation of bishops on the subject of slavery.

This conference never took place, it appears. Nonetheless, a few within the church were concerned enough to ask further questions. Beilby Porteus, bishop of Chester and a close associate of Baron Grantham, commenced inquiries into the character of Caribbean slavery in these months; his inquiry would culminate in a consequential partnership with the West Indian activist the Reverend James Ramsay. Antislavery ideas received

58. Sharp to John Sharp, March 1779, in Hoare, *Memoirs,* 186; Commonplace Book C, 38, and Diary G (spring 1779), 90–94, both in Granville Sharp Papers, D3549 13/4/2.

regular airing at Cambridge in the years following Granville Sharp's private appeals. Hinchliffe and Richard Watson invited Sharp to the university in the spring of 1781 to discuss with them ideas for promoting ameliorative reform. The slave trade doomed Africans "to daily misery," "inexpressible cruelty," "unceasing torments," and "an untimely death," declared university vice-chancellor Peter Peckard in a public sermon in 1784. It was, he added, "the disgrace of our country." Peckard would set the examination question in 1785—Is it lawful to make slaves of others against their will?—that would move the twenty-five-year-old Thomas Clarkson to investigate the conditions of the British slave trade.[59] In this indirect way, Granville Sharp would have a decisive impact on the crystallization of antislavery impulses in certain circles within the Church of England.

The intensity of these efforts, however, must be set along- [IV] side the modesty of the results. If Sharp raised consciousness, he did not start a movement. The tireless cajoling of the bishops produced few genuine converts. Most had no desire to take a public position on a question of commercial policy. Even John Hinchliffe never publicized his antislavery views. Among the many vices the clergy condemned in the dozens of fast-day sermons delivered during the American war, colonial slavery and the British slave trade figured in only the rarest instances.[60] On these occasions, personal probity was a more common concern than matters of policy. Entirely representative was the Reverend David Wilson's menu of transgressions: "the practice of gross immoralities," "neglect of the word of God,"

59. Diary G (March, April 1781), 106–114, Granville Sharp Papers, D3549 13/4/2; Sharp to bishop of Peterborough, Mar. 17, 1781, in Hoare, *Memoirs,* 189; Beilby Porteus Notebooks MS 2099 (Feb. 11, 1783), 57, Lambeth Palace Library; Arthur Herbert Bayse, *The Lords Commissioners of Trade and Plantations Commonly Known as the Board of Trade, 1748–1782* (New Haven, Conn., 1925), 211; Anstey, *The Atlantic Slave Trade and British Abolition,* 246n; Peter Peckard, *Piety, Benevolence, and Loyalty Recommended in a Sermon Preached before the University of Cambridge, January 30, 1784* (Cambridge, 1784), 4, 5; John Gascoigne, *Cambridge in the Age of Enlightenment: Science, Religion, and Politics from the Restoration to the French Revolution* (Cambridge, 1989), 222–224.

60. A conclusion I draw from a careful reading of 58 of the 143 extant fast-day sermons published in Britain during the American Revolution, as listed in Thomas R. Adams, *The American Controversy: A Bibliographical Study of the British Pamphlets about the American Dispute, 1764–1783,* 2 vols. (Providence, R.I., 1980).

"formality and hypocrisy," "unfruitfulness under the means of grace," "incorrigibleness under lesser strokes of judgment," "confidence in the arm of flesh," "apostasy from God and his ways," and "covenant breaking." When more specific, clergy inveighed against quotidian vices—"the taverns, the playhouses, the card-tables, and the sinful amusements of the present age"—and preached up daily virtues.[61] Too few in England owned slaves or shares in slave ships for either to be a compelling object for renunciation.

Slavery not only lacked immediacy. There was no mechanism for action, no vehicle for mobilizing antislavery opinion. Sharp himself offered nothing for potential abolitionists to do. Even with the example of the petitioning counties at hand, Sharp seems never to have considered establishing a similar association to promote the antislavery cause. And so he allowed the clergy to express disapproval of the slave system without securing from them a commitment to a particular measure or a specific course of action. James Yorke had at hand a copy of *The Law of Retribution* when composing his sermon for the Society for the Propagation of the Gospel in 1779 but, nonetheless, uttered not a word from the pulpit about colonial slavery or the Atlantic slave trade when the time came for him to speak. "The powers of custom, indolence, and interest, are violent oppugners of reformation," he privately advised Sharp. Nonetheless, he would heartily join with "abler advocates than myself, at any favourable moment, in the advancement of so liberal and Christian a cause." Yorke agreed to follow, in other words, but would not lead. A similarly qualified pledge came from Edmund Keene, bishop of Ely: "If any thing in favour of the Slave Trade should be brought into the House of Lords," he vowed to Sharp, "he *would certainly go down to the House on purpose to oppose it.*"[62]

Sharp seems not to have appreciated the difficulty of working for moral reform through the Church of England. Deep commitment to the spiritual

61. David Wilson, *National Calamities Procured by National Sins; or, The Tokens of Wrath, from the Lord upon a Sin-full People, Considered; in Three Discourses from Ezekiel vii. 12* (London, 1777), 40, 45, 47, 49, 51, 55, 56, 58; John Kello, *God's Departure from a People the Most Dreadful Judgment; a Sermon, Preached to the Congregation of Protestant Dissenters, at Bethnal Green, December the 13th, 1776* (London, 1776), 19.

62. James Yorke (bishop of St. Davids) to Sharp, Mar. 14, 1779, and Sharp to John Hinchliffe (bishop of Peterborough), Mar. 17, 1781, both in Hoare, *Memoirs*, 187, 188, 189.

authority of the episcopacy dulled his otherwise powerful impulse to confront institutional resistance. From the bishops, and only the bishops, he
would accept professions of goodwill at face value. There was no reason to
suppose, Sharp insisted, "that any of [the bishops] will refuse their concurrence and assistance in this matter." Benezet had complained that John
Green's SPG sermon of 1768 seemed to justify slavery, contravening the
spirit of the widely noticed antislavery sentiments expressed by the bishop
of Gloucester, William Warburton, two years before. Whatever Green's
views then, Sharp insisted in 1781, "sure I am, that he was afterwards fully
convinced of the bad consequences of the Slave Trade." On a recent
Sunday morning after services at Saint Paul's Cathedral, Sharp explained,
"before all the vergers and many other persons that were passing in the
aisle," Green declared that the slave trade was "a very abominable thing"
and "ought to be abolished." Such pronouncements, the less credulous
American Quaker abolitionist William Dillwyn knew, were for effect, not
to effect change. And Dillwyn was of the far more accurate opinion that
only a series of "calamities" would drive the bishops into supporting slave
trade abolition.[63] However, the grandson of the archbishop of York har-
bored an idealized view of the Church of England. It may have been
reasonable to hope that the custodians of the public faith would take a
stand on a matter that concerned the spiritual welfare of the nation. But it
was unreasonable, if not naive, to expect the keepers of orthodoxy and
bulwarks of the establishment to take the lead in advocating changes to the
status quo, especially on matters of trade.[64] The bench of bishops, with
several important exceptions, stood in support of the British slave trade
until the date of its abolition.

In some respects, Granville Sharp was ill suited to lead an antislavery

63. Sharp to Hinchliffe, Mar. 17, 1781, in Hoare, *Memoirs,* 190; Benezet to George
Dillwyn, 1783, in Brookes, *Friend Anthony Benezet,* 374.

64. Granville Sharp also attempted to recruit several bishops into the parliamentary
reform movement to restore "the due *limitations* of the Crown." He told John Hinchliffe
that the bishops, those "solemnly consecrated Rulers and Overseers in the Kingdom of
God," had sufficient "Faith and knowledge" to comprehend fully the "truly loyal Doctrine concerning *the absolute necessity of limiting all temporal Powers by the obedience
which we owe to the kingdom of God, and his righteousness.*" Sharp to bishop of Peterborough, Mar. 30, 1781, Granville Sharp Correspondence, D3549 13/1/P23, GRO.

movement. He had no gift for or patience with the pragmatics of politics. Consistently, he refused to align himself with the political factions through whom he could have exercised greater influence, even when he embraced the substance of their agendas. He wrote tracts for the Society for Constitutional Information but would not attend the meetings and never became a member. Only reluctantly would Sharp agree to serve as the figurehead of the Society for Effecting the Abolition of the Slave Trade at its inception in 1787. And in every instance, he declined to serve as the chair.[65] A censorious piety accompanied this diffidence. A good-natured riposte to Benjamin Rush's materialistic philosophy of morals thinly disguised an unshakable faith in the eminence of the Holy Spirit.[66] Virulent denunciations of "apostates"—"Deists, Arians, Socinians, and others, who deny the Divinity of Christ, and of the Holy Ghost"—surely distanced some Dissenters.[67] Sharp spent a decade trying to convert Anthony Benezet from the "dangerous errors" of Quakerism.[68] Granville Sharp could be intolerant and aloof as well as humane, compassionate, and principled. Unlike William Wilberforce, who would moderate his religious fervor to persuade the less devout, Granville Sharp neither found nor sought a way to frame his views so that they could win broad assent. The "excessive purity" of his opinions, conceded his first biographer, were "often conceived to be eccen-

65. Drinkwater-Lunn, "John Cartwright, Political Education, and English Radicalism," 88; Sharp to J. Sharp, Nov. 3, 1787, Granville Sharp Papers, D3549 13/1/S9.

66. Sharp wrote, "This 'Suspension of the Moral Faculty' is not allways [sic] occasioned, I fear, by mere physical causes and bodily infirmities:—the influence of invisible spiritual Enemies is too often to be apprehended." Sharp to Rush, Oct. 31, 1774, in Woods, ed., "The Correspondence of Rush and Sharp," *JAS,* I (1969), 12.

67. Sharp, *The Just Limitation of Slavery in the Laws of God,* 26n. Sharp was not a latitudinarian. He opposed the move by liberal Anglicans like John Jebb to nullify the laws requiring subscription to the Thirty-nine Articles, or tests of faith, prescribed by the Church of England. The drift by Joseph Priestley and other Presbyterians toward Unitarianism led Sharp to comment on "how necessary it is for the preservation of any religious Society that they severally ordain a Subscription to the particular form of Doctrine, or principles which they respectively profess." Sharp to Rev. Robert Findlay, Mar. 16, 1773, Granville Sharp Letterbook, fols. 101–102.

68. Sharp to Benezet, Nov. 18, 1774, Granville Sharp Papers, D3549 13/1/B19; "Dangrous errors" of Quakerism: Sharp to Findlay, July 1, 1772, Granville Sharp Letterbook, fol. 89.

tric and visionary."[69] Sharp refused compromises on what he regarded as matters of "right" and "righteousness." He held an unyielding view of Christian duty. This was the source of his unwavering stance against colonial slavery and the Atlantic slave trade. Unlike his contemporaries, he never could regard human bondage in anything other than moral terms. Ardor helped him wring from the bench of bishops verbal commitments to support an antislavery movement. Nonetheless, he was not the sort of person around whom a political movement could coalesce.

These prejudices perhaps would have mattered less if Granville Sharp had been more focused on promoting the antislavery cause. The kind of single-minded determination that he displayed in fighting slaveholding in England could have forced slave trade abolition or emancipation to the forefront of public debate in the last years of the American war. But Sharp had started to consider colonial slavery, the transatlantic slave trade, the coercion of America, and the corruption of the legislature as just so many species of state-sanctioned tyranny. As he explained to Hinchliffe, Christian duty called the righteous "to put a Stop to further bloodshed, to abolish slavery, and to restrain the dangerous influence of the crown." He recalled in 1781 that his first motive for supporting constitutional reform "was, an earnest desire to promote *peace with America;* the two subjects being connected with each other, and both with that of tolerating Slavery."[70] In the end, Sharp's protests against oppression in its varied expressions scattered his efforts and diminished their force.

Several historians have made much of the selectivity of later abolitionists, of their focus on distant abuses and their inattention to injustices in British society closer to home.[71] Yet with respect to slavery, Sharp perhaps was not selective enough. If he was the most determined British opponent of slavery during the Revolutionary era, antislavery never mattered more to him during these years than the protests against the American war or the campaign to reform the legislature. "*The corruption of Parliament,*" he wrote in 1782, "is the real source of all our national calamities and griev-

---

69. Hoare, *Memoirs,* 175.

70. Granville Sharp Papers, D3549 13/1/P23; Hoare, *Memoirs,* 191.

71. The merits of such assessments are a central theme in the excerpts and essays published in Thomas Bender, ed., *The Antislavery Debate: Capitalism and Abolitionism as a Problem in Historical Interpretation* (Berkeley, Calif., 1992).

ances."[72] Sharp seems not to have considered pushing abolitionism on the county associations, despite his close engagement with the campaign for political reform. On the subject of slavery, he never developed a scheme for the national dissemination of propaganda, although he contributed to a similar program conducted by the Society for Constitutional Information. Granville Sharp published seven separate tracts on parliamentary reform and another seven on the virtues of replacing a standing army with a free militia between 1777 and 1786. He wrote one on slavery.[73]

What was true of Sharp was true as well of the various opposition movements that emerged at the end of the American war. Of the issues on the reform agenda, the ethics of the slave system was always less than pressing. Sharp's close association with London radicals generated in these circles only tepid enthusiasm for antislavery organizing. The issue of slavery never became more than of marginal importance to the Society for Constitutional Information. Its members found the salve of humanitarianism no substitute for reforming the political system and ending an expensive, ruinous war. Indeed, the politicians who favored peace defended the interests of slaveholders when doing so could embarrass the ministry or help conclude the conflict. The Rockingham Whigs, for example, roundly criticized Lord North for allowing British commanders to liberate slaves owned by American rebels. It was the only position the Rockinghams or their like-minded associates took with any consistency on slavery during the course of the war.[74] One of their number, David Hartley, did speak out against the Atlantic trade in Africans. When in 1777 Lord North presented

72. [Granville Sharp], *The Claims of the People of England*, 2d ed. (London, 1782), 8.

73. See the complete list of Sharp's works published in Hoare, *Memoirs*, 487–496.

74. See, for example, Edmund Burke, "Speech on Conciliation with America," "Address to the King," "Address to the Colonists," and "Speech on the Use of Indians," each in Paul Langford, ed., *The Writings and Speeches of Edmund Burke* (Oxford, 1981–), III, 130, 267, 281, 359–361; Simmons and Thomas, eds., *Proceedings and Debates of the British Parliaments respecting North America, 1754–1783*, VI, 597 (May 22, 1776, speech of General Conway); [Willoughby Bertie], [fourth] earl of Abingdon, *Thoughts on the Letter of Edmund Burke, Esq.; to the Sheriffs of Bristol, on the Affairs of America*, 6th ed. (Oxford, [1777]), 56; Newcome Cappe, *A Sermon Preached on Friday the Fourth of February, 1780; the Late Day of National Humiliation, to a Congregation of Protestant-Dissenters, in Saint-Saviour-Gate, York, and Published at the Request of the Audience* (York, 1780), 24.

the annual motion to grant thirteen thousand pounds to the Company of Merchants Trading to Africa for the upkeep of the coastal trading forts, Hartley rose to add that the Board of Trade should act to mitigate the evils of slavery. Months later, on the floor of the House of Commons, he displayed handcuffs used on British merchant ships to protest the trade in slaves. By 1781, though, Hartley thought slavery reform far less urgent than suing for peace and resolving the constitutional crisis at home. "The greatest of all evils *now*," Hartley declared, "that which requires instant remedy, is the American war: A war which has had its rise in pride, and now derives its nourishment from corruption." Even he regarded putting "poignards into the hands of negroes" as barbaric.[75]

Because of its origins in a collective sense of crisis, there was a chance that enthusiasm for reform would subside once the era of anxiety passed, after the establishment of peace and the formation of a stable ministry that enjoyed public and royal support. In the former colonies, the purported commitment to emancipation dissolved once the new nation secured independence. And in England, Granville Sharp's declining attention to the antislavery cause during the 1780s hints that even ardent abolitionists might need the pressure of events to sustain their commitment. Public attention could have focused again on the inconsistency and hypocrisy of American slaveholders, even as more became attentive to the ways the nation depended on the exploitation of Africans. In 1785, essayists were still condemning American slavery and celebrating British free soil. Certainly Richard Price elected to ignore Sharp's appeal for collective self-scrutiny when he smugly recommended that Americans look to Britain for an example of commitment to freedom for Africans.[76]

75. Cobbett and Hansard, *The Parliamentary History of England*, XVII, 1042–1056, XIX, 315–316; David Hartley, *An Address to the Committee of Association of the County of York, on the State of Public Affairs* (London, 1781), 41; Hartley, *Letters on the American War Addressed to the Right Worshipful the Mayor and Corporation of the Town of Kingston upon Hull*, 3d ed. (London, 1778), 77.

76. See the *Daily Universal Register*, Jan. 8, 1785, cited in Gretchen Gerzina, *Black London: Life before Emancipation* (New Brunswick, N.J., 1995), 200, and Richard Price, *Observations on the Nature of the Importance of the American Revolution, and the Means of Making It a Benefit to the World . . .* (London, 1785), 83–84. South Carolina statesman Henry Laurens took it upon himself to set Price straight. "Britain is the fountain from whence We have been supplied with Slaves for upwards of a century. Britain passed Acts

The enthusiasm for constitutional reform did wane, inside Parliament and outside it, after the younger William Pitt and his followers triumphed at the polls in 1784. As the Reverend Wyvill would observe in 1787, "The prospect of happier times had produced a disposition to acquiesce." The tendency to dwell on the moral character of the empire, however, would be a lasting consequence of the American war. "It is the duty of the British government," Antiguan exile Charles Crawford insisted in 1783, "if she is willing to avert the further indignation of Heaven . . . to bring a Bill into Parliament for the discontinuance of the slave-trade throughout all the British dominions." "We shall never prosper as a nation until that execrable traffic [the slave trade] be abolished," Gilbert Wakefield of Liverpool would tell a friend in 1783. Several months later Wakefield would take the occasion of the day "Appointed for a General Thanksgiving on Account of the Peace" to observe that British subjects held Africans in "the profoundest ignorance" under an "unrelenting Spirit of Barbarity." No wonder enemies had been raised to "punish our Disobedience." Only "Acts of Benevolence and Righteousness," Wakefield would declare, could save Britain from "the Pit of Destruction, into which we have been gradually sinking." The American war, several would agree, had exposed the sins of empire and established the urgency of reform. To Cambridge philosopher and theologian William Paley, the loss of North America proved that Britain had grown too proud after the conquests in the Seven Years' War. It was wrong for a free people to rule vast territories and hold men and women in slavery. When abolitionism reached a fever pitch in 1787 and 1788, campaigners would still recall the humbling experience of the American war. An Oxford clergyman would remark wistfully, "The Western Empire is gone from us, never to return; it is given to another more righteous than we; who consecrated the sword of resistance declaring for the abolition of slavery."[77]

---

of Parliament for encouraging and establishing the Slave Trade. . . . Nor is it quite a decided fact that the moment a negro sets his foot on British Ground, he becomes a free Man." Laurens to Price, Feb. 1, 1785, in W. Bernard Peach and D. O. Thomas, eds., *The Correspondence of Richard Price*, II, *March 1778–February 1786* (Durham, N.C., 1991), 263. The case for a rapid return to stability in British political culture after the American war is argued forcefully in Eliga Gould, *The Persistence of Empire: Political Culture in the Age of the American Revolution* (Chapel Hill, N.C., 2000), 148–180.

77. C. Wyvill to William Pitt, July 29, 1787, in Christopher Wyvill, ed., *Political*

This emerging concern with how the British conducted themselves overseas would first center on the East India Company, not the Atlantic slave trade in African captives. In the 1780s, the treatment of native populations on the subcontinent became the subject of sustained official questioning. The apparent mismanagement of relations with the nawab of Arcot exposed the returned Madras governor, Sir Thomas Rumbold, to government investigation and a failed prosecution. In February 1781, a select committee of the House of Commons opened an inquiry into miscarriages of justice in Bengal, an inquiry broadened a year later into an examination of how British possessions in India may be governed "with the greatest Security and Advantage to this Country," and by what means "the Happiness of the Natives may be best promoted." The resulting reports detailed questionable practices by East India Company servants and occasioned a sustained harangue in the House of Commons against British despotism in the East. Edmund Burke famously declared in 1783 that "all political power which is set over men . . . ought to be some way or other exercised ultimately for their benefit"; every species of political dominion is "in the strictest sense a *trust;* and it is of the very essence of every trust to be rendered *accountable*." To this end, he led from 1786 until 1795 a dramatic if unsuccessful attempt to convict former Bengal governor Warren Hastings for corruption and oppression.[78]

Papers, Chiefly respecting the Attempt of the County of York, and Other Considerable Districts, Commenced in 1779 . . . to Effect a Reformation of the Parliament of Great-Britain, 4 vols. (London, [1794–1802]), IV, 32; [Charles Crawford], *Liberty: A Pindaric Ode* (Philadelphia, 1783), 15n (first printed in Tunbridge Wells, Canterbury, Maidstone, and London, 1783); Gilbert Wakefield to Rev. George Gregory, Sept. 2, 1783, in Arnold Wainwright and John Towill Rutt, eds., *Memoirs of the Life of Gilbert Wakefield,* 2 vols. (London, 1804), I, 500; Gilbert Wakefield, *A Sermon Preached at Richmond in Surry on July 29th, 1784, the Day Appointed for a General Thanksgiving on Account of the Peace* (London, 1784), 17–18; William Paley, *The Principles of Moral and Political Philosophy* (London, 1785), 196; William Agutter, *The Abolition of the Slave Trade Considered in a Religious Point of View; a Sermon Preached before the Corporation of the City of Oxford, at St. Martin's Church, on Sunday, February 3, 1788* (London, 1788), 26.

78. Langford, ed., *The Writings and Speeches of Edmund Burke,* V, 18; Edmund Burke, "Speech on Fox's East India Bill," ibid., 385; Frederick G. Whelan, *Edmund Burke and India: Political Morality and Empire* (Pittsburgh, Pa., 1996), 24, 52. On official queries into East India affairs in the early 1780s, see James Phillips, "Parliament

The examinations of the East India Company reflected the new inclination after the American war to consider imperial practices a national concern and a legitimate area of official inquiry. No instance reflects more
clearly the emerging attention in Britain to the ethics of overseas enterprise
than the evolving preoccupations of Thomas Parker, a lawyer at Lincoln's
Inn. Parker had published in 1775 a vast compendium of British legislation
and court records pertaining to transoceanic commerce, which served at
once as a work of reference for merchants and a tribute to the wealth and
power of the British Empire. Just seven years later, though, in 1782, he
came forward with a very different text, one deeply marked by the struggles
that attended the years of crisis. This was an examination of "our national
conduct" around the globe, from the end of the Seven Years' War to the
surrender of Cornwallis at Yorktown. This most recent era, from Parker's
perspective, had been an unqualified disaster, not only because of British
losses in North America, but also because of the ethos that had accompanied the expansion of empire. Parker devoted the bulk of his critique to
developments in India, where greed, he insisted, had led to unforgivable
atrocities. But what made Parker's work distinctive was how he linked what
he described as tyranny in India to British crimes elsewhere. He thought a
lust for wealth and power within the British state had led to the loss of the

---

and Southern India, 1781–3: The Secret Committee of Inquiry and the Prosecution of Sir
Thomas Rumbold," *Parliamentary History,* VII (1988), 81–97; P. J. Marshall, *The
Impeachment of Warren Hastings* (Oxford, 1965), 1–17; Langford, ed., *The Writings and
Speeches of Edmund Burke* (Oxford, 1981–), V; Marshall, "Burke and India," in Ian
Crowe, ed., *The Enduring Edmund Burke* (Wilmington, Del., 1997), 39–47; and Mar-
shall, "Edmund Burke and India: The Vicissitudes of a Reputation," in Rudrangshu
Murkherjee and Lakshimi Subramanian, eds., *Politics and Trade in the Indian Ocean
World: Essays in Honor of Ashin Das Gupta* (Delhi, 1998), 250–269. See also Lucy S.
Sutherland, *The East India Company in Eighteenth-Century Politics* (Oxford, 1952), and
Conway, *The British Isles and the War of American Independence,* 337–346. On public
doubts regarding the virtue of the British Empire in the last years of the American war,
see the comments by Wilson, *The Sense of the People,* 269–284. For the increasingly
important role of Parliament in the investigation and oversight of overseas enterprise
before and after the American war, see P. J. Marshall, "The British State Overseas," in
Bob Moore and Henk F. K. van Nierop, eds., *Colonial Empires Compared: Britain and
the Netherlands, 1750–1850: Papers Delivered to the Fortieth Anglo-Dutch Historical
Conference, 2000* (Aldershot, Eng., 2003), 177–181.

thirteen colonies. The pursuit of wealth, he wrote, had also caused the enslavement of tens of thousands of African men, women, and children. And after the Seven Years' War, the fever for sugar cultivation had led British speculators to seize lands from the Caribs on the newly acquired island of Saint Vincent. "Our conduct," Parker declared, "contains every injury which the people of one country can well do to another." The British government had abandoned the people of Corsica in their time of need, during their attempt to win independence from France. The state had conspired to assist Russia in the partition of Poland in 1772, a dismemberment that many in Britain had regarded as a tragedy. All of this had taken place without protest by the British people, and with minimal dissent in Parliament. These violations of what Parker called "natural justice" inexplicably went unpunished. It was his belief, in 1782, that only a public commitment to imperial reform could restore the reputation of the British government and redeem the character of British overseas enterprise.[79]

These concerns contributed, during the 1780s, to the emerging idea of trusteeship, to the view that morals should figure in imperial policy, that rule should be exercised "for the benefit of the governed" as well as the governors, "that where Britain's power / Is felt," poet William Cowper wrote in 1785, "mankind may feel her mercy too."[80] Those who thought about imperial questions long had assumed that Britain did not rule overseas at all, that the colonies were composed of peaceful, settler communities, with colonists who enjoyed the rights of freeborn Englishmen and who possessed a preeminent commitment to trade rather than dominion. The results of the Seven Years' War had begun to challenge this self-image, and the outcome of the Revolution revealed the many ways that the interests associated with imperial rule could conflict with the preservation of

79. Thomas Parker, *The Laws of Shipping and Insurance, with a Digest of Adjudged Cases: Containing the Acts of Parliament relative to Shipping, Insurance, and Navigation . . . with the Determinations of the Courts of Justice on Trials concerning Shipping, Insurance . . . from Trinity Term, 1693, to Michaelmas Term 1774 . . .* (London, 1775); Parker, *Evidence of Our Transactions in the East Indies: With an Enquiry into the General Conduct of Great Britain to Other Countries, from the Peace of Paris, in 1763* (London, 1782), citation on iv.

80. William Cowper, *The Task* (London, 1785), as cited in James G. Basker, ed., *Amazing Grace: An Anthology of Poems about Slavery, 1660–1810* (New Haven, Conn., 2002), 297.

established rights and liberties. Among a broader public, during the American war, there arose, too, a desire for Britain to rule in a way consistent with the nation's self-ascribed reputation for a commitment to freedom. In the end, few would embrace Granville Sharp's suggestion that injustices abroad would bring down the British Empire. Confidence in national virtue ran too high for such pessimism to be effective for long. But preserving pride in British institutions required some form of adjustment. Instead of abandoning the myth that the nation possessed an empire of liberty, the British would look for ways to make the facts conform more closely to the national myth.

PART III

The Search for Solutions

CHAPTER 4

British Concepts of Emancipation in the Age of the American Revolution

Of the obstacles that would face those first Britons who hoped to bring the injustice of slavery or the slave trade forward for public debate, few presented greater difficulties than the customary association of slavery with imperial wealth and power. To the many with an investment in the colonial economy or concerned with Britain's standing among European rivals, an empire without slavery was simply unthinkable. As trade theorist Malachy Postlethwayt asserted in 1746, "The *Negroe-Trade* and the natural Consequences resulting from it, may be justly esteemed an inexhaustible Fund of Wealth and Naval Power to this Nation."[1] Even those moved to denounce slavery in print often conceded that colonial slavery made Atlantic commerce and overseas settlement possible. When British chroniclers of American colonization, for example, reflected during the 1770s on the failed experiment to prohibit slavery in the infant colony of Georgia several decades earlier, they emphasized the folly of attempting to produce export crops without slaves. However humane the motives, William Russell maintained, banning slavery in the fledgling colony was "a species of oppression." John Huddleston Wynne found slaveholding distasteful, thought it corrupted the morals of British settlers, and feared it would end in bloody insurrections. Yet, even with his misgivings, Wynne could not bring himself to advocate slave trade or slavery abolition. The "very short experience" in Georgia showed a ban on slavery to be "an impractical measure." "The want of hands to cultivate the southern plantations" made slavery "a necessity," wrote Wynne. Further, he noted, echoing an opinion held even by many of slavery's professed opponents, "Africans,

1. Malachy Postlethwayt cited in David Brion Davis, *The Problem of Slavery in Western Culture*, 2d ed., rev. (Oxford, 1988), 150; for further discussion on this point, see 151–154. Note also in this context the verdict rendered by Seymour Drescher: "The essential rationale for British-sponsored slavery, from first to last, was its apparent contribution to the collective wealth and power of the empire." Drescher, *Capitalism and Antislavery: British Mobilization in Comparative Perspective* (London, 1987), 20.

or their descendants, are better able to support severe labour in hot countries than any of European blood."[2]

For Granville Sharp and the other early proponents of antislavery initiatives, the challenge lay not only in the power of vested interests but also in the limited ways that those troubled by slavery could imagine the future development of the American colonies. The fruits of long-standing practice and the imperatives of international competition made a strong case for resisting radical change. Moreover, the experience of American colonization indicated few alternatives to slave labor. As best as anyone in Britain could judge, an Atlantic empire required human bondage, a belief that not only weakened the impact of antislavery argument but also inhibited the possibility of organizing concerted action for change. For how does one rally support for a goal—an empire without slaves—that few could conceptualize or articulate, that almost no one in the British Isles had thought viable, and that, as it must have seemed to even the most hopeful, resided in the realm of fantasy?

Several of the first antislavery propagandists in England simply dismissed pragmatic questions and rejected slavery on principle. "It is impossible," John Wesley wrote in 1774, "that it should ever be necessary, for any reasonable creature to violate all the laws of Justice, Mercy, and Truth." If empire required slavery, Wesley suggested, then empire ought to be renounced. This kind of moral absolutism, however laudable in principle, could win little sympathy from those responsible for colonial governance and scarcely more from a public invested in the fruits and majesty of empire. Wesley himself seems to have understood the futility of his position. "Should we address ourselves to the Public at large?" he asked rhetorically. "What effect can this have? It may inflame the world against the guilty, but is not likely to remove the guilt. Should we appeal to the *English* nation in general? This is also striking wide. . . . As little would it

2. William Russell, *The History of America, from Its Discovery by Columbus to the Conclusion of the Late War; with an Appendix, Containing an Account of the Rise and Progress of the Present Unhappy Contest between Great Britain and Her Colonies*, 2 vols. (London, 1778), II, 305; [John Huddleston] Wynne, *A General History of the British Empire in America: Containing, an Historical, Political, and Commercial View of the English Settlements; Including All the Countries in North-America, and the West-Indies, Ceded by the Peace of Paris*, 2 vols. (London, 1770), II, 540, 541, 545.

in all probability avail, to apply to the Parliament. So many things, which *seem* of greater importance lie before them that they are not likely to attend to this." Wesley resigned himself to espousing the unpromising strategy British Quakers also settled on during the late 1760s and early 1770s: a direct appeal to merchants, planters, and captains of slave ships to change their ways.[3]

An antislavery movement did not have to happen in Britain. There had never been one before. But if antislavery argument was to have effect, moralists would have to do more than simply declare that slavery was wrong. Many Britons could accept the moral argument, as we now know.[4] The real burden lay in rethinking the relationship between coerced labor and empire, disassociating the institution of slavery from prevailing assumptions about the purposes of overseas colonies, and developing practical, attainable, compelling alternatives. What would an alternative to colonial slavery entail? To pose the question hints at the magnitude of the task.[5] Reformers would not only have to devise new schemes for the recruitment, organization, and management of labor. They also would have to uproot

3. John Wesley, *Thoughts upon Slavery*, 3d ed. (London, 1774), 19, 23, 24–27; Minutes of the Meeting for Sufferings, XXXII (May 29, 1767, Aug. 31, Nov. 2, 1770, Jan. 11, 1771), 69, 408, 424, 444, Library of the Society of Friends, London. More than a dozen years earlier, in a seminal passage from his *System of the Principles of the Laws of Scotland*, Scottish jurist George Wallace had also recommended surrendering empire if empire required exploitation of slave labor. See David Brion Davis, "New Sidelights on Early Antislavery Radicalism," *William and Mary Quarterly*, 3d Ser., XXVIII (1971), 589. On the public embrace of empire, see Kathleen Wilson, *The Sense of the People: Politics, Culture, and Imperialism in England, 1715–1785* (Cambridge, 1995); Bob Harris, " 'American Idols': Empire, War, and the Middling Ranks in Mid-Eighteenth-Century Britain," *Past and Present*, no. 150 (February 1996), 111–114; and H. V. Bowen, "British Conceptions of Global Empire, 1756–1783," *Journal of Imperial and Commonwealth History*, XXVI, no. 3 (1998), 1–5.

4. See generally Davis, *The Problem of Slavery in Western Culture*, pts. 2 and 3; Drescher, *Capitalism and Antislavery*, 12–24; Robin Blackburn, *The Overthrow of Colonial Slavery, 1776–1848* (London, 1988), 35–66; and Moira Ferguson, *Subject to Others: British Women Writers and Colonial Slavery, 1670–1834* (New York, 1992), chaps. 1–5.

5. Note also the comments by David Brion Davis on the challenges involved in abolishing slavery in those regions where slavery was of limited import: Davis, *The Problem of Slavery in the Age of Revolution, 1770–1823* (Ithaca, N.Y., 1975), 86–92.

customs fundamental to enterprise throughout the British Atlantic. A program to end slavery, for example, either would have to lure slaveholders into surrendering their slaves voluntarily or would have to divest slaveholders of their human chattel through force. The second approach necessarily would require from the state an unprecedented invasion of customary, nearly sacred rights in property and therefore would present daunting, if not insurmountable, constitutional, political, and logistical hurdles. Indeed, any plan for emancipation presented the specter of enhanced imperial authority, if not a formal shift of power from the colonial assemblies to Parliament. Even a scenario involving a gradual voluntary end to slavery would demand institutions empowered to mediate between former slaves and former slaveholders. How else, in the absence of mass revolt by the enslaved, could emancipation be secured and enforced throughout the colonies?

Furthermore, in addition to threatening to dispossess colonists of their property and aggrandize the imperial state, emancipation promised revolutionary social change. Slavery established status in British America as well as a scheme for labor. If the enslaved would no longer be slaves, who exactly, in civic terms, would they be? Abolishing slavery would seem to present one of two prospects: an incorporation, in some form, of liberated slaves into colonial society or, alternatively, relocation of hundreds of thousands of freed slaves to the frontiers of the British Empire or outside the realm. A genuine challenge to slavery thus entailed far more than a challenge to slave labor. It necessitated, as well, an engagement with fundamental questions regarding property, imperial governance, and social organization. At bottom, those who would abolish slavery required an alternative concept of empire.

This chapter directs attention to the first British proposals to end colonial slavery, delineates their character, accounts for their timing, and explains their failure to win public attention and political influence, with the aim of illuminating aspects of the relation between antislavery opinion and evolving definitions of imperial mission between the Seven Years' War and the American Revolution. The challenge of ruling the diverse populations brought within the empire in the 1760s inspired among policy makers a paternalistic ethos centered on pacifying His Majesty's new subjects and restraining the ambitions of British settlers. The broader impulse to extend royal protection to outsiders encouraged several British writers, and particularly writers concerned with imperial administration, to conceive of slaves as British subjects as well as the property of slaveholders. And this willingness, among a select few, to think of slaves as subjects of George III assisted the formulation of the first tentative emancipation schemes, which are situated and explained here within the context of the wide-ranging, public discussion of imperial policy that took place during the Revolutionary War. Because envisioning the British American provinces without slavery, more generally, required novel ways of thinking about empire, substantive debate about colonial governance had the potential to facilitate unconventional thoughts about the future of slavery and the slave trade in the British Atlantic. The first emancipation schemes served and reflected the broader-based aim to solidify and refurbish faltering British control in North America. In important ways, slavery reform proposals were entwined with attempts to bolster metropolitan authority. This nascent ideal of imperial stewardship, premised on a centralization of power and a policing of social relations in overseas possessions, offered a framework for an antislavery campaign. But the vision was vulnerable to the scope and novelty of its ambitions in the 1770s and, in the event, undone and discouraged by the unfavorable results of the American war for independence.

"These papers will contain a proposal for the extension of [I] the future power and commerce of Great Britain." This unlikely introduction opened an anonymously published essay printed in 1772 with the title *Plan for the Abolition of Slavery in the West Indies,* the first British publication to offer a concrete, if quixotic, emancipation scheme. The author suggested that the state purchase each year several dozen African boys and girls from the slaving forts along the eastern Atlantic coast, instruct and train the children in England, and settle them at the age of sixteen as colonists in the Pensacola district in the new British province of West Florida. The resulting colony of free Africans, the author argued, would encourage manumissions by giving British settlers a place to send liberated slaves while inducing "a spirit of industry and achievement" among the enslaved by opening the prospect for freedom. Furthermore, the West Florida settlement would present, for southern climes, a competing model of labor and social relations. Customary practices are hard to change in established colonies, the author conceded. By contrast, new and (from a British perspective) underpopulated provinces offered unusual opportunities for experimentation, perhaps "a nursery of some good intentions, which may hereafter be extended with facility into the other colonies, or into Great Britain itself." The Pensacola colonists would demonstrate that free laborers could cultivate export crops and that Africans would produce them even if not held as slaves. Eventually, by necessity, the older colonies would abandon slavery to compete with their more successful southern neighbor. Over time, in Pensacola, "the settlers will increase, they will cultivate, they will trade, they will overflow; they will become labourers and artizans in the neighbouring provinces; they will, being freemen, be more industrious, more skillful, and, upon the whole, work cheaper than slaves . . . and slavery will thereupon necessarily cease." This, then, was an imaginative, if ingenuous plan to "check the progress of slavery" by exposing its disadvantages, by displaying the merits of free labor and the capacities of Africans, and by allowing "time and management," not a sudden shift in policy, to effect change. Through prudent, incremental steps, cooperation between blacks and whites in the Americas would replace the enmity bred by racial slavery.[6]

If the proposal seemed whimsical, it originated in a considered, knowledgeable inquiry into American governance. The author, Maurice Morgann, served William Fitzmaurice Petty (second earl of Shelburne) as private secretary and, in this capacity, sometime adviser on colonial administration.[7] Unlike Granville Sharp or John Wesley, Maurice Morgann participated actively in the formulation of imperial policy. Morgann not only embraced empire. He spent much of his career trying to make the empire work. During Shelburne's tenure as president of the Board of Trade in the spring and summer of 1763, Morgann assisted his patron in drafting measures for the organization and management of American territories ac-

6. [Maurice Morgann], *Plan for the Abolition of Slavery in the West Indies* (London, 1772), 4, 7, 13, 15, 25.

7. Morgann perhaps is best known for his discerning *Essay on the Dramatic Character of Sir John Falstaff* (London, 1777). Daniel A. Fineman identifies Morgann as the author of *Plan for the Abolition of Slavery in the West Indies,* but without supporting documentation. See Fineman, ed., *Maurice Morgann: Shakespearean Criticism* (Oxford, 1972), 6–7. In his private correspondence, Granville Sharp makes several references to the proposal by "the ingenious Mr. Morgan." See, for example, Granville Sharp to earl of Macclesfield, Feb. 20, 1773, and Sharp to Col. James, Apr. 8, 1773, both in Granville Sharp MS Letterbook, fols. 176, 180, York Minister Library (YML).

quired at the Peace of Paris. In July 1766, when Shelburne joined the Chatham administration as secretary of state for the Southern Department, Morgann received the post of undersecretary responsible for American affairs. Seventeen months later, in December 1767, Shelburne designated Morgann to serve as the cabinet emissary to Quebec, where, three years after conquest, the rights of His Majesty's French Catholic subjects and the arrangements for government and revenue remained unresolved and, in both Quebec and Britain, bitterly contested. Morgann returned from Canada in January 1770 to find the Chatham ministry dissolved, his patron out of favor, and his influence accordingly curtailed. Shelburne's dozen years in opposition left Morgann without a role in imperial administration during the Revolutionary War. And American independence robbed Morgann of the three-hundred-pound sinecure he enjoyed as absentee secretary for the province of New Jersey. But when Shelburne returned to office briefly as secretary of state for the Home Department in 1782, he tapped Morgann to serve in New York as executive secretary to Sir Guy Carleton at British army headquarters, where Morgann reluctantly administered the retreat of British forces from the thirteen former colonies.[8]

8. Morgann's career in imperial governance is described in Fineman, ed., *Maurice Morgann*, 4–9. A substantial collection of his policy memoranda is preserved in the Shelburne Papers at the William L. Clements Library, Ann Arbor, Mich. From published sources, further detail on his work for Shelburne may be gleaned from R. A. Humphreys, "Lord Shelburne and the Proclamation of 1763," *English Historical Review*, XLIX (1934), 245–250; Humphreys, "Lord Shelburne and British Colonial Policy, 1766–1768," *Eng. Hist. Rev.*, L (1935), 259n; Franklin B. Wickwire, *British Subministers and Colonial America, 1763–1783* (Princeton, N.J., 1966), 93–94, 96–97n; Michael G. Kammen, *A Rope of Sand: The Colonial Agents, British Politics, and the American Revolution* (Ithaca, N.Y., 1968), 279–280; and Jack M. Sosin, *Whitehall and the Wilderness: The Middle West in British Colonial Policy, 1760–1775* (Lincoln, Nebr., 1961), 151–152, 157–158. Morgann's mission to Quebec is best followed in two collections of reprinted documents: Adam Shortt and Arthur G. Doughty, eds., *Documents relating to the Constitutional History of Canada, 1759–1791*, I (Ottawa, 1907), 199–201, and W. P. M. Kennedy and Gustave Lanctot, eds., *Reports on the Laws of Quebec, 1767–1770* (Ottawa, 1931). The Quebec colony's attorney general, Francis Maseres, was unimpressed by Morgann's grasp of the constitutional questions at issue, writing privately, "He is a well-bred agreeable man but not a lawyer; and he has a pompous way of talking that seems borrowed from the house of commons cant about the constitution etc., without having

In these positions, Morgann wrote expansively on imperial policy, in each instance with the overarching aim to harness the colonies to metropolitan authority. "The Colonists," he asserted in 1763, "are merely Factors for the Purposes of the Trade." The same year he suggested, among other draconian measures, revoking the charters held by the several American provinces. In one scholar's judgment, Morgann's policy recommendations in the months after the Seven Years' War were "probably harsher than the spirit of any British legislation toward America before the passage of the Boston Port Bill."[9] This rigid authoritarianism softened after the Stamp Act crisis, by which time both Shelburne and Morgann had concluded that coercive policies would harm trade and incite rebellion. Still, although favoring conciliatory measures thereafter, Morgann never ceased to regard America as "mere colonies planted in subservience to the Interest of Great Britain and calculated to increase its commerce its Wealth and its power." British might derived from its western empire, the erstwhile subminister believed. Throughout the American war, even after the defeat of Lord Cornwallis at Yorktown in 1781, he held out hope for reconciliation and an imperial union. In 1786, three years after peace with the independent United States, Morgann still clung to the dream of restoring British sovereignty in North America, confident, recorded loyalist diarist William Smith, that no government "the Offspring of Theoretic premeditation" could long survive.[10]

---

precise Ideas of what he would say." Maseres to Fowler Walker, Aug. 31, 1768, in W. Stewart Wallace, ed., *The Maseres Letters, 1766–1768* (Toronto, 1919), 119. Morgann was at Carleton's side at Tappan in May 1783 when the British commander informed George Washington that slaves liberated by British forces would not be returned to their masters. Paul R. Reynolds, *Guy Carleton: A Biography* (New York, 1980), 144–146. The variety and extent of Morgann's work in New York may be followed in the papers of British Army Headquarters, which Morgann held in private possession until 1789. See volumes II through IV of Great Britain, Royal Commission on Historical Manuscripts, *Report on American Manuscripts in the Royal Institution of Great Britain . . .* , 5 vols. (London, 1904–1909).

9. "On American Commerce and Government Especially in the Newly Acquired Territories," Shelburne Papers, LXXXV, fols. 26, 29; Wickwire, *British Subministers and Colonial America*, 94–95.

10. Fineman, *Maurice Morgann*, 4–6; Humphreys, "Lord Shelburne and British Colonial Policy," *Eng. Hist. Rev.*, L (1935), 268–269; "On the Right and Expediency of Taxing America" [c. 1765], Shelburne Papers, LXVVV, fol. 73; L. F. S. Upton, ed., *The*

Several writers had proposed amelioration of slavery, and many had denounced the institution on principle, but before Morgann wrote in 1772, no one in England had devised a scheme for gradual emancipation. His *Plan for the Abolition of Slavery in the West Indies* bespoke a sharp contempt for racial bigotry, animated, in this instance, by the case of *Somerset v. Steuart*, which, as it did for several others, moved Morgann to publish his opinions on slavery and race. However, the Florida scheme took shape first as a policy memorandum, as a privately distributed document, not as antislavery propaganda. It surfaced from Morgann's immersion in the minutiae of American governance, not from the public debates surrounding the Somerset case. Although the plan was published in 1772, Morgann hatched the idea of colonizing free Africans in Pensacola nine years earlier, "soon after the conclusion of the late Peace," he explained in the preface.[11] Initially, he had appended the plan to a manuscript titled "On American Commerce and Government Especially in the Newly Acquired Territories," one of several documents drafted for Shelburne late in the spring of 1763, months before the Board of Trade advertised the sale of Florida land grants, months before Georgia agent William Knox circulated his influential "Hints respecting the Settlement of Florida," indeed, more than a year before ministers had a decent map of the Pensacola district.[12] Morgann's

---

Diary and Selected Papers of Chief Justice William Smith, 1784–1793, II, *The Diary, October 6, 1785, to May 18, 1787* (Toronto, 1965), 105.

11. [Morgann], *Plan for the Abolition of Slavery in the West Indies,* 1.

12. The manuscript copy of Morgann's plan does not survive, but an unambiguous reference to the scheme appears in his "On American Commerce and Government" (1763): "It may appear whimsical to propose that a certain Number of boys and girls about 8 or 10 years old should be annually brought from affrica, educated here 'till 15; and then sent over to Florida and Louisiana as Settlers: Yet an enterprising farmer would perhaps pursue, in respect to the animal creation, some plan of this nature for improving his Estate. If even one of the Islands was to be so settled, by way of Experiment only, I believe future ages would bless so generous a policy, and Brittain be for ever remembered as the Parent of Freedom." On early schemes for Florida settlement, see Bernard Bailyn, *Voyagers to the West: A Passage in the Peopling of America on the Eve of the Revolution* (New York, 1986), 432–433. For British want of information on the West Florida district, see Board of Trade secretary Thomas Pownall's "Sketch of a Report concerning the Cessions in Africa and America at the Peace of 1763," printed in Humphreys, "Lord Shelburne and the Proclamation of 1763," *Eng. Hist. Rev.,* XLIX (1934), 262.

manuscript addressed problems of administration, revenue, and defense. A settlement for freed Africans in the heart of the British Empire, he added, would further long-standing objectives: expanding trade, fortifying British North America's southern border, settling barren territories without the loss to England of productive laborers, enlarging the pool of consumers for British products, and developing a channel through which to funnel trade with the Spanish colonies. Africans could serve the empire better, he hypothesized, if not held as slaves.

Morgann offered, instead, a novel concept of community within the British Empire. Racial difference resulted from environment, he explained, and as a consequence had utility. Morgann accepted that Europeans perished in tropical climates and that in those regions, therefore, only Africans and their descendants could cultivate the land. But to him, these "facts" recommended the incorporation of Africans into civil society, not enslavement and social death. If the frontier imposed by climate marked the perimeter of British power, it also indicated where Africans could best serve as agents of British expansion. Maurice Morgann may have known of the British use of (enslaved) black manpower in military expeditions against Cartagena (1741), Martinique (1759), Guadeloupe (1759), and Havana (1762), but his proposal shared rather more with the liberationist imperialism first promoted in the late sixteenth century by the younger Richard Hakluyt. African allies and auxiliaries, if encouraged to settle the underdeveloped territories in the Floridas and the Caribbean, Morgann insisted, could themselves produce staple crops for European markets and conduct trade, on behalf of the British Empire, with Spanish America. Similarly, if nurtured and adequately supported, alliances with sovereigns along the coast of Africa could help extend commerce "through the very heart" of the continent, where Britons lacked the capacity and constitution to settle.[13]

Abolition of slavery, then, rather than compromising empire, was the proper measure for a "free and generous government" inclined to "views of empire and domination" that were "worthy of ambition." Unleashed from the disgrace of slavery and no longer "restrained by climate," the British Empire would stand on "the sure foundations of equality and justice." Morgann envisaged an absorption of the "black subjects of Britain" into the

13. [Morgann], *Plan for the Abolition of Slavery in the West Indies*, 27.

imperial corpus. In due time, Morgann assured, the former slaves would
"talk the same language, read the same books, profess the same religion,
and be fashioned by the same laws." Through marriages with Europeans in
the new settlements, variations in skin color would "wear away" by steady,
imperceptible "degrees." "The whites will inhabit the northern colonies,"
and "to the south, the complexions will blacken by regular gradation."
Then, with "one tongue," a "united people" would "commemorate the
auspicious aera of universal freedom" while "the sable arm" of British
authority would reach "through every region of the Torrid Zone," "shake
the power of Spain to its foundations," and elevate Great Britain "to the
seat of unenvied and unlimited dominion."[14]

After the Jacobite rebellion of 1745, to discourage further uprisings
in Scotland Parliament enacted legislation that would transform "savage"
Highlanders into assimilated, productive, loyal Britons.[15] With a similar
end in view, Morgann's plan gradually would acculturate Africans, award
them a stake in the empire, and thereby discourage insurrections and the
threat of what he predicted to be "a general" and "merited carnage." And
just as Scottish soldiers helped make possible the conquests of the Seven
Years' War, blacks would help secure British supremacy in the Americas.
Civilize, liberate, incorporate, and unite. This was Morgann's formula for
achieving uncontested rule in the Americas, ending slavery, and in the
process "restoring the integrity of the British government, and vindicating
the credit and honour of our common nature."[16] In viewing Africans as
potential allies rather than internal enemies, as subjects of the crown rather

14. Ibid., 25, 26, 33. On the British use of slaves and free blacks in mid-eighteenth-
century military expeditions, see Peter Voelz, *Slave and Soldier: The Military Impact of
Blacks in the Colonial Americas* (New York, 1993), 77–81. For reference to Hakluyt's
proposal of 1579 to colonize the Straits of Magellan with escaped Spanish slaves and
English convicts, see Edmund S. Morgan, *American Slavery, American Freedom: The
Ordeal of Colonial Virginia* (New York, 1975), 16–17.

15. Linda Colley, *Britons: Forging the Nation, 1707–1837* (New Haven, Conn., 1992),
119–120. See also Eric Richards, "Scotland and the Uses of the Atlantic Empire," in
Bernard Bailyn and Philip D. Morgan, eds., *Strangers within the Realm: Cultural Margins of the First British Empire* (Chapel Hill, N.C., 1991), 106–112, and T. M. Devine,
Scotland's Empire and the Shaping of the Americas, 1600–1815 (Washington, D.C.,
2003), 204–213.

16. [Morgann], *Plan for the Abolition of Slavery in the West Indies*, 32.

than the property of slaveholders, Morgann pictured an empire defined by neither ethnicity nor religion—in fact, on nothing more than allegiance.

Maurice Morgann wrote creatively about slavery because, in part, as a matter of employment, he ruminated routinely on imperial policy. And his decision to describe enslaved Africans as imperial subjects reflected a characteristic and intensifying concern among British administrators to enhance the presence and extend the influence of the crown in the American territories. The cessions of the 1760s brought an unprecedented number and variety of peoples within British dominions. Never had England or Britain seized more land at once. "In the multitude of people is the king's honour," the Book of Proverbs taught. Assessed in more utilitarian or mercantilist terms, the crown had acquired an almost countless number of new cultivators, consumers, and dependents. By contemporary estimates, in 1763, the twenty-five-year-old George III could now claim authority over an additional seventy-five thousand French Canadians, approximately thirty thousand planters, slaves, and Caribs in the Ceded Islands, perhaps one hundred thousand Native Americans, a smattering of Spanish colonists in the Floridas, and, it was believed, anywhere between ten and twenty million people in Bengal.[17] In theory, by conquest or capitulation, each had become subjects of the crown, as the propagandists of the empire repeatedly averred. Foreigners settling in British dominions "are to be considered in the same light of obedience as natural born subjects," asserted scribe and agriculturist Arthur Young. "The inhabitants [of India]," wrote William Knox, "are British subjects, tho' governed by their own laws, or laws

17. Contemporary estimates of population presented in P. J. Marshall, "Empire and Opportunity in Britain, 1763–1783," Royal Historical Society, *Transactions,* 6th Ser., V (1995), 112, and, for the Ceded Islands, Lawrence Henry Gipson, *The British Empire before the American Revolution,* IX, *The Triumphant Empire: New Responsibilities within the Enlarged Empire, 1763–1766* (New York, 1956), 238, 240, 255–256. On mid-eighteenth-century views of the benefits of populousness, see especially Frederick G. Whelan, "Population and Ideology in the Enlightenment," *History of Political Thought,* XII (1991), 34–72. Also helpful are Edgar S. Furniss, *The Position of the Laborer in a System of Nationalism: A Study in the Labor Theories of the Later English Mercantilists* (Boston, 1920); Klaus E. Knorr, *British Colonial Theories, 1570–1850* (Toronto, 1944), 68–81; James Bonar, *Theories of Population from Raleigh to Arthur Young* (New York, 1966); and Daniel Statt, *Foreigners and Englishmen: The Controversy over Immigration and Population, 1660–1760* (Cranbury, N.J., 1995).

framed by the East India Company." In the aftermath of British incursion on Carib lands in Saint Vincent, John Campbell insisted that the natives were still "intitled to Justice and Humanity, more especially when considered as Subjects of the Crown of Great Britain." To Campbell, the point was important enough to repeat: the Caribs must be "treated with Justice and Lenity, to which as Men, and Subjects of the Crown of Great Britain, they are surely entitled."[18]

In the eighteenth century, the meaning of subjectship retained the quasi-medieval connotations of a personal bond between individual and lord. Subjectship could be natural or acquired, that is, a consequence of birth within the sovereign's domain or of absorption through naturalization or conquest. In either case, subjectship was understood as natural, perpetual, and immutable, a civic analogue of the relation between parent and child. The relationship entailed obligations: the monarch owed the subject pro-

18. [Arthur Young], *Political Essays concerning the Present State of the British Empire; Particularly respecting: I. Natural Advantages and Disadvantages, II. Constitution, III. Agriculture, IV. Manufactures, V. The Colonies, and VI. Commerce* (London, 1772), 36; [William Knox], *The Present State of the Nation: Particularly with respect to Its Trade, Finances, etc. etc. Addressed to the King and Both Houses of Parliament*, 3d ed. (London, 1768), 85; John Campbell, *A Political Survey of Britain: Being a Series of Reflections on the Situation, Lands, Inhabitants, Revenues, Colonies, and Commerce of This Island; Intended to Shew That We Have Not Yet Approached Near the Summit of Improvement, but That It Will Afford Employment to Many Generations before They Push to Their Utmost Extent the Natural Advantages of Great Britain; in Two Volumes* (London, 1774), II, 682n, 684n. Gregory Evans Dowd has argued that British officials found it difficult to think of Native Americans, and other non-Europeans, as subjects of the crown. Dowd, *War under Heaven: Pontiac, the Indian Nations, and the British Empire* (Baltimore, 2002), 174–212. Most of his evidence, though, derives from the records produced by imperial officials residing in the colonies. The view from London seems to have been more varied, since several writers and state officers do seem to have used the language of subjectship to describe the status of the various nations and peoples. These were ideological claims to possession far more than descriptions of the character of British relations with others in this period. The concept of subjectship, moreover, unlike citizenship, does not imply equality. In any case, the point here is that expanded definitions of subjectship were available and current among British observers in the early 1760s, when Maurice Morgann conceived his scheme, although they may not have been typical.

tection, while the subject owed allegiance. The relationship also conveyed membership: although subjects could and did hold different ranks, in theory, each could rightfully claim certain privileges, not the least of which was the right to hold real property and the right to equal consideration under the law.[19] In this respect, the increasingly multiethnic, polyglot empire presented difficult if not unfamiliar questions, specifically, the extent to which the new subjects would affirm their subordination by avowing allegiance to the crown and the extent to which those who pledged their allegiance should enjoy the same rights as natural-born subjects.

British officials responsible for imperial governance looked to encourage trade and generate further revenue for a depleted treasury after the Seven Years' War. At the same time, they aimed to keep British colonists from antagonizing the established residents in the acquired territories. In several instances, in the laws and policies authorized for Quebec, in the investigations into the actions by East India Company officials in Bengal, and in the regulation of trade and settlement in the North American hinterland, ministers attempted to solidify authority over foreign peoples in a way that thwarted the ambitions of speculators fixed to exploit ceded lands.[20] The

19. James H. Kettner, *The Development of American Citizenship, 1608–1870* (Chapel Hill, N.C., 1978), 3–8, 51; P. J. Marshall, "Britain and the World in the Eighteenth Century, IV: The Turning Outwards of Britain," Royal Hist. Soc., *Trans.*, 6th Ser., XI (2001), 3–4.

20. This paragraph and the next build on and extend several of P. J. Marshall's articles: "Empire and Authority in the Later Eighteenth Century," *Jour. Imperial and Commonwealth Hist.*, XV, no. 2 (1987), 105–122; "A Nation Defined by Empire, 1755–1776," in Alexander Grant and Keith J. Stringer, eds., *Uniting the Kingdom? The Making of British History* (London, 1995); "Parliament and Property Rights in the Eighteenth-Century British Empire," in John Brewer and Susan Staves, eds., *Early Modern Conceptions of Property* (London, 1995), 530–544; and "Britain and the World in the Eighteenth Century," Royal Hist. Soc., *Trans.*, 6th Ser., XI (2001), 5–15. See also H. V. Bowen, *Elites, Enterprise, and the Making of the British Overseas Empire, 1688–1775* (London, 1996), 173–193; Eric Jarvis, "His Majesty's Papist Subjects: Roman Catholic Political Rights in British West Florida," *Gulf South Historical Review*, XVI (2000), 6–19; and J. Russell Snapp, "An Enlightened Empire: Scottish and Irish Imperial Reformers in the Age of the American Revolution," *Albion*, XXXIII (2001), 388–403. The problem of managing foreign peoples residing within British dominions, it must be emphasized, predated the Seven Years' War. The ethos of cosmopolitan authoritarianism, with its

Royal Proclamation of 1763 recognized Native American possession of the lands west of the Appalachians and prohibited British settlement there. The Quebec Act dashed the hopes of newly arrived British merchants in the colony who wished to codify a Protestant ascendancy and establish uncontested rule for themselves. The Privy Council obliged British settlers in Grenada to admit French Catholic planters to the council, assembly, and judicature. In part, such measures reflected the ideal of paternalism fundamental to the monarchical ethos. To the new subjects, the stepchildren in the imperial family, the king owed and thereby pledged to provide protection. However, honoring the property of conquered peoples and tolerating institutions and practices alien to British law also represented a politic accommodation to circumstance. In some regions, imposing the British

---

characteristic emphasis on state supervision of overseas enterprise, was extended rather than originated in the 1760s. Elizabeth Mancke, "Another British America: A Canadian Model for the Early Modern British Empire," *Jour. Imperial and Commonwealth Hist.*, XXV, no. 1 (1997), 1–36.

From the sizable historiography on the territories Britain acquired in the Seven Years' War, the following bear particularly on the present discussion. Quebec: Philip Lawson, *The Imperial Challenge: Quebec and Britain in the Age of the American Revolution* (Montreal, 1990), and David Milobar, "Quebec Reform, the British Constitution, and the Atlantic Empire: 1774–1775," *Parliamentary History*, XIV, pt. 1 (1995), 65–88. India: P. J. Marshall, *Bengal: The British Bridgehead: Eastern India, 1740–1828* (Cambridge, 1991); Bowen, "British India, 1765–1813: The Metropolitan Context," in P. J. Marshall, ed., *The Oxford History of the British Empire, II, The Eighteenth Century* (Oxford, 1998), 530–551; and Marshall, "Transactions of the Royal Historical Society Presidential Address: Britain and the World in the Eighteenth Century, III: Britain and India," Royal Hist. Soc., *Trans.*, 6th Ser., X (2000), 1–16. The North American hinterland: Sosin, *Whitehall and the Wilderness;* Peter Marshall, "Colonial Protest and Imperial Retrenchment: Indian Policy, 1764–1768," *Journal of American Studies*, V (1971), 1–17; Richard White, *The Middle Ground: Indians, Empires, and Republics in the Great Lakes Region, 1650–1815* (Cambridge, 1991), 269–365; J. Russell Snapp, *John Stuart and the Struggle for Empire on the Southern Frontier* (Baton Rouge, La., 1996); Eric Hinderaker, *Elusive Empires: Constructing Colonialism in the Ohio Valley, 1673–1800* (Cambridge, 1997), 161–175; and Dowd, *War under Heaven*, 213–224. Grenada: Gipson, *The Triumphant Empire*, 268–272, and Andrew Jackson O'Shaugnessy, *An Empire Divided: The American Revolution and the British Caribbean* (Philadelphia, 2000), 124–126. For an interregional perspective, see Robin F. A. Fabel, *Colonial Challenges: Britons, Native Americans, and Caribs, 1759–1775* (Gainesville, Fla., 2000).

constitution, as a practical matter, was out of the question; this was certainly the case in Bengal and nearly so in Quebec. Elsewhere, the effort and expense required to support effective administration could be elusive, as Whitehall would learn between 1764 and 1768, when a shifting set of administrations half-heartedly attempted imperial regulation of the trans-Appalachian west.

Even more important, permitting British colonists to seize the property and land of existing residents risked inciting armed conflict, as officials in Britain learned the hard way during and after the Seven Years' War. Recurring violence threatened both to invite the interference of European rivals, especially in the Caribbean, and to generate further costs to maintain peace. It made more sense to assuage and incorporate potential enemies living within British dominions. When advisers favoring toleration of Catholicism and a restoration of French civil law argued on behalf of the Quebec Act, for example, they stressed that securing the loyalty of the Canadian majority would both aid the defense of the western frontier and decrease the threat of a French *revanche*. There was nothing new about attempts to pacify and acculturate American Indians. But after 1763, after Pontiac's War, an accommodationist strategy served to answer as well the imperatives resulting from territorial expansion. When John Stuart, His Majesty's superintendent for the southern district, proposed to the Board of Trade in 1764 strict imperial regulation of colonists who traded with Indians, a bureaucracy to ensure enforcement of the new laws, and, in the words of historian J. Russell Snapp, "a color-blind judicial system," he hoped to prevent settlers from fomenting a backcountry war.[21] With Native Ameri-

21. Snapp, *John Stuart and the Struggle for Empire on the Southern Frontier*, 63. In 1769, Alexander Cluny advocated alliances with Indians in West Florida to achieve ends with which Maurice Morgann would have concurred. First, "they would take that labor upon them, which from the difference of climate we are unequal to." Second, voluntary labor would have the salutary effect of liberating Americans from the "Necessity and Danger of importing the untractable Negroes of *Africa,* whose numbers hourly threaten the Safety of our Colonies, as their Expence is an heavy burthen upon their Trade." Third, cultural assimilation and social harmony would follow; the natives "would soon learn our Manners, and incorporating themselves with us, become a part of our own people." [Alexander Cluny], *The American Traveller; or, Observations on the Present State, Culture, and Commerce of the British Colonies in America, and the Further Improvements of Which They Are Capable; with an Account of the Exports, Imports, and*

cans, with Canadians, with French planters in the West Indies, with the peoples of Bengal, with Highlanders, and perhaps, too, with Africans as Maurice Morgann suggested, accommodation, absorption, and metropolitan oversight and regulation seemed the best way to further trade, decrease expenditures, and preserve peace.

To be sure, the British used force, too. The crown honored the property rights only of those who took oaths of allegiance. Those who rejected subjectship faced the prospect of relocation or extermination, as many Native Americans came to learn. When the Caribs of Saint Vincent insisted in 1772 on independence from British authority and prevented settlement of their lands, ministers sent two regiments from North America to compel their submission. But, in contrast to the removal of the Acadians from Nova Scotia in 1755, a vocal but significant minority in Parliament and out-of-doors denounced expropriating the property of the established inhabitants. In 1755, clearing Acadia of "subversives" could be framed as a necessary bulwark against French and Indian aggression in North America. Extirpating the Caribs, by contrast, looked more like an expensive and dishonorable gift to rapacious land-grabbers.[22] The new governor appointed in 1773, Valentine Morris, thought more might be gained from an alliance with the Caribs, and their employment as auxiliaries in colonial forces, than

---

*Returns of Each Colony Respectively, —— and of the Numbers of British Ships and Seamen, Merchants, Traders, and Manufacturers Employed by All Collectively: Together with the Amount of Revenue Arising to Great-Britain Therefrom; in a Series of Letters, Written Originally to the Right Honourable the Earl of ********* by an Old and Experienced Trader* (London, 1769), 112.

22. This assessment of the Carib War draws on Gipson, *The Triumphant Empire,* 260–266; Bernard Marshall, "The Black Caribs: Native Resistance to British Penetration into the Windward Side of St. Vincent, 1763–1773," *Caribbean Quarterly,* XIX, no. 4 (December 1973), 4–19; Michael Craton, *Testing the Chains: Resistance to Slavery in the British West Indies* (Ithaca, N.Y., 1982), 145–153; Peter Hulme, *Colonial Encounters: Europe and the Native Caribbean, 1492–1797* (London, 1986), 242–249; Michael Craton, "Planters, Imperial Policy, and the Black Caribs of St. Vincents," in Craton, *Empire, Enslavement, and Freedom in the Caribbean* (Kingston, Jamaica, 1997), 117–132; and Fabel, *Colonial Challenges,* 156–186, 200–204. For a considered overview of the expulsion of the Acadians, see Naomi E. S. Griffiths, *The Contexts of Acadian History, 1686–1784* (Montreal, 1992), 62–94, and Geoffrey Plank, *An Unsettled Conquest: The British Campaign against the Peoples of Acadia* (Philadelphia, 2001), 140–157.

from antagonizing them through war. On balance, after the Seven Years' War, intermittent protests notwithstanding, Whitehall did not permit British entrepreneurs to enjoy free rein in the new territories. Ministers preferred managed subjugation to naked exploitation, if only to secure the submission of His Majesty's new subjects.

These developments, the addition of new peoples to the empire and the disposition to conceive the relation in terms of allegiance and protection, help make sense of otherwise incongruous moments when writers treating imperial affairs, such as Maurice Morgann, cast slaves as subjects of George III. Absentee slaveholder William Knox presents the most unlikely case. Former provost-marshal of Georgia, briefly London agent for Georgia and East Florida, substantial plantation owner, sometime adviser to the Society for the Propagation of the Gospel, undersecretary of state in the American department from 1770 to 1782 (the same office previously held by Maurice Morgann), Knox emerged during the first years of the British antislavery movement of the late 1780s and early 1790s as a stalwart defender of the slave trade.[23] Yet, if Knox thought slavery necessary to empire, he could not approve, in 1768, cruel treatment of "so vast a multitude of his [majesty's] own subjects." In his view, British colonists' property right in slaves was local, not absolute, because the colonial assemblies granting the right themselves were subordinate to the "supreme magistrate" of king-in-council. Slaveholders may have a legal claim to a slave's service, but, as British subjects, as with apprentices in England, slaves had a claim to "an impartial dispensation of the laws." In this argument, Knox was as interested in asserting the principle of imperial sovereignty, specifically the authority of Parliament to legislate for the colonies, as ensuring humane treatment of the enslaved. He recommended similar programs of intervention to supervise relations with Indians in North America and Catholics in Ireland and Quebec. What matters here is the off-handed, casual way with which Knox identified slaves as subjects and, in this designation, allowed a right to

---

23. Leland J. Bellot, *William Knox: The Life and Thought of an Eighteenth-Century Imperialist* (Austin, Tex., 1977). For Knox's support of the slave trade, see Great Britain, Royal Commission on Historical Manuscripts, *Report on Manuscripts in Various Collections*, VI, *The Manuscripts of Miss M. Eyre Matcham; Captain H. V. Knox; Cornwallis Wykeham-Martin, Esq., etc.* (Dublin, 1909), 202, 203, 222, 291–292, and [Knox], *A Letter from W. K., Esq. to W. Wilberforce, Esq.* (London, 1790).

protection from the crown. "It is most reproachful to this country," he declared, "that there are more than five hundred thousand of its subjects, for whom the legislature has never shewn the least regard." He hoped ministers would examine the slave codes and require the colonies to report on measures taken to ensure the slaves' "legal rights."[24]

Few adopted William Knox's notion of slaves as subjects, it should be emphasized. In this period, Britons rarely paused to reflect on the civil status of enslaved Africans or to consider slaves as any more than the property of British colonists.[25] Yet, when Maurice Morgann proposed enlisting liberated Africans in imperial expansion, or when, several years later, James Ramsay characterized slaves as industrious, "valuable sub-

24. [William Knox], *Three Tracts respecting the Conversion and Instruction of the Free Indians and Negro Slaves in the Colonies, Addressed to the Venerable Society for the Propagation of the Gospel in Foreign Parts* [London, 1768], 27, 32, 33. Leland J. Bellot provides the most extensive overview of Knox's attitudes toward slavery and race but, regarding slavery, fails to recognize the conflicted character of Knox's thought and overlooks the subminister's concern to impose imperial oversight. See Bellot, "Evangelicals and the Defense of Slavery in Britain's Old Colonial Empire," *Journal of Southern History,* XXXVII (1971), 19–40. A brief but more penetrating assessment of Knox and his views on slavery appears in David Waldstreicher, *Runaway America: Benjamin Franklin, Slavery, and the American Revolution* (New York, 2004), 186–192. For Knox's views on problems of empire, more generally, see Snapp, "An Enlightened Empire," *Albion,* XXXIII (2001), 390–395.

25. "Under the English slave system in the West Indies," Elsa V. Goveia concluded, "the slave was not regarded as a subject, but rather as property; and when the English humanitarians attempted to take the view that he was a subject, they were advocating a theoretical and practical innovation which only slowly gained acceptance in the controversies over amelioration and emancipation." Goveia, *The West Indian Slave Laws of the Eighteenth Century* (Barbados, 1970), 20–21. During his crusade against slaveholding in England, Sharp insisted that slaves brought to the British Isles became subjects of the crown and, hence, "absolutely secure in his or her personal liberty." In an extended footnote buried in his first antislavery tract, he added, "Every inhabitant of the British colonies, black as well as white, bond as well as free, are undoubtedly *the King's subjects,* during their residence within the limits of the *King's dominions,* and as such, are entitled to personal protection, howsoever bound in service to their respective masters." Granville Sharp, *A Representation of the Injustice and Dangerous Tendency of Tolerating Slavery, or of Admitting the Least Claim of Private Property in the Persons of Men, in England . . .* (London, 1769), 72n.

jects" deserving succor and patronage, or in 1775, when Lord Dunmore promised freedom to Virginia slaves willing to assist the crown suppress an incipient colonial rebellion, they each drew on concepts of inclusion, allegiance, and protection that were strengthened, if not generated, by the accession of hundreds of thousands of aliens to the British Empire.[26] It may be that the idea of slaves as subjects could only have suggested itself when, more generally, as a consequence of the Seven Years' War, the governance and incorporation of strangers had become, inescapably, the subject of extensive discussion.

[II]   As it happens, *Plan for the Abolition of Slavery in the West Indies* was the first of several British emancipation schemes circulated in the 1770s. In 1776, Granville Sharp publicized what he called the "Spanish Regulations," the colonial custom of *coartación*, which enabled and encouraged Spanish Caribbean slaves to purchase their freedom in installments.[27] In 1778, a Newcastle essayist appended a similar proposal to a pamphlet assaying prospects for retaining the North American empire. That same year, after a decade of frustrated struggles with the Leeward Islands elite, the Reverend James Ramsay from the island of Saint Christopher submitted to the bishop of London and the archbishop of Canterbury a memorial outlining "a plan for the education and gradual emancipation of slaves in the West Indies." In 1780, Edmund Burke composed a seventy-

26. James Ramsay, *An Essay on the Treatment and Conversion of African Slaves in the British Sugar Colonies* (London, 1784), 113–114. For Dunmore, see Benjamin Quarles, *The Negro in the American Revolution* (Chapel Hill, N.C., 1961), 19–32, and Sylvia R. Frey, *Water from the Rock: Black Resistance in a Revolutionary Age* (Princeton, N.J., 1991), 76–77.

27. On *coartación*, see H. S. Aimes, "Coartacion: A Spanish Institution for the Advancement of Slaves into Freedmen," *Yale Review*, XVII (1909), 412–431; Herbert S. Klein, *African Slavery in Latin America and the Caribbean* (Oxford, 1986), 194–195; and Alan Watson, *Slave Law in the Americas* (Athens, Ga., 1989), 50–57. Sharp advocates the "Spanish Regulations" several times in private correspondence between 1772 and 1781. He endorses them in print in *The Just Limitations of Slavery in the Laws of God, Compared with the Unbounded Claims of the African Traders and British American Slaveholders; with a Copious Appendix: Containing, an Answer to Rev. Mr. Thompson's Tract in Favor of the African Slave Trade . . . A Proposal on the Same Principle for the Gradual Enfranchisement of Slaves in America . . .* (London, 1776), 54–55.

two-point "Negro Code" that provided for metropolitan oversight and administration of the British slave trade and slavery in the American colonies. Less than a year later, with Granville Sharp's encouragement, John Hinchliffe, bishop of Peterborough, drafted a bill based on the "Spanish Regulations" that would "soften and gradually reduce the Slavery in the West Indies."[28]

These proposals have escaped scholarly notice.[29] Roughly drawn and often inadequate to their professed ends, they scarcely attracted attention in their own day. In several instances, the authors withheld the texts from publication or, like Morgann, released them many years after the initial composition, in some cases anonymously. James Ramsay began work on

28. *Essays, Commercial and Political, on the Real and Relative Interests of Imperial and Dependent States, Particularly Those of Great Britain, and Their Dependencies; Displaying the Probable Causes of, and a Mode of Compromising the Present Disputes between This Country and Her American Colonies; to Which Is Added an Appendix, on the Means of Emancipating Slaves without Loss to Their Proprietors* (Newcastle, Eng., 1777); "Memorial Suggesting Motives for the Improvement of the Sugar Colonies Particularly of the Slaves Employed in Their Culture, and Offering Reasons for Encouraging the Advancement of These Last in Social Life and Their Conversion to Christianity; Extracted from a Manuscript Composed on That Subject by James Ramsay, Minister in the Island of St. Christopher, and Author of a Plan of Reunion between Great Britain and Her Colonies published by Murray No 32. Fleet Street," cataloged as: "Memorial on the Conversion of Slaves in the Sugar Colonies by James Ramsay," Fulham Papers, XX, fol. 80, Lambeth Palace Library (for the copy addressed to the bishop of London, see Society for the Propagation of the Gospel Papers, XVII, fols. 221–223, Lambeth Palace Library); Edmund Burke, "Sketch of a Negro Code," in Paul Langford, ed., *The Writings and Speeches of Edmund Burke* (Oxford, 1981–), III, 562–581. Evidence concerning Hinchliffe's scheme is preserved in Granville Sharp's diaries, although the document itself appears not to survive. See Diary G (Feb. 7, Mar. 12, 19, Apr. 7, 1781), fols. 106, 108, 110, Granville Sharp Papers, D3549 13/4/2, Gloucestershire Record Office (GRO).

29. Although see the comments interspersed through Eve W. Stoddard, "A Serious Proposal for Slavery Reform: Sarah Scott's *Sir George Ellison*," *Eighteenth-Century Studies*, XXVIII (1995), 379–396. Remarkably, the weighty corpus of Burke historiography has ignored his "Negro Code" almost entirely. Robert W. Smith provides an extended but ultimately inconclusive background in "Edmund Burke's Negro Code," *History Today*, XXXVI (1976), 715–723. See also James Coniff, "Burke on Political Economy: The Nature and Extent of State Authority," *Review of Politics*, XLIX (1987), 507–511.

his manuscript in 1768, completed an initial draft in 1771, extended it
further by 1776, then abandoned the text for several years before publishing
a substantially revised version in 1784 as *An Essay on the Treatment and
Conversion of African Slaves in the British Sugar Colonies*.[30] Edmund
Burke kept the "Negro Code" to himself for more than a decade before
sharing it with Home Secretary Henry Dundas in 1792. John Hinchliffe
refrained from distributing his emancipation scheme for nearly eight years;
only the establishment of the Society for Effecting the Abolition of the Slave
Trade gave him the courage to bring it forward for wider scrutiny.[31] Those
proposals that were published failed, almost entirely, to influence public
debate. The leading literary journals thought Sharp's *Just Limitations of
Slavery in the Laws of God* unworthy of review. Few seem to have noticed
the Newcastle author's suggestions for reform.[32] Similarly, no one took
seriously Maurice Morgann's Pensacola project. Shelburne, his patron,
seems to have ignored it, as did the imperial administrators who recommended recruiting German and Swiss colonists from Louisiana and Protestants from France, but not liberated Africans, to settle West Florida.[33] The
plan fared scarcely better with the public when published in 1772. Even
Granville Sharp seems to have found only the warnings against future slave

30. The significance of Ramsay's revisions to his original text is discussed in the
following section of this chapter.

31. Edmund Burke to Henry Dundas, Apr. 9, 1792, in *The Works of the Right
Honourable Edmund Burke,* 8 vols. (London, 1792–1827), V, 197; Fair Minute Books of
the Committee for Effecting the Abolition of the Slave Trade (Feb. 12, 1788), I, 37–38,
British Library, Add. MSS 21254.

32. The principal literary journals, the *Monthly Review* and the *Critical Review,*
elected not to comment on Sharp's tract. In surveying writing on slavery during the
Revolution and in the decade after, I have yet to encounter reference to or commentary
on the Newcastle pamphlet.

33. There is no reference to Morgann's plan in the several reports completed by the
Board of Trade on the territories acquired in 1763. On subsequent proposals for West
Florida colonization, see Cecil Johnson, *British West Florida, 1763–1783* (New Haven,
Conn., 1943), 31–33; J. Barton Starr, "Campbell Town: French Huguenots in British
West Florida," *Florida Historical Quarterly,* LIV (1976), 532–547; Bailyn, *Voyagers to the
West,* 478–479; Jarvis, "His Majesty's Papist Subjects," *Gulf So. Hist. Rev.,* XVI (2000),
13; and Gabriel B. Paquette, "The Image of Imperial Spain in British Political Thought,
1750–1800," *Bulletin of Spanish Studies,* LXXXI (2004), 206–213.

insurrections worthy of comment.[34] The *Monthly Review,* typically sympathetic to antislavery sentiment, characterized the pamphlet as "visionary and romantic" and noted the author's advocacy of mongrelized American settlements with thinly masked bemusement.[35]

In the study of ideas and ideologies, though, the value of marginal texts lies in their capacity to elucidate broader patterns in thought and argument, and sometimes less with their immediate influence or affect on contemporaries. The emancipation schemes circulated in the 1770s, taken together, mark a transitional moment, a qualitative shift, a conceptual leap in British antislavery thought. The authors went beyond condemnations of slavery. They offered alternatives. They envisioned what had been unthinkable: an empire without slaves, worked by free black men and women vested with certain limited rights and liberties traditionally enjoyed by British subjects. The Georgia trustees' prohibition of slavery provided a precedent of sorts. But the reformers of the 1770s hoped to go further, looking less to prevent the expansion of slavery than to end human bondage where it existed. In retrospect, the British emancipation schemes of the Revolutionary era matter most, in fact, *because* of their limited influence. Students of British antislavery sometimes have written as if the movement's focus on slave trade abolition was foreordained, as if an unbroken line could be traced from Anthony Benezet's early publications condemning the slave trade in the 1760s to the formation of the Society for Effecting the Abolition of the Slave Trade in 1787. The evolution of abolitionism in Britain, however, was neither linear nor destined to assume a particular direction. The initial concern of the first antislavery activists, these emancipation schemes make clear, was colonial slaveholding itself, far more than the Atlantic slave trade. They bring to light, when taken together, a forgotten moment in early Anglo-American abolitionism, a period when a small but well-placed few devised schemes for comprehensive reform that, in breadth and reach,

34. In republishing a brief extract from Morgann's tract, Sharp selected only those passages alluding to the threat of slave revolts. Granville Sharp, *An Essay on Slavery, Proving from Scripture Its Inconsistency with Humanity and Religion* (London, 1773), 62–64. This was the focus as well of a review printed in the *Gentleman's Magazine* in July 1772. James G. Basker, " 'The Next Insurrection': Johnson, Race, and Rebellion," *The Age of Johnson: A Scholarly Annual,* XI (2000), 43.

35. *Monthly Review,* XLVI (1772), 535.

would not be equaled again until after the French Revolution and the Napoleonic Wars.

Why did several writers in these years promote emancipation when no one in Britain had thought to do so before? Each possessed an acute hostility to slavery, of course, and they wrote at a time when intellectuals elsewhere in Europe and the Americas also entertained the idea of fundamental reform to colonial slavery. In 1765, two years after Maurice Morgann composed his sketch for a free colony in Pensacola, the French political economist Abbé Baudeau suggested sending liberated Africans to till the vast tracts of land west of the Mississippi. Several years earlier, in 1758, a Lisbon-born lawyer and priest residing in Bahia, Manuel Ribeiro Rocha, advocated abolishing slavery in Brazil in favor of indentured labor. "Antislavetrader," writing in the *Pennsylvania Gazette* in 1768, called for a petition to George III "to grant some of the ceded islands to the southward, for a Negro Colony" so that the next generation of blacks could be "sent thither at a suitable age at the expense of the government." Pennsylvania Quaker Anthony Benezet in 1771 recommended abolition of the British slave trade, a limited time of servitude for those already held in slavery, oversight of freed slaves by county supervisors, substitution of white indentured servants for slaves, and the establishment of a free colony for blacks west of the Appalachians. More generally, the burgeoning revolution against imperial rule in North America occasioned a variety of proposals for a comprehensive emancipation.[36]

36. Davis, *The Problem of Slavery in Western Culture*, 429–430; Celia M. Azevedo, "Rocha's *The Ethiopian Redeemed* and the Circulation of Anti-Slavery Ideas," *Slavery and Abolition*, XXIV, no. 1 (April 2003), 101–126; Darold D. Wax, "Reform and Revolution: The Movement against Slavery and the Slave Trade in Revolutionary Pennsylvania," *Western Pennsylvania Historical Magazine*, LVII (1974), 410; Anthony Benezet, *Some Historical Account of Guinea, Its Situation, Produce, and the General Disposition of Its Inhabitants with an Inquiry into the Rise and Progress of the Slave-Trade, Its Nature and Lamentable Effects* . . . (Philadelphia, 1771), 139–141; Jacob Green, *A Sermon Delivered at Hanover (in New-Jersey), April 22, 1778, Being the Day of Public Fasting and Praying throughout the United States of America* (Chatham, 1779); John Saillant, ed., " 'Some Thoughts on the Subject of Freeing the Negro Slaves in the Colony of Connecticut, Humbly Offered to the Consideration of All Friends to Liberty and Justice,' by Levi Hart; with a Response from Samuel Hopkins," *New England Quarterly*, LXXV (2002), 107–128.

Yet, on balance, these contemporaneous initiatives, which sometimes received limited circulation even in their original languages, appear not to have informed British writings.[37] Instead, the British emancipation schemes reflected, in part, the broader tendency among European thinkers to apply in theory the lessons drawn from the emerging science of human society. The would-be emancipators chose to exploit, and their schemes indicate an unqualified faith in the validity of, cultural assumptions prevailing among many of the late-eighteenth-century intelligentsia. British reformers assumed that individuals worked more productively if moved by incentive rather than force. They held sacred the right to self-possession. And they had an unshakable confidence in the human capacity for moral development. In important respects, these writers aimed to bring colonial practice in line with what they thought to be universal truths about humanity and the good society. So, to a degree, the late-eighteenth-century idea of emancipation reflected an "enlightened" interest in guiding American plantation societies into conformity with "civilized" norms.[38] Yet if the idea of an empire worked by free labor was informed by an optimistic ambition to

37. The Newcastle essayist, however, did build explicitly on New Jersey Quaker William Dillwyn's *Brief Considerations on Slavery and the Expediency of Its Abolition; with Some Hints on the Means Whereby It May Be Gradually Effected; Recommended to the Serious Attention of All, and Especially of Those Entrusted with the Powers of Legislation* (Burlington, N.J., 1773). See *Essays, Commercial and Political*, 130–135. Of the writers under consideration here, only Granville Sharp seems to have possessed extensive familiarity with the antislavery publications printed in the North American colonies on the eve of the War of Independence. The works of these British projectors reflected and participated in the broader intensification of antislavery sentiment and circulation of antislavery literature after midcentury but, as strategies for substantive change, presented a departure from earlier work. The slavery reforms proposed by Abbé Raynal and his colleagues in *Histoire philosophique et politique des établissemens et du commerce des Européens dans les deux Indes* (Amsterdam, 1770) seem not to have influenced these schemes. The English historian William Russell appropriated several of Raynal's passages on slavery for his own *History of America* but advocated only an amelioration of slavery, adding tentatively that he looked forward to colonies "gradually conferring liberty on the negroes." Russell, *The History of America*, I, 579–583, citation on 583.

38. Davis, *The Problem of Slavery in Western Culture*, 400–438; Steven Mintz, "Models of Emancipation during the Age of Revolution," *Slavery and Abolition*, XVII, no. 2 (August 1996), 1–21.

make the world anew, emancipationism in Britain also took shape under the tangible pressures of a specific juncture in imperial history. Like Maurice Morgann, those who would reform slavery had in view the ways emancipation could sustain, and even advance, colonial enterprise. Rather than abstract and vague expressions of principle or fantastic projections of future change, the schemes, on the whole, exhibited concrete, if ultimately unworkable, attempts to restore accord and security within the empire at a moment of threatened dissolution, an agenda most evident when the sum effect of shared principles comes into view.

Begin with the proposed work regimes. British emancipationists accepted the need to sustain the productivity of colonial plantations. However, they questioned the labor model upon which those economies relied. Domestic experience, successful practices in the British Isles, seemed to establish axiomatic truths about human psychology applicable to workers in every society, truths enshrined in Adam Smith's influential passage on the advantages of wage labor in book 3 of *The Wealth of Nations*. James Ramsay urged slaveholders to consider "the state of workers in free countries," who, he asserted, execute "in the same time, thrice the labour of slaves." Consider, too, the work slaves and free laborers actually performed, the Newcastle essayist observed: "Men conscious of being free, will, even for moderate wages, engage themselves in labour that appear the most intolerable to slaves." That colonial experience failed to verify such propositions worried these reformers not at all. Planters may require African labor, Morgann and others agreed, but they did not require slave labor. How, then, to effect a transfer from slavery to liberty without infringing the property rights of slaveholders? Permit slaves to purchase their freedom from their owners by allowing wages for work completed during, as the Newcastle pamphleteer put it, "leisure hours." Schemes for self-purchase, as established by customs like the "Spanish Regulations," "give such encouragement to industry," enthused Granville Sharp, "that even the most indolent are tempted to exert themselves."[39] In this arrangement, slaves

39. Ramsay, "Memorial Suggesting Motives for the Improvement of the Sugar Colonies," fol. 79; *Essays, Commercial and Political*, 137, 143; Sharp, *The Just Limitation of Slavery in the Laws of God*, 55. As Seymour Drescher has stressed, the idea that free labor was cheaper and more productive than slave labor predated publication of *The Wealth of Nations*. Drescher, *Capitalism and Antislavery*, 133. For instructive overviews

gradually would acquire freedom, plantations would retain their workforce, and slaveholders would take a dual return on their investment—receiving both labor and a refund on the price paid for the freed slave. In effect, in exchange for liberty, slaves would bear the cost of their initial purchase and, presumably, perform the same work with greater efficiency. The emancipators did not intend simply to set slaves free. Instead, they would have the manumitted labor as before, but to draw wages rather than at the instigation of the whip.

To this end, emancipationists sought to protect slaves' earnings and ensure to them control over its use.[40] Burke's code, for example, would allow the enslaved to bequeath property to descendants and prohibit its seizure or appropriation by slaveholders. Such provisions would initiate, even where bondage remained, transfer of proprietorship away from the slaveholder and toward the self. In this transition to self-possession, the reformers considered fundamental an inviolable right to family relations. The Newcastle essayist would require slaveholders to sell enslaved children to their free parents who presented sufficient funds. Burke's code contained several provisions designed to recognize, encourage, and protect slave marriages. Similarly, the various proposals would vest slaves with claims to land. Granville Sharp would have "spare" lands divided into *"compact little Farms"* and slaves settled as peasants. In Burke's regime, married slaves resident on a plantation for more than twelve months could not be sold away.[41] In addition, then, to a right of self-purchase, the projectors would

---

on the pre-Smithian discussions of the role of incentive in promoting industriousness, see A. W. Bob Coats, "Changing Attitudes to Labour in the Mid-Eighteenth Century," in Coats, *British and American Economic Essays,* I, *On the History of Economic Thought* (London, 1992), 63–84, and Donna T. Andrew, *Philanthropy and Police: London Charity in the Eighteenth Century* (Princeton, N.J., 1989), 136–146.

40. In nearly every instance, metropolitan commentators appear to have assumed, perhaps understandably, that slaves in British America always lacked claims to property. Generally, British antislavery writers knew nothing of the variety of labor systems embraced by the institution of slavery. Specifically, they were unaware of the prevalence of task-labor in the North American lowcountry. Nor were they aware of the existence or character of the internal economies in slave societies in British America or elsewhere. For an introduction to these topics, see Philip D. Morgan, *Slave Counterpoint: Black Culture in the Eighteenth-Century Chesapeake and Lowcountry* (Chapel Hill, N.C., 1998).

41. Burke, "Sketch of a Negro Code," in Langford, ed., *The Writings and Speeches of*

establish for slaves a prior right to property and family, in effect, delineating a civil and domestic sphere for the enslaved upon which slaveholders could not intrude. If the emancipation schemes resisted ceding the enslaved full autonomy, they chipped away at the custom of slaves as alienable chattel. Masters would retain, for a time, rights to their human property, but not unlimited discretion to dispose of that property as they saw fit.

For the enslaved, compliance with prescribed cultural norms would be the price of the ticket to self-possession. If slaves were to be freed, the emancipators insisted, they would have to adopt British mores. Reform schemes espoused slave marriages, for example, less to honor slaves' desires than to foster civility. Admission to society required hewing to the patriarchal ethos. Because, in Burke's words, the "state of matrimony and the Government of family" best formed "men to a fitness for freedom, and to become good Citizens," he made marriage a precondition of liberty. Indeed, in his plan, slaveholders would provide "a Woman" to enslaved men over the age of twenty-one on the "requisition" of crown-appointed colonial officials. Those male slaves "fitted" for "the Offices of Freemen" would have reached thirty years, fathered no fewer than three children "born to him in lawful Matrimony," and earned a certificate from a parish minister attesting to "regularity in the duties of Religion, and of . . . orderly and good behavior." James Ramsay also positioned proper morals and manners as the bridge to liberty. To Ramsay, absolute dependence in slavery left the unfree worse than savages: "A savage in all his efforts, acts for himself, and the advancement of his proper concerns; but a slave is the bare appendage of a man, he has nothing to call his own." To free slaves without moral instruction, he reasoned, would leave them without the facility for self-advancement, which, to Ramsay's way of thinking, entailed fidelity to "the good of the community." To instill the values of social responsibility, Ramsay would have slaves judge each other's conduct "in the manner of juries."[42] In this way, slaves would grasp the importance of normative behavior and thereby acquire a stake in preserving the social order.

Edmund Burke, III, 577–579; John A. Woods, ed., "The Correspondence of Benjamin Rush and Granville Sharp, 1773–1809," *JAS,* I (1967), 15.

42. Burke, "Sketch of a Negro Code," in Langford, ed., *The Writings and Speeches of Edmund Burke,* III, 577, 578, 580; Ramsay, "Memorial Suggesting Motives for the Improvement of the Sugar Colonies," fol. 79.

A persisting concern for stability, commerce, and civic harmony, then, figured prominently in these schemes. The emancipationists envisioned an ordered and orderly transition to freedom, a transition that, they optimistically presumed, would bring extensive benefits at negligible costs. Replacing slave labor with free labor would increase wealth because slave labor was inefficient. It would bring, they contended, an explosive growth in colonial consumption, as freedmen able to earn and acquire would purchase British manufactures in greater quantities. Best of all, slave labor would transform mutual contempt and violence among black and white in British America into a perpetual, fraternal peace. "To the public," Ramsay aphorized, "the difference between the slave and the citizen is immense, the one being the strength, the other being the weakness of the state." "Should we continue to keep nearly the whole race as slaves, and not encourage and assist them to liberate themselves," the Newcastle essayist warned, "the epocha of their universal freedom, and ruin of their present masters, may be at no very distant period." How foolish was this, when emancipation, properly administered, could serve *"state policy"*? In a scheme that expedited self-redemption, Africans *"must either be looked on as an accession of so many subjects, or as the means of such a national acquisition of property as they have paid for their emancipation."*[43] For the first time, the argument from necessity was being turned on its head. Understood correctly, the gradual extension of liberty held the best prospects for preserving imperial wealth and power. "Police and public utility," Ramsay professed, "join their voices with religion and humanity."[44] The interests of slaves are the interests of masters. The interests of both are the interests of empire.

This notion, implausible and to most contemporaries demonstrably false, issued from a variety of sources, not from a coherent movement. Although they shared certain assumptions, the schemes reveal a hodgepodge of priorities and expectations. Some advocated immediate liberation. Oth-

43. Ramsay, "Memorial for Suggesting Motives for the Improvement of the Sugar Colonies," fol. 80; *Essays, Commercial and Political,* 143–144, 147.

44. Ramsay, "Memorial for Suggesting Motives for the Improvement of the Sugar Colonies," fol. 79. In a similar vein, Maurice Morgann had written: "This world is not, in truth, so imperfectly constituted, as that men are ever tempted, by real interest, to deviate from the principles of humanity and justice." [Morgann], *Plan for the Abolition of Slavery in the West Indies,* 10.

ers favored gradual emancipation over several generations. In a few instances, the schemes would have coerced planters into carrying out reforms. In others, the schemes depended on slaveholders' cooperation. With the exception of Burke's code, they betrayed a pronounced lack of system. Measures designed to reduce dependence on slavery most typically failed to arrange for reducing or eliminating the slave trade, for example. Indeed, Morgann, Burke, and the Newcastle pamphleteer seemed to assume that the slave trade would continue. Moreover, these first emancipation proposals were not the work of a particular party, interest, or network. The authors held disparate allegiances. The group included the chief propagandist for the Rockingham Whigs (Burke), a prelate sympathetic to American resistance (Hinchliffe), a clerk at the Board of Ordnance who fraternized with disaffected London radicals (Sharp), a provincial political economist (the Newcastle essayist), an undersecretary in the Chatham administration (Morgann), and a Scottish slaveholder residing in the island of Saint Christopher who would serve in the Caribbean as a spy for the British navy during the American war (Ramsay). They were largely unknown to one another and, evidently, drafted their schemes independently.[45] However, they shared—by virtue of experience, employment, or disposition— an active engagement with imperial questions.[46] The first proponents of

45. Granville Sharp, however, was responsible for informing John Hinchliffe of the "Spanish Regulations."

46. The contributions of Edmund Burke to the debate on America may be traced in Langford, ed., *The Writings and Speeches of Edmund Burke,* III. For Granville Sharp, see Colin Bonwick, *English Radicals and the American Revolution* (Chapel Hill, N.C., 1977); Robert E. Toohey, *Liberty and Empire: British Radical Solutions to the American Problem, 1774–1776* (Lexington, Ky., 1978), 36–52; and the previous chapter in this volume. I have discussed Morgann above; Ramsay's obsession with the revolution in North America figures in the pages that follow. Erstwhile Massachusetts governor Thomas Hutchinson referred to John Hinchliffe as "the only Bishop who has interested himself in American affairs." Hutchinson cited in Paul Langford, "The English Clergy and the American Revolution," in Eckhart Hellmuth, ed., *The Transformation of Political Culture: England and Germany in the Late Eighteenth Century* (Oxford, 1990), 276n6. J. Russell Snapp has drawn attention to the provincial origins of the most ardent promoters of imperial reform in the era after the Seven Years' War. See Snapp, "An Enlightened Empire," *Albion,* XXXIII (2001), 389–390. Only two of the six writers under consideration here were Englishmen, and those Englishmen, comparatively, showed rather less

emancipation not only factored imperial interests into their proposals; they were themselves active in debating and rethinking colonial governance and administration.

The British not only thought more about their North American colonies during the Revolutionary era. They thought about those colonies differently. Writing about the colonies addressed a range of subjects before 1760: religion, theology, and church government; the experience of migration; the ends and means of commercial policy; the consequence of encounters with native peoples; the outcome of explorations in geography and science; the experience of travel and adventure.[47] These topics retained their importance. But after 1760, they were supplemented by now urgent, if long-standing questions regarding the standing of colonies and colonists within the empire, the structure of political authority, and the techniques by which colonies should be defended, financed, administered, and governed. Who should pay for empire and how? Did colonists reside within or outside the realm? What limits, if any, were there to the sovereignty of king-in-parliament in British America? Such questions prompted even more general public musing on the advantages and disadvantages of encouraging overseas settlement. Why have colonies? What purpose did they serve, in theory and in practice? Did faltering authority over North America recommend, more generally, new techniques of control elsewhere in the empire? These questions, powerfully raised by the expansion of the empire after 1763, acquired a growing importance in the late 1760s and 1770s.

---

enthusiasm for antislavery proposals that made explicit the importance of state intervention in colonial affairs. Nonetheless, the sample from which this discussion is drawn is far too small to offer even tentative conclusions about the link between provincial origins and a commitment to antislavery reform. This is just one of many questions that would benefit from further research.

47. R. C. Simmons, ed., *British Imprints relating to North America, 1621–1760: An Annotated Checklist* (London, 1996), xiii–xx. As Bob Harris has emphasized, attention to empire through the Seven Years' War tended to concentrate on the rivalry with France. The focus seems to have shifted to affairs in North America in the years that followed, at least until France entered the War of American Independence in 1778. Harris, "War, Empire, and the 'National Interest' in Mid-Eighteenth-Century Britain," in Julie Flavell and Stephen Conway, eds., *Britain and America Go to War: The Impact of War and Warfare in Anglo-America, 1754–1815* (Gainesville, Fla., 2004), 13–40.

They generated an extensive literature that revealed considerable diversity of opinion.[48]

Colonial slavery and the Atlantic slave trade remained far less vulnerable while agreement prevailed on the means and ends of empire, as long as custom validated established practice. While priorities remained fixed, few opportunities arose to rethink the relation between empire and slavery. But the American controversy put the imperial project to question and inspired a variety of creative and sometimes comprehensive plans to rework its structure. Exponents of parliamentary supremacy entertained the possibility of admitting American representatives to Westminster, for example. Political economist Josiah Tucker, who articulated the first doubts about the merits and necessity of possessing American provinces, suggested that Britain declare independence from the thirteen colonies. The radical political theorist John Cartwright proposed a "Grand British League and Confederacy" of self-governing states.[49] With regard to theorizing about empire, it was a time of experimentation. To an unusual degree, in this period, the British chose to examine received premises about overseas dominion, about its peoples, and about their relationship to each. The years of crisis opened a space for the reconsideration of imperial policy. And in this space those who intensely disliked slavery had an unforeseen opportunity not only to express antislavery sentiment but to develop novel alternatives.

[III]   If the emancipation schemes of the 1770s, as an intellectual exercise, presented a sharp break from customary ways of conceiving the relation between slavery and empire, as potential policy initiatives they raised provocative questions regarding the exercise of power. Reducing the

48. On this literature, see Thomas R. Adams, *The American Controversy: A Bibliographical Study of the British Pamphlets about the American Disputes, 1764–1783*, 2 vols. (Providence, R.I., 1980), and Martin Kallich, ed., *British Poetry and the American Revolution: A Bibliographical Survey of Books and Pamphlets, Journals and Magazines, Newspapers, and Prints, 1755–1800*, 2 vols. (Troy, N.Y., 1988). These questions and debates are placed in their broadest context in Bowen, "British Conceptions of Global Empire," *Jour. Imperial and Commonwealth Hist.*, XXVI, no. 3 (1998), 5–27.

49. J. G. A. Pocock, "Josiah Tucker on Burke, Locke, and Price: A Study in the Varieties of Eighteenth-Century Conservatism," in Pocock, *Virtue, Commerce, and History: Essays on Political Thought and History, Chiefly in the Eighteenth Century* (Cambridge, 1985), 157–191; Toohey, *Liberty and Empire*, 36–52, citation on 47.

power masters held over slaves required, in some way, reducing the power slaveholders possessed in the governance of colonial societies. It was one thing for British projectors to propose alternatives to slavery but something else to impose such alternatives on colonial slaveholders. The first anti-slavery crusaders regarded the challenge of reorienting imperial policy as nearly insurmountable, it is true. Yet the more fundamental problem was constitutional, not political. Even if emancipationists could generate momentum for slavery reform, did the crown or Parliament have the standing and resources to make such measures enforceable law? To frame the question in more general terms, who, if anyone, possessed the requisite authority to abolish slavery, and how, as a practical matter, could the proper authorities implement and sustain substantive change to colonial practices?

In the eighteenth-century British Empire, there was no precedent for imperial management of colonial slavery and no infrastructure to give such a design administrative life. Indeed, metropolitan officials capable, in theory, of shaping slavery in British territories had chosen, in effect, to ignore human bondage in the British colonies. From the first years of colonization forward, legal historian Jonathan Bush has stressed, neither the Privy Council, Parliament, nor the common law courts at Westminster attempted to write slave laws for the colonies or revise the codes enacted by colonial assemblies. This neglect followed from the broader custom of conceding to British settlers extensive autonomy in governing their internal affairs.[50] The Privy Council did negate prohibitive duties on slave imports and instruct royal governors to secure legislation protecting slaves from murder and "inhumane" severities.[51] Yet, in practice, imperial sovereignty

50. Jonathan A. Bush, "Free to Enslave: The Foundations of Colonial American Slave Law," *Yale Journal of Law and the Humanities*, V (1993), 417–470; Jack P. Greene, *Peripheries and Center: Constitutional Development in the Extended Polities of the British Empire and the United States of America, 1607–1788* (Athens, Ga., 1986), 1–76; Greene, "Negotiated Authorities: The Problem of Governance in the Extended Polities of the Early Modern Atlantic World," in Greene, *Negotiated Authorities: Essays in Colonial Political and Constitutional History* (Charlottesville, Va., 1994), 1–24; Greene, "Transatlantic Colonization and the Redefinition of Empire in the Early Modern Era: The British-American Experience," in Christine Daniels and Michael V. Kennedy, eds., *Negotiated Empires: Centers and Peripheries in the Americas, 1500–1820* (New York, 2002), 269–282.

51. W. E. B. Dubois, *The Suppression of the African Slave Trade to the United States of*

proved less decisive than the consistency with which British ministers honored colonial legislation that provided for property in and the governance of slaves. Metropolitan officials proceeded as if the local custom of slavery established a private right upon which they would not intrude. And this tradition of near purposeful neglect instilled an unspoken belief among American slaveholders that imperial administrators *could not* interfere in the possession and management of slaves in the British colonies. Paradoxically, then, colonial slavery, with the almost feudal autonomy it granted British settlers, resided *sub silentio*. It lay outside imperial oversight, while still, in principle, in the realm of imperial authority.

In important respects, this situation was unique among European states with colonies in the Americas. Roman civil law provided an analytic and theoretic framework for slavery in the Spanish Empire, the Code Noir instituted by royal edict for the French colonies in 1685, and the regulations obtaining in Brazil. Rather than a patchwork of provincial codes, Britain's rivals appeared to possess uniform laws of slavery, developed and administered in the metropolis and either extended or applied to dominions in America. And unlike the British American slave laws, which were concerned almost exclusively with policing the slave population, the civil law tradition governed relations between master and slaves, particularly as it related to the rights of the enslaved to self-purchase. The differences should not be overstated. Appearances could be deceiving. Settlers elsewhere in the Americas, like British colonists, instituted coercive local ordinances, took responsibility for the enforcement of the laws, and therefore could hinder the operation of protective regulations. In most instances, there was

---

America, 1638–1870, ed. A. Norman Klein (1896; rpt. New York, 1969), 7–37; Leonard W. Labaree, ed., *Royal Instructions to British Colonial Governors, 1670–1776*, 2 vols. (1935; rpt. New York, 1967), II, 505–508. The Board of Trade and the Privy Council at times acted more aggressively and decisively when slaveholders threatened unusually severe actions against free blacks. In 1739, the Privy Council prevented the Antiguan legislature from using slave testimony to prosecute two freedmen accused of aiding a conspiracy to revolt. Similarly, imperial officials in 1761 prohibited the assembly of Bermuda from expelling from the colony free blacks suspected of inspiring slave unrest. See David Barry Gaspar, *Bondsmen and Rebels: A Study of Master-Slave Relations in Antigua, with Implications for Colonial British America* (Baltimore, 1985), 43–62; PRO CO 37/19, fols. 54–64.

a limited capacity for and commitment to inspection and oversight.[52] But to British observers the regulations in the Spanish, Portuguese, and French colonies seemed by comparison to ensure enlightened administration and a measure of justice. Formally, at least, their codes placed slavery under law. To the proponents of gradual emancipation, the problem in British America was not so much the inadequacy of colonial law than what looked like no law at all. Granville Sharp likened American planters to Turkish despots. The slaveholder, he said, was "an arbitrary monarch, or rather a lawless Basha in his own territories." With disgust, James Ramsay reported to church prelates, "There is not a single law, I had almost said a single Custom that operates effectually in the [slaves'] favour. Every man may beat, abuse, ill treat, maim and starve them, at the suggestion of his lust, his avarice, his malice, his caprice."[53]

The custom of colonial autonomy, then, presented a formidable block to prospects for emancipation, as it did more generally to the exercise of imperial authority. A metropolitan attempt to seize and manage an institution traditionally administered exclusively by the colonial assemblies threatened, by necessity, profound constitutional change. This reluctance to interfere with customary rights to property and self-rule would help inhibit legislative action to end slavery in the established sugar colonies for another half century, until 1833, when the West Indian interest, cognizant of overwhelming public pressure for emancipation, secured from Parliament a

52. Gouveia, *West Indian Slave Laws;* Alan Watson, *Slave Law in the Americas* (Athens, Ga., 1989); Klein, *African Slavery in Latin America and the Caribbean,* 190–196; Alejandro de La Fuente, "Law: Latin American Law," in Seymour Drescher and Stanley L. Engerman, eds., *A Historical Guide to World Slavery* (New York, 1998), 253–255. For instances of the complexities in the application of these laws see, for example, Gilbert C. Din, *Spaniards, Planters, and Slaves: The Spanish Regulation of Slavery in Louisiana, 1763–1803* (College Station, Tex., 1999); Malick W. Ghachem, "Montesquieu in the Caribbean: The Colonial Enlightenment between *Code Noir* and *Code Civil*," *Historical Reflections/Réflexions historiques,* XXV, no. 2 (Summer 1999), 189–207; and A. J. R. Russell-Wood, " 'Acts of Grace': Portuguese Monarchs and Their Subjects of African Descent in Eighteenth-Century Brazil," *Journal of Latin American Studies,* XXXII (2000), 307–332.

53. Sharp, *A Representation of the Injustice and Dangerous Tendency of Tolerating Slavery,* 82; Ramsay, "Memorial Suggesting Motives for the Improvement of the Sugar Colonies," fol. 79.

twenty-million-pound buyout of their slave property.[54] For a brief period, though, in the late 1760s and 1770s, limiting colonial self-governance had particular appeal within certain circles in the British government. The tentative emancipation schemes of the 1770s arose with and complemented the new priorities that took shape after the Stamp Act crisis, after British Americans explicitly challenged Parliament's authority to legislate for the colonies, as ministers tried to sustain and enforce colonial subordination. By instituting new taxes, by suspending recalcitrant assemblies, by policing with more vigor the acts of trade, and by reforming colonial administration, policy makers worked to affirm imperial sovereignty, in principle and in fact. To the few inclined to muse at length on the subject of colonial slavery, the apparently unlimited, inviolable right in British America to property in persons proved that the colonists possessed, already, far too much independence. Even evident, egregious abuses lay beyond the power of the British state to prevent. For those opponents of slavery who believed that Parliament should legislate aggressively on colonial questions, antislavery measures promised not only to redress moral wrongs; they promised as well to assist in the rehabilitation of metropolitan authority.

No writer defined this agenda with greater clarity than the Reverend James Ramsay. Ramsay understood that slavery reform could occur only by centralizing sovereign power in the British Empire, a step that, anyway, he thought urgent to preserving command of the North American colonies. More than others at this time, Ramsay made explicit the assumption implicit in the slavery reform schemes of this period. He directly confronted the problem presented by the almost complete independence enjoyed by colonial plutocrats. From the unpublished work Ramsay completed in the 1770s emerges a detailed picture of how antislavery opinion could foster hostility to colonial independence and how, in turn, reservations about colonial autonomy could deepen an opposition to colonial slavery. His unpublished manuscripts illustrate the affinity between assertions of parliamentary supremacy and the attempt to limit those customary rights that in-

54. See generally David Brion Davis, *Slavery and Human Progress* (New York, 1984), 174–175, 178–179, 345–346, and for further detail, D. J. Murray, *The West Indies and the Development of Colonial Government, 1801–1834* (Oxford, 1965). Only in the crown colonies, which lacked legislative assemblies, did the Colonial Office institute ameliorative reforms.

sulated colonial slavery from external attack. James Ramsay had too much savvy to avow explicit support for enlightened absolutism. Yet his case against American slavery and colonial rebellion bore a pronounced, if unintended, resemblance to the absolutist arguments that sixteenth-century theorist Jean Bodin conceived when French nobles threatened to resuscitate personal servitude and Huguenot ideologues espoused resistance to monarchical authority: only a strong state headed by an indivisible sovereign could protect the dispossessed from oppression and ensure social harmony and political order.[55]

To an extent, Ramsay's reform proposals reflected a wider desire among certain planters in the British Caribbean to place colonial slavery on a more secure footing, an aim animated in part by an intensifying fear of slave insurrections.[56] However, where several of his contemporaries in the Caribbean recommended the amelioration of slavery, Ramsay wanted coerced labor abolished over time. Margaret Middleton, the pious spouse of his

55. On Bodin and slavery, see Davis, *The Problem of Slavery in Western Culture*, 111–114, and Henry Heller, "Bodin on Slavery and Primitive Accumulation," *Sixteenth Century Journal*, XXV (1994), 53–65.

56. For the Jamaica revolt of 1760 that deepened these anxieties, see Craton, *Testing the Chains*, 125–139, and Peter Linebaugh and Marcus Rediker, *The Many-Headed Hydra: Sailors, Slaves, Commoners, and the Hidden History of the Revolutionary Atlantic* (Boston, 2000), 221–224. Ramsay wrote several years after Antiguan planter Colonel Samuel Martin espoused treating slaves with "justice and tenderness," after the first British governor of Saint Vincent detailed publicly a regime for the "treatment, care, and protection" of imported Africans, and more than a decade after James Grainger urged benign, gentle "slave management" in the widely read *Sugar-Cane: A Poem*. Samuel Martin, *An Essay upon Plantership, Humbly Inscribed to His Excellency, George Thomas, Esq., Chief Governor of the Leeward Islands*, 4th ed. (London, 1765), 4; [Sir William Young], *Considerations Which May Tend to Promote the Settlement of Our New West-India Colonies, by Encouraging Individuals to Embark in the Undertaking* (London, 1764), 48. On Martin and Grainger, see Davis S. Shields, *Oracles of Empire: Poetry, Politics, and Commerce in British America, 1690–1750* (Chicago, 1990), 71–82; Richard B. Sheridan, "Samuel Martin, Innovating Sugar Planter of Antigua, 1750–1776," *Agricultural History*, XXXIV, no. 3 (July 1960), 126–139; John Gilmore, *The Poetics of Empire: A Study of James Grainger's "The Sugar-Cane"* (London, 2000), 1–65; and Shaun Irlam, "'Wish You Were Here': Exporting England in James Grainger's *The Sugar Cane*," *ELH*, LXVIII (2001), 385–389.

patron Charles, had written Ramsay in the 1760s to encourage religious instruction on the Saint Kitts plantations. In considering this request, Ramsay found himself addressing at length the character of Caribbean society and the impoverished state of the colonial church. By the spring of 1771, he had completed a lengthy letter in reply that recommended independent financing for the Caribbean clergy, a step he thought essential to fostering religious life in the colonies.[57] The building crisis in the North American colonies, however, helped Ramsay understand these primarily religious concerns in their political context. It led him to see colonial autonomy as a structural flaw in the imperial constitution, a flaw that enabled the abuse of labor and the neglect of religion throughout the plantation colonies. His original manuscript thus evolved during the 1770s into "something like a system for the regulation and improvement of our sugar colonies, and the advancement and conversion of their slaves." In these years, gradual emancipation became Ramsay's explicit aim.[58]

57. Ramsay printed Margaret Middleton's letter, without identifying her as its author, in the preface to the first of his published antislavery tracts. See *An Essay on the Treatment and Conversion of African Slaves,* viii–xiv. For a brief but vivid treatment of Charles and Margaret Middleton, see John Pollock, *Wilberforce* (London, 1977), 49–54. They receive more extended discussion in I. Lloyd Phillips, "The Evangelical Administrator: Sir Charles Middleton at the Navy Board, 1778–1790" (D.Phil. thesis, Oxford University, 1975). See also chapter 6 in this volume. For Ramsay's lengthy reply, which first laid out ideas developed in his published work, see James Ramsay to Margaret Middleton, Mar. 20, 1771, Noel Papers, DE 32124/322/1, Leicestershire Record Office.

58. Ramsay, *An Essay on the Treatment and Conversion of African Slaves,* iii. The Leicestershire manuscript, completed in 1771, explicitly rejects gradual emancipation as a realizable goal. "It would perhaps be difficult for government to form a plan, which would give full liberty, and thereby impart due importance and utility to the slaves in the West India colonies, without injuring or even entirely ruining the fortunes of their proprietors, and with them the trading part of the nation connected with them in business and interest." He continued: "The slaves in our little spot would at a very equitable appraisement amount to thirteen hundred and fifty thousand pounds sterling. And in all our sugar colonies they cannot be less in value than twenty millions. And as the slaves, in our colony alone, are part of a stock of four millions, and as they alone give life effect and use to that stock the fruits of their labour being worthy yearly to the consumers above seven hundred thousand pounds sterling, it will easily be apparent that an immense change, or rather loss of property, would be occasioned by such a scheme, at once

By the mid-1770s, that manuscript consisted of two books. The first treated "the powers of government to improve the state of the colonies." After a first chapter comparing British slavery unfavorably with ancient and modern slave regimes, Ramsay addressed the necessity, in all states, of centralized authority, how this principle related to the administration of the American colonies, and the importance of religious establishments to effective governance. In the second book he discussed the "Powers of Government exercised in improving the condition of Colony Slaves." There he described the native capacities of Africans, the difficulties faced by those seeking to bring slaves to Christianity, and the likely benefits to colonial society that successful efforts at conversion would yield. He concluded with a comprehensive scheme for administrative reform.[59] From the origi-

---

taking into effect in all our colonies. Nor would it be easy to find the masters an equivalent." The futility of pursuing emancipation he developed further several pages later: "A state of absolute freedom is a state of things, which we are rather to wish for than expect. It supposeth a regard for religion, a neglect of immediate profit, and a soundness of policy, very foreign to the estimation and opinion of the present age. And to make the plan effectual it would need to take place in all the European settlements. An event so little to be looked for in the course of things, that a man would hardly venture the imputation of so much extravagance as the bare suggestion of it would be deemed. For could so many clashing interests be made to agree in one point. And would not that great object of European policy, the balance of trade, be supposed to be in danger, if any partial innovation were to take place." Ramsay to Middleton, Mar. 20, 1771, Noel Papers, DE 3214/322/1.

59. British Library, Add. MSS 27621. The manuscript lacks a formal title. The title assigned by the British Library, which is the same as the title Ramsay gave his first antislavery pamphlet, simply misleads, as the contents differ dramatically. Here and throughout, I employ the phrase Ramsay used when describing his manuscript to the bishop of London: "Motives for the Improvement of the Sugar Colonies." The manuscript also presents problems for citing specific pages from the volume. As now preserved, the text of the reform scheme is bound with approximately three dozen pages of Ramsay's manuscript notes and commentaries on slavery-related subjects. As a consequence, two different systems for numbering pages appear in the volume, one of which, however, has been partially defaced by a subsequent slash through the figures inscribed on the top of each page. For the sake of consistency, the page numbers to be given here follow the "clean" series as presented in the manuscript, although this series does not correspond with the actual sequence of manuscript pages contained within the volume.

nal manuscript, he extracted the sections addressing governance and colonial administration and early in 1778 published them anonymously, in revised form, as *Plan of Re-Union between Great Britain and Her Colonies,* a text heretofore attributed to William Pulteney, second earl of Bath.[60] The opening chapter of the first book and the entirety of the second Ramsay revised, expanded, and published in 1784 as *An Essay on the Treatment and Conversion of African Slaves in the British Sugar Colonies,* a landmark treatise in the nascent campaigns of the 1780s.[61] Although Ramsay published on the subjects separately, in an earlier incarnation his critique of slavery served, in part, as an attack on colonial autonomy.

Recent scholarship has given extensive attention to the character of British conservative thought in the era of the American Revolution.[62] In every important respect, Ramsay was strictly orthodox in his views. With regard to politics, he revered properly constituted authority and insisted on the supremacy of Parliament and the indivisibility of sovereignty. To a patrician's suspicion of popular politics he joined an active detestation of

60. For example, Vincent T. Harlow, *The Founding of the Second British Empire, 1763–1793,* I, *Discovery and Revolution* (London, 1952), 215–216. In addition to the conclusive evidence of Ramsay's authorship in the British Library manuscript, Ramsay took credit for *Plan of Re-Union* in his petition to the bishop of London, "Memorial on the Converson of the Slaves," fol. 79.

61. Folarin Shyllon provides an especially detailed account of Ramsay's influence on early abolitionism in Britain. See his *James Ramsay, the Unknown Abolitionist* (Edinburgh, 1977), 42–96.

62. Particularly instructive are: Margaret E. Avery, "Toryism in the Age of the American Revolution: John Lind and John Shebbeare," *Historical Studies* (Melbourne, Australia), XVIII, no. 70 (April 1978), 24–36; Paul Langford, "Old Whigs, Old Tories, and the American Revolution," *Jour. Imperial and Commonwealth Hist.,* VIII, no. 2 (1980), 106–130; J. C. D. Clark, *English Society, 1688–1832: Religion, Ideology, and Politics during the Ancien Regime* (Cambridge, 1985), 199–247; James E. Bradley, "The Anglican Pulpit, the Social Order, and the Resurgence of Toryism during the American Revolution," *Albion,* XXI (1989), 361–388; Langford, "The English Clergy and the American Revolution," in Hellmuth, ed., *The Transformation of Political Culture,* 275–308; James J. Sack, *From Jacobite to Conservative: Reaction and Orthodoxy in Britain, c. 1760–1832* (Cambridge, 1993); and Peter N. Miller, *Defining the Common Good: Empire, Religion, and Philosophy in Eighteenth-Century Britain* (Cambridge, 1994).

political factions, such as the Rockingham Whigs, which he thought compromised the natural unity of the state. Ramsay viewed society as organic,
not contractual. He believed that individuals could enjoy true liberty and
security only through the advancement of the common good, which the
state had the sole responsibility to protect. The church served as a bulwark
to social order. So Dissenters and others who "affect to exalt the individual
at the expence of the community" posed a threat, in Ramsay's view, to
"decency, religion, and law." Two decades of residence in the British Caribbean left Ramsay hostile toward its ruling oligarchs. He took issue with the
way colonists placed what he called the "Kingdom of I" above the interests
of society as a whole. Slavery in British America displayed the consequences of such an ethos. Here was evidence of the tyranny spawned by
unrestricted freedom. "Every where in every age," Ramsay noted, "the
chain of slavery has been fashioned by the hand of liberty." Although
positioned to bring slavery within the compass of law, the culprits, the
colonial assemblies that licensed license and oppression, were "neither
competent, or inclined, to introduce such reformation as humanity so-
licites." Indeed the slave codes the assemblies enacted led to "the negation
of the law," since the end of law in every society, Ramsay wrote, was to
secure "the equal protection of its citizens."[63] That slaves were not citizens
was irrelevant to Ramsay where the right to legal protection was concerned.
As laborers for the British state, slaves were members of society; and as
members of society, slaves had a claim to the rights on which society, as
such, existed to guarantee. Those colonial assemblies that refused to honor
the rightful claims of each member to legal protection had forfeited, in
principle, their right to legislate. For Ramsay, the wickedness of British
American slavery clinched the case against colonial self-governance.

If the problem, then, lay with the imperial constitution, the self-evident
solution was to "unhinge the present method of managing the colonies,"
end "the absurdity and contradiction of various, jarring legislators," recognize Parliament as the "supreme legislature," and reduce the power of
colonial assemblies. A host of improvements to the sugar colonies, including a reformation of slavery, could follow, Ramsay explained. No longer
should the colonies govern themselves with minimal oversight from Lon-

63. "Motives for the Improvement of the Sugar Colonies," xii, 27, 39, 44, 44n, 69.

don. And no longer should the Privy Council have the responsibility of reviewing colonial legislation. Instead, Ramsay recommended, each measure written in British America should be reviewed by a committee of Parliament, composed in part by delegates appointed by the several colonies. These procedural reforms would then clear the way for a substantive revision of colonial laws. Imposts, as far as possible, Ramsay wished to equalize. For law to have authority, for it to command assent, for it to unite an empire, it had to eliminate "particular exemptions." Those colonial taxes that regulated trade Ramsay wished to have levied in a uniform fashion, with the revenue earmarked for the navy, trading posts, and debts amassed from the "defence of trade and the colonies." All other colonial taxes would be "annihilated." Britain would pay for the civil and ecclesiastical establishments in the colonies. Customhouse officials in British America would receive salaries from the Treasury, to make unnecessary the uneven, costly fees and perquisites they imposed on traders. The crown's duties on enumerated goods exported from "the Old Charibee colonies" would be required from each colony in the British Caribbean; no longer would Jamaica or the Ceded Islands receive a dispensation. A portion of the resulting income would support additional clergy for the West Indies, thereby liberating ministers from dependence on the patronage of slaveholders. An independent clergy could then devote themselves to instructing slaves and, Ramsay hoped, mediating between slaves and masters. In cooperation with London-appointed judges to be charged with adjudicating conflicts between slaves and masters, the clergy would acquire reputations as the Africans' advocate. Clerical benevolence would draw the enslaved to Christianity. And as enslaved Africans attained a stake in society, as they established "proper" marriages, secured claims to their families, were attached to the land on which they worked, they would be prepared to contemplate the fate of their souls and the obligations of each individual to the good of society as a whole.[64]

This was how slaves would be brought to the gospel and ultimately, perhaps, to freedom: first, by establishing parliamentary supremacy; second, by restructuring colonial administration; third, by funding positions for independent clergy in the West Indies; fourth, by gradually incorporating slaves into civil society; and, fifth, by ensuring to them the protection

64. Ibid., 73–93, 154–167, citations on 72, 74, 77, 76.

of the law. Fundamental, overdue reforms to empire would also result. Through a "timely interposition of the legislature," through an extension of levies on West Indian produce, Britain would "acquire a considerable accession of strength; have its trade and taxes improved, and a large number of useful fellow subjects, now sunk in misery and bondage made happy here, and capable of happiness hereafter."[65]

If James Ramsay had published his original text, interpreters of the British antislavery movement perhaps would have recognized the ties between the first aspirations for slavery reform and attempts at imperial reorganization. However, from the antislavery tracts Ramsay published in the 1780s, it is difficult, if not impossible, to detect his commitment to administrative reform and the indivisible sovereignty of king-in-parliament. And that is because James Ramsay deliberately suppressed the broader agenda that shaped his antislavery proposals. Ironically, the original manuscript, itself a product of the Anglo-American conflict, was a casualty of colonial rebellion. War in America demonstrated the likely consequences of heavy-handed attempts to impose imperial rule. It was far better, some British politicians concluded (particularly after the defeat at Saratoga in the fall of 1777) to cede legislative autonomy to potentially mutinous colonies in exchange for continued allegiance to the crown, preservation of commercial ties, and maintenance of a united front against European rivals. Lord North offered such terms to Congress through the Carlisle peace commission of 1778, and the Irish Parliament accepted such an arrangement from the Shelburne ministry in 1782. So Ramsay's proposal to strengthen imperial authority, which he seems to have completed in 1776, ran counter to the drift of informed opinion among those responsible for colonial governance.[66] His friends of "rank and learning," he would later explain, ap-

---

65. Ibid., 168.

66. Harlow, *The Founding of the Second British Empire*, I, 493–557. I date Ramsay's manuscript on the basis of a statement presented in the introduction to his *Plan of Re-Union* (1778). "The outlines of the following Plan are taken from a manuscript on the improvement of the sugar-colonies, which the author has had in hand these ten years. It has been extracted and fitted for a temporary publication, in hopes of its contributing something to elucidate the rights of Britain, deserted and betrayed as she is, by too many of her ungrateful sons. It was prepared, in another form, for publication two years ago." [Ramsay], *Plan of Re-Union between Great Britain and Her Colonies* (London, 1778), v.

proved of gradual abolition but advised him "with one voice" to strike from the manuscript "every part that tended to introduce those political questions, which must be unavoidable in treating the state of the colonies, and their dependence on a mother country."[67] Therefore, when Ramsay published the revised version of the manuscript in 1784 as *An Essay on the Treatment and Conversion of African Slaves in the British Sugar Colonies,* he removed each section and passage relating to sovereignty, legislatures, religious establishments, and taxes. The antislavery tract explained why slavery should be reformed and identified which reforms were necessary but not how those reforms should be authorized, implemented, or enforced. Retained was the plan for appointing additional clergy in the colonies, but extracted from the text was the scheme to fund their salaries. His antislavery treatise called for new laws that would allow slaves a semblance of legal protection, but it did not specify which legislature should act or, more to the point, which had the authority to act. In short, Ramsay's published work dodged the sensitive question of legislative power, upon which the original manuscript turned.

An elastic concept of subjectship and a perceived need to bring the enlarged empire under ministerial control helped make schemes for slavery reform possible. At the same time, the inability to translate theoretic authority into actual power helped make their enactment (political hurdles aside) nearly impossible and even their publication ill advised. James Ramsay mangled his original manuscript with reluctance. Factious demagogues had so captured public opinion, he later grumbled, that "it had become a sort of treason to express any attachment to the laws of government or religion in our country, or stand in vindication of their claims." As noted, Ramsay did publish his proposals for reorganizing the empire, but anonymously in 1778 as *Plan of Re-Union between Great Britain and Her Colonies,* a misleading title for a work concerned to annul "all the little colony-systems" rather than shape an amicable peace.[68] He longed for an earlier era when, he claimed, colonies accepted their subordination to the mother country and when the state and the church possessed unquestioned authority.

67. Ramsay, *An Essay on the Treatment and Conversion of African Slaves,* iii–iv.
68. [Ramsay], *Plan of Re-Union between Great Britain and Her Colonies,* xv.

Twenty years ago, things might have been assumed as axioms, that are now become objects of grave discussion. This is not, in common, the age of establishing, but of unsettling first truths . . . "Every man his own legislator," is a phrase which when applied to created Being, contains blasphemy too horrid to be imagined, or nonsense, that mocks explanation. Yet it is powerful enough to annihilate every law of God, either respecting religion or adopted authority. And with them it has pulled down family, society, an established religion, all that men ever fought or bled for.[69]

James Ramsay hated slavery, but he may have hated the American rebels more. He despised their leading men in Congress ("atheistical profligate bankrupts"), the actions of their army ("numerous scenes of horror, oppression, inhuman murders, and unrelenting cruelty, in every possible dress"), their constitutional principles ("laid in profligacy, Atheism, ingratitude, and oppression"), and the "consummate effrontery" of their friends in Britain, particularly the Rockingham Whigs.[70] In the end, Ramsay would have to console himself with an attack on slavery alone. Those efforts would bring him notoriety and influence. James Ramsay would be the first to fix British attention on colonial slavery in a way that had lasting effect. With this success, though, he failed utterly in what he initially set out to do, to assist in preserving and reconstructing the American empire.

The nascent British interest in slavery reform during the [IV] Revolutionary era must not be divorced from the ultimately unsuccessful metropolitan efforts to reconstitute imperial authority. When William Knox suggested that slaves, like indentured servants, should be eligible for an "impartial dispensation of the laws," he stressed that "no authority, but that of parliament," could institute such a measure. Of slavery, Maurice Morgann wrote, "The evil is wholly imputable to the state; and the remedy can be obtained only by its assuming different maxims and a better policy" for the empire as a whole. Provide America with a new constitution, Methodist minister Thomas Vivian advised Lord Dartmouth, the former secretary of

69. Ibid., xv.

70. Ibid., 52n, 53n, 135n. On the near visceral hatred of philosophes and political radicalism among the orthodox, see Sack, *From Jacobite to Conservative*, 38.

state for British America, and let that constitution "be similar to our own" under "the same Supreme Legislature." The price of political equality, Vivian added, should conform with metropolitan standards of civility and justice: "Why not compleat the resemblance or union as much as possible by abolishing slavery among them?" Emancipation, he added, would rescue enslaved Africans from oppression, contribute to uniting the empire under uniform laws, and, importantly, ensure the dependence of the colonies. Even if Americans surrendered their arms, Vivian observed, "they would still be glad to embrace the opportunity of becoming independent." Only divesting Americans of their bondsmen would permanently "weaken" their strength.[71]

By 1778, the commanders of the British army in America had reached the same conclusion and, in liberating slaves owned by colonial patriots as a matter of policy, effected in practice the abstract aims articulated by emancipation theorists—an assertion of imperial rule through the appropriation of human property possessed by rebellious British colonists.[72] No one spelled out the way emancipation could shift the balance of power in North America with more candor than Sir William Draper: "Proclame *Freedom* to their Negroes," he advised in 1774, "then how long would they be a people? They would soon cry out for pardon, and *render unto* CAESAR *the Things which are* CAESAR's." Samuel Johnson presented a similar suggestion one year later. "If they are furnished with fire arms for defense, and utensils for husbandry, and settled in some form of government within the country, they may be more grateful and honest than their masters."[73]

The self-styled British friends of American liberty who favored slavery reform hid from the authoritarian implications of the antislavery measures they espoused at the cost of incoherence. David Hartley wanted Parliament to enact a law protecting slaves from their owners but opposed metropolitan attempts to legislate for the colonies. Granville Sharp campaigned

---

71. [Knox], *Three Tracts,* 25; [Morgann], *Plan for the Abolition of Slavery in the West Indies,* 13; Thomas Vivian to earl of Dartmouth, Jan. 16, 1777, Dartmouth Papers, D(w) 1778/II/1733, Staffordshire Record Office.

72. See generally Frey, *Water from the Rock,* 45–171.

73. [Sir William Draper], *The Thoughts of a Traveler upon Our American Disputes* (London, 1774), 21; Basker, " 'The Next Insurrection,' " *The Age of Johnson,* XI, 48.

ardently early in the Revolutionary War on behalf of colonial autonomy yet
hoped that the crown would prevent colonists "from oppressing their *poor
Brethren.*" This, he declared, was an "essential purpose of Regal Government."[74] Edmund Burke, too, wrestled with conflicting principles. In 1778,
he renounced the imperious maxims enshrined in the Declaratory Act of
1766, which he had a hand in producing.[75] Yet the provisions of his Negro
Code of 1780 would have charged an army of administrators with policing
each component of the slaving network in the British Atlantic. Indeed, if
enacted, it would have established a colonial bureaucracy more extensive
than even the most ambitious plans of imperial administration for North
America proposed to date. A slave ship would require clearance from a
"searcher of the Port" to depart from England. At the British forts on the
African coast, state-appointed inspectors would supervise and approve
slave sales. Britons intending to trade inland in Africa would require a
license from the governor, whom Burke would vest with the power to
prosecute unscrupulous traders. The commander of the naval fleet sta-
tioned off Africa would have the power to inspect slave ships "as often as he
shall see occasion." In the West Indies, Burke would appoint for each
island an "Attorney General, Protector of Negroes," whose responsibilities
would include, among other duties, receiving complaints from slaves, pros-
ecuting slaveowners for felonious assaults, and purchasing the freedom of
slaves who "shall appear to him to excel in any mechanical Art or other
knowledge or practice." In addition to bringing the enslaved under the care
of state-appointed officials, Burke would have placed the British Atlantic
slaving network within the jurisdiction of the common law. Traders who
kidnapped slaves in Africa would be jailed in London, Bristol, Liverpool, or Glasgow and prosecuted "as if the Offenses had been committed

74. George Herbert Guttridge, *David Hartley, M.P., an Advocate of Conciliation,
1774–1783* (Berkeley, Calif., 1926), 327–328; Granville Sharp to Lord North, Feb. 18,
1772, in Prince Hoare, *Memoirs of Granville Sharp . . .* (London, 1820), 78–80; Granville
Sharp, *The Law of Retribution; or, A Serious Warning to Great Britain and Her Colonies, Founded on Unquestionable Examples of God's Temporal Vengeance against Tyrants,
Slave-Holders, and Oppressors* (London, 1776), 183n.

75. Burke, "Speech on Repeal of the Declaratory Act," in Langford, ed., *The Writings and Speeches of Edmund Burke,* III, 373–374.

within" those "Cities and Towns." Even more radically, "in all cases of injury to Member or life" in the colonies, "the offenses against a Negro," Burke recommended in an echo of William Knox, "shall be deemed and taken . . . as if the same were perpetrated against any of his Majesty's subjects."[76] Burke, like Knox and Ramsay before him, championed the "indiscriminating supremacy of law" throughout British dominions, law that, he and others were coming to believe, should admit the claims of the enslaved.

The proposals to superintend colonial slavery through new metropolitan bureaucracies comported with wider attempts to fortify and extend in the Americas the administrative machinery of the state. They marked a faith in the advantages of centralizing power within the empire. And they reflected an emerging preference to assert greater control over the far-flung settlements and conduct policy in a way that assuaged and "improved" the diverse peoples residing within. In the schemes for slavery reform lie, not only the germs of an abolitionist ethos, but also the seeds of the nineteenth-century imperial mission that lauded Christianity, civilization, and commerce.[77] But dissolution of the North American empire interrupted efforts to extend imperial rule. With faith lost in the ability of the government to command consent in the western Atlantic, interest in concrete measures for slavery reform waned along with broader attempts to strengthen metropolitan control in colonies governed by representative assemblies. In their initial, unguarded incarnations, the innovative schemes for gradually abolishing slavery composed by John Hinchliffe, James Ramsay, and Edmund Burke would remain unpublished.

The British government lacked a compelling political or economic reason to abolish colonial slavery in the era of the American Revolution. And, as British military strategy during the French Revolutionary and Napoleonic wars would show, ministers would continue to place a priority on securing, sustaining, and, if possible, extending the West Indian plantation

---

76. Burke, "Sketch of a Negro Code," ibid., 562–581, citations on 564, 570, 572, 580.

77. Marshall, "Empire and Authority in the Later Eighteenth Century," *Jour. Imperial and Commonwealth Hist.*, XV, no. 2 (1987), 105–122; Eliga H. Gould, "American Independence and Britain's Counter-Revolution," *Past and Present*, no. 154 (February 1997), 107–146.

economy. Typically, between 1776 and 1815, Britain resisted the temptation to incite slave revolts. Regiments of slave soldiers were established in the 1790s to defend Caribbean slavery rather than spark its overthrow.[78] Yet even if ministers had wanted to act against slavery, the American conflict seemed to establish that neither Parliament nor the crown held a clear authority to do so. Commanders in the American theater, of course, could free the slaves of belligerents who placed themselves outside the crown's protection. Those slaveholders loyal to the king, though, retained their customary right to self-governance and chattel slavery. By successfully resisting restrictions on colonial autonomy, the North American rebels discouraged future attempts at comprehensive imperial reform. In this respect, they unintentionally insulated slavery in the existing sugar colonies from metropolitan interference for several decades to come. If, as it has been argued, the American Revolution improved the prospects for a general emancipation by confining slavery to those colonies unable to revolt against imperial rule, the conflict also reinforced long-standing limits on Parliament's power to intervene in the internal affairs of the British settlements in the western Atlantic.[79]

The first British activists failed in their effort to promote antislavery measures, in part, because they lacked a viable program of reform. The plans they devised required from the imperial state powers that it appeared not to possess. In the end, alternatives would have to appear possible to make possible campaigns for an alternative. Subsequently, in the 1780s, reformers would shift their attention to abolishing the slave trade, which Parliament had an unquestioned authority to regulate and which, before the Revolutionary War, American patriots had highlighted as an emblem of British tyranny in America. The individuals who first made slave trade abolition seem plausible, by advocating trade with Africa in staple crops

78. Michael Duffy, "World-Wide War and British Expansion, 1793–1815," in P. J. Marshall, ed., *The Oxford History of the British Empire,* II, *The Eighteenth Century* (Oxford, 1998), 184–195; Roger Norman Buckley, *Slaves in Red Coats: The British West India Regiments, 1795–1815* (New Haven, Conn., 1979).

79. David Brion Davis, "American Slavery and the American Revolution," in Ira Berlin and Ronald Hoffman, eds., *Slavery and Freedom in the Age of the American Revolution* (Charlottesville, Va., 1983), 262–280; O'Shaughnessy, *An Empire Divided,* 245.

instead of slaves, numbered among the theorists and commentators on imperial affairs.[80] Moral commitment and public sentiment would provide the energy for abolitionism. Yet, as with programs for slavery reform in the decade before, the campaign to abolish the slave trade in the 1780s would build on a more general rethinking of how the empire ought to work, in this instance, under the very different conditions presented by national humiliation, massive debt, diplomatic isolation, and population and territorial losses in America. This is a central theme of the chapter that follows.

In the schemes treated here, there was an underlying confidence in the capacity of enlightened officials to guide and regulate colonial affairs. In the last years of the American war, by contrast, anxieties regarding imperial expansion, always present but less prominent before 1775, acquired new importance. Before the war, policy makers thought too little had been done to secure British rule in America. After successive defeats and the heightened threat of French invasion, a broader public came to believe that ministers had perhaps tried too much. If the idea of concerted action against the Atlantic slaving system first gestated in the attempts to wield control over British overseas settlements, the deepening conviction that action must be taken against the slave trade matured with doubts regarding the virtue of rapid overseas expansion. Where, to a few in the 1770s, the iniquities of the slave system first signaled administrative neglect, by the early 1780s, to many, it would begin to symbolize, instead, what one clergyman called in 1781 the declining "moral state of the British Empire."[81]

80. See, for example, Josiah Tucker, *Reflections on the Present Matters in Dispute between Great Britain and Ireland . . .* (London, 1785).

81. Samuel Stennett, *National Calamities the Effect of Divine Displeasure; a Sermon, Preached in Little Wild-Street, Near Lincoln's-Inn-Fields, on Occasion of the General Fast, February 21, 1781* (London, [1781]).

CHAPTER 5

Africa, Africans, and the Idea of Abolition

The "traffic" in "rational beings" will continue until the "pecuniary interests of Europeans can be diverted into another channel." This was the advice the elderly Quaker doctor John Fothergill shared with his protégé John Coakley Lettsom shortly before his death in 1780, after a dozen years of intermittent and unsuccessful lobbying against the Atlantic slave system. The eminent English physician had been instrumental in 1767 in arranging for the first London reprints of Anthony Benezet's publications.[1] In 1768 Fothergill had read in manuscript the research Granville Sharp had begun to assemble against the practice of slaveholding on English soil. Fothergill had given Sharp financial and moral support four years later, in 1772, when the case of James Somerset lay before Lord Mansfield and the Court of King's Bench. In the subsequent months, he had hosted the American Quaker abolitionist John Woolman and had introduced Benezet's colleague William Dillwyn to Granville Sharp and other antislavery enthusiasts in England. Fothergill, moreover, had studied the emancipation schemes that circulated during the 1770s with great interest. He had expressed enthusiasm for the "Spanish Regulations," which Granville Sharp had shared with the sympathetic during the American war. Perhaps inspired by Maurice Morgann's *Plan for the Abolition of Slavery in the West Indies,* Fothergill in 1772 had written optimistically (though in private) of colonizing liberated slaves in the Americas, perhaps, he suggested, in the new British colonies of Tobago or Saint Vincent.[2]

1. John Coakley Lettsom, ed., *The Works of John Fothergill . . .* , 3 vols. (London, 1783–1784), III, xlvi–xlvii. The Benezet pamphlet was first published as *A Caution and Warning to Great Britain and Her Colonies in a Short Representation of the Calamitous State of the Enslaved Negroes in the British Dominions: Collected from Various Authors, and Submitted to the Serious Consideration of All, More Especially of Those in Power* (Philadelphia, 1766). For John Fothergill's role in shepherding the text through publication by the Society of Friends in England, see MS Minutes of the Meeting for Sufferings, XXXII (May 22, 1767), 68, Library of the Society of Friends (LSF), London; MS Minutes of the Committee on Friends Books (n.d., 1767), 39, LSF.

2. John Fothergill to Granville Sharp [1768?], [1772?], MS Granville Sharp, Received

John Fothergill, then, had enough experience by 1780 to recognize the challenges that aspiring antislavery activists faced. He knew that the works of Benezet had failed to generate an antislavery movement in Britain before the American Revolution, even among his brethren within the Society of Friends, among whom, he remarked sadly in 1779, there was "a sort of lethargy prevailing among too many." With David Hartley and other proponents of conciliation, Fothergill had labored unsuccessfully in 1775 to work out an amicable peace between Britain and the colonies. So he understood, as James Ramsay did by 1778, that the moment for benevolent intervention in the American colonies had passed, that the successful rebellion in North America would compel British opponents of slavery to abandon schemes for a comprehensive emancipation. "It is not a time," he confessed to Sharp in 1779, "to hope much good to liberty."[3] Most of all, Fothergill recognized the decisive influence of "pecuniary interests." He knew that a profitable trade would be abolished only if abolition could be characterized persuasively as improving and enhancing British trade rather than diminishing it. He understood that moral appeals needed to be balanced by attention to economic interests and the needs of state.

John Fothergill was a scientist as well as an abolitionist and, therefore, often in the company of cosmopolitan men dedicated to the promotion of useful knowledge. In collaboration with Joseph Banks and other naturalists in 1771, he had commissioned an entrepreneur, Henry Smeathman, to study the flora and fauna on the Grain Coast of Africa. During the four years that he spent in Sierra Leone, Smeathman became convinced that the soil and the climate could support commercial agriculture, that crops like sugar, indigo, and cotton traditionally cultivated in the Americas could

---

Letterbook, 1768–1772, Historical Society of Pennsylvania (HSP), Philadelphia; Fothergill to Sharp, Feb. 2, 1772, in Betsy C. Corner and Christopher C. Booth, eds., *Chains of Friendship: Selected Letters of Dr. John Fothergill of London* (Cambridge, Mass., 1971), 374–375; Sharp to Fothergill, Feb. 8, 1772, MS Granville Sharp Letterbook, fols. 46–48, York Minster Library (YML); Sharp to Anthony Benezet, Jan. 7, 1774, Granville Sharp MSS, D3549 13/1/B19, Gloucestershire Record Office (GRO); Fothergill to John Pemberton, Aug. 29, 1772, Pemberton Papers, XXXIV, fol. 165, HSP.

3. Fothergill to Pemberton, June 14, 1779, Portfolio MSS, XXXVIII, fol. 113, LSF; R. Hingston Fox, *Dr. John Fothergill and His Friends: Chapters in Eighteenth Century Life* (London, 1919); Fothergill to Sharp, Mar. 11, 1779, in Prince Hoare, *Memoirs of Granville Sharp* . . . (London, 1820), 188.

instead be acquired from Africa, and that Africans might be taught, as he saw it, the value of a hard day's work. Smeathman also became intrigued with attaining power and influence on the coast, and he married three daughters of local rulers in quick succession. He left Sierra Leone in 1775 for Grenada in the British West Indies at the behest of sugar planters who hired him to exterminate ants; the self-styled "flycatcher" had become in Africa an expert on insects. There, too, he took to the study of plantation agronomy, certain, he told Fothergill, that with a suitable mixture of skills and labor he could produce staple crops along the Atlantic coast of Africa for export to Europe, if given the chance to return. These reports persuaded the aged Quaker physician by the late 1770s that slave trade abolition might be described as promoting, rather than reducing, Atlantic commerce. The way to end slavery in the colonies, Fothergill told Lettsom after the Smeathman expedition, was to transfer British sugar production from the Caribbean to Africa, "where it seems to have been indigenous, and thrives luxuriantly," and where "the natives" might "be employed as servants for hire, and not as slaves compelled to labour by the dread of torture."[4] Here was the alternative channel through which the pecuniary interests of Europe might be diverted. Here was a way to attain the produce of the Americas without a dependence on the Middle Passage.

The development of alternatives to the Atlantic slave trade in the late eighteenth century, in every instance, depended on the hope of encouraging a trade in African commodities rather than human bodies, although the character and content of the proposals would vary. Dreams of reordering

4. Smeathman's expedition is now detailed splendidly in Deirdre Coleman, *Romantic Colonization and British Anti-Slavery* (Cambridge, 2005), 28–37. See also Stephen J. Braidwood, *Black Poor and White Philanthropists: London's Blacks and the Foundation of the Sierra Leone Settlement, 1786–1791* (Liverpool, 1994), 6–12, and discussion in notes on 35–37; and Henry Smeathman, *Proposals for Printing by Subscription, Voyages and Travels in Africa and the West-Indies, from the Year 1771 to the Year 1779 Inclusive* [London, 1780]. For Lettsom's account of Fothergill's advice, see John Coakley Lettsom, *Memoirs of John Fothergill, M.D., etc.*, 4th ed. (London, 1786), 69–70. Lettsom published this idea anonymously in 1780s, in the weeks before Fothergill's death. *Gentleman's Magazine, and Historical Chronicle*, L (1780), 458. Lettsom confessed to be the author of this essay several years later. Lettsom to Dr. Cuming, Oct. 20, 1787, in Thomas Pettigrew, ed., *Memoirs of the Life and Writings of J. C. Lettsom, with a Selection from His Correspondence*, 3 vols. (London, 1817), II, 135.

the Africa trade, of stimulating staple crop production along the West African coast, waxed and waned during the eighteenth century but revived forcefully for a time in the early 1780s as certain British entrepreneurs looked for new opportunities and resources after the American war. The new British settlement in Sierra Leone established in 1786 as an asylum for black loyalists represented the most concrete result of this intensified interest in the West African coast. It also marked the meeting point for several crystallizing impulses and agendas fundamental to the making of organized abolitionism in the 1780s.

Surprisingly, the formulation of the Sierra Leone scheme rarely figures in accounts of early British antislavery. As has long been clear, the Sierra Leone experiment represented more than one outcome of a long-standing colonizationist fantasy. The project arose in part from the self-assertion of fugitive slaves escaping from the United States after the American War of Independence. Its early history brings to light the strategies and aims of free blacks within the British Empire in the crucial years before organized abolitionism emerged in Britain. The occasion for the scheme indicates also a subtle but significant shift in how some British officers and politicians regarded men and women of African descent residing in the British Empire. In the context of the American Revolution and its aftermath, affording protection to black loyalists seemed to advance the needs of state, even when that assistance sacrificed the concerns of propertied and commercial interests discomfited by the prospect of legal rights for liberated slaves. Last, the Sierra Leone experiment indicates, also, an emerging tendency among antislavery enthusiasts to seek in Africa solutions to the problem of slavery in the Americas, to reform enterprise in the western Atlantic by reordering operations in the eastern Atlantic. In each of these ways—as the distant offspring of an expansionist fantasy, as a refuge for free blacks escaping from slaveholding in the Americas, as an instance of an emerging interest in the ideal of trusteeship among decision makers within the British government, and as an indirect challenge to the slave system itself—the Sierra Leone settlement occupies a crucial though often overlooked place in the development of the antislavery movement in Britain.

[I]   In key respects, the roots of the Sierra Leone settlement lay deep in the history of British enterprise in Africa. It evolved from the hopes of a persistent few who in the eighteenth century wished to establish a more permanent British presence along the African coast, who wanted to found colonies of settlement that promoted commercial agriculture, not merely a trade in human bodies, who aimed to enhance the state's role in the management of African enterprise. The Restoration governments of the late seventeenth century had tried to restrict British commerce in the eastern Atlantic to chartered joint stock corporations. From 1660 to 1698, the Royal Adventurers to Africa and its successor, the Royal Africa Company, held an exclusive right to transport captive Africans to the British colonies. But freebooters, the "separate traders," proved far more effective in providing the American colonies with a sufficient supply of slaves and, after 1713, won from Parliament unfettered access to the coast.[5] Thereafter, limited metropolitan oversight was the rule in the African trades. By the early eighteenth century, the initiative in African waters had shifted to individual traders and investors willing to hazard fortunes on uncertain ventures. Parliament in 1730 assumed from the Royal Africa Company the costly obligation to maintain trading forts and thereby ensure British influence on the coast. The forts, however, played only a marginal role in the trade. Ships arriving from England regularly skirted these stations to deal directly with African sellers. From the Gold Coast to the Bight of Benin, the African trade often took on the character of an open, unpoliced bazaar. British ships routinely sold to African buyers goods produced by European rivals when in competition for the purchase of human cargoes. British factors in Africa sometimes boarded enslaved men and women on French and Dutch ships.[6] This last practice was common particularly along the banks of the

5. K. G. Davies, *The Royal African Company* (London, 1957), esp. 97–152; James A. Rawley, *The Transatlantic Slave Trade: A History* (New York, 1981), 141–169. For the challenge to the Royal Africa Company's monopoly, see Tim Keirn, "Monopoly, Economic Thought, and the Royal African Company," in John Brewer and Susan Staves, eds., *Early Modern Conceptions of Property* (London, 1996), 427–466; Kenneth Morgan, ed., *The British Transatlantic Slave Trade*, II, *The Royal African Company* (London, 2003), x–xxiv; and James A. Rawley, "Richard Harris, Slave Trader Spokesman," in Rawley, *London, Metropolis of the Slave Trade* (Columbia, Mo., 2003), 57–70.

6. A. P. Newton, "British Enterprise in Tropical Africa," in J. Holland Rose, A. P. Newton, and E. A. Benians, *The Cambridge History of the British Empire*, 8 vols. (1929–1959; rpt. Cambridge, 1961), II, 633–635; Davies, *The Royal African Company*, 121–122, 259–262; Nigel Tattersfield, *The Forgotten Trade: Comprising the Log of the Daniel and Henry of 1700 and Accounts of the Slave Trade from the Minor Ports of England, 1698–*

Gambia, Sierra Leone, and Sherbro Rivers, where British firms established private trading posts, especially after the final demise of the Royal Africa Company in 1750. Historian David Hancock reports that from 1763 to 1783 Grant, Oswald, and Company provided from their Bance Island fort 4,847 men, women, and children to French ships dispatched from Honfleur.[7] On the African coast, self-interest prevailed routinely over corporate or national interests. Perhaps nowhere in the Atlantic was the mercantilist system more widely abandoned in practice.

The British merchants operating in Africa sought assistance from the state only when fulfilling their ambitions required the muscle of state authority. Gold, not slaves, first had brought the English (like other Europeans) to the African coast. Deep into the eighteenth century the prospect of substantial returns in gold would continue to enthrall British men who traveled to Africa, even as gold exports declined. Those who dreamed of locating an African El Dorado hoped above all to enrich themselves. Yet they understood that they would need state support to exploit and profit from their claims. Private interests were described as public interests when private interests needed state funding. In 1757, for example, an entrepreneur name Thynne proposed to instruct Fantee laborers in what he characterized as Brazilian techniques of gold mining if the crown first would secure land rights along the Gold Coast for British nationals. George Glas,

---

1725 (London, 1991), 78; Margaret Priestley, *West African Trade and Coast Society* (London, 1969), 75.

7. David Hancock, *Citizens of the World: London Merchants and the Integration of the British Atlantic Community, 1735–1785* (Cambridge, 1995), 172–220. This practice had early eighteenth-century precedents. London slave trader Humphry Morice dealt extensively in Dutch wares and frequently sold slaves to Dutch and Portuguese agents along the coast. James A. Rawley, "Humphry Morice: Foremost London Slave Merchant of His Time," in Rawley, *London, Metropolis of the Slave Trade*, 45–46, 48, 50. For Miles Barber and Co., which operated from the Sherbro River, see Walter Rodney, *A History of the Upper Guinea Coast, 1450–1800* (Oxford, 1970), 251–253, and Melinda Elder, *The Slave Trade and the Economic Development of Eighteenth-Century Lancaster* (Halifax, Eng., 1992), 59–60. In 1763, former company factor Richard Brew constructed a "castle" of his own in the shadows of the English fort at Annamaboe. Priestley, *West African Trade and Coast Society*, 55–113. For further evidence of such privately owned slave trading stations, see Conrad Gill, *Merchants and Mariners of the Eighteenth Century* (Westport, Conn., 1961), 74–91.

a slave trader, sought from the king in 1764 an exclusive claim to a discovery he advertised as "the greatest that has been made in commerce" since 1492—a West African harbor positioned to divert gold caravans away from the Sahara and toward the Atlantic coast and British merchants. When lobbying for support, these speculators often resorted to the vocabulary of imperial power. They predicted increased revenue for the Treasury, enlarged markets for British manufactures, and growth of the merchant marine. And they warned darkly of the consequences if Britain should "be too late in her application to Negroe princes" for the rights to inland gold fields. The French, they predicted, would be the first to exploit the natural resources of the continent should the state fail to act quickly.[8] These warnings about the dangers presented by French power, in one instance, transformed British enterprise on the coast. The merchants Samuel Touchet and Thomas Cuming wanted access to the French-controlled trade in gum arabic, an item used in the refinement of silks and other textiles. So in 1758 they successfully urged on the elder William Pitt an expedition to capture the French trading base at Saint Louis, selling the plan to the first minister as a means of reducing the economic power of a bitter rival.[9]

For all the wealth the slave trade produced, some familiar with the coast thought the potential for commerce with Africa scarcely tapped. This view prevailed particularly among those unsuccessful in the competition to procure slaves for the American colonies. In sporadic fits of enthusiasm, the Royal Africa Company asked its agents to promote the export trades in

8. Robin Law and P. E. H. Hair, "The English in Western Africa to 1700," in Nicholas Canny, ed., *The Oxford History of the British Empire,* I, *The Origins of Empire: British Overseas Enterprise to the Close of the Seventeenth Century* (Oxford, 1998), 251–256; "Proposal for Working the Gold Mines on the Gold Coast of Guinea," PRO CO 267/6; "Petition of George Glas to the Lords Commissioners of Trade and Plantations (The Board of Trade)," PRO PC 1/7/96; [George Glas], *A Scheme for Opening a Trade between the European and the Inhabitants of the Inland Parts of Africa* (London, 1764).

9. James L. A. Webb, Jr., "The Mid-Eighteenth Century Gum Arabic Trade and the British Conquest of Saint-Louis du Senegal, 1758," *Journal of Imperial and Commonwealth History,* XXV, no. 1 (1997), 37–58; Joseph E. Inikori, *Africans and the Industrial Revolution in England: A Study in International Trade and Economic Development* (Cambridge, 2002), 397–399; Maxine Berg, "In Pursuit of Luxury: Global History and British Consumer Goods in the Eighteenth Century," *Past and Present,* no. 182 (February 2004), 137–140.

cotton, indigo, pepper, medicines, and potash. The company at times took the further step of sending to the coast seeds, mills, and technicians to set up its own plantations. The Royal Africa Company attempted indigo along the Sherbo River in the 1690s and again, with brief success, at Cape Coast Castle early in the eighteenth century. These modest achievements owed much to the initiative of Sir Dalby Thomas, the energetic and ambitious chief factor at Cape Coast Castle from 1703 and probably the first British official to espouse agricultural "improvement" in West Africa. Before his death in 1711, he wrote officials in London about supplementing the several acres of indigo at Cape Coast with corn, cotton, and sugar worked by slave labor, in the hope that, in time, the region could support a British colony. These ideas continued to circulate long after Thomas left the scene. In 1715 the Royal Africa Company funded a short-lived project to seek gold mines near the coast. In 1718 they considered manufacturing rum. Exploration of the African interior figured in the fiction of Daniel Defoe, who published two defenses of the Royal Africa Company in the 1710s, and sent his fictional Captain Singleton on a transcontinental trek through southern Africa. James Brydges, the duke of Chandos and a prominent voice in company affairs, renewed plantation schemes a decade later, convinced that Africa could "become as beneficial to England as America is to Spain." Under his leadership, in the early 1720s, the Royal Africa Company sent to Cape Coast Castle gins to foster an export trade in cotton and teams of Cornish miners to draw ores from Akan gold fields.[10]

10. David Eltis, *The Rise of African Slavery in the Americas* (Cambridge, 2000), 241–244; Robin Law, "King Agaja of Dahomey, the Slave Trade, and the Question of West African Plantations: The Embassy of Bulfinche Lambe and Adomo Tomo to England, 1726–1732," *Jour. Imperial and Commonwealth Hist.*, XIX, no. 2 (1991), 155–158; Davies, *The Royal African Company,* 132–133, 220–221, 344–345; Rodney, *A History of the Upper Guinea Coast,* 167–170; Tattersfield, *The Forgotten Trade,* 91–92; Kwame Yeboa Daaku, *Trade and Politics on the Gold Coast, 1600–1720: A Study of the African Reaction to European Trade* (Oxford, 1970), 45–46; Colin Palmer, *Human Cargoes: The British Slave Trade to Spanish America, 1700–1739* (Urbana, Ill., 1981), 36; Tim Keirn, "Daniel Defoe and the Royal African Company," *Bulletin of the Institute of Historical Research,* LXI (1988), 243–247; Roxann Wheeler, *The Complexion of Race: Categories of Difference in Eighteenth-Century British Culture* (Philadelphia, 2000), 107–109; Larry Stewart, *The Rise of Public Science: Rhetoric, Technology, and Natural Philosophy in Newtonian Britain, 1660–1750* (Cambridge, 1992), 320–324; Joseph E. Inikori,

These projects, both real and imagined, were doomed by the inability of the British to establish ascendancy anywhere in Africa. Like other Europeans, British visitors suffered from high mortality on the coast. Military and political authority, moreover, rested unambiguously with African elites. Until the capture of Senegal in 1758, the British could claim no territory in Africa. Factors, soldiers, traders, and artisans in the hundreds occupied the scattered forts during the eighteenth century. But these establishments were little more than trading posts held at the pleasure of local rulers to whom the British paid tribute or annual rent. The British garrisons kept the commerce open to British ships. African political and commercial elites in the coastal towns, however, prevented the formation of sizable British settlements, an opposition that the slave traders were neither equipped nor inclined to overcome. The hundreds of independent British merchants who outfitted ships for Africa found returns in the slave trade far more enticing than uncertain long-term investments in commercial agriculture, where they lacked secure claims to land and insufficient wealth to compete against the American colonists in the market for slave labor.[11]

The Chaining of a Continent: Export Demand for Captives and the History of Africa South of the Sahara, 1450–1870 (Mona, Jamaica, 1992), 47–50, Chandos cited on 48; Inikori, Africans and the Industrial Revolution in England, 385–388. The account presented in this paragraph and the pages that follow touch on a vast subject that deserves a more extended discussion than it can receive here. Readers should be aware that comparable ambitions developed elsewhere in Europe during the eighteenth century, with comparably limited results. The international history of schemes for plantations, colonies, and legitimate commerce in Africa before the 1780s remains unwritten. For the Dutch, see Inikori, Africans and the Industrial Revolution in England, 385–388. For the French, see William B. Cohen, The French Encounter with Africans: White Response to Blacks, 1530–1880 (Bloomington, Ind., 1980), 155–166.

11. For general statements on European vulnerability in Africa during the eighteenth century, see J. D. Fage, "African Societies and the Atlantic Slave Trade," Past and Present, no. 125 (November 1989), 97–115, and Robin Law, " 'Here Is No Resisting the Country': The Realities of Power in Afro-European Relations on the West African 'Slave Coast,' " Itinerario, XVIII (1994), 50–64. The isolated conditions endured by Britons at work on the coast are evoked in Hancock, Citizens of the World, 195–198, David Henige, " 'Companies Are Always Ungrateful': James Phipps of Cape Coast, a Victim of the African Trade," African Economic History, IX (1980), 27–47, and Ty M. Reese, "The Drudgery of the Slave Trade, 1750–1790," in Peter A. Coclanis, ed., The Atlantic Econ-

The Royal Africa Company, in theory, was better suited to attempt projects that would not yield quick returns. But its weak political standing in England, outsized debt, and unreliable agents hindered even its modest attempts to expand the trade in staple crops. Its successor, the Company of Merchants Trading to Africa, suffered as well from limited funds. Even more, though, it never established more than nominal control over its employees on the coast. The organizations responsible for overseeing the Africa trade struggled to maintain the forts, provision the garrisons, and instill a semblance of discipline. They stood no chance of setting up plantations in Africa on their own.[12] The Board of Trade added to these difficulties after 1750 by discouraging private efforts to plant British colonists anywhere along the coast. In 1752 the board forbade officials at the Gold Coast from reviving cotton and indigo plantations on the grounds of Cape Coast Castle, in part because cultivation in Africa could harm the profitability of colonial settlements in the Americas by offering them competition. The board did express an interest in Thynne's plan to capture Fantee gold mines for British nationals. But it decided that any attempt to exercise command in Africa would entangle merchants in local politics and undermine the Atlantic slave trade.[13] Caution prevailed. The state neither supervised the African trade nor blessed efforts to expand its compass.

---

omy during the Seventeenth and Eighteenth Centuries: Organization, Operation, Practice, and Personnel (Columbia, S.C., 2005), 277–280. Mortality rates among Royal Africa Company employees are treated in K. G. Davies, "The Living and the Dead: White Mortality in Africa, 1684–1732," in Eugene Genovese and Stanley Engerman, eds., Race and Slavery in the Western Hemisphere: Quantitative Studies (Princeton, N.J., 1975), 83–98. The difficulty of competing with the American plantations is considered in Inikori, Africans and the Industrial Revolution in England, 388–389, 393.

12. On the weaknesses of Royal African Company oversight, see Law, "King Agaja of Dahomey, the Slave Trade, and the Question of West African Plantations," Jour. Imperial and Commonwealth Hist., XIX, no. 2 (1991), 157–158, and Davies, The Royal African Company, 344–349. For the Company of Merchants Trading to Africa, see Eveline Christiana Martin, The British West African Settlements, 1750–1821: A Study in Local Administration (London, 1927), 43–56.

13. Consider excerpts from the board's report on Thynne's application to discover and work gold mines near the coast: "England has not in Africa, like Portugal in the Brasils, Property in the Soil, or Sovereignty over its Inhabitants. On the contrary, the British interest, both in Possessions and Commerce, depends chiefly, if not entirely, on

This restricted if judicious definition of national interest infuriated those enamored with grandiose fantasies of establishing British imperial power in Africa, notably Malachy Postlethwayt, a commentator too frequently neglected in histories of British antislavery thought. Students of the eighteenth-century empire know Postlethwayt as the chief propagandist for the Royal Africa Company and, as such, as a leading apologist for the Atlantic slave trade in the 1740s. Few, though, have noticed his more general commitment to extending the reach of the British state deep into the African hinterland or the consequences of that commitment to his evolving view of the Atlantic slave trade, a shift evident in his later publications.[14] Postlethwayt believed that great wealth awaited the nation that

---

the good Will and friendship of the Natives, who do not allow Us even those Possessions limited as they are to the bare Spots on which Our Forts and Factories are situated without the Payment of an annual Quitrent, by way of acknowledgement of their Right. The whole of the British Commerce also, as well in Slaves, as in Elephants Teeth and Gold Dust, passes thro' the hands of the Natives, who have ever expressed great Jealousy at every attempt made by Europeans to discover the Nature and Produce of their Country and particularly their Gold. . . . When these circumstances are considered, it must be submitted whether it be adviseable to give Encouragement to such an Undertaking. . . . Whether there is any reasonable hope of Succeeding in it; and whether on the contrary, there is not great Reason to fear, that the very attempt might, by embroiling us with the Natives, and thereby affording the most favourable Opportunity to the designs of our Enemies who have Settlements on the Coast, be productive of such Consequences, as may endanger the British Possessions, and the valuable Branches of Commerce which we now carry on in that Country." "Lords of Trade Report to William Pitt on Mr. Thynne's Proposal to Work Gold Mines on the Coast of Africa," Jan. 23, 1758, PRO CO 267/6. See also Martin, *The British West African Settlements,* 24–25. For India, see P. J. Marshall, "The British in Asia: Trade to Dominion, 1700–1765," in Marshall, ed., *The Oxford History of the British Empire,* II, *The Eighteenth Century* (Oxford, 1998), 498. The concern to protect West Indian cultivators of tropical crops is discussed briefly in Inikori, *Africans and the Industrial Revolution in England,* 389–392, and Daaku, *Trade and Politics on the Gold Coast,* 46. North American and West Indian lobbyists almost certainly campaigned to prevent the development of plantation agriculture in West Africa. Regrettably, that history remains unwritten.

14. Little of Postlethwayt's correspondence appears to survive, but much can be gleaned about his life from his several publications. See also Peter N. Miller, *Defining the Common Good: Empire, Religion, and Philosophy in Eighteenth-Century Britain* (Cam-

secured for itself a commerce in the natural products of Africa. For this reason, it was not enough to allow the independent merchants to predominate in the Africa trade. If these individual traders succeeded well in securing profits for themselves, they had not and would not do enough to advance the nation's strategic interests in Africa as a whole. The state, he argued, needed to promote what later generations would come to know as "legitimate commerce," in particular by deepening official investment in the Royal Africa Company. Its declining fortunes he regarded as symptomatic of a more general failure among politicians to grasp the national importance of the Africa trade or its possibilities.

Postlethwayt had a personal interest in keeping the Royal Africa Company afloat. He served on its Court of Assistants for more than a dozen years before it was disbanded in 1750. In three increasingly alarmist pamphlets published in the 1740s, he warned that abandoning the company would mean throwing the slave trade into the arms of European competitors. As it was, he stated, the exclusive privileges enjoyed by the Compagne des Indes enabled France to supply its colonies with slaves at a cheaper price, permitting the cultivation of sugar at a lower cost, allowing French sugar to undersell British sugar in European markets, and in turn strengthening the French merchant marine. Whereas France kept the purchase price of slaves low by restricting the number of French ships on the African coast, British merchants drove up their own costs through reckless bidding wars on each cargo. Only the Royal Africa Company, Postlethwayt insisted,

---

bridge, 1994), 163–169; William Darity, Jr., "British Industry and the West Indies Plantations," in Joseph E. Inikori and Stanley L. Engerman, eds., *The Atlantic Slave Trade: Effects on Societies, Economies, and Peoples in Africa, the Americas, and Europe* (Durham, N.C., 1992), 270–273; Philip D. Curtin, *The Image of Africa: British Ideas and Action, 1780–1850* (Madison, Wis., 1964), 70; and E. A. J. Johnson, *Predecessors of Adam Smith: The Growth of British Economic Thought* (New York, 1937), 185–205. Only a handful of studies have been alert to the way Postlethwayt's published views shifted over time. See James Robert Constantine, "The African Slave Trade: A Study of Eighteenth Century Propaganda and Public Controversy" (Ph.D. diss., Indiana University, 1953), 45–51; David Brion Davis, *The Problem of Slavery in Western Culture*, 2d ed., rev. (Oxford, 1988), 160–161; Angelo Costanzo, ed., *The Interesting Narrative of the Life of Olaudah Equiano; or, Gustavus Vassa, the African, Written by Himself* (Peterborough, Ont., 2001), 25–26, 300–303; and Philip Gould, *Barbaric Traffic: Commerce and Antislavery in the Eighteenth-Century Atlantic World* (Cambridge, Mass., 2003), 21–24.

could discourage such free-for-alls by negotiating for all British traders a set price from African suppliers. Furthermore, only sufficient funding for the company's forts in Africa could keep the French from encroaching on British trade in the Gambia River and prevent the Dutch from seizing control of traffic along the Gold Coast. Postlethwayt accepted that independent merchants would predominate in the carrying trade across the Atlantic. He proposed for the Royal Africa Company a sphere of activity better suited to its coastal establishment. In addition to warehousing captives for British merchants, the forts could serve as stations from which to carry "*British* Produce and Manufactures into the very heart of Africa, where they have not yet reached." Only a joint-stock company could perform this task. And the prospects, he added parenthetically, were limitless. "It certainly is our own Fault," he declared, "if we do not render the *African Trade* as valuable to Great Britain as the *Mines* of *Peru, Mexico,* and the *Brazils* are to the *Spaniards* and *Portuguese*."[15]

Few before the American Revolution went further than Postlethwayt in imagining West Africa as a future seat of British power. The idea of a British empire in Africa figured prominently in his several publications on trade and commercial policy even after the Royal Africa Company lost its charter. Increasingly, he looked with hope to the East India Company, which already had routine access to the textiles most valued by African consumers. Even more, Postlethwayt explained, the East India Company possessed the capital required to build forts and factories in the interior and, thereby, forge alliances with "negro princes." In time, he predicted trade with Africa

15. [Malachy Postlethwayt], *The African Trade, the Great Pillar and Support of British Plantation Trade in America . . .* (London, 1745), 45. See also Postlethwayt, *The Importance of Effectually Supporting the Royal African Company of England . . .* (London, 1745), and Postlethwayt, *The National and Private Advantages of the African Trade Considered: Being an Enquiry, How Far It Concerns the Trading Interest of Great Britain, Effectually to Support and Maintain the Forts and Settlements in Africa; Belonging to the Royal African Company of England . . . with a New and Correct Map* (London, 1746). The first of these tracts the English Short Title Catalog wrongly attributes to Charles Hayes, director of the Royal Africa Company. Postlethwayt identifies himself as the author in his *In Honour to the Adminstration; the Importance of the African Expedition Considered: with Copies of the Memorials . . . the Whole as Planned and Designed by Malachy Postlethwayt . . . to Which Are Added, Observations, Illustrating the Said Memorials* (London, 1758), 270–273.

would surpass commerce with Asia and the Americas. Postlethwayt described Africans as "savages." But he also thought their extensive trading networks evidence of great wealth and stable polities. Commerce, Postlethwayt insisted, would civilize Africans as it had American Indians and, in turn, instill a dependence on British goods. Sending out British colonists to the coast in substantial numbers would inspire the peoples of Africa to embrace European tastes and manners. They would "become so civilized as to clothe, and live more and more according to the European mode." The desire for imported manufacturers, in turn, would move Africans to offer up precious commodities and clear the way, on the continent, for the cultivation of crops valued in European markets. Postlethwayt waxed rhapsodic contemplating the possibilities. "None except the Portuguese," he remarked, "have made any use of all the land, the fruitful soil lies waste, a very established country, pleasant vallies, banks of rivers, spacious plains capable of cultivation to unspeakable benefit, in all probability will remain fallow and unnoticed."[16] Postlethwayt considered the West African hinterland a vast, unimproved common. His plans for commercial agriculture represented a grand scheme of enclosure.

As his enthusiasm for a British empire in Africa intensified, Postlethwayt's support for the slave trade seems to have diminished. The erstwhile propagandist for the Royal Africa Company turned against the slave trade in later publications, including his *Britain's Commercial Interest Explained* (1757) and the several editions of his *Universal Dictionary of Trade and Commerce*. These works not only expounded on the commercial returns that the colonization of Africa could yield. They also suggested that a British empire in Africa could liberate the continent from the horrors of the Atlantic slave trade. Christian Europe stood to gain more from "a friendly, humane, and civilized commerce" with Africa than a "trifling portion of trade upon their sea-coasts." But civilized commerce had become impossible because of the disorder in West African societies caused by the colonial demand for slaves. While this situation persisted, Europeans could never "travel with safety into the heart of Africa" or "cement" "commercial friendships." If the

16. Postlethwayt, *In Honour to the Administration*, 59, 85, 93. Similar passages appear in the 1757 and 1766 editions of Postlethwayt's *Universal Dictionary of Trade and Commerce* (London) and *Britain's Commercial Interest, Explained and Improved in a Series of Dissertations*, 2 vols. (London, 1757).

slave trade ended, however, "a fair and honourable commerce" could take its place and "civilize" the "natives." At that point, white laborers could be recruited from Europe to work the Caribbean sugar colonies as servants in the place of enslaved Africans. This attempt to justify British colonies in Africa led Postlethwayt to reconsider some of his earlier statements. His later works insisted on the human equality of African peoples, who he thought possessed the same "rational faculties" and were "as capable of mechanical and manufactural arts and trades" as Europeans. Postlethwayt described the Atlantic slave trade as ruinous for Africa. His publications may have been among the first to argue that it led to the continent's "underdevelopment." "The whole country was captive," he observed in his *Universal Dictionary of Trade and Commerce,* "and produced its treasures, merely for the use and benefit of the rest of the world, and not at all for its own." In 1757, three decades before the formation of the Society for Effecting the Abolition of the Slave Trade, indeed, four years before the Quakers renounced participation in the slave trade, Postlethwayt was hoping that his publications would "rouse some noble and benevolent christian spirit to think of changing the whole system of the Africa trade."[17]

17. Postlethwayt, *The Universal Dictionary of Trade and Commerce* . . . , 2 vols., 3d ed. (London, 1766), I, vii, 25, 727. Postlethwayt the publicist was recognized at the time and since as a "literary pirate" who liberally appropriated the ideas of others, especially in his *Universal Dictionary.* See Richard Yeo, *Encyclopaedic Visions: Scientific Dictionaries and Enlightenment Culture* (Cambridge, 2001), 21; Elspet Fraser, "Some Sources of Postlethwayt's Dictionary," *Economic History,* III (1938), 25–32; and Fritz Redlich, "The Earliest English Attempt at Theoretical Training for Business: A Bibliographical Note," *History of Political Economy,* II (1970), 199–204. For these reasons, it may seem possible that the antislavery views published in the *Universal Dictionary* were silently extracted from the work of others, and not Postlethwayt's own. The work of this important author desperately needs more extensive study. There are, nonetheless, at least three reasons to believe that antislavery opinions published in his work were in fact his own views. First, they also appear in his works written to confront specific junctures in British imperial affairs, notably *Britain's Commercial Interest, Explained and Improved.* The antislavery statements in the *Universal Dictionary* were not, then, mere transcriptions to which the author attributed minimal importance. He also included them in his other publications. Second, the introduction to the third edition of the *Universal Dictonary* specifically identifies the passages on the Africa trade as the special contribution of the author. "Would it not be far more beneficial for all the trading European states, rather to

Malachy Postlethwayt contemplated antislavery measures in the 1750s and 1760s, it must be emphasized, as a means of enlarging the British Empire more than of promoting a revolution in attitudes toward slavery. There were limits, therefore, to how far he would push his antislavery views. Postlethwayt never strayed far from his first concern with expanding the reach of British trade. Outside his bulky tomes on British commerce, there is no evidence that he lobbied privately or publicly for slave trade abolition. For him, the cause of humanity never mattered more than extending the sphere of British power. Indeed, he tended to conflate the two, assuming that colonization of the coast would be an unambiguous good for the peoples of West Africa, about whom he actually knew little. What seemed to bother Postlethwayt most about the slave trade, in fact, were the ways it prevented the development of what he thought would be more lucrative branches of commerce.[18] Early abolitionists writing in the 1780s—notably Thomas Clarkson and Olaudah Equiano—would draw on his writings extensively (and selectively) to bolster their case against the slave trade. Until his death, though, in 1766, Postlethwayt's principal concern would remain with finding new ways to capture Africa's natural wealth.

Those ambitions to diversify British enterprise on the coast would become increasingly common in the decade after the Seven Years' War with

---

endeavour to cultivate a friendly, humane, and civilized commerce, with those people, into the very center of their extensive country, than to content themselves only with skimming a trifling portion of trade upon their sea-coasts? Has not the author of this performance, to no purpose yet, many years since suggested ways and means, whereby this might be done to the immense benefit of the British empire?" (vii). Finally, those passages in the *Universal Dictionary* that were most critical of the Atlantic slave trade were featured in sections set off as "remarks," sections in the dictionary where Postlethwayt shifted from narrative and description to opinion and prescription, a tendency especially pronounced on topics concerned with the national interest. Redlich, "An Eighteenth Century Business Encyclopedia as a Carrier of Ideas," *Harvard Library Bulletin*, XIX (1971), 80, 83, 87, 97–98. Postlethwayt's reasons for condemning the slave trade were complex, as the analysis in these pages should suggest, but the critique itself appears sincerely meant. Postlethwayt, moreover, was not alone in imagining African colonization as a route to slave trade abolition at the close of the Seven Years' War. See the anonymously published *Plan for Improving the Trade at Senegal* (London, 1763), as cited in Coleman, *Romantic Colonization and British Anti-Slavery*, 208n2.

18. Postlethwayt, *The Universal Dictionary of Trade and Commerce*, I, 685.

the seizure of French trading posts along the Senegal River. The new province of Senegambia, formally established in 1765, presented the possibility of extending British commerce beyond what Postlethwayt had mocked as a mere coasting trade. Parliament seemed to anticipate this possibility by granting the new colony a governor, council, courts, and constitution in the same years that it was authorizing new governments in the captured territories in Canada, the Caribbean, and the Floridas. British appointees recognized the opportunities for profit, too, as they conspired to transform Senegambia into personal fiefdoms in the same years that their peers pursued similar prospects for speculation in those parts of the Americas opened up by British conquest. Senegambia seemed to allow for the founding of a permanent beachhead on the African coast. Within a year of arrival, Governor Charles O'Hara had devised plans to establish white colonists several hundred miles up the Senegal River, near what he thought to be extensive gold mines and "prodigious quantities of Rice, Wax, Cotton, Indigo, and Tobacco." His successor, Matthias McNamara, would try to arrange for a colony of convicts along the Senegal in 1776. Among commentators in Britain, too, the new colony of Senegambia, like the new territories in North America and the Caribbean, generated grand (even grandiose) expectations. Thomas Whateley thought that it opened the way for an "Improvement in Power, in Commerce, and in Settlement, to a Degree, perhaps, of Colonization." Arthur Young espoused the introduction of "European customs and refinements" to create a demand for British manufactures in what most regarded as an immensely populous region. John Campbell fastened on the commodities that might be acquired and proposed encouraging "the Natives" to settle near the forts and cultivate export crops. O'Hara predicted that, in time, Senegambia would become "one of the richest Colonies, belonging to his Majesty," that British colonists would "extend over every part of this Continent that was worth while to settle."[19]

---

19. Martin, *The British West African Settlements*, 80–102; J. M. Gray, *A History of the Gambia* (1940; rpt. London, 1966), 234–275; H. A. Wyndham, *The Atlantic and Slavery* (London, 1935), 51–58; Frederick Madden and David Fieldhouse, eds., *Select Documents on the Constitutional History of the British Empire and Commonwealth: The Foundations of a Colonial System of Government*, III, *Imperial Reconstruction, 1763–1840: The Evolution of Alternative Systems of Colonial Government* (Westport, Conn., 1985), 491–505; Charles O'Hara to earl of Dartmouth and Board of Trade, 1765, July 26,

A British empire in Africa, however, was more easily imagined than accomplished in the eighteenth century. The eighteen years of British "rule" in Senegambia turned out to be an unqualified failure for the British and a disaster for the Wolof peoples of Senegal. Without colonists, Senegambia was a colony only in name. The elaborate constitution proved wholly inappropriate for a province that never boasted more than a few dozen British residents. Charles O'Hara, governor from 1765 to 1776, moreover, had little interest in and no skill for civil administration. He managed to increase the volume of the slave trade by instigating wars upriver. But because he terrorized the Francophone African creoles residing along the Senegal, Britain never reaped the full benefits of the gum trade. Dissension, backbiting, and corruption plagued the first British "province" in Africa. With the exception of the traders who imported gum from Senegal, few in England mourned the loss when the French captured Saint Louis in 1779 during the American Revolution.[20] The settlement did succeed, however,

---

1766, PRO CO 267/1; [Arthur Young], *Political Essays concerning the Present State of the British Empire; Particularly respecting: I. Natural Advantages and Disadvantages, II. Constitution, III. Agriculture, IV. Manufactures, V. The Colonies, and VI. Commerce* (London, 1772), 527–528; John Campbell, *A Political Survey of Britain: Being a Series of Reflections on the Situation, Lands, Inhabitants, Revenues, Colonies, and Commerce of This Island; Intended to Shew That We Have Not Yet Approached Near the Summit of Improvement, but That It Will Afford Employment to Many Generations before They Push to Their Utmost Extent the Natural Advantages of Great Britain; in Two Volumes* (London, 1774), II, 633; Thomas Whateley, *Considerations on the Trade and Finances of This Kingdom, and on the Measure of Administration, with Respect to Those Great National Objects since the Conclusion of the Peace*, 3d ed. (London, 1766), II, 129–130.

20. The earlier history by Martin, Gray, and Wyndham carefully avoid mention of O'Hara's depredations. His military career is outlined in William D. Griffin, "General Charles O'Hara," *Irish Sword*, X, no. 40 (1972), 179–187. For his subsequent role fighting in North America and the Caribbean during the American Revolution, see George C. Rogers, Jr., ed., "Letters of Charles O'Hara to the Duke of Grafton," *South Carolina Historical and Genealogical Magazine*, LXV, no. 3 (July 1964), 158–180, and Andrew Jackson O'Shaughnessy, *An Empire Divided: The American Revolution and the British Caribbean* (Philadelphia, 2000), 232. Brief but more balanced assessments of O'Hara's administration appear in James F. Searing, *West African Slavery and Atlantic Commerce: The Senegal River Valley, 1700–1860* (Cambridge, 1993), 114, 153, and Boubacar Barry, *Senegambia and the Atlantic Slave Trade* (Cambridge, 1998), 67–68, 87.

in producing a constituency in Britain for the colonization of Africa. Despite the obvious hazards, despite the undistinguished results of the first experiment, those who had resided in Senegambia for any length of time returned to Britain convinced that on the African coast, if given another chance, they could build a fortune for themselves, and perhaps for the nation, too.

The British defeat in the American war gave the Senegambia veterans additional arguments for a second attempt at colonization. The familiar lures remained: the mysteries of the unexplored interior, the likely market in Africa for British goods, the potential for commodity production in a tropical climate. What made the proposals of the 1780s different, what accounts for their quantity and variety, were the still uncertain consequences of American independence. The loss of the thirteen North American colonies threatened to rob the empire of American consumers, a vast supply of staple crops, and the principal source of foodstuffs for Caribbean plantations. In the end, of course, American independence proved less detrimental to the imperial economy than was feared. After the American war, British Atlantic trade would enter a period of explosive growth; at its close, though, no one could know what the future held. It seemed possible that Britain would need to look elsewhere for markets, for commodities, for provisions to supply the West Indian colonies. If the American rebellion succeeded, Senegambia governor John Clarke predicted in 1777, "the remaining Provinces of the Empire may rise in their Claims to public attention." The Gambia River district, the opposition gadfly Temple Luttrell declared in 1777, might provide "every valuable production we receive from America." "With proper care," he argued, "the advancement of the general trade to Africa" might "save the *debris* of this once mighty empire, when America shall be no longer ours." "The improvement of your marine nurseries, and an extension of your commerce to Africa," he told the House of Commons, "may yet maintain the British realm in splendor and prosperity, when her colonies on the other side of the Atlantic are totally separated from her empire."[21]

21. John Cannon, "The Loss of America," in H. T. Dickinson, ed., *Britain and the American Revolution* (London, 1998), 244–246; Gov. John Clarke to Lord George Germain, Sept. 12, 1777, in Madden and Fieldhouse, eds., *Select Documents,* III, *Imperial Reconstruction,* 504; William Cobbett and T. C. Hansard, *The Parliamentary History of*

Empire in Africa, several entrepreneurs agreed, could compensate for losses in America. Between 1783 and 1788, more than a dozen schemes materialized to transform or expand British enterprise on the African coast. Returned Senegambia administrators came forward with plans to colonize the Gambia River district, to which Britain retained exclusive trading rights at the peace. The British government struggled during and after the American war to find a place to dump felons sentenced to transportation. Charles O'Hara led a delegation to Whitehall that proposed a convict colony several hundred miles up the Gambia River. A rival, Edward Morse, bombarded the government in the same years with schemes to populate the region with British settlers and diversify the export trade. He stressed not only the likely take in staple crops. A colony on the Gambia, he argued, might also provision the Caribbean islands with "lumber, corn, and other Necessaries which heretofore they received from America." In a similar report, Daniel Houghton, a returned Senegambia soldier and future explorer of the Gambia, urged that Africa could supply crops no longer available within British territories. He recommended particularly the great quantity and high quality of Gambia cotton as a substitute for the plantations lost with the return of Tobago to France at the peace of 1783.[22]

England from the Earliest Period to the Year 1803, from Which Last-Mentioned Epoch It Is Continued Downwards in the Work Entitled "Hansard's Parliamentary Debates" . . . , 36 vols. (London, 1806–1820), XIX, 307, 308, 314, 315. The relation between the loss of America and fantasies of possession in Africa is described well in Coleman, *Romantic Colonization and British Anti-Slavery,* 2–3, 5, 20–22.

22. "Minutes of the Committee of the House of Commons Respecting a Plan for the Transporting of Felons to the Island of Le Maine in the River Gambia," PRO HO 7/1; Alan Frost, *Convicts and Empire: A Naval Question, 1776–1811* (Oxford, 1980), 8–9, 28–37; Frost, *Botany Bay Mirages: Illusions of Australia's Convict Beginnings* (Melbourne, 1994), 101–109; Patrick Webb, "Guests of the Crown: Convicts and Liberated Slaves on McCarthy Island, the Gambia," *Geographical Journal,* CLX (1994), 136–142; Edward Morse to Lord Sydney, Mar. 6, 1783, PRO CO 267/7; Morse, "A Comparative Statement of the Advantages and Disadvantages to Be Expected from the Territory of the River Gambia in the Hands of the African Company or Erected in a Colony," PRO CO 267/8; Daniel Francis Houghton to Thomas Townshend, Feb. 24, 1783, PRO CO 267/20; Robin Hallett, *The Penetration of Africa: European Exploration in North and West Africa to 1815* (New York, 1965), 219–224. The reader should keep in mind that the West African coast was just one of several regions considered for British colonization after the

British adventurers nominated almost every region in West Africa for exploration or colonization by the British during the 1780s. The government considered sending felons to Sierra Leone, São Tomé, and Cape das Voltas before settling in 1786 on the South Pacific and Botany Bay.[23] An army lieutenant in 1785 urged William Pitt to reorganize the Gold Coast establishment by vesting authority for the forts in the crown, instituting agriculture in the place of the transatlantic slave trade, dispatching convicts to Cape Coast Castle to serve as colonists, and acquiring African labor for the settlements by redeeming slaves destined for the Middle Passage.[24] All of these schemes were ambitious. Some bordered on the sublime. With the loss of North America, advised an adventurer named Henry Trafford, Britain had to look to the eastern Atlantic to secure its economic future. In 1783, he pestered the Shelburne ministry with what he called a "Plan of an Universal Revolution of Commerce," premised on a "re-transplantation of East and West Indian, North and South American Trades, into Africa." He looked forward to the day, he wrote, when Africa would be "traded, travelled and traversed, with the same efficacy and security as Europe." These were the same months in which Henry Smeathman, the originator of the Sierra Leone scheme, sought patrons for his plans to "civilize Africa," imagining himself, in each instance, as the founder of a new nation, a "Romulus, or Mahomed," perhaps, or, as he wrote to John Coakley Lettsom, "almost a Penn."[25]

American war. This was a moment when entrepreneurs also pushed expeditions against Panama, Peru, and Chile, expeditions conceived as voyages of conquests that might yield a British empire in South America. See Alan Frost, "Shaking Off the Spanish Yoke: British Schemes to Revolutionise America, 1739–1807," in Margarette Lincoln, ed., *Science and Exploration in the Pacific: European Voyages to the Southern Oceans in the Eighteenth Century* (Woodbridge, Suffolk, Eng., 1998), 27–32.

23. Frost, *Convicts and Empire*, 37–49; Frost, *Botany Bay Mirages*, 17–18. A House of Commons committee appointed to consider the convict question noted that Cape Das Voltas could serve as a home for British loyalists. A. G. L. Shaw, *Convicts and the Colonies: A Study of Penal Transportation from Great Britain and Ireland to Australia and Other Parts of the British Empire* (London, 1966), 47.

24. The Papers of William Pitt, first earl of Chatham, PRO 30/8/363.

25. Henry Trafford to Lord Grantham, Mar. 5, 1783, Grantham Papers, L29/340/341, Bedfordshire Record Office; Trafford to earl of Shelburne, Mar. 5, 1783, Shelburne Papers, CLII, fol. 75, William L. Clements Library, Ann Arbor, Mich.; "Plan of an Universal Revolution of Commerce," Feb. 14, 1783, ibid., fols. 152, 177 ff.; Henry Smeath-

In some quarters, the assessment of economic interest was more sober. The prospect of new sources for raw cotton intrigued several merchants. London trader Richard Oswald in 1783 directed factors at his Bance Island fort to "buy all the Cotton Wool you can get . . . in this trade with the Natives, and endeavour to learn whether it may not be possible to persuade those people to increase the culture of that article, as a commodity of exchange and commerce." To support his ambitions for Sierra Leone, Henry Smeathman quietly lined up two London investors willing to back the project in exchange for potential returns in raw cotton.[26] Manchester manufacturers seem not to have troubled themselves with the proposals to colonize the African coast. But some did display a particular interest in obtaining high-quality cotton from the continent. In 1786, the Privy Council Committee for Trade and Plantations began a series of initiatives designed to increase the volume of raw cotton produced within the empire in order to liberate the nation from a continued dependence on foreign suppliers and meet the exploding demand in Britain and Europe for Lancashire textiles.[27] Ultimately, Mancunians would draw the bulk of their cotton supplies from India, the British Caribbean, and the southern United States. In 1787, though, when the subject was still in question, seventeen Manchester firms were pushing for the Gambia and Cape Coast Castle as "the most likely place to try the Experiment" in cotton planting since, "upon the

---

man to Lettsom, July 16, 1784, in Pettigrew, ed., *Memoirs of the Life and Writings of J. C. Lettsom*, III, 275–276. George Chalmers, an official at the Board of Trade, dismissed Trafford as "a madman or an Ideot." Chalmers cited in Coleman, *Romantic Colonization and British Anti-Slavery*, 15.

26. Richard Oswald to Captain Griffiths, July 4, 1783, in Sheila Lambert, ed., *House of Commons Sessional Papers of the Eighteenth Century*, LXVIII, *Minutes of the Evidence on the Slave Trade, 1788 and 1789* (Wilmington, Del., 1975), 283; Braidwood, *Black Poor and White Philanthropists*, 94. Oswald took some interest, briefly, in Smeathman's proposals following the American war. Smeathman to Lettsom, July 16, 1784, in Pettigrew, ed., *Memoirs of the Life and Writings of J. C. Lettsom*, 272.

27. Caribbean governors were directed to encourage cotton planting in the British West Indies. At the recommendation of Joseph Banks, Polish scientist Anton Hove was dispatched to India to study cotton cultivation on the subcontinent. Vincent Harlow, *The Founding of the Second British Empire, 1763–1793*, II, *New Continents and Changing Values* (London, 1964), 280–293; David Mackay, *In the Wake of Cook: Exploration, Science, and Empire, 1780–1801* (London, 1985), 144–167.

African continent," "it grows . . . spontaneously." And in 1789, almost two years after the city's residents assembled thousands of signatures for its petition to Parliament on behalf of abolition, the Manchester writer John Lowe, Jr., argued publicly for, in the words of critic Deirdre Coleman, "the practicability as well as profitability of substituting for the slave trade a trade in African products." Lowe insisted that Africa could "make us amends, ten thousand fold," for the loss of the American colonies.[28]

Several scholars have discussed these proposals—notably Philip Curtin and Vincent Harlow—but their importance, wrongly, has been measured only in terms of their limited impact on policy and practice instead of their consequences for black loyalists and abolitionists. With the important exception of the Sierra Leone scheme, these plans were nonstarters. Holding European rivals at bay, keeping trade open to British merchants, minimizing costs—these remained the primary concerns in the African trade, and for many decades after. Otherwise, the state delegated oversight to the slave traders, who seem not to have cared about colonies or the prospects for commercial agriculture. This hands-off policy resembled the stance government had taken toward the East India Company. But, because of its sizable revenues and, after 1757, large territorial possessions, politicians had started to take a direct interest in Indian affairs by the 1780s. The African trade, by contrast, failed to win the sustained attention of a particular office or official. The British presence on the coast tended to rank low in the hierarchy of bureaucratic priorities. Lord George Germain ordered two regiments to Cape Coast Castle to defend British headquarters and to destroy the Dutch trading station at Commenda during the American war. But to avoid a drain on manpower, he sent a regiment of convicts that proved more successful at antagonizing African allies than achieving their modest military objectives.[29] Always, ministers of state treated Africa like a

28. William Frodsham to the Lords Committee of the Privy Council of Trade, Nov. 30, 1787, PRO BT 6/140; Coleman, *Romantic Colonization and British Anti-Slavery*, 16; John Lowe, Jr., *Liberty or Death; A Tract, by Which Is Vindicated the Obvious Practicability of Trading to the Coasts of Guinea, for Its Natural Products, in Lieu of the Slave-Trade* (Manchester, Eng., 1789), citation on 17.

29. Wilfrid Oldham, *Britain's Convicts to the Colonies,* ed. W. Hugh Oldham (Sydney, 1990), 72–80. Records of the British attack on the Dutch fort at Commenda in 1781 may be traced in PRO CO 267/7.

backwater. There was little in the way of policy or strategy, rarely evidence of vision or initiative. Politicians often were embarrassingly uninformed about the coast. Parliament established a committee in 1785 to consider a government plan to abandon felons on an isolated island more than three hundred miles up the Gambia River. That committee soon learned, to its astonishment, that the Pitt ministry lacked even the simplest information about the intended destination.[30] Several entrepreneurs outside the halls of power formulated plans for a British empire in Africa at the end of the American war. Where decisions were made, though, delivering slaves to the American colonies would remain the primary concern.

[II]   The West African coast held out a rather different promise to free blacks looking to escape North American slavery and racism, hoping to find an asylum for liberty. There, somewhere on the African coast it seemed, they might acquire land, security, and autonomy, a refuge from discrimination, dependence, and want. Their interest in the region differed from the ambitions and aspirations of men like Henry Smeathman, Malachy Postlethwayt, or Charles O'Hara. They did not care about reorganizing British trade. They expressed little interest in the promotion of Atlantic commerce. Nor did they lobby for slave trade abolition, a comprehensive emancipation, or other far-reaching plans of reform. They hoped, instead, to improve on the situation in which they found themselves. Their concerns were more immediate, their aims more pragmatic, the projects more personal. As early as 1773, four black freedom-seekers in Massachusetts declared a desire "to transport ourselves to some part of the Coast of *Africa*" to found "a settlement." After the war, free blacks in Rhode Island and Massachusetts explored opportunities to emigrate as a way of promoting a sense of nationhood. The free black preacher John Marrant told his Nova Scotia congregation in the late 1780s that on the coast of Africa they could establish a Christian utopia and an independent black state. Henry Smeathman in 1786 would, at last, find a constituency for his Sierra Leone scheme among the black loyalists in London hoping to start life anew on

30. See the testimony of Evan Nepean in "Minutes of the Committee of the House of Commons respecting a Plan for Transporting Felons to the Island of Le Maine in the River Gambia," fols. 4–12; Oldham, *Britain's Convicts to the Colonies,* ed. Oldham, 95–104.

the African coast. These Africans who would colonize Africa were not merely objects of charity, although their resettlement would require private and public patronage. By deciding to settle in Africa, they fought to determine their fate. The black loyalists in London resisted in 1786 those who would send them to Nova Scotia or the Bahamas instead. Those in Nova Scotia, several years later, demanded the opportunity to migrate to resettle in Sierra Leone, to escape from the white settlers who denied them land and equality. To them, the colonization of the African coast meant something altogether different from what it had meant to an adventurer like Henry Smeathman or what it would mean to abolitionists like Granville Sharp. The coast presented an opportunity for independence, freedom, and self-sufficiency.[31]

In the development of antislavery initiatives in late eighteenth-century Britain, black self-assertion had been and could be decisive. Fugitive slaves had effectively ended slaveholding in Britain one decade after the Seven Years' War by making slaveholding untenable. When they fled from involuntary servitude in a "land of liberty," they made slavery the subject of scrutiny. They obliged slaveholders to assert their authority through a show of force. That determination to win freedom had led as well to the abolition of slavery in Scotland in 1778. Inspired by the success of James Somerset, the enslaved Joseph Knight initiated the pivotal contest in the Scottish courts by escaping from the home of absentee planter John Wedderburn. Thereafter, the vigilance of free blacks would make it difficult for slaveowners to deport enslaved men and women from British soil. In one important instance, black initiative had transformed the Atlantic slave trade into a public scandal. In the spring of 1783 the sailor and former slave Olaudah

---

31. The petition of Peter Bestes, Sambo Freeman, Felix Holbrook, and Chester Joie, Apr. 20, 1773, in Gary B. Nash, *Race and Revolution* (Madison, Wis., 1990), 174; Floyd J. Miller, *The Search for a Black Nationality: Black Emigration and Colonization, 1787–1863* (Urbana, Ill., 1975), 4–28; W. Bryan Rommel-Ruiz, "Atlantic Revolutions: Slavery and Freedom in Newport, Rhode Island, and Halifax, Nova Scotia" (Ph.D. diss., University of Michigan, 1999), 302–311, 366–367; Braidwood, *Black Poor and White Philanthropists,* 98–102; John Saillant, "Antiguan Methodism and Antislavery Activity: Anne and Elizabeth Hart in the Eighteenth-Century Black Atlantic," *Church History,* LXIX (1999), 103, 106–107; Saillant, " 'Wipe Away All Tears from Their Eyes': John Marrant's Theology in the Black Atlantic, 1785–1808," *Journal of Millennial Studies,* I, no. 2 (1999). Web site: http://www.mille.org/publications/winter98/saillant.PDF.

Equiano drew Granville Sharp's attention to the infamous case of the slave ship *Zong*, from which Captain Luke Collingwood in 1781 tossed 132 enchained Africans into the Atlantic in order to claim insurance for lost cargo. Sharp responded to Equiano's report by trying (and failing) to have the ship captain and his crew prosecuted for murder and by impressing on those in power "*the necessity* (incumbent upon the whole nation) to put an immediate stop to the *Slave Trade*."[32] The incident caused a minor furor in the press and would be remembered by later antislavery campaigners as crucial to exposing the horrors of the slave trade. Black self-assertion after the American war, in sum, continued attempts to secure rights and liberties in the years before, although the aims and strategies would change in crucial ways.

Researchers still know far too little about the approximately ten thousand men and women of African descent who lived in the British Isles in the era of the American Revolution. Key questions remain unanswered and, to a degree, unanswerable. Like the great majority of laboring peoples in the early modern era, most black men and women living in Britain could neither read nor write. With several notable exceptions, they did not publish. Letter books do not survive. As a result, scholars have few opportunities to know in detail what blacks were thinking and saying in these crucial years. Access to what Africans were doing is also elusive. The strategies social historians

32. For black freedom struggles in England during the eighteenth century, see especially Douglas A. Lorimer, "Black Slaves and English Liberty: A Re-Examination of Racial Slavery in England," *Immigrants and Minorities*, III (1984), 121–150, as well as the works cited in chapter 1 of this book. The most thorough account of both *Knight v. Wedderburn* and of the case of the slave ship *Zong* appear in F. O. Shyllon, *Black Slaves in Britain* (London, 1974), 177–183, 184–199. For Granville Sharp's response to Equiano, see Hoare, *Memoirs*, 236, 241–244; Diary H (Mar. 19, 20, 21, May 19–22, 1783), 1, 4, Granville Sharp MSS, D3549 13/4/2; Sharp to William Lloyd Baker, May 22, 1783, ibid. The papers Granville Sharp assembled on the *Zong* incident are preserved as "Volume of Bound Manuscripts: Documents Relating to the Case of the Ship Zong, 1783. Entirely in Granville Sharp's Hand," National Maritime Museum, sec. 6: Rec/19. From this collection, see especially Sharp to duke of Portland, July 18, 1783. Sharp's early exchange of information with Equiano is referenced in Vincent Carretta, "Phillis Wheatley, the Mansfield Decision of 1772, and the Choice of Identity," in Klaus H. Schmidt and Fritz Fleischmann, eds., *Early America Re-Explored: New Readings in Colonial, Early National, and Antebellum Culture* (New York, 2000), 210.

have used to reconstruct the experience of the English poor provide little help in this instance. No institution before 1783 took a prolonged interest in the several thousands living in or near London. The state, the church, and local governments did not treat the small community of Africans in Britain as a distinctive group. The British government neither enacted legislation that bore specifically on the black population nor established administrative units charged with special oversight. No occupations, moreover, were assigned exclusively to black workers. Blacks represented, instead, a small proportion of the much larger class of sailors, servants, and domestics. For all of these reasons, Britain's black population is difficult to study in the aggregate. Indeed, historians may never have more than very rough estimates of the number of blacks in London, where the African population was comparatively large and concentrated, and perhaps most measurable. The fragments that scholars have culled from disparate sources—from the diaries and correspondence of slaveholders, from portraits, parish registers, court records, wills, and runaway advertisements—allow only for anecdotal (if often elegant) histories that, unavoidably, focus heavily on the more exceptional figures.[33]

33. In addition to those cited above, the key works are: K[enneth] Little, *Negroes in Britain: A Study of Racial Relations in English Society*, rev. ed. (London, 1972); James Walvin, *Black and White: The Negro and English Society, 1555–1945* (London, 1973); Folarin Shyllon, *Black People in Britain, 1555–1833* (London, 1977); Peter Fryer, *Staying Power: The History of Black People in Britain* (London, 1984); James Walvin, *England, Slaves, and Freedom, 1776–1838* (Jackson, Miss., 1986), 26–68; Keith A. Sandiford, *Measuring the Moment: Strategies of Protest in Eighteenth-Century Afro-English Writing* (London, 1988); Gretchen Gerzina, *Black London: Life before Emancipation* (New Brunswick, N.J., 1995); Norma Myers, *Reconstructing the Black Past: Blacks in Britain, c. 1780–1830* (Portland, Ore., 1996); and James Walvin, *An African's Life: The Life and Times of Olaudah Equiano, 1745–1797* (London, 1998). Compare with Sue Peabody, *"There Are No Slaves in France": The Political Culture of Race and Slavery in the Ancien Regime* (Oxford, 1996). Myers's painstaking research on late eighteenth- and early nineteenth-century London has established a minimum population figure of ten thousand with perhaps five thousand in London. Her systematic attempt to make the best of unsystematic sources hints that a more precise estimate, in the absence of new evidence, may be unattainable. Ian Duffield, rightly, has drawn attention to the underused naval records as likely sources for learning about those blacks who resided in England for a time during the late eighteenth century. Sailors and port workers almost certainly constituted

The exceptional figures matter quite a bit, though, to the history of British antislavery. The writings of Boston captive Phillis Wheatley and London grocer Ignatius Sancho, in particular, figured in the evolving antislavery debate in Britain during the 1770s and 1780s, particularly as it concerned the intellectual capacities of Africans and their descendants. White opponents of slavery described the accomplishments of these two black authors as a rebuke to racist assumptions, as evidence of African competence, talent, and promise. From Boston, the Reverend Thomas Woolridge wrote breathlessly to the earl of Dartmouth about Wheatley and her talents. To him, she was a marvel. "I was astonish'd and could hardly believe my own Eyes" when she sat to write, he effused. The contemporary debate on the significance and meaning of race shaped the reaction to Sancho's letters, too. His would embarrass those "half-informed philosophers" and "superficial investigators of human nature," declared the *Monthly Review* in 1784, who insist that "*Negers* as they are vulgarly called, are inferior to any white nation in mental abilities." Reactions of this kind fulfilled the hopes of his editor, Frances Crewe, who in 1782 had gathered Sancho's letters for publication with the express purpose of encouraging antislavery sentiment. Sancho's writings, she stated in the preface to his *Letters,* should prove "that an untutored African may possess abilities equal to an European." During the 1780s several British opponents of slavery—including Charles Crawford, Thomas Clarkson, George Gregory, William Dickson, and Joseph Woods—would seize on both Wheatley and Sancho as proof that Africans were capable of moral and cultural improvement. In this way, as symbols of black accomplishment, these early black writers assisted British arguments against slavery at a crucial moment in their development.[34]

---

the largest occupational class for black men in this period. Ian Duffield, " 'I Asked How the Vessel Could Go': The Contradictory Experiences of African and African Diaspora Mariners and Port Workers in Britain, c. 1750–1850," in Anne J. Kershen, ed., *Language, Labour, and Migration* (Aldershot, Eng., 2000), 121–154.

34. Thomas Woolridge cited in James Rawley, "The World of Phillis Wheatley," *New England Quarterly,* L (1977), 670; the *Monthly Review* and Frances Crewe are cited in Vincent Carretta, ed., *Letters of the Late Ignatius Sancho, an African* (New York, 1998), xvii, 4. Introductions to these works that place them in their cultural milieu are provided by Sandiford, *Measuring the Moment,* 43–72, and Carretta, *Unchained Voices: An Anthology of Black Authors in the English-Speaking World of the Eighteenth Century* (Lexington,

Wheatley and Sancho, though, were not mere symbols. They contributed to the antislavery discourse of the period. Both denounced the slave system explicitly. Wheatley wrote of being "snatch'd from *Afric's* fancy'd happy seat." Sancho condemned those who would vouch for Wheatley's talent but not her right to liberty. As early as 1766, he inveighed against the "cruel and capricious tyrants" prevailing in the sugar colonies.[35] Recent assessments, moreover, have unveiled the political opinions sometimes masked behind Wheatley's neoclassical verse and Sancho's playful Shandyean prose. In different ways, the works of both challenged the social and moral order that made slaveholding possible. Moreover, Wheatley and Sancho undoubtedly expressed a degree of contempt for slavery in private that surpassed in vehemence what ended up in print. The Sancho that readers had in the 1780s (as now) is the Sancho that Frances Crewe chose to produce. He emerges from his letters to Laurence Sterne as an unthreatening and unchallenging figure.[36] Researchers may never know if Crewe withheld from publication other letters that would have cast Sancho

---

Ky., 1996), 1–16. My discussion in this paragraph and the two that follow draws from the large and growing literature on Phillis Wheatley and Ignatius Sancho. I have benefited particularly from the following. Sancho: Paul Edwards and Polly Rewt, eds., *The Letters of Ignatius Sancho* (Edinburgh, 1994); Reyahn King, ed., *Ignatius Sancho: An African Man of Letters* (London, 1997); and Markman Ellis, "Ignatius Sancho's Letters: Sentimental Libertinism and the Politics of Form," in Vincent Carretta and Philip Gould, eds., *Genius in Bondage: Literature of the Early Black Atlantic* (Lexington, Ky., 2001), 199–217. Wheatley: Mukhtar Ali Isani, "The British Reception of Wheatley's *Poems on Various Subjects*," *Journal of Negro History*, LXVI (1981), 144–149; William H. Robinson, *Phillis Wheatley and Her Writings* (New York, 1984); David Grimsted, "Anglo-American Racism and Phillis Wheatley's 'Sable Veil,' 'Length'ned Chain,' and 'Knitted Heart,'" in Ronald Hoffman and Peter J. Albert, eds., *Women in the Age of the American Revolution* (Charlottesville, Va., 1988), 338–444; Frank Shuffleton, "On Her Own Footing: Phillis Wheatley in Freedom," in Carretta and Gould, eds., *Genius in Bondage*, 175–198; Kirstin Wilcox, "The Body into Print: Marketing Phillis Wheatley," *American Literature*, LXXI (1999), 1–29; [Helen Thomas], *Romanticism and Slave Narratives: Transatlantic Testimonies* (Cambridge, 2000), 201–225.

35. Wheatley, "To the Right Honourable William, Earl of Dartmouth, His Majesty's Principal Secretary of State for North-America, etc.," in Carretta, *Unchained Voices*, 66; Carretta, ed., *Letters of the Late Ignatius Sancho*, 74.

36. Carretta, ed., *Letters of the Late Ignatius Sancho*, 7.

in a different light. Self-censorship among black writers probably mis-shapes the archival record, too. For many years, it had seemed to scholars that the mixed-race New England theologian Lemuel Haynes took no interest in the institution of slavery until much later in life, until many years after American independence. When historian Ruth Bogin in 1983 produced an unpublished antislavery manuscript that Haynes wrote in 1776, the discovery forced a reassessment of Haynes's history and early black antislavery thought. As the historian John Saillant has now shown in exquisite detail, Haynes took the occasion of the Declaration of Independence to circulate among his friends a challenge to the narrow definition of liberty that prevailed within the patriot cause. "The oppression inherent in slavery," he wrote, was "a much greater oppression" than what the colonists experienced and "which they, themselves, impose on another." Almost certainly there were other black men and women in this period who drafted antislavery manuscripts that they could not or would not publish.[37]

These silences, in their own way, are crucial pieces of evidence. They help clarify what made black protests in Britain during the 1780s different from black antislavery initiatives in the decades before. Before the American Revolution, both external and self-imposed constraints limited what black activists could achieve. The forms they chose and the styles they adopted in these texts would prove far less influential as antislavery polemic than the works that Ottobah Cugoano and Olaudah Equiano would compose in the 1780s. The earlier publications succeeded more as interventions in ongoing debates about the capacities of the African race than as attempts to influence the political future for colonial slavery. Because Wheatley wrote about slavery obliquely and, in most instances, without reference to concrete injustices, her British readers, in 1773, could fixate on the hypocrisy of American slaveholders, as they were inclined to do, rather than scrutinize the slave trade that first brought her to Boston. The British treated her as a wonder rather than a thinker. Because Sancho assumed the persona of the jocular exile, his letters could be and were read in England as

37. Ruth Bogin, " 'Liberty Further Extended': A 1776 Antislavery Manuscript by Lemuel Haynes," *William and Mary Quarterly*, 3d Ser., XL (1983), 83–105. For Haynes, see the rich and complex study by John Saillant, *Black Puritan, Black Republican: The Life and Thought of Lemuel Haynes* (Oxford, 2003), Haynes cited on 16.

effusions of sentiment rather than as protests against empire and slavery.[38] Black men and women like Sancho and Wheatley—those who had acquired the cultural knowledge necessary to acquire an audience for their words—must have despised Atlantic slavery almost uniformly. But before the 1780s, they seem not to have agitated publicly and explicitly for slave trade abolition or a comprehensive emancipation. A similar conclusion may be offered for the several thousand African men and women in Britain before and during the American war whose voices the surviving records do not report. The runaway ads attest to their desire for freedom. Through flight, they helped end slaveholding in Britain. Among blacks in Britain there must have been countless protests against the slave system during the eighteenth century that went unrecorded or remain undiscovered. But there is no evidence of a coordinated, organized campaign among blacks in England before the 1780s to abolish slavery in the colonies or slave trading in the Atlantic. If such a campaign did exist, it left no mark.

Events transpired differently during the 1770s in New England, where Africans and their descendants did organize a public campaign to abolish slavery in the region. In the years before the Revolutionary War, enslaved people across New England petitioned the colonial governments for their liberty. In Massachusetts, particularly, that campaign showed coordination, savvy, and persistence. It represented an extension of earlier attempts by some individuals to achieve liberty through freedom suits in the colony's courts, where slaves, unusually, had long enjoyed limited rights under the law. There, in Massachusetts, the enslaved lobbied for province-wide emancipation at least three times in 1773, twice in 1774, and again in 1777. These efforts were carefully orchestrated. Organizers launched the 1773 initiative through a kind of steering committee, perhaps modeled on the committees of correspondence that their white neighbors had formed when

38. About Wheatley, the *Monthly Review* mused on how "this ingenious young woman is yet a slave." "The people of Boston," it observed, "boast themselves chiefly on their principles of liberty. One such act as the purchase of her freedom would, in our opinion, have done more honour than hanging a thousand trees with ribbons and emblems." *Monthly Review*, XLIX (1773), 458–459. See also Isani, "The British Reception of Wheatley's *Poems on Various Subjects*," *Jour. Negro Hist.*, LXVI (1981), 144–149; Wilcox, "The Body into Print," *Am. Lit.*, LXXI (1999), 1; and Carretta, ed., *Letters of the Late Ignatius Sancho*, xv–xx.

mobilizing against British authority. They distributed antislavery circulars to state legislators and town governments throughout the province. The Somerset case seems to have sparked the first antislavery petition in 1773. "Felix," the author, alluded vaguely to the hopes raised among blacks in New England who had learned of Mansfield's decision. Thereafter, though, the momentum for political organizing owed most to the broader spirit of rebellion in the colonies. A petition of April 1773 appealed explicitly to the honor of Massachusetts patriots, to "men who have made such a noble stand" for liberty. Two months later, with growing confidence, black petitioners invoked a claim to natural rights. By 1774, campaigners such as the "African" writing to the *Massachusetts Spy* were giving increasing attention to the hypocrisy of their white neighbors. Compare your experience with ours, insisted Caesar Sarter in the *Essex Journal and Merrimack Packet*. "Now if you are sensible that Slavery is in itself, and in its consequences, a great evil; why will you not Pity and relieve the poor, distressed, enslaved Africans?" By the time Prince Hall led a dozen black petitioners to the legislature in 1777, he and his colleagues had come to link American liberty with freedom for Africans in America: in petitioning for rights, we have acted as you acted, Prince Hall and his colleagues explained; like you, we have waited patiently for our grievances to be addressed; our peaceable requests too have been ignored; if your cause is legitimate, so is ours; "every principle from which America has acted in the Cours of their unhappy Deficulties with Great Britain pleads stronger than a thousand arguments in favour of your petitioners." Hall and his associates did not threaten violence. But the logic of the argument in 1777 pointed to the possibility of even more direct forms of resistance.[39]

39. *The Appendix; or, Some Observations on the Expediency of the Petition of the Africans, Living in Boston etc. Lately Presented to the General Assembly of This Province; to Which Is Annexed, the Petition Referred to; Likewise, Thoughts on Slavery; with a Useful Extract from the Massachusetts Spy, of January 28, 1773, by Way of an Address to the Members of the Assembly; by a Lover of Constitutional Liberty* (Boston, [1773]), 13–15; James Swan, *A Disuasion to Great-Britain and the Colonies, from the Slave-Trade to Africa,* 2d ed. (Boston, 1773), ix–x; John Allen, *An Oration on the Beauties of Liberty, or the Essential Rights of the Americans; Delivered at the Second Baptist-Church in Boston, upon the Last Annual Thanksgiving, Dec. 3d, 1772, Dedicated to the Right Honorable the Earl of Dartmouth; Published by the . . . Request of Many; by a British Bostonian,* 4th ed. (Boston, 1773), 75–78; Sidney Kaplan, *The Black Presence in the Era of the American*

"If they could seize opportunity, they could not create it." So C. L. R. James wrote of enslaved men and women in Saint Domingue on the eve of the Haitian Revolution. Slave insurrections in the Americas often occurred in moments of political crisis or in time of war. The Stono Rebellion that unsettled white South Carolina in 1739 broke out the same weekend England declared war on Spain. The aborted conspiracy by Africans and Irish to burn Manhattan to the ground in 1741 took shape when the city stood vulnerable to the threat of Spanish invasion. Tacky's revolt in Jamaica, one of the bloodiest to occur in the British Caribbean during the eighteenth century, started in 1760, shortly after soldiers typically assigned to the slave patrols left to assist the British invasion of French Guadeloupe during the Seven Years' War. An insurrection scare occurred in Jamaica again in 1776, not long after the British government ordered a regiment from the island to assist the army in North America. Thousands of enslaved men and women escaped their bondage during the American Revolution.[40] Later, perhaps

Revolution, 1770–1800, 2d ed. (Washington, D.C., 1989), 12, 15, 16, 103; Thomas J. Davis, "Emancipation Rhetoric, Natural Rights, and Revolutionary New England: A Note on Four Black Petitions in Massachusetts, 1773–1777," *NEQ*, LXII (1989), 248–263; *Massachusetts Spy*, Feb. 10, 1774; *Essex Journal and Merrimack Packet*, July 20, 1774; Emily Vanessa Blanck, "Revolutionizing Slavery: The Legal Culture of Slavery in Revolutionary Massachusetts and South Carolina" (Ph.D. diss., Emory University, 2003), 70, 93–98, 128–129, 149–150, 223–225. For the significance of freedom suits in New England between the Seven Years' War and the American Revolution, see John Wood Sweet, *Bodies Politic: Negotiating Race in the American North, 1730–1830* (Baltimore, 2003), 228–239. See also Patricia Bradley, *Slavery, Propaganda, and the American Revolution* (Jackson, Miss., 1998), 66–80, for reception and reaction in New England and elsewhere to the Somerset Case. For examples of freedom petitions in Connecticut and New Hampshire, see Gwendolyn Evans Logan, "The Slave in Connecticut during the American Revolution," *Connecticut Historical Society Bulletin*, XXX (1965), 73–78, and Roger Bruns, ed., *Am I Not a Man and a Brother: The Antislavery Crusade of Revolutionary America* (New York, 1977), 452–453.

40. C. L. R. James, *The Black Jacobins: Toussaint L'Ouverture and the San Domingo Revolution* (New York, 1938), 25; Merton L. Dillon, *Slavery Attacked: Southern Slaves and Their Allies, 1619–1865* (Baton Rouge, La., 1990), 23–25; Thomas J. Davis, *A Rumor of Revolt: The "Great Negro Plot" in Colonial New York* (New York, 1985); Michael Craton, *Testing the Chains: Resistance to Slavery in the British West Indies* (Ithaca, N.Y., 1982), 125, 127, 138, 174; Richard B. Sheridan, "The Jamaican Insurrection Scare of 1776

most famously, the slave insurrection that culminated in the Haitian Revolution began when the overthrow of the French monarchy and divisions among elites in Saint Domingue destabilized the authoritarian regimes that discouraged slave rebellion. Without the American Revolution, without colonial resistance to imperial rule, it might have taken much longer for black men and women in New England to find an opportunity to campaign for a general emancipation. Organized resistance among the enslaved during the eighteenth century (and at other times, too) is less a measure of their desire to be free (which was constant) than an index to their shifting sense of the possible, to an awareness of broader changes in the social and political order.

A sustained challenge to established institutions frequently requires the prospect of success, however distant, or the presence of useful allies. Otherwise, inequities of power, the force of custom, and a limited sense of alternatives can conspire to discourage persistent attempts to promote permanent change. It can be difficult, in retrospect, to keep the novelty of abolitionism in view. In the 1780s, the British had few precedents for the kind of mass organizing later generations could take for granted. The British public had never mobilized previously around a cause centered on the welfare of foreigners overseas. Even the most concerned—like Granville Sharp, James Ramsay, Anthony Benezet, and John Fothergill—would long be inhibited by the immensity of the task, by the apparent necessity of the slave system and the dearth of ways to halt its progress. The antislavery movement would depend, ultimately, on a broad base of public support. Yet it could never have commenced without the leadership of those whom sociologists sometimes term "early risers," those individuals and groups positioned to conceive a political program and win access to those in power.[41] Anyone, hypothetically, could have originated an antislavery movement in Britain. In the abstract, perhaps, enslaved men and women could have taken the lead in defining the agenda in Britain and mobilizing public support. To have a strong chance of success, though, a

---

and the American Revolution," *Jour. Negro Hist.*, LXI (1976), 293, 300–301, 305–306; Andrew J. O'Shaughnessy, *An Empire Divided: The American Revolution and the British Caribbean* (Philadelphia, 2000), 53, 153; Sylvia R. Frey, *Water from the Rock: Black Resistance in a Revolutionary Age* (Princeton, N.J., 1992).

41. Sidney Tarrow, *Power in Movement: Social Movements and Contentious Politics*, 2d ed. (Cambridge, 1998), 71–90.

nascent movement first would need political entrepreneurs who possessed the status and resources sufficient to sustain a novel undertaking through its first tentative stages, through the period when even the sympathetic would regard the cause as futile. Any number of groups or coalitions in the British Isles could have qualified for this role. But the small, impoverished, socially dependent, politically powerless, and culturally marginal black population in Britain, though, may have been among the least equipped.

It would have been difficult for black men and women in Britain to do any more than they did before the American war. Few had the leisure to study the structure of the Atlantic slave system and draw up schemes for reform. And few possessed the social and economic independence required to canvass for legislative change. Not many could have imagined for themselves the role of "abolitionist" before the 1780s, when, with the exception of Granville Sharp, there was no such thing in Britain as an "abolitionist." The daily work of survival imposed far more limited horizons and suggested more restricted ambitions. Even Ignatius Sancho, among the most educated and cosmopolitan black men living in England before the Revolutionary War, would do little more than address sentimental appeals to Laurence Sterne. The great majority, like Ukawsaw Gronniosaw, battled more regularly with the everyday indignities of poverty, isolation, and despair. Olaudah Equiano was one of the fortunate few with sufficient earnings, autonomy, and patronage to agitate for reform. And even he appears not to have considered campaigning for slave trade abolition until the mid-1780s, after the beginning of the Quaker campaign in England and the publication of James Ramsay's *Essay* in 1784. As late as 1779, Equiano was making plans to serve as an Anglican missionary on the African coast, an indication perhaps of where the concerns of some literate blacks lay in the decade before the Society for Effecting the Abolition of the Slave Trade formed.[42]

42. Carretta, ed., *The Letters of the Late Ignatius Sancho*, 331; James Albert Ukawsaw Gronniosaw, *Wonderous Grace Displaye'd in the Life and Conversion of James Albert Ukawsaw Gronniosaw, an African Prince, Giving an Account of the Religion, Customs, Manners, etc., of the Native of Zaara, in Africa; as Related by Himself* (Bath, 1772); Carretta, ed., *Olaudah Equiano: The Interesting Narrative and Other Writings* (New York, 1988), 220–223. Equiano took an interest in serving as an Anglican missionary on the coast at the encouragement of Matthias McNamara, who in 1775 had succeeded Charles O'Hara as the British governor of Senegambia.

Antislavery organizing among blacks in New England emerged from the opportunities that followed from colonial resistance to imperial authority. In a similar way, antislavery organizing among blacks in Britain would develop during the late 1780s as new allies surfaced and new openings became apparent. The era of the Revolutionary War left many free blacks convinced that they had earned recognition as loyal subjects of the crown. At the Court of King's Bench, they had received from Lord Mansfield in 1772 the right to protection from involuntary exile. The British army in North America had granted liberty to enslaved men and women who expressed their "allegiance" to the king by fleeing from colonists in rebellion. Some fugitives had won protection from the British state after the American war and escaped with the British army to Nova Scotia or London. A coalition of London philanthropists, the Committee for the Relief of the Black Poor, had formed in 1786 to care for those black loyalists in the city that suffered from want of work, shelter, and sustenance. In these years, moreover, the British government took small but important steps toward formalizing its commitments to its free black subjects. The liberated found that they could declare a corporate identity that had legitimacy in the eyes of the state. They were "Dunmore's Regiment" or "the Black Pioneers." Brigadier General Samuel Birch in New York City presented black loyalists with passports granting them the right to leave North America with the British army. Black loyalists in London destined for Sierra Leone each secured from the state certificates that declared the bearer a "faithful Loyal Subject" and "a *Freeman* of the Colony of Sierra Leona." London philanthropists designated as "corporals" the representatives elected by "the Black Poor."[43]

This inclination to grant recognition and protection invited free blacks to make claims on the imperial state. It encouraged free blacks throughout

43. Benjamin Quarles, *The Negro in the American Revolution* (Chapel Hill, N.C., 1961), 19–33; Todd W. Braisted, "The Black Pioneers and Others: The Military Role of Black Loyalists in the American War for Independence," in John W. Pulis, ed., *Moving On: Black Loyalists in the Afro-Atlantic World* (New York, 1999), 11–18; James W. St. G. Walker, *The Black Loyalists: The Search for a Promised Land in Nova Scotia and Sierra Leone, 1783–1870* (1976; rpt. Toronto, 1992), 11; Braidwood, *Black Poor and White Philanthropists*, 91–93, 103–104. This paragraph and the two that follow are informed throughout by Saillant, "Antiguan Methodism and Antislavery Activity," *Church Hist.*, LXIX (1999), an important essay that covers far more than its title indicates. As Saillant shows, recognition by the state and an orientation toward state power were crucial for

the postwar empire to negotiate the terms on which their loyalty would be based. Because the British government had begun to think of black loyalists as wards of the state, black loyalists started to think of themselves as an interest group. Once recognized as royal subjects, it would be hard to deter free blacks from acting as other loyal subjects would. They fought to have their understanding of British commitments manifest in practice. Increasingly, during the 1780s, they brought their grievances directly to the British government. The Nova Scotia settlers lobbied the governors of the province and thereafter the administration of William Pitt to insist on the land and supplies they had been promised on embarking from New York. When that did not work, they petitioned for transportation to Sierra Leone. The elected leaders of "the Black Poor" insisted on Sierra Leone as the ideal setting for resettlement and then, months later, fought the scheme as they became concerned about the government's true intentions in shipping them to the coast.[44]

A formal relationship with the state seemed to allow a right to be heard. Olaudah Equiano turned his position as a government functionary into a platform from which to criticize his employers. Administrators at the British naval board in 1786 appointed Equiano as "Commissary of Provisions and Stores for the Black Poor to Sierra Leona." He was to serve, in effect, as a British emissary. But Equiano became unsettled by the mismanagement and corruption that plagued the planning for the expedition and its launch. British officials responded by treating Equiano like a troublesome functionary. They dismissed him and then compensated him for his service. Importantly, he presented those protests, and himself, in explicitly racial terms. He stood forward as the spokesman for a constituency, not merely himself, and denounced the abuse of African migrants as disconcerting evidence of British treachery.[45]

---

allowing certain black writers to tackle the problem of slavery comprehensively and collectively (100–115). See also James W. St. G. Walker, "Myth, History, and Revisions: The Black Loyalists Revisited," *Acadiensis,* XXIX (1999), 99.

44. Gary B. Nash, "Thomas Peters: Millwright and Deliverer," in Nash and David G. Sweet, *Struggle and Survival in Colonial America* (Berkeley, Calif., 1981), 77–84; Walker, "Myth, History, and Revisions," *Acadiensis,* XXIX (1999), 88–89; Braidwood, *Black Poor and White Philanthropists,* 129–143; Rommel-Ruiz, "Atlantic Revolutions," 354–357.

45. Carretta, ed., *Olaudah Equiano,* 226–231; Braidwood, *Black Poor and White*

Black leaders like Equiano who emerged in London during the 1780s increasingly took public positions on what the imperial state ought to do. They took advantage of the emerging antislavery movement to claim a public voice for themselves. The campaign against the British slave trade transformed Equiano's life even as he helped to shape it. In 1785 Equiano had seen the progress of Quaker antislavery movements in Philadelphia. Later in the year, he led a delegation of eight Africans to Grace Church Street Meeting in London to thank the Society of Friends for publishing antislavery tracts. He conducted a spirited attack on proslavery writers in the daily press in the winter of 1788, when the first antislavery petitions descended on the House of Commons. In those months, he headed a committee of free blacks in sending public letters of praise to allies like Granville Sharp and avowed sympathizers in Parliament such as William Pitt, Charles James Fox, and William Dolben. Equiano was almost certainly the most famous black person in England by 1788, even before the publication of the now classic narrative of his own life in 1789. But he represented just one of many blacks in England who took the opportunity presented by the developing antislavery movement to denounce human bondage and tell their own story.[46]

If the British antislavery movement helped Africans attain a place on the public stage, it could not impose a script. The emerging class of African leaders sometimes pushed the antislavery cause far beyond the aims of its British organizers. In some respects, Ottobah Cugoano's *Thoughts and Sentiments on the Evil of Slavery* (1787) represented a pastiche of earlier works by Anthony Benezet, James Ramsay, and Thomas Clarkson, pamphlets that Quaker abolitionists in London subsidized and republished. He paraphrased their tracts liberally. In other respects, though, Cugoano took an unusually broad view of the problem of slavery. Most British antislavery writers avoided sweeping critiques of the imperial project when trying to win support for slave trade abolition. Cugoano, by contrast, described the exploitation of Africans as symptomatic of the larger crimes attending

---

Philanthropists, 102–103, 149–158. This aspect of Equiano's career is also treated at length in Walvin, *An African's Life,* 141–149.

46. Carretta, ed., *Olaudah Equiano,* 224–225, 326–348; *Morning Chronicle,* Feb. 20, 1788; Donna T. Andrew, comp., *London Debating Societies, 1776–1797,* London Record Society, *Publications,* XXX (1994), records 1312, 1318, 1513.

European expansion, a point that he developed through lengthy quotations from William Robertson's *History of America*, which detailed Spanish depredations in the Indies. No less unusual was the pronounced emphasis Cugoano placed on the sovereign authority of divine law. At a time when most abolitionists in Britain favored reasoned arguments over impassioned jeremiads, Cugoano drew on Granville Sharp's Revolutionary era quartet to cast reform as a Christian duty and moral obligation. If Cugoano drew inspiration from the Society for Effecting the Abolition of the Slave Trade, he displayed no fidelity to their restricted goals. The committee would never have endorsed Cugoano's bold denunciations of the crown, the Church of England, and Parliament for licensing oppression. Nor would the abolitionists have embraced his call for a "total abolition of slavery," or "a universal emancipation of slaves." Cugoano understood the antislavery potential of an imperial state vested with expansive powers of enforcement. He may have been the first of any color to recommend that the Royal Navy patrol the Atlantic Ocean and intercept merchants trafficking in slaves. His *Thoughts and Sentiments* represented the most radical antislavery publication printed in Britain before 1788.[47]

The emerging antislavery campaigns of the 1780s, then, broadened the sense of the possible among some exiled Africans. Thereafter, black radicals like Robert Wedderburn would hold forth publicly on the "Horrors of Slavery," and sometimes with a directness that would make white abolitionists uncomfortable.[48] The difference in tone, spirit, content, and form that separates the works of Ignatius Sancho in the 1760s from Ottobah Cugoano in the 1780s hints at the sharp break separating the moments in which they wrote. Before the 1780s, before the antislavery movements crystallized,

47. Keith Sandiford provides an especially nuanced treatment of Cugoano in *Measuring the Moment*, 93–177. See also Paul Edwards's introduction to Ottobah Cugoano, *Thoughts and Sentiments on the Evils of Slavery*, ed. Paul Edwards (London, 1969) [Originally published as Ottobah Cugoano, *Thoughts and Sentiments on the Evil and Wicked Traffic of the Slavery and Commerce of the Human Species . . .* (London, 1787)]. On Cugoano's invocation of state power, see Saillant, "Antiguan Methodism and Antislavery Activity," *Church Hist.*, LXIX (1999), 108–109.

48. Iain McCalman, ed., *The Horrors of Slavery, and Other Writings by Robert Wedderburn* (Edinburgh, 1991); Peter Linebaugh and Marcus Rediker, *The Many-Headed Hydra: Sailors, Slaves, and Commoners, and the Hidden History of the Revolutionary Atlantic* (Boston, 2000), 287–326.

blacks in Britain had far more modest goals, goals that reflected the situations in which they found themselves and the possibilities they could conceive. Most often, they aspired less to abolish slavery than escape from its clutches. They tried to secure autonomy and personal security for themselves rather than influence the course of parliamentary politics. Like nearly everyone else in Britain, blacks in the British Isles could scarcely imagine a successful campaign to abolish the British slave system before the American war. Until the late 1780s, and for very many long after, they organized pro-liberty movements far more than abolitionist movements. As late as the summer of 1786, there was as much interest in going to Africa as going to Parliament.

[III]   Sir Guy Carleton learned a good deal about black pro-liberty movements during the fourteen months he commanded British forces in North America at the close of the Revolutionary War. His predecessor, Henry Clinton, had offered freedom to slaves who deserted patriot owners and then organized the escaped into labor and auxiliary corps. As a result, when Carleton arrived in New York in May 1782, he found more than three thousand black loyalists residing in the vicinity of British army headquarters. Some had participated in the campaigns against the American rebels. Others had exploited the chaos of war to find refuge behind British lines. Carleton also knew of similar aspirations among the far larger body of runaways who had fled to the British army in the South. During the months before Carleton arrived in North America, the "spirit and enterprise" of black freedom-seekers had inspired British and loyalist officers there to propose ambitious plans for reconquering the rebellious colonies with regiments of liberated soldiers. Put ten thousand black men in arms, advised the South Carolina loyalist John Cruden in 1782. This would "bring the most violent" of the rebels "to their senses."[49]

---

49. Quarles, *The Negro in the American Revolution,* 19–32, 111–157; Ellen Gibson Wilson, *The Loyal Blacks* (New York, 1976), 62–65; Frey, *Water from the Rock,* 63–172; Braisted, "The Black Pioneers and Others," in Pulis, ed., *Moving On,* 7–25; Graham Russell Hodges, "Black Revolt in New York City and the Neutral Zone: 1775–1783," in Paul A. Gilje and William Pencak, eds., *New York in the Age of the Constitution, 1775–1800* (Cranbury, N.J., 1982), 20–47; Judith Van Buskirk, "Crossing the Lines: African-Americans in the New York City Region during the British Occupation, 1776–1783," in

Carleton took charge of the North American command too late to consider establishing an army of former bondsmen. The British government intended to negotiate a peace in 1782, not prolong the war. In conducting the retreat, though, Carleton had a free hand and thus decisive influence on the fate of fugitive slaves who had come to the British seeking protection and liberty. The seventh article of the preliminary peace terms circulated in the spring of 1783 required Britain to withdraw from the United States "without causing any destruction or carrying away any Negroes or other Property of the American inhabitants," as South Carolina merchant-planter Henry Laurens had advised. By the time word of the agreement reached North America, the British already had evacuated from Georgia and South Carolina as many as ten thousand black men, women, and children, many of whom were destined for enslavement to British loyalists in the Floridas or the Caribbean. Re-enslavement also would have been the fate of the black loyalists residing in New York if Carleton had chosen to honor the American interpretation of the peace treaty. At a pivotal meeting at Orangetown, New York, on May 6, 1783, Carleton informed a shocked George Washington of his intention to take the liberated slaves living in New York to Nova Scotia. British proclamations had freed the rebels' slaves from servitude, Carleton explained. They could no longer be considered property. Carleton and his entourage (which included the emancipationist Maurice Morgann) took great pleasure, it is clear, in posturing as liberators before the commander in chief of the Continental Army. Washington and his aides insisted that all escaped slaves should be regarded as property and therefore returned to their rightful owners. With equal passion, the British delegates maintained that they had a moral duty to honor their promise to the black men and women who had earned protection from the crown.[50]

Explorations in Early American Culture, supplemental issue to *Pennsylvania History,* LXV (1998), 74–100; Graham Russell Hodges, *Root and Branch: African Americans in New York and East Jersey, 1613–1863* (Chapel Hill, N.C., 1999), 147–153; John Cruden to earl of Dunmore, Jan. 5, 1782, in George Livermore, *An Historical Research respecting the Opinions of the Founders of the Republic on Negroes as Slaves, as Citizens, and as Soldiers; Read before the Massachusetts Historical Society, August 14, 1862* (Boston, 1862), 186.

50. The Orangetown meeting is described in Wilson, *The Loyal Blacks,* 47–57, and Paul R. Reynolds, *Guy Carleton: A Biography* (New York, 1980), 145–146. For the transportation of British slaves owned by loyalists from North America to the British Caribbean, see Frey, *Water from the Rock,* 182; Michael Craton, "Loyalists Mainly to

By standing his ground, Carleton determined British policy toward the black loyalists in New York. "The English had compassion upon us," recalled the Methodist preacher and South Carolina fugitive Boston King. True to his word, Carleton provided for their transportation to Nova Scotia with twenty-three thousand other American loyalists and tried to arrange for their proper settlement in the province.[51] Although Carleton had acted on his own, his actions received the blessing of His Majesty's ministers. In the words of first minister Lord North, who returned to office in April 1782, the government deemed the policy "an act of justice" and "perfectly justifiable." Secretary of State Charles James Fox declared that returning the former slaves after offering "a Promise of Liberty" during the war would be a cause for shame for a "Man of Honour to execute." Home Office secretary Thomas Townshend (Lord Sydney) in 1784 directed Nova Scotia governor John Parr to give "protection and favour" to the black emigrants. When they evaded these orders in the late 1780s, Nova Scotia administrators, in the end, would incur the wrath of the Pitt ministry. The black veteran Thomas Peters traveled to London in 1791 to expose the way Canadian officials mistreated black families and conspired to exploit their poverty. William Pitt's government responded with a curt directive that ordered Nova Scotia administrators to award the former slaves the land and provisions they were due. "In consideration of their Services," Henry

---

Themselves: The 'Black Loyalist' Diaspora to the Bahamas, 1783–c.1820," in Verene A. Shepherd, ed., *Working Slavery, Pricing Freedom: Perspectives from the Caribbean, Africa, and the African Diaspora* (New York, 2002), 44–68; John W. Pulis, "Bridging Troubled Waters: Moses Baker, George Liele, and African American Diaspora to Jamaica," in Pulis, ed., *Moving On,* 183–219.

51. "I recommend them to your protection, and beg you will apply to Governor Parr, that in case they settle near any of the towns they have a town lot as at Shelburne, and about twenty acres in vicinage, granted them; and if as towns at a distance, their grant may be extended to over one hundred acres." Guy Carleton to Charles James Fox, Oct. 21, 1783, in Great Britain, Royal Commission on Historical Manuscripts, *Report on Historical Manuscripts in the Royal Institution of Great Britain* (London, 1909), IV, 420. See also Graham Russell Hodges, ed., *The Black Loyalist Directory: African Americans in Exile after the American Revolution* (New York, 1996), xvi; "Memoirs of the Life of Boston King, a Black Preacher; Written by Himself, during His Residence at Kingswood-School," *Methodist Magazine* (March 1798), in Carretta, ed., *Unchained Voices,* 356.

Dundas explained, George III was "anxious that they should be grati-fied."[52] The British government backed these commitments with money—the Treasury spent more than thirty thousand pounds transporting black loyalists from Nova Scotia and London to Sierra Leone between 1786 and 1792.[53] Of equal importance, successive administrations refused to return to America those who had sought freedom with the British army and refused to compensate United States slaveowners for the laborers they had lost, as the peace treaty of 1783 seemed to require.[54]

The protection that British authorities extended to the black loyalists would seem to indicate a measure of official sympathy for the "Negro." But there was a less heartening story here, too. If British commanders some-times acted like liberators, they did not usually behave like humanitarians. Slaves of loyalists before the American war remained slaves of loyalists after the American war. Enslaved men and women seized as "contraband" dur-ing the conflict faced an uncertain fate. Loyalists appropriated some as compensation for their lost property. Others seem to have been shipped to the Caribbean and sold as slaves, though the exact numbers may never be known. Black freedom-seekers, moreover, often suffered egregiously from the sometimes dire conditions in British military camps. Countless thou-sands died from disease and inadequate provisions. Many found them-selves left behind during the British evacuations at war's end. Cornwallis, alone, expelled and then abandoned more than two thousand black men, women, and children when leaving Yorktown in the summer of 1782. Even the liberated who left with the British often fared poorly. Black loyalists in Nova Scotia received the smallest, least promising lots and suffered the

52. Lord North to Sir Guy Carleton, Aug. 8, Dec. 4, 1783, Lord Sydney to John Parr, Oct. 5, 1784, and Henry Dundas to Parr, Aug. 6, 1791, all in Walker, *The Black Loyalists,* 17n30, 21, 26, 115; North to Carleton, Dec. 4, 1783, in Wilson, *The Loyal Blacks,* 60n45; Charles James Fox cited in Philip M. Hamer et al., eds., *The Papers of Henry Laurens,* 16 vols. (Columbia, S.C., [1968]–2003), XVI, 231n1.

53. On the initial Sierra Leone expedition organized in 1786 and 1787, the Treasury disbursed £14,747 13s. 9d. The exodus from Nova Scotia cost nearly £15,592 13s. Braidwood, *Black Poor and White Philanthropists,* 161; Walker, *The Black Loyalists,* 135–136, 143n59.

54. Arnett G. Lindsay, "Diplomatic Relations between the United States and Great Britain Bearing on the Return of the Negro Slaves, 1788–1828," *Jour. Negro Hist.,* V (1920), 391–419.

longest delays in having their claims to land fulfilled. If the Treasury made an effort to find a home for the exiles in Sierra Leone, it also rushed the first group of settlers out of England on an ill-prepared expedition that led to the death of nearly all the colonists.[55]

This record of disregard, this frequent tendency among British officials to neglect the interests of black fugitives, makes the less common instances of charity even more perplexing. Agents of the crown treated poorly most black men and women who came under their control. Under the circumstances, though, it may be surprising that they did not treat them worse. Britain had far more to gain from abandoning the black loyalists entirely. All of the former slaves could have been sent to the Caribbean to make up for the labor shortage that affected certain West Indian islands in the last years of the American war. All of the escaped could have been "given" to those British Americans who had remained loyal to the crown and clamored for compensation for the property they lost during the war.[56] Further, returning the runaways to their owners in the new United States, as the peace treaty prescribed, would have provided a way to expedite the repayment of prewar debts to British merchants. In material terms, Britain had little to gain by securing the liberty of the black loyalists in Nova Scotia.

What, then, were British officials doing when they guaranteed freedom and protection to escaped slaves in the years after the American war concluded? And what do these actions suggest about British attitudes toward blacks in the years when abolitionism first took shape? Many in Britain thought extreme those writers who denied the very humanity of Africans. David Hume and Edward Long stood out for the lengths they went to degrade the black race. Far more acceptable at the time was the image of the "Negro" as the exemplar of primitive ignorance and innocence, a view that

55. Frey, *Water from the Rock*, 107, 127–128, 141–142, 148, 155–156, 159–160, 170–171, 175, 182; Walker, *The Black Loyalists*, 18–63; Rommel-Ruiz, "Atlantic Revolutions," 351–354; Braidwood, *Black Poor and White Philanthropists*, 136–161; Philip Ranlet, "The British, Slaves, and Smallpox in Revolutionary Virginia," *Jour. Negro Hist.*, LXXXIV (1999), 217–226. For a revisiting of the number of enslaved men and women who escaped to the British, see Cassandra Pybus, "Jefferson's Faulty Math: The Question of Slave Defections in the American Revolution," *WMQ*, 3d Ser., LXII (2005), 243–264.

56. J. R. Ward, *British West Indian Slavery, 1750–1834: The Process of Amelioration* (Oxford, 1988), 283; O'Shaughnessy, *An Empire Divided*, 166.

reflected a nostalgia for a precommercial world civilized Europe had lost and, at the same time, reassured Britons of their cultural superiority. Perceptions and reactions varied. In England, Africans could provoke ridicule or anxiety or affection or contempt or pity, or some combination of all of these at once. Few in Britain, though, seem to have thought of Africans as natural slaves. There were too many reservations about slavery, considered in the abstract, to regard bondage as natural to anyone. But the prevailing state of "barbarism" in Africa, in the view of many, did seem to leave its peoples equipped only for servile labor. If there had to be slaves, and that might be regretted, it perhaps was to be expected that those slaves would be Africans. The British, generally, assumed the pertinence of racial difference, rather than insisting on its importance.[57]

If the British thought of blacks as inferiors, practices in the Atlantic were shaped as much by experiences *with* Africans as attitudes *toward* Africans. Although most in Britain held Africans in low regard, they could not always indulge in fantasies of superiority. In too many parts of the Atlantic, they had no control over the black people with whom they came in contact. In North America and most of the Caribbean, where the British held Africans as slaves and servants, colonists had the freedom to establish racial hierarchies. In other instances, though, British migrants sometimes had to accede to their own political or military weakness. In the Americas, this was most apparent in relations with maroon communities, whom British colonists sometimes treated as sovereign states. Jamaican maroons secured near complete independence from British colonists in 1739 after several decades of intermittent conflict. British settlers negotiated with the Caribs of Saint Vincent after an unsuccessful attempt in 1773 to seize their lands for plantation agriculture. When white men found themselves fighting alongside black men while at war, allegiance could at least temporarily take precedence over race. In the marketplace as well, the British sometimes had to treat with blacks on equal terms. Historian Michael Jarvis has described how Jamaican planters, for example, found themselves negotiating the sale of ship cargoes with enslaved sailors employed as agents for Bermuda merchants. Long-standing personal relationships between merchants in Bristol and Liverpool and the Ekpe of Old Calabar facilitated the expansion

57. From the large and varied literature on this subject, I am indebted here particularly to Wheeler, *The Complexion of Race.*

of the British slave trade in the Bight of Biafra in the late eighteenth century. The Ekpe traders sent their children to Liverpool to reside temporarily with British merchants so that they could build and strengthen connections with prominent families in the trade. The correspondence that resulted from these exchanges between British and Old Calabar merchants was "permeated," according to one study, by "the language of sociability."[58]

British traders on the West African coast depended entirely on the good-will of their hosts. There, no matter how much they may have disliked black people, Englishmen could not afford the luxury of racism. The English derived their influence in Africa from their ability to provide wanted goods, including firearms, to African purchasers. So British traders placed a priority on cultivating peaceable relations with local merchants and sovereigns in the hopes of keeping commerce open and on favorable terms. Atop the slaving forts dotting the coast, armaments pointed seaward. English traders were in no position to wage war on the peoples with whom they traded. But they had a particular interest in keeping merchants from other European nations from intruding on the sections of the coast they regarded as their own. Such attempts at monopoly, though, were rarely successful. African traders appreciated the importance of playing competitors off one another,

58. Craton, *Testing the Chains,* 61–96, 151–152; Michael Craton, "Planters, British Imperial Policy, and the Black Caribs of St. Vincent's," in Craton, ed., *Empire, Enslavement, and Freedom in the Caribbean* (Kingston, Jamaica, 1997), 129; Robin F. A. Fabel, *Colonial Challenges: Britons, Native Americans, and Caribs, 1759–1775* (Gainesville, Fla., 2000), 195–198; Philip D. Morgan, "British Encounters with Africans and African Americans, circa 1600–1780," in Bernard Bailyn and Philip D. Morgan, eds., *Strangers within the Realm: Cultural Margins of the First British Empire* (Chapel Hill, N.C., 1989), 188–190; Michael J. Jarvis, "Maritime Masters and Seafaring Slaves in Bermuda, 1680–1783," *WMQ,* 3d Ser., LIX (2002), 607; Paul E. Lovejoy and David Richardson, "Trust, Pawnship, and Atlantic History: The Institutional Foundations of the Old Calabar Slave Trade," *American Historical Review,* CIV (1999), 333–355, "the language of sociability" cited on 344. See also Lovejoy and Richardson, "Letters of the Old Calibar Slave Tade, 1760–1789," in Carretta and Gould, eds., *Genius in Bondage,* 89–115, and Madge Dresser, *Slavery Obscured: The Social History of the Slave Trade in an English Provincial Port* (London, 2001), 63–64. April Lee Hatfield makes a similar point about the ways experience and circumstances shaped attitudes in "A 'Very Wary People in their Bargaining' or 'Very Good Marchandise': English Traders' Views of Free and Enslaved Africans, 1550–1650," *Slavery and Abolition,* XXV, no. 3 (December 2004), 1–17.

and did so exceedingly well. For this reason, British agents in Africa fretted incessantly about their fragile position on the coast.[59] Within the Company of Merchants Trading to Africa, there was a preoccupation with accommodating the needs and interests of their African partners. British slave traders, for example, opposed government plans to transport large shipments of English convicts to Cape Coast Castle in the early 1780s because they feared the scheme "would render the British Nation odious to the Natives of the Country, and be thereby a Means of greatly injuring the African Trade."[60] The Fantees and Commendas lost several hundred soldiers helping the British seize the Dutch trading fort of Elmina in 1780 during the American Revolution. When the British returned the fort to the Dutch at the close of the war, their angered allies at Commenda, "exasperated to the point of Madness" by 1786, threatened to halt all trade with English merchants until they were compensated for the soldiers needlessly sacrificed in what looked, in the aftermath, to be a frivolous expedition.[61]

The British shipped tens of thousands of Africans across the Atlantic each year by the end of the eighteenth century. When the wrong Africans ended up enslaved, however, extravagant attempts to atone for the error often followed. An act of Parliament prohibited British traders from kidnapping Africans from the coast and selling them into slavery in the colonies. And the Company of Merchants Trading to Africa routinely directed its employees to prevent illegal seizures.[62] But these measures could not

59. [Tweed], *Considerations and Remarks on the Present State of the Trade to Africa; with Some Account of the British Settlements in That Country, and the Intrigues of the Natives since the Peace; Candidly Stated and Considered in a Letter Addressed to the People in Power More Particularly, and the Nation in General; by a Gentleman, Who Resided Upwards of Fifteen Years in That Country* (London, 1771); John Peter Demarin, *A Treatise upon the Trade from Great-Britain to Africa: Humbly Recommended to the Attention of Government* (London, 1772).

60. Thomas Rutherford to Thomas Townshend, Oct. 2, 1782, PRO T 70/69, fol. 153; Oldham, *Convicts to the Colonies*, ed. Oldham, 73, 80–81.

61. See, for example, Horace Riggs Popham to Edward Thompson, Jan. 10, 1786, PRO T 1/633.

62. "The castle Slaves are so closely connected with the people of the country by Marriages and other social Ties, that an attempt to remove any of the former would infalliably occasion very great Disturbances and Insurrections among the Natives; and render the Safety of the forts and Settlements highly precarious, as their Defence de-

stop unscrupulous ship captains from ensnaring free persons or castle slaves supposedly fixed to the coast. In 1777 Captain Benjamin Hughes of Liverpool sold into slavery two freemen he had hired at Annamaboe to assist in navigating his ship to the West Indies. Several years earlier, the prince of Badagry on the Slave Coast had responded to a similar stunt by Captain James Johnson also of Liverpool by taking nine British hostages from a later ship in retaliation. To head off a similar conflict, the Company of Merchants Trading to Africa went to unusual lengths to assuage the injured parties at Annamaboe. First, they arranged passage to Jamaica for a kinsman, Cofee Aboan, so he could identify the surviving captive, Quamino Amissah. The committee then brought Aboan and Amissah back to England and, on Amissah's behalf, filed a suit against Captain Hughes. Considerable effort was made to return Amissah home in good health. Damages recovered in the suit were sent forward to Annamaboe in the hope of making restitution.[63] Throughout the ordeal, the committee of merchants made a point of alerting Amissah's "Friends and Relations" to "the Pains the Committee have taken to see Justice done to him." The reason for these pains, they made explicit: "His safe Arrival in Africa, is of great importance to the trade of this Country." Because Amissah's compatriot, Aboan, had shown some reluctance to leave England, the committee called on the governor at Cape Coast Castle to see that Aboan returned home to his kin, "lest his absence should be attended by any bad consequence to the trade." On such matters, where profits were at stake, the Company of Merchants Trading to Africa displayed exceptional vigilance. Four years after the fact, and long after the nine English hostages had perished, the committee was still trying to bring Captain James Johnson to justice.[64]

---

pends more on the attachment of the Slaves, than on their feeble Force in Civil and Military Servants." Rutherford to William Knox, Sept. 23, 1778, PRO T 70/69, fol. 130.

63. Samuel Poirer to Samuel Green, Dec. 21, 1776, Feb. 1, 6, 1777, Poirer to Charles Hope, Dec. 25, 1776, Company of Merchants Trading to Africa to governor at Cape Coast Castle, Jan. 2, 1777, Dec. 30, 1778, Rutherford to Benjamin Hughes, Aug. 27, Sept. 3, 1777, Rutherford to Capt. Thomas Eagles, May 27, Oct. 21, Nov. 11, 1778, Rutherford to Guion Forbes, Mar. 3, 1779, and Rutherford to Capt. Joseph Roberts Wood, Mar. 3, 1779, all in PRO T 70/69, fols. 122–125, 129, 130, 132, 133, 134.

64. Company of Merchants Trading to Africa to governor and council, Cape Coast Castle, Dec. 30, 1778, Rutherford to Capt. Thoburn, Mar. 5, 1779, Rutherford to governor and council at Cape Coast Castle, Mar. 11, 1779, Rutherford to James Clegg, Aug. 9,

The British were in no position to treat all black people alike. Each situation required prudent adjustments to circumstance. In the new colony of Senegambia the Francophone Africans forced the recall of the chief British officer from the coast in 1775. The *habitants*, as the traders were known, charged that British governor Charles O'Hara had destroyed their property, appropriated their slaves, banned Catholicism, and instigated inland wars on peaceful villages to generate captives for the transatlantic trade. Secretary of State Lord George Germain recalled O'Hara a year later, because he worried that further alienating the local elites would undermine British enterprise on the Senegal River.[65] Those Francophone blacks and mulattoes less likely to subvert British interests, however, received far less protection from the British crown. In 1777 Bruono Largarite organized a committee of free blacks in the Caribbean island of Dominica to petition George III against colonial laws that stripped them of rights they had enjoyed under French rule. The Board of Trade expressed sympathy for the petitioners and asked the colonial assembly to mitigate the harsher provisions of the recently enacted laws. But the board thought it far more important to back British settlers attempting to develop the sugar economy on the newly acquired island than to honor the complaints of the established black and mulatto inhabitants.[66]

1780, Rutherford to Green, Aug. 9, 1780, and Rutherford to Messrs. Clegg and Williamson, Aug. 17, 1780, all ibid., fols. 133, 134, 139, 140. There is still much to be learned from these cases in which the "wrongfully enslaved" were returned to the West African coast. For additional instances, see Lovejoy and Richardson, "Trust, Pawnship, and Atlantic History," *AHR,* CIV (1999), 91, 98; Lovejoy and Richardson, "Letters of the Old Calabar Slave Trade," in Carretta and Gould, eds., *Genius in Bondage,* 345–346; and Randy J. Sparks, "Two Princes of Calabar: An Atlantic Odyssey from Slavery to Freedom," *WMQ,* 3d Ser., LIX (2002), 555–584.

65. "A Petition Present. by the Inhabitants of Senegal Request. for a Redress of the Injustice Done to Them by His Excellency. Gov. O'Hara at Difft. Times. Senegal, 22 August, 1775," PRO CO 267/1; Searing, *West African Slavery and Atlantic Commerce,* 114; Barry, *Senegambia and the Atlantic Slave Trade,* 68.

66. "Petition of the Free Negroes, Mullatos, and Mustees of Dominica against an Act Passed There for Regulating the Manumission of Slaves [1774–1775]," "Petition of Bruono Largarite [1777]," and "Petition of Bruono Largarite [1778]," all in PRO CO 71/1; "Report of the Lord Commissioners of Trade to the Committee of Council for Plantations on the Dominica Manumission Law, the Petition of Free Blacks of Dominica,

A similar pragmatism and careful weighing of interests was evident in the way the British dealt with the recruitment of black soldiers. Opinion varied among commanders and shifted from situation to situation. Most important, no strict principle determined policy for any length of time anywhere in the British Empire. On-the-spot decisions were the rule. British officers opposed arming blacks until they found a reason to be for it. On his appointment in 1765, Charles O'Hara was directed by the Board of Trade to incorporate black soldiers into his garrisons in Senegal as vacancies occurred. O'Hara refused to follow through on what he described as the "impolitic" suggestion because it would "destroy that subordination," which, he thought "the Negroes" were obliged to accept. Less than a dozen years later, though, when the French threatened to overrun the British outpost at Saint Louis, O'Hara's successor, Matthias McNamara, recommended the purchase of five dozen adolescent Senegalese boys to fortify His Majesty's forces.[67] Similar reversals occurred elsewhere. Acting on his own, the earl of Dunmore in 1775 established a regiment of escaped slaves to quell rebellion in Virginia. Less than two years later, when William Howe arrived in New York and found black men serving in loyalist regiments, he ordered all "Negroes, Mollattoes, and other Improper Persons" discharged in 1777 in order to put the provincial forces on "the most respectable footing." But this was a year after Sir Henry Clinton in North Carolina and East Florida governor Patrick Tonyn had begun to form corps of black pioneers and militia to assist the war effort in the South. Clinton, as commander of British forces, offered freedom to rebel-owned slaves in 1779, though he resisted the temptation to follow Dunmore in establishing slave regiments.[68]

---

and the Petitions of Bruono Largarite," PRO PC 1/60; Board of Trade to Privy Council Committee for Plantation Affairs, May 6, 1777, PRO CO 271/2, fol. 405.

67. Charles O' Hara to earl of Dartmouth and Board of Trade, c. 1765, and Lt. Gov. Matthias McNamara to Board of Trade, Jan. 26, 1776, both in PRO 267/1. In these years, there was a similar record of ambivalence about arming slaves at Cape Coast Castle, the administrative headquarters for the Company of Merchants Trading to Africa. Reese, "The Drudgery of the Slave Trade," in Coclanis, ed., *The Atlantic Economy during the Seventeenth and Eighteenth Centuries*, 290.

68. Orderly Book Collection, King's American Department Orderly Book, William L. Clements Library; Alexander Innes to Sir Henry Clinton, Nov. 9, 1779, in Alfred E. Jones, ed., "A Letter regarding the Queen's Rangers," *Virginia Magazine of History and Biography*, XXX (1922), 368–372.

Yet Clinton issued the Phillipsburg Proclamation just one year after his superior, Lord North, had promised the parliamentary opposition an official investigation into Dunmore's decision to arm slaves against American rebels. It took some time for official policy to catch up with actual practice.[69] Andrew J. O'Shaughnessy has shown that both the army and colonial legislatures armed blacks in great numbers in the British Caribbean during the American war. But only with the pressing needs of the war with France, more than a decade later, during the revolutions of the 1790s, did the British formally establish slave regiments.[70]

A wider view of these measures diminishes their apparent novelty. The British had employed slaves in the Caribbean earlier in the century to wage war against European rivals, as they would again during the American Revolution. There was little new, more generally, in using foreign troops to advance imperial ends. "Military multiculturalism," as Linda Colley has dubbed the practice, had become common by the late eighteenth century. The East India Company used sepoy armies for its victories in Bengal during the 1750s and to sustain its authority on the subcontinent thereafter. Controversially, British commanders armed Native Americans against colonial rebels in the early stages of the American Revolution.[71] British officials were more committed to keeping the empire under British control than establishing racial purity. Which is better? John Cruden asked rhetorically in reference to his proposal to arm ten thousand slaves, "to make this vast continent become an acquisition of power, strength, and consequence to

69. Braisted, "Black Pioneers and Others," in Pulis, ed., *Moving On*, 11–12, 19. The promised investigation does not appear to have taken place.

70. O'Shaughnessy, *An Empire Divided*, 174–181; Roger Norman Buckley, *Slaves in Red Coats: The British West India Regiments, 1795–1815* (New Haven, Conn., 1979). For additional details on this complex history in the Anglo-American context during the long eighteenth century, see Andrew O'Shaughnessy and Philip D. Morgan, "Arming Slaves during the American Revolution," in Christopher Leslie Brown and Philip D. Morgan, eds., *Arming Slaves: From Classical Times to the Modern Age* (New Haven, Conn., 2006).

71. Peter M. Voelz, *Slave and Soldier: The Military Impact of Blacks in the Colonial Americas* (New York, 1993); O'Shaughnessy, *An Empire Divided*, 45–46; Marshall, "The British in Asia," in Marshall, ed., *Oxford History of the British Empire*, II, *The Eighteenth Century*, 499; Colin G. Calloway, *The American Revolution in Indian Country: Crisis and Diversity in Native American Communities* (New York, 1995).

Great Britain again, or tamely give it up to France, who will reap the fruits of American Independence, to the utter ruin of Britain?"[72] British commanders, as Maurice Morgann and others had anticipated, did not regard blacks only as a source for labor or the object of police, as their American brethren did. These officers, therefore, proved less committed to strict racialized thinking. It was not difficult for British officers to think of blacks, in some contexts, as British subjects, as more than simply labor or the property of British colonists. Like Native Americans or Indians in Bengal, blacks in America represented a reservoir of manpower that might be harnessed to the cause of state power, that might be enlisted as allies in the service of empire. Such practices made sense to military men aware of the broad changes taking place throughout British dominions. Lieutenant Colonel Benjamin Thompson liked to refer to the Independent Troop of Black Dragoons he directed in South Carolina as his "Sepoy Troop."[73]

The service blacks rendered the crown during the American Revolution impressed British officers like Benjamin Thompson. If enslaved men and women deserted American plantations and households to help themselves, their assistance during the war took on special importance to British commanders in America. The escaped seemed to display loyalty to the crown at a time when many American colonists were renouncing their allegiance to the throne. And the ex-slaves offered themselves to the British army in large numbers just as British officers grew disillusioned with the quality of assistance from white loyalists. The South Carolina command wished to establish black regiments at the end of the war because they thought it the only way to recover North America. But what recommended the enlistment of black soldiers in particular was evidence of their desire to be faithful subjects. The former slaves, Dunmore explained in 1782, were "not only better fitted for service in this warm climate than white men, but they are also better guides, may be got on much easier terms and are perfectly attached to our sovereign." Lieutenant General James Moncrief wrote, too, of the "great advantages" to be gained by "embodying a Brigade of Negroes in this Country," particularly because of the "confidence in which they have placed in us." Several officers left North America convinced that the former slaves deserved the privileges of British liberty. In London, returned com-

---

72. Cruden to Dunmore, Jan. 5, 1782, in Livermore, *Historical Researches*, 184.

73. Braisted, "Black Pioneers and Others," in Pulis, ed., *Moving On*, 22.

manders stood forward on behalf of former slaves who had served the crown with distinction. Stephen Norris, the deputy commissioner for provisions in New York, reported that John Thompson "was under arms and very active with the King's Regimt." The black loyalists who received compensation from the Commission of Claims held letters of recommendation from the earl of Dunmore for their service in the Ethiopian Regiment. Henry Clinton in 1791 introduced Nova Scotia emissary Thomas Peters to Lord Grenville as formerly "a very active Serjt. in a very usefull Corps."[74]

The British liberated to win a war, not to promote emancipation. Yet once they had cast themselves as liberators, they became less willing to compromise self-imposed commitments. The protection the British state offered to some black loyalists in the aftermath of the Revolutionary War represented a partial attempt to honor obligations. "I had no right to deprive them of that liberty I found them possessed of," Guy Carleton explained to George Washington. Carleton won approbation in some quarters for the assistance he gave to black freedom struggles. "In this, as in every thing else," stated one loyalist, he "has acted with Openness and Candor." In every instance, the evacuation of black loyalists from New York was characterized as fulfilling a national promise. "It would be inhuman to the last Degree and a base Violation of Public Faith to send those Negroes back to their Masters who would beat them with the utmost Cruelty." A contributor to the *Public Advertiser* condemned the way that black loyalists in London had been "left to perish by famine and cold in the sight of that people for whom they have hazarded their lives, and even (many of them) spilt their blood." White loyalists who had lost property during the war had been compensated. "Shall these poor humble assertors of [Britain's] rights be left to the agonies of want and despair?" Henry Clinton worried in 1791 that the black loyalists of Nova Scotia "seem to be the only Loyalists that have been neglected."[75]

74. Dunmore to Clinton, Feb. 2, 1782, in Livermore, *Historical Resarches*, 187; James Moncrief to Clinton, Mar. 13, 1782, James Moncrief MS Letterbook, William L. Clements Library; Walker, "Myth, History, and Revisions," *Acadiensis*, XXIX (1999), 90n; Braisted, "Black Pioneers and Others," in Pulis, ed., *Moving On*, 4–5; Mary Beth Norton, "The Fate of Some Black Loyalists of the American Revolution," *Jour. Negro Hist.*, LVIII (1973), 406; Wilson, *The Loyal Blacks*, 179.

75. Walker, "Myth, History, and Revisions," *Acadiensis*, XXIX (1999), 90, 92; Cath-

In this way, moral purpose emerged from an entirely amoral set of decisions. British commanders did not set out to undermine North American slavery. Yet, once they started the process, they often found little incentive to reverse course. The British government never authorized manumissions en masse. But once the practice began, the North ministry made almost no effort to prevent it. Expedients determined practice. Practice determined policy. And policy, over time, drifted toward becoming a matter of principle. Recognizing the liberty of those who had fought for the crown became an end in itself by the early 1780s. If the British stood to gain little in material terms by guaranteeing the liberty of the escaped, there seemed no reason to squander the moral capital their emerging reputation for benevolence produced. A note of self-approbation suffused the postwar attempts to establish black loyalists on a secure footing. Gestures of fidelity to wartime allies served as a kind of psychic compensation for the prestige the war sacrificed. Indeed, in a less explicit way, the patronage extended to black loyalists functioned much as the Somerset verdict had. If the Americas were to be a zone of slavery, those who sought protection from the crown might expect to benefit from British liberty. Some agents of the crown such as Guy Carleton felt morally obliged to the slaves the king's forces had freed. But they also liked what the fulfillment of those obligations said about the character of the British government. As early as 1784, William Pitt was explaining to U.S. emissary John Adams that the British had protected black loyalists "in obedience to the dictates of the higher law of humanity."[76] By the end of the American war, the British government had learned that displays of benevolence toward liberated Africans could help sanctify the pursuit of national interest.

---

erine S. Crary, *The Price of Loyalty: Tory Writings from the Revolutionary Era* (New York, 1973), 362; "Z" from *Public Advertiser,* Jan. 19, 1786, cited in Braidwood, *Black Poor and White Philanthropists,* 68; Wilson, *The Loyal Blacks,* 55–56. As Kathleen Wilson correctly observes, there also was public hostility to the black loyalists in England. Not everyone agreed that allegiance mattered more than nation. Wilson, *The Island Race: Englishness, Empire, and Gender in the Eighteenth Century* (London, 2003), 46–48.

76. John Chester Miller, *The Wolf by the Ears: Thomas Jefferson and Slavery* (New York, 1977), 112.

FIGURE 4. *Reception of the American Loyalists by Great Britain, in the Year 1783.*
Engraving by H. Moses after an inset in the portrait of John Eardley Wilmot by
Benjamin West (1812). Circa 1815. From John Eardley Wilmot, *Historical View of the
Commissioners for Enquiring into the Losses, Services, and Claims of the American
Loyalists, after the Close of the War between Great Britain and Her Colonies in 1783*
(1815), ed. George Athan Billias (Boston, 1972).

    *Among those receiving Britannia's protection are two Africans, far left, who are
represented as "looking up to Britannia in grateful remembrance of their emancipation
for slavery," in the words of the former loyalist claims commissioner John Eardley
Wilmot (vii).*

[IV]   If generosity toward certain "needy" Africans could serve
the needs of state, such gestures might also ennoble *commercial* ventures,
Henry Smeathman concluded in the aftermath of the American war. Indeed, this looked like the only way to salvage his languishing hopes of establishing a colonial settlement under British authority near Sierra Leone.
Few in Britain had taken an interest in the journal of his travels along the
African coast. Unable to attract sufficient subscribers, he could not publish
his memoirs. The mercurial adventurer, nonetheless, was determined to
find a sponsor. "I must and will go to Africa," he would tell John Coakley
Lettsom in 1784. And so he readied himself the next year to travel to the
coast as a manager for "an eminent African merchant house in the city" to
oversee "a very important enterprise of commerce and agriculture." Yet he
had understood as early as 1783 that a "humanitarian" enterprise would
win more consistent patronage in the postwar era than a strictly commercial
venture, a suspicion borne out by the unexpected backing he received from
Treasury officials looking to establish a new home for the black loyalists
three years later. He could sense the emerging attention, in 1783, to the
exploitation of Africans and the problem of slavery. Smeathman knew that
Fothergill and Lettsom had recommended sugar production on the West
African coast as a substitute for plantations in the West Indies. He knew
that the Society of Friends had petitioned Parliament for an abolition of the
slave trade in June 1783. So he lobbied Quakers that fall, and for many
months after, for funds to establish a free labor experiment in Sierra Leone.
This would give him the opportunity, it must have seemed to the ambitious
Smeathman, for wealth, power, fame, and respect.[77]

The colonization of Africa could serve moral as well as commercial
ends, Smeathman would tell the Society of Friends. It could transform
empire into an agent of civilization, justice, and mercy as well as an engine
of wealth. The Senegambia veterans had emphasized the prospects for
British profit. Smeathman, by contrast, thought a free labor settlement
strategically placed could transform Africa itself, although he never lost

___

77. Smeathman to Lettsom, Apr. 17, July 16, 1784, Oct. 15, 1785, and Elizabeth
Smeathman to Lettsom, Jan. 3, 1787, all in Pettigrew, ed., *Memoirs of the Life and
Writings of J. C. Lettsom*, III, 261, 270, 275–276, 281–287; Curtin, *The Image of Africa,*
95–97.

sight of the ways he might profit personally. In this way, Smeathman's plan recalled the expansionist aims promoted at midcentury by Malachy Postlethwayt, perhaps more than the more limited efforts to promote commercial agriculture in Africa. The peoples of the Grain Coast, Smeathman observed, failed to value private property and thus neglected the land's natural bounty. Rather than exploiting their potential wealth, "their strength is in general exhausted upon silly and trivial exertions." Smeathman did not attribute these shortcomings to a natural deficiency among black peoples. Indeed, he denounced those who regarded Africans as inferior to Europeans. "Laziness," he explained, resulted from debilitating customs. This meant, of course, that "good government and education would change them wonderfully." Therein lay the value to Africa of a British colony; it promised to teach Africans better habits. In 1783 Smeathman wanted to gather for his settlement outcasts from around the British Atlantic world— white craftsmen from England, black loyalists from America, and captives redeemed from slave stations at Goree and Senegal. He hoped that free "people of colour" in the West Indies would migrate to the colony to "enjoy those privileges never allowed them in a government framed solely by white people." At the same time, across West Africa, the defenseless and dispossessed, he predicted, would flock to Sierra Leone in search of protection and liberty. "Very soon" the colony would "civilize the country, and gradually absorb all the petty tyrannies, and change them into subordinate free states, by offering advantages to all ranks too inviting to be resisted." The result in Sierra Leone would be a "free commonwealth," "a sanctuary for the oppressed people of colour," which, by emancipating several thousand slaves every year, would "gradually abolish the slave trade in the human species." The American Revolution, he understood, had established a new standard. Within a generation or two, he predicted, the Sierra Leone settlement would extend "a saving influence . . . wider than even *American Independence*."[78]

78. "Substance of Two Letters Addressed to Dr. Knowles of London, on the Productions and Colonization of Africa" [1783], and *Substance of a Plan of a Settlement, to Be Made near Sierra Leone, on the Grain Coast of Africa, Intended More Particularly for the Service and Happy Establishment of Blacks and People of Colour to Be Shipped as Freemen, under the Direction of the Committee for Relieving the Black Poor, and under the Protection of the British Government; by Henry Smeathman Who Resided in That*

London Quakers, as a group, refused Smeathman's request for funding in 1783 and 1784. They doubted his integrity and intentions. As pacifists, they preferred not to participate in the founding of an armed settlement. And they disliked Smeathman's declared plan to purchase the slaves he would liberate; they thought this an encouragement to the slave trade, not a challenge.[79] These features of the Smeathman scheme troubled Granville Sharp, too. Ten years of unsuccessful campaigning against the British slave trade, though, had left him more open to considering new possibilities, regardless of their origin or the character of their proponents. Sharp, therefore, embraced the fundamentals of the Sierra Leone project at once. In the fall of 1783 he commented publicly on how the proposed settlement, properly conceived, could serve the cause of liberty. New colonies, Granville Sharp observed, presented the unusual opportunity to design public institutions from scratch. Sharp hoped to revive and transplant to West Africa the archaic Anglo-Saxon system of franklpledge, which he thought the only form of government capable of guaranteeing authority, order, and liberty. Like the Georgia trustees a half century earlier, Sharp wanted to forbid the engrossment of land in the new colony. He proposed a ban on private landholdings and recommended a day's labor as the medium of exchange, so debtors could clear obligations by service to public works. In great detail, he prescribed the forms of worship he thought most likely to encourage the propagation of the gospel among settlers in West Africa. Because Sharp had given the subject some thought, and because he had a

---

Country Near Four Years (London, 1786), both printed in C. B. Wadstrom, *An Essay on Colonization, Particularly Applied to the Western Coast of Africa* . . . , II, pt. 2 (London, 1794), 197–209, citations on 200, 201, 203, 204.

79. Smeathman to Lettsom, July 16, 1784, in Pettigrew, ed., *Memoirs of the Life and Writings of J. C. Lettsom,* III, 275–276. As Deirdre Coleman has pointed out, Smeathman seems to have been either deeply ambivalent or thoroughly inconsistent about the ethics of slaving. In letters to patrons in England, he described in lurid detail the heart-wrenching misery of captives aboard ships bound for the Americas. At the same time, he seems to have been a sometime participant in the slave trade, catching slaves for sale in the years he was catching termites to study. His emancipation scheme promised liberty and opportunity for the unfree and dispossessed. Yet he hoped to create a settlement of industrious, malleable workers who, as refugees and exiles, had lost all moorings to family, custom, or culture. Coleman, *Romantic Colonization and British Anti-Slavery,* 30, 32, 38–39, 49–51.

well-earned reputation as an advocate for former slaves, he would have substantial influence over the regulations established for the "Black Poor" sent to Sierra Leone in 1787. Although he took steps to encourage the cultivation of export crops in the colony, his primary concern was to establish an exemplary polity in the eastern Atlantic, "A Province of Freedom" that could serve as a model for the rest of the British Empire.[80] By 1787 Granville Sharp had transformed a primarily commercial enterprise into a philanthropic venture that aimed to advance an antislavery agenda.

Antislavery colonization had other advocates as well in the mid-1780s. Before and after Henry Smeathman's death, the Quaker ingenue William Thornton promoted a similar project as an antislavery initiative on both sides of the Atlantic. The native of Tortola in the Virgin Islands first took to the idea in 1784, when he kept company in Paris with Smeathman, who just then was looking for patrons for his Sierra Leone fantasy. In London, a year later, Thornton talked up the plan among his Quaker brethren as a sure way to abolish the slave trade. In New York and Rhode Island, where he resided in the late 1780s, he put the scheme before free blacks looking to migrate to an independent settlement of their own. Like Smeathman, Thornton hoped to combine commerce and philanthropy, though, in this case, his philanthropy seems to have been more sincerely meant. Thornton placed less emphasis on the wealth the colony would produce for investors and rather more on the resources it might make available to all merchants operating in the Atlantic. He envisioned his new settlement as an eastern Atlantic entrepôt, a free port open without discrimination to all ships sent from Europe and the Americas seeking to purchase tropical produce. Like Smeathman, Thornton proposed to redeem from bondage enslaved Africans destined for sale into the Atlantic slave trade. But he had the good sense not to compare himself, at least on paper, to Muhammad or William Penn. The principal difference between their plans, though, related to the identity of the proposed settlers. Smeathman hoped to attract a menagerie

80. Granville Sharp, "Memorandum on a Late Proposal for a New Settlement to Be Made on the Coast of Africa, 1 August 1783," in Sharp, *An Account of the Constitutional Polity of Congregational Courts*, 2d ed. (London, 1786), 263–281; Sharp, *Short Sketch of Temporary Regulations (Until Better Shall Be Proposed) for the Intended Settlement on the Grain Coast of Africa, Near Sierra Leona* (London, 1786); Curtin, *The Image of Africa*, 99–102; Braidwood, *Black Poor and White Philanthropists*, 16–18, 185–186.

of castoffs from around the British Atlantic. Thornton, by contrast, hoped to bring over to Africa those slaves who had been manumitted in the Americas.[81]

These proposals differed in aim and purpose from the colonization plans that dominated antislavery efforts in the United States several decades later, during the early nineteenth century. Abolitionists in the early Republic would hope to encourage manumissions in America by reassuring their fellow citizens that liberated slaves would leave the nation's shores once free. Some colonizationists in the United States did care about the welfare of black Americans. The projects tended to gain political support in the early Republic, however, because they seemed to solve the problem of slavery by ridding the nation of black men and women, perhaps entirely. British colonizationists also hoped that liberated slaves would migrate from the plantation colonies to establish new free settlements in Africa. Smeathman, Sharp, and Thornton, though, had no desire to cleanse the British Caribbean colonies of its black population. The British public and the British state, they knew, worried far more about the preservation of wealth and power than the promotion of racial purity in the sugar islands. Colonization, to these British idealists, represented an effort to reconceive the definition of national interest and the orientation of imperial trade. It represented an attempt to put empire on what they considered a more politically favorable because a more morally defensible footing. The Reverend George Gregory in 1785 paired an emancipation scheme for the British West Indies with a proposal to establish a colony of English and black settlers on the African coast. As slavery was phased out in the Caribbean, he argued, new sources

81. Thornton sent details of his scheme in 1789 to the Society for Effecting the Abolition of the Slave Trade and the Societie des Amis des Noirs, hoping that abolitionists would help defray the initial costs. Even with their lack of support, Thornton gave up on the project grudgingly. In 1792, he shifted his energies toward sketching a design for the new United States Capitol in the District of Columbia, for which he is best known by students of the early American Republic. But as late as 1791, while in Tortola, his birthplace, he was petitioning the governing council of the British Virgin Islands to express enthusiasm for a free settlement in Africa. These activities are now splendidly detailed in C. M. Harris, ed., *Papers of William Thornton*, I, *1781–1802* (Charlottesville, Va., 1995), 19–62, 70–85, 99–117, 123–127, 129–130. For an early version of Thornton's Africa scheme, see Thornton, "General Outlines of a Settlement on the Tooth or Ivory Coast of Africa," ibid., 38–41.

of wealth could flow into the British Isles from the eastern Atlantic. In the long run, he insisted, this made good economic sense. "It will hardly be believed," he wrote of the Atlantic slave trade, "that a commercial nation extended itself so strenuously to destroy and exterminate those people who might have been excellent customers."[82]

The peculiar character of the chief promoters injured the reputation of these initiatives at the time and since. A coarse and grandiose adventurer (Smeathman), a self-absorbed and immature Quaker (Thornton), and an eccentric philanthropist (Sharp) numbered among the most committed proponents of antislavery colonization. Acquaintances often doubted their judgment. Smeathman was "always in a hurry," Lettsom reflected in 1787, "unfortunate in his projects, and disappointed in most of his schemes." The Reverend Samuel Hopkins of Rhode Island considered William Thornton "flighty and unsteady," as did most of the free blacks in Newport and Boston to whom Thornton failed to sell his scheme.[83] The sympathetic, it seems, respected Sharp's ardor more than his good sense. This was not, on the whole, an auspicious collection of leaders for what was, in any case, a difficult undertaking. The colonization schemes, moreover, left an undistinguished legacy. They would prove ineffective as an antislavery strategy, as both British and American experience in the nineteenth century would show.[84] The future of the British antislavery movement, it may seem apparent in retrospect, lay with an attack on the slave trade, not with the modest and unsuccessful attempts to colonize Africa in the decades that followed.

But understanding what did not happen (once again) is as important as detailing what did. The variety of antislavery measures floated in the 1770s and 1780s—from comprehensive emancipation to the colonization of Africa—underscores the uncertainty with which the first antislavery activists proceeded. No one knew which antislavery strategy would have the

82. G[eorge] Gregory, *Essays Historical and Moral* (London, 1785), 326–328.

83. Diary of Thomas Wilkinson, n.d., 1785, Lettsom to William Thornton, Nov. 28, 1786, and Samuel Hopkins to Moses Brown, Mar. 7, 1787, all in Harris, ed., *Papers of William Thornton*, 29n, 36, 57n, 58n.

84. Seymour Drescher, *The Mighty Experiment: Free Labor versus Slave Labor in British Emancipation* (Oxford, 2002), 88–100. Subsequent antislavery colonization projects are discussed in detail in Coleman, *Romantic Colonization and British Anti-Slavery*, chaps. 2 and 3.

best chance of success. Every imaginable means of bringing down the slave system looked unpromising. Establishing a "Province of Freedom" on the West African coast may look wholly inadequate in retrospect. But when Smeathman and Sharp published their colonization schemes in the mid-1780s, few expected that slave trade legislation could become the subject of popular agitation in a matter of years or that the British government could be persuaded to enact abolitionist agitation two decades later. Indeed, for all their limits, this was one clear advantage of the colonization schemes. They could be launched by private subscription and with limited state assistance. They did not require, necessarily, the coercive force of legislation or a direct confrontation with vested interests.

Colonization, moreover, made sense in the context of what its proponents thought they knew at the time. They simply assumed that the "luxuriant" African soil would support agricultural "improvement." They felt certain that local elites in Sierra Leone would accept the presence of colonial settlers, if those settlers traded peaceably and refrained from participation in the slave trade. The antislavery potential of these schemes followed a logic comprehensible to utopian reformers in the late eighteenth century. Like Maurice Morgann before them, the planners thought change would be most easily achieved by modeling alternatives, by allowing the force of example to argue against established practices. They intended these schemes as pilot initiatives, as opportunities to instruct Africans and Europeans alike about their own best interests. West Africans would learn of the European demand for staple crops. European merchants would discover the riches to be drawn from the African soil. And all of Europe and America would be persuaded by the productivity and efficiency of free labor in a tropical climate. The colonizationists were naive in thinking that lucrative practices like the Atlantic slave trade and colonial slavery would be surrendered voluntarily. They were far too optimistic about how quickly change could be accomplished this way. The planners, moreover, overlooked or ignored the obvious obstacles. They disregarded the mortality rates suffered by migrants to the coast. They recognized only gradually the problem of controlling the actions of the men and women they sent to Sierra Leone. They showed little appreciation of the touchy diplomatic questions that would arise over relations with local elites. And they severely underestimated the financial costs that such an experiment would require. The vague, unspecific manner in which they invoked the idea of "Africa" betrayed the ways that the imagination had outraced actual information.[85] Yet these shortcomings, and their consequences, proved far more evident in retrospect than at the time. Granville Sharp nearly exhausted his personal wealth to sustain the floundering venture in 1788 because he thought the Sierra Leone project "the most effectual means of destroying the *slave trade*." The more level-headed Evangelicals gathered around Member of Parliament William Wilberforce would endorse the antislavery potential of the Sierra Leone experiment in 1791 by securing from Parliament a government-chartered company to place the project on a more secure financial footing.[86]

The nascent campaign against the British slave trade, in fact, shared much with the proposals to plant a British empire in Africa. They both assumed Africa possessed substantial natural wealth that could find a profitable market in Europe. They both aimed at the same ultimate goal: the overthrow of slavery in British America. And the chain of effects they predicted derived from similar judgments about the power of economic incentive. Outlawing the Atlantic slave trade, abolitionists argued, necessarily would clear the way for legitimate commerce with Africa and encourage manumission in the British West Indies, predictions that proved nearly as naive as the faith colonizationists placed in the far-reaching effects that would follow from a tiny settlement in Sierra Leone. The programs differed less in assumptions, goals, or rationale than in how and where their proponents elected to intervene. If colonizationists looked with hope to experiments at the margins of the empire, the abolitionists chose to challenge established interests at the center. If colonizationists planned to model alternatives to slavery, abolitionists hoped to cripple human bondage in the colonies by preventing planters from purchasing new slaves.

Slave trade abolition, as a political agenda, had certain advantages over the emancipation schemes considered in the previous chapter. No one contested the right of Parliament to regulate British overseas trade. Abolition did not require, as emancipation would, a protracted struggle with the colonial legislatures. Still, as an intervention in colonial policy, abolition presented problems of its own. It entailed, it seemed to contemporaries, far

85. The limits to British understanding of Africa in this period are summarized clearly in Curtin, *The Image of Africa*, 115–119.

86. Sharp to Lettsom, Oct. 13, 1788, in Harris, ed., *Papers of William Thornton*, 90.

more than the elimination of the Middle Passage. It also threatened a diminished labor force in the British West Indies, a decline in colonial trade, the sacrifice of African markets, an accession of wealth and power for European rivals, and a loss of prestige for Britain in the eastern Atlantic. For these reasons, it would not be enough to argue that the slave trade *should* be abolished. Campaigners would also need to show that the slave trade *could* be abolished, that tropical crops *could* be produced without the transportation of Africans to the Americas, that British products might be sold in Africa without purchasing slaves in return. The moral case *against* the slave trade was familiar, by the mid-1780s, and easy to rehearse. But if they wanted to be heard, if they wanted to influence commercial policy, those intending to stand against the slave trade would have to stand *for* something else. The early abolitionists, then, needed what men like Henry Smeathman had in abundance: the capacity to imagine the future as radically different from the past, a vision for enterprise in Africa focused on agricultural exports rather than on the transportation of African people. They had to present a moral cause in the language of commercial and national interest.

The early efforts to diversify the Africa trade, the black loyalist campaign for independence, the government and state support for the Sierra Leone scheme—in different ways, each helped make the reordering of British enterprise in Africa a plausible project. They provided the context that allowed slave trade abolition to become not merely a humane wish but a viable political program. The abolitionist movement "constituted one major impulse leading to British imperialism in Africa," as has long been clear.[87] But it is just as true that aspirations for an empire in Africa contributed "one major impulse," in its own way, to the campaign against the slave trade.

The first abolitionists leaned heavily on those authorities like Malachy Postlethwayt who had envisioned radically different ways of organizing the Africa trade. Anthony Benezet drew his portrait of Africa from a variety of sources, most of which he generously cited. In tone and substance, though, key passages seemed to owe an unacknowledged debt to the work of

87. Ralph A. Austen and Woodruff D. Smith, "Images of Africa and British Slave-Trade Abolition: The Transition to an Imperialist Ideology, 1787–1807," *African Historical Studies,* II (1969), 83.

Postlethwayt, the erstwhile propagandist for the Royal Africa Company. Benezet dwelled at length on the fertility of the African soil in his three major publications on the slave trade, first printed in 1762, 1767, and 1771, respectively. The continent produced "vast quantities of rice and other grain," he wrote in *Some Historical Account of Guinea,* and "plenty of fruits and roots; palm wine and oyl, and fish in great abundance with much tame and wild cattle." Benezet intended these statements to show that European demand for slave labor destroyed otherwise peaceful and productive societies. Benezet was far more consistently the moralist. But he followed Postlethwayt closely when describing how the Atlantic slave trade harmed African societies and the welcome consequences that would follow from its abolition. Benezet regretted that by breeding "Confusion and Bloodshed, and all the Extremities of temporary Misery," British traders had instilled in Africans "a general Detestation and Scorn of the Christian Name." If Europeans would honor their faith, the "cruel wars amongst the blacks" would end and, he added, again following Postlethwayt, "a fair and honourable commerce, in time, take place throughout that vast country." Benezet, in truth, had only the most limited interest in the growth of Atlantic commerce or imperial power. The Quaker schoolteacher tended to be suspicious of the profit motive. Yet he believed that even the statesmen unmoved by appeals to humanity could not ignore the fact that Africa held "vast treasures of materials necessary for the trade and manufactures of Great-Britain" and could supply "most of the commodities" typically imported from the colonies.[88]

88. Anthony Benezet, *Some Historical Account of Guinea, Its Situation, Produce, and the General Disposition of Its Inhabitants; with an Inquiry into the Rise and Progress of the Slave Trade, Its Nature, and Lamentable Effects; Also a Republication of the Sentiments of Several Authors of Note, on This Interesting Subject; Particularly an Extract of a Treatise Written by Granville Sharp* (London, 1772), 22–23, 68, 144; Benezet, *A Caution and Warning to Great Britain and Her Colonies in a Short Representation of the Calamitous State of the Enslaved Negroes in the British Dominions* (Philadelphia, 1767), 20. Several commentators have noted the way Benezet could be cagey about his sources. David Brion Davis called attention to Benezet's choice to avoid reference to insurrections and sympathy for slave insurrections in his antislavery tracts. Maurice Jackson has suggested convincingly that Benezet likely drew much of his information about Africa from the enslaved men and women he instructed at his school in Philadelphia. Davis, "New Sidelights on Early Antislavery Radicalism," *WMQ,* 3d Ser., XXVIII (1971), 590–

Boston abolitionist James Swan also emphasized the benefits the empire stood to win from a reorganization of the Africa trade. In a conscious echo of Anthony Benezet, he described in 1772 how the Atlantic slave trade fomented war in Africa, discouraged agriculture, and depopulated the continent. And he agreed with Benezet that Britain, therefore, missed an opportunity to propagate the Christian religion in Africa. Swan, however, was less hesitant than Benezet to embrace the idea of a commercial empire in Africa. Nor did Swan have qualms about openly praising Postlethwayt and his writings. For too long, Swan agreed, the British slave trade had blinded British merchants to their true interests, so that they "never once think of such commodities as *Europe* might consume." Writing during the Seven Years' War, Postlethwayt had been unwilling to espouse slave trade abolition outright. Despite his growing reservations, he understood its importance to imperial trade. In 1772, in the midst of the Revolutionary movement in colonial America, Swan felt able to dispense with such caution. He called on European merchants to give up the slave trade entirely. In its place, he offered a variation on Postlethwayt's initial proposal: an establishment of incorporated trading companies that would export European and American manufactures to the coast in exchange for crops and minerals drawn from the African soil.[89]

These economic arguments on behalf of abolition went unnoticed in Britain before the Revolutionary War. British commentators before 1775 preferred to castigate American colonists for owning slaves. They cared rather less about the Atlantic slave trade in African labor. That inclination dissipated as American abolitionists began to point out the hypocrisy of British critics of colonial slavery, as the experience of defeat in Britain prompted more careful scrutiny of imperial institutions and practices. Moreover, the postwar schemes to colonize Africa, as we have seen, facilitated the evolution of abolitionist argument. If Henry Smeathman proved unable to persuade the Society of Friends to support the colonization of Sierra Leone in 1783, he showed them how to link antislavery with schemes to improve British enterprise in Africa. The Quaker leadership broached

594; Maurice Jackson, " 'Ethiopia Shall Soon Stretch Her Hands unto God': Anthony Benezet and the Atlantic Antislavery Revolution" (Ph.D. diss., Georgetown University, 2001), 196–197.

89. Swan, *A Disuasion to Great-Britain and the Colonies,* 29.

the issue gingerly in their opening salvo against the slave trade in 1783, alluding vaguely to the "rich" "vegetable and mineral productions" of Africa and the "advantages" to be expected from a "well-regulated commerce."[90]

James Ramsay of Teston, however, was the first in Britain to describe in detail how abolition could promote British commercial growth. His second antislavery publication—*An Inquiry into the Effects of Putting a Stop to the African Slave Trade, and of Granting Liberty to the Slaves in the British Sugar Colonies* (1784)—dealt with the subject at length. In several respects, the pamphlet simply repackaged ideas that others had floated before. Ramsay argued that Britain should lead the way in civilizing Africa thereby, promoting a taste for and dependence on European goods. The slave trade, he maintained, harmed the national interest. Ramsay deplored a system that allowed British traders operating on the West African coast to provide thousands of slaves each year to French and Dutch merchants. On this matter, Ramsay could be quite arch. "If we deliberately contribute to our rivals' naval importance, shall we deserve pity when we are crushed under it?" Here was yet another instance in which private interests had been permitted to undermine the public good. Ramsay was certain that a commodity trade with Africa held out far better prospects for the development of national wealth. Staple crop production in the eastern Atlantic, moreover, would prevent further dependence on the strategically vulnerable Caribbean colonies. As a start in this direction, he recommended the introduction of sugar, tobacco, and indigo in the former Portuguese island colony of São Tomé, where the inhabitants, he noted, already were acculturated to Christianity and European mores. From there, "negroe teachers and artisans" might be sent to the African mainland to "instruct and improve the heathen."[91]

In 1784 James Ramsay still aimed first at the amelioration and reform of colonial slavery. He regarded the abolition of the slave trade as a means

90. Society of Friends, London Meeting for Sufferings, *The Case of Our Fellow-Creatures, the Oppressed Africans, Respectfully Recommended to the Serious Consideration of the Legislature of Great-Britain, by the People Called Quakers* (London, 1783), 5.

91. James Ramsay, *An Inquiry into the Effects of Putting a Stop to the African Slave Trade, and of Granting Liberty to the Slaves in the British Sugar Colonies; by the Author of the Essay on the Treatment and Conversion of African Slaves in the British Sugar Colonies* (London, 1784), 21, 40.

toward that end. It seemed to him, and others, that abolition of the slave trade would force planters to take better care of the men, women, and children in their charge. In this way, abolition might accomplish the kind of gradual emancipation that he now accepted lay outside the power of Parliament to effect. But if Ramsay had decided to live with the limits on imperial authority, he remained angered by the audacity of the North American rebels. And in this, his second antislavery treatise, he made no effort to disguise his irritation. Ramsay acknowledged that slave trade abolition might drive the West Indian colonies into a union with the new United States. His own opinion was that a second American Revolution in the Caribbean was unlikely since the comparatively expensive sugar produced in the British West Indies could only find a market in Britain, where it did not have to compete with cheaper French sugar and where consumers were accustomed to its artificially inflated price. But if the West Indian colonies did pursue independence, Ramsay added truculently, they should be permitted to go. Instead, Britain should turn to Africa where it might enjoy an extensive and free trade without the inflation-producing monopolies favored by the West Indian sugar producers or the unpaid debts of Caribbean landholders. Indeed, Ramsay seemed to think this, in the long run, the best way of responding to American independence. If the sun was setting on the western empire, he thought there dawned in the east hopes for new enterprise unburdened by ungrateful British colonists.[92]

The reevaluation of commercial policy after the American war helped those hostile to slavery locate new avenues for attack. Josiah Tucker took the occasion of the debate in 1785 on Irish trade duties to call for a restructuring of the sugar trade. And he cast his antislavery proposals as part of a broader protest against the restraints imposed on British commerce by mercantilist regulations. Josiah Tucker wanted the slave trade abolished and thought the hidden hand of free markets could do the work. "All the reasonings, moral arguments, or eloquence in the world" would achieve little, he wrote in an echo of John Fothergill, "till some other method can be devised for supplying Europe with sugars, and other produce of the southern climates at a *cheaper rate* than what we receive through the medium of slavery." Tucker had long thought free labor cheaper than slave labor. Foreign colonies produced sugar at less expense, he wrote in 1785, because

92. Ibid.

the institution was less brutal and more carefully regulated by metropolitan authorities. Free workers in India, he noted, produced the cheapest sugar of all. This proved that "the inhabitants of Great Britain are tied down at present to such exorbitant prices as the monopolizing planter or his agent shall be pleased to extort from them" and verified "that of all the monopolies, slavery is the most prejudicial to the true interests of a great trading nation." Liberalization of Irish trade, then, presented an opportunity to expose the irrationalities of the mercantilist system. Free markets would increase the demand for cheaper sugars grown by free labor. Unable to fix prices, British Caribbean planters would no longer be able to compete. Then imports could be drawn from Africa instead, where, Tucker thought, they would be found cheapest of all, since "the sugar-cane grows spontaneously," and "rice, cotton, indico, and other articles of great value, may be raised with very little trouble." In less than half a century, as a consequence, "not only Great Britain and Ireland, but also all of Europe may be supplied (if they please) with sugars and all the products of the warmer climates, without slavery, without colonies, without governments and placemen, without fees and perquisites, without forts and guarda-costas, without contracts, and without jobbs."[93]

In the nineteenth century, the antislavery movement came to serve the broader attack on mercantilism and the promotion of what historians know as free trade imperialism, just as Josiah Tucker had hoped. In the late eighteenth century, though, most antislavery campaigners displayed only the most limited interest in the emerging science of political economy. Instead, insofar as possible, the abolitionists embraced established orthodoxies. They did not want to appear as if they would innovate too much. Indeed, in the first years of the campaign, the Committee for Effecting the Abolition of the Slave Trade declared a commitment to the essential principles of mercantilism. Its publicists professed a fidelity to maxims earlier antislavery enthusiasts had rejected, ignored, or slighted: sugar cultivation was vital to British interests; naval strength should remain a priority; competitive advantage should be sought over European rivals; and British goods ought to be carried in British ships. To these maxims, the abolitionists added two correctives: slavery neither was the only nor the best way to

93. Josiah Tucker, *Reflections on the Present Matters in Dispute between Great Britain and Ireland* . . . (London, 1785), 9, 13, 14, 16, 17.

cultivate sugar, and the slave trade interfered with the nation's true commercial interests in Africa.

These arguments received their most complete elaboration in the work of Thomas Clarkson, the driving spirit behind the Committee for Effecting the Abolition of the Slave Trade at its founding in 1787 and, in the early years, its chief propagandist. His *Essay on the Impolicy of the African Slave Trade* (1788) represented the first British antislavery tract to pass over the moral problem of slavery entirely and confine itself exclusively to the political and economic case for abolition. It synthesized and publicized the wide range of arguments on behalf of legitimate commerce that had circulated in Britain since Postlethwayt published in the 1750s, if not before. Indeed, Clarkson explicitly cited Postlethwayt to show that even erstwhile defenders of the slave trade preferred an export trade in tropical produce once they understood the vast gains that abolition would yield. Clarkson departed from his predecessors, however, by putting empirical meat on the theoretical bones of abolitionist argument. He armed himself with specifics. He tabulated the potential value to British manufacturers of African woods, spices, dyes, and medicines; he calculated the advantage of purchasing rice, indigo, and tobacco from Africa rather than America; he recounted, one individual at a time, the loss of twenty-two of the twenty-five British sailors employed on a recent slaving voyage; he cited twenty-six plantations where planters cultivated sugar without purchasing new slaves; and he relayed anecdote after anecdote evidencing that good treatment and plentiful provisions resulted in productive and less rebellious workers. All of the data served to buttress the key claim: abolishing the slave trade would further commerce, promote manufactures, and bolster national strength.[94]

By the time Clarkson published in the summer of 1788, just five years after Smeathman first circulated his colonization scheme, the potential benefits of legitimate commerce had become a familiar talking point in abolitionist circles. Baptist minister Robert Robinson told his Cambridge congregation that "the numerous emoluments of African commerce are capable of amazing augmentation." In Birmingham, Joseph Priestley spoke of purchasing sugar from Africa with British manufactures and "without

94. T[homas] Clarkson, *An Essay on the Impolicy of the African Slave Trade* (London, 1788), Postlethwayt cited on 25–26.

the expense of settling and defending plantations of our own." A black writer in Britain cataloged for Charles Jenkinson, the first minister of trade, the many benefits that slave trade abolition might bring. "A commercial Intercourse with Africa," Olaudah Equiano explained, "opens an inexhaustible Source of Wealth to the manufacturing interest of Great Britain; and to all which the Slave Trade is a physical Obstruction." "The Population, Bowels, and Surface of Africa abound in valuable and useful Returns; the hidden treasures of Countries will be brought to light and Circulation." "Industry, Enterprise, and Mining will have their full Scope, proportionably as they civilize. In a Word, it lays open an endless Field of Commerce to the British Manufacturer and Merchant Adventurer."[95]

In retrospect, Equiano's enthusiasm for British expansion into Africa may seem deeply ironic, if not tragic. Later generations in West Africa and elsewhere would have their doubts about extractive economies and commercial dependence, what would come to be known in the nineteenth century as informal empire. But few, in the 1780s, including Equiano, could anticipate the injustices that would ensue from the ideas all abolitionists embraced. Even if foreseen, very few in the eighteenth century had a language with which to critique practices that remained, at this juncture, fantasies more than institutions. The abolitionists did not intend to exchange one form of exploitation for another. They took up the ideas of profiteers like Henry Smeathman to make slave trade abolition viable, so they could lobby skeptical politicians and an uncertain public. In the process, though, they succeeded where men like Postlethwayt had consistently failed, in popularizing the purported benefits of enhancing British power on the West African coast. Postlethwayt had been sure that opening new channels of trade with Africa would aid merchants and the state. He could not have guessed that the opponents of the slave trade would make this case more effectively than those like him, concerned, above all, with the

95. Robert Robinson, *Slavery Inconsistent with the Spirit of Christianity; a Sermon Preached at Cambridge, on Sunday, Feb. 10, 1788* (Cambridge, 1788), 37–38; Joseph Priestley, *A Sermon on the Subject of the Slave Trade; Delivered to a Society of Protestant Dissenters, at the New Meeting, in Birmingham* (Birmingham, Eng., 1788), 28; Gustavus Vassa, late commissary for the African settlement, to Right Honourable Lord Hawkesbury, Mar. 13, 1788, in Carretta, ed., *Olaudah Equiano*, 333–334.

assertion of imperial authority and the expansion of British commerce. In the eighteenth century, abolitionists would need the vision of men like Postlethwayt to make the case for slave trade abolition. In the nineteenth century, British merchants would need the moral capital accrued during the abolition campaign to make the colonization of Africa conform to new definitions of imperial purpose.[96]

96. Curtin, *The Image of Africa,* pts. II and III; Howard Temperley, *White Dreams, Black Africa: The Antislavery Expedition to the River Niger, 1841–1842* (New Haven, Conn., 1991); T. C. McCaskie, "Cultural Encounters: Britain and Africa in the Nineteenth Century," in Andrew Porter, ed., *The Oxford History of the British Empire,* III, *The Nineteenth Century* (Oxford, 1999), 664–689.

The Conflict Resolved

British Evangelicals and Caribbean Slavery after the American War

Until quite recently, accounts of the British antislavery movement told only the efforts of its leaders, with William Wilberforce and the other Clapham Sect Evangelicals cast as the heroes. In this interpretive tradition, their labors, struggles, and triumphs in Parliament provided the principal theme.[1] In the past quarter century, however, the focus has shifted. The lines of analysis have multiplied and extended, and with welcome results. Now we have assessments that emphasize the role of extraparliamentary agitation, the influence of slave resistance, the pertinence of social and economic change, and the social meanings of "humanitarianism" in late Georgian England. Attention to antislavery elsewhere—in the United States, France, the Netherlands, Brazil—has clarified what made British antislavery British. From this more recent work, abolitionism emerges as a stabilizing force in an era of revolutionary change, as one aspect of a "democratic revolution," as a consequence of an intensifying market economy, or as a unifying factor in the forging of the British nation.[2] These themes, what-

1. The best of this work includes R[eginald] Coupland, *Wilberforce: A Narrative* (Oxford, 1923); Coupland, *The British Anti-Slavery Movement* (1933; rpt. New York, 1964); and Roger Anstey, *The Atlantic Slave Trade and British Abolition, 1760–1810* (London, 1975).

2. See, respectively, David Brion Davis, *The Problem of Slavery in the Age of Revolution, 1770–1823* (Ithaca, N.Y., 1975); Seymour Drescher, *Capitalism and Antislavery: British Mobilization in Comparative Perspective* (London, 1987), 155; Thomas L. Haskell, "Capitalism and the Origins of the Humanitarian Sensibility, Part 1," *American Historical Review*, XC (1985), 339–361, and Haskell, "Capitalism and the Origins of the Humanitarian Sensibility, Part 2," ibid., 547–566; Linda Colley, *Britons: Forging the Nation, 1707–1837* (New Haven, Conn., 1992), 350–355. For comparative analyses, see several articles by Seymour Drescher: "Brazilian Abolition in Comparative Perspective," *Hispanic American Historical Review*, LXVIII (1988), 429–460; "British Way, French Way: Opinion Building and Revolution in the Second French Slave Emancipation," *AHR*, XCI (1991), 709–735; and "The Long Goodbye: Dutch Capitalism and Antislavery in Comparative Perspective," ibid., XCIX (1994), 44–69.

ever else may be said of them, improve on those accounts that presented abolition and emancipation as the work of a noble few. If these studies have not always treated the foundations of abolitionism with care, the history of the antislavery movement now finds a more secure place within the interpretive frameworks that organize the history of late Georgian Britain. With an expanded concept of politics, the "Saints," as contemporaries derisively tagged the Clapham Sect, emerge merely as one of many groups committed to antislavery projects at the end of the eighteenth century.[3]

Ironically, however, these correctives have sustained, in one respect, the hagiographies they intended to displace. Most recent assessments neglect, avoid, or dismiss the Evangelicals, leaving unrevised the facile encomiums many readers justifiably now find inadequate. Perhaps some remain spooked by the specter of a resurrected Whig history, by the unsettling prospect of a return to the anodyne chronicling of virtuous men engaged in a righteous crusade, a narrative long associated with the justification of imperial rule. As a consequence, the central question begged by the traditional accounts remains unresolved: why, in the late 1780s, did certain Evangelicals within the Church of England assume a leadership role in the developing campaign to abolish the British slave trade? Any treatment of Evangelical initiatives, to be sure, encounters at least two interpretive problems. There is first the challenge of evaluating with fairness the actions of a

3. James Walvin, "The Public Campaign in England against Slavery," in David Eltis and Walvin, eds., *The Abolition of the Atlantic Slave Trade: Origins and Effects in Europe, Africa, and the Americas* (Madison, Wis., 1981), 65–79; Walvin, "The Rise of British Popular Sentiment for Abolition, 1787–1832," in Christine Bolt and Seymour Drescher, eds., *Anti-Slavery, Religion, and Reform: Essays in Memory of Roger Anstey* (Folkestone, Kent, Eng., 1980), 149–162; Drescher, "Public Opinion and the Destruction of British Colonial Slavery," in Walvin, ed., *Slavery and British Society, 1776–1846* (London, 1982), 22–48; Drescher, *Capitalism and Antislavery;* Drescher, "Whose Abolition? Popular Pressure and the Ending of the British Slave Trade," *Past and Present,* no. 143 (May 1994), 136–166; David Turley, *The Culture of English Antislavery, 1780–1860* (London, 1991); Clare Midgley, *Women against Slavery: The British Campaigns, 1780–1870* (London, 1992); Midgley, "Slave Sugar Boycotts, Female Activism, and the Domestic Base of British Anti-Slavery Culture," *Slavery and Abolition,* XVII, no. 3 (December 1996), 137–162; J. R. Oldfield, *Popular Politics and British Anti-Slavery: The Mobilisation of Public Opinion against the Slave Trade, 1787–1807* (Manchester, Eng., 1995); Judith Jennings, *The Business of Abolishing the British Slave Trade, 1783–1807* (London, 1997).

group that inspired great passions, sympathetic and hostile, at the time and since. Wilberforce and his associates tend to invite polarized reactions. It becomes difficult, for this reason, to find an interpretive space between reverent reportage and cynical derision. The second (and related) problem involves judging the Evangelicals' motivations. Careful students of anti-slavery often declare motivations inscrutable, "a shadowy subject even for the most insightful biographers," David Brion Davis has written.[4] Such warnings have their place, but honored in practice they tend to close off investigation precisely where it needs to begin. When we ask why abolition-ism, why did individuals and groups organize against the slave trade, we are asking not only about macrohistorical processes and contexts. We are asking also about motivations, about decisions to act. This problem cannot be dodged. If an answer to questions about motivation must be incomplete, as it must, dodging the problem encourages, as it has in most published work on the abolitionists, implied or perfunctory explanations of individual and collective behavior that merely assume or assert the noble (or con-temptible) motivations of the figures in question.

The aim here is neither to condemn William Wilberforce and his associ-ates nor to rehabilitate their reputations. Instead, to get at the problem of motivation, we need to revisit the Evangelicals' intentions. Understanding *why* the Evangelicals acted first involves clarifying what they were *trying to do*. This approach means, necessarily, that less can be said here about the consequences of their choices. But a separation of intentions from conse-quences is useful anyway, since, too often, and wrongly, the *results* of the Evangelicals' labors have been read backward as *sources* for, or *explanations* of, their projects. Outcomes provide only an imprecise guide to motiva-tions. The Evangelicals, it will become apparent, did not set out to become abolitionists. They were concerned about slavery but not, initially, with promoting abolition or emancipation. What mattered to them was the promotion of Evangelical religion, both within the British Isles and across the British Empire. The Evangelicals not only had religious *motives*. They also had religious *objectives*.

4. David Brion Davis, "The Perils of Doing History by Ahistorical Abstraction: A Reply to Thomas L. Haskell's *AHR Forum* Reply," in Thomas Bender, ed., *The Anti-slavery Debate: Capitalism and Abolitionism as a Problem in Historical Interpretation* (Berkeley, Calif., 1992), 306.

[1]   Evangelical abolitionism has long defied easy explanation. Roger Anstey, the last to study the topic with care, concluded that Evangelical antislavery originated in the peculiar features of Evangelicalism itself. It sprang, he proposed, from the dynamics of spiritual rebirth, from the convulsive experience of conversion to "vital Christianity." He identified the crucial elements as, first, a deepened awareness of personal sin and, second, a renewed faith in the saving grace offered by God and conferred through Christ's atonement on the cross. The institution of slavery, Anstey explained, looked different to those men and women who experienced a spiritual awakening. The second-born sensed acutely the horror of evils such as slavery, "because they had come to see its enormity in themselves." The assurance that through divine grace they were freed from sin placed in them a "consequential assurance that they could overcome the sin of and in other men." For the converted, good works followed from salvation, from a gratitude for redemption. Evangelicals did not perform good works to be saved, since salvation, they believed, could come only through faith. Instead, thankfulness propelled them into active propagation of the gospel, so that others could recognize the sin within themselves and then choose to surrender themselves to God. Furthermore, because Evangelicals conceived of sin as a form of bondage, liberation from sin led the reborn to understand the importance of liberation from enslavement in this world. For these reasons, Anstey wrote, "in the very warp and woof of Evangelical faith, slavery, of all social evils, stood particularly condemned." Evangelical theology, "by reason of the very elements which composed it, had to mark down slavery, and, in the immediate, the slave trade, as the object of attack."[5]

The difficulties for this thesis lie not only with the varied reactions to

---

5. Anstey, *The Atlantic Slave Trade and British Abolition,* 184–199, esp. 193, 198; Anstey, "Slavery and the Protestant Ethic," in Michael D. Craton, ed., "Roots and Branches: Current Directions in Slave Studies," in *Historical Reflections/Réflexions historiques,* VI, no. 1 (Summer 1979), 165. In this vein, see also Edith F. Hurwitz, *Politics and the Public Conscience: Slave Emancipation and the Abolitionist Movement in Britain* (London, 1973). On the defining features of British Evangelicalism in the eighteenth century, see particularly D. W. Bebbington, *Evangelicalism in Modern Britain: A History from the 1730s to the 1980s* (London, 1989), 1–17, 34–66, and G. M. Ditchfield, *The Evangelical Revival* (London, 1998), 24–38.

slavery among Evangelicals in the Americas, but with the manifest indifference among British Evangelicals to the enslavement of Africans during the first half century of the revival, from the 1730s into the 1780s. As a social movement, the Evangelical revival did not stir antislavery organizing, even in the British Isles where, unlike Anglo-America, slaveholders could not determine social values. The midcentury progenitors of Anglican Evangelicalism—individuals such as Samuel Walker, William Grimshaw, William Romaine, and Thomas Adam—left no record of opposition to slavery in their deeds or words. Several prominent British Evangelicals, in fact, had a vested interest in human bondage. Profits from his Caribbean plantations enabled the Reverend Martin Madan to build a chapel for London Evangelicals at the Lock Hospital for Penitent Prostitutes. George Whitefield infamously espoused the introduction of slavery in Georgia and later employed slaves in the colony's Bethesda orphanage. Slave ship captain John Newton continued in the Atlantic trade several years after his first conversion to vital religion and publicly opposed the slave trade only after William Wilberforce asked him to do so in 1788. Until the 1770s, moreover, those Evangelicals in England who took an interest in the enslaved focused exclusively on the Africans' spiritual welfare. Like many American revivalists, Anne Dutton, an English follower of Whitefield, urged slaves to accept their bondage and concentrate on the improvement of their souls. A recent biographer writes that George Whitefield's patron, Selina Hastings, countess of Huntingdon, "considered slavery in a Christian establishment preferable to freedom without religion." She more than doubled the number of slaves at the Bethesda orphanage in the years after George Whitefield's death, even as she promoted the testimony of free black Christians like Ukawsaw Gronniosaw, John Marrant, and Phillis Wheatley.[6] For the early

6. Victor N. Paananen, "Martin Madan and the Limits of Evangelical Philanthropy," Wesley Historical Society, *Proceedings*, XL, no. 3 (October 1975), 57–68; William A. Sloat III, "George Whitefield, African-Americans, and Slavery," *Methodist History*, XXIII (1994), 3–13; David Brion Davis, *The Problem of Slavery in Western Culture*, 2d ed., rev. (Oxford, 1988), 148; Edwin Welch, *Spiritual Pilgrim: A Reassessment of the Life of the Countess of Huntingdon* (Cardiff, Wales, 1995), 5, 133–134; Marcus Wood, *Slavery, Empathy, and Pornography* (Oxford, 2003), 28–31, 41–53; Stephen J. Stein, "A Note on Anne Dutton, Eighteenth-Century Evangelical," *Church History*, XLIV (1975), 485–491; Boyd Stanley Schlenther, " 'A Great Mother in Israel': Selina Hastings, Countess of Huntingdon: The Delineation of an Eighteenth-Century Enthusiast," *Studies on Voltaire*

revivalists, a commitment to rescuing the wayward from sin did not lead to an interest in liberating the enslaved from bondage. David Brion Davis's conclusion remains apt: "The main thrust of eighteenth-century revivalism ended with the missionary, not the abolitionist."[7]

It does seem possible, in retrospect, that the Methodists could have coalesced into an antislavery lobby in Britain during the Revolutionary era. John Wesley displayed courage and resolve with his vigorous pronouncements in *Thoughts upon Slavery*, which went through three printings in 1774; he hoped in 1778 that the slave trade—"this . . . worse than pagan abomination"—would be "removed from us forever." John William Fletcher, one of Wesley's lieutenants, worried publicly over the consequences of national sins such as slavery in the first months of the American war. The Reverend Thomas Vivian of Cornwood privately urged Lord Dartmouth to advocate freedom for slaves in North America during the conflict. The Reverend Thomas Rankin had told a gathering of followers in Maryland in 1775 that "the cause of all our misery" was "the sins of Great Britain and her colonies," "the buying and selling the souls and bodies of the poor Africans" in particular.[8] Briefly, after the American war, Methodists in the new United States followed the Quakers' lead and formally

----

and the Eighteenth Century, CCCIII (1992), 303, 447; Schlenther, *Queen of the Methodists: The Countess of Huntingdon and the Eighteenth-Century Crisis of Faith and Society* (Durham, N.C., 1997), 91; Adam Potkay and Sandra Burr, eds., *Black Atlantic Writers of the Eighteenth Century: Living the New Exodus in England and the Americas* (New York, 1995), 4. A brisk and effective overview of John Newton's career in the slave trade and subsequent rejection of the traffic appears in James A. Rawley, *London, Metropolis of the Slave Trade* (Columbia, Mo., 2003), 108–122.

7. Davis, *The Problem of Slavery in Western Culture*, 388.

8. John Wesley cited in William E. Phipps, *Amazing Grace in John Newton: Slave-Ship Captain, Hymnwriter, and Abolitionist* (Macon, Ga., 2001), 176; [John William] Fletcher, *American Patriotism Farther Confronted with Reason, Scripture, and the Constitution: Being Observations on the Dangerous Politics Taught by the Rev. Mr. Evans, M.A. and the Rev. Dr. Price; with a Scriptural Plea for the Revolted Colonies*, 2d ed. (London, 1777), 109; Thomas Vivian to earl of Dartmouth, Jan. 16, 1777, Dartmouth Papers, D(W) 1778/II/1733, Staffordshire Record Office; Thomas Rankin cited in Cynthia Lynn Lyerly, *Methodism and the Southern Mind, 1770–1810* (Oxford, 1998), 24. The composition of *Thoughts upon Slavery* is described in Warren Thomas Smith, *John Wesley and Slavery* (Nashville, Tenn., 1986), 90–97.

banned slaveholders from the religious fellowship. These initial stirrings could have had far-reaching consequences in Britain, if Methodist leaders had mobilized their membership against slavery. They could have originated a national (even transatlantic) campaign at least a decade before the Society for Effecting the Abolition of the Slave Trade took shape. When Wesley published *Thoughts upon Slavery* in 1774, he had more than twenty-five thousand adherents and a centralized structure for disseminating literature and organizing his followers. Yet Methodists in the British Isles made no attempt to realize the potential for collective action. The question of slavery was never brought before the annual conference of Methodist ministers in Britain. The *Arminian Magazine,* the chief literary organ of the Methodist movement, largely ignored human bondage, though it did, at times, celebrate the conversion of individual Africans to Christianity. Only with the establishment of the Society for Effecting the Abolition of the Slave Trade in 1787, and not before, did the Wesleyans lobby actively for antislavery measures. The Wesleyans, like other Evangelicals, aimed to save souls, not change laws. They insisted that evangelizing need not interfere with the claims of church, state, or property. Even after Wesley issued a fourth edition of *Thoughts upon Slavery* in 1787, and even after several years of widespread abolition petitioning (in which Methodists participated), Wesley's man in America, Thomas Coke, would assure Caribbean planters in the 1790s that Methodist ministers proselytizing among slaves presented no threat to slavery.[9]

The Wesleyans' inclination to accept the established political and social order reflected a more general pattern in the British revivals of the eighteenth century. The domain of the Lord, not the powers of the state or the private claims of individuals, concerned pietists until the late 1780s. "I meddle not with the disputes of party," John Newton wrote in 1775, "nor concern myself about any political maxims, but such as are laid down in

---

9. On Thomas Coke, see Drescher, *Capitalism and Antislavery,* 119–120. The number of followers is drawn from Gordon Rupp, *Religion in England, 1688–1791* (Oxford, 1986), 405. On the conservative politics of the Methodist movement, see David Hempton, *The Religion of the People: Methodism and Popular Religion, c. 1750–1900* (London, 1996), 77–90. For an example of the reporting of African conversions in the *Arminian Magazine,* see Randy Sparks, *The Two Princes of Calabar: An Eighteenth-Century Atlantic Odyssey* (Cambridge, Mass., 2004), 136.

scripture." "It was not our call to [inter]meddle in affairs of state," Moravian missionaries explained to the governor of the Leeward Islands in 1782. "If there was a positive political demand in the teaching of the divines," historian Ian Bradley has written, "it was one of absolute submission to the government of the day."[10] There were few Evangelicals in politics during the eighteenth century. The higher ranks of society were typically resistant to the "religion of the heart," if not skeptical and openly hostile. Evangelicals remained very much in the minority among the "better sort" in the 1780s.[11] Even where Anglican Evangelicals gathered, they rarely shaped the character of a community, as John Newton did in Olney before he moved to London in 1780. Evangelical clergy within the Church of England found posts in scattered locales. They never attained persistent strength in a particular city, county, or region. Those outside the Wesleyan flock did not have, and did not feel the need for, a unifying structure or leadership.[12]

10. Ian Campbell Bradley, "The Politics of Godliness: Evangelicals in Parliament, 1784–1832" (D.Phil. thesis, Oxford University, 1974), 7; J. C. S. Mason, *The Moravian Church and the Missionary Awakening in England, 1760–1800* (Woodbridge, Suffolk, Eng., 2001), 113; John Newton cited in Bebbington, *Evangelicalism in Modern Britain*, 72–73. The brothers Thornton (Samuel, Robert, and Henry) do not appear to have promoted a religious politics until slave trade abolition became an issue in the House of Commons; on this, see Standish Meacham, *Henry Thornton of Clapham, 1760–1815* (Cambridge, Mass., 1964), 71–72.

11. The unusual career of Selina, countess of Huntingdon, presents the instructive exception. The pious aristocrat helped sustain Calvinist Evangelicalism in its first decades by serving as a patron for George Whitefield and other Evangelical clergy, by securing chapels, and by establishing a college in Wales for lay ministers. Unlike John Wesley, she sought to convert the upper classes, acquiring private chapels in such resort towns as Brighton and Bath and inviting the nobility to her drawing rooms to hear her ministers preach. Her decision in 1782 to register her chapels as Dissenting churches cost the countess the support of previously sympathetic clergy who wished to stay within the Church of England. The hostility of polite society to Evangelicalism is referenced in Bebbington, *Evangelicalism in Modern Britain*, 22–23, 25. For the countess of Huntingdon, see L. E. Elliott-Binns, *The Early Evangelicals: A Religious and Social Study* (Greenwich, Conn., 1953), 134–142; Bebbington, *Evangelicalism in Modern Britain*, 29–30; Gordon Rupp, *Religion in England, 1688–1791* (Oxford, 1986), 462–464, 467–471; and more generally Edwin Welch, *Spiritual Pilgrim*, and Schlenther, *Queen of the Methodists*.

12. This overview largely draws on the following: G. R. Balleine, *A History of the Evangelical Party in the Church of England* (London, 1933), 50–134; Elliott-Binns, *The*

Marginal, dispersed, fragmented, limited in reach, Anglican Evangelicalism lacked not only a political agenda but also the prestige, organization, and ambition to acquire political clout.

The Evangelicals who guided slave trade abolition through Parliament between 1788 and 1807, therefore, differed from their predecessors. They enjoyed social prominence and political standing. Moreover, they exploited their position in ways that the small number of Evangelical statesmen before them would not. In particular, they used their public stature to put what they regarded as moral questions on the agenda of Parliament. What needs explanation, then, is not only why Evangelicals championed abolition, which Evangelicalism, as such, cannot explain, but, more generally, why Evangelicals took to politics at all, why a new ethos developed that enlarged the traditional concern with saving souls into a broader effort to reshape the nation and the empire. The customary but anachronistic focus on the activities of the Clapham Sect, in these years, necessarily misleads. The Clapham Saints did lead the abolition campaign in Parliament, but they did not originate the antislavery campaign among Evangelicals within the Church of England. There was no Clapham Sect in 1787, when William Wilberforce encouraged the formation of the Society for Effecting the Abolition of the Slave Trade. At the time, James Stephen and Zachary Macaulay still resided in the West Indies. Charles Grant and John Shore served the East India Company in Bengal. Of those subsequently linked with the Clapham Sect in the early nineteenth century, only the aged Evangelical patron John Thornton resided in Clapham as of 1787. His son Henry Thornton would not purchase Battersea Rise, the estate that became Claphamite headquarters, until 1792.[13]

More important to the early history of abolitionism was the coterie of devout Anglicans gathered at Barham Court, the principal estate in the

---

Early Evangelicals, 418–457; Kenneth Hylson-Smith, *Evangelicals in the Church of England, 1734–1984* (Edinburgh, 1989), 19–57; and D. Bruce Hindmarsh, *John Newton and the English Evangelical Tradition: Between the Conversions of Wesley and Wilberforce* (Oxford, 1996), 298–331.

13. Elliott-Binns, *The Early Evangelicals,* 449–450. Ernest Marshall Howse provides the evidence but fails to draw the conclusion. See Howse, *Saints in Politics: The "Clapham Sect" and the Growth of Freedom* (Toronto, 1952), 10–16. As explained in chapter 3, Granville Sharp should not be considered as a member of the Clapham Sect.

village of Teston, more than two dozen miles east and south of Clapham. In Teston, the Reverend James Ramsay completed his influential pamphlets on slavery in the British West Indies. In Teston, in the fall of 1786, a youthful Thomas Clarkson pledged his energies to a national campaign for slave trade abolition. And in Teston, weeks later, William Wilberforce first agreed to bring the cause before Parliament. Teston, not Clapham, became the first headquarters for Evangelical abolitionism. In 1789, in the weeks before he introduced in the House of Commons the first motion for slave trade abolition, Wilberforce "and the whole Junto of Abolitionists," Hannah More reported, were "locked up" at Barham Court, "*slaving* till two o'clock every morning," noting subsequently that "they had walked out but once in the three weeks they had been there." "The great charter of African liberty" would be completed at Teston, More predicted. The village would be remembered, she said, as the "Runneymeade of the negroes."[14] The prediction, of course, was wrong. Emancipation in the British Empire would occur more than four decades later, and as a consequence of actions and actors in the Caribbean (both enslaved and free) as well as in the British Isles, all of whom lay beyond the effective control of Evangelical politicians. Hannah More was wrong, too, about Teston's place in historical memory. Few now remember the village as the place where Evangelical abolitionists first formed their plans.

Life at Barham Court remains shaded in obscurity, illuminated only by several letters Hannah More composed during visits to Teston in the mid-1780s. In these years, More gradually distanced herself from polite literary circles, where her skills as a poet and dramatist first brought her acclaim. Instead, as she gravitated toward a more intense devotional life, she dedicated her pen to religious themes.[15] If John Newton guided Hannah More through her spiritual awakening, in Teston she first found religious fellowship. There her new commitments took full shape. Barham Court belonged to the charitable recluse Elizabeth Bouverie, Lady Bounti-

14. Hannah More to her sister, n.d., 1789, May 1789, both in William Roberts, ed., *Memoirs of the Life and Correspondence of Mrs. Hannah More*, 2d ed., 4 vols. (London, 1834), II, 154, 156.

15. M. G. Jones, *Hannah More* (Cambridge, 1952), 86–91; Charles Howard Ford, *Hannah More: A Critical Biography* (New York, 1996), 45–82; Anne Stott, *Hannah More: The First Victorian* (Oxford, 2003), 68–70, 79–86, 91–92.

ful incarnate. As a benefactress, she embraced the ideals of patronage in a landed society, extending munificence to the poor in exchange for defer-ence. Bouverie's philanthropies, wrote Hannah More, were "boundless." She was the principal donor to the Teston charity school. In the manicured park encircling Barham Court she kept a "Chamber for sick beggars, poor vagrant ones come there to lie in . . . houseless wretches frequently come there and die." Because of Bouverie's good works, More wrote, "there is nothing like want or dirt in the whole village. . . . Poverty here is quite lovely and going to Church is so pleasant that it hardly looks like a duty." Bouverie shared Barham Court with her childhood friend, the devout Lady Margaret Middleton, and Sir Charles Middleton, comptroller of the navy and, as of 1784, member of Parliament for Rochester. Like Bouverie, Hannah More explained, Lady Middleton was distinguished by her "feeling and compas-sion"; "her philanthropy extends to every animal."[16]

These two women, Elizabeth Bouverie and Margaret Middleton, estab-lished the commitment to piety and charity that gave Barham Court its distinctive character. Here, in Teston, Hannah More found a model for how wealthy Evangelicals, and wealthy Evangelical women in particular,

---

16. More to [Ann Kennicott], June 7, 1784, Hannah More MSS, Correspondence, binder no. 1, William Andrews Clark Library, Los Angeles; More to her sister, n.d., 1784, and Memoir entry, June 4, 1786, both in Roberts, ed., *Memoirs of Mrs. Hannah More,* I, 360, II, 24; Teston Village School Subscription Book, Gambier MSS, U194 Q10, Center for Kentish Studies, Maidstone, Eng. For Margaret Middleton, see Georgina Chatterton, ed., *Memorials Personal and Historical of Admiral Lord Gambier . . . ,* 2d ed., 2 vols. (London, 1861), I, 139–145; John Knox Laughton, ed., *Letters and Papers of Charles, Lord Barham, Admiral of the Red Squadron, 1758–1813,* I, Naval Records Society, *Publications,* XXXII (London, 1907), xxii–xxiv; I. Lloyd Phillips, "The Evangelical Administrator: Sir Charles Middleton at the Navy Board, 1778–1790" (D. Phil. thesis, Oxford University, 1975), 12–20. Illustrative detail appears in John Pollock, *Wilberforce* (London, 1977), 49–50. For Elizabeth Bouverie, in addition to these materials, see the genealogical and biographical data included in Edward Hasted, *The History and Topo-graphical Survey of the County of Kent; Containing the Antient and Present State of It, Civil and Ecclesiastical; Collected from Public Records, and Other Authorities: Illustrated with Maps, Views, Antiquities, etc.,* 2d ed., V (1798; rpt. East Ardsely, Wakefield, Eng., 1972), 126–136. On the idea of "Lady Bountiful," see Dorice Williams Elliott, " 'The Care of the Poor Is Her Profession': Hannah More and Women's Philanthropic Work," *Nineteenth-Century Contexts,* XIX (1995), 180.

might live. Here, at Barham Court, seemed to be the dedication to religion and philanthropy that More shortly after would help idealize as women's work and the basis for women's activism in the relief of social problems. That ideal, an ideology in succeeding decades, would shape the cultural world of middle-class Victorians in the early nineteenth century. In the 1780s, at Barham Court, that ethos appeared in embryo, at a midpoint between the sentimental charity Sarah Scott celebrated in her fictional *Millennium Hall* and the vigorous philanthropy the Claphamites actualized through the popular success of their campaign against the slave trade. Hannah More wrote enthusiastically about her visits to Barham Court because she knew that what she found there was unusual. The letters she sent from Teston applaud the priority her hosts placed on the spiritual life and the sacred. "Nothing can exceed the goodness of the inhabitants whose lives are spent in acts of beneficence," she enthused, "such an enchanted Country, such Books! Such nightingales! Such Roses! Then within doors such goodness, such Charity, such Piety! I hope it is catching and that I shall bring away some of the odour of sanctity about me."[17]

The men of Barham Court worshipped with reverence, observed the duties prescribed by scripture with constancy, and defended religious causes with zeal. Yet there is less evidence, in their papers, of a pronounced concern with their own sinfulness or of a transformative conversion or awakening. Of the reticent Sir Charles Middleton, Hannah More wrote only that he "adhered to the stern and simple virtues of the old school." In his own words, he owed to Lady Middleton "all I possess of religion."[18]

17. More to [Kennicott], June 7, 1784, Hannah More MSS, Correspondence, binder no. 1. My discussion here is informed especially by Catherine Hall, "The Early Formation of Victorian Domestic Ideology," in Sandra Burman, ed., *Fit Work for Women* (New York, 1979), 21–30; Dorice Williams Elliott, *The Angel Out of the House: Philanthropy and Gender in Nineteenth-Century England* (Charlottesville, Va., 2002), 1–80; and Anne K. Mellor, *Mothers of the Nation: Women's Political Writing in England, 1780–1830* (Bloomington, Ind., 2000), 13–38. The judgment of Ian Bradley is relevant here, too: "The most important agents in the spread of Evangelical religion among the upper classes seems . . . to have been the female members of the families. It was nearly always through wives and daughters that seriousness was introduced into aristocratic households." Bradley, *The Call to Seriousness: The Evangelical Impact on the Victorians* (London, 1976), 40.

18. Memoir entry, June 4, 1786, in Roberts, ed., *Memoirs of Mrs. Hannah More*, II, 24; Sir Charles Middleton cited in Pollock, *Wilberforce*, 50.

Similarly, private memoranda written between 1777 and 1808 do not detail, as they would for a true Evangelical, the spiritual odyssey of Beilby Porteus, bishop of Chester, incumbent in the nearby parish of Hunton, and intimate friend of both the Middletons and Hannah More. Bishop Porteus, in fact, kept a politic distance from the Evangelical clergy. His religious opinions expressed themselves, instead, in programs to invigorate the Church of England. No late eighteenth-century prelate promoted public obedience to scriptural injunctions with greater ardor. Hannah More identified him in 1783 as her favorite bishop. In 1781, Porteus introduced a bill in the House of Lords to suppress Sunday evening social clubs masquerading, he complained, as "Theological Societies." Of the measure, he wrote, "it takes away . . . no other liberty, but the liberty of burlesquing Scripture, and making religion a public amusement, and a public trade, which I was inclined to think . . . [God] would not consider essential marks of freedom."[19] In a similar vein, Sir Charles Middleton directed his sense of Christian duty into various improving projects. His scheme to reorganize the Royal Navy after the American war included a program to improve the morals of impressed sailors. At the same time, he led a life of disciplined probity. He rigorously honored the Sabbath, refusing to write letters on Sunday, and denouncing the performance of Sunday concerts and theater.[20]

The Teston circle shared the concerns and priorities of Evangelicals and

19. More to Kennicott, Apr. 22, 1783, Hannah More MSS, Correspondence, binder no. 1; John H. Overton and Frederic Relton, *A History of the English Church*, VII, *The English Church: From the Accession of George I to the End of the Eighteenth Century (1714–1800)* (London, 1906), 238, 251–254; M. Quinlan, *Victorian Prelude: A History of English Manners, 1700–1830* (New York, 1941), 52; Robert Hodgson, "The Life of The Right Reverend Beilby Porteus, D.D., Late Bishop of London," in Hodgson, ed., *The Works of the Right Reverend Beilby Porteus . . .* , 6 vols. (London, 1811), I, 71–82, citation on 82; Bob Tennent, "Sentiment, Politics, and Empire: A Study of Beilby Porteus' Anti-Slavery Sermon," in Brycchan Carey, Markman Ellis, and Sara Salih, *Discourses of Slavery and Abolition: Britain and Its Colonies, 1760–1838* (New York, 2004), 158–159. Porteus describes his estate at Hunton and neighbors in Teston in Porteus, *A Brief Account of Three Favorite Country Residences, to Which Is Added Death, a Poetical Elegy First Printed at Cambridge in the Year 1759* (London, 1808).

20. Phillips, "The Evangelical Administrator," 12–30; John E. Talbott, *The Pen and Ink Sailor: Charles Middleton and the King's Navy, 1778–1813* (London, 1998), 12–15, 115–129.

social reformers elsewhere in England. They assumed the poor should remain poor, but suffer less, worship more, and behave better. The Testonites joined in the rapidly spreading Sunday school movement, an initiative designed to provide instruction in the gospel to children of the poor and curb profanation of the Sabbath. Porteus instructed the clergy of his Chester diocese to aid the schools, describing them "as the only expedient we can with confidence look up to for a reformation of manners among the common people."[21] His concern with the manners of the poor reflected more general desires that took shape after the American war to restrain such prosaic vices as vagrancy, blasphemy, and drunkenness. In 1787 he assisted William Wilberforce in securing from George III a proclamation against vice and immorality, a declaration aimed at spurring magistrates to enforce existing laws with greater vigor. Sir Charles Middleton joined Porteus and Wilberforce in recruiting noblemen and bishops for the voluntary society they formed to ensure attention to the king's proclamation. In encouraging gospel instruction, in promoting moral reform through the prosecution of everyday sins, and in enlisting a broad spectrum of respectable society in these schemes, the Teston circle stood in the mainstream of and helped channel the reform currents that shaped the cultural landscape in Britain during the years after the war with the United States.[22]

A preoccupation with slavery in the British West Indies distinguished the Teston clan from their contemporaries, a preoccupation that originated in their long association with the Reverend James Ramsay, the Teston

21. Beilby Porteus, *A Letter to the Clergy of the Diocese of Chester, concerning Sunday Schools* (London, 1786), printed in Hodgson, ed., *The Works of Beilby Porteus*, VI, 237. On the early Sunday school movement, see R. A. Soloway, *Prelates and People: Ecclesiastical Social Thought in England, 1783–1792* (London, 1969), 351–358; Thomas Walter Laqueur, *Religion and Respectability: Sunday Schools and Working Class Culture, 1780–1850* (New Haven, Conn., 1976), 4–9, 190–192; and Donna T. Andrew, *Philanthropy and Police: London Charity in the Eighteenth Century* (Princeton, N.J., 1989), 170–172.

22. "Occasional Memoranda and Reflexions," Aug. 5, 1787, fols. 160–162, Porteus MSS 2099, Lambeth Palace Library, London. A full assessment of the Proclamation Society appears in Joanna Innes, "Politics and Morals: The Reformation of Manners Movement in Later Eighteenth-Century England," in Eckhart Hellmuth, ed., *The Transformation of Political Culture: England and Germany in the Late Eighteenth Century* (Oxford, 1990), 57–118.

parish vicar as of 1781. Ramsay owed his career to Teston patronage, and the good offices of Charles Middleton in particular. Middleton's sponsorship had enabled Ramsay to take up the Saint Christopher livings of Saint John's Capisterre in 1762 and Christ Church and Nicola Town in 1763. Through Middleton's influence, in 1777 Ramsay had received an introduction to American secretary Lord George Germain, to whom he sent intelligence reports on the war in the Caribbean through the summer of 1781. And through Middleton's influence in April 1778 Ramsay had been appointed chaplain on the *Prince of Wales,* commanded by Admiral Samuel Barrington, who that summer would take charge of British forces in the Leeward Islands. On the encouragement of Charles Middleton, Elizabeth Bouverie presented Ramsay with the Teston vicarage and the rectory of the neighboring church of Nettlested in the fall of 1781. Shortly thereafter, Middleton obtained for Ramsay a two-hundred-pound-per-year salary to serve as his confidential secretary at the navy board.[23] In this post, Ramsay contributed actively in the work of his benefactor. He aided Sir Charles Middleton in the remodeling of naval laws and regulations. For Middleton he devised strategies to increase the numbers of British sailors and suggested schemes for ensuring readiness for war in times of peace. In addition, he drafted a proposal for the establishment of Sunday schools in rural parishes.[24]

Like Hannah More, James Ramsay denounced what he regarded as the secularizing spirit of the times. "The bold and free spirits of the age," he

23. The most reliable biographical sketch on Ramsay's early career appears in Sir James Watt, "James Ramsay, 1733–1789: Naval Surgeon, Naval Chaplain, and Morning Star of the Anti-Slavery Movement," *Mariner's Mirror,* LXXXI (1995), 156–170. See also Folarin Shyllon, *James Ramsay: The Unknown Abolitionist* (Edinburgh, 1977), 3–13; *Encyclopedia Britannica,* XV (Edinburgh, 1797), 791–794; and Eric Duncan, "James Ramsay, 1733–1789—Abolitionist," *Aberdeen University Review,* CLXXXII (1989), 127–135. For Ramsay's service in the Royal Navy, see "Statement of Public Services Performed by the Reverend James Ramsay, Vicar of Teston, in Kent," enclosed in a letter from P. Mitchell to Middleton (aka Barham), July 20, 1787, in John Knox Laughton, ed., *Letters and Papers of Charles, Lord Barham, Admiral of the Red Squadron, 1758–1813,* II, Navy Records Society, *Publications,* XXXVIII (London, 1909), 252–255. For Charles Middleton's naval service during the American war, see ibid., I, viii–xxvi.

24. Ramsay MSS, fol. 88, Rhodes House Library, Oxford; Laughton, ed., *Letters and Papers of Charles, Lord Barham,* II, 251, 280–286.

stated in an early draft preface to his antislavery manuscript, "have so successfully combated all the old prejudices respecting government, and country, annihilated intellect, stripped revelation of all wonder of divine love, and even prescribed to the Deity, not only how he was to govern his own creation, but the very manner in which he may be pleased to exist." One consequence was a loosening of the bonds that held society together. Ramsay had little patience with the cult of sensibility. He thought it a poor substitute for an active commitment to moral duty. "Philosophers," as he derisively tagged Joseph Priestley and David Hume, had substituted "theoretical, lifeless notions of universal benevolence" for the more sturdy connections of "family, friends, and country." "At present," he added, "nothing claims applause but a moonshine glow of sentiment, in which the heart has no share, that neither enlivens the affections, or invigorates the conduct."[25] The results of this lassitude were evident, Ramsay thought, in the "fatal consequences" experienced in the American war. At sea, he had witnessed "unhappy divisions" between officers and officers, and officers and sailors. In his view, the Royal Navy was rife with disobedience and disorder. The solution, he said, lay with intensifying the influence of the church at sea, improving the morals of sailors through the instruction of the gospel.[26] As with Charles Middleton and Beilby Porteus, in Ramsay's surviving papers there is no evidence of a conversion or spiritual awakening. Yet like the rest of the Teston clan he wanted to see religion hold broader sway in private and public life. This was the only way, Ramsay thought, to respond to the disappointments of the preceding decade.

The failures of the West Indian church and problems of imperial gover-

25. British Library, Add. MSS 27621, fol. 8. For Hannah More's critique of Enlightenment writers, see M. J. Crossley Evans, "The English Evangelicals and the Enlightenment: The Case of Hannah More," *Stud. Voltaire*, CCCIII (1992), 458–462.

26. Ramsay wrote, "The courage that may be depended on at all times; the exertion that shrinks not at danger, and yields not to despair must be founded in the love of God, and the hopes and fears of another life. Persuade a seaman, that God has fixed him at his post and he looks for his manly exertion in it, he will smile at danger, he will endure fatigue, he will even fear with patience undeserved ill-treatment. For he does his duty to God and not to men; and from God and not from men doth he expect his reward." Ramsay MSS, fol. 21. Ramsay wrote these words for the preface of a planned second edition of his *Sea Sermons; or, A Series of Discourses for the Use of the Royal Navy* (London, 1781), an edition that ultimately went unpublished.

nance, it is now clear, shaped Ramsay's assessment of and prescriptions for Caribbean society. He hoped to promote the reorganization of empire through the reformation of slavery. In a more immediate sense, though, Ramsay's antislavery writings represented the culmination of an extended exchange with Margaret Middleton. If Charles Middleton advanced Ramsay's career, Margaret Middleton fostered and nurtured his commitment to moral reform. She posed the initial query that led Ramsay to write on the British Caribbean plantations. And she pursued the subject avidly with him until his *Essay on the Treatment and Conversion of Africans* went to press in 1784. Ramsay later told Thomas Clarkson that on this subject "her importunities were great" and that "he had on this account, and in obedience also to his own feelings" begun work in the late 1760s on his proposal to improve slavery in the West Indies. Margaret Middleton, in fact, had a decisive impact on the more general development of antislavery commitments at Barham Court. She insisted that Barham Court serve as a space for conversations about slavery. It seems likely that she pressured not only Ramsay but Charles Middleton and Porteus, too, especially after the American Revolution. Hannah More in 1791 told Lady Middleton in private correspondence that "you have the first title to every prize on the whole slave subject." Christian Ignatius Latrobe, a leading figure in the Evangelical Moravian Church who spent nearly four months at Barham Court in 1786, reported to his daughter thirty years later that the "abolition of the slave trade was . . . the work of a *woman*." Margaret Middleton "was the honored instrument of bringing the monster within range of the artillery of the executive justice of this kingdom."[27]

Regrettably, the specifics of Margaret Middleton's role in early Anglican Evangelical antislavery remain difficult to document in detail. The Middletons made a habit of destroying their correspondence. Yet, as the recent research on the political work of aristocratic women makes clear, not only did women like Margaret Middleton act as "political facilitators," in the

27. Thomas Clarkson, *The History of the Rise, Progress, and Accomplishment of the Abolition of the African Slave-Trade by the British Parliament*, 2 vols. (London, 1788), I, 222–223; Pollack, *Wilberforce*, 53–54; Christian Ignatius Latrobe, *Letters to My Children . . . Containing a Memorial of Some Occurrences in My Past Life . . .* (London, 1851), 24; More to Lady Middleton, n.d., 1791, Noel Papers, DE 3214/304/13, Leicestershire Record Office.

words of historian Elaine Chalus, they frequently shaped the definition of political projects and determined their importance. Middleton's appeals to Ramsay are consistent with a more general commitment among some elite women to affect politics through the agency of others. The Evangelical Sarah Osborn, of Newport, Rhode Island, who also took a special interest in the religious education of African men, women, and children, seems to have exercised a similar influence over the Reverend Samuel Hopkins, who became an ardent abolitionist in the 1770s through her encouragement. What literary historian David Grimstead has written of Sarah Osborn applies equally well to Margaret Middleton. "Probably Osborn would not mind that the world little noticed her efforts; she often fretted, as the saintly must, about motives of vanity and pride mingling with her truly caring impulses. To some degree her triumph lay in finding a male authority figure to carry on her work so that the issues involving salvation and black potential would not be clouded with what she saw as empty controversy over who or what sex acted."[28]

Margaret Middleton's concerns centered on the moral and religious obligations of the slaveholders, on the masters' responsibility to care for the spiritual welfare of his servants. Middleton rejected the suggestion that gospel preaching would interfere with the accumulation of profits. She insisted that the gospel, in fact, "would be the most profitable means of making slaves diligent and faithful; for it would awaken conscience within

28. Elaine Chalus, "Elite Women, Social Politics, and the Political World of Late Eighteenth-Century England," *Historical Journal*, XLIII (2000), 669–697, citation on 685; David Grimsted, "Anglo-American Racism and Phillis Wheatley's 'Sable Veil,' 'Length'ned Chain,' and 'Knitted Heart,'" in Ronald Hoffman and Peter J. Albert, eds., *Women in the Age of the American Revolution* (Charlottesville, Va., 1989), 381. See also Sheryl A. Kujawa, "'The Path of Duty Plain': Samuel Hopkins, Sarah Osborn, and Revolutionary Newport," *Rhode Island History*, LVIII (2000), 74–89. Of Evangelical women preachers in this period, Anne K. Mellor has written that "they had claimed and achieved the right to comment on the rectitude or unrighteousness of the government, the military, the professions of law and medicine, and especially of commerce, and to condemn in the name of the highest authority—God and Scripture—the sins of the males who surrounded them." Mellor, *Mothers of the Nation*, 71. See also Helen M. Jones, "A Spiritual Aristocracy: Female Patrons of Religion in Eighteenth-Century Britain," in Deryck W. Lovegrove, *The Rise of the Laity in Evangelical Protestantism* (London, 2002), 85–90.

them, to be a strict overseer, and a severe monitor, whom they could not evade." Middleton, however, was not especially concerned, in this context, with promoting social control. She wanted to establish, instead, the power of divine providence, the extent of God's intervention in human affairs. "A sparrow falls not to the ground," she wrote, "without his permission." "A cup of cold water given for his sake, doth not escape his notice, nor go without its reward." This, to her, was the most powerful reason why planters should accept a small sacrifice of labor in the fields.

> Without working a manifest miracle, God may give success to our endeavours in a thousand ways, which shall seem to be the natural effects of industry, or of that unknown direction of human affairs, which in common accent is called chance. He may make us skilful in managing occasions, sagacious in forseeing events. He may preserve us from expansive illness, guard us from mischievous neighbors.

"Endless are the methods," she added, by which, "in an unperceived manner, he can turn the common accidents of life to reward men who prefer duty to present advantage, who cooperate with his benevolence in promoting the happiness of their fellow-creatures." Caribbean planters could see for themselves that overworking enslaved men and women led to the death of their laborers and, thereby, destroyed their investment. "Do not such men acknowledge in this, strong traces of Divine justice, punishing cruelty and thirst of gain by the most natural means, by making them counteract and defeat their own purpose?" "May we not expect Providence to prosper by means as natural our humane, benevolent attention to wretches, whom the crimes and avarice of selfish men have placed in our power?" "We cannot hold ourselves blameless," she concluded. "If we forbear using our best endeavours to communicate the knowledge of [religion] to every one within our reach."[29] The sanctification of slavery was her dearest hope.

For Margaret Middleton and the Teston circle, the antislavery impulse, therefore, did not spring from the logic of the conversion experience. Instead, it originated in frustrated aspirations to propagate the gospel in the

29. The undated letter, which appears to have been written in 1768, appears in James Ramsay, *An Essay on the Treatment and Conversion of African Slaves in the British Sugar Colonies* (London, 1784), viii–xiv.

British West Indies. Their efforts were informed by the dispiriting experience of James Ramsay in Saint Kitts. They gestated and matured in the
context of abiding friendship, religious fellowship, and shared purpose.
James Ramsay brought his project of West Indian reform with him to
Barham Court when he took up residence there in the last months of 1781.
The Teston clan, in turn, by recommending revisions to succeeding drafts,
would help refine the unfinished text for public consumption. The values
and priorities of the Teston clan decided what they saw in James Ramsay's
manuscript and what they took from it. In its final form, as it came to
completion under the guidance of the Teston clan, the *Essay on the Treatment and Conversion of African Slaves in the British Sugar Colonies* contained less on gradual emancipation than Ramsay initially intended and
nothing at all on the imperial constitution. This, his first and most influential antislavery tract, would reflect instead Barham Court's sensibilities and
agenda. From James Ramsay, they learned that Caribbean elites luxuriated
in tyranny and vice, disregarded the human dignity of the enslaved, and
suffered heathens to remain in spiritual darkness. The Teston clan responded in predictable fashion. They called for, in the words of Beilby
Porteus, the institution of "fixed laws" and "police" to restrain abusive
slaveholders and for initiatives that would provide the enslaved "protection, security, encouragement, improvement, and conversion."[30]

[II]   No one promoted the Ramsay plan with more ardor than
Beilby Porteus. His personal campaign within the Church of England to
promote Christian instruction in the Caribbean displays at once the ambitions of the Teston clan and their limits. The moral character of the British
West Indies represented a new area of interest for the bishop of Chester in
the 1780s. Before the American war, he gave no indication of his later hope
of expanding the influence of the Church of England overseas.[31] The

30. Beilby Porteus, *Bishop of Chester's Sermon before the Incorporated Society for the
Propagation of the Gospel in Foreign Parts; at Their Anniversary Meeting in the Parrish
Church of St. Mary-le-Bow, on Friday, February 21, 1783,* 2d ed. (London, 1784), 16.

31. Porteus served as chaplain to the archbishop of Canterbury, Thomas Secker, when
the Quaker abolitionist Anthony Benezet wrote Secker in 1768 asking the church to
lobby Parliament for antislavery legislation. William Knox, who worked as an adviser for
Secker in 1768, claimed years later that Porteus wrote for the archbishop the now

American Revolution, however, had caused Porteus, like others, to reflect on the means and ends of empire. In the process, he became convinced, in the last years of the war, that the Church of England needed to take greater responsibility for the spiritual welfare of enslaved men and women in the British Caribbean colonies. Already, by the time Ramsay settled in Teston in 1781, Porteus had grown troubled with the way Europeans treated Indians and Africans in the colonies. He was greatly affected by William Robertson's *History of America* (1777), which detailed Spanish and Portuguese atrocities in the conquest of the Indies. Porteus was moved, too, by Granville Sharp's insistence in 1779 that war in North America could only be understood as divine punishment for national wrongdoing. More than once, in the early 1780s, Porteus accosted Sharp with questions about the godlessness prevailing in the British West Indies. Porteus, therefore, responded with enthusiasm when he learned of Ramsay's plan to improve the British Caribbean colonies. James Ramsay later told the young activist Thomas Clarkson that he had finally sent his long withheld manuscript to press in 1784 because Bishop Porteus insisted that he should. For the first time in a half century, since the early years of Edmund Gibson's tenure as bishop of London in the 1720s, a highly placed official within the Church of England was taking a sustained interest in the character of Caribbean slavery.[32]

In February 1783, Porteus delivered the annual sermon for the Society for the Propagation of the Gospel in Foreign Parts. Typically, these sermons presented formulaic statements about sustaining the strength of the overseas church. Rarely did the speaker state that particular institutions or cus-

---

infamous reply that refused assistance to American abolitionists. William Knox to Lord Chancellor (Thurlow), May 26, 1789, Great Britain, Commission on Historical Manuscripts, *Report on Manuscripts in Various Collections,* VI, *The Manuscripts of Miss M. Eyre Matcham; Captain H. V. Knox; Cornwallis Wykeham-Martin, Esq., etc.* (Dublin, 1909), 203.

32. Hodgson, "The Life of Beilby Porteus," in Hodgson, ed., *The Works of Beilby Porteus,* I; Porteus to Baron Grantham, Dec. 24, 1777, Grantham Papers, L30/1/315/0, Bedfordshire Record Office; "Occasional Memoranda and Reflections," Dec. 13, 1777, fol. 34, Porteus MSS 2098; Prince Hoare, *Memoirs of Granville Sharp* . . . (London, 1820), 189–190, 236; Anstey, *The Atlantic Slave Trade and British Abolition,* 246n; Clarkson, *History of the Rise, Progress, and Accomplishment of the Abolition of the African Slave-Trade,* I, 233.

toms demanded urgent action. Porteus, however, came to the meeting with an agenda—to insist on new and more determined attention to the spiritual welfare of enslaved Africans in the West Indies. In doing so, Porteus drew heavily on Ramsay's still-unpublished manuscript. He echoed Ramsay's complaints against the sugar plantations: "The slaves are in general considered a mere machine and instruments to work with, as having neither understandings to be cultivated nor souls to be saved"; never are they encouraged to keep the Sabbath; scandalously, "nothing has been done by the Church to instruct them in Christianity"; so, "they give themselves up freely to the grossest immoralities, without so much as being conscious that they're doing wrong." Porteus accepted Ramsay's opinion on the best way to proceed: "A certain degree of improvement and civilization has been always found necessary to prepare the mind for the admission of the divine truths of Revelation." The bishop's proposed remedy followed Ramsay's almost to the letter: "We must first give them some of the benefits and blessings of society and civil government. We must as far as possible, attach them and their families to the soil . . . and even allow a certain number of the most deserving to work out their freedom by degrees . . . as a reward of superior merit and industry, and of uncommon progress in the knowledge and practice of Christianity."[33]

Beilby Porteus followed this well-noticed sermon the next year with a campaign to inspire the SPG into a more active commitment to missionary work in the Caribbean. To a meeting on March 19, 1784, Porteus brought a lengthy plan for instructing the enslaved on the SPG's Codrington estates in Barbados. The proposal addressed directly what looked like the primary obstacles to successful evangelizing. The SPG's Codrington agents cared too little about instructing the enslaved. So Porteus suggested recruiting experienced, dedicated, skilled clergy and awarding them sizable salaries to ensure that the work went forward. The demands of sugar cultivation took from the enslaved the time they might devote to attending lessons. So Porteus called on the Codrington managers to set aside specific hours each week for Christian instruction. Codrington slaves had shown no desire for Christianity because Christians routinely had oppressed them. So Porteus

---

33. Porteus, *Bishop of Chester's Sermon*, 9, 11, 22–23. Bob Tennant describes the occasion evocatively in "Sentiment, Politics, and Empire," in Carey, Ellis, and Salih, *Discourses of Slavery and Abolition*, 162–171.

emphasized the importance of ameliorating slavery, and protecting the interests of slaves, so that they would think better of Christian ministers. Carnal sins in the slave quarters—fornication, adultery, polygamy, and rape—contravened Christian mores. So, to facilitate conversions, slaves should be required to live as married couples, as if the church had blessed their unions. Potential converts on the SPG estates suffered from exposure to the bad example set by neighboring plantations and to the constant contact with "heathens" imported from Africa. This was a reason, Porteus argued, to make SPG plantations self-sufficient—to encourage births on the estate and forgo slave imports and to discourage contacts between the Codrington slaves and those on other plantations not brought up in the Christian faith.[34]

Porteus found the traditional objections to instructing slaves in Christianity unpersuasive. Caribbean planters long had insisted that blacks lacked the mental capacity to be more than nominal Christians. Yet, when set against the evidence of Ramsay's experience in the Leeward Islands, those claims had begun to look false and self-serving. Ramsay had detailed at great length in his manuscript the ways the French tended to the spiritual welfare of the enslaved in their Caribbean colonies. In the Danish West Indies and in Antigua more recently, Ramsay affirmed, the Moravians had converted several thousand enslaved Africans, with the effect, Porteus emphasized, of rendering them "remarkably serious, attentive, devout, and edifying."[35] These reports only touched on the truth. With hindsight and a wider perspective, historians now know that black men and women throughout much of North America and in some parts of the Caribbean were beginning to embrace Protestant Evangelicalism during the last half of

34. Beilby Porteus, *An Essay towards a Plan for the More Effectual Civilization and Conversion of the Negro Slaves in the Trust Estate in Barbadoes, Belonging to the Society for the Propagation of the Gospel in Foreign Parts, First Written in the Year 1784, and Addressed to the Society; and Now Considerably, Altered, Corrected, and Abridged*, in Hodgson, ed., *The Works of Beilby Porteus*, VI, 167–217.

35. Porteus, *Bishop of Chester's Sermon*, 30n. For further details on Porteus and the importance of the Moravians' example to Teston Clan initiatives more generally, see J. C. S. Mason, *The Moravian Church and the Missionary Awakening in England, 1760–1800* (Woodbridge, Suffolk, Eng., 2001), 92–95, 117–119, and Jon F. Sensbach, *Rebecca's Revival: Creating Black Christianity in the Atlantic World* (Cambridge, Mass., 2005), 243–244.

the eighteenth century and, in the process, to transform the meaning of the Christian gospel.[36] About these developments, the Teston clan knew more than most in Britain, primarily because of their association with Ramsay. Therefore, they sensed that in certain parts of the Caribbean attempts to convert the enslaved to Christianity had started to achieve, from the standpoint of Protestant missionaries, unprecedented success. The fact was, as Anglican clergy in the Caribbean began to understand in the 1780s, the Church of England was falling behind in an undeclared competition for potential churchgoers. In Antigua, the influence of Wesley disciple Nathaniel Gilbert had spread Methodism to the slave quarters. Baptist revivals had begun to stir in Jamaica in 1784, with the arrival of itinerant minister and former Virginia slave George Liele. This work, commenced by Protestant Evangelicals outside the Church of England, led some Anglican clergymen in the West Indies to take missionary work more seriously. Antigua minister John Shepherd asked the Associates of Dr. Bray in 1781 for "books of devotion" to distribute among the enslaved in his parish. He was inspired, Shepherd explained, because the Methodists' slaves were "of a more sedate and composed deportment and of a more meek and modest behavior towards their superiors."[37]

The prospect of doing good and the evidence of sectarian competition, however, made little impression on the leadership of the SPG. No amount of persuading could convince the bench of bishops to invest further in the Christian instruction of enslaved Africans on the Codrington estates. For a time, Porteus expected that he might lead his brethren to see the matter as he did. At least five—Moore, Markham, Moss, Barrington, and Hurd—agreed that "something certainly *ought* to be done for the Negroes in

36. From a very large literature, see Sylvia R. Frey, *Water from the Rock: Black Resistance in a Revolutionary Age* (Princeton, N.J., 1991), 284–325; Frey and Betty Wood, *Come Shouting to Zion: African American Protestantism in the American South and the British Caribbean to 1830* (Chapel Hill, N.C., 1998), chaps. 4 and 5; Mason, *The Moravian Church and the Missionary Awakening*, 106–113; and Sensbach, *Rebecca's Revival*.

37. Edgar N. Thompson, *Nathaniel Gilbert: Lawyer and Evangelist* (London, 1960); Thomas J. Little, "George Liele and the Rise of Independent Black Baptist Churches in the Lower South and Jamaica," *Slavery and Abolition*, XVI, no. 2 (August 1995), 188–204; Minutes of the Meetings of the Associates of the Late Dr. Bray [MiDAB], Feb. 8, 1781, USPG Papers, Bray Associates MSS, vol. f3, fols. 87–89, Rhodes House Library.

the Society's Estate." Like Granville Sharp before him, though, Porteus learned quickly that there was a vast gulf between concessions on principle and commitments to active doing. His concrete proposal exposed the confessions of goodwill as empty gestures. Rationalizations for inaction abounded. Those invested in the West Indian economy, according to Porteus, thought that instructing the Codrington slaves in Christianity would violate the terms of the trust. Those with ties to North America worried that increased funding for Caribbean projects would lessen the resources available to the church elsewhere.[38] Porteus first had perceived the inattention to the Codrington slaves as thoughtless neglect. After the opposition he faced at the meeting in March 1784, he saw more clearly that, despite its declared mission, the SPG simply did not want to bother with converting enslaved men and women to Christianity.

This indifference within the Anglican Church to the fate of the Anglican faith in the British West Indies enraged Beilby Porteus. He thought this obstinacy an embarrassment to the British nation and its church. For him, the treatment of British slaves had become by 1784 a measure of collective virtue. Missions, he confided to his diary, were an undertaking "in which our Credit, our reputation, our Interest and the Interest of Religion are . . . essentially concerned." And he regarded the refusal to support such projects as emblematic of the troubling tendency in Britain to sacrifice godliness before the altar of temporal gain. Before the war, perhaps, the size of the American empire had prevented the SPG from funding the Barbados missions properly. With its various commitments, the society may have been spread too thin. Yet surely, he insisted, this argument had no force after American independence. The growing number of Protestant settlers in Canada would require SPG assistance, to be sure. Yet their situation, Porteus insisted, was not as "deplorable and destitute" as the conditions endured by blacks in the British Caribbean. The Canadians, he noted, "are

38. "Occasional Memoranda and Reflections," Mar. 19, 1784, fols. 82–94, Porteus MSS 2099. John Warren, bishop of Bangor, did back Porteus publicly three years later. In the published version of his sermon of 1787 to the SPG, Warren agreed that the society had an obligation to set an example to British slaveholders elsewhere in the Caribbean. John Warren, Lord Bishop of Bangor, *A Sermon Preached before the Society for the Propagation of the Gospel in Foreign Parts at Their Anniversary Meeting . . . on Friday, February 16* (London, 1787), xvi.

not heathens, they are not slaves; they have some Christianity, some morality exists among them." West Indian slaves held out to the church the most
pressing need in what remained of the British Americas. Thirteen of the
fifteen "provinces" had been lost to the empire, Porteus mused privately.
"When will the Negroes be attended to if not now?" The bishop of Chester
scarcely could contain his disgust. In a manner of minutes, and with limited
discussion, the SPG simply had discarded its declared purpose of propagating the gospel in foreign parts. "It is not *small* Difficulties, it is not *great*
Difficulties that should have deterred us," Porteus wrote to himself, "Nothing less than an absolute demonstrable *impossibility* should have discouraged us from the *attempt*."[39]

The intransigence of the SPG in 1784 enhanced the importance of the
Associates of Dr. Bray, a charitable society that had funded several schools
for black children in North America before the War of Independence and
that had figured importantly in the founding of Georgia earlier in the
century. The Associates of Dr. Bray differed from the SPG in several ways.
Among the clerical elite, the SPG enjoyed a far higher profile. Bishops
predominated on the governing board. The Associates of Dr. Bray, by
contrast, drew from a restricted and far more modest pool of donors.
Porteus in 1784 estimated the SPG's budget at three thousand pounds a
year. The Bray Associates operated on a fraction of that sum. The SPG
served as the organizing agency for the Anglican Church in the colonies, a
charge broad enough to allow for routine evasion of its apparent responsibility to baptize slaves in the colonies. The Associates of Dr. Bray, by
contrast, possessed the far more specific mission to provide religious books
to provincial libraries and instruct slaves in the Christian religion, a mission
the organization pursued diligently in North America, although on a limited scale. This restrictive definition of their work and their relative independence from episcopal oversight enabled the associates to act aggressively on the newly perceived needs of the West Indies. The American
Revolution, already, had forced the associates to reconsider their priorities,
before Porteus began to influence their choices. The loss of thirteen colonies took from the Associates of Dr. Bray their principal field of endeavor.
In 1777, they had closed their schools in the middle colonies and donated

39. "Occasional Memoranda and Reflections," Mar. 19, 1784, fols. 82–94, Porteus
MSS 2099.

their limited funds to a charity school in Gloucestershire. Only Canada and the Caribbean colonies remained within the empire when the associates could finally renew their primary mission to sponsor schools for black children in the Americas. In the fall of 1781, in response to evidence of Methodist inroads in Antigua, the associates sent "to each clergyman in the West Indies" fifty copies of Josiah Waring's *Letters to an American Planter,* an essay first published by the associates in 1770 to further Anglican conversions on the North American plantations.[40]

The Associates of Dr. Bray led the new effort in the 1780s to provide Caribbean churchmen with devotional literature. In the process, the organization attracted new members and new subscribers including several already active in antislavery and moral reform campaigns. James Oglethorpe and Granville Sharp became associates in 1785. Elizabeth Bouverie gave five-pound donations to the society in 1786 and 1787. Charles Middleton joined the associates in 1788. Bennet Langton, the Lincolnshire landowner known for his "evangelical virtue," had been a regular subscriber since 1783.[41] These gifts facilitated the new Caribbean initiatives. In July 1783, months after Porteus spoke before the SPG, the associates forwarded to the clergy of Barbados 800 copies of Waring's *Letters,* along with 160 copies of Thomas Bacon's sermons for American slaves.[42] The contributors pro-

40. Ibid., Mar. 19, 1784, fol. 90; John C. Van Horne, *Religious Philanthropy and Colonial Slavery: The American Correspondence of the Associates of Dr. Bray, 1717–1777* (Urbana, Ill., 1985); MiDAB, Apr. 1, 1777, Sept. 27, 1781, Bray Associates MSS, vol. f3, fols. 77, 93.

41. Account Book of Dr. Bray's Associates, II, June 6, 1785, Feb. 6, Apr. 11, 1786, Feb. 27, 1787, Bray Associates MSS; Annual Report of the Associates of the Late Dr. Bray (London, 1788), ibid.; MiDAB, Sept. 27, 1781, vol. f3, fol. 93, ibid. Samuel Johnson once commented that, though he admired Langton, he thought him "too ready to introduce religious discussions upon all occasions." For this and an additional reference to Langton's "evangelical virtue," see George Birkbeck Hill, ed., *Boswell's Life of Johnson . . . ,* 6 vols., rev. and enl. (Oxford, 1934–1950), IV, 216, 280. In the spring of 1787, Bennet Langton would host the famous dinner at which William Wilberforce and others would encourage the formal establishment of the Society for Effecting the Abolition of the Slave Trade.

42. Thomas Bacon, *Two Sermons, Preached to a Congregation of Black Slaves, at the Parish Church of S. P. in the Province of Maryland; by an American Pastor* (London, 1782); [John Waring], *Letters to an American Planter, from His Friend in London* (London, 1781). A similar package of tracts was sent to Anguilla, Saint Martin, Tortola,

vided their expertise as well. James Oglethorpe in 1785 prepared for the associates a revised edition of Bishop Thomas Wilson's *Essay towards an Instruction for the Indians*. The same year, Beilby Porteus procured for the associates a tract titled *Christian Directions and Instructions for the Negroes*.[43] The associates distributed both publications widely in the British West Indies. The charity benefited also from the recalcitrance of the SPG. An anonymous female donor (perhaps Bouverie or Margaret Middleton) presented Porteus in 1785 with £82 11s. "for the purpose of civilizing, instructing, and converting the Negroes" on the Codrington estates. Knowing that the SPG would neglect the opportunity, Porteus sent the gift instead to the Associates of Dr. Bray, who used the money in 1786 to establish a charity school for black children in Saint Thomas Parish, Barbados.[44]

These Anglican activists felt certain that the planters neglected their true interests. British slaveholders believed that Christian instruction would destroy the social order in the Caribbean plantations. "The precepts and doctrines of the Gospel," reformers like Porteus explained in reply, "would be the best possible means of keeping [the Negroes] to their duty, and of rendering them industrious, honest, sober, faithful and obedient to their masters." With such statements, those zealous for Christian conversion came close to defending the institution of slavery. When Porteus, for example, described spiritual slavery as "much worse" than chattel slavery, he articulated a characteristic and long-standing tendency in the devotional literature distributed by those who would promote plantation missions—a commitment to salvation of the soul and a passing interest in the personal liberty of the person.[45] Beilby Porteus disliked slavery, actually. He wrote

---

Saint Vincent, and Dominica in October 1783. MiDAB, July 7, Oct. 19, 1783, vol. f3, fols. 102, 103–105, Bray Associates MSS.

43. Thomas Wilson, *The Knowledge and Practice of Christianity Made Easy to the Meanest Capacities; or, An Essay towards an Instruction for the Indians . . .* (London, 1787); *Christian Directions and Instructions for Negroes* (London, 1785). At this time, James Ramsay also published *A Manual for African Slaves* (London, 1787), though this pamphlet appears not to have been distributed by the Associates of Dr. Bray.

44. "Occasional Memoranda and Reflections," Feb. 28, 1785, fol. 118, Porteus MSS 2099; MiDAB, Mar. 3, 1785, vol. f3, fol. 112, Bray Associates MSS.

45. Porteus, *An Essay towards a Plan for the More Effectual Conversion and Civilization of the Negro Slaves*, in Hodgson, ed., *The Works of Beilby Porteus*, VI, 213; Porteus, *Bishop of Chester's Sermon*, 12.

hopefully of a distant day for emancipation.[46] Yet he understood that advancing the cause of religion required a compromise with propertied interests. He realized that the promotion of Christianity in the West Indian plantations meant avoiding, suppressing, and even denying the existence of an antislavery agenda. Porteus was elevated in 1787 to the diocese of London, which gave him direct authority over the Anglican ministers in the British West Indies and elsewhere in the American empire. Months later he sent a forceful letter to the Caribbean clergy, directing them to commence programs for religious instruction of the enslaved. He asked them to establish schools in each parish for black girls and boys. He told the ministers that "it would be a labour truly evangelical" to follow in Christ's footsteps and preach to the poor. Even in the midst of the campaign against the slave trade, though, he wrote nothing about abolition.[47]

The political logic that informed these choices becomes most apparent when the Caribbean initiatives are compared with the Sunday school movement that took shape in England during the same years. The two campaigns were of a piece. Driven by similar impulses, faced with similar challenges, they adopted similar strategies to achieve similar goals. Both took place against the backdrop of competition from Evangelical revivals outside the church. Both confronted a traditional disregard among the privileged for the spiritual welfare of the working classes and dispossessed. The Sunday school and Anglican missionary programs tried to ease the fears of those suspicious of religious enthusiasm and uneasy about teaching the poor to read. Providing for the spiritual welfare of the poor meant, first, mollifying the anxieties of the elite. To this end, they stressed the social utility of Christian instruction: religion, promoters explained, would make laborers work better; it would make them more docile and easier to control. Both programs held forth the promise of a harmonious, unified society in which social conflicts would be subsumed beneath a shared reverence for God, nation, and the established order. Their ideal postreform societies were nearly indistinguishable. At its establishment in 1785, the Sunday School Society stated that it aimed "to encourage industry and virtue—to dispel the darkness of ignorance—to diffuse the light of knowledge—to

---

46. Porteus, *Bishop of Chester's Sermon*, 24n.

47. Beilby Porteus, *A Letter to the Clergy of the West-India Islands* (London, 1788), 5, 8; also see Mason, *The Moravian Church and the Missionary Awakening*, 126–132.

bring men cheerfully to submit to their stations—to obey the laws of God and their country—to make that part of the community, the country poor, happy—to lead them in the pleasant paths of religion here, and to endeavour to prepare them for a glorious eternity."[48] Beilby Porteus imagined his proposed "NEW SCHOOL FOR PIETY AND VIRTUE in the Atlantic Ocean" in precisely the same terms.

> A spectacle no less singular in its kind, than honourable to us and our religion, a little society of truly Christian Negroes, impressed with a just cause, and living in the habitual practice, of the several duties they owe to God, to their masters, to their fellow labourers and to themselves; governed by fixed laws, and by the exactest discipline, yet tempered with gentleness and humanity; enjoying some little share of the comforts and advantages of social and domestic life . . . performing their daily tasks with alacrity and fidelity; looking up to their masters as their friends; their protectors and their benefactors; and consoling themselves for the loss of their liberty and their native land, by the care taken to "make their yoke, easy, and their burden light," to civilize their manners, to enlarge their understanding, to reform their hearts, and to open to them a prospect into a better and happier country where all tears shall be wiped from their eyes, and where sorrow and slavery shall be no more.

Porteus prescribed for the West Indies a benign Christian paternalism, not much different from what he and other moral reformers at the time were recommending for England, only Porteus would appoint for each district "a Guardian of the Negroes."[49]

Beilby Porteus and the rest of the Teston clan initially showed little interest in the slave trade or its abolition. If left to their own impulses, they might never have become abolitionists. From the beginning, they evaded a direct challenge to political and commercial institutions. And from the beginning, their interest in colonial slavery focused particularly on the

48. Laqueur, *Religion and Respectability,* 34. See also Betsy Rodgers, *Cloak of Charity: Studies in Eighteenth-Century Philanthropy* (London, 1949), 95–111, and Soloway, *Prelates and People,* 349–358.

49. Porteus, *An Essay towards a Plan for the More Effectual Civilization and Conversion of the Negroe Slaves,* in Hodgson, ed., *The Works of Beilby Porteus,* VI, 215; Porteus, *Bishop of Chester's Sermon,* 28–29.

promotion of Christianity and the moral improvement of the British Caribbean plantations. Margaret Middleton first queried James Ramsay about
the character of West Indian society because she thought inattention to the
spiritual welfare of the enslaved disgraceful. In their several incarnations,
the long-delayed Ramsay manuscripts aimed above all to elevate and fortify
the Anglican Church in the British Caribbean. When Beilby Porteus tried
to transform Ramsay's ideas into action, he directed his efforts particularly
toward support for the colonial clergy. In their public and private writings,
moreover, the Teston clan made little mention of the slave trade or the need
for its abolition before the summer of 1784. Indeed, Ramsay would alarm
the otherwise sympathetic in his *Essay* with the suggestion that the slave
trade might provide a way to rescue Africans from slavery and heathenism
in their native land, a long-familiar claim favored by apologists for the slave
trade. Wilberforce later recalled that initially he hoped only to improve the
treatment of the enslaved in the West Indies.[50] In the early 1780s, the
Teston clan displayed only the most limited interest in more aggressive antislavery measures. Ramsay still favored schemes for a very gradual emancipation. Porteus spoke and wrote favorably about the "Spanish Regulations." Hannah More had disparaged the slave trade when among her
acquaintances.[51] Yet these were gestures rather than commitments. Their
efforts might easily have culminated with an intensified missionary movement, not unlike the abbreviated scheme the SPG attempted to inspire
much earlier in the 1710s and the 1720s. The program of Christian reform
for the Caribbean colonies agreed far more with the Testonites' shared
priorities: enlarging the sphere of influence for the church, combating sin,
and harmonizing relations among the ranks. All of this seemed necessary

50. Ramsay, *An Essay on the Treatment and Conversion of African Slaves in the
British Sugar Colonies;* Robert Isaac and Samuel Wilberforce, *The Life of William
Wilberforce,* 5 vols. (London, 1838), I, 149. Porteus did refer to the slave trade as
"opprobrious" and noted that the British led all other European nations in the traffic.
The obligations these facts entailed, though, were less to lobby for abolition than to
"soothe and alleviate" their "temporal bondage" "as much as possible, and by endeavour-
ing to rescue them from the still more cruel bondage of ignorance and sin." Porteus,
Bishop of Chester's Sermon, 33–34.

51. Porteus, *Bishop of Chester's Sermon,* 23; Porteus, *An Essay toward the More
Effectual Civilization and Conversion of the Negroe Slaves,* in Hodgson, ed., *The Works of
Beilby Porteus,* VI, 201–202.

and eminently sensible to them. And yet in England, as well as in the West Indies, they faced obstruction from those who wished well to commerce but not religion and from those who held leadership positions in the Church of England but would not lead in the ways these reformers thought church officials should.

[III]   The Teston circle hoped to stimulate Anglican missions in the sugar colonies. The public conversation that Ramsay inspired, however, would center instead on questions of humanity and justice. James Ramsay's *Essay on the Treatment and Conversion of African Slaves in the British Sugar Colonies* (1784) introduced a new set of issues for consideration. By calling attention to West Indian practices and, in effect, away from North American hypocrisy, the text caused a dramatic shift in the public discussion of antislavery measures. The pamphlet produced a prolonged exchange about the character of British Caribbean slavery, the nature of metropolitan responsibility for the sugar colonies, and the prospects for rectifying the horrors of human bondage. Many had written critically about the British West Indies before 1784, and in various registers and different formats. Yet, in terms of impact, no previous text approached the importance and influence of the Ramsay treatise. Beilby Porteus would recall in 1803 that the discussion created by the *Essay* "contributed perhaps more than any other to the parliamentary enquiry" into the slave trade.[52] Its influence, indeed, extended beyond the subjects it explicitly addressed. For the ensuing controversy had a decisive effect on James Ramsay himself, who would be affected deeply by the public reaction to what he wrote.

The *Essay* differed from previous commentaries on Caribbean slavery in several ways. First, there was its scope and ambition. The volume stretched over three hundred pages. A long first chapter ranged across the history of slavery from ancient times to the end of the Revolutionary War. Subsequent sections elaborated with great care arguments for civilizing the enslaved, the advantages to be gained from instructing them in Christianity, and the intellectual abilities of African peoples. It offered a plan for their "improvement and conversion." Second, there was its authority. The product of nearly two decades of living, writing, and thinking in the West Indies, the

52. Porteus's comment printed in Hodgson, ed., *The Works of Beilby Porteus,* II, 401n–402n.

author possessed an unusual command of his subject. Many British men and women who published antislavery statements in the eighteenth century had never seen plantation slavery for themselves. Ramsay not only had lived in the Caribbean. He was himself a former slaveholder, like many Anglican clergy who had lived in the West Indies. These experiences allowed Ramsay to describe the mores of British Caribbean society in detail, to dispense with the moving but generic narratives established by the legends of stock characters such as Oroonoko or Inkle and Yarico. He replaced those fictional archetypes with concrete examples of how enslaved men and women lived, how sugar plantations functioned, what West Indian society was like. Third, there was the effusive praise from the critics. When published in 1784, the *Essay* received special treatment from the press. The *Critical Review* printed a two-part assessment in May and June. The June issue of the *Monthly Review* devoted the lead article to Ramsay's treatise. Both journals lauded its achievements. "The treatment of the slaves in the West Indies is a subject which has been often regretted by men of humanity," the *Critical Review* wrote, "but never discussed with such precision, care, and ability."[53]

More than a decade had passed since spokesmen for the West Indian interest last felt obliged to justify Caribbean slavery. At that time, several had tried to contain the implications of the Somerset case in 1772, so that the popular support for the verdict in the British Isles would not evolve into a concerted attack on colonial practices.[54] Thereafter, defenders

53. *Monthly Review,* LXX (1784), 409–418; *Critical Review,* LVII (1784), 381–386, 449–452, citation on 381.

54. John Peter Demarin, *A Treatise upon the Trade from Great-Britain to Africa: Humbly Recommended to the Attention of Government* (London, 1772); Samuel Estwick, *Considerations on the Negro Cause Commonly So Called, Addressed to the Right Honourable Lord Mansfield, Lord Chief Justice of the Court of King's Bench, by a West Indian* (London, 1772); Edward Long, *Candid Reflections upon the Judgment Lately Awarded by the Court of King's Bench, in Westminster-Hall, on What Is Commonly Called the Negro Cause* (London, 1772); Edward Long, *The History of Jamaica; or, General Survey of the Ancient and Modern State of That Island . . .* , 3 vols. (London, 1774), I, 5, II, 267–271, 390–402; Tho[mas] Thompson, *The African Trade for Negro Slaves, Shewn to Be Consistent with Principles of Humanity, and with the Laws of Revealed Religion* (Canterbury, [1772]); Samuel Martin, *An Essay upon Plantership, the Fifth Edition, with Many Additions, and a Preface upon the Slavery of Negroes in the British Colonies* (London,

of slavery returned to public debate only when sufficiently alarmed by what they interpreted as a genuine threat. In this regard, they set the bar high. They ignored Granville Sharp's quartet of pamphlets published in 1776. They took little notice of the countless antislavery statements that emerged in pamphlets and the press, poetry and prose, during and after the American Revolution. Even the *Case of Our Fellow-Creatures* (1783), which marked the beginning of a new Quaker antislavery campaign in Britain, drew no reply.

The *Essay on the Treatment and Conversion of African Slaves,* however, was another matter entirely. It left the West Indian interest apoplectic. The volume drove them into paroxysms of outrage. Each one of the nine proslavery tracts published in Britain from the summer of 1784 through 1787 represented either an explicit or implicit reaction to Ramsay's *Essay*. The proslavery interest developed a fixation with the erstwhile minister from Saint Kitts. Three replies appeared within a year of the *Essay*'s publication, each denouncing Ramsay and defending slavery in almost equal measure.[55] Ramsay responded quickly in turn, with one publication in 1785 and another early in 1786. The first presented an exhaustive and exhausting point-by-point refutation of his critics. The second offered the insights of a naval captain familiar with the West Indies and able to corroborate Ramsay's

---

1773); *A Supplement to Mr. Wesley's Pamphlet Entitled Thoughts upon Slavery* (London, 1774); Samuel Martin, *A Short Treatise on the Slavery of the Negroes in the British Colonies; Shewing That They Are Much Happier Than in Their Native Country . . .* (Antigua, 1775). See also Srividhya Swaminathan, "Developing the West Indian Pro-slavery Position after the Somerset Decision," *Slavery and Abolition,* XXIV, no. 3 (December 2003), 46–50.

55. *Remarks on a Pamphlet Written by the Rev. James Ramsay, M.A., under the Title of Thoughts on the Slavery of the Negroes, in the American Colonies* (London, 1784); *An Answer to the Reverend James Ramsay's Essay, on the Treatment and Conversion of Slaves, in the British Sugar Colonies* (Basseterre, 1784); *Cursory Remarks upon the Reverend Mr. Ramsay's Essay on the Treatment and Conversion of African Slaves in the Sugar Colonies* (London, 1785). Three others appeared shortly after: *Letters to a Young Planter; or, Observations on the Management of a Sugar-Plantation; to Which Is Added, the Planter's Kalendar; Written on the Island of Grenada, by an Old Planter* (London, 1785); Sir Philip Gibbes, *Instructions for the Treatment of Negroes, etc., etc., etc.* (London, 1786); and [Gordon Turnbull], *An Apology for Negro Slavery; or, The West-India Planters Vindicated from the Charges of Inhumanity* (London, 1786).

depiction of British West Indian slavery.[56] Replies piled on top of replies thereafter. James Tobin of Nevis answered in 1787 with a *Short Rejoinder to the Reverend Mr. Ramsay's Reply*. Ramsay came back a month later with *A Letter to James Tobin*, to which Tobin quickly retorted with *A Farewell Address to Rev. Mr. James Ramsay*. As this exchange concluded, in 1788, another commenced. A "West Indian planter" came forward with disapproving *Considerations on the Emancipation of Negroes and on the Abolition of the Slave Trade*. In reply, Ramsay wrote back with one of his more effective tracts: *Objections to the Abolition of the Slave Trade with Answers*. The erstwhile Caribbean churchman worried the West Indian interest because he could describe systematic abuses, because he could elaborate a well-thought-out strategy for reform, because he could do more than invoke sentiment or moral principles.[57]

The British public knew surprisingly little about the character of Caribbean society when this debate commenced in 1784. The curious could gather a basic understanding of West Indian society and economy from the available histories and geographies; Edward Long's three-volume *History of Jamaica* (1774), well known for its arch defense of slavery and its Negrophobia, represented the most familiar work. Before 1784, however, few

56. James Ramsay, *A Reply to the Personal Invectives and Objections Contained in Two Answers; Published by Certain Anonymous Persons . . .* (London, 1785); John Samuel Smith, *A Letter from Capt. J. S. Smith to the Revd Mr Hill on the State of the Negroe Slaves; to Which Are Added an Introduction, and Remarks on Free Negroes, etc.* (London, 1786).

57. Defending the reputation of Caribbean society would remain a concern for the West Indian interest, even after antislavery campaigns turned their attention to the slave trade and its abolition rather than slavery and its emancipation. In 1788, alone, there appeared three pamphlets purporting to render a "true" picture of slavery in Jamaica. William Beckford, Jr., *Remarks upon the Situation of the Negroes in Jamaica, Impartially Made from a Local Experience of Nearly Thirteen Years in That Island* (London, 1788); [Peter Marsden], *An Account of the Island of Jamaica, with Reflections on the Treatment, Occupation, and Provisions of the Slaves; to Which Is Added a Description of the Animal and Vegetable Productions of the Island; by a Gentleman Lately Resident on a Plantation* (Newcastle, Eng., 1788); Hector McNeill, *Observations on the Treatment of the Negroes, in the Island of Jamica, Including Some Account of Their Temper and Character, with Remarks on the Importation of Slaves from the Coast of Africa, in a Letter to a Physician in England* (London, 1788).

published accounts detailed relations between masters and slaves or the circumstances in which the enslaved lived and worked. Alarm in Britain at the idea of human bondage rarely implied an in-depth knowledge about social conditions on the ground. Beilby Porteus, for example, confessed in his sermon of 1783 that he drew the bulk of his information from men like James Ramsay, who had lived in or traveled to the West Indies. As late as 1787, Porteus still was gathering evidence to support Ramsay's "Assertions and Facts Representing the Treatment of the Negroes."[58] The *Monthly Review* wound itself in knots trying to sort out conflicting evidence. In June 1784, the editors responded with enthusiasm to Ramsay's *Essay* and quoted at length his unsparing criticism of the West Indian proprietors. A year later, though, they reversed their stance when evaluating the proslavery pamphlet *Cursory Remarks,* which convinced them that the condition of the slaves was "by no means as intolerable as we had conceived it to be." This statement drew an angry retort from James Ramsay, who charged the *Monthly Review* of siding with the proslavery interest.[59] Chastened, the editors thereafter chose to excuse themselves from the dispute and refused to render an opinion regarding the "facts" in question.

For James Ramsay and other antislavery campaigners, however, starting the debate served almost as well as winning it. The West Indian interest owed its political strength in part to the tendency within the British Isles to view the slave system as a necessity, even as doubts festered about its justice and virtue. The exploitation of slave labor remained secure as long as it escaped close questioning. More than any other publication, Ramsay's *Essay* exposed West Indian society for what it was, thereby cutting through the almost willful ignorance that insulated Caribbean slavery from public scrutiny. He understood correctly that the immediate benefit of his work lay in the questions it raised about the slave system. The *Essay,* he wrote in 1785, "obliged people to examine prejudices which before they took on

58. Porteus, *Bishop of Chester's Sermon;* "Occasional Memoranda and Reflections," Aug. 2, 1784, Apr. 13, 1787, fols. 99, 154–158, Porteus MSS 2099.

59. *Monthly Review,* LXX (1784), 409–418; ibid., LXXIII (1785), 269; undated letter from James Ramsay to the editors of the *Monthly Review* written in 1785 published as an attachment with separate pagination in James Ramsay, *A Reply to the Personal Invectives,* 1–3; Ramsay, *A Letter to James Tobin, Esq., Late Member of His Majesty's Council in the Island of Nevis* (London, 1787).

trust."[60] Antislavery writers still needed to make a case for abolition or emancipation, as before. But after 1784, slave traders and the West India interest needed to explain, as well, why questionable practices should escape improvement. Convincing a metropolitan readership to tolerate colonial slavery they found a delicate task. It put them in the position of justifying what, on moral grounds, looked incapable of justification.

Apologists could and did fall back on the sanctity of private property, the economic value of slave labor, and the national interest in sustaining valuable Atlantic trades. Otherwise, though, they found nearly every line of argument closed. Few felt comfortable defending "slavery" before a public that prided itself on its commitment to "liberty." Advocating human bondage seemed like confessing, in the same moment, to a want of civility and sensibility. Sometimes, as a consequence, proslavery writers put less energy into defending slavery than defending themselves. One writer stressed that planters were, on the whole, "remarkable for urbanity of manners, liberality of sentiment, and generosity of disposition." James Tobin of Nevis insisted that West Indian slaveholders were as "worthy, as useful, as loyal, but as *misrepresented* a set of subjects as any in the dominions of Great Britain." To allay suspicions that they had become hardened to the inhumanity of slavery, proslavery writers often avowed a personal distaste for human bondage. Almost every proslavery pamphlet published between 1784 and 1788 contains such concessions: "that slavery is an evil no man will deny"; "for the abolition of slavery none can be a greater advocate than myself"; "no man condemns, as an abstract proposition, more than I the command over the lives and properties of their fellow creatures." The author of the *Cursory Remarks* opened (insincerely) with the hope that "the blessings of freedom will in due time, be equally diffused over the face of the whole globe."[61]

In these almost farcical attempts to embrace enlightened moral standards, the West Indians revealed the same status anxiety that haunted

---

60. Ramsay to Thomas Lyttleton, n.d., Ramsay MSS, fol. 62.

61. [Trumbull], *An Apology for Negro Slavery*, 34; *Considerations on the Emancipation of Negroes and on the Abolition of the Slave-Trade*, 2; *Remarks on a Pamphlet Written by the Rev. James Ramsay*, 22; *Thoughts on Civilization and the Gradual Abolition of Slavery in Africa and the West Indies . . .* (London, 1789), 1; *Cursory Remarks upon the Reverend Mr. Ramsay's Essay*, 5.

North American slaveholders on the eve of the War of Independence. They did not want to give up slavery and yet did not wish to be thought of as vicious tyrants either. North Americans had tried to solve this problem by shifting the burden of responsibility to the British Isles, by highlighting British hypocrisy, by blaming the British government and British merchants for the Atlantic slave trade. But the West Indian interest could not adopt this strategy, not with any conviction. Unlike some of their North American brethren, they needed the slave trade to continue. So, rather than condemn imperial policies that had and still served them well, several drew attention to what they characterized as the comparably inhumane institutions in British society. Before the American Revolution, a few North American patriots, Benjamin Franklin most famously, had pointed out the distressing conditions endured by Scottish coal miners and English day laborers. James Grainger and Edward Long had experimented with such comparisons, too.[62] After 1784, the sufferings of the British poor became a recurring theme in proslavery literature. James Tobin, for example, drew the contrast between "nominal" liberty in England and slavery in the Caribbean. "Emaciated, squalid, and heart-broken" workers in England "are absolutely bound either to work, or starve" while, in the West Indies, "a sober, industrious negro is seldom without a good suit or two of cloaths to his back, and a few dollars in his pocket."[63]

Neither Ramsay nor his patrons at Barham Court intended to encourage comparisons between West Indian slaves and the English poor. They wanted servitude in the colonies to be Christian and lawful, just like, they implied, labor in the British Isles. Yet, by making physical sufferings an index of injustice, they inadvertently exposed to scrutiny the exploitation of workers at home. It gave antislavery writers like Ramsay no trouble to identify the formal differences between Caribbean slavery and British servitude. The editors of the *Times* summed up the position well in 1788 when

---

62. James Grainger, *The Sugar Cane: A Poem; in Four Books; with Notes* (London, 1764), book IV, lines 165–182, as published in John Gilmore, *The Poetics of Empire: A Study of James Grainger's "The Sugar-Cane"* (London, 2000), 150; Long, *The History of Jamaica*, II, 402.

63. *Cursory Remarks upon the Reverend Mr. Ramsay's Essay*, 89, 96, 98n. For additional examples from the press, see *St. James Chronicle*, Mar. 22–25, 25–27, 1788, and *Whitehall Evening Post*, Mar. 11–13, 20–22, 27–29, 1788.

they wrote that "slavery does not consist in what a man *suffers,*—but in a power existing in another man to encrease or decrease those sufferings at pleasure."[64] Yet, in the long run, drawing such distinctions failed to insulate Ramsay and his allies from the same kind of challenge they presented to slaveholders. They found themselves obliged to justify institutions and practices that they long had taken for granted. As a consequence, in attempting to contain the application of their moral principles, they unintentionally compromised the image of the movement at its inception, through the nineteenth century, and, later, in twentieth-century historiography. Characterizing an economic and social system as a moral problem, the abolitionists would learn, encourages moral criticism in return. It invites the accused to respond by levying retaliatory accusations. The British antislavery movement had its start this way, as now should be clear—British denunciations of North American slaveholding circled back to Britain, in the Revolutionary era, in the form of North American protests against the Atlantic slave trade. In a similar way, British denunciations of Caribbean slaveholding returned to Britain in the form of questions about daily injustices in England. Propagandists might control what they wrote but rarely what their writings would come to mean or what those writings would help others notice. Shifts in moral perception, new questions about the ethical character of customary practices, sometimes depended less on the march of ideas and, at times, more on the dynamics of political conflict.

The West Indian interest experimented with other arguments. A few turned to the Bible for scriptural defenses of human bondage.[65] Some suggested that the slave trade "rescued" Africans from the barbarity of their native land.[66] In the end, though, defenders relied on the more sturdy assistance provided by claims of national interest. The appropriate question, one wrote of the slave trade in 1788, "is not whether the traffic in

---

64. *Times,* Mar. 8, 1788.

65. See, for example, *An Answer to the Reverend James Ramsay's Essay on the Treatment and Conversion of Slaves,* and Raymund Harris, *Scriptural Researches on the Licitness of the Slave-Trade, Shewing Its Conformity with the Principles of Natural and Revealed Religion, Delineated in the Sacred Writings of the Word of God* (Liverpool, 1788).

66. Thomas Maxwell Adams, *A Cool Address to the People of England, on the Slave Trade* (London, 1788), 32.

Negroes shall cease or not; but whether Great Britain shall or shall not retain her power."[67] Proslavery writers made almost no attempt to defend slavery in the abstract. Moreover, as if to underscore the concession, they frequently put forward modest schemes for reform or improvement, several of which, in substantive terms, differed little from what Ramsay himself had suggested. One agreed that forcing slaves to work on the Sabbath was indefensible, though he held the clergy rather than the planters responsible for the practice. Another recommended a reduction in the number of slaves carried on each slave trading ship, a provision of adequate food and water, and prosecution of slave traders who murdered human cargo. The Jamaica Assembly passed a Regulating Act in 1788 that consolidated and rephrased its slave codes to give the impression that slaves, like the English, enjoyed the protection of the laws.[68] From the tone of the debate, after Ramsay published, it seemed as if the question at issue was less the need for change than which changes should take place, how, and when. To this extent, proslavery writers seemed to lose the argument in the moment it began.

For James Ramsay, however, this initial success came at a private cost. The controversy transformed him into a public figure and exposed him to personal attack. Ramsay anticipated, he claimed after, that disclosing the character of Caribbean slavery would stir the ire of the planter class. He

67. *Considerations on the Emancipation of the Negroes*, 27.

68. *Cursory Remarks upon the Reverend Mr. Ramsay's Essay*, 100–101; [Turnbull], *An Apology for Negro Slavery*, 53–56. On the Jamaica law, see J. R. Ward, *British West Indian Slavery, 1750–1834: The Process of Amelioration* (Oxford, 1988), 2, and Lowell Joseph Ragatz, *The Fall of the Planter Class in the British Caribbean, 1763–1883: A Study in Social and Economic History* (New York, 1928), 266–267. Such gestures in favor of modest reform seem to have been common among French proslavery writers before the French Revolution as well. Malick W. Ghachem, "Montesquieu in the Caribbean: The Colonial Enlightenment between *Code Noir* and *Code Civil*," *Historical Reflections/ Réflexions historiques*, XXV, no. 2 (Summer 1999), 197. These concessions to public opinion hint at the vulnerability felt by the West Indian interest when forced to debate slavery publicly. What they decided not to say was as revealing as what they did. Few in the 1780s attempted racial justifications for slavery, undoubtedly because they presumed that such argument would make them appear unenlightened and illiberal. Two early writers explicitly denounced previous suggestions in 1774 by Jamaican planter Edward Long that blacks were a separate species. See *Cursory Remarks upon the Reverend Mr. Ramsay's Essay*, 141, and [Trumbull], *An Apology for Negro Slavery*, 34.

had predicted, he stated later, that several would besmirch his character. "When I suffered myself to be prevailed upon to give my thoughts to the public, I threw my own reputation into the bargain. I knew my antagonists well enough to expect only the basest, the most unmanly treatment in return. I have not been disappointed." The first of the replies to the *Essay* from unnamed writers in his former home of Saint Kitts leaned heavily on ad hominem attacks, charging him, as Ramsay summarized: "of not being a Christian; of having been a Presbyterian; a harsh surgeon; a violent politician; a cruel master; a grasping avaricious man; a bad neighbour; he preached his people out of church; he mocked God's judgments; he was a corrupt magistrate," and so on. "In short, such a monster never before appeared on paper."[69] If these attacks were extreme, so was Ramsay's reaction. His *Reply to the Personal Invectives* of 1785 and his *Letter to James Tobin* of 1787 stood out for their rushed composition and bitterness. In these texts, Ramsay corrected misrepresentations of his *Essay* and exposed the weak arguments of his opponents. But the venom in his replies often undermined an otherwise powerful case. His second and third tracts showed none of the care and moderation that distinguished the *Essay*, which the Teston clan had given such careful review. The Teston clan would not have encouraged Ramsay to dwell at length on each minute point raised by his antagonists, a choice that made the *Reply* of 1785, in particular, tiresome and unreadable. Nor could they have thought well of Ramsay's decision to chastise the *Monthly Review* for recommending the opinions of certain proslavery writers.[70] Ramsay's ardor in defending himself contributed to the growing view in some quarters that abolitionists, too often, allowed enthusiasm to overpower sound judgment. Ramsay risked losing his audience by descending into vituperative screeds that seemed to tell as much about the personality of the author as the problem of slavery in the Caribbean.

The controversy caused by the *Essay* propelled Ramsay into a new career. It turned the parish minister and naval board clerk into a polemicist. With all that had been written about slavery in the British colonies by 1784,

69. Ramsay, *A Reply to the Personal Invectives and Objections*, 2; Ramsay to the *Monthly Review*, n.d., 1785, as printed ibid., app., 2.

70. Folarin Shyllon has detailed the tedious exchange between Ramsay and his opponents in his fine biography. Shyllon, *James Ramsay*, 42–74.

FIGURE 5. The Reverend James Ramsay. By Carl Frederik von Breda. 1789.
Courtesy, National Portrait Gallery, London

the antislavery cause in England still lacked a champion singularly dedicated to the cause. Granville Sharp had at times devoted himself to antislavery lobbying. Yet Sharp tended to spread himself thin among various
reforming causes and, more, was too erratic to persist in a specific line of
political labor. In England, in the early 1780s, there still was no one comparable to Anthony Benezet, who from the late 1760s until his death in 1784
insistently kept the issue of slavery before the North American public,
particularly in the middle colonies. Ramsay's dedication to the improvement of slavery dated back to the 1760s, his first years in Saint Kitts. But
that private commitment first attained public importance in 1784. After the
attacks he endured in 1784 and 1785, Ramsay considered his fate as connected with the welfare of slaves in the West Indies. Like them, he thought
himself unjustly persecuted. And he tended to link their redemption with
the redemption of his reputation. Because his publications had made him
an object of contempt, Ramsay found it impossible to divorce his sense of
self from the opinions he held.[71] He could vindicate himself only through
the vindication of his cause. By personalizing the contest, by reacting
venomously to a comprehensive proposal to ameliorate slavery, the West
Indian interest helped create what they needed least—a passionate opponent determined to make the antislavery cause a personal crusade.

James Ramsay had not planned, at first, to campaign against the slave
trade. Yet, as he learned of Quaker plans to promote abolition in 1784, and,
as he considered the ways slave trade abolition could make West Indian
slavery less brutal, he began to take an active interest in the transatlantic
traffic. The *Inquiry into the Effects of Putting a Stop to the African Slave
Trade* appeared shortly after the *Essay* and offered, as argued in the previous chapter, the first sustained attempt in twenty years to describe abolition as wise commercial policy. From 1785 to 1787, in the same years he

---

71. Consider two statements: (1) "The author should intitle this publication, An
Apology for his Life and Opinions; for his character as a man, and his reasoning as an
author, as if they could stand or fall together, are so blended, as to force him to blend also
their vindication"; (2) "But my character assumes an importance when connected with
the cause of liberty, which I have undertaken. The public will excuse a solicitude about it,
when it has been inseparately blended with the merits of an object, that ought to interest
every human feeling." Ramsay, *A Reply to the Personal Invectives and Objections*, iii;
Ramsay, *A Letter to James Tobin*, v–vi.

defended his *Essay* and himself, Ramsay called repeatedly for an investigation of the Atlantic trade.[72] These appeals differed little from those put forward by other antislavery writers. The Quakers, in particular, lobbied actively for parliamentary action between 1783 and 1786. Ramsay, however, seems to have settled rather early on the course that such an investigation should take.

William Jolliffe, the member of Parliament for Petersfield in Huntingdon, had served on the Board of Trade during Lord North's ministry. He liked the *Essay* and wrote to Ramsay, in the fall of 1784, looking for advice on "a bill for granting protection to the African Slaves in our Sugar Colonies." "There are few things on which I have more frequently thought," Ramsay wrote in reply, "but I fear Parliament has done many things lately that disclaim a legislative authority over its dependencies"—an unambiguous reference to American independence and the substantial legislative autonomy Ireland won from the Rockingham and Shelburne ministries in 1782. "The best foundations to go upon," Ramsay advised, "would be a committee in the House of Commons to inquire into the nature and extent of our African trade." Here perhaps Ramsay had in mind the kind of investigations recently conducted into the behavior of East India Company officials in Bengal. Hearings of this kind, he continued, "will expose such scenes of oppressive cruelty, and such schemes of wretched policy, as even without a law must have its effect on the opinion and practice of the public." He recommended an inquiry into all aspects of the trade: the numbers of ships and sailors employed; the value of the goods traded to West Africa; the methods of procuring slaves and the conditions of the Middle Passage; the volume of the slave trade to British and foreign colonies; and the conditions of the trade during and immediately after the war with America.[73] More than two years before the formation of the Society for Effecting the Abolition of the Slave Trade, James Ramsay had in hand the strategy that would help push slave trade abolition to the top of the political agenda in 1788.

Ramsay's notoriety attracted a widening circle of abolitionists to Barham

72. Ramsay, *A Reply to the Personal Invectives and Objections,* 52–53, 61, 100; Smith, *A Letter from Capt. J. S. Smith to the Revd Mr Hill,* 49–51; Ramsay, *A Letter to James Tobin,* vii.

73. Ramsay to Mr. Joliffe, Jan. 6, 1785, Ramsay MSS, fol. 1.

Court after 1786. A pilgrimage to Teston became a rite of passage for the emerging abolitionist leadership. Margaret Middleton would insist that the antislavery cause remain a constant subject of debate among the guests at Barham Court. Ramsay could provide years of experience and the example of personal commitment. Charles Middleton, with his position at the naval board, could help abolitionists attain unusual access to information pertaining to the British slave trade. In the fall of 1786, the Teston clan received a visit from Thomas Clarkson, who had just published his *Essay on the Slavery and Commerce of the Human Species*. Clarkson went to Teston at the invitation of James Ramsay, who learned of Clarkson's work through the publisher they shared, the Quaker printer James Phillips. During his stay at Barham Court, Clarkson declared an intention to dedicate his life to slave trade abolition. These meetings decided the political agenda along the lines Ramsay had proposed. Margaret Middleton called on Charles to introduce an abolition bill in the House of Commons. A poor orator, Charles thought he could not do the cause justice, so he suggested that they solicit William Wilberforce, the young member of Parliament for Yorkshire, just then in the throes of a turbulent crisis in faith.[74]

The most recent generation of scholarship typically has   [IV] found it hard to embrace the Evangelicals. Frequently, and not incorrectly, these modern assessments tend to characterize the pious reformers as a repressive and reactionary elite. The reputed limits of Evangelical philanthropy have become almost legendary. In the same years they fought for the abolition of the slave trade and colonial slavery, some have observed, they neglected or obstructed efforts to better the condition of the working classes or advance the cause of political reform. These accounts, it might be observed, rehearse the views of the Evangelicals' opponents at the time. In their own day, the Evangelicals inspired a host of ardent enemies. Radicals loathed their defense of the established order. The clerical establishment viewed the Saints as a fanatical fifth column conspiring to conquer the Church of England for the cause of Methodism. The polite thought them philistines for their strictures against the theater, literature, and music. Nearly everyone outside the blessed circle resented their arrogance. In the

74. Clarkson, *History of the Rise, Progress, and Accomplishment of the Abolition of the African Slave-Trade*, I, 222–223; Pollock, *Wilberforce*, 53–54.

first three decades of the nineteenth century, as Evangelicals began to exercise a disproportionate influence on British culture, their critics routinely derided them as censorious, bossy, condescending, and smug. Wilberforce biographer Reginald Coupland recalled the words of William Cobbett, who in 1818 found in his involuntary exile from England some comfort in the distance he would gain from the Saints and their exasperating self-righteousness. America, he wrote in 1818, had "No Wilberforces. Think of *that!* No Wilberforces."[75]

No Wilberforce. For more than a generation, interpreters have sought to write the history of British antislavery with "no Wilberforce." The last serious attempts to consider the antislavery labors of the Evangelical statesman and his associates appeared in 1975.[76] If certain aspects of *Capitalism and Slavery* some now regard as dated and dubious, Eric Williams continues to influence the way scholars understand and approach the antislavery leadership. *Capitalism and Slavery* revived in 1944 most of the charges levied against the Clapham Sect more than a century before. Williams described the Saints as conniving and hypocritical. And he resurrected the personal animosities that had come to prevail in early Victorian politics. Wilberforce was not merely insincere and ineffective: "With his effeminate face [he] appears small in stature. There is a certain smugness about the man, his life, his religion."[77] That strain of interpretation has left a powerful legacy. In the most recent generation of research, there is an almost obses-

75. Eric Williams, *Capitalism and Slavery* (1944; rpt. Chapel Hill, N.C., 1994), 144. There appears to be no standard work on the religious and political opposition to Anglican Evangelicals for this period, but see generally Coupland, *Wilberforce*, 421–426, citation on 422; Ford K. Brown, *Fathers of the Victorians: The Age of Wilberforce* (Cambridge, 1961), 156–183, 187–233, 285–316, 363–377; Bradley, *The Call to Seriousness*, 26–31, 63–70, 109–113, 154–155; Doreen M. Rosman, *Evangelicals and Culture* (Beckenham, Eng., 1984); Hylson-Smith, *Evangelicals in the Church of England*, 67–68; Wood, *Slavery, Empathy, and Pornography*, 153–154, 165–171, 224; and Alan Harding, *The Countess of Huntingdon's Connexion: A Sect in Action in Eighteenth-Century England* (Oxford, 2003), 109–117.

76. Anstey, *The Atlantic Slave Trade and British Abolition*, pts. III and IV; Davis, *The Problem of Slavery in the Age of Revolution*, esp. 404–462, although see also the essays by James Walvin, Fiona Spiers, and Ian Bradley in Jack Hayward, ed., *Out of Slavery: Abolition and After* (London, 1985).

77. Williams, *Capitalism and Slavery*, 178–196, citation on 181.

sive fear of being duped into uncritical adulation. Some, following Williams, proudly confess to distaste for the Clapham Sect. Dale H. Porter, for example, opened his study of 1974 candidly: "To most readers it will be plain that I have not been sympathetic to William Wilberforce's evangelical style of argument. While recognizing his eloquence and determination, I grew annoyed by his over-riding insistence, session after parliamentary session, on his own solution to the problem of the slave trade." "If in my account Wilberforce and his friends appear hasty, narrow-minded, or even ignorant, it is because the members of Parliament and the public often saw them that way, and said so."[78] Others have preferred to emphasize what Evangelical abolitionists failed to do. This approach received its most sophisticated expression in the work of David Brion Davis, who famously proposed in 1975 that class interests helped Evangelicals and other elites embrace antislavery measures and disregard more radical projects of reform.[79] In most instances, though, the current assessments have dispensed with the Evangelicals altogether. Historians of British religious history still describe abolition and emancipation as Clapham Sect achievements. Historians of antislavery, by contrast, tend now to treat the Evangelicals as of marginal interest and limited consequence.[80]

This lack of sympathy for the Evangelicals, if in many ways understandable, has made it difficult to understand them. By choosing not to take the Evangelicals seriously, too many have underestimated what they were up against and, therefore, what they were up to. Generally, antislavery histories have presented too static a picture of the Evangelicals within the Church of England. Most fail to appreciate the social and cultural context in which their actions first took shape. Too often, characteristic features of the mature campaign in the early nineteenth century are projected back on the infant initiatives of the late 1780s. So, for example, the Clapham Sect wins credit for launching the abolition campaign even though the Clapham Sect, as such, had yet to form. And Evangelicals are described as targeting the

---

78. Dale H. Porter, *The Abolition of the Slave Trade in England, 1784–1807* ([Hamden, Conn.], 1970), xi.

79. Davis, *The Problem of Slavery in the Age of Revolution*, 343–385, 453–468.

80. The work on popular abolitionism, particularly, has dropped the Evangelicals almost entirely. See Oldfield, *Popular Politics and British Anti-Slavery,* and the various publications by Seymour Drescher and James Walvin.

slave trade from the first when, in truth, initially, they hoped only to "improve" slavery and promote Anglican Protestantism in the slave quarters. In a similar way, and for similar reasons, the spirit in which Evangelical politicking originated has been misjudged. The Clapham Sect earned a reputation by the early nineteenth century for almost limitless self-assurance. Their Teston predecessors, however, started from a very different place. Their peculiar brand of Christian politics had more tentative, more uncertain beginnings, a point of special importance if their eventual commitment to slave trade abolition is to be fully understood.

There looked to be no place for Evangelicals in British politics during the first half century of the revival, from the conversion of Wesley to the conversion of Wilberforce. Aristocrats who embraced "vital Christianity" exposed themselves to ridicule and contempt. Satirists made frequent sport of Lady Huntingdon. Sir Richard Hill, for several years the lone Methodist in Parliament, inspired only derisive laughter when he quoted scripture on the floor of the House of Commons.[81] The earl of Dartmouth, a more savvy politician, understood that colleagues would tolerate his religious enthusiasm only if he divorced his politics from his piety. With the exception of the countess of Huntingdon, no member of the laity worked more assiduously to advance the careers of Evangelical ministers within the Church of England. Yet, during his long and significant career in Parliament, Dartmouth would not use his office as a platform from which to advance his religious opinions. Indeed, he confused and horrified his pious friends in 1774 by introducing the Quebec Act (and its measures licensing Catholicism) in the House of Lords. Dartmouth compromised his principles not only on the issue of slavery. Routinely, he cordoned off his political work from (to him) the no less important work of promoting the Evangelical revival.

It would have taken exceptional courage to do otherwise. Evangelicalism in the late eighteenth century lacked the social cachet it would acquire early in the nineteenth. Before the "age of Wilberforce," religious enthusiasm made the polite and respectable deeply uncomfortable. No one had forgotten the civil wars that arose from religious divisions a century before. To some, the emphasis that Evangelicals placed on the natural depravity of

---

81. Schlenther, *Queen of the Methodists,* 120–123; Brown, *Fathers of the Victorians,* 65–68. See also Edwin Sidney, *The Life of Sir Richard Hill, Bart., M.P. for the County of Shropshire* (London, 1839).

human beings, the necessity of divine grace for redemption, and the spiritual legitimacy of sudden "conversions" looked like a recrudescence of Puritanism. The Church of England taught a moderate, rational Christianity during the eighteenth century. Evangelicals undermined these teachings by emphasizing the sublime joys that attended the total immersion in a life of faith. The ecclesiastical structure faced an implicit challenge from the revival, too. Itinerant preachers ignored the custodial authority of the parish curates. John Wesley's Methodists took the "irregularities" of the revival furthest: by appointing lay, female, and illiterate preachers; proselytizing among the poor; questioning the faith of the established clergy; fostering civic disturbances; promoting puritanical discipline; and, it was alleged, inconsistently, licensing sexual orgies. These were the disturbing practices the respectable associated with new religious movements propagating "serious Christianity."[82]

At the time the abolition movement began, polite society still looked down on religious enthusiasm. To introduce religious topics on social occasions showed poor taste and bad manners. Some sense of the stigma attached to fervid piety comes through in the memoirs and correspondence of Hannah More, who completed a gradual conversion from dramatist to didact in the 1780s. More proclaimed a distaste for Methodists, befitting her social status. At the same time, she regretted even more the way social conventions among her peers forced a bottling up of religious feeling and religious conversation. She would come to agree with her friend Ann Kennicott, who thought the name "methodistical" a "bugbear word" conceived "to frighten people from expressing those sentiments which they both ought to cherish and avow." Consider a letter More wrote to Lady Margaret Middleton in 1786. "I believe there are many among our acquain-

---

82. J. D. Walsh, "The Anglican Evangelicals in the Eighteenth Century," in Marcel Simon, ed., *Aspects de L'Anglicanisme: Colloque de Strasbourg (14–16 juin 1972)* (Paris, 1974), 87–102; Walsh, "Methodism and the Mob in the Eighteenth Century," in G. J. Cuming and Derek Baker, eds., *Popular Belief and Practice: Papers Read at the Ninth Summer Meeting and the Tenth Winter Meeting of the Ecclesiastical History Society*, Studies in Church History 8 (Cambridge, 1972), 237–257; David Hempton, "Methodism and the Law," in Hempton, *The Religion of the People*, 145–157; T. B. Shepherd, *Methodism and the Literature of the Eighteenth Century* (London, 1940), 207–247; Mary Thale, "Deists, Papists, and Methodists at London Debating Societies, 1749–1799," *History*, LXXXVI (2001), 338–341.

tances who withstand the flesh and the devil very courageously, who yet have not the resolution to resist the *world*. Modesty, the dread of singularity, and the fear of exciting suspicions of their sincerity, chain the tongues of some whose hearts burn within them." The utterance of words such as "*regeneration, new birth, Divine influence,* and *the aids of the spirit*" should not be feared or censored, said More. They are not "methodistical nonsense, but the sober language of the new testament." Why, then, should it be wrong to speak of "the Lord" in polite company? "Where the mind is deeply imbued with a subject it naturally falls into the language of it." So did not this prevailing discomfort with religious enthusiasm indicate, in fact, a break from spiritual moorings? "Should we not talk of [religion] as often we do of money, business, beauty, pleasure or wit?" These were the questions of a woman trying to withdraw from a corrupt society while maintaining the regard of the circles she felt a need to resist. More was not, in her words, "palliating cant," she assured Margaret Middleton, "but I think still that religion is in more danger from our frozen moderation than from the ill-judged zeal" of revivalists. Those unable to tolerate the earnestness of Methodism, in her view, possessed only a half-hearted commitment to the faith. Genuine Christians, she insisted, would not find threatening the Methodists' "indiscreet dialect": "When we cannot forgive anything because it is perfectly discrete as to time and place, and perfectly elegant in its expression, we should be afraid that our zeal is falling to the freezing point."[83]

Biographies detailing the conversion of William Wilberforce and Hannah More often give inadequate attention to the social transgression entailed by their "awakening." Unlike most converts, Wilberforce and More had public reputations. When Wilberforce set off on a transformative tour of Europe with the Reverend Isaac Milner, he was the newly elected member for the largest constituency in England and the close friend of the king's new first minister, the younger William Pitt. When she met John Newton in 1787, Hannah More was a renowned figure in London literary circles. What would be the social and political consequences of their turn to "Methodistical" religion? Each wrestled with conflicting impulses. They could turn

83. Mrs. Kennicott to More, n.d., 1782, in Roberts, ed., *Memoirs of Mrs. Hannah More,* I, 259–260; More to Margaret Middleton, June 14, 1786, in Chatterton, ed., *Memorials of Admiral Lord Gambier,* I, 155–158.

away from the temptations of the "world" to nurture their emerging spiritual commitments. Or they could keep their position in society and, potentially, compromise their religious scruples. No one else in the Teston clan faced this choice. Beilby Porteus and Charles Middleton sympathized with the Evangelical movement. But they did not experience themselves the trauma of a spiritual awakening and thus never felt conflicted about retaining a place in public life. Margaret Middleton and Elizabeth Bouverie were more ardent in their faith. But their inclination to withdraw from the world was facilitated by social conventions that encouraged women to regard the home as their "proper" sphere. The choice for Wilberforce and More was far more difficult. They already had public lives. They were reluctant to surrender their public prominence. At the same time, conscience would not permit either to live as others did.

This had been Lord Dartmouth's predicament. Can one be a serious Christian and retain public standing? Can a serious Christian act in the world without compromising faith? The questions haunted William Wilberforce in the winter of 1785–1786 as he sought to reconcile his awakened faith in God's saving grace, his growing distaste for polite diversions, and a conflicting desire to retain the esteem of his peers. And the questions haunted his friends who wished him to stay in public life. William Pitt received the change in Wilberforce with undisguised regret. In a warm but stern letter written in early December 1785, Pitt warned Wilberforce of "deluding yourself into principles" that would "render your virtues and your talents useless both to yourself and mankind." Why "this preparation of solitude, which can hardly avoid tincturing the mind either with melancholy or superstition"? "Surely the principles as well as the practice of Christianity are simple, and lead not to meditation only but to action."[84] Or so Pitt tried to argue. Yet he knew that, typically, Evangelicalism directed converts less to useful labor than to withdrawal, meditation, and eccentricity. At least that seemed, to the unsympathetic, the fate that Evangelicals usually selected.

The Reverend John Newton helped persuade Wilberforce and Hannah More to remain in public life. Like Pitt, he thought their prominence an opportunity to enlarge the realm of the sacred and the good. In Wilber-

---

84. William Pitt to William Wilberforce, Dec. 2, 1785, in A. M. Wilberforce, ed., *Private Papers of William Wilberforce* (London, 1897), 13.

force, he saw "very considerable" "abilities," Newton confided to William Cowper in 1786. The young convert's "situation and connections" were "likely to afford him ample scope for usefulness in public life," both "as a Christian and as a statesman." After he moved from Olney to London in 1780, Newton had grown certain that though such talents rarely "coincide" they were "not incompatible."[85] Hannah More found only incomplete comfort from the country retreat she created for herself, she worried. Newton explained that he had found his mission among the multitude, that to find peace in faith one had to find a principle of action. He put the apparently stark choice between faith and society in an unfamiliar light. "So far as our hearts are right," he advised Hannah More, "all places and circumstances which his wise and good providence allots us are nearly equal." She internalized the lesson. Religion does not, as some supposed, "encourage men to fly from society, and hide themselves in solitudes: to renounce the generous and important duties of active life, for the visionary, cold, and fruitless virtues of an Hermitage, or a cloyster." "The mischief arises not from our living in the world," More wrote in 1788, "but from the world living in us; occupying our hearts, and monopolizing our affections. Action is the life of virtue, and the world is the theatre of action."[86] The true challenge, then, lay in erasing the stigma attached to fervid piety, in creating a space for godliness in public life. Newton understood the difficulty of the task. "The Christian life is a warfare," he admitted to Hannah More. "Much within us and much without us must be resisted." Yet he assured Wilberforce in 1787 that "there are some persons at this time, who would be more open and explicit in their Religious profession than they are, were it not for a . . . fear of being reported Methodists."[87]

What might a Christian politician do to alter how the elite looked at the devout? The question preoccupied William Wilberforce and the Teston clan in the same months that the Society for Effecting the Abolition of the

85. John Newton cited in Phipps, *Amazing Grace in John Newton,* 180.

86. John Newton to Hannah More, n.d., 1787, in Roberts, ed., *Memoirs of Mrs. Hannah More,* II, 91; [Hannah More], *Thoughts on the Importance of the Manners of the Great to General Society* . . . (London, 1788), 96–97.

87. Newton to More, n.d., 1787, in Roberts, ed., *Memoirs of Mrs. Hannah More,* II, 93; Newton to Wilberforce, Nov. 1, 1787, Wilberforce Adds., Papers of William Wilberforce, c. 49, fol. 14, Bodleian Library, Oxford University.

Slave Trade first took shape. In the summer of 1787, as Thomas Clarkson made his subsequently famous tour of the slave ports, Wilberforce was making a similar journey, criss-crossing the nation to recruit supporters for the Society for Enforcing His Majesty's Proclamation against Vice and Immorality. In addition to suppressing sin, in addition to invigorating the enforcement of laws against vice, the Anglican Evangelicals wanted to foster piety among the "better sort," among those who, in More's words, already lived free "from gross vice." Enlisting the intended converts in the leadership of moral reform projects seemed like one way to win them over. Another lay in changing public opinion about what piety meant, in elevating the status of religion in private and public life. At the heart of the Teston program stood an attempt to make piety fashionable, to "do within the Church, and nearer the throne," as Wilberforce would put it, "what Wesley has accomplished in the meeting and amongst the multitude."[88]

This was the purpose of Hannah More's *Thoughts on the Importance of the Manners of the Great,* published anonymously in the spring of 1788, an essay historian Ford Brown aptly characterized as the Evangelical "manifesto." More went beyond advising aristocrats to avoid sin. She aimed as well at assumptions prevailing among those she regarded as nominal Christians, at the notion that communicants need only abide by the letter of the faith and need not embrace its spirit. In one respect, she urged a greater degree of self-consciousness. She asked her readers to recognize the pedestrian vices they committed from "habit and want of reflection." In another respect, though, she called for a loosening of restraints, a liberation of religious feeling among those who cherished the Cross but felt ashamed to admit it. No longer, More wrote, should it be thought "ill-bred and indiscreet that the escapes of the tongue should now and then betray the 'abundance of the heart.'" She directed those who "acknowlege the truth of the Christian doctrines" to give voice to their faith, to desist in, to use an anachronistic expression, silencing themselves.[89]

This text, like James Ramsay's *Essay on the Treatment and Conversion of*

88. More to Sir Charles Middleton, July 31, 1787, in Chatterton, ed., *Memorials of Admiral Lord Gambier,* I, 165; Wilberforce cited in Anthony Armstrong, *The Church of England, the Methodists, and Society* (London, 1973), 133.

89. Brown, *Fathers of the Victorians,* 98; [More], *Thoughts on the Importance of the Manners of the Great,* 77, 80.

the African Slaves, emerged from an extended conversation that had been taking place among the Teston clan. Hannah More wrote *Thoughts upon the Manners of the Great,* but her friends at Barham Court helped decide its form, content, and approach. The idea for the pamphlet, she told Charles Middleton privately, was "entirely the result of two or three conversations I had with you . . . and with Mr. Wilberforce." Of an early draft, she continued, "I wish it to be seen only by Lady Middleton, Mrs. Bouverie, and Mr. Wilberforce." Those three would provide editorial advice. If the result seemed suitable for publication, "I should wish to entreat the Bishop of Chester with it, and to ask his judgment on the subject."[90] This tight-knit group—More, Wilberforce, Porteus, Bouverie, the Middletons—wished to enlarge faith's dominion in private and public life, harness the secular to the sacred, and, in the process, recast godliness as respectable and appropriate for the well placed and polite. This would have the additional benefit, they believed, of instilling in both the higher and the lower ranks an attendance to their reciprocal duties.

This commitment to advancing Evangelical Protestantism gave the developing campaign against the slave trade special value to the Teston clan. Abolitionism furthered their fundamental aims in ways that now should be clear. They expected that abolition of the slave trade would coerce planters into treating the enslaved with greater care, perhaps opening the way to Christian instruction in the colonies. The research of Thomas Clarkson showed the commerce in captured Africans to be a national vice, a perspective that could help them connect the Atlantic slave trade to the other sins they thought besetting the nation. Because few in Britain participated personally in the slave trade, vilifying the practice would prove less threatening than asking the public to reconsider how they spent their Sunday afternoons. Abolitionism could establish an appetite for moral reform without, first, requiring the sacrifice of familiar pleasures. For the Evangelicals,

90. More to Middleton, July 31, 1787, in Chatterton, ed., *Memorials of Admiral Lord Gambier,* I, 165. As Jane Nardin has observed, the correspondence between Hannah More and the Teston circle often reveals the most about her various projects and purposes. She emerges, for example, as a more pointed critic of the social order in this correspondence than in her published works. See Nardin, "Hannah More and the Problem of Poverty," *Texas Studies in Literature and Language,* XLIII (2001), 270–275, 278, 280–282.

moreover, the emerging campaign offered one way to both act in the world and face down its corruptions. Slave trade abolition provided an initial focus for their far-reaching ambitions. Coupland was almost certainly correct when he suggested that "Wilberforce would not have stayed long in politics if the shadow of the slave trade had not fallen across his path." In the correspondence of the Teston clan, there is palpable relief in finding a specific program of action. The enthusiastic letter Hannah More sent to her sister in the spring of 1788, during the first months of the campaign, is representative: "The other day, just as I was going to dinner, arrived Lady Middleton, saying, I must at all events come away with her immediately to dine with Mr. Wilberforce at her home. We had four or five hours of most confidential and instructive conversation, in which we discussed all the great objects of reform which they have in view."[91] Abolitionism gave the Evangelical reformers something concrete to do.

Most of all, the campaign against the slave trade allowed the Evangelicals a chance to win over those otherwise suspicious of campaigns against vice. Antislavery sentiment had grown fashionable by the 1780s. It had become associated with politeness, sensibility, patriotism, and a commitment to British liberty. By leading an abolition movement, the Evangelicals could draw on those more positive associations to give a benevolent, less repressive cast to their broader crusade for moral reform. They could align themselves with the promotion of justice, mercy, humanity, and virtue as well as the promotion of religion. Abolitionism, for these reasons, could operate as an opening wedge, a Trojan horse that might breach the walls of infidelity for the cause of godliness. It seemed to the Teston clan that more direct approaches would fail. In 1789, after the Society for Effecting the Abolition of the Slave Trade had won nationwide support, Wilberforce still thought it best to withhold an essay that detailed his religious opinions. He knew that "the dread of an over-righteous man would deter people from cooperating with me ... were I to express all I think I should be deemed an enthusiast."[92] With abolition, no such concern—a campaign against the slave trade could bring together a variety of groups both in Parliament and

91. Coupland, *The British Anti-Slavery Movement,* 73; More to her sister, [spring 1788], in Roberts, ed., *Memoirs of Mrs. Hannah More,* II, 106–107. Note here, again, the influence attributed to Margaret Middleton by her friends.

92. Wilberforce cited in Robin Furneaux, *William Wilberforce* (London, 1974), 144.

out-of-doors, even if those groups had little sympathy for the Evangelicals' religious agenda. Abolitionism could help make moral reformers (and perhaps moral reform) palatable. Like no other issue, it could carve out new space for religious action in the public arena, and it could give political standing to the devout while vesting them with moral authority.

Indirection was the only way to proceed, Hannah More believed. The prey must be stalked. A more aggressive approach would only frighten off the quarry. These had been her assumptions when writing the well-received *Thoughts upon the Manners of the Great.* "All one can do in a promiscuous society," More explained to her sister, "is not so much to start religious topics, as to extract from common subjects some useful and awful truth." And she adopted this strategy when looking for other ways that might make abolition serve the reformation of manners. The erstwhile playwright stopped attending the theater out of moral scruple early in the 1780s. She thought it a progenitor of vice. But, for this reason, its popular and sordid character made it the ideal arena in which to dramatize the evils of slavery. "I know of no place but the play house," she observed to Margaret Middleton, "where three thousand people meet every night. Many people go to a play who never go to Church, and if they do go to church," she added in a swipe at the clergy, "few preachers except the Bishop of Chester and Mr. Ramsay will vindicate the right of slaves."[93] Opening a production that inspired sympathy for Africans would not only propagate the antislavery gospel; it would clean up the character of the theater by transforming the stage into a pulpit for moral improvement.

Abolition of the slave trade for the Evangelicals always was an end in itself, never merely an instrument. Their horror at the trafficking and enslavement of human bodies was genuine. Yet what gave the issue particular importance to the Evangelicals, what accounts for the peculiar energy they invested in the campaign, were the edifying habits that might follow from righteous labor, the moral lessons they hoped men and women would draw from fighting public sins. The Evangelicals' turn against the slave trade was not simply an eruption of benevolence. It was also a considered, strategic choice, an opening salvo in a wider campaign against nominal Christianity

93. More to her sister, n.d., 1788, in Roberts, ed., *Memoirs of Mrs. Hannah More,* II, 96; More to Margaret Middleton, Sept. 10, 1787, in Chatterton, ed., *Memorials of Admiral Lord Gambier,* I, 169–170.

that they advanced at once on several fronts. Anglican Evangelicals could not have foreseen the influence they would wield in the early nineteenth century. They could never have dreamed in 1787 that they would be remembered as the progenitors of a cultural movement. But they did hope that abolitionism would provide a way to bring morals into politics. Catherine Hall observed many years ago that "the campaign on manners and morals would undoubtedly have been far less effective if the antislavery movement had not been such a success."[94] By trying to explain how the Clapham Sect gave rise to abolitionism in Britain, too many accounts have missed the ways that abolitionism gave rise to the Clapham Sect.

What often has mattered most to later historians mattered rather less to the Evangelicals. Both contemporaries and later commentators have judged the Saints by the degree to which they served the cause of liberty, a confusion the Evangelicals themselves deliberately bred. In this respect, their critics—from Cobbett to Williams—would be correct: the Saints were uncertain champions of liberty, at best. But liberty had never been and would never be the preeminent aim of the Anglican Evangelicals. From the beginning, among themselves, these aspiring moral and religious crusaders evaluated their work on different terms. For them, in all of their projects, in the dozens of initiatives they coordinated in the decades that followed, the spread of gospel preaching, the inculcation of "vital Christianity," marked the true measure of success. Evangelical abolitionists were selective in 1787, and not a little deceptive, but they were not hypocrites. Their primary aim was not abolition of the slave trade, the promotion of free labor, or social control—though they came to embrace these causes, too. Above all, they wanted to make the British people sincere Christians without making themselves pariahs.

94. Hall, "The Early Formation of Victorian Domestic Ideology," in Burman, ed., *Fit Work for Women*, 30.

CHAPTER 7

The Society of Friends and the Antislavery Identity

"The Negro has two classes of Friends," James Ramsay wrote in 1784, "one that looks chiefly to liberty, while the other regards only religion."[1] If Ramsay's friends in Teston numbered among those primarily concerned with religion, the Quakers who published his work were establishing themselves by 1784 as the foremost champions of liberty for enslaved Africans. Many in Britain had come to question the morality of the Atlantic slave trade by the end of the American war, but the Society of Friends, from 1783 to 1787, stood nearly alone in the attempt to organize a political crusade. No other group before 1787 labored with comparable intensity. Quakers delivered the first abolition petition to the House of Commons (1783), established the first antislavery committees and associations in the British Isles (1783), and initiated the systematic circulation of antislavery literature (1783, 1784). Until the formation of the Society for Effecting the Abolition of the Slave Trade in 1787, what the British read about the wrongs of the slave trade they learned, primarily, from Quaker writers or Quaker publicists. Almost every author who protested the traffic in the 1770s and 1780s drew heavily, if not entirely, on the seminal works of Philadelphia Friend Anthony Benezet. And almost every significant antislavery tract printed in England, between 1783 and 1787, including James Ramsay's *Essay*, came off the presses of Quaker publisher James Phillips. In these crucial transitional years, Friends arranged for the distribution of tens of thousands of abolitionist books, pamphlets, and newspaper essays. When British men and women rallied behind the standard of the Society for Effecting the Abolition of the Slave Trade in 1787, they enlisted in what had been, initially, a Quaker campaign.

At first glance, the leadership of Friends would seem easy to explain. The Quaker campaign in England continued the Quaker campaign in

1. James Ramsay, *An Inquiry into the Effects of Putting a Stop to the African Slave Trade, and of Granting Liberty to the Slaves in the British Sugar Colonies* (London, 1784), 10.

North America. It extended the efforts in the colonies to rid the sect of slaveholders and rewrite the slave laws enacted by provincial legislatures. For this reason, the first initiatives by Friends in England are often described as the consequence of transatlantic influence, as a manifestation of what David Brion Davis has called "the antislavery international."[2] Yet the concept of influence may serve better as a description of events than as an explanation of behavior. The theme tends to cast transatlantic influence as inherently influential. It leaves little room for the possibility of conflict or disagreement among Quakers over ends and means. And, as a result, it often discourages examination of the ways Friends differed from each other, differences manifest not only between Quakers in North America and Quakers in England but among English Quakers themselves. If we resist subscribing unreflectively to the Quakers' reputation for philanthropy, and if we look more closely at the history and character of English Quakers in the eighteenth century, their pioneering role in the British antislavery movement becomes more perplexing, less logical, more curious.

The crucial fact has gone unremarked. When English Quakers initiated a campaign against the Atlantic slave trade in the 1780s, they acted entirely out of character. During the eighteenth century, Quakers generally took no interest in public policy. Indeed, the ethos of the sect in this period encouraged withdrawal and separateness to reinforce the Friends' sense of themselves as a peculiar people. English Quakerdom in the eighteenth century had little of the crusading spirit characteristic of the founding era a century earlier. Quaker ministers, both women and men, stressed the value of turning from the world, suppressing the will, and abandoning "creaturely" striving in human affairs. In these years, Quaker historian Rufus Jones has written, Friends had "no outer history." They "saw no way to remake the world or establish the Kingdom of God in the earth on any great scale," so Friends became "timid and conservative in their relation to public questions."[3] Antislavery organizing thus would require from Friends in England a substantial reorientation in values, a redirection of energies outward,

2. David Brion Davis, *The Problem of Slavery in the Age of Revolution, 1770–1823* (Ithaca, N.Y., 1975), 213–254. See also Betty Fladeland, *Men and Brothers: Anglo-American Antislavery Cooperation* (Urbana, Ill., 1972), 16–33.

3. Rufus M. Jones, *The Later Periods of Quakerism*, 2 vols. (London, 1921), II, 12, 30–31, 314–315.

away from sectarian concerns and toward a confrontation with the society in which they lived. It required from Friends a new institutional commitment, a willingness to labor on behalf of those outside the religious society. Abolitionism would demand, as well, a subtle but significant shift in the character of their public testimonies, from peaceable religious witness to political advocacy. In addition to adhering to vows to do no harm, Quakers would have to commit themselves to the more difficult mission of stopping harms performed by others. For a program of this kind, Friends in England had few precedents. Never before in the eighteenth century had they tried as a group to shape national legislation through a public crusade. Indeed, taking a stand on moral questions broke with their established habit of leaving sinful neighbors to their devices. And standing forth publicly deviated from their scruples against political activism. Quaker ministers long had regarded a preoccupation with temporal affairs harmful to cultivating the "inner plantation of the spirit." The Religious Society of Friends in 1782 had no overarching public purpose. They did not aspire, generally, to transform the society in which they lived. Abolitionism, then, did not evolve inexorably from Quaker values or from the sect's fundamental priorities and purposes. Indeed, it would force upon Friends a shift in the way that they thought of themselves and their place in the larger society.

In charting this transformation from quietism to activism and, with it, the translation of moral scruples into organized protest, this chapter proposes that Quaker abolitionism in England took shape from conflicts *within* the Society of Friends, conflicts that made the cost of *not acting* against the slave trade unbearable. The decisive influence that sustained persistent campaigning by Friends in England, however, lay *outside* the Society of Friends. And it is here that the overlapping ambitions, initiatives, and contexts elucidated earlier in this book attain their full salience. "Contentious politics is produced," sociologist Sidney Tarrow has written, "when political opportunities broaden, when they demonstrate the potential for alliances and when they reveal the opponents' vulnerability."[4] The American Revolution created opportunities for antislavery organizing, first for Friends in North America before the war, and then for Friends in England in its aftermath. The politics of the Revolutionary War exposed

4. Sidney Tarrow, *Power in Movement: Social Movements and Contentious Politics,* 2d ed. (Cambridge, 1998), 23.

the slave system to critical scrutiny and designated complicity in slavery as evidence of collective vice. The temporary loss of confidence in officials and institutions in the last year of the American war fostered an intense interest in the moral health of the nation. These were the conditions that helped inspire emancipationist, colonizationist, and amelorationist schemes during the 1770s and 1780s (see chapters 4–6). In practice, though, political opportunities are more perception than fact. They become opportunities only when conceived as such by potential actors, only when those actors have an occasion to find them.

English Quaker abolitionism in the 1780s emerged out of tensions within the Society of Friends, tensions that the antislavery movement itself would help to heal. It drew strength from the unexpected discovery of an opportunity to act, and to act in such a way that was consistent with Quaker values and answered Quaker needs. The Quaker campaign that commenced in 1783 reveals how political opportunities can produce political actors, how the prospect of success can draw otherwise passive observers into action. And it shows how the commitment to act can lead individuals and groups to new self-definitions, to new ideas of themselves. A dialectic was at work after 1783 between the Society of Friends and the movement they originated. Abolitionism made abolitionists in the same moment that abolitionists made abolitionism. The movement forged a new identity for the Religious Society of Friends in England as the Friends shaped a new campaign. And that identity and that reputation would provide a model for others who hoped both to contribute to the effort and to redefine themselves, to promote slave trade abolition and embody virtue in practice. In the evolution of Quaker antislavery lies an important truth about how "moral perception," in the words of Moses Finley, "becomes effective in action."[5] On controversial topics, taking a stand becomes easier when it means standing out without standing alone.

[1]   The Religious Society of Friends had confronted the problem of slavery during the third quarter of the eighteenth century by refusing to have further part in it. They banned slave trading among their members and, over time, slaveholding, too. Those who refused to cooper-

---

5. M. I. Finley, "The Idea of Slavery," *New York Review of Books*, Jan. 26, 1967, 6–10, citation on 8.

ate they disowned. This antislavery campaign represented one aspect of a broader program in the reformation of American Quakerism, which had commenced during the era of the Seven Years' War. It had required political agitation, but within the sect and among Friends, instead of outside the religious society. When the London Yearly Meeting banned Friends from participating in the slave trade in 1761, it established a new standard of discipline for its members rather than registering a public protest against human commerce. Distancing themselves from the slave system gave further meaning to the obligations of the religious fellowship. If Quaker actions indicated what they thought true Christians should do, that was a conclusion others would need to draw for themselves. The leaders of the reformation within the Society of Friends in Britain did not, at first, push the antislavery campaign beyond the boundaries of the sect.

By the mid-eighteenth century, the Quakers had long since abandoned the hope that the gospel of Christian love would turn a fallen world away from sinful practices. Instead, they had come to think of themselves as representing a "spiritual remnant," among the "unconvinced," in the words of Quaker historian Rufus Jones, "as bearers of truths and ideals for which this world was not ready." Friend Issac Fletcher of Cumberland thought of the Quaker church as "encamped in the wide extended plain of the world, under the direction and command of the great Captain and Leader and surrounded as it were in their tents with the impregnable walls of their discipline."[6] This self-conception placed great value on the preservation of

6. Jones, *The Later Periods of Quakerism*, I, 157. Sydney V. James, *A People among Peoples: Quaker Benevolence in Eighteenth-Century America* (Cambridge, Mass., 1963), 30–32, 86, 101, 317; Jack D. Marrietta, *The Reformation of American Quakerism* (Philadelphia, 1984), 36; Angus J. L. Winchester, ed., *The Diary of Isaac Fletcher of Underwood, Cumberland, 1756–1781*, Cumberland and Westmorland Antiquarian and Archaeological Society, Extra Ser., XXVII (1994), xxi. In 1997 historian H. Larry Ingle wrote that "from the very end of the seventeenth century to the very end of the eighteenth, English Quaker history is pretty much of a void." Ingle, "The Future of Quaker History," *Journal of the Friends' Historical Society*, LVIII (1997), 10. An up-to-date history of British Friends in the eighteenth century remains very much a need, although the survey by James Walvin provides good coverage of the period. See Walvin, *The Quakers: Money and Morals* (London, 1997). Since Ingle reached this judgment, though, there has been an upsurge of new work on the religious life of the Society of Friends, much of which attends carefully to the work of the Quaker ministry, both men and women who served as

sectarian customs and testimonies, but rather less on converting those outside the religious society to Quaker principles or codes of conduct. Indeed, in a perverse way, Friends needed the moral failings of their neighbors, if only to give purpose to their ethic of distancing and distinguishing themselves from other Protestants. Quakers in England, generally, did not attempt to proselytize among those outside the Society of Friends. They would have been pleased, to be sure, to find their neighbors adopting Quaker mores, but they no more expected contemporaries to cease slave trading than they expected them to forswear war, abolish tithes, or renounce oath-taking. Somehow, then, the one group in British society whose creed demanded an avoidance of contentious political issues came to lead in the late 1780s what would evolve into the prototype for nineteenth-century reform movements.

Anthony Benezet of Philadelphia differed from the other Friends active in the antislavery movement before the American Revolution. Unlike his contemporaries, he looked beyond the borders of the Society of Friends. Several in North America did become regional leaders in the campaigns against the slave trade and slavery during the 1770s—Moses Brown in Rhode Island, Robert Pleasants and Edward Stabler in Virginia, William Dillwyn, Samuel Allinson, and David Cooper in New Jersey. But only Benezet considered the question in its broadest imperial and Atlantic contexts. From his first writings, in 1760, he sought a wide audience for his work, appealing not only to the conscience, like his friend John Woolman,

---

"Public Friends." This work suggests that Rufus Jones was too pessimistic in his assessment of the spiritual history of the Quakers in this period. See particularly Bonnelyn Young Kunze, "'Vesells Fitt for the Masters Us[e]': A Transatlantic Community of Religious Women, the Quakers, 1675–1753," in Kunze and Dwight D. Brautigam, eds., *Court, Country, and Culture: Essays on Early Modern British History in Honor of Perez Zagorin* (Rochester, N.Y., 1992), 177–197; Rebecca Larson, *Daughters of Light: Quaker Women Preaching and Prophesying in the Colonies and Abroad, 1700–1775* (New York, 1999); Phyllis Mack, "Religion, Feminism, and the Problem of Agency: Reflections on Eighteenth-Century Quakerism," *Signs: Journal of Women in Culture and Society*, XXIX (2003), 161–174; and Helen Plant, "'Subjective Testimonies': Women Quaker Ministers and Spiritual Authority in England: 1750–1825," *Gender and History*, XV (2003), 296–318. It still seems clear, however, that an orientation toward social and religious reform *outside* the religious society did not develop among Quaker men or Quaker women in Britain until the last two decades of the eighteenth century.

but also to sentiment and the intellect. In each of his works he presented individual horrors as the specific consequences of systematic injustice. He was among the first to describe the separate efforts throughout North America to curtail the Atlantic slave trade as a single "movement." And he was among the first to conceive the diverse testimonials against the slave trade from an earlier era as constituting an antislavery tradition. In the last years of the colonial era, Anthony Benezet acted as the leading propagandist for slave trade abolition and its chief instigator. His tracts reached every colony on the eastern seaboard north of the Carolinas. He kept isolated activists across North America abreast of progress elsewhere. During the last two decades of his life, he kept up a continual attack on the slave trade, refusing to believe that minds and practices could not be changed. He never let the issue rest, a quality that set him apart. "Its [sic] tiresome," the Quaker grandee Israel Pemberton once said of Benezet, "to hear Anthony always saying the same thing."[7]

Quakers professed to believe that the light of God resided in all men and women, but few gave the principle more concrete expression than Anthony Benezet. Human equality to Benezet was an ontological fact rather than a philosophical doctrine or maxim. He faithfully exhibited in practice the social and moral obligations that followed from these values. A son of Huguenot refugees, he took special interest in the welfare of the dispossessed, of Indians, uprooted Acadians, and the Philadelphia poor, as well as enslaved Africans. Of the Nova Scotian exiles who settled in Pennsylvania in 1755, Deborah Logan recalled, Benezet was "almost their only friend." Through the Friendly Association, Benezet intervened in the formation of colonial and imperial policy as it related to the treatment of Native American neighbors. The Quaker crusader insisted on the human capacity for improvement. And at a time and in a place where the educational opportunities were few for girls and even more limited for Africans,

---

7. The best introduction to the life and labors of Anthony Benezet remains George S. Brookes, *Friend Anthony Benezet* (Philadelphia, 1937). See also Nancy Slocum Hornick, "Anthony Benezet: Eighteenth-Century Social Critic, Educator, and Abolitionist" (Ph.D. diss., University of Maryland, 1974), and Maurice Jackson, " 'Ethiopia Shall Soon Stretch Her Hands unto God': Anthony Benezet and the Atlantic Antislavery Revolution" (Ph.D. diss., Georgetown University, 2001). Israel Pemberton cited in Anthony Benezet to George Dillwyn, Sept. 11, 1779, in Brookes, *Friend Anthony Benezet,* 337.

Benezet opened his doors and gave ceaselessly of his time to the instruction of both. He tried to experience the world through the eyes of others, less to achieve sympathetic identification than to know how he ought to act. In 1756, when Pennsylvanians girded themselves for war against neighboring Indians, Benezet visited with several Delaware chieftains to learn how they understood and experienced the actions of backcountry settlers. Rather than judge, Benezet preferred to educate those who opposed or disagreed with him. He placed great stress on how experience and habit formed character. Benezet tended to regard surrender to the baser instincts as reflecting a broader failure in the moral instruction rendered by society rather than the pronounced fault of the sinner. Therefore, the role of education was to prepare boys and girls, Europeans and Africans, to live a useful life and ward off the lures of idleness, selfishness, and ignorance.[8]

Like other moral reformers within the Society of Friends, Benezet's opposition to slavery drew substantially on his doubts about the pursuit of wealth. Slaveholding, to him, reflected the tendency to regard the rewards of the world above the rigors of the spiritual life, "toiling years after years, enriching themselves, and thus getting fuel for our children's vanity and corruption." But unlike his peers, Benezet never thought it sufficient to turn inward, away from society, and away from corrupting practices. To nurture true godliness, it was not enough to avoid sin and escape the snares to living ethically. A complete suppression of human pride could be fully achieved only through a commitment to do good. "Charity," Benezet offered to Burlington, New Jersey, Friend John Smith in 1760, "would be the most likely way to remove that selfishness which is the parent of obduracy of heart and of most other vital evils." Because "true charity" could cure the spiritual impoverishment plaguing Friends, Benezet diagnosed its absence

8. Benezet to Samuel Fothergill, Nov. 27, 1758, cited in Jackson, "'Ethiopia Shall Soon Stretch Her Hands unto God,'" 31; James, *A People among Peoples,* 201–205; Nancy Slocum Hornick, "Anthony Benezet and the Africans' School: Toward a Theory of Full Equality," *Pennsylvania Magazine of History and Biography,* XCIX (1975), 399–421; Roger A. Bruns, "A Quaker's Antislavery Crusade: Anthony Benezet," *Quaker History,* LXV (1976), 88; William C. Kashatus III, "A Reappraisal of Anthony Benezet's Activities in Educational Reform, 1754–1784," *Quaker History,* LXXVIII (1989), 26–34; Maurice Jackson, "The Social and Intellectual Origins of Anthony Benezet's Antislavery Radicalism," Supplementary edition to *Pennsylvania History,* LXVI (1999), 86–112; Brookes, *Friend Anthony Benezet,* 45–49, 64–73, Deborah Logan cited on 67.

as "in a great measure the cause of the declension which prevails." Too often, among Friends, avowals of sympathy for sufferers like Acadians supplanted genuine benevolence. Doctrines "declared in the gallery," he lamented, "are too much contradicted in practice, and but little the topic of discourse." "The appellation of *Steward* is what we often take upon ourselves, but indeed, in the mouth of many it is but cant, unmeaning expression." It was indefensible to preach up the Golden Rule and yet withhold sustenance, security, and justice from those in need. The Society of Friends suffered not only from an entanglement in worldly concerns, in Benezet's view. More generally, Friends had grown deaf to the call of godliness. They had allowed the desire for wealth to choke the dictates of the conscience. Hewing to piety required vigilance, and vigilance could be best nurtured and sustained through the exercise of charity, since "the bent of nature is always reconciling back toward self, and the spirit of the world." Without the godliness instilled through the daily practice of charity, "Christianity becomes more a matter of opinion than a fructifying root."[9]

In some ways, Benezet's interests mirrored the broader social reform program taking shape elsewhere in the North American colonies and in the British Isles. When he promoted temperance and pushed for the establishment of schools and hospitals, he took part in the growing commitment among the middling classes on both sides of the Atlantic to campaign for moral and social improvement. What distinguished Benezet from his peers was his belief that charitable service should define the identity of the Society of Friends. Benezet envisioned a new mission for the sect. Friends did need to enforce sectarian discipline, he agreed. But, even more, they needed to manifest their sanctity through the way they engaged the world, through a philanthropic ethos, rather than withdrawal and separateness. Anthony Benezet first would help to formulate the public role that Friends would assume in the new United States during the years that followed the American war. If Friends could no longer dominate formal politics in Pennsylvania, they might instead provide the colony with moral leadership. This would have the virtue of making Quaker men and women better people.[10]

9. Benezet to John Smith, Aug. 1, 1760, in Brookes, *Friend Anthony Benezet*, 241–242.

10. For the crisis of the Revolutionary era as generating a service ethic within the Society of Friends in the Delaware Valley, see James, *A People among Peoples*, 240–334.

The Benezet campaign against the slave trade evolved gradually and somewhat haphazardly, not from a deliberate scheme. Like most successful entrepreneurs, he was an opportunist. When drafting his publications, Benezet raided the works of other authorities to document how the Atlantic slave trade destroyed African societies. But, even more, he seized on and attempted to exploit those situations that promised to expand the constituency for antislavery measures. During the Seven Years' War, he compared for nervous Pennsylvanians the theft of people from Africa with the kidnapping of Europeans on the frontier. Shortly after the Stamp Act crisis he began to cast antislavery as the logical extension of the colonial defense of liberty.[11] He recruited prominent patriots, Benjamin Rush most successfully, to serve as abolitionist pamphleteers. Slaveholding politicians, such as Patrick Henry, who confessed doubt about the justice of slave labor, Benezet harangued to change their ways. In the years before the American war, Benezet urged those colonies inclined to halt the slave trade because of prudence or politics to consider, in addition, the moral case against the traffic in men, women, and children. When he learned of abolitionist agitation in Massachusetts in the early 1770s, the Quaker campaigner considered traveling to New England to give the emerging antislavery impulses his support.[12]

Before 1766, before the Stamp Act crisis, Benezet had shown little interest in British attitudes toward slavery. He had regarded North Americans as his primary audience. Although he had grown increasingly critical of the British slave trade in the early 1760s, he tailored his antislavery arguments to change the behavior of American slave buyers and slave-

11. Anthony Benezet, *A Caution and Warning to Great Britain and Her Colonies in a Short Representation of the Calamitous State of the Enslaved Negroes in the British Dominions* (Philadelphia, 1767). Benezet's rhetorical strategies receive analysis in Jackson, "The Social and Intellectual Origins of Anthony Benezet's Antislavery Radicalism," 93–104; David L. Crosby, "Anthony Benezet's Transformation of Anti-Slavery Rhetoric," *Slavery and Abolition,* XXIII, no. 3 (December 2002), 39–58.

12. Benezet to Robert Pleasants, Apr. 8, 1773, Pleasants to Benezet, Feb. 22, 1774, Benezet to Samuel Allinson, Oct. 23, 1774, and Benezet to Henry Laurens, December 1776, all in Brookes, *Friend Anthony Benezet,* 298–302, 425–426, 321–322, 324–325; Benezet to Moses Brown, May 9, 1774 [visit to New England], in Roger A. Bruns, *Am I Not a Man and a Brother: The Antislavery Crusade of Revolutionary America, 1688–1788* (New York, 1977), 308–313.

holders rather than British traders.[13] Benezet decided to write for a British audience as well in 1766, after he read the antislavery statements published in the annual sermon to the SPG by William Warburton, bishop of Gloucester. In the months after, Benezet sent a stream of letters to English Quakers and a select list of religious leaders, including John Wesley, the countess of Huntingdon, and the archbishop of Canterbury.[14] The same year he persuaded Philadelphia Meeting for Sufferings to publish several hundred copies of his new work, *A Caution and Warning to Great Britain and Her Colonies,* and forward those pamphlets to its London counterpart. In these letters, and in the Philadelphia Meeting for Sufferings epistle sent with the package of tracts, his message was the same. The slave trade required "deep consideration." Only ignorance of its true nature, he declared charitably, could have allowed those in authority to sanction such "prodigious wickedness." He hoped that copies of *A Caution and Warning* would be placed in the hands of "those in power" to alert them to the injustice. After completing a longer tract on the slave trade in 1771, Benezet spelled out his ambitions more explicitly. Friends in England could not be "innocent" if they remained "silent" spectators of atrocities like the slave trade. Since Friends were "acquainted with the prodigious iniquity," since Friends in their own Yearly Meeting epistle to their churches had "declared their abhorrence of it," it was now their duty, "either as a people, or by their principle members, to endeavour for its removal" by a representation to Parliament.[15]

13. See [Anthony Benezet], *A Short Account of That Part of Africa Inhabited by the Negroes* (Philadelphia, 1762).

14. William Warburton, bishop of Gloucester, *A Sermon Preached before the Incorporated Society for the Propagation of the Gospel in Foreign Parts, at Their Anniversary Meeting in the Parish Church of St. Mary-le-Bow on Friday, 21 February 1766* (London, 1766); Benezet to the Society for the Propagation of the Gospel, Apr. 26, 1767, Benezet to Thomas Secker, archbishop of Canterbury, n.d. [1767], and Benezet to John Wesley, May 23, 1774, all in Brookes, *Friend Anthony Benezet,* 272–273, 273–274, 318–321; Benezet to countess of Huntingdon, Mar. 10, 1775, in Bruns, *Am I Not a Man and a Brother,* 379–384.

15. Benezet to Sophia Hume, July 25, 1767, MSS, CLXIII, fol. 25, Library of the Society of Friends (LSF), London; Benezet to David Barclay, Apr. 29, 1767, MSS Portfolio XXXVIII, fol. 87 [typescript], LSF; Benezet to Richard Shackleton, June 6, 1772, and Benezet to Granville Sharp, May 14, 1772, both in Brookes, *Friend Anthony Benezet,* 295–296, 290–293.

To a degree and for a time, Friends in England responded constructively to these requests. In May 1767 the London Meeting for Sufferings reprinted fifteen hundred copies of *A Caution and Warning* and distributed them to each member of Parliament. With additional copies still on hand in the fall of 1770, Meeting for Sufferings sent the remainder to more than one hundred merchant houses in London. Quaker trader William Rathbone circulated several dozen copies of Benezet's tract in Liverpool. Additionally, London Meeting for Sufferings appointed a temporary committee to follow the progress of the antislavery address the Virginia legislature sent to George III in 1772. That October, London Meeting for Sufferings went so far as to encourage a similar petition from the provincial government of Pennsylvania. The wealthy Quaker merchant David Barclay led a delegation of Friends to the Board of Trade in the spring of 1773 in a behind-closed-doors attempt to win a favorable reception for colonial antislavery petitions. In their epistles of 1772 and 1774, London Yearly Meeting made a point of applauding Friends' efforts in the colonies to halt the slave trade to North America. It was encouraging to find, they proclaimed in 1774, that "our testimony" against the slave trade "had some happy influences on the minds of considerate people of other denominations."[16]

The theme of Anglo-American influence, then, would seem to suit the history of Quaker antislavery lobbying before the American war. Friends in England could serve as a conduit for the exchange of correspondence and publications between antislavery activists in the colonies, like Benezet, and potential allies in the British Isles. The governing bodies of English Quakerdom—the London Yearly Meeting and the London Meeting for Sufferings—were positioned to reprint, promote, and circulate the antislavery testimony published by Quakers in North America. Networks,

---

16. Minutes of the Committee on Friends Books, n.d., 1767, Nov. 25, 1768, Sept. 14, 1770, n.d., 1770, fols. 39, 53, 64, 69–72, LSF; London Meeting for Sufferings to Philadelphia Meeting for Sufferings, Oct. 2, 1772, MS Letters Which Passed betwixt the Meeting for Sufferings in London, and the Meeting for Sufferings in Philadelphia, I, fol. 86, LSF; Minutes of the London Meeting for Sufferings, July 31, Sept. 25, Oct. 9, Dec. 4, 1772, Jan. 8, Feb. 5, 12, Mar. 26, 1773, XXXIII, fols. 127–128, 153, 161, 184, 202, 218, 221, 233, LSF; *Epistles from the Yearly Meeting of Friends, Held in London, to the Quarterly and Monthly Meetings in Great Britain, Ireland, and Elsewhere, from 1681 to 1857 . . .* (London, 1858), I, 19–20.

FIGURE 6. David Barclay. Engraving by Earlom from a print by Houghton. [1809].
Courtesy, The Library of the Religious Society of Friends, London.

The Quaker merchant and banker endorsed antislavery efforts in North America but would discourage antislavery lobbying in the British Isles.

however, sometimes fail. The power to facilitate could operate, too, as the power to obstruct. Because London Meeting for Sufferings held a preeminent position within the Anglo-American community of Friends, it could also, if it chose, inhibit the antislavery campaign of colonial Friends by modifying, muffling, or withholding those views it considered impolitic or not in the interest of the religious society. This kind of suppression of internal dissent had retarded the progress of antislavery inclinations within the Society of Friends in North America until 1758. If London Friends could serve as the metropolitan agents for Quaker abolitionists in the colonies, they could also serve as the gatekeepers to access and influence in Britain.

English Friends, in fact, cooperated rather less than first appears. The London leadership evinced no more than a hesitant embrace of colonial abolitionism, despite their supportive words. London Meeting for Sufferings formally followed through on American requests for assistance, but often half-heartedly and with great caution. Consistently, they construed their responsibility to American abolitionists in the most limited and narrow fashion. Never did they take the opportunity to present individual colonial petitions as a more general complaint against the slave system itself. The terse minutes describing the visit of 1773 to the Board of Trade revealed a strikingly tentative approach. The delegation spoke with the board about stopping importation only "to those provinces" that had petitioned. They requested favorable attention "to such Applications to Government as may be made by those Colonies to discourage the further Importation of Negroes among them." In this report, they said nothing of standing against the slave trade in general and on principle, as Benezet had recommended. In describing their actions to Friends in America, London Quakers gave no evidence, furthermore, of assuming a crusading ethos. David Barclay produced an especially odd report on the heels of his conference with Lord Dartmouth in February 1773. Since Dartmouth already intended to discourage the British slave trade to Virginia, Barclay explained, a formal application to the Board of Trade from the Society of Friends "did not appear necessary."[17] This was bizarre advice to give just weeks after that same Board of Trade had disallowed a modest 5 percent duty on slaves shipped to Virginia, which the assembly had instituted the previous year.

17. Minutes of the Meeting for Sufferings, Feb. 5, Mar. 26, 1773, XXXIII, fols. 218, 233, LSF.

In the same months that Barclay assured the London Meeting for Sufferings that Lord North's ministry would permit American colonists to curtail the Atlantic slave trade, Lord Dartmouth candidly was informing Granville Sharp that slave trade abolition, of any kind, stood no chance of approval. It was almost as if David Barclay hoped that an optimistic report about what the North ministry might do would forestall more aggressive campaigning by Friends in North America.

London Friends, in truth, approached the question of abolitionism with timidity and ambivalence in the years of the American crisis. Their efforts from 1770 to 1782 were feeble and half-hearted. Consider how they described their labors to their brethren in Philadelphia. "We have not been inattentive to your Request in regard to the Slave Trade," they stressed, as if to suggest that they had done more than they had, or were willing, to do. The truth, as the defensive double negative indicated, was rather less than what campaigners in North America such as Benezet would have hoped. Most revealingly, Quakers in England wholly ignored Anthony Benezet's call for Friends, individually or as a group, to petition Parliament for slave trade abolition, which they would not do until after the American war. Benezet remembered in 1783 that, of the many Quakers in Britain to whom he wrote soliciting assistance in the years before the first shots were fired in Lexington, not one had bothered to reply.[18]

Too many accounts of early Quaker antislavery overlook, and thus leave unexplained, the vast gulf between the reluctance of English Quakers to act in the 1770s and their enthusiasm for abolitionism in the years after the American war. Making sense of this substantial and dramatic shift, though, is not easy, since neither at the time nor after did English Quakers explain their very qualified support of North American abolitionists. In the voluminous records of the Society of Friends, there is no evidence of internal discussion or debate about American antislavery efforts or Benezet's appeals. The absence of correspondence on the matter hints that, at the time, or after, Friends in England made a point of keeping their counsel on what must have been a touchy subject.

18. London Meeting for Sufferings to Philadelphia Meeting for Sufferings, Dec. 10, 1773, MS Letters Which Passed betwixt the Meeting for Sufferings in London, and the Meeting for Sufferings in Philadelphia, I, fol. 97; Benezet to Dillwyn, n.d., 1783, in Brookes, *Friend Anthony Benezet*, 374.

The paralysis of English Quakers would seem to have stemmed from several sources. Wealthy Friends dominated the London leadership, which proved largely uninterested in the movement to strengthen discipline within the religious society. Discomfited by the zeal of religious reformers, they tended to disapprove of those who would draw attention to the sect by challenging the status quo, even within the Society of Friends. The courtly Quaker patriciate in London thought the saintly John Woolman an embarrassment rather than a source for inspiration. Many of these wealthy Friends, moreover, still held a stake in the slave system in the 1760s and 1770s. Although Friends no longer participated directly in the slave trade, the leadership of London Meeting for Sufferings included several prominent North American merchants heavily invested in the Atlantic economy. So it would have been a surprise, perhaps, to find giants in the Chesapeake tobacco trade—men such as David Barclay, John and Capel Hanbury, and John Eliot—assisting attempts to curtail the supply of slave labor to Virginia, even though several had begun to shift their capital into banking and domestic industries. An economic explanation, however, can only take us so far. The concern for profits surely mattered much less to the many Friends without a stake in staple crop production, who also chose to disregard Benezet. For his own part, the Philadelphia activist thought he detected in Britain what he knew in America as "that unfeeling disposition for the miseries of others, which so much prevails, in this age." Privately, Benezet expressed to Benjamin Franklin a fear that Friends in England lacked the courage to take a stand "in so unpopular a cause," despite its evident merits.[19]

In important respects, the institutional culture of the Society of Friends

19. Henry J. Cadbury, *John Woolman in England: A Documentary Supplement* (London, 1971); Jacob M. Price, *Capital and Credit in British Overseas Trade: The View from the Chesapeake, 1700–1776* (Cambridge, Mass., 1980), 71–75; Price, "The Great Quaker Business Families of Eighteenth-Century London: The Rise and Fall of a Sectarian Patriciate," in Richard S. Dunn and Mary Maples Dunn, eds., *The World of William Penn* (Philadelphia, 1986), 363–399; Price, "English Quaker Merchants at War and Sea, 1689–1783," in Roderick A. McDonald, ed., *West Indies Accounts: Essays on the History of the British Caribbean and the Atlantic Economy in Honour of Richard Sheridan* (Kingston, Jamaica, 1996), 65; Benezet to Benjamin Franklin, Apr. 27, 1772, in Leonard W. Labaree et al., eds., *The Papers of Benjamin Franklin*, 37 vols. to date (New Haven, Conn., 1959–), XIX, 112–116.

in England did not lend itself to the kind of campaign Anthony Benezet espoused. The religious society rarely took political risks. Quakers held an anomalous position in British society. In exchange for loyalty to the Hanoverian regime, the state tolerated the distinctive features of Quaker religious observance. Government exempted Friends from military service. In civil proceedings, Quakers were permitted to make a declaration of allegiance rather than swear oaths. Justices of the peace employed summary rulings to exact tithes from Quaker households unwilling to pay taxes "voluntarily" to support the Church of England. To protect these privileges, as well as the interests of Quakers in the Americas, London Meeting for Sufferings kept careful watch over proceedings in Parliament. Among the Quakers attending to parliamentary affairs were several of London's most substantial merchants, such as Barclay, the Hanburys, and Daniel Mildred. The Quaker patriciate thus wielded at Whitehall a degree of influence disproportionate to the size of the Society of Friends and without equal among the various sects of Protestant Dissenters. But this special relationship with the state depended on the consistency with which Friends, as an interest group, confined their lobbying efforts to the defense of their distinctive religious liberties. Predictably, when Quakers in Pennsylvania sought assistance from London Meeting for Sufferings during the trials of the Seven Years' War, the London Friends advised them to resign from the assembly rather than expose the sect, as a whole, to public criticism. First and foremost, the Quaker leadership in England aimed to steer the religious society away from controversy, the better to devote their energies, collectively and individually, to protecting their distinctive customs, traditions, and place.[20]

The prospect of civil war within the empire put the Quakers' tenuous legal standing at risk. War always exposed the Quakers to resentment, since they would neither serve in nor fund the military. The conflict with America exacerbated these difficulties by forcing Friends to side either with the crown or with the American patriots. Throughout the years of crisis,

20. N. C. Hunt, *Two Early Political Associations: The Quakers and the Dissenting Deputies in the Age of Sir Robert Walpole* (Oxford, 1961), 1–112; Alison Gilbert Olson, "The Lobbying of London Quakers for Pennsylvania Friends," *Pennsylvania Magazine of History and Biography*, CXVII (1993), 131–149; James, *A People among Peoples*, 146–147.

Friends in England enjoined Quakers in the colonies to practice strict neutrality. They urged Quaker politicians in Pennsylvania to sue peacefully for a redress of grievances and to calm the impulse toward radical agitation among their neighbors. If they counseled against participation in the "tumults and riots" against British rule, they advised as well against obsequious displays of loyalty to the crown. "Studiously avoid everything adverse either to Administration here, on one side—or to the Congress on the other side," English Friend John Fothergill warned Philadelphia merchant and Quaker leader James Pemberton in 1775. "Submission to the prevailing power must be your duty." If many Friends in England had grave reservations about the coercion of America, they did not participate as a group in the public protests against the American war. When the Reverend Christopher Wyvill organized county associations to promote parliamentary reform in late 1779, London Meeting for Sufferings hurriedly distributed a circular to the regional monthly meetings directing Friends to "be upon their guard . . . and not be drawn in to unite in the Associations, Petitions, Protests, or Subscriptions, now carrying on in various places, and for different purposes." "To lead a quiet peaceable life, in all godliness and honesty," the London Meeting for Sufferings advised English Friends in 1780, "is our Christian and incumbent duty: and as we keep this in our remembrance, studying to mind our proper business, we may be happily preserved from the many evils that are in this world."[21] Politic as these injunctions were, this ethic helped discourage Friends from confronting the Company of Merchants Trading to Africa or state support for the Atlantic slave trade.

Benezet succeeded better in raising up Quaker abolitionists in the North American colonies, in part, because the Revolutionary movement proved amenable to the propagation of antislavery principles. Friends could hook abolitionist arguments to the libertarian rhetoric the patriots employed against imperial rule. And political mobilization across North America cre-

---

21. Olson, "The Lobbying of London Quakers for Pennsylvania Friends," *PMHB*, CXVII (1993), 149–152; John Fothergill to James Pemberton, Mar. 17, 1775, and Fothergill to Henry Zouch, Oct. 8, 1779, both in Betsy C. Corner and Christopher C. Booth, eds., *Chain of Friendship: Selected Letters of Dr. John Fothergill of London* (Cambridge, Mass., 1971), 446, 492–493; Society of Friends, London Meeting for Sufferings, *To Friends in the Several Counties and Places . . .* [Jan. 29, 1780] (London, 1780).

ated a climate conducive to the enactment of antislavery legislation. In Pennsylvania and Rhode Island, Quakers grafted antislavery appeals onto the Revolutionary movement and in New Jersey and New York won support from patriots engaged in broader efforts to overturn imperial authority. Historian Sydney James perhaps overstated the case when he suggested that Friends pursued abolitionism, in part, to endear themselves to the leaders of the Revolutionary movement.[22] But certainly the widespread questioning of the slave system that took place in the North American colonies on the eve of rebellion gave Friends in America the unforeseen opportunity to shift their stance against slavery from sectarian reform to public advocacy. Quakers in England might have reacted differently to Benezet's appeals in the 1770s, if their first attempts at antislavery lobbying in 1767 had brought a more enthusiastic response from politicians or the public, if canvassing for abolition had required less courage.

Still, economics, the institutional culture of the Society of Friends, and Revolutionary era politics—taken together they do not explain the passive, lukewarm way that London Friends reacted to Quaker abolitionism in North America. As Benezet knew, several Quaker elders in England did, in fact, dabble in politics, usually to protect the peculiar privileges of the religious society, but sometimes, too, in the pursuit of more secular ends. If Quakers eschewed politics as a group, individual Friends participated energetically in the familiar agitational repertoire of lobbying, pamphleteering, and petitioning. Quaker traders, for example, stood at the head of British merchant opposition to the Stamp and Townshend Acts. David Barclay led the Committee of North American merchants in its campaign for Stamp Act repeal. With a similar end in view, tobacco trader Capel Hanbury led the animated politicking conducted by the Merchant Venturers of Bristol. During the House of Commons hearings on the Stamp Act in the spring of 1766, Barclay, Hanbury, and Quaker dry goods trader Daniel Mildred presented the merchants' case for appeasement and repeal. David Barclay, in particular, blurred the otherwise firm boundaries British Friends drew between religion and politics. If the Quaker patrician could not approve of the more radical opposition in England and North America to imperial policy, he nonetheless labored assiduously to discourage the British government from

22. James, *A People among Peoples,* 219–239; Marietta, *The Reformation of American Quakerism,* 124–125.

punishing the colonies. Barclay spent several hours cloistered with Lord North in 1775 unsuccessfully trying to talk him out of closing the Newfoundland fisheries to Massachusetts ships. With Benjamin Franklin and sympathetic members of Parliament, he toyed with several schemes to negotiate a peace. Barclay's partner in this behind-the-scenes canvassing, John Fothergill, exploited his service to Lord Dartmouth as personal physician to explore opportunities for an amicable settlement with the thirteen colonies. Exhaustive research by historian Arthur J. Mekeel in fact suggests that English Friends, both women and men, conducted an extensive campaign for peace on the eve of war. Rachel Wilson and Frances Dodshon presented private addresses against coercing America to George III in 1775. If Friends in England proved reluctant to campaign for abolition, they had no difficulty lobbying for peace.[23]

Quietism accounts only in part for the tepid reaction of British Quakers to Benezet's antislavery crusade, since, at bottom, Benezet asked Friends to do for Africans what Friends were already doing on behalf of peace with America: testify on principle for a change of imperial policy. If they could privately harangue ministers and the king, if they could publish tracts anonymously against enforcing imperial rule, prominent Friends in London also should have found a way to bring the horrors of the slave trade to public notice. The truth was, as Benezet came to realize, Friends in England did not care much for abolitionism once abolitionism required more than voicing support for North American attempts to change North American laws. John Fothergill met with Dartmouth to discuss the slave trade in the early 1770s, introduced Benezet's colleague and former pupil William Dillwyn to Granville Sharp, and helped offset the expenses incurred by counsel for James Somerset. He ruminated on strategies for discouraging the slave trade in the years before his death, as we have seen. Otherwise, though, before the Revolutionary War, British Friends left a trail of missed opportunities. They passed up most every chance to promote abolitionism at a time when such a campaign might first have come to fruition. Quakers

23. Arthur J. Mekeel, *The Relation of the Quakers to the American Revolution* (Washington, D.C., 1979), 23–25, 139, 142; P. D. G. Thomas, *British Politics and the Stamp Act Crisis: The First Phase of the American Revolution, 1763–1767* (Oxford, 1975), 36; Corner and Booth, eds., *Chain of Friendship*, 27–29; R. Hingston Fox, *Dr. John Fothergill and His Friends: Chapters in Eighteenth-Century Life* (London, 1919), 343–344, 400–403.

chose not to exploit the popularity of Lord Mansfield's decision in the Somerset case, although the case concluded in the same months Benezet peppered them with tracts and missives. From the extensive records documenting Granville Sharp's activities during the 1770s, there is almost no evidence of Quaker participation or assistance. Sixteen years passed between the first antislavery pamphlet published by English Friends (Benezet's *Caution and Warning*, 1767) and the second (*The Case of Our Fellow-Creatures*, 1783). The slave system figured not at all in the several anonymous essays published on behalf of colonial liberties by Thomas Crowley or John Fothergill. Joseph Woods served actively on various Quaker abolition committees in the 1780s. But his short-lived periodical, the *Monthly Ledger*, offered not a word against the slave system from 1773 to 1775.[24] If Quaker elders had wanted to stir public sentiment against colonial slavery, they would have agreed to print John Woolman's *Considerations on the Keeping of Negroes* in the British edition of his published works. As Yorkshire Friends pointed out, to no avail, Woolman had urged Quakers in England to campaign among the great for abolition of the slave trade in the weeks before his death in 1772.[25]

24. [Thomas Crowley], *Observations and Propositions for an Accommodation between Great Britain and Her Colonies* (London, 1768); Crowley, *Dissertation on the Grand Dispute between Great-Britain and America* (London, 1774); Crowley, *Letters and Dissertations on Various Subjects, by the Author of the Letter Analysis A. P. on the Disputes between Great Britain and America* (London, 1776?); Crowley, *Letters to the King from an Old Patriotic Quaker* (London, 1778); *Monthly Ledger, or Literary Repository* . . . , 3 vols. (London, 1773–1775).

25. In the preface to the second edition of Woolman's posthumous *Works*, the editors explained that "as many weighty arguments and pertinent advices, relating to slavery and oppression of the Negroes in the Plantations, are contained in the Journal, it was therefore apprehended that two small Tracts on the subject might be omitted in the Abridgement." John Woolman, *Works of John Woolman; in Two Parts*, 2d ed. (London, 1775), iv. The Friends gathered at the Quarterly meeting in Yorkshire, where Woolman died in 1772, objected to this abridgment of his work and asked for a reprinting in England of the more extensive edition first published in Philadelphia in 1774. After considering the question, the Morning Meeting of Elders, which was responsible for overseeing the Quaker press, advised the Meeting for Sufferings that some of Woolman's concerns "did not appear so particularly to relate to the state of things in this Nation, as they may to some other places," an unambiguous reference to Woolman's critique of slaveholding. As

The American Revolution has been described as interrupting Quaker abolitionism. It did indeed temporarily halt their antislavery campaigns in North America. The war put a hold on Benezet's until then extensive correspondence, postponed the antislavery labors of Moses Brown and Rhode Island Friends, inhibited further Quaker petitions to the legislatures of New York and New Jersey, and delayed, briefly, Friends' efforts to liberalize manumission laws in Virginia and North Carolina. Among English Friends, though, there was hardly an antislavery movement to interrupt. Indeed, in a sense, the American Revolution gave English Quakers temporary relief from the burden of Anthony Benezet's incessant appeals, which, until 1782, they had made a point of ignoring.

[II]   The Society of Friends in England could dodge North American requests for antislavery organizing as long as individuals like Anthony Benezet presented those requests, rather than official bodies like the Philadelphia Meeting for Sufferings. Inaction would prove harder to defend once the Quaker leadership in Pennsylvania began to issue more formal appeals. The Philadelphia Meeting for Sufferings sent gentle admonitions three times in the last years of the American war. In January 1780, they presented the patriot critique of the British slave trade. At a moment when "trouble and distress so surround . . . the very foundations of a mighty Empire," "ought not an Enquiry individually and as a Nation to go forth—Why is this with us? Is there not a cause?" They lamented "an Evil so derogatory to the dignity of Christianity and the true interests of a people who value themselves on their professions and sentiments of Liberty." Surely this was "a subject highly worthy the serious, and deliberate attention of the rulers in your Nation." Surely the time had come for Quakers to give their witness against the slave trade "more general prevalence in the world."[26]

---

late as 1775, the ownership of slaves could still be dismissed as an American concern that had no bearing on British society or mores. Minutes of the Morning Meeting of Elders, Feb. 13, 20, 27, July 24, Aug. 28, 1775, VI, fols. 224–225, 234, 237, LSF; Minutes of the Meeting for Sufferings, July 21, Sept. 8, 1775, XXXIV, fols. 114, 136.

26. Philadelphia Meeting for Sufferings to London Meeting for Sufferings, Jan. 20, 21, 1780, in MS Letters Which Passed betwixt the Meeting for Sufferings in London, and the Meeting for Sufferings in Philadelphia, I, fols. 168–169.

The London Meeting for Sufferings refused to take the hint. They praised Quaker antislavery efforts in the colonies yet would neither acknowledge the British slave trade as a subject of special concern nor accept a responsibility to act. The Philadelphia Meeting tried a second time in November 1781, explaining that no one in Britain or North America could escape the burden of continued injustice to Africans, that this was not merely a colonial question, that testimony against the slave trade was a sacred duty even in the face of opposition from the powerful. The London Meeting for Sufferings did not reply to these gentle admonitions, so, the following year, Pennsylvania Friends took a more direct approach. "The trade to the African coast is still supported by authority on your side," they bemoaned. Friends in England, therefore, had an obligation to "embrace all opportunities of promoting the discouragement of it." Eight months later, London Meeting for Sufferings answered with characteristic fatalism, predicting "the greatest opposition from the combination of interested parties" and warning that "the part we can contribute" was "small." But such pessimism, they recognized, would no longer suffice as a response, so in April 1783 they promised to present the question for "solid consideration" to the London Yearly Meeting, the annual June gathering of British Friends. If this was a modest step, it went much further than the London leadership would have traveled by themselves, without the push from Philadelphia.[27]

The new pressure from the Philadelphia Meeting for Sufferings followed from two developments among Quakers in the United States during the American war. In the first place, Friends had become optimistic about the prospects for a comprehensive attack on American slavery. Before and during the war, they had watched with guarded optimism as colonial legislatures and then the Continental Congress seemed to turn against the Atlantic slave trade. Actions taken by the newly independent states hinted that even more profound transformations lay in the near future. The Penn-

27. Philadelphia Meeting for Sufferings to London Meeting for Sufferings, Nov. 15, 1781, Aug. 15, 1782, and London Meeting for Sufferings to Philadelphia Meeting for Sufferings, Dec. 29, 1780, Apr. 4, 1783, all in MS Letters Which Passed betwixt the Meeting for Sufferings in London, and the Meeting for Sufferings in Philadelphia, I, fols. 168–169, 180, 188, 198–199; Dillwyn to James Pemberton, May 6, 1783, Pemberton Papers, Parish Collection, Historical Society of Pennsylvania (HSP), Philadelphia.

sylvania assembly surprised Friends by enacting a gradual emancipation law in 1780. Persistent application by Quakers in Virginia led the legislature in 1782 to abolish codes that discouraged slave manumissions. The British Parliament might also be persuaded to act, Philadelphia Meeting for Sufferings reasoned, if the "Light of Truth" could break through on the banks of the Chesapeake and in other places where "temporal considerations, and long accustomed prejudices" had led to "obdurate blindness."[28] To the Quaker leadership in North America, it seemed as if the time for public antislavery lobbying had arrived. This new impulse to organize resulted, in the second place, from transformations within the Society of Friends. The Philadelphia Meeting for Sufferings had started to believe, by the early 1780s, that they had a religious duty to instruct all Americans on moral questions. Anthony Benezet had called on Friends during the Seven Years' War to become leaders in charity as a substitute for formal politics. But only with their sufferings during the Revolution did Friends look for new ways to serve the broader communities in which they lived. A winnowing of the ranks contributed to the new orientation. The years of conflict rid American Quakerdom of its more worldly members. Only the most ardent Friends remained within the religious society by the end of the war. The enhanced position of reformers within the society gave more weight to the views of those like Benezet who thought Friends should revive the prose-lytizing spirit of their seventeenth-century predecessors.[29]

When Philadelphia Meeting for Sufferings pushed abolitionism on Friends in England, the group was also attempting to revive in the British Isles greater attention to sectarian discipline. After the peace, thirteen Quaker ministers from the former colonies journeyed to England in 1783 and 1784 to extend and expand the campaign against worldliness within the Society of Friends. Of those Americans present at the Yearly Meeting in 1783, no one exercised greater influence than John Pemberton of Phila-

28. Philadelphia Meeting for Sufferings to London Meeting for Sufferings, Aug. 15, 1782, MS Letters Which Passed betwixt the Meeting for Sufferings in London, and the Meeting for Sufferings in Philadelphia, I, fol. 198; Thomas E. Drake, *Quakers and Slavery in America* (New Haven, Conn., 1950), 83–89.

29. James, *A People among Peoples*, 241–267; Marietta, *Reformation of American Quakerism*, 232–261; Richard Bauman, *For the Reputation of Truth: Politics, Religion, and Conflict among the Pennsylvania Quakers, 1750–1800* (Baltimore, 1971), 155–187.

delphia, who had more than a quarter century of experience in the North American crusade to promote religious purity. Pemberton had been a leading light in the reformation of American Quakerism since the era of the Seven Years' War. More than five hundred families in the Philadelphia area had received visits from Pemberton and Daniel Stanton in the late 1750s, as Quaker ministers sought to enforce fidelity to the "little things" that distinguished the truly pious. Pemberton had figured prominently in the canvassing of Quaker slaveholders in the 1760s and 1770s, when the spiritual leaders pushed their less strict brethren to recognize their sins. And John Pemberton had been among the nearly two dozen prominent Friends sent into exile in southwestern Virginia in 1777 and 1778 for failing to sympathize sufficiently with the Revolutionary cause. Pemberton, like other Quaker reformers, believed that this suffering had fostered a new sense of purpose among Friends in North America and had encouraged a greater attention to their religious testimonies. Without a similar set of experiences in England, he and other North American ministers feared further backsliding among English Friends, especially the London leadership, and a deepening rift between pious Quakers in the United States and worldly Quakers in the British Isles. In a kind of spiritual apprenticeship, Pemberton had traveled with colonial Quaker minister John Churchman through the British Isles during the 1750s in an early crusade against impiety within the religious society. With a similar end in view, to forward the reformation, Pemberton in 1783 returned to England, and found his labors very much in need. At Hertford, Friends ignored strictures against the paying of tithes. In Norwich, lax members routinely arrived late to meetings for worship. Too often, the grandees of the Grace Church Street Meeting in London failed to attend at all. Elsewhere, Pemberton predicted, monthly meetings would soon close because only a few Friends remained. "So much barrenness prevails," Pemberton noted privately to himself, "that I sometimes think it scarcely quits cost to travel."[30]

30. Margaret Hope Bacon, "The Establishment of London Women's Yearly Meeting: A Transatlantic Concern," *Jour. Friends' Hist. Soc.*, LVII (1995), 158; Jones, *The Later Periods of Quakerism*, I, 26; Marietta, *The Reformation of American Quakerism*, 75, 81, 89; Jean R. Soderlund, *Quakers and Slavery: A Divided Spirit* (Princeton, N.J., 1985), 171; W. H. Hodgson, ed., *The Life and Travels of John Pemberton . . .* (London, 1844), 48, 120–123.

John Pemberton and the other Quaker ministers from America set the less strict London patriciate on edge. Quaker elders in England did not take well to what they thought of as a challenge to their spiritual and temporal authority. "Thy well meaning Countrymen are come here as *Reformers*," an irritated David Barclay wrote to James Pemberton, John's brother, two weeks after the Yearly Meeting of 1783, and "with an Impetuosity that several of our most valuable Friends have termed *over driving*." "It has fallen to my lot," Barclay explained, "to *openly* dissent from the opinions of your countrymen, and to express the sentiments of some of our most weighty valuable Friends." "The chief points they seem to have in view," Barclay continued, referring to the American visitors, "are to overset the practice of Friends in paying Taxes that may be partially applied to military purposes, and to make the Mg. Of Ministers and Elders independent of the mgs. Of discipline[,] to impress an idea that the present day is more enlighten'd than those of our ancient Friends; (Fox, Barclay, Penn etc.) and in *all cases* to lay aside what they term *worldly wisdom*." He regarded the first scruple as impractical and the second ill considered. The third and fourth concerns he thought overzealous. "I have been told not to quote Wm. Penn," he wrote with astonishment, "because he had dealt or approved the dealing in Slaves." An address to government in favor of slave trade abolition, he added, was "*stamped so high* by [thy Countrymen], and some few others, that a Committee was appointed to draw it up."[31] Barclay may have exaggerated the impact of "outside agitators" on deliberations at the Yearly Meeting. He may also have minimized unduly the "few others" among the English who stood with the American ministers. His angry testimony, nonetheless, discloses the existence of sharp divisions within the Society of Friends at the pivotal gathering of 1783. The proposed campaign for slave trade abolition, therefore, constituted one part of a broader and deeper set of questions concerning religious discipline, reform, the role of female ministers in Quaker governance, and the very meaning of Quakerism in the aftermath of war, revolution, and American independence.

Thanks to the work of Quaker historian J. William Frost it becomes possible to identify some of those "few others" in London who sided with Pemberton and other American ministers in 1783 on behalf of abolitionism and religious reform, more generally. His republication of *The Records and*

31. Barclay to Pemberton, July 2, 1783, Pemberton Papers, XXXIX, fols. 51–52.

Recollections of James Jenkins permits unrivaled insight into the personalities of Quaker leaders in the moment when the abolitionist campaign began within the Society of Friends. The memoir sheds light especially on tensions within the religious society in the last years of the American war. Jenkins, a trader of modest means, resented the "notoriously tythe-paying meeting of Grace Church Street" and denounced the "chains of aristocratic bondage" in which Quaker leaders like Barclay bound the Society of Friends. Jenkins described how "an Aristocracy of Elders ruled with an almost exclusive sway" and "always expected, and often obtained, the obsequious obedience of their humbler brethren." A small group of "feudal chiefs" presided over meetings for business. Younger men were discouraged from participating in discussions of discipline. And on questions of conduct, prominent Friends occasionally received unusual leniency. Such was the case in 1777, when Joseph Talwyn, an elder of Ratcliff Monthly Meeting, refused to accept the decision of two separate sets of Quaker arbitrators in a dispute over his deceased brother's will. Flouting the sect's custom of finding a negotiated settlement to legal disputes, Talwyn forced the case onto the agenda of the London Yearly Meeting in 1782, where "a few rich friends," Jenkins remembered with disgust, sided with Talwyn.[32]

The Talwyn affair, Jenkins recalled, commenced "a great Revolution among us." A number of young men "whose naturally-good abilities had been greatly improved by liberal education" challenged the "all powerful chieftains." They inspired, in turn, those unaccustomed to speaking out on matters of discipline to voice their anger at Talwyn's breach of contract and duty. These men—Jenkins singled out Joseph Gurney Bevan, James Phillips, Wilson Birkbeck, Jonathan Hoare, and Samuel Hoare, Jr.—"whose powers of disputation had been thus accidentally called into practice, continued speakers, and they neither would be kept down, as they had hitherto been in their respective monthly-meetings; and hence arose a change in the external government of our society in London."[33] The last years of the American war, then, seem to have marked a transitional moment for the leadership of the Society of Friends in England. The "great Revolution" occurred just one year before the pivotal London Yearly Meeting of 1783.

32. J. William Frost, *The Records and Recollections of James Jenkins* (New York, 1984), 128–129, 131–132, 158, 280n.

33. Ibid., 133, 134.

Each of the young Friends who came to prominence during the Talwyn affair would assume an influential role in organizing the Quaker campaign against the slave trade during the years that followed. Joseph Gurney Bevan and publisher James Phillips would labor with unusual diligence on the Meeting for Sufferings subcommittee on the slave trade. Samuel Hoare, Jr., would join with William Dillwyn and four other Friends in the summer of 1783 to establish an antislavery propaganda committee. Their partners in this venture—George Harrison, John Lloyd, Dr. Thomas Knowles, and Joseph Woods—may not have numbered among the young Friends who stood forward in the Talwyn affair. (James Jenkins provides only a partial list.) But each possessed a "liberal education" or had shown themselves uncomfortable with the established leadership within the Society of Friends. Harrison had studied at Warrington Academy under the patronage of John Fothergill and had been exposed there to the rationalist traditions within Protestant dissent. The two years John Lloyd spent in North America at the beginning of the American war left him enamored with the secular philosophy of natural rights. Thomas Knowles attracted the ire of London elders because of his frequent recourse to "head knowledge" when challenging their authority. Joseph Woods, who had published the *Monthly Ledger* in the mid-1770s, took pleasure in the circulation of ideas and the promotion of useful knowledge. With William Dillwyn, he served as London agent for the Library Company of Philadelphia.[34]

John Pemberton and the other American ministers who promoted abolitionism at the Yearly Meeting of 1783 benefited, then, from generational and philosophical rifts that emerged within the Society of Friends in the early 1780s. On one side stood the "weighty friends," the group David Barclay described as disturbed by the "impetuousity" of American reformers. The men he named—Isaac Sharpless, Thomas Corbyn, the elder William Rathbone, and Edmund Gurney—certainly would have numbered among those Jenkins characterized as "feudal chiefs." On the other side stood a younger set of Friends, more cosmopolitan in their tastes and less deferential to

34. For the Quaker slave trade committees established in 1783, see the discussion that follows. For biographical sketches of these figures, see Judith Jennings, *The Business of Abolishing the British Slave Trade, 1783–1807* (London, 1997), 6, 9, 12; Humphrey Lloyd, *The Quaker Lloyds in the Industrial Revolution* (London, 1975), 189; and Frost, *The Records and Recollections of James Jenkins*, 129.

established authorities within the religious society, more inclined to back slave trade abolition in the manner American reformers proposed.[35] They may not have embraced every aspect of the call for religious discipline. They seem to have been more enthusiastic about various programs of social reform. But they agreed with those like Benezet and Pemberton who thought the Society of Friends should conceive of itself as a force for good in the world, not merely a refuge from its temptations.

The Society of Friends does not minute their deliberations, so historians probably will never know who said what about the slave trade at the London Yearly Meeting of 1783. Fortunately, though, a manuscript account written by one in attendance briefly hints at the nature of the exchange. After a reading of the epistle of 1782 from the Philadelphia Meeting for Sufferings, "many words were gone into . . . all seeming to be well intended but full of the Arts and contrivances." These arts and contrivances the writer does not detail. Several of the London elders probably stood forward to praise the visiting Friends for their labors against slavery in America and applaud their desire to see the slave trade abolished. Perhaps they added a hope that one day an "opening," as Friends put it, would allow for an end to so horrible a practice. But the private and national interests in the slave trade were great, and formidable enough to defeat any application put forward by a tiny religious minority, these more cautious Friends likely explained. Preserving the safety and security of the religious society was their first responsibility. Why sacrifice the peaceable reputation of the Society of Friends by taking up a futile venture destined to rile up a nest of antagonists? Opponents of abolitionist organizing, like David Barclay, probably offered words such as these. Those seem to have been the objections London Friends raised privately among themselves in prior years.[36]

35. The age differences are particularly striking. In the year of the Talwyn affair, David Barclay was 69, Isaac Sharpless was 75, Thomas Corbyn was 66 or 67, Isaac Wilson was 60, Edmund Gurney was 56, and William Rathbone was 51. By contrast, Joseph Gurney Bevan was 24, James Phillips was 34, Wilson Birkbeck was 23, and Samuel Hoare, Jr., was 26. I have been unable to determine the age of Jonathan Hoare. From the antislavery publicity committee established in 1783, John Lloyd was 26, Thomas Knowles was 43, Joseph Woods was 39, and George Harrison was 30. Ages determined from Frost's annotations in *The Records and Recollections of James Jenkins* and the typescript Dictionary of Quaker Biography, LSF.

36. Journal of Yearly Meeting, 1783, MS box 10, 2 (15), LSF.

The format of the London Yearly Meeting, however, did not lend itself to domination by the "feudal chiefs." Discouraging abolitionism would prove far more difficult when the question of the slave trade lay open for discussion by scores of Friends at the general meeting. In a setting in which anyone could speak, it would be hard to silence the vocal minority that wanted Friends to act aggressively. The pragmatic conservatism of the London patriciate, in such circumstances, competed unfavorably with the enthusiasm of those hoping to renew the Quaker commitment to principled moral witness, perhaps especially those from Yorkshire who in 1772 had wanted to see Woolman's antislavery tracts published with his collected works. The debate on abolition put the proponents of inaction in an awkward position. The obstructionists did not want to defend the slave trade. They abhorred the traffic, in all likelihood. It must have unsettled the grandees to find themselves positioned as allies of the African interest. But what they feared most were the consequences that would follow from opposing the slave trade publicly. A Quaker meeting for worship, however, was a poor place to recommend prudence over piety. When John Pemberton, William Dillwyn, and sympathetic English Friends spoke, their more cautious and more pragmatic opponents must have found it difficult to produce compelling replies. The Quaker custom of achieving a consensus about "the sense of the meeting" would seem to have driven the skeptical like Barclay into a grudging acquiescence. "A degree of awful solemnity gradually spread itself over the Meeting," the diarist in attendance wrote, "as this prevailed the contrary nature fell under it . . . this encreased more and more over the meeting so that the glorious all powerful dominance of the blessed Truth was witnessed."[37]

A similar dynamic seems to have taken place a quarter century earlier in Pennsylvania, when the question of slaveholding and slave trading among Friends first came before the Philadelphia Yearly Meeting. Quaker elders worried in 1758 that antislavery strictures would offend prominent members within the religious society and undermine the unity of the fellowship. The exchange between abolitionists and defenders of the status quo proceeded as it must have in London in 1783. "None did openly justify the practice of slave-keeping in general," John Woolman observed of this earlier meeting. That would have been difficult to do, given Quaker principles.

37. Ibid.

FIGURE 7. *Gracechurch Street Meeting*. Painting in oil. Artist unknown. Circa 1770. Courtesy, The Library of the Religious Society of Friends, London.

Quaker elders in London would find it difficult to silence Friends from America who urged action against the slave trade in 1783.

But several had maintained "that if the Friends patiently continued to exercise[,] the Lord in his time might open a way for the deliverance of these people." To the preference for gradualism, Woolman replied in the same way that John Pemberton probably responded in 1783 when confronting similar reservations at the London Yearly Meeting.

> Many slaves on this continent are oppressed, and their cries have reached the ears of the Most High. Such are the purity and certainty of his judgments, that he cannot be partial in our favor. In infinite love and goodness he hath opened our understanding from one time to another concerning our duty towards this people, and it is not a time for delay. Should we now be sensible of what he requires of us, and through a respect to the private interest of some persons, and through a regard to some friendships which do not stand on an immutable foundation, neglect to do our duty in firmness and constancy, still waiting for some extraordinary means to bring about their deliverance, God may by terrible things in righteousness answer us in this matter.

Pemberton's message in 1783 undoubtedly differed on the specifics. But the appeal to Quaker values, to how Quakers understood their relationship to one another and to the world in which they lived, made inaction impossible. In 1783, as in 1758, religious reformers exploited the size and solemnity of a Yearly Meeting to bully reluctant elders into accepting new antislavery commitments. At the conclusion of the meeting in 1758, Woolman wrote, many "said that they believed liberty was the negro's right; to which, at length, no opposition was *publicly* made."[38]

On June 16, 273 Quaker men signed a petition to the House of Commons that declared the "suffering situation" of "the enslaved Negroes" "a subject calling for the humane Interposition of the legislature" and asked members to consider an abolition of the slave trade. The politicians surprised Friends with their response. "Favourably received," a relieved David Barclay told the London Meeting for Sufferings several days later. "Well received," William Dillwyn recorded in his diary. If he had attended, Edmund Burke told Irish Quaker Richard Shackleton, he would have given a magnificent speech in favor of abolition. Another "distinguished member" expressed to John Pemberton "his hearty willingness to afford any assistance he could in this matter." Pemberton noted to himself candidly, "This is more encouragement than was expected." The official account transcribed in the Book of Cases, the repository of legal judgments affecting the Society of Friends, provided a similar assessment. A delegation from the London Yearly Meeting, John Lloyd reported, visited Lord North and Lord John Cavendish, "who receiv'd them very respectfully, and expressed their approbation of the petition." Unable to find Charles James Fox, the delegates left a copy of the petition for him at home. In the lobby of Westminster, they met Sir Cecil Wray, member of Parliament for Westminster who had opposed the American war and who had espoused constitutional reform. Wray agreed, at their request, to present a motion on the floor of the House. In introducing the petition, Wray announced, "he hoped to see the day when not a Slave should remain in the Dominions of this Realm." Lord North seconded Wray's motion, declaring that the petition's "object, and tendency, ought to recommend it to every humane breast."[39]

38. Frederick B. Tolles, ed., *The Journal of John Woolman, and a Plea for the Poor* (Gloucester, Mass., 1971), 86, 87, 88, my emphasis.

39. Minutes of the Meeting for Sufferings, June 20, 1783, XXXVI, fol. 417; typescript

This apparent sympathy for abolition needs explaining since, at first glance, it would seem to conflict with the official support members of Parliament gave to the slave trade in the 1780s before the formation of the Society for Effecting the Abolition of the Slave Trade. Much of the interest generated by the Quaker petition arose from its novelty. John Lloyd observed that several members studied the petition with "great attention" at the close of the day's session.[40] Antislavery tracts had been published in Britain. Private attempts had been made to lobby bishops and cabinet ministers. Colonial legislatures had sent antislavery addresses to the Board of Trade and to the king. But no one before 1783 had sent an abolition petition to the House of Commons. Friends caught the attention of members of Parliament recovering from the shock of a lost empire. Some, like Lord North, genuinely thought well of the principles the Quakers invoked. Several months later North was urging Sir Guy Carleton to provide for the black loyalists destined for Nova Scotia. More important, though, the politicians had few reasons to speak ill of the Quaker petition. The Society of Friends gave them an opportunity to voice their support for liberty and humanity. It cost them nothing and committed them to little more than praising Friends for their noble gesture. In 1783, as throughout the eighteenth century, it was easy to oppose the slave trade in theory and back the slave trade in practice.

With respect to abolition, it is true, the Friends' petition made no impact on parliamentary politics or government policy. Lord North warned the petitioners that the slave trade, "in a Commercial View[,] was become necessary to almost every nation in Europe." But Friends experienced these events as a step forward, and a spur to action, rather than a setback. On the heels of its "favourable reception" in the House of Commons, the Meeting for Sufferings appointed a standing committee of twenty-two Friends, including David Barclay, "to embrace all opportunities to promote the Intention of the Yearly Meeting respecting the Slave Trade." That committee included William Dillwyn, Thomas Knowles, Joseph Lloyd, and James Phillips, as well as more than a quarter of the male elders of the

---

calendar of the diaries of William Dillwyn, June 17, 1783, II, fol. 24, LSF; Hodgson, ed., *The Life and Travels of John Pemberton,* 128; John Pemberton to James Pemberton, June 27, 1783, Pemberton Papers, XXXIX, fol. 38; The Book of Cases, June 27, 1783, III, fol. 196, LSF.

40. The Book of Cases, June 27, 1783, III, fol. 196.

Morning Meeting. The apparent encouragement from Parliament helped Friends overcome the cautious instincts that had hindered Quaker abolitionism in England for nearly two decades. In a short pamphlet published in December 1783 for distribution to each member of Parliament, the Meeting for Sufferings explained on behalf of the Society of Friends that their stand against the slave trade had been inspired by the belief that many in both the Lords and Commons would prove "friends to civil and religious liberty." "This persuasion," they continued, "joined to the favourable reception of our last yearly-meeting to the House of Commons, encourages us to address you . . . on this important subject."[41]

[III]   Praise made all the difference. It left Friends enthusiastic not only about abolition but what abolitionism could mean for the Society of Friends. David Barclay found that the petition of 1783 "gained the Society universal approbation." On the floor of the House of Commons, politicians lauded Friends "as the most benevolent society in the universe."[42] These tributes encouraged Friends to picture themselves as moral campaigners, to assume the mantle of crusaders for justice and virtue. Before the summer of 1783, dim prospects for success had intimidated Friends into inaction. Thereafter, their willingness to take up a difficult task seemed, instead, to mark Quakers off as unusually virtuous, as distinctively philanthropic, as peculiarly sensitive to the interests of humanity and charity. In this way, in their own eyes especially, Friends could restore their tradition of conscientious Christian witness. A lifeless fidelity to stale customs stripped of symbolic significance characterized too much of the spiritual life within the Society of Friends, reform-minded Quakers believed. Abolitionism looked like one way to give renewed meaning and focus to their religious fellowship. And it seemed to address the persistent tension between the need for religious purity and social acceptance. By embracing

41. Ibid.; Minutes of the Meeting for Sufferings, June 20, 1783, XXXVI, fol. 417; Society of Friends, London Meeting for Sufferings, *The Case of Our Fellow-Creatures, the Oppressed Africans, Respectfully Recommended to the Serious Consideration of the Legislature of Great-Britain, by the People Called Quakers,* 2d ed. (London, 1784), 4–5.

42. Barclay to James Pemberton, July 2, 1783, and Daniel Mildred to Pemberton, June 27, 1783, both in Pemberton Papers, XXXIX, fols. 39, 51; The Book of Cases, June 27, 1783, III, fol. 196.

abolitionism, Friends in England could advance the religious reformation of Anglo-American Quakerism without surrendering entirely to the highly scrupulous prescriptions pushed by Quaker ministers from the colonies. A campaign against the slave trade provided one way to denounce avarice without sacrificing material abundance. And canvassing for abolition could help Quakers forge ties with those outside the Society of Friends while sustaining and strengthening their sectarian identity. Indeed, in the end, abolitionism would help Quakers become, at once, better Quakers and more acceptable to society.

The Religious Society of Friends in Britain directed its substantial institutional resources to the promotion of slave trade abolition in the fall of 1783. Few issues received more sustained attention from the London Meeting for Sufferings. An ad hoc subcommittee stood poised after the summer of 1783 to exploit further opportunities to canvass Parliament for antislavery measures. With this aim in mind, that subcommittee prepared in the fall a brief statement, *The Case of Our Fellow-Creatures, the Oppressed Africans,* which called for the abolition of the slave trade and "relief of those already in bondage."[43] Shortly after the victory of William Pitt and his followers at the polls in the spring of 1784, Jacob Hagen, Daniel Mildred, and John Townsend visited with the new ministry. The politicians again praised Friends for their benevolence and "declared their hearty concurrence" with Friends in principle, "but thought the time was not yet come to bring the Affair to maturity, wch they never the less wished and are ready to promote when opportunity offers." In the past, an evasive response of this kind usually discouraged further activity. This time London Friends reacted by launching an extensive and, in Britain, unprecedented propaganda campaign against the slave trade and colonial slavery. If ministers could not be moved to act through gentle persuasion, then pressure would be brought to bear through public opinion, by what Friends later described as "a Call on Government so general and so laud as to be availing."[44]

43. Society of Friends, *The Case of Our Fellow-Creatures, the Oppressed Africans,* 14.

44. Barclay to James Phillips, Dec. 19, 1783, Thompson-Clarkson Illustrations, III, fol. 121, LSF; Minutes of the Meeting for Sufferings Committee on the Slave Trade (MiMSCST), May 14, 20, 24, 27, 1784, fols. 5–8, 11, LSF; LMS to PMS, Nov. 3, 1786, MS Letters Which Passed betwixt the Meeting for Sufferings in London, and the Meeting for Sufferings in Philadelphia, I, fol. 262.

Quaker propagandists shaped the information available to the reading public after 1783. "The contempt in which [blacks] are held, and the remoteness of their sufferings from the notice of disinterested observers," London Yearly Meeting concluded, "have occasioned few advocates to plead their cause." It surprised American Friends, particularly, to find how little those in England knew about the character of the Atlantic slave trade or its consequences. William Dillwyn hoped in 1783 that the Zong case would go some way toward exposing the inhumanities of the traffic. But he recognized that only a concerted effort to detail the daily operations of the slave trade and colonial slavery would have lasting effect. Philadelphia Quakers had found that, when they published antislavery opinion, others in North America would follow suit. So they advised Friends in London to set an example for all in Britain by putting the subject before the public, by drafting antislavery essays of their own, and by reprinting the best of those works first published in North America.[45]

Ready access to the press was crucial. An antislavery pamphlet written in 1773 by the Philadelphia patriot Benjamin Rush never went to press in England in the mid-1770s because its sponsor, Granville Sharp, could not find a London publisher willing to risk poor sales. British abolitionists faced no such problems in the 1780s. Every major antislavery tract printed in England from 1783 through 1787 came off the presses of Quaker printer James Phillips. Without the largesse of the Society of Friends, Phillips would have had fewer tracts to publish. London Meeting for Sufferings subsidized the publication of *The Case of Our Fellow-Creatures*. On the encouragement of Anthony Benezet, Friends produced a London edition of *A Serious Address to the Leaders of America* (1783) by Quaker David Cooper of New Jersey. A private subscription collected from Friends made possible the anonymous publication of *Thoughts on the Slavery of the Negroes* by Joseph Woods in 1784. In the same year, the Meeting for

45. The 1784 epistle of the London Yearly Meeting printed in *Epistles from the Yearly Meeting of Friends,* II, 57; John Pemberton to James Pemberton, May 14, July 16, 1783, Pemberton Papers, XXXVIII, fol. 164, XXXIX, fol. 70; Dillwyn to James Pemberton, May 6, 1783, Parish Collection, I, Pemberton Papers; James Pemberton to Phillips, July 22, 1784, MSS Portraits, VI, fol. 152, LSF; James Pemberton to John Pemberton, Aug. 27, 1783, Pemberton Papers, XXXVIII, fol. 89.

Sufferings arranged for a second London printing of Benezet's *Caution and Warning to Great Britain and Her Colonies*. Phillips also shepherded through the press several major tracts by crusaders outside the Society of Friends. Quakers received permission to republish the antislavery sermon Beilby Porteus delivered to the Society for the Propagation of the Gospel in 1783. Each of James Ramsay's antislavery tracts came off the Quaker press, including the landmark *Essay on the Treatment and Conversion of African Slaves in the Sugar Colonies* of 1784. And Friends published the major works of Thomas Clarkson, first in 1786 and then after. Most of these texts were printed in substantial quantities and often distributed for free.[46]

Friends not only published antislavery pamphlets. They acted aggressively to see that men of influence possessed them. No well-read person could have been unaware of *The Case of Our Fellow-Creatures* by the late 1780s. London Meeting for Sufferings provided for the publication of two thousand in November 1783, and ten thousand more in June 1784. In August 1784, they called on the regional quarterly meetings to distribute *The Case of Our Fellow-Creatures* throughout the counties they served. These tracts, Meeting for Sufferings stressed, were neither "addressed to, nor intended for, the members of our society." Instead, they should be presented to "such other persons . . . as are in a situation which may afford them an opportunity of discouraging the traffic." Similar instructions accompanied a second request six months later to circulate copies of Benezet's *Caution and Warning*. "Success of a labor of this kind," London Friends reiterated, "depends on a diligent care to put them into proper hands." Because of these circulars, distribution committees took shape across British Quakerdom. Some were very small. Joseph Fry, John Lury, and Thomas Scantlebury took responsibility for distributing Benezet's pamphlet in Bristol. Others could be quite large. A committee of twenty-

46. Sharp to Benjamin Rush, Feb. 21, 1774, and Benezet to John Pemberton, Aug. 10, 1783, both in Brookes, *Friend Anthony Benezet*, 355–359, 446–447; MiMSCST, Sept. 26, Oct. 3, 23, 1783, fols. 3–4; Phillips to James Pemberton, June 15, 1784, and Dillwyn to John Pemberton, Nov. 6, 1783, both in Pemberton Papers, XLI, fol. 150; Marcus Wood, "'The Abolition Blunderbuss': Free Publishing and British Abolitionist Propaganda, 1780–1838," in James Raven, ed., *Free Print and Non-Commercial Publishing since 1700* (Aldershot, Eng., 2000), 68–71.

seven Quaker men fanned out across Yorkshire to place copies of *The Case of Our Fellow-Creatures* with county grandees.[47]

The activities of the distribution committees that canvassed London survive in rich detail. These Friends took care to target men positioned to shape commercial and imperial policy. The London and Middlesex Quarterly Meeting earmarked hundreds of pamphlets for the principal bankers, insurers, and merchants in London, including major investors in the East India Company, the Company of Merchants Trading to Africa, and the Committee of West Indian Merchants. Both Anglican and Protestant Dissenting clergy received dozens of copies of both *The Case of Our Fellow-Creatures* and *A Caution and Warning*. They targeted nearly every official in the local and national government, from county justices of the peace to the commissioners of the navy and the customs. Quaker agents made an effort to visit every general and colonel in the British army residing in London and every admiral and captain living in the vicinity.[48] The distribution campaign, then, was exceptionally thorough. Dozens of Quakers across England devoted countless hours in 1784 and 1785 to placing antislavery literature in the proper hands.

To attain some sense of what these labors may have meant to those involved, it helps to imagine pairs of Quakers canvassing door-to-door, copies of *The Case of Our Fellow-Creatures* in hand. For most of these antislavery missionaries, it would have been the first time that they had solicited those outside the Society of Friends for their patronage of a political cause. "A Quaker cannot go out of doors, but he is reminded of his own singularity or of his difference . . . from his fellow citizens," Thomas Clarkson observed two decades later. Because the polite often regarded Quakers as insular and dour, some Friends probably approached the work with

47. Joseph Row to John Pemberton, Nov. 29, 1783, and Phillips to James Pemberton, June 15, 1784, both in Pemberton Papers, XXXIX, fol. 176, XLI, fol. 180; London Meeting for Sufferings, *To the Quarterly Meeting of Friends . . . 27 August 1784* (London, 1784), vol. G, p. 22, box 32, LSF; London Meeting for Sufferings, *To the Quarterly Meeting of Friends . . . 25 February 1785* (London, 1785), vol. G, p. 24, box 32, LSF; Minutes of the Bristol Monthly Meeting, July 1, 1785, XI, fol. 509, SF/A1/15, Bristol Record Office; Minutes of the Yorkshire Quarterly Meeting, Sept. 29–30, 1784, Mic 301, LSF.

48. Minutes of the Committee of the Quarterly Meeting relative to Distributing the Case of the Poor Enslaved Africans (1784–1786), MS box E1/9B, LSF.

trepidation. The difficulty of the task likely sobered some, too. By directing Friends across England to participate in this campaign, however, the Meeting for Sufferings made opposition to the slave trade an essential aspect of what it meant to be Quaker. Laboring against "the avarice of unrighteous men" reinforced the religious fellowship and instilled a collective sense of purpose. The London distribution committee, in the fall of 1785, decided to leave copies of Benezet's pamphlet with the heads of "divers public Schools in this Metropolis," including Harrow, Charterhouse, Eton, and Westminster. Friends returned from these meetings pleased to find that the campaign met with "general approbation and concurrence, the business everywhere proving an easy introduction and furnishing great satisfaction" to those engaged. In distributing antislavery pamphlets among the British elite, Friends advocated for themselves as they advocated for enslaved Africans. The campaign to do good showed that they valued more than doing well.[49]

In recent years, some historians have dismissed the efficacy of Quaker labors, and stressed instead the more conclusive influence of public opinion. "As long as the Quakers concentrated on addressing only the powerful," Seymour Drescher has written, "they had, after more than three years of quiet lobbying, succeeded in converting two or three MPs to the idea of Parliamentary action." This assessment not only underestimates the difference Quakers made but misdescribes what Friends did. If Quakers lobbied men in power, they also tried to change opinion out-of-doors. In the summer of 1783, in the same months that the Meeting for Sufferings appointed a standing committee to lobby "those who count," a smaller body worked surreptitiously to litter the British press with selections from antislavery literature. William Dillwyn, George Harrison, Samuel Hoare, Jr., John Lloyd, Thomas Knowles, and Joseph Woods purchased space to print antislavery notices in the London and provincial press. They concen-

---

49. Thomas Clarkson, *A Portraiture of Quakerism; Taken from a View of the Education and Discipline, Social Manners, Civil and Political Economy, Religious Principles, and Character, of the Society of Friends*, 3 vols. (New York, 1806), III, 173. London Meeting for Sufferings, *To the Quarterly Meeting of Friends . . . 25 February 1785;* Minutes of the Committee of the Quarterly Meeting relative to Distributing the Case of the Poor Enslaved Africans (1784–1786), Aug. 15, 1785, fol. 9, MS box E1/9B; Minutes of the Subcommittee on Benezet's Caution, Jan. 2, 1786, fol. 17, ibid.

trated especially on two London triweeklies, the *General Evening Post* and *Lloyd's Evening Post,* both of which possessed a wide circulation in the metropolis and the counties. "The Slave Association," as Dillwyn referred to this surreptitious committee of six, selected excerpts from a variety of tracts and treatises. They took passages from familiar antislavery texts by Benezet, Porteus, Rush, Warburton, and Ignatius Sancho. They extracted descriptions of the slave trade from the travel narratives of Adanson, Astley, Sloan, and John Hamilton Moore. They drew on the intellectual authority of such renowned philosophers as Montesquieu, Hume, and Adam Smith. Recent critiques of the Spanish, French, and British empires the Slave Association clipped from histories written by John Campbell, Abbé Raynal, and Thomas Parker.[50]

The variety of works selected hints at a defining feature of the Quaker publicity committee. Friends in general, and the "Slave Association" in particular, proceeded with unusual guile. By selecting excerpts from a variety of genres and authorities, they tried to create the impression that hostility to slavery was widespread. Moreover, this approach allowed them to disguise the extent to which the sudden appearance of antislavery sentiment in the press reflected a Quaker initiative. Throughout the early 1780s, Friends deliberately masked their contribution to the dissemination of abolitionist literature. John Coakley Lettsom in 1780 sent a letter to the *Gentleman's Magazine* recommending the transfer of sugar production from the West Indies to Africa. To give the impression that he was an enlightened slaveholder, rather than an ardent Quaker, the native of the Virgin Islands signed his essay as "A West Indian." John Pemberton anonymously slipped an American antislavery essay into the Bristol press in 1783.[51] The Slave Association subsidized the publication of two thousand copies of Joseph Woods, *Thoughts on the Slavery of the Negroes,* yet produced the work without attribution to Woods and without reference to funding by the Society of Friends. With respect to abolitionism, then,

50. Seymour Drescher, *Capitalism and Antislavery: British Mobilization in Comparative Perspective* (London, 1987), 63–64; Minutes of the "Slave Association," Thompson-Clarkson Illustrations, II, fol. 9; typescript calendar of the diary of William Dillwyn, Sept. 15, 1783, II, fol. 27.

51. *Gentleman's Magazine, and Historical Chronicle,* L (1780), 458; John Pemberton to James Pemberton, July 16, 1783, Pemberton Papers, XXXIX, fol. 70.

British newspapers and periodicals published from the summer of 1783 to the spring of 1787 need to be read with caution. Historians will never know how many of the antislavery statements that appear in the British press in this period resulted from Slave Association sponsorship. What sometimes looks like an upsurge of antislavery argument and commentary in the press occasionally represented little more than the initiative of a clever Quaker propagandist. Friends not only attempted to generate antislavery opinion. They tried to create the appearance of an emerging public consensus on behalf of abolition more than two years before that support materialized in full.

The sum of Quaker efforts between 1783 and 1787, from the canvassing of the elite to the dissemination of antislavery literature, profoundly affected the political and cultural landscape. Veterans of the movement for parliamentary reform embraced abolitionism as an extension of their aims. Sir Cecil Wray, a London ally of Yorkshire reformer Christopher Wyvill, presented the Quaker petition of 1783 to the House of Commons. Months later the Society for Constitutional Information (SCI), in which Wray served as president, arranged for the petition's publication in the London press. The following year, the SCI published an antislavery essay written by one of their number, Thomas Day. A petition to the House of Commons calling for an abolition of the slave trade emerged from the town of Bridgewater in the spring of 1785, just months after the Quakers had started to circulate copies of *The Case of Our Fellow-Creatures* and *A Caution and Warning* to local governments. The Bridgewater organizer John Chubb had worked with Wray and others in the organization of the extraparliamentary movement for political reform. Antislavery writers relied heavily on Quaker networks and resources. Friends not only published the works of like-minded enthusiasts like James Ramsay and Beilby Porteus. They encouraged antislavery initiatives in quarters where they had developed slowly or not at all. Henry Smeathman cast his Sierra Leone plan as an antislavery scheme because of the Quaker example. The leadership of Friends seems to have expedited the publication of James Ramsay's *Essay*. A young Thomas Clarkson could get his Latin thesis on the slave trade published in 1786 because Friends actively sought out manuscripts that would advance the cause. Their propaganda campaign, London Friends reported proudly in 1785, had impressed "many sensible minds of various denominations," "who till lately had never contemplated the weighty subject." "This iniquitous practice need only be known to be detested," the Quaker publisher James Phillips declared.[52]

The problem, of course, was that detesting the slave trade was not the same as being committed to its abolition. The Quaker propaganda campaign made a difference, but it did not, in the immediate, make a movement. Informed opinion, alone, was not enough to make antislavery a vital political issue, Friends began to realize in the final months of 1785. In the halls of power, there was "an approbation of our benevolence . . . but little prospect of success," since "deep rooted ideas of interest" made antislavery measures seem impractical. "Men of liberal minds," particularly those who taught in the public schools, agreed with the justice of the cause but feared the consequences of manumission and emancipation for the British Caribbean and the empire. For this reason, London Quakers sought from their American brethren in December 1785 some evidence that liberation of the enslaved had proved a positive good in the northern and middle states. Philadelphia Friends reminded them, in reply, that the antislavery cause should be decided only on the grounds of righteousness. To introduce temporal concerns or more narrow considerations of material interest was to honor the dubious moral standards of slaveholders and their allies. But Friends in England, after more than a year of canvassing, knew that a campaign based on religious principle would never make much progress with the public or Parliament, as Granville Sharp might have told them if they had asked. While London Friends watched the mails waiting for advice from Philadelphia, they struggled with how best to proceed. The standing committee of the Meeting for Sufferings met just twice in the fourteen months between October 1785 and February 1787. And attendance at those meetings was low.[53]

52. Eugene Charlton Black, *The Association: British Extraparliamentary Political Organization, 1769–1793* (Cambridge, Mass., 1963), 112–115; Minutes of the Society for Constitutional Information, Aug. 15, 22, 1783, June 4, 11, 1784, fols. 24, 25, 44, 74, Treasury Solicitor's Series 11/961, PRO; LMS to PMS, Jan. 28, 1785, MS Letters Which Passed betwixt the Meeting for Sufferings in London, and the Meeting for Sufferings in Philadelphia, I, fol. 232; Phillips to James Pemberton, June 15, 1784, Pemberton Papers, XLI, fol. 150.

53. Diary of Elihu Robinson, June 13, 1785, MS box R3/2, LSF; London Meeting for Sufferings to Philadelphia Meeting for Sufferings, Dec. 2, 1785, Nov. 3, 1786, and Philadelphia Meeting for Sufferings to London Meeting for Sufferings, May 18, 1786, all in MS

The problem with Quaker efforts was not so much that they were lobbying the wrong people but that they were lobbying the right people unsuccessfully, and perhaps in the wrong way. The distinctive qualities that helped make Friends pioneers in the antislavery movement—their tradition of principled witness, their separation from church and state, their marginal place in British society—handicapped their campaign. Their distance from polite society at once insulated them from the values and biases that facilitated the toleration of slavery and isolated them from those they hoped to mobilize. The "take-off" of Quaker abolitionism ultimately depended on the cooperation of allies outside the Society of Friends.

Thomas Clarkson's 1807 history of the abolition move-   [IV]
ment details the key events that transformed the Quaker campaign into a national movement. It has long served as the basic source for understanding the crucial shifts in 1786 and 1787 that led to the formation of the Society for Effecting the Abolition of the Slave Trade. For these critical months, the archival record is exceptionally thin otherwise. Without Clarkson's account, scholars now would know almost nothing about how the Society for Effecting the Abolition of the Slave Trade took shape. But Clarkson's *History* is a problematic source. He prepared the text in the early nineteenth century from his own memory and from records in his possession. It is, therefore, at once a history and a memoir. As a major figure in the events he described, he found it necessary to write about himself, sometimes at length, and this emphasis drew unfavorable commentary at the time.[54] Clarkson's firsthand knowledge of people and events

---

Letters Which Passed betwixt the Meeting for Sufferings in London, and the Meeting for Sufferings in Philadelphia, I, fols. 245–246, 255–261, 262; MiMSCST, Aug. 11, 14, 1786, fols. 30–31.

54. The Moravian leader Christian Ignatius Latrobe noted in 1815 that Clarkson had been "charged with egotism by many reviewers." "No one can read his work," he added, "without the impression left upon his mind, that the author takes great merit to himself, and almost makes himself out to be the main spring and chief instrument in bringing about that great event." "He makes a kind of apology for this" in the text, Latrobe acknowledged, but this "appeared to me pretty lame." Christian Ignatius Latrobe, *Letters to My Children . . . Containing a Memorial of Some Occurrences in My Past Life . . .* (London, 1851), 13.

gives the book unusual authority. As a result, some historians have been tempted to render these decisive months in Clarkson's terms, as the consequence of his awakening to the problem of slavery and his "fateful" decision, in the fall of 1786, to devote his life to abolishing the slave trade. Clarkson's *History* is in part a deeply personal statement, a confession he wrote to describe how, through providence, he discovered his life's mission. This tendency in his work makes it easy to cast Clarkson as an uncaused cause who arrived heroically on stage to lead the abolition campaign when the time was ripe. Those unhappy with this mode of explanation, with its stress on the providential intervention of an individual actor, often have preferred to minimize or even ignore Clarkson rather than retell the history of these years from his perspective.

But neither uncritical repetition nor abrupt dismissal will do if we are to understand what Clarkson did, what he was up to, or, more broadly, how organized abolitionism finally crystallized in Britain in 1787. Thomas Clarkson did matter. He did have a decisive impact on the established Quaker campaign. He enlarged its ambitions and improved its prospects by serving as a liaison between London Friends and the Teston Evangelicals. If not for Clarkson, the separate Quaker and Evangelical antislavery initiatives easily could have remained distinct in approach and limited in consequence. In 1786, with all the reform schemes that had been proposed and discussed, the prospect for a sustained political movement against the slave trade or colonial slavery still looked remote. Nonetheless, Clarkson did make too much of himself in his *History*. The self-aggrandizing chapters in the narrative must be read with care. But Clarkson still must be taken seriously, indeed almost as seriously as he took himself. For therein lies a crucial clue to the source of his peculiar commitment and the nature of his influence. Clarkson brought special qualities to the Quaker abolitionist movement in 1786, qualities it needed and lacked. He embodied and encouraged a style of self-consciousness essential to the campaign's eventual success.

In crucial respects, Thomas Clarkson differed little from the opponents of slavery who preceded him. He first took an interest in the Atlantic slave system because of an unexpected and unsettling exposure to its horrors. Granville Sharp began to fight slaveholding in England during the 1760s after an absentee slaveholder sued him for defending the rights of liberated Africans residing on English soil. James Ramsay started to muse on the injustice of West Indian slavery after experiencing the arrogance of sugar planters firsthand. For Clarkson, the defining encounter came through vicarious experience, from studying and musing carefully on the work of Anthony Benezet in 1785, which the London Meeting for Sufferings had republished just months before. Cambridge vice-chancellor Peter Peckard invited undergraduates competing for a university essay prize in 1785 to consider, "Is it right to make slaves of others against their will?" In preparing an answer, Clarkson later recalled, Benezet's *Historical Account of Guinea* provided "almost all I wanted." Like other highly sensitive men and women in Britain, he found the facts outrageous once he understood them. Both brooding and idealistic, Clarkson found it difficult, like Granville Sharp, to accept a compromise on "what should be" for the sake of "how things were." Impetuous and zealous, Clarkson was quick to act and slow to quit. Practical considerations tended not to deter him. Like James Ramsay, he tackled his pursuits with a dogged thoroughness. His compulsive single-mindedness became legendary. If Benezet irritated other Friends because he was "always saying the same thing," Clarkson to Samuel Taylor Coleridge was a kind of "moral steam-engine," "the Giant with one idea."[55]

His personality and personal experience helped Clarkson become an opponent of slavery, but the historical moment and his social position allowed him to become an abolitionist. A campaign against the Atlantic slave trade had become easier to contemplate by 1785, the year he wrote his Cambridge thesis. Unlike Benezet, Sharp, or Ramsay, Clarkson did not have to start from the beginning. He could build on the progress that others had made, using their knowledge, experience, and networks. Clarkson had not suffered, at this point, through long years of frustration and defeat, and

55. Thomas Clarkson, *The History of the Rise, Progress, and Accomplishment of the Abolition of the African Slave-Trade by the British Parliament*, 2 vols. (London, 1808), I, 205–209. Coleridge cited in Ellen Wilson, *Thomas Clarkson: A Biography* (New York, 1990), 1. A compelling portrait of Clarkson's personality and character appears in J. R. Oldfield, *Popular Politics and British Antislavery: The Mobilisation of Public Opinion against the Slave Trade, 1787–1807* (Manchester, Eng., 1995), 70–91. Peckard's choice of topics almost certainly reflected one consequence of his conversations with John Hinchliffe, bishop of Peterborough, a fellow of Cambridge University and erstwhile proponent of Granville Sharp's "Spanish Regulations." In a sermon of 1784 Peckard had condemned colonial slavery and declared the British slave trade "the disgrace of our country." See my discussion on pp. 194–195, above.

so it was easier for him to proceed with optimism. Nearly two decades of conflict with the slaving interest had left the idealistic Granville Sharp discouraged, if not cynical. Coming to the subject in 1785, Clarkson, by contrast, was more inclined to see opportunity. Assisting this more hopeful outlook was a marked advantage in place and access. Clarkson would remain aware that he lacked a noble upbringing, that he possessed neither the power nor the wealth to attain a position among the heads of state. Still, he was better placed and better prepared to lead and influence others. As an ordained clergyman in the Church of England, he escaped the stigma that marginalized abolitionists within the Society of Friends. A native of East Anglia, he never suffered the ostracism that tended to restrict the ambitions of the much older Scot and returned West Indian James Ramsay, who, despite his connections to the Teston clan, seems never to have been comfortable among "the great." Clarkson, the son of a schoolteacher, could struggle with his self-esteem when in the company of the powerful. But because of his schooling among the elite and preparation for the ministry, he had enough confidence to seek out aristocratic patrons and sufficient interpersonal skills to attain a genuine hearing.[56] Clarkson, in short, benefited from opportunities and personal resources that previous campaigners had lacked.

Yet what most distinguished Clarkson was the character of his commitment. Others in Britain had cared and did care a great deal about the sins of slaving, but no one else—not Sharp, not Ramsay, not Wilberforce—gave their lives to the antislavery cause in the way Clarkson did. For the others, antislavery represented one of many concerns. Thomas Clarkson, by contrast, made antislavery causes his purpose in life. That inclination, to focus on one task, originated in the peculiar quirks of his personality. But his

56. On Clarkson's exchange with potential patrons in 1786, see Clarkson, *History of the Rise, Progress, and Accomplishment of the Abolition of the African Slave-Trade,* I, 218–222, 226, 235–236. For reasons that have bedeviled biographers, Clarkson proved exceptionally shy in 1786 and 1787 when in the company of William Wilberforce, a fact that Wilberforce himself noted in 1788: "Clarkson is a very modest man, and you must encourage him and pat him on the Head or he will never venture and come near you, or speak his mind with the requisite freedom." Wilberforce to William Wyndham Grenville, Nov. 23, 1788, fol. 141, BM Add. MSS 69038. For Clarkson's youth, see Wilson, *Thomas Clarkson,* 4–9.

preoccupation with abolitionism, as opposed to some other cause, became possible because of the profound change in what the Atlantic slave system had come to mean in the British Isles during and after the American Revolution. By the 1780s, for the first time, antislavery looked like the kind of cause that deserved a personal commitment. To condemn slavery in principle and colonial institutions in practice had become by the 1780s the mark of an enlightened, humane Christian. Since the midcentury, novelists like Sarah Scott and Laurence Sterne had presented the man and woman of feeling, with their characteristic sympathy for the African, as the exemplar of moral virtue. It required only a small step to see that active opposition to slavery could be used as a way to demonstrate individual moral worth, once such aims lost their association with hopeless idealism. Robert Robertson had anticipated this possibility in the 1730s when he referred to a campaign against the slave trade as "a path to true glory."[57] Yet it took almost a half century for that possibility to be fully grasped. Until the 1770s, those who expressed concern for the enslaved concentrated almost exclusively on making colonial slavery more Christian. The American patriots seeking liberation from parliamentary sovereignty were the first to exploit the ennobling power of antislavery gestures. That example helped moralists and politicians in Britain during the Revolutionary era recognize the moral capital to be gained, more generally, from attending to the ethics of empire, as the impeachment of East India Company governor Warren Hastings showed. By the time Thomas Clarkson came of age, the moral character of overseas enterprise had become a regular subject of public concern. Clarkson could choose abolitionism in the 1780s because imperial reform had become, more generally, a legitimate subject for official and public inquiry.

The American Revolution, moreover, had helped popularize a new kind of heroism. To some idealistic young men, it seemed that valor might be proved through dramatic displays of service to injured humanity, as well as through courage on the battlefield. The elevated spirit of the Revolutionary movement, its invocation of universal principles, its preoccupation with virtue and honor, its professed interest in the good of humankind, inspired ambitious youths around the Atlantic world to seek out comparable fields

57. Markman Ellis, *The Politics of Sensibility: Race, Gender, and Commerce in the Sentimental Novel* (Cambridge, 1996), 49–128; [Robert Robertson], *A Letter to the Right Reverend the Lord Bishop of London* (London, 1730), 70.

of heroic action. The Revolutionary and post-Revolutionary era is replete with young men looking to win public regard through spectacular feats of charity to the enslaved. John Laurens of South Carolina wanted desperately to lead a regiment of liberated black soldiers into battle in the cause of American independence in part because he thought it would bring him fame, regard, and esteem. At the end of the American war, looking for further ways to prove his merit, the marquis de Lafayette tried to establish a colony for liberated slaves in Central America. In founding a new colony in Sierra Leone, Henry Smeathman imagined himself as the founder of nations, as a Romulus or a Penn, he wrote. He predicted that in the long term the project would prove more consequential than American independence. The grand drama of revolutionary struggle captivated these aspiring liberators. William Thornton wanted to establish a colony in Africa for freed slaves from the Americas primarily because he felt guilty about the wealth his family earned from their sugar estates in Tortola. Nonetheless, he envisioned his proposed colony, and by extension himself, as a potential savior to humanity. He wanted nothing less than to found a second independent republic in a world of European empires.[58] Each of these projects, significantly, was imagined as a solitary mission rather than as a cooperative enterprise. The exponents seemed as interested in how they would

58. Gregory D. Massey, "The Limits of Antislavery Thought in the Revolutionary South: John Laurens and Henry Laurens," *Journal of Southern History*, LXIII (1997), 501, 509–518; Liliane Willens, "Lafayette's Emancipation Experiment in French Guiana, 1786–1792," *Studies on Voltaire and the Eighteenth Century*, CCXLII (1986), 345–362; Henry Smeathman to John Coakley Lettsom, July 16, 1784, in Thomas Pettigrew, ed., *Memoirs of the Life and Writings of J. C. Lettsom*, 3 vols. (London, 1817), III, 275–276; "Substance of Two Letters Addressed to Dr. Knowles of London on the Productions and Colonization of Africa," [n.d., 1783], in C. B. Wadstrom, *An Essay on Colonization, Particularly to the Western Coast of Africa* . . . (London, 1794), 198; William Thornton to Lettsom, Nov. 18, 1786, and "General Outlines of a Settlement on the Tooth or Ivory Coast of Africa," 1786, both in C. M. Harris, ed., *The Papers of William Thornton*, I, *1781–1802* (Charlottesville, Va., 1995), 30–34, 38–41. Once again, the similarity in age would seem important. With the exception of Smeathman, each of these antislavery romantics came of age during the American Revolution: Laurens was born in 1754; Lafayette was born in 1757; Thornton, Pitt, and Wilberforce were born in 1759; and Thomas Clarkson was born in 1760.

be remembered as in the potential of their experiments to work. A self-aggrandizing hubris was characteristic. "I know of no other person," Thornton wrote of himself, "who will make the same sacrifice of family, friends, fortune, and an expensive education, with the most precious years in the prime of life, to live with the rejected and despised part of mankind, and in an unhealthy climate." He was "willing to attempt," he boasted, "what I know many would startle at."[59]

Thomas Clarkson had a more sober and practical bent than men like Laurens, Smeathman, and Thornton. But, like them, he had a profound commitment to finding proof of his own genius. In his *History* Clarkson freely confessed to the ambitions that drove him as a student and shaped his choices. He cherished his reputation at Cambridge for superior scholarship and took great pride, he recalled, in winning first prize for the best Latin dissertation in 1784. He entered a similar competition the next year (on the subject of slavery) with the hope of repeating his previous success. So the intense way he attacked the question of slavery at first had as much to do with a will to win, with a desire to stand out, as with a profound concern for humanity. When questioned by Quakers in 1786, Clarkson admitted that he had written, initially, in hopes of "obtaining literary honour," because he had "the wish of being distinguished." This preoccupation with attaining the regard of others he later described, in a telling revelation, as an albatross. It nearly prevented him, he remembered, from pledging his life to abolition. In choosing to make antislavery a career, he recalled anticipating several obstacles: it would be hard to find information on the slave trade, locate powerful sympathizers, and attract the funds necessary to keep an antislavery campaign afloat. But he had worried most, he remembered, about the likely consequences for his career, about surrendering opportunities for preferment and distinction within the Church of England in pursuit of what looked to be a quixotic goal. He had worried that by becoming an abolitionist he would have to sacrifice his ambitions for himself.[60]

59. Thornton to Lettsom, May 20, 1787, in Harris, ed., *The Papers of William Thornton,* I, 56, 57.

60. Clarkson, *History of the Rise, Progress, and Accomplishment of the Abolition of the African Slave-Trade,* I, 205–206, 214, 227–229.

FIGURE 8. Thomas Clarkson. By Carl Frederik von Breda. 1788.
Courtesy, National Portrait Gallery, London

In 1807 Clarkson chose to think of the commitment he made twenty-one years before as a surrender to God's will, as the fulfillment of divine providence. The writings of Anthony Benezet, he decided, had opened to him his true purpose in life. But, in truth, Clarkson seems less to have surrendered his ambitions than discovered a new outlet for their expression. Rather than achieving renown in a conventional manner, he found a way to distinguish himself through his courageous devotion to the abolition of the slave trade. The pleasure that he derived from demonstrating his moral commitment helped him select a far less conventional path than advancement in the church could provide. Thomas Clarkson did care about the enslaved. His humanitarianism was genuine. But a man that had his need for acclaim could never have given his life to a particular mission unless, in a profound sense, it also enabled him to display who he thought he was and to appear to others how he wished to seem. Like Laurens, Thornton, Smeathman, Lafayette, and even Wilberforce, the young Clarkson decided that antislavery activism offered a chance for distinction, a sublime sense of purpose. Grand in ambition, visionary in aim, demanding in execution, and nearly impossible to achieve, yet principled in purpose, altruistic in spirit, and a pleasure to contemplate—what could be more heroic than a life devoted to the abolition of the slave trade and an end to slavery?

This romantic sense of self set Clarkson apart from his predecessors, who cared about the slave trade and slavery but not at all about how opposition to slavery reflected on themselves. Like most Quakers, Anthony Benezet showed little interest in self-promotion. Unprepossessing and lacking in charisma, he had a greater interest in charity than in burnishing his reputation. Granville Sharp seems to have gone out of his way to avoid the limelight. Eccentric and erratic, he often shunned opportunities for public leadership. The women of Barham Court—Elizabeth Bouverie and Margaret Middleton—hid their substantial influence on the emergence of Evangelical antislavery, preferring to honor and, indeed, reify the social codes that established politics as "men's work" and the promotion of religion as the special province of women. Because he cared more than Clarkson about his position within the Church of England, Bishop of Chester Beilby Porteus approached slave trade abolition cagily. Although an opponent of the slave trade, he took few political risks and would not identify himself overtly with the antislavery cause. More than most, James Ramsay found an identity in his opposition to slavery, particularly in his courageous battles with the West Indian interest after 1784. But Ramsay tended to regard himself as a martyr instead of a hero, a perhaps predictable choice for a man who spent much of his career disaffected and besieged. Among Clarkson's peers, only William Wilberforce possessed an equally romantic sense of self. Wilberforce, significantly, committed himself to slave trade abolition shortly after William Pitt warned him that someone else would lead the way and earn the credit unless he acted soon. Yet Wilberforce, the Evangelical, had two missions, the promotion of Christianity and slave trade abolition. The second constituted one aspect of the first. Clarkson, by contrast, seems to have had a single purpose in mind. He imagined himself as the redeemer of African liberty.

If Thomas Clarkson had thought less of himself, if he had less confidence in his abilities, if he had been unable to imagine himself leading a national crusade, he might never have pledged his life to abolitionism. Students of Anglo-American antislavery movements have become familiar with the dark side of charitable causes, with the ways that high ideals could degenerate into self-serving behavior or serve as a mask for self-interest. But they have tended to miss the ironic ways that self-aggrandizing impulses, in some instances, can facilitate the emergence of idealistic behavior.[61] The Quaker antislavery campaign of the mid-1780s stalled not only because Quakers lacked political standing. It had slowed almost to a halt because the Quaker circulars had failed to capture the public imagination, because their preference for conscientious witness and humble moral appeals could foster a moral consensus but not sustained fervor or collective action. When operating on their own, Friends made no attempt to depict what a public campaign against slavery might look like to observers or feel like to participants. They neither wrote nor thought about the ways an antislavery movement could commence a national renewal or facilitate collective redemption. And this inability to describe slave trade abolition in elevated terms was the direct result of an inability to imagine themselves in a heroic role, to think of themselves as conquering agents of change. Friends were willing to lobby politicians and other men with political influence. They anonymously slipped antislavery notices into the London and provincial

61. Here I have benefited from the work of sociologist Colin Campbell, especially *The Romantic Ethic and the Spirit of Modern Consumerism* (Oxford, 1987), 207–216.

press. As a group and as individuals, though, they lacked that peculiar blend of egotism and idealism characteristic of those who inspire and lead.

The new abolition society, it is true, bore strong traces of its Quaker origins. The Society for Effecting the Abolition of the Slave Trade inherited the unspent funds donated to the Quaker "Slave Association" as well as five of its key members. At its inception, two-thirds of the governing committee were members of the Society of Friends.[62] Moreover, in the ordinary business of the society, Quakers did almost all of the work. Thomas Clarkson spent the first months of the campaign of 1787 away from London gathering evidence. Granville Sharp served as the chair of the abolition society but rarely attended. At the first twenty-four meetings of the Society for Effecting the Abolition of the Slave Trade, during the first seven months of its labors, Quakers always stood in the majority.[63] When preparing for the campaign in the provinces, the abolition society relied heavily on Quaker networks. Ninety percent of the men invited to serve as corresponding agents of the Society for Effecting the Abolition of the Slave Trade belonged to the Society of Friends. More than a third had served in a similar capacity for the Meeting for Sufferings just three years before.[64] Pre-

62. Dillwyn, Harrison, Hoare, Lloyd, and Woods continued on from the "Slave Association." They were joined by Quakers John Barton, Joseph Hooper, and James Phillips, as well as Clarkson, Sharp, Richard Phillips, and Philip Sansom. I have calculated the assets of the abolition society from the running list of donations reported by Hoare (the treasurer) in the committee minute books. For the first list of subscribers, see Society for Effecting the Abolition of the Slave Trade, "At a Meeting for the Purpose of Taking the Slave Trade into Consideration . . ." (list of subscribers with accompanying circular) (London, 1787), LSF. This list was published between July 5 and 17. Fair Minute Books of the Society for Effecting the Abolition of the Slave Trade (MiAbS), July 5, 17, 1787, I, fols. 7–8, BM Add. MSS 21254.

63. The governing committee of the abolition society acquired greater balance after the addition of James Martin, M.P., William Morton Pitt, M.P., John Vickris Taylor, and Josiah Wedgwood in December 1787. Society for Effecting the Abolition of the Slave Trade, "Encouraged by the Success Which Has Attended the Publication of Sundry Tracts against Slavery . . ." (with list of subscribers, December 1787), Antislavery Tracts, box 291, LSF.

64. Compare MiAbS, July 17, 1787, I, fols. 9–11, with MiMSCST, Mar. 30, 1784, fols. 17–24.

dictably, provincial support emerged first where Friends possessed an unusual degree of local influence. The Gurneys of Norwich made the county of Norfolk an early center of abolitionist enthusiasm. The Lloyd family achieved similar results in the manufacturing town of Birmingham.[65] Friends not only administered the Society for Effecting the Abolition of the Slave Trade. They also kept it solvent. In the first two months of the campaign, approximately 60 percent of the subscribers belonged to the Society of Friends. More than a year later, Quakers still represented no less than a quarter of the contributors and had donated no less than a fifth of the money raised.[66] In the first year of the movement, and after, Friends did the mundane labor that made abolitionism work.

If Quakers provided the infrastructure, though, the movement derived its character from the elevated aspirations of its originator and its political sponsor, from Thomas Clarkson and William Wilberforce. They helped give the campaign a grandeur it previously had lacked. From the beginning, they intended to encourage the expression of the national will, both to apply pressure to Parliament and to convert the nation to the abolitionist cause. Privately, Clarkson complained of the Quakers' "caution" and "prudence" in the first months after the formation of the London committee. Because the Quakers had been concerned only with legislation, they had focused primarily on influencing "those who count" and reshaping public

65. Norfolk, not Manchester, as Seymour Drescher has proposed, was the first district outside London to contribute substantially to the antislavery cause. As of September 4, 1787, Norfolk subscribers (more than half of whom were Quakers) represented a fifth of all subscribers to the abolition society and made up 60 percent of all provincial donors. Subscribers connected with the wealthy Gurney family included Bartlett Gurney, Joseph Gurney, John Gurney, Thomas Bland, Samuel Alexander, Hannah Gurney, Abel Chapman, and Richard Gurney. Society for Effecting the Abolition of the Slave Trade, "List of Subscribers Reported as of September 11, 1787," J. W. Johnson Collection of Printed Ephemera, "Slavery," Bodleian Library, Oxford University. Few if any of the nineteen Norfolk subscribers that enlisted after 1787 appear to have been members of the Society of Friends. On Birmingham, see MiAbS, Sept. 18, Oct. 30, 1787, fols. 15, 22; *Aris' Birmingham Gazette*, Jan. 7, 1788; and Lloyd, *The Quaker Lloyds in the Industrial Revolution*, 201.

66. Compare the subscription list printed in July 1787 with Society for Effecting the Abolition of the Slave Trade, *A List of the Society Instituted in 1787 for Effecting the Abolition of the Slave Trade . . . 12 August 1788* (London, 1788).

opinion. Clarkson and the Teston clan wanted to generate a public campaign, so they looked for ways to promote not only public opinion but also public involvement.[67] Wilberforce had participated actively in the Yorkshire Association and, to a degree, owed his seat in Parliament to the influence of Christopher Wyvill's political machine. From the outset of its labors, and perhaps on the advice of Wilberforce, the London committee encouraged town and county meetings across Britain to send antislavery petitions to Parliament. Those who had hoped that the loss of the American colonies would result in the remodeling of the British constitution participated in large numbers. If Parliament could not be reformed, then perhaps the empire could. The leaders of the Yorkshire Association between 1780 and 1784 resurfaced in 1787 and 1788 as subscribers to the abolition society.[68] Early donors included several founders of the Society for Constitutional Information, including Thomas Day and Richard Price. Fourteen members of Parliament gave money to the abolition society during its first year. All fourteen in 1783 or in 1785 had cast votes in favor of

67. Hannah More to Lady Middleton, Sept. 10, 1787, in Georgina Chatterton, ed., *Memorials Personal and Historical of Admiral Lord Gambier . . .* , 2d ed., 2 vols. (London, 1861), I, 169. "Sorry am I to be obliged, by truth, to unsay the good I have been saying of the Quakers," More wrote to Middleton. "I have a natural predilection for them, and having been accustomed to see some of them whenever I saw Mr. Clarkson, I believed, because I wished that they were warm promoters of the great cause he has in hand. But when I came to talk with him alone, I had the mortification to find that nothing could be more lukewarm, cautious, and worldly-wise than they are. *Talking* humanely, perhaps, but when anything is to be *done,* or any assistance given, they are as cold and prudent as the most discreet and money-loving churchman. Clarkson desires us to canvass for him from the Member of Parliament down to the common seaman; he wishes to turn the tide of public affection in favour of this slave business." This was, to be sure, too bleak a picture of Quaker commitments. But it does reveal the tensions in strategy and style between the Society of Friends and the more brash and ambitious Clarkson. It is significant that More refers here to the "slave business" as Clarkson's cause. In the course of his research in Liverpool and Bristol in the summer of 1787, Clarkson obtained pledges to petition from residents of Bridgewater, Monmouth, Bristol, Gloucester, Worcester, Shrewsbury, and Chester. MiAbS, Oct. 16, 1787, I, fols. 16–17.

68. Those subscribers included Christopher Wyvill, Richard Monckton Arundel (Viscount Galway), the Rev. William Mason, Gamaliel Lloyd, John Fountayne (the dean of York), Samuel Shore, the Rev. James Wilkinson, and Samuel Tooker.

parliamentary reform, at a time when the supporters of such measures remained in a substantial minority.[69]

Abolitionism seems to have had special appeal to groups just learning to find a voice in public affairs. The General Chamber of Manufacturers (GCM) represented midland and northern industrial interests in the years when William Pitt and his cabinet considered new terms of trade after the Revolutionary War. It was formed in 1785 to oppose plans to equalize trade duties with Ireland, a move the manufacturers feared would harm English industrialists. The GCM provided provincial magnates with a platform from which to pursue their political interests. Its officers included Thomas Walker of Manchester, Samuel Garbett of Birmingham, John Wilkinson of Sheffield, and Josiah Wedgwood of Staffordshire.[70] These leaders of the manufacturing interest would become leaders of provincial abolitionism in 1787. The campaign developed rapidly along the lines of communication established by the commercial and industrial lobbies during the three years before. In 1785 Quaker printer James Phillips had represented the book-sellers in the General Chamber of Manufacturers. In the summer of 1787, on behalf of the Society for Effecting the Abolition of the Slave Trade, he offered to correspond with Walker of Manchester and Wedgwood of Staffordshire, since he had worked with them before. By the end of the summer, Wedgwood had agreed to serve as a member of the executive committee of the Society for Effecting the Abolition of the Slave Trade, while Walker had taken the lead in promoting the antislavery cause in Manchester. For these provincial leaders, the opportunity to win promi-

69. These fourteen were: Isaac Hawkins Browne, Baron Thomas Dimsdale, Joshua Grigsby, Paul Le Mesurier, Richard Monckton Arundel (Viscount Galway), Henry Duncombe, James Martin, William Morton Pitt, William Smith, Henry Thornton, Robert Thornton, Samuel Thornton, Samuel Whitbread, and William Wilberforce. For political biographies of these figures, see Sir Lewis Namier and John Brooke, *The History of Parliament: The House of Commons, 1754–1790,* 3 vols. (New York, 1964), II, III.

70. The best accounts of this coalition of industrial interests, organized in 1785 as the General Chamber of Manufacturers, appear in Witt Bowden, *Industrial Society in England towards the End of the Eighteenth Century,* 2d ed. (London, 1965), 181–193. See also J. M. Norris, "Samuel Garbett and the Early Development of Industrial Lobbying in Britain," *Economic History Review,* X (1958), 450–460; Vivian Eve Dietz, "Before the Age of Capital: Manufacturing Interests and the British State, 1780–1800" (Ph.D. diss., Princeton University, 1989), 124–136.

nence and esteem provided a further reason to encourage the developing movement. Thomas Walker, and the other Manchester delegates in the GCM, had drawn national attention in 1785 and 1786 by defeating a tax on cottons. They had been hailed as heroes in Manchester on their return from London. Still giddy with this experience and emboldened by their success, they flexed their muscles again in 1787 on behalf of the Society for Effecting the Abolition of the Slave Trade. In January 1788 they published a call to arms in every major newspaper in the nation, encouraging fellow citizens to act as they had, to make slave trade abolition a national cause.[71]

71. MiAbS, July 1787, I, fol. 11; Frida Knight, *The Strange Case of Thomas Walker: Ten Years in the Life of a Manchester Radical* (London, 1957), 26–34; *Merchants and Manufacturers Magazine of Trade and Commerce* (1785), I, 21; E. M. Hunt, "The North of England Agitation for the Abolition of the Slave Trade, 1780–1800" (master's thesis, University of Manchester, 1959), 72. The involvement of midland and northern commercial lobbyists in antislavery organizing seems to have been especially pronounced. John Wilkinson of Sheffield, who had given an exceptionally large donation to the General Chamber of Manufacturers in 1785, numbered among the first subscribers to the Society for Effecting the Abolition of the Slave Trade in 1787. His banking house in London— Dorset, Johnson, and Wilkinson of New Bond Street—was one of two banks that agreed in December 1787 to receive subscriptions on behalf of the society. The other belonged to Sir Herbert Mackworth, a significant investor in Welsh copper and coal mining, the lone member of Parliament to join the General Chamber of Manufacturers and a substantial donor to the Society for Effecting the Abolition of the Slave Trade. Thomas Clarkson singled Mackworth out as "particularly interested in the cause" of abolition. MiAbS, Dec. 18, 1787, fol. 23; Society for Effecting the Abolition of the Slave Trade, *A List of the Society, Instituted in 1787* . . . (London, 1787); Clarkson, *History of the Rise, Progress, and Accomplishment of the Abolition of the African Slave-Trade,* I, 236. Four of the five delegates sent to London in 1785 to fight for repeal of a new excise tax on fustians subscribed to the Manchester Abolition Committee two years later—Thomas Walker, Thomas Richardson, James Entwistle, and Samuel Rawlinson. Eight of the eleven members of the Manchester committee of fustian traders also gave to the Manchester abolition committee. Six of the eleven men who served on the Birmingham Commercial Committee—Samuel Garbett, George Humphreys, Samuel Glover, William Russell, William Turner, William Welch—subscribed to the Birmingham abolition committee. Matthew Boulton and James Watt, the owners of the largest factory in the county, contributed to the Birmingham subscription, too. Hunt, "The Anti-Slave Trade Agitation in Manchester," Lancashire and Cheshire Antiquarian Society, *Transactions,* CXXVI (1977), 52; "Minute Book of the Proceedings to Obtain the Repeal of the Act

Within six months, the House of Commons received more than one hundred petitions from across the nation in support of slave trade abolition. Petitioners in Chesterfield and Nottingham thanked the London and Manchester leaders for "the zeal, activity, and manly firmness which they have manifested in this noble cause," as the Nottingham committee expressed it. For most towns and counties, drawing up a petition represented an opportunity to join a movement already in motion. Abolitionists in Bristol thought it proper to correspond with the "other Associations in this Kingdom formed for the same purpose." Birmingham abolitionists observed "that similar petitions are already prepared and preparing." The Leeds petitioners referred to the "christian philanthropy, which hath of late diffused through these realms." Plymouth supporters "embrace[d] the opportunity of joining in a measure which breathes so laudable a spirit of humanity." A Newbury advocate argued that failure to support abolition would be an embarrassment to the town: "Shall we alone be silent, or be the last in the cause of HUMANITY?" Wilberforce took steps to ensure that Yorkshire would be well represented. "I sh'd be sorry," he wrote to Wyvill, "if our little kingdom should be backward in its endeavours to rescue our fellow creatures from misery and dishonour." As the last of the petitions filtered in, Presbyterian minister George Walker of Nottingham appealed to the pride of Yarmouth minister William Manning. "Why has not Yarmouth joined the National Voice in the cause of human liberty? It will succeed, and nothing in my whole experience has given me more reason to think well of my country. It is not too late for you to come in for your share of the honour."[72]

Imposing Duty on Bleached Cotton Goods," MS 336.27 M9, Manchester Central Reference Library; G. Henry Wright, *Chronicles of the Birmingham Chamber of Commerce, A.D. 1813–1913, and of the Birmingham Commercial Society, A.D. 1783–1812* (Birmingham, Eng., 1913), 14. The Society for Effecting the Abolition of the Slave Trade in 1787 and 1788 was not dominated by a coalition of capitalist interests, as Eric Williams proposed in 1944. At the same time, it is clear that several prominent lobbyists for the manufacturing interest exercised leadership roles in the nascent campaign in the provinces. This seems to have followed more from interregional networks of communication than careful assessments of an opportunity for profit. Not one of these petitioners or subscribers made an economic case for abolition, which they perhaps had good reason to offer, if they had one. At the very least, they did not think slave trade abolition would harm their specific economic interests.

72. *St. James Chronicle*, Feb. 12–14, 1788; *Morning Chronicle*, Feb. 26, 1788; *Bir-*

As George Walker understood, and as certain abolitionists had hoped, the public campaign against the slave trade boosted collective dignity and self-esteem. The Edinburgh presbytery petitioned because they wished "to see their country distinguished by the righteousness which exalteth a nation." Wilberforce expected that it would "retrieve our national character from the foulest dishonour." Abolitionism allowed the British to reestablish their devotion to liberty, which had been called into question by American independence, without embracing the radicalism of the American rebels. The Reverend Robert Boucher Nickolls hoped abolition would show the American states "that we are no less friendly to liberty than they." Indeed, when Britons learned in 1788 that the Constitutional Convention at Philadelphia had decided to allow the slave trade to continue until 1807, they recognized an opportunity to distinguish themselves. "To the first nation in the scale of liberty," wrote the editors of the *General Evening Post,* "the rest have a right to look for such an example." Abolitionism became an occasion for the expression of patriotism. William Cowper knew what he was doing in 1788 when he set his poem "The Negro's Complaint" to the tune of "Admiral Hosier's Ghost," the patriot ballad originally composed in 1739 and 1740 during the war with Spain. Abolition, the *Morning Chronicle* was pleased to report, "like the celestial fire, appears to electrify every worthy spirit amongst all bodies and societies of people." In the aftermath of the American war, this coming together was regarded as salutary for Britain as well as for the antislavery cause. A Manchester propagandist hoped that "extending Emancipation to other Parts of the Empire . . . would counterbalance Years of Military disgrace, and civil Dissension."[73]

---

mingham Gazette, Jan. 28, 1788; *Leeds Intelligencer,* Mar. 4, 1788; *General Evening Post,* Apr. 8–10, 1788; *Reading Mercury and Oxford Gazetteer,* Mar. 24, 1788; Wilberforce to Christopher Wyvill, Jan. 25, 1788, Wilberforce Add. MSS D. 56, fols. 14–15, Bodleian Library; George Walker to William Manning, June 6, 1788, Thompson-Clarkson Illustrations, II, fol. 99.

73. *Public Advertiser,* Mar. 20, 1788; Wilberforce to Wyvill, Jan. 25, 1788, Wilberforce Add. MSS D. 56, fol. 15; Robert Boucher Nickolls, *A Letter to the Treasurer of the Society Instituted for the Purpose of Effecting the Abolition of the Slave Trade* (London, 1787); *General Evening Post,* Jan. 22–24, 1788; James King and Charles Ryskamp, eds., *The Letters and Prose Writings of William Cowper,* 5 vols. (Oxford, 1979–1986), III, 127n; *Morning Chronicle,* Feb. 14, 1788; *Manchester Mercury,* Oct. 9, 1787.

In material terms, little had changed in 1788. The slave trade continued to expand and profit merchants in London, Liverpool, and Bristol. Plantations owners in the British Caribbean continued to purchase and work slaves to produce the staple crops that British men and women consumed. And the imperial economy, more generally, remained dependent on the productivity of the slave system and its capacity to supply markets and revenue. Yet the stance of the British public toward a campaign against these practices had changed entirely. Long unconcerned with the Atlantic slave trade or overseas slavery, the nation suddenly had turned against the institutions that had served it well. The men and women who gave life to this movement originated the campaign in the process of pursuing a variety of ends, to cleanse their society of sin and corruption, to renew its power and dignity, or to prove themselves holy or worthy or brave. The enthusiastic public response to their campaign, however, may be more easily explained. To a people that wished to think of themselves as Christian, moral, and free, the abolitionists presented an opportunity to express their reverence for "liberty, justice, and humanity," and at little cost to themselves. Who besides those with a personal stake in the slave system could object to that?

Moral Capital

How important, therefore, was the American Revolution? In the end, what difference did American independence make? Let us suppose that this history had been slightly different, that instead of war in 1775 and independence by 1783, there had been an uneasy peace that, at least temporarily, forestalled the secession of the thirteen North American colonies from the British Empire. Perhaps if Parliament had responded differently to the troubles of the East India Company, for example, perhaps if the government of Lord North had decided against the Tea Act, it might have been possible in 1773 and after to postpone the march to war. What, then, would have been the consequences for antislavery impulses within the British Isles? No answer, of course, can be more than informed guess-work. Speculating about futures that did not happen necessarily places us on shaky ground. In truth, the only reliable answer to such a question is that we do not and cannot know. And yet the thought experiment may be worthwhile, less because it helps "prove" the suggestions in this book (which it cannot) than because it may help clarify, in a rather different way, certain lines of historical development that I have emphasized throughout this book.[1] It may help make explicit certain counterfactual claims that have remained only implicit thus far. For, in fact, any attempt to explain how one set of historical events and circumstances influences another implies a counterfactual; it supposes that an agent of change really did matter. If, for example, we are to assign the American Revolution an important place in the making of British abolitionism, then we must also accept, at least implicitly, that the history of antislavery in Britain would have been very different without the American Revolution. The interesting questions, therefore, are how different, and in what ways?

---

1. For a similar, but more elaborate, imagining of an alternative future for slavery without the American Revolution that starts from a very different premise—British victory in the American War of Independence—see David Brion Davis, "American Slavery and the American Revolution," in Ira Berlin and Ronald Hoffman, eds., *Slavery and Freedom in the Age of the American Revolution* (Charlottesville, Va., 1983), 262–280.

Antislavery opinion, as we have seen, had numerous sources, the great majority of which had nothing to do with American resistance or independence. Men and women disliked slavery during the eighteenth century for any number of reasons. The enslaved, of course, resented their enslavement because, among other reasons, it destroyed lives, mangled bodies, uprooted communities, ruptured families, and degraded its victims. Free men and women of African descent often identified with the sufferings of those in bondage. They worried as well about the fragility of their own claims to freedom. A small number of British men and women in the colonies and in the British Isles, moreover, developed sympathy for individual slaves. Rather more learned to feel pity for unjustly enslaved nobility, such as the fictional Oroonoko. There were a few on both sides of the Atlantic who expressed concerns about the specific conditions in which enslaved peoples lived and worked. Some British men and women detested the very principle of slavery in the abstract and found it difficult to accept its institutionalization in the colonies. The slave system, it seemed, failed to acknowledge the humanity of Africans or their sanctity as fellow creatures, as children of God. Slavery, moreover, inhibited the spread of Christianity. It discouraged or prevented Africans from acknowledging Christ and living as Christians. It promoted sin among the free. Slavery gave encouragement to pride and greed. It fostered laziness and debauchery. Some disliked slavery because it led to luxury or because it turned labor into a commodity. And some hated slavery because it provided the basis for the social power and political power of the planter class, a nouveau riche that threatened to reorder traditional markers of social status and sidestep the established routes to political power. In a more formal sense, slavery seemed to compromise the rule of law. It made unrestrained violence a common feature of colonial life. Opponents of slavery feared the prospect of insurrection. They worried about the impact of slavery on the social order. They noted the tensions between the ideology of British liberty and the realities of colonial slavery.

Those who disliked slavery could register their distaste in any number of ways. They could protest individually or collectively by declaring their disapproval. This could take place in a variety of forms, through essays, poetry, and novels, on the stage, in scientific treatises, philosophical literature, or travel narratives. They could demonstrate their opposition through their own choices by refusing to hold slaves, purchase slaves, or sell slaves, or by refusing to have a stake in the slave system itself. More radically, they could distance themselves from the slave system by establishing communities or jurisdictions in which slave traders, slaveholders, and the enslaved themselves would not be welcome. Some opponents of slavery in the eighteenth century elected to alleviate particular instances of suffering through charitable gifts, gestures of concern and respect, attempts to educate, convert, or elevate, through decisions to manumit. Some even devised more systematic programs for Christian conversion, amelioration, colonization, abolition, or emancipation. Several shifted from one strategy to another over the course of their lives. A few pursued a variety of objectives at once. Before the era of the American Revolution, however, no one had attempted to impose antislavery values through parliamentary legislation. Antislavery initiatives, instead, targeted the behavior of particular individuals and communities rather than the public laws of the colonies or the state.

An organized antislavery campaign, perhaps, could have developed in the British Atlantic world without the American Revolution, even if British authorities and American elites had arranged and sustained an uneasy peace from 1773. There were indications that significant antislavery commitments already had begun to take shape in both Britain and North America. The Quaker withdrawal from slaveholding and slave trading on both sides of the Atlantic, for example, owed little to the imperial crisis. In North America, especially, Friends probably would have stood forward as opponents of the slave trade with or without American independence. Moreover, the Middle Atlantic and New England colonies probably still would have tried to restrict or prohibit the transportation of enslaved Africans to their shores during the 1770s, even if a settlement between the colonial assemblies and the British government had been reached. Granville Sharp still would have campaigned against slavery on English soil, as he did between 1767 and 1772. And Maurice Morgann still would have published his *Plan for the Abolition of Slavery* in 1772. Each of these initiatives reflected reactions to the social and political conditions prevailing in the British Empire after the Seven Years' War. They did not depend, initially, on the crisis within the empire that led to American independence. Metropolitan distaste for colonial slavery, more generally, owed little to political events. Without the American Revolution, a culture of sensibility still would have existed in the British Isles that stigmatized slaveholders and expressed sympathy for Africans. The Evangelical revival, additionally, still would have pushed slaveholders to allow conversion of the enslaved on the plantations. James Ramsay developed his plans for West Indian social and religious reform in 1768, several years before the consequences of North American resistance became clear. The American Revolution did not cause active opposition to the British slave system. Several had explored opportunities for substantive change before the conflict itself took full shape and could have continued (and probably would have continued) to do so in its absence.

What were the prospects for these initiatives without the American Revolution, if the British Empire had remained intact? Antislavery movements, of a kind, still might have developed in any number of ways. Tensions between slaveholders and Christian missionaries in the southern colonies and the Caribbean could have led by the end of the eighteenth century to a more general questioning of the slave system itself by the religious itinerants and their metropolitan supporters. In those places where slaveholders refused to permit Evangelicals to preach, a conflict between planters and missionaries might have led to a wider contest over the character of colonial slavery. An antislavery program could have emerged, as well, out of conflicts within the British Isles. The Somerset case made clear that the power of slaveholders would be vastly curtailed if not void entirely when those slaveholders brought their slaves to the metropolis. If the American Revolution had not intervened, that tension between colonial custom and metropolitan law could have become even more pronounced and controversial. Hostility toward slaveholders would only have deepened in Britain if those slaveholders had sought a fugitive slave law from Parliament or if, in time, slaves in the British colonies had more regularly found ways to seek refuge in the British Isles. If New England colonies, such as Massachusetts, for example, had followed the British precedent, as seems possible, and outlawed slaveholding in the province, free soil in the northern provinces could have set the stage for a prolonged controversy in North America over the return of fugitive slaves, a controversy that perhaps would have required mediation by the imperial government.

A third possibility involves conflicts over the slave trade. The colonial attempt to regulate the British slave trade after the Seven Years' War could have evolved into a call for its abolition. Anthony Benezet and other Quakers in North America almost certainly would have added moral arguments to the pragmatic case against the slave trade in the Middle Atlantic and New England colonies, as they did, in fact, in the years before the American Revolution. That campaign, without doubt, would have found some support in Britain among the unusually sensitive like Granville Sharp and the still small but vocal few hostile to the British slave trade and the Company of Merchants Trading to Africa. Under these circumstances, it is not hard to imagine the development of a transatlantic lobby rooted in Philadelphia, Boston, and London (and perhaps even Williamsburg) committed to reducing or even eliminating the Atlantic slave trade. An antislavery lobby of this kind probably would have attracted significant public support in both Britain and the northern colonies.

The political meaning of antislavery organizing, however, would have been very different in a united empire, without the American Revolution. The diverging interests of the northern and southern colonies in North America would have emerged, instead, within the framework of empire rather than in the context of a federal union. It is not hard to imagine the development of a British planter lobby forming in response, a lobby designed to unite the slaveholding interest from Maryland to Tobago. With this kind of conjoined opposition, the abolitionists would have faced a much more difficult task. Indeed, it is fair to ask, if, under these circumstances, many of the concerned would have made the attempt at all. Who in a position of authority, and how many in the political nation, would have elected to alienate the British planter class just years after a war for independence had been narrowly averted? This planter interest would have found it difficult to seek independence, to be sure, though one can imagine southern and Caribbean slaveholders entertaining the possibility of an alliance with a European rival, as some Saint Domingue planters did during the early years of the Haitian Revolution. Undoubtedly, southern and Caribbean propagandists would have tried to recruit northern assistance by portraying the challenge to the slaving interest as a threat to the rights of all the American colonies, both those with slaves as well as those with none. Under these circumstances, an attack on slaveholders or slave traders might have seemed needlessly provocative and dangerously divisive to those in Britain and North America sympathetic to antislavery impulses but wary of precipitating a renewed debate over taxation and representation, imperial sovereignty, and the rights of colonies. North Americans did not want to pay a modest tax on imported tea, as they would show in 1773, because they feared the creep of parliamentary authority. One may imagine the likely response if Parliament had tried to liberate their slaves.

Without the American Revolution, then, without American independence, it would have been difficult for an antislavery movement to develop as a national movement, as it did in the British Isles during the 1780s. It would have emerged, instead, as a contest between North Atlantic lobbyists contemptuous of the planter class and a (wealthy) southern and Caribbean interest intensely protective of its liberties. Within a unified empire, the abolitionists would have seemed like agents of division rather than moral patriots aiming to restore the character of the nation and the empire. Emancipation perhaps would have come sooner than 1863 to North America in a united British Empire, if the imperial state had been willing and able to enforce the principle of parliamentary supremacy. But it perhaps would have come at the cost of a bloody civil war, with an intrusive imperial government trying to impose its will on far-flung plantation societies rapidly expanding both in the Caribbean and toward the Mississippi River. Or it might have encouraged a North American version of the Great Trek. In these circumstances, abolitionism would have been associated in Britain and elsewhere with the threat of disunion and the promotion of authoritarian rule rather than with national unity, moral prestige, and the advance of liberty.

Herein lies the importance of American independence (and the American independence movement) to the evolution of antislavery sentiment in the British Isles. The American Revolution did not cause abolitionism in Britain as much as it transformed the political and cultural significance of antislavery organizing. The divide within the empire transformed the ways that antislavery opinion could be used and enhanced the reputation of antislavery initiatives. Because of the political conflict, American patriots and their British sympathizers could interpret colonial attempts to restrict slave imports as principled resistance to British tyranny, as well as a prudent adjustment to immigration laws. British defenders of imperial rule could interpret Mansfield's verdict in the Somerset case as a rejection of colonial mores, as well as a vindication of English liberty. Military officers could understand black assistance to British armed forces during the Revolutionary War as instances of allegiance from royal subjects, as well as service from colonial laborers. The American empire, itself, could be seen as a testing ground for the moral authority to rule, as well as a source of wealth and power. Its character could be seen as cause for self-scrutiny, as well as a reason for national pride. And organized opposition to the slave system could be seen as a basis for collective reform and renewal, as well as a threat to commerce and property. None of these new ways to interpret antislavery organizing had been as clearly available before the American war.

Political scientist John Kane has defined moral capital as "moral prestige—whether of an individual, organization or cause—in useful service." This emphasis that Kane places on "useful service" is critical. Moral capital —like economic, social, cultural, or intellectual capital—is a resource. It derives its worth not solely from its value but also from its utility, from those moments when "moral prestige" is mobilized "for the sake of tangible, exterior returns."[2] The concept of moral capital draws attention to the ways that moral distinction can become a source for power in the world, the ways that it facilitates and legitimates action. The ends that moral capital enables, moreover, need not be political ends. Moral capital can serve a variety of purposes—cultural, intellectual, social, emotional, or interpersonal. What matters is that moral capital, as capital, is employed in a way that sustains the moral prestige of the actor, that draws from the accumulated stock of moral credit without depleting it. For moral capital reproduces itself continually, when expended with discretion. It not only sustains and enhances the reputation of an actor or actors. A cause that has earned moral capital becomes, itself, a source of moral capital for other causes; the association with people or causes that possess moral capital becomes a strategic benefit for those in search of moral standing or moral influence. William Wilberforce and Hannah More, for example, understood that their leadership in the abolition movement would bring credit to other projects that lacked the same moral prestige. And those hoping to sanctify personal ambitions or more parochial purposes would associate themselves with the antislavery movement to give those aims legitimacy. This became especially apparent, for example, a century later. European governments and adventurers intent on seizing power in Africa at the end of the nineteenth century, most famously, would justify their partition of the continent and its subjection to imperial rule as one aspect of their war on slavery.

2. John Kane, *The Politics of Moral Capital* (Cambridge, 2001) 7.

This moral prestige, however, and the capital it produces, is hard to acquire and easy to lose, since it depends entirely on the perceptions of others. It accrues to those whose choices are not merely virtuous but appraised as virtuous by their contemporaries. It belongs to those who display "fidelity, commitment, and able action in the service of publicly valued goals."[3] The abolitionist movement had come to enjoy moral prestige by 1788 because antislavery sentiment, by then, had become uncontroversial *and*, more unusually, because antislavery organizing had come to seem worthy of esteem. If, by contrast, abolitionism had been construed primarily in negative terms—as irrational, futile, naive, or quixotic—it perhaps would have attracted a few committed devotees, but it would not have accumulated public approbation or moral prestige. The campaign against the slave trade (or any other antislavery initiative) could not have crystallized unless the campaign had become an indicator of individual and collective merit. At the most basic level, this was how the American Revolution mattered in the making of the antislavery movement in Britain at the end of the eighteenth century. It produced an environment in which organized opposition to slavery, for the first time, could seem worthy of praise.

Antislavery argument became useful during the era of the American Revolution, and thereafter. Its political utility meant that attacks on the slave system could serve a range of purposes at once. They could function both as ends in themselves as well as means toward other ends. Several of the colonial assemblies wanted to limit the number of enslaved Africans entering North America *and* blame the British government for the Atlantic slave trade. Granville Sharp wanted to overthrow human bondage *and* establish liberty of the subject as an inviolable right in British law. The proponents of gradual emancipation, like James Ramsay, aimed to eliminate slavery *and* strengthen the role of Parliament in overseas governance. Sir Guy Carleton and other British commanders wanted to protect the freedom of liberated slaves *and* establish the state as a benevolent authority that honored its commitments. The proponents of British colonies in Africa wanted to diminish the slave trade *and* enhance British power on the West African coast. Free blacks in Britain hoped to expose the horrors of the slave trade *and* assert their claim to the rights and liberties possessed by other free subjects of the crown. The Teston circle hoped to promote

3. Ibid., 41.

Christianity in the British West Indies *and* make Evangelicalism socially acceptable in the British Isles. Quakers in England tried to abolish the slave trade *and* renew their claim to preeminence in discerning sacred truths. In each instance, the moral authority that attended antislavery commitments assisted projects that lacked comparable moral status, projects that stood to benefit from an association with opposition to human bondage.

For too long, assessments of abolitionist initiatives have foundered on false binaries: the organizers and their constituencies were either selfless *or* self-interested; they were either humanitarians *or* hypocrites. But the motives that shape political behavior are rarely so simple. Social movements that draw a great number of followers from many quarters, in particular, must be varied and complex in their origins. Indeed, the emerging antislavery movement would attract broad support precisely because of its capacity to mean different things to diverse participants. The movement enjoyed public success because it expressed values that held wide appeal *and* served more parochial interests, because it invoked notions of justice or humanity *and* brought moral capital to its adherents. Antislavery sentiments failed to ignite comparable antislavery movements elsewhere in western Europe or in the Americas, in these years, perhaps because antislavery organizing seemed to bring little credit and few benefits to the activist, because alienation rather than approbation was likely to result. In those circumstances it would take special courage to act. Abolitionists in the United States would fail to acquire the same kind of moral prestige in the mid-nineteenth century because their cause, inescapably, threatened dissolution of the nation. Antislavery opinion had wide currency among the French *philosophes* by the time of the American Revolution. French commentators condemned colonial slavery with a force, vigor, and frequency that rivaled the British. But, for reasons that need further exploration, abolitionism did not confer opportunities, status, or further benefits to its proponents in France. After 1788, in fact, its association with British reform briefly tainted antislavery activism. That stigma soon lost its power during the French Revolution, to be sure. The emancipation decree of 1794 at once expressed Jacobin values *and* met the strategic imperative of winning support from black insurgents in the Caribbean. But the new association of abolitionism with Jacobinism would mean that antislavery would be linked with turmoil and violence in France and Haiti after the restoration of the French monarchy. French abolitionists in the first half of the nineteenth century would have to contend not only with the proslavery interest but also with the negative associations that antislavery had acquired after Haitian independence.

I have been suggesting, then, that understanding how abolitionist movements began means understanding not only changing attitudes toward slavery but also, and even more, changing attitudes toward antislavery. Antislavery sentiments alone did not cause antislavery commitments. Aspiring reformers were influenced as well by the prospects before them, by their sense of opportunities, by the possibilities for effective assistance from others, by the likelihood (however distant) of some degree of success, by how they thought they would be judged. Their interpretation of what contemporaries would think of them affected what they chose to do and how they chose to do it. It helped decide, in fact, whether they acted at all. The Society of Friends, for example, might have behaved very differently before the American Revolution if they had thought that public lobbying against the slave trade would reflect well on them. James Ramsay perhaps would have come forward in the early 1770s with his proposal for slavery reform if he had thought his plan would win a hearing. In this way, the history of antislavery organizing becomes not only a history of networks and initiatives and not only a history of antislavery sentiments but also a history of opportunities and agendas, public perception and self-perception— a history of the way the image of antislavery action and the image of the abolitionists changes over time.

Scholars tend to understand better now the shortcomings of the British antislavery movement, its limited ambitions, its self-aggrandizing character, its narrow definition of "slavery," its selective philanthropy, its paternalism in the guise of humanitarianism, its insufficiency as a strategy for social reform, its complicity with new forms of imperial supremacy and domination. Such shortcomings, in fact, inhere in most political causes that trade on their moral virtue, that advertise their commitment to principles that transcend self-interest. These declarations of moral purpose sometimes say less about what the cause is about than what its proponents hope to acquire from their involvement and how they hope others will interpret its aims. They often speak most eloquently to how a political movement needs to present itself when its declared end also operates as a vehicle for other ends. If the abolitionists, and their countless supporters, had sought abolition only, they would not have demanded recognition of their moral virtue. They would not have had to parade their reputation for sincerity and special merit. Abolition, and then emancipation, would have been enough, as they were, indeed, for Granville Sharp, who never learned to make his opposition to slavery politically useful or the basis for public importance.

The esteem enjoyed by the British opponents of slavery was rare, as a comparative study of the image of abolitionists likely would show. The perception of antislavery organizing could shift rapidly with events, as the case of France and the French Revolution makes clear. I have argued in this book that the American Revolution touched off a transformation in the public perception of antislavery action in the British Isles, as well as in the North American colonies. It gave new pertinence to what had been a question of marginal interest. It left conceivable a program that had seemed a fantasy, at best. It inspired urgency in quarters where an unfocused hope for gradual improvement had tended to prevail. It helped antislavery activists seem like moral exemplars rather than utopian fanatics, as idealists hoping to restore the honor of the British Empire rather than drive it into division and ruin. And yet that moment of opportunity could have passed without consequence. The opening that arose in the 1780s easily could have been missed. An antislavery movement in Britain that coalesced in May 1791, instead of May 1787, soon would have been associated with revolution in France and insurrection in Saint Domingue rather than patriotism and Christianity, an association that would have hindered the prospects for a successful appeal to Parliament and the public for decades to come. What would have been the fate of antislavery impulses in and around the Atlantic world during the nineteenth century without the ideological support provided by a well-established antislavery movement in the British Isles, without its reputation for moral excellence, and without its evidence of success?

Too often, the British campaigns of the late eighteenth century have been presented as the predictable outcome of the era, as the logical result of cultural trends, social change, political shifts, or economic forces, as a consequence of human progress. Yet the story of how the British antislavery movement began suggests more strongly that the campaign itself was fortuitous, that it need not have developed when it did, as it did, and with the popularity that it acquired. In the end, what is remarkable about abolitionism in Britain is not that it took so long to emerge, that it was politically ineffective for many years, or that it was limited in its ambition and selective in its scope. Such movements often are. What is truly surprising about British abolitionism is that such a campaign ever should have developed at all.

Aboan, Cofee, 306

Abolitionism: defined, 17–18, 20

Absolutism, 155, 161, 245

Acadians, 225, 397, 399

Adam, Thomas, 337

Adams, John, 108, 172, 312

Adanson, Michel, 430

Address to the Inhabitants of the British Settlements, An (Rush), 148

Africa, 262–282, 314–322, 324, 330

Akan, 266

Albornoz, Bartolome de, 39

Allinson, Samuel, 396

Amelioration, 28, 70–71, 73, 77, 217, 244n, 245, 325–326, 328, 355, 363, 364, 372, 375, 386

American Revolution, 2, 13, 27, 29, 160, 182–185, 188, 202, 204–206, 213, 216, 251, 253, 256–257, 262, 277, 294, 298, 303, 314, 326–327, 346, 358, 393–394, 407–409, 412, 414–416, 423, 437–438, 449, 451–462

Americans against Liberty (Serle), 119

Amissah, Quamino, 306

Anglicanus, 95

Annamaboe, 306

Anstey, Roger, 336

Answer to the Declaration of the American Congress, An (Lind), 133

Antigua, 66, 73, 76, 202, 242n, 355, 356, 359

Antislavery: defined, 17, 19

Antislavery campaigns (British Isles): and American example, 110–137, 151–152, 202, 320–330, 333–334, 364–377, 387, 402, 443–450; politics of, 185–187; obstacles to, 196, 209–212, 258, 260, 292, 322;

free blacks in, 283–284, 288–289, 292–293, 297–298, 300, 311; Anglican Evangelicals in, 341–342, 386–389; Quakers in, 425–434, 442–444

Antislavery campaigns (North America), 105–108, 110, 114, 135–138, 143, 201, 400, 409, 412–414; and ideology of revolution, 105–107, 110–111, 113, 137–143, 202, 232, 288, 324, 400, 408–409, 413–414, 437–438; politics of, 137–151, 159, 257; Granville Sharp and, 159, 164–168; and British campaigns, 167–170, 202, 233; black abolitionists in, 288–290, 294

Antislavery colonization, 108, 213–214, 217–220, 232, 259, 262, 314–321, 394, 438

Appalachians, 223, 224

Arcot, nawab of, 203

Arianism, 172, 198

Arming slaves: American, 108, 131, 438; British, 113, 131–132, 200–201, 218, 228, 254, 257, 294, 308–310

Arminian Magazine, 339

Armitage, David, 52

Army, British, 308–311; blacks in, 95, 294, 298, 308–311; in North America, 125, 140, 215, 299, 308–310; in British West Indies, 291, 309

Arundel, Richard Monckton (Viscount Galway), 445n, 446n

Associated Counties, 186–187, 196, 200, 408

Associates of Dr. Bray, 61, 64–65, 72, 80, 356, 358–360

Astley, Thomas, 430

Atkins, John, 41

Axtell, James, 58

Bacon, Anthony, 128

Bacon, Thomas, 65, 359

Bacon's Rebellion, 43

Badagry, prince of, 306

Bahamas, 283

Baldwin, Ebenezer, 106

Bance Island, 264, 280

Banks, Joseph, 260

Baptists, 66, 124, 328, 356

Barbados, 43, 49, 61–62, 66, 69, 71–72, 76, 78, 88–89, 354, 357, 359–360

Barclay, David, 66, 402, 404–407, 409–410, 416–417, 419–420, 423–424

Barham Court, 341–345, 349, 352, 370, 376–377, 386, 441

Barre, Issac, 157

Barrington, Samuel, 347

Barrington, Shute, 356

Barton, Joseph, 443n

Bath, 340

Battersea Rise, 341

Battle of Brandywine, 120

Baudeau, Abbé, 232

Baxter, Richard, 57, 70

Beckford, William, 94

Beckles, Hilary, 42

Bedford Whigs, 183

Bellamy, Joseph, 178

Benezet, Anthony, 4, 24, 39, 91, 99, 118, 137, 140, 164–165, 168, 174n, 197, 198, 231–232, 259–260, 292, 296, 322–323, 352n, 375, 396–397, 400–402, 405–412, 426–427, 435, 441; influence of, 40, 324, 391, 435, 441; social concerns of, 397–399; and Society of Friends, 399, 414, 430

Bengal, 157, 203, 220, 222–223, 235, 309–310, 341, 376

Bentham, Jeremy, 132

Berkeley, George, 79–80

Bermuda, 42, 49, 79, 242n, 303

Bevan, Joseph Gurney, 417–418

Bight of Benin, 263

Bight of Biafra, 304

Birch, Samuel, 294

Birkbeck, Wilson, 417

Birmingham, 328, 444, 446, 447n, 448

Black Pioneers. *See* Dunmore's Regiment

Blacks, free: in West Indies, 242n, 303, 307, 356; in England, 262, 282–284, 286–289, 293–298, 310–312, 319, 337; in North America, 303, 315, 317, 337

Board of Trade, 63, 144, 194, 201, 213–214, 217, 242n, 268, 307, 308, 376, 402, 404, 423

Bodin, Jean, 245

Bogin, Ruth, 288

Bolzius, Johann Martin, 85–87

Book of Cases (Quaker), 422

Book of Proverbs, 220

Boston, 53, 87, 99, 107, 121, 165, 286, 288, 319, 324

Boston Port Bill, 167, 216

Botany Bay, 279

Boulton, Matthew, 447n

Bouverie, Elizabeth, 342–343, 347, 359–360, 383, 386, 441

Bradley, Ian, 340

Bray, Thomas, 60–61, 70–71. *See also* Associates of Dr. Bray

Brazil, 11, 49, 171, 232, 242

Breitenbach, William, 179

Brew, Richard, 264n

Bridgewater, 431, 445

Brighton, 340

Bristol, 53, 54n, 100, 255, 303, 427, 430, 445n, 448, 450

Britain's Commercial Interest Explained (Postlethwayt), 272

Brown, Ford, 385

Brown, Moses, 396, 412

Browne, Isaac Hawkins, 446n

Bryan, Hugh, 66–67

Brydges, James (duke of Chandos), 266

Burgh, James, 146

Burke, Edmund, 123, 203, 228–230, 235–236, 238, 255–256, 422

Burlington, 398
Burnaby, Rev. Andrew, 122–123
Bush, Jonathan, 241
Butler, Jon, 75

Calvinists, 87, 178–180, 194, 195
Cambridge, 328
Cambridge University, 1, 194–195, 202, 435, 439
Campbell, John, 221, 275, 430
Canada, 108, 215, 224, 275, 357–359
Canterbury, archbishop of, 94, 194, 228, 352, 401
Cape Coast Castle, 266–268, 279–281, 305–306
Cape das Voltas, 279
Capitalism and Slavery (Williams), 12–14, 16, 18, 378–379
Captain Singleton (Defoe), 266
Capuchins, 39
Caribs, 156, 170, 176, 205, 220–221, 225, 303
Carleton, Guy, 215, 298–300, 311–312, 425
Carlisle Peace Commission, 251
Carlyle, Thomas, 10
Cartagena, 39, 74, 218
Cartwright, John, 146, 161, 188–192, 240
Case of Our Fellow-Creatures, The (Society of Friends), 366, 411, 424–428, 431
Catholic Church, 39, 55, 66, 68, 186, 224, 307, 380
Caution and Warning to Great Britain and Her Colonies, A (Benezet), 401, 402, 411, 427, 429
Cavendish, Lord John, 422
Ceded Islands, 220, 232
Chalmers, George, 280n
Chalus, Elaine, 349–350
Charles II, 34
Charleston, S.C., 64
Chatham ministry, 215, 238. *See also* Pitt, William, earl of Chatham
Chesapeake, the, 66, 68–69, 120

Chesterfield petitions, 448
Children (African): and unfree status, 45; schools for, 61, 64, 358–361, 397–398; liberation of, 108, 213, 232; and enslaved parents, 235–236, 250
Chile, 171, 279
Choctaws, 170
Christian Directions and Instructions for the Negroes (anon.), 360
Christian missions to Africa, 293, 316
Christian missions to slaves (Catholic), 39, 60, 68, 71, 355
Christian missions to slaves (Protestant), 28, 33, 48, 56–66, 68–75, 80, 89, 245–247, 250, 316, 325, 337–339, 350–364, 379–380; and antislavery impulses, 37, 55, 57–59, 62–63, 66–75, 78, 91–92, 250, 350–351, 354–355, 386; African resistance to, 58, 66, 354; results of, 62, 63, 66, 68–69, 72, 75, 355–356. *See also* Church of England; Methodists
Chubb, John, 431
Churchman, John, 415
Church of England, 146, 150, 169, 172–174, 184, 192–199, 297, 345, 348, 352–363, 377, 381; in the colonies, 33, 35–36, 40–41, 60–61, 64–74, 354, 356, 361, 363, 365, 372
Clapham, 342
Clapham Sect (the Saints), 171–172, 333–335, 341, 344, 378–380, 389
Clarke, John, 277
Clarkson, Thomas, 1, 3–9, 24, 70, 195, 274, 286, 296, 328, 342, 349, 353, 377, 385–386, 427–428, 431, 433–445, 447n
Climate, 86, 209–210, 218, 224n, 234, 310
Clinton, Henry, 298, 308–309, 311
Cluny, Alexander, 224n
Coachmaker's Hall, 187
Coartación ("Spanish Regulations"), 194, 228–229, 234, 259, 363, 435
Cobbett, William, 9, 14, 378, 389
Code Noir, 242

Codrington Plantations, 61–62, 72–73, 354–357, 360

Coercive Acts, 167

Coke, Thomas, 339

Coleman, Deirdre, 281

Coleridge, Samuel Taylor, 8, 435

Colley, Linda, 309

Collingwood, Luke, 284

Commenda, 281

Commendas, 305

Committee for Relief of the Black Poor, 294, 317

Committee of North American Merchants, 409

Committee of West Indian Merchants, 428. *See also* West India interest

Common good, 81, 120, 126, 137–138, 175, 236, 249–250, 325

Common law, 44, 46–47, 55–56, 93–94, 96–98, 180, 188, 241, 255–256

Common Sense (Paine), 125

Compagne des Indes, 270

Company of Merchants Trading to Africa, 140, 150, 201, 268, 305–306, 408, 428

Compton, Henry, 60

Cone, Carl, 149

Connecticut, 106–107, 135

Considerations on the Emancipation of Negroes and on the Abolition of the Slave Trade (anon.), 367

Considerations on the Keeping of Negroes (Woolman), 411

Constitutional Convention, 449

Continental Congress, 120, 136, 142, 251, 253, 408, 413

Convicts, 45, 49, 82, 124–125, 275, 278–279, 281, 305

Cooper, David, 396, 426

Coram, Thomas, 79

Corbyn, Thomas, 418

Cork (Ireland), 53

Cornwallis, Lord, 203, 216, 301

Corsica, 171, 205

Cotton, 266, 278–281

Counter-Enlightenment, 172

Coupland, Reginald, 9, 21, 378, 387

Cowper, William, 205, 384, 449

Crawford, Charles, 202, 286

Creek Indians, 82, 170

Crewe, Frances, 286–287

Critical Review, 365

Cropper, James, 14

Crowley, Thomas, 411

Cruden, John, 298, 309–310

Cuba, 11, 39, 95, 218

Cugoano, Ottobah, 288, 296–297

Cumberland, 395

Cuming, Thomas, 265

Cursory Remarks upon the Reverend Mr. Ramsay's Essay on the Treatment and Conversion of African Slaves in the Sugar Colonies (anon.), 368–369

Curtin, Philip, 281

Dalrymple, John, 128

Danbury, Conn., 107

Danish West Indies, 355

Darien, Conn., 84

Dartmouth, William Legge, earl of, 119, 145, 165, 169, 175–177, 189, 253, 286, 338, 340n, 380, 404–405, 410

Davies, Samuel, 66

Davis, David Brion, 41n, 48, 107, 177, 335, 338, 379, 392

Day, Thomas, 118, 431, 445

Declaration of Independence, 120, 133, 142, 143, 145, 288

Declaration of the People's Natural Right to a Share in the Legislature (Sharp), 161, 167

Declaratory Act, 161, 255

Decline thesis, 13–16, 18

Defoe, Daniel, 266

Deists, 198

Delaware, 136

Delaware Indians, 398

Demarin, John Peter, 145

Denny, Thomas, 138

Dickson, William, 286

Dillwyn, William, 24, 197, 259, 396, 410, 418, 420, 422–423, 426, 429–430, 443n

Dimsdale, Baron Thomas, 446n

Dodshon, Frances, 410

Dolben, James, 296

Dominica, 307

Draper, Sir William, 254

Drescher, Seymour, 21, 51, 110, 429, 444n

Duncombe, Henry, 446n

Dundas, Henry, 230, 300–301

Dunmore, earl of (John Murray), 131–133, 228, 309, 310

Dunmore's Regiment, 294, 308–309, 311

Dutch in North America, 125

Dutch West India Company, 40

Dutton, Anne, 337

East India Company, 53, 156–158, 203–204, 221–222, 271, 281, 309, 341, 376, 428, 437

East Indian sugar, 11–14

East Jersey, 89

Ebeneezer, Ga., 85

Edmundson, William, 43, 57, 88

Edwards, Jonathan, 177–179

Edwards, Jonathan, the younger, 178

Effingham, earl of (Thomas Howard), 188

Egmont, earl of (John Perceval), 79

Ekpe, 303–304

Eliot, John, 406

Elmina, 305

Eltis, David, 20, 50, 51n

Emancipation: in the British Empire, 9, 14, 112, 243–244, 342; endorsement of, 28, 165, 170, 231–232, 297, 326, 338, 360–361, 363; schemes for, 108, 147, 194, 213–214, 217–220, 228–240, 246, 249–251, 318, 352, 394; in the northern United States, 108–109, 141, 414; as imperial reform, 212–213, 217n, 218–219, 226–227,

232, 234–237, 244–246, 248–256, 298–299, 308–312

Empire (British): perceptions of, 26, 52–53, 119–121, 155–161, 202–206, 214, 239–240; defense of, 120–122, 125, 127–133, 144–145, 148, 216, 248–250; antislavery as rejection of, 138–145, 159, 169–170; critics of, 156–157, 162–164, 170–171, 175, 177, 191, 202, 204, 205, 225, 297, 430; proposals for the improvement of, 161, 189, 210, 212–213, 216, 219–220, 222–228, 231, 240, 242–243, 249–251, 253, 257–258, 264–265, 269, 271–272, 274–275, 277–279, 282, 307, 309–310, 318, 324, 326, 329–330, 335, 341; antislavery as aid to, 185, 218–219, 234, 237, 244–245, 251, 254–255, 297, 309–310, 349–375; Africans as agents of, 218–220, 225, 226, 254, 298–310; antislavery as threat to, 322

Enfield, Conn., 107

Enlightenment, 20, 23, 37, 41n, 47–48, 51, 52, 52n, 98, 111, 174–175, 233

Entwistle, James, 447n

Equiano, Olaudah, 24, 95n, 274, 284, 288, 293, 295–296, 329

Erskine, Rev. John, 149

Essay in Vindication of the Continental Colonies in America, An (Lee), 115

Essay on the Impolicy of the African Slave Trade, An (Clarkson), 328

Essay on the Slavery and Commerce of the Human Species, An (Clarkson), 377

Essay towards an Instruction for the Indians, An (Wilson), 360

Essex Journal and Merrimack Packet, 290

Estwick, Samuel, 97–98

Eton, 429

Evangelical revival (Great Awakening), 37, 58, 65–66

Evangelicals (Church of England): as critics of slavery, 1, 4, 19, 28–29, 106, 149, 160, 167, 171–172, 321, 333–335, 341–342, 344, 379, 386–389; critics of, 10–11, 14, 340,

377–386; abolitionism among, 19–20, 26, 41n, 336, 341; and politics, 28, 339–343, 380, 383; and polite society, 28, 345, 348, 388; toleration of slavery by, 176, 337–338, 350–351, 360; women as lay leaders among, 343–344, 349–350, 385–386, 441; cultural legacies of, 380, 389. *See also* Teston Circle

Evans, Caleb, 146

Fairfax County, Va., 139

Fantee, 264, 268, 305

Farewell Address to Rev. Mr. James Ramsay, A (Tobin), 367

Farmer, John, 89

Ferguson (ship captain), 119

Fielding, John, 94

Finley, Moses, 394

Fleetwood, William (bishop of Saint Asaph), 63

Fletcher, Isaac, 395

Fletcher, John William, 121, 129, 185, 189, 192, 338

Floridas, 218, 220, 232, 275, 299; West Florida, 170, 213–214, 217, 224n, 230; East Florida, 226, 308

Folkestone, Viscount (William Bouverie), 157

Fothergill, John, 259–261, 292, 314, 326, 408, 410–411, 418

Fountayne, John (dean of York), 445n

Fox, Charles James, 296, 300, 422

Fox, George, 57, 58, 70, 416

France, 143, 159, 171, 205, 245; empire of, 82, 171, 285, 430; as British rival, 182, 239, 265, 270–271, 279, 309–310, 326; in the Atlantic slave trade, 264, 270; antislavery in, 282; and slaveholding in the Americas, 372. *See also* Code Noir

Franklin, Benjamin, 116–118, 135, 146–148, 370, 406, 410

Frankpledge, 316

Fredericksburg, Va., 64, 108

Free labor, 19–20, 214, 218, 234–235, 237, 320, 326–327

Freeman, F., 95

Free Soilers, 79

Free trade, 13–14, 317, 326–327

French colonists in the Americas, 125, 220, 223–226, 230, 355

Friendly Association, 397

Frost, J. William, 416

Fruchtman, Jack, 172

Fry, Joseph, 427

Galley slavery, 127

Gambia River, 41, 264, 271, 277, 278, 280, 282

Garbett, Samuel, 446, 447n

Garden, Alexander, 64

Gazetteer, 118

General Chamber of Manufacturers, 446–447

General Evening Post, 430, 449

Gentleman's Magazine, 33, 35, 94, 95, 148, 430

George II, 82

George III, 131, 136, 142, 145, 162, 164–165, 183, 213, 220, 226, 232, 297, 301, 307, 346, 402, 410

Georgia, 64, 66, 73, 91, 107, 116, 217, 226, 299, 337, 358; and ban on slavery, 78, 83–85, 187, 209, 231

Georgia Trust, 79–88, 91, 100, 231, 316

Germain, George, 157, 183, 281, 307, 347

Germans in North America, 125, 230. *See also* Salzburgers

Germantown protest, 87

Gibbs, Isaac, 84

Gibson, Edmund, 63, 72, 353

Gilbert, Nathaniel, 356

Glas, George, 264–265

Glasgow, 255

Gloucester, 445n

Glover, Samuel, 447n

Godwin, Morgan, 43, 57, 69–71, 73–75

Gold Coast, 263, 264, 268, 271, 279
Goodricke, Henry, 128
Goree, 315
Grace Church Street Meeting, 296, 415, 417
Grain Coast, 260, 315
Grainger, James, 245n, 370
Grant, Charles, 341
Grant, David, 184
Grant, Oswald, and Company, 264
Green, John, 197
Gregory, George, 286, 318–319
Grenada, 223, 261
Grenville, William Wyndham, 311
Grigsby, Joshua, 446n
Grimshaw, William, 337
Grimstead, David, 350
Gronniosaw, Ukawsaw (James Albert), 95, 99, 293, 337
Guadeloupe, 218, 291
Gum arabic, 265, 276
Gurney family of Norwich, 418, 444

Hagen, Jacob, 425
Haitian Revolution, 14, 188, 291, 292
Haklyut, Richard, the younger, 218
Hall, Catherine, 389
Hall, Prince, 290
Hammon, Jupiter, 95n
Hanbury, Capel, 406–407
Hanbury, John, 406–407
Hancock, David, 264
Hargrave, Francis, 96
Harlow, Vincent, 281
Harrison, Brian, 114
Harrison, George, 418, 429, 443n
Hart, Levi, 178
Hartley, David, 146–148, 165, 186, 189, 200–201, 254, 260
Haskell, Thomas, 20, 152
Hastings, Selina (countess of Huntingdon), 176, 337, 340n, 380, 401
Hastings, Warren, 203, 437
Havana, 218

Haynes, Lemuel, 288
Hazard, Tom, 88
Henry, Patrick, 400
Hepburn, John, 89
Hertford, 415
Hey, Richard, 127
Hill, Sir Richard, 380
Hillsborough, earl of (Wills Hill), 119
Hinchliffe, John, 194–195, 199, 229–230, 238, 256, 435n
Historiography of British antislavery, 8–22, 25–26, 29–30, 40, 41n, 46, 62, 111–113, 136–137, 231, 299, 333–336, 377–379, 389, 392, 405, 429, 433–434, 439
History of America (Robertson), 297, 353
History of America (Russell), 122
History of Jamaica (Long), 367
History of the Rise, Progress, and Accomplishment of the Abolition of the African Slave-Trade (Clarkson), 3–9, 18, 30, 433–434
Hoare, Jonathan, 417
Hoare, Samuel, Jr., 417, 418, 429, 443n
Hodgson, John, 73
Hollis, Thomas, 146
Honest Whigs (Friends of America), 118, 126, 132, 145–152, 161–165, 169, 188–191, 238, 253–255, 260
Honfleur, 264
Honor: of the thirteen colonies, 106–107, 109, 113, 138–143, 167–168, 202, 437; of Britain, 112–113, 185–186, 202, 219, 299–300, 311–312, 449
Hooper, 443n
Hooton, Elizabeth, 89
Hopkins, Samuel, 178, 319, 350
Houghton, Daniel, 278
House of Commons, 1, 125, 146, 156, 184, 186, 191, 192, 194, 201, 203, 215n, 296, 342, 376–377, 380, 409, 422–424, 431, 448
House of Lords, 380
Howe, Richard, 120

Howe, William, 308
Hughes, Benjamin, 306
Huguenots, 245, 397
Humanitarianism, 4–18, 21, 23–27, 57–58, 91, 93, 113, 119–120, 129, 142, 149, 156, 200, 226, 250–251, 301, 314, 318, 333, 351, 437–438, 441
Hume, David, 158–159, 302, 348, 430
Humphreys, George, 447n
Huntingdon, 376
Hutchinson, Thomas, 139, 238n

Ilchester, 125
Impartial History of the Present War in America, An (Murray), 151
Impressment, 44, 77n, 117, 188
Indentured servants, 42–43, 45, 86, 232
Independents (sect), 124
India, 156–158, 162, 203–205, 220, 280, 327
Inkle and Yarico, 365
Innes, William, 124–126, 128
Inquiry into the Effects of Putting a Stop to the African Slave Trade, An (Ramsay), 325, 327–328, 375
Inquisition, 127
Insurrections (slave), 33, 34, 42, 51, 66, 75–76, 291–292; abolitionist perspectives on, 33, 180n, 219, 237, 327; encouragement of, 43, 131–133; European fears of, 75–78, 81–82, 86, 88, 138, 209, 224n, 230–231, 237, 245, 421
Ireland, 226, 326–327, 446
Irish in North America, 34, 43, 50, 125, 162, 291

Jacobite rebellion (1745), 219
Jamaica, 33, 66, 72, 73, 76, 77n, 87, 145, 177, 245, 291, 306, 356, 367n, 372
James, C. L. R., 12, 291
James, Sydney, 409
Jarvis, Michael, 303
Jebb, John, 146, 149, 161, 189, 191, 198n
Jefferson, Thomas, 142–143, 148

Jenkins, James, 417, 418
Jenkinson, Charles, 329
Johnson, James, 306
Johnson, Samuel, 121–122, 129, 134, 151, 159, 166, 254, 359n
Jolliffe, William, 376
Jones, Rufus, 392, 395
Jury trials for slaves, 147, 148, 236
Just Limitation of Slavery in the Laws of God, The (Sharp), 180, 230

Keene, Edmund, 196
Keith, George, 89
Kennicott, Ann, 381
Kennicott, Benjamin, 173n
Kerr, James, 93
King, Boston, 300
Knight, Joseph, 283
Knowles, Thomas, 418, 423, 429
Knox, William, 217, 220–221, 226–227, 253, 256, 352n–353n

Lafayette, marquis de, 438, 441
Lagos, 39
Lamb, Matthew, 144
Langton, Bennet, 359
Largarite, Bruono, 307
Latrobe, Christian Ignatius, 349, 433n
Laurens, Henry, 106, 141–142, 201n–202n, 299
Laurens, John, 116n, 141, 438, 439, 441
Law of Liberty, The (Sharp), 180, 190
Law of Passive Obedience, The (Sharp), 180
Law of Retribution, The (Sharp), 180, 187, 190, 193, 196
Lay, Benjamin, 70, 89, 90
Lee, Arthur, 115–118, 134–135, 139, 147–148
Leeds, 448
Leeward Islands, 61, 228, 340, 347, 355
Legislative Rights of the Commonalty Vindicated, The (Sharp), 190
Legitimate commerce, 257–258, 260–262, 265–272, 274–275, 277–281, 314–315, 317,

319–330, 430. *See also* Slave trade (British): alternatives to

Leicester, Mass., 107, 138, 139n

Le Jau, Francis, 69

Le Mesurier, Paul, 446n

Letters to an American Planter (Waring), 359

Letter to James Tobin, A (Ramsay), 367, 373

Lettsom, John Coakley, 259, 261, 279, 314, 319, 430

Liberty (English): ideology of, 46–49, 52, 53, 56, 91, 96–98, 100–101, 105, 117–121, 125–126, 128–129, 133, 149–150, 152, 155, 161–162, 186, 206, 215n, 310, 369; and American slavery, 116–121, 125–126, 129, 201; and America, 120–122; threats to, 158, 161–162, 164, 166, 167, 171, 192; and British slave trade, 412; and abolitionism, 449

Library Company of Philadelphia, 418

Liele, George, 356

Lincoln's Inn, 190, 204

Lind, John, 121, 130–133, 145, 151, 166

Lisle, David, 93

Liverpool, 53, 100, 202, 255, 303–304, 306, 402, 445n, 450

Lloyd, Gamaliel, 445n

Lloyd, John, 418, 422, 423, 429

Lloyd family, 444

Lloyd's Evening Post, 430

Locke, John, 119

Lock Hospital for Penitent Prostitutes, 337

Lofft, Capel, 189–190

Logan, Deborah, 397

London, 91, 100, 116–119, 121, 156, 184, 187, 188, 200, 255, 340, 428, 431, 450; blacks in, 94–96, 99, 283–285, 289, 293–296, 310–311

London Chronicle, 94–95

London Common Council, 190

London Evening Post, 156

London Foundling Hospital, 79

London Magazine, 40

London Meeting for Sufferings, 401–402, 404–408, 411, 413, 417, 424, 427; and subcommittee on the slave trade, 418, 423–427, 429, 432, 447

London Yearly Meeting, 395, 401–402; and petitions for abolition, 413–414, 417, 419–424, 431

Long, Edward, 95, 97–98, 302, 367, 370, 372n

Lorimer, Douglas A., 92

Louisiana, 230, 232

Lowe, John, Jr., 281

Loyalists: British, 120, 216, 298–302, 309–311; black, 216, 262, 281–283, 294–295, 298–302, 310–315, 322, 423

Lury, John, 427

Luttrell, Temple, 277

Macaulay, Catherine, 146

Macaulay, Zachary, 341

Mackworth, Herbert, 447n

McNamara, Matthias, 275, 293n, 308

Madan, Martin, 337

Madras, 203

Maine, 79

Manchester, 280–281, 444n, 446–449

Mansfield, Lord (William Murray), 97–99, 117, 119, 259, 290, 294, 411

Manumission, 88, 91, 105, 118, 432; endorsement of, 68, 89, 107; promotion of, 213, 234–235, 242, 318, 321, 354, 412, 414

Markham, William, 356

Maroons, 33, 42–43, 303

Marrant, John, 282, 337

Marriage, 92, 219, 235–237, 250, 355

Martin, James, 443n, 446n

Martin, Samuel, 245

Martinique, 95, 218

Maryland, 60, 64, 66n, 120, 122, 135

Maseres, Francis, 215n

Mason, Rev. William, 445n

Massachusetts, 78, 79, 87, 99, 106–108, 116,

136, 138, 139, 148, 167, 180, 282, 289, 410; abolitionism in, 400

Massachusetts Spy, 290

Mather, Cotton, 57, 58

Medford, Mass., 107

Mein, John, 121

Mekeel, Arthur, 410

Menouca, Lourenco da Savila de, 39n–40n

Mercado, Tomas de, 39

Merchant Adventurers of Bristol, 409

Merchants: in Atlantic trade, 34–35, 53, 106–108, 114, 124, 139, 142–145, 168, 182, 246n, 302–303, 314, 320, 324, 402, 406, 409. *See also* Slave trade (British)

Methodists, 66, 73, 121, 172, 185, 253–254, 300, 338–339, 356, 359, 377, 380–382

Mexico, 155

Middleton, Sir Charles, 245–246, 343–349, 359, 377, 383, 386

Middleton, Lady Margaret, 24, 245–246, 343–345, 349–351, 360, 363, 377, 381–383, 386–388, 441, 445n

Mildred, Daniel, 407, 409, 425

Millennium Hall (Scott), 344

Milner, Isaac, 382

Miners, British, 44, 117, 266, 370

Miscegenation, 95–96, 219

Moncrief, James, 310

Montesquieu (Charles-Louis de Secondat), 127, 430

Monthly Ledger, 411, 418

Monthly Review, 231, 286, 289n, 365, 368, 373

Montserrat, 43

Moore, Rev. John, 356

Moore, John Hamilton, 430

Moravians, 66, 73, 87, 340, 349, 355, 433

More, Hannah, 24, 342–345, 347, 349, 381–388, 445n

Morgan, Cadwalader, 88

Morgann, Maurice, 214–220, 224n, 225–227, 229–230, 232, 234, 238, 259, 299, 310, 320

Morice, Humphry, 264n

Morning Chronicle, 449

Morning Meeting of Quaker Elders, 410n–411n, 423–424

Morris, Valentine, 225

Morse, Edward, 278

Moss, Charles, 356

Murray, James, 150–152

Muslim slave traders, 50

Nabobs, 158

National identity, 52–53, 56, 117–120, 123–124, 155–157, 160, 182; and antislavery, 185–186, 333, 387, 444, 447–450. *See also* Liberty (English): ideology of

Native Americans (Indians), 69, 81, 125, 130–131, 155, 162, 164, 170, 220, 223–225, 226, 272, 309–310, 353

Natural rights, 39, 105, 113, 118, 120, 126, 128–130, 133, 164, 185, 290, 418

Navy, Royal, 44, 53, 95n, 209, 238, 255, 297, 343, 345, 347–348, 377

Negro in the Caribbean, The (Williams), 12

Nettlestead, 347

Nevis, 33, 367, 369

Newbury, 448

Newcastle, 150, 228, 230, 234, 235, 237, 238

New Divinity, 178–180

Newfoundland fisheries, 410

New Jersey, 108, 116, 135, 165, 215, 396, 398, 409, 412, 426

Newport, R.I., 53, 89, 317, 350

Newspapers, 429–430, 442–443, 447

Newton, John, 176, 337, 339–340, 342, 382–384

New York City, 53, 64, 76, 87, 107–108, 116, 120, 136, 165–166, 215, 291, 294, 295, 298–299, 308, 311, 317, 409, 412

Nichols, Robert Boucher, 449

Niles, Nathaniel, 106, 178

Norfolk, 64, 444n

Norris, Stephen, 311

North, Frederick, 164, 169, 175, 183, 200–201, 251, 300, 309, 410, 412, 422–423
North Carolina, 87, 308, 412
Northfield, Mass., 87
North ministry, 125, 133, 183, 187, 200, 312, 376, 405
Norwich (Eng.), 415, 444
Norwich, Conn., 107
Notes on the State of Virginia (Jefferson), 143
Nottingham petitions, 448
Nova Scotia, 79, 225, 282, 283, 294–295, 299–302, 311, 423. *See also* Loyalists: black

Objections to the Abolition of the Slave Trade with Answers (Ramsay), 367
Observations on Civil Liberty (Price), 126, 150, 157
Oglethorpe, James, 79–80, 83–84, 187–188, 190n, 359, 360
O'Hara, Charles, 275–276, 278, 282, 293n, 307–308
Old Calabar, 303–304
Old Light, 87
Old Whig, 38
Olney, 176, 340, 384
Oroonoko, 365
Orphans, English, 44, 50
Osborn, Sarah, 350
O'Shaughnessy, Andrew J., 309
Oswald, Richard, 280
Ottolenghe, Joseph, 64
Ottoman Empire, 132
Oxford University, 202

Paine, Thomas, 125
Paley, William, 202
Pamphlets: proslavery, 33, 36, 98, 366–369; antislavery, 43, 69, 94, 99, 110, 115–116, 134, 137, 148, 166, 168, 177, 180–182, 200, 213–214, 217, 259, 288, 296–297, 323, 328, 364–369, 373, 375, 377, 400–402, 411, 420, 423, 425–427, 430–431; and

American crisis, 114, 121–122, 126–134, 239–240
Panama, 279
Paris, 188, 317
Parker, Thomas, 203–204, 430
Parliament (English), 47, 63, 79, 83–85, 96n, 119–121, 125–128, 130, 133, 144, 146–147, 149–151, 156–158, 161–165, 169, 171–172, 182–183, 189, 191–192, 199, 202, 205, 211–212, 219, 225–226, 240–241, 244, 248–254, 257, 275, 282, 296–297, 314, 326, 333, 339, 341, 376, 379–380, 401, 402, 407, 412–413, 416, 423–425, 427, 429; licensing of slave trade by, 55, 135, 141, 149–150, 169, 181, 201, 202n, 263, 305, 321, 423
Parliament (Irish), 162, 182, 186, 251, 376
Parliamentary reform: and abolitionism, 26, 29, 190–192, 431, 445–446; advocates of, 161, 162, 183–184, 186, 188–192, 197n, 199–202
Parr, John, 300
Paternalism, 58, 75, 362
Paul (apostle), 58
Peace treaty (1783), 216n, 292, 302
Peckard, Rev. Peter, 195, 435
Pemberton, Israel, 397
Pemberton, James, 408, 416
Pemberton, John, 24, 414–416, 418, 420–422, 430
Penn, William, 42, 279, 416
Pennsylvania, 42, 88–90, 107–108, 116, 164, 165, 168, 232, 397–398, 400, 402, 407–408, 420
Pennsylvania Assembly, 135, 140, 402, 407, 413–414
Pennsylvania Executive Council, 140–141
Pennsylvania Gazette, 232
Peru, 155, 279
Peters, Thomas, 300, 311
Petersfield, 376
Petitions for abolition: British, 1, 39n–40n, 281, 296, 314, 391, 416, 422–424, 431,

447–449; North American, 139–140, 164–165, 168, 170, 181

Philadelphia, 53, 89, 90, 107–108, 140, 143, 296, 391, 396, 406, 408, 414–415, 426, 449

Philadelphia Meeting for Sufferings, 401, 405, 412–413, 419, 432

Philadelphia Yearly Meeting (1758), 420–422

Phillips, James, 377, 391, 417–418, 423, 426–427, 431–432, 443n, 446

Phillips, Richard, 443n

Phillipsburg Proclamation, 309

Pitt, William, earl of Chatham, 158, 190n, 215, 238, 265

Pitt, William, the younger, 14, 202, 279, 296, 312, 425, 442; ministry of, 282, 295, 300–301, 382, 383, 446

Pitt, William Morton, 443n, 446n

Plan for the Abolition of Slavery in the West Indies (Morgann), 213–214, 217–220, 228, 230–231, 259

Plan of Re-Union between Great Britain and Her Colonies (Ramsay), 248, 252

Pleasants, Robert, 396

Plymouth, 448

Poland, 132, 205

Poniatowski, Stanislaw, 132

Pontiac's War, 224

Poor (English): as subject to unfree labor, 44, 46n, 50; attitudes toward, 79, 343, 346, 361; relief of, 79–80, 82, 86–87, 342–343, 346, 361–362, 397; and Sierra Leone, 315; and slaves in the colonies, 370–371; and Methodists, 381

Porter, Dale H., 379

Porteus, Beilby, 24, 194, 345, 346, 348, 349, 352–364, 368, 383, 386, 388, 427, 430–431, 441

Portsmouth, 98

Portuguese Empire, 38–39, 171, 188, 271, 325

Postlethwayt, Malachy, 209, 269–275, 282, 315, 328; and Atlantic slave trade, 272–274, 324, 328, 329; and abolitionists, 322–324, 328, 330

Presbyterians, 66, 124, 127, 131, 198, 448–449

Presbytery of Edinburgh, 449

Price, Richard, 126–128, 130, 132, 146, 149–150, 157, 172, 185, 201, 445

Priestley, Joseph, 172, 198n, 328, 348

Primitivism, 51, 303

Prince of Wales (ship), 347

Privy Council, 136, 139, 144, 164, 223, 226, 241, 242n, 250, 280

Problem of Slavery in Western Culture, The (Davis), 41n

Proclamation against vice and immorality (1787), 346, 385

Proclamation of 1763, 223

Progress, 40–41, 47–48, 52, 233

Propagande de Fide, 39n–40n

Proslavery: argument and opinion of, 33–36, 52, 58, 72, 75, 84, 97–98, 117, 365–372; assumptions of, 49–54, 110, 141, 240, 432

Protestant refugees, 82, 85–87, 91, 230. *See also* Huguenots

Providence, R.I., 107

Providence Island, 42, 49

Public Advertiser, 311

Public Ledger, 121

Pulteney, William, earl of Bath, 248

Puritans, 69, 381

Pyle, Robert, 88

Quakers. *See* Society of Friends

Quebec, 215, 222–223, 226

Quebec Act, 223, 224, 380

Race, 49n, 50–52, 59, 69, 87, 96n, 115–116, 119, 124, 130, 213, 217–218, 247, 267, 272–273, 286, 288, 302–305, 307–310, 312n, 315, 318, 355, 364, 367, 372n, 397

Radnor County, 88

Ramsay, James, 1, 24, 39, 74, 145, 194, 227–230, 234, 236–238, 243–253, 256, 260,

292–293, 296, 325–326, 342, 346–350,
352–356, 360n, 363–368, 370–377, 385,
388, 391, 427, 431, 434–436, 441–442
Ratcliff Monthly Meeting, 417
Rathbone, William, 402, 418
Rawlinson, Samuel, 447n
Raynal, Abbé, 159, 233n, 430
*Records and Recollections of James Jenkins,
The* (Frost), 416–417
Regulating Act of 1788 (Jamaica), 372
*Reply to the Personal Invectives and Objec-
tions, A* (Ramsay), 373
*Representation of the Injustice and Dan-
gerous Tendency of Tolerating Slavery, A*
(Sharp), 99, 174, 190
Resistance: of slaves, 75–77, 85, 91–93, 99,
262, 289–291, 297–298, 308, 333
Rhode Island, 42, 88, 89, 107, 135, 282, 317,
319, 350, 396
Richardson, Thomas, 447n
Richmond, duke of, 189, 190n
Rishworth, Samuel, 42
Robertson, Robert, 33–36, 39, 48, 71–72,
92, 437
Robertson, William, 297, 353
Robinson, Robert, 328
Robinson, Thomas (Baron Grantham), 194
Rocha, Manuel Ribeiro, 232
Rockingham Whigs, 183, 200, 238, 249,
253, 376
Roebuck, John, 128
Romaine, William, 337
Roman Empire: and British Empire, 158
Royal Adventurers to Africa, 263–264
Royal Africa Company, 38, 63, 263–266,
268–272, 323
Rozbicki, Michal, 46
Rumbold, Sir Thomas, 203
Rundle, Thomas, 38
Rush, Benjamin, 140, 148, 164, 167, 198,
400, 426, 430
Russell, William, 122, 209, 233n, 447
Russia, 205

Saillant, John, 288
Sailors: in British slave trade, 53, 209, 267,
328, 376; black, 94–95, 98, 119, 283–285,
285n–286n, 303, 306
Saint Christopher (Saint Kitts), 39, 74, 145,
228, 238, 347, 352, 366, 373, 375
Saint Domingue, 291, 292
Saint George's Fields, 158
Saint John's, Cambridge University, 1
Saint Louis (Senegal), 265, 279, 308
Saint Paul's Cathedral, 197
Saint Vincent, 156–158, 170, 175, 176, 205,
221, 225, 245n, 259, 303
Salem, Mass., 107, 148
Salzburgers, 85–87, 91
Sancho, Ignatius, 286–287, 289, 293, 297,
430
Sandiford, Ralph, 89–90
Sandoval, Alonso de, 39, 74
Sandwich, Lord (John Montagu), 183
Sandwich, Mass., 107, 139n
Sansom, Philip, 443n
Sâo Tomé, 279, 325
Saratoga, 251
Sarter, Caesar, 290
Savannah, Ga., 83–85
Savile, Sir George, 157
Scantlebury, Thomas, 427
Scots Highlanders, 84, 219, 225
Scots in the Americas, 125, 238
Scott, Sarah, 344, 437
Secker, Thomas, 352
Seeley, John, 8
Senegal River, 267, 274–276, 307, 315
Senegambia, 275–278, 293n, 307–308
Sensibility, 23, 37, 40, 41n, 43–44, 48, 51–
52, 63, 69, 71, 98–99, 113, 116, 134, 178–
179, 187, 288–289, 293, 344, 348, 370,
387, 396–397, 437
Sepoys, 309–310
Serious Address to the Leaders of America, A
(Cooper), 426
Serle, Ambrose, 119–121, 129, 170

Sermons: and Christian missions to slaves, 63–65, 68; fast-day, 184, 191, 195; antislavery, 195; presented to the SPG, 196, 197, 353–354, 357n, 359, 360, 401, 427

Servant labor: in the colonies, 34, 46, 76, 82, 137–138, 146, 162, 218; in England, 44, 93; in Africa, 261, 315

Seven Years' War, 90, 94, 105, 144, 219, 239n, 400, 407, 414, 415; legacies of, 156–160, 202, 204–205, 212–213, 216, 217, 220–226, 239–240, 274–275

Sewall, Samuel, 78

Shackleton, Richard, 422

Sharp, Granville: and slavery in the empire, 1, 4, 24, 99–100, 210, 214, 230–231, 243, 259–260, 283–284, 292–293, 296–297, 353, 357, 359, 366, 405, 410–411, 426, 432, 435–436, 443; and slaveholding in England, 93–97, 99, 227n, 434; personal limitations of, 96n, 197–200, 314, 375, 441; and antislavery as reply to national crisis, 160, 164, 169–171, 175–176, 180–182, 185, 192–195, 199, 201, 206, 284; at the Board of Ordnance, 161, 177, 190, 238; and institutional reform in England, 161–162, 188–190, 197n, 199–200; as critic of empire, 161–165, 167, 170–171, 175, 197, 254–255; and American abolitionists, 165–169, 233n; religious views of, 171–182, 193, 198–199; as emancipation theorist, 227n, 228–231, 234–235; as colonization theorist, 316–321

Sharp, James, 93

Sharp, John, 172

Sharp, Thomas, 172

Sharp, William, 93

Sharpless, Isaac, 418

Shebbeare, John, 121, 127, 131, 151, 166, 170

Sheffield, 446

Shelburne, earl of (William Fitzmaurice Petty), 214–217, 230; followers of, 183; ministry of, 194, 251, 279, 376

Shepherd, John, 356

Sherbro River, 264, 266

Shipley, Jonathan, 146

Shore, John, 341

Shore, Samuel, 445n

Short Rejoinder to the Reverend Mr. Ramsay's Reply, A (Tobin), 367

Shrewsbury, 445n

Sierra Leone, 260–262, 264, 279–282, 294–295, 301, 314–317, 320–322, 431, 438

Sierra Leone Company, 321

"Sketch of a Negro Code" (Burke), 228–230, 235–236, 238, 255–256

Slave Association, 429–431, 443

Slave Coast, 306

Slave codes, 43, 55, 69, 77, 164, 227, 241–243, 249, 372

Slaveholders: exoneration of, 33–36, 71, 114, 117–118, 141, 142, 149–151, 169; identity of, 33–36, 71, 115–118, 123, 141, 367n, 369–370; absentee, 94, 158, 226, 283, 434; property interests of, 108, 132, 147, 212, 219–220, 226–227, 234–236, 240–242, 246n–247n

Slaveholding (colonies): criticism of, 33–39, 41, 42, 44, 48, 57, 59, 62–63, 67, 69–71, 75, 78–79, 81–84, 86–91, 93–97, 100, 114–118, 120–127, 131–135, 138, 140, 159, 164, 166–167, 169, 175, 179–182, 186n, 187–188, 202, 209, 224n, 226, 243, 246, 249, 287–288, 297, 324, 326–327, 342, 351, 360, 363–365, 376, 398, 435; legitimacy of, 39, 47, 88, 98, 105, 116, 130, 147; and personal advancement, 42, 49, 83, 85, 87, 337, 357; as an innovation in English practice, 44–46, 49; as outside the rule of law, 45–48, 92–93, 95, 119, 166, 243–244, 257; as peculiar to the colonies, 49, 96, 98, 101, 115, 117, 120, 121, 123–127, 151–152, 201, 233, 312, 411–412; as remote from British concerns, 51–52, 100, 114, 117, 170; as beyond imperial regulation, 55–56, 62–63, 92, 100, 240–244, 246, 252, 257, 326; renunciation of, 68,

106, 108, 138, 140-143, 148, 167, 168, 181, 211, 339; prevention of the extension of, 78, 83, 96; as embarrassment, 105-107, 170; and the American character, 115, 118, 120-126, 129-131, 133-134; and resistance to British authority, 116, 118, 123-126, 134, 150-151, 166-168, 249

Slaveholding (England), 91-101, 151, 164, 227, 434; resistance to, 91-93, 283, 289; opposition to, 93-97, 259; legality of, 117-120, 129, 135, 181, 201; criticism of, 166; rarity of, 196

Slave labor: as a necessity in the Americas, 33-34, 49, 82, 84, 86, 209-210, 292; as cheaper than free labor, 34, 84, 86, 327; as less advantageous than free labor, 41, 84, 137, 214, 237; eligibility of the English for, 46n, 50; and national wealth, 47-48, 51, 53-54, 63, 114-115, 117, 160, 209, 246n, 368-369; assertion of rights of, 92, 105, 107-108, 130-131, 141, 147, 164, 226-227, 235-236, 241, 249-256, 262, 354, 355, 362, 376, 434; alternatives to, 224n; as aid to imperial expansion, 266, 279

Slave patrols, 88, 291

Slave petitions, 37, 42, 92-93, 99, 108, 289-290, 306

Slavery: defined, 126-128, 132, 149, 371

Slave trade (British): administration of, 34, 55, 63, 143, 194, 213, 255, 257, 263, 267, 269, 281-282, 304-305, 321, 372; denouncement of, 35-38, 41, 44, 57, 84, 114, 118, 135, 138-140, 142, 149, 151, 167-169, 171, 176, 180-181, 186n, 191, 195, 200-201, 202n, 205, 211, 260, 272-274, 284, 287, 318-319, 322-330, 338, 354, 363-364, 376, 386, 388, 391, 397, 400-401, 412-413, 429, 435n; merchants in, 49, 117, 263-264, 267, 269n, 270-271, 281, 303-307, 325; impact of, in Africa, 50, 186n, 272-273, 276, 307, 319, 323-324, 400; impact of, on society, 51, 94-97, 138-140, 224, 355; as a source of wealth and power,

53, 141, 209, 371-372, 376, 450; defenses of, 54, 84, 145, 168, 226, 269, 363, 371-372; restrictions on, in North America, 76, 83, 135-136, 144, 151-152, 355, 397, 405-406, 413; opposition to, in North America, 106-107, 135-138, 140-142, 144-145, 148, 165, 232, 400, 404, 423, 427; negation of colonial duties on, 135-136, 139, 144-145, 149-150, 168-169, 177, 181, 241, 404; alternatives to, 261-263, 271-273, 318-319, 322-329

Slave trade (Dutch), 40-41, 271, 281, 305

Slave trade (Portuguese), 38-39

Sloane, Hans, 430

Smeathman, Henry, 260-261, 279-280, 282-283, 314-320, 322, 324, 328-329, 438-439, 441

Smith, Adam, 115-116, 134-135, 152, 158-159, 234, 430

Smith, John, 398

Smith, William (loyalist), 216

Smith, William (member of Parliament), 446n

Snapp, J. Russell, 224

Snelgrave, William, 37

Society for Constitutional Information and Abolitionism, 189, 198, 200, 431, 445

Society (Committee) for Effecting the Abolition of the Slave Trade, 19, 24, 70, 71, 198, 230-231, 273, 293, 297, 327-328, 339, 341, 359n, 376, 384, 387, 391, 423, 433, 443-446, 448

Society for the Propagation of the Gospel, 61-64, 68, 70, 72-73, 196-197, 226, 353-360, 363-364, 401, 423

Society for the Relief of Free Negroes Unlawfully Held in Bondage, 108

Society of Friends (British Isles): as abolitionists, 1, 4, 19, 23-24, 28-29, 160, 211, 259-261, 279, 293, 296, 314, 316, 324-325, 366, 375-377, 391-392, 394, 402, 411, 418, 422-433, 436, 439, 442-443; renunciation of the slave trade by, 90-91,

273, 395; image of, 124, 198, 428–429; and antislavery schemes, 316–317, 324, 405, 408, 410, 412; and Friends in America, 391–392, 401–403, 411–415, 418–419, 426; and politics, 392–393, 396, 407–411, 419, 425; conflicts within, 393–394, 406, 416–421; identity of, 393–396, 424–425, 428–429

Society of Friends (colonies), 66, 69; as abolitionists, 4, 40, 42, 57, 70, 87–91, 99, 105, 108, 118, 135, 138, 140, 197, 232, 259, 296, 391, 408–409, 412–414, 420–421, 426; disownment of slaveholders by, 78, 338–339, 415, 420–421; and sectarian reform, 90–91, 100, 138, 392, 394–395, 398–399, 414–415, 418–419; and Friends in Britain, 391–392, 401–403, 411–415, 424–426

Socinians, 198

Some Historical Account of Guinea (Benezet), 323, 435

Somerset, James, 96, 97

Somerset v. Steuart, 78, 96–98, 105, 164, 259, 365, 410–411; legacies of, 98–101, 117–120, 135, 217, 283, 290, 294, 312

Sons of Liberty, 120

South Carolina, 64, 66, 75, 76, 81, 83, 85, 87, 90, 106, 136, 144, 202n, 291, 298–300, 310, 438

South County, R.I., 88

South Sea Company, 79

Sovereignty, 121, 126, 128, 132–133, 143–145, 147, 161, 164, 167, 216, 220, 226, 239–245, 248–253

Spanish Empire, 39, 49, 52, 60, 82, 84, 155–158, 171, 194, 218–219, 242–243, 266, 271, 279, 291, 353

Stabler, Edward, 396

Staffordshire, 446

Stamp Act crisis, 116, 122, 124, 125, 142, 144, 216, 244, 400, 409

Stanley, Hans, 157

Stanton, Daniel, 415

Staten Island, 120

Stephen, James, 341

Sterne, Laurence, 287, 293, 437

Stono Rebellion, 291

Straits of Magellan, 219

Strong, Jonathan, 93

Stuart, John, 224

Subjectship, 212, 220–223, 225–228, 262; and Africans, 217–220, 226–228, 231, 237, 249–253, 255–256; defined, 221–222; and rights of free blacks, 294–295, 310; and black loyalists, 299–300, 310–311

Summary View of the Rights of British America, A (Jefferson), 148

Sunday schools, 346–347, 361–362

Sunday School Society, 361

Swan, James, 324

Tacky's revolt, 291

Talwyn, Joseph, 417–418

Tarrow, Sidney, 393

Taxation No Tyranny (Johnson), 122

Taylor, John Vickris, 443n

Temperley, Howard, 20

Teston Circle, 325, 341–353, 356, 373, 377, 380, 383, 391, 434, 436; as ameliorationists, 362–364, 380; religious agenda of, 384–386; and abolitionism, 386–389; on Quakers, 444–445, 445n

Thomas, Sir Dalby, 266

Thompson, Benjamin, 310

Thompson, John, 311

Thornton, Henry, 34, 172, 446n

Thornton, John, 183, 341

Thornton, Robert, 446n

Thornton, Samuel, 446n

Thornton, William, 317–319, 438–439, 441

Thoughts and Sentiments on the Evil of Slavery (Cugoano), 296–297

Thoughts on the Importance of the Manners of the Great (More), 385–386, 388

Thoughts on the Slavery of the Negroes (Woods), 426, 430

Thoughts upon Slavery (Wesley), 181, 338, 339
Thynne (African trader), 264, 268
Times, 370–371
Tobin, James, 367, 369, 370
Tonyn, Patrick, 308
Tooker, Samuel, 445n
Tortola (Virgin Islands), 317, 318n, 438
Touchet, Samuel, 265
Townsend, John, 425
Townsend, Thomas, 300
Townshend Acts, 144, 409
Trafford, Henry, 279
Trecothick, Barlow, 156
Trelawney, Edward, 77n
Trusteeship, 203, 205, 213, 256, 262
Tryon, Thomas, 43, 78
Tucker, Josiah, 129, 158–159, 240, 326
Tucker, St. George, 143
Turner, William, 447n

Unitarianism, 198
Universal Dictionary of Trade and Commerce, The (Postlethwayt), 272–273
University of Edinburgh, 115

Valeri, Mark, 179
Vibert, Faith, 64
Villeinage, 44, 93
Virginia, 43, 49, 57, 64, 66, 69, 75, 76, 88, 108, 114, 119, 122, 131, 132, 136–137, 139, 144, 151, 168, 191, 228, 308, 356, 396, 402, 404, 412, 414
Virginia Gazette, 142
Virgin Islands, 430
Vivian, Thomas, 176, 185, 253–254, 338
Volunteers (Ireland), 182
Von Reck, Philip Baron, 87

Waalo, 276
Wachovia, 87
Wakefield, Gilbert, 202
Walker, George, 448, 449

Walker, Samuel, 337
Walker, Thomas, 446–447
Wallace, George, 211n
Walpole, Horace, 44, 124
Walsh, Robert, 143
Warburton, William, 197, 401
Waring, Josiah, 359
Warren, John, 357
Warrington Academy, 418
Washington, George, 216n, 299, 311
Watson, Richard, 191, 195
Watt, James, 447n
Wealth of Nations, The (Smith), 158, 234
Wedderburn, John, 283
Wedderburn, Robert, 297
Wedgwood, Josiah, 187, 443n, 446
Welch, William, 447n
Wesley, John, 121, 127, 129–130, 132, 172, 176, 181, 210–211, 214, 338–339, 340n, 356, 380–381, 385, 401
West India interest, 10–12, 54, 112, 135n, 191, 243–244, 326, 365–372, 375, 428
Westminster, 422
Wharton, Thomas, 73
Whateley, Thomas, 275
Wheatley, Phillis, 24, 99, 286–288, 337
Wheeler, Granville, 173
Wheelock, Matthew, 122, 123, 128
Whitbread, Samuel, 446n
Whitefield, George, 66–67, 70, 176, 337, 340n
Wilberforce, William, 1, 14, 24, 172, 176, 184, 198, 321, 333, 335, 337, 341–342, 347, 359n, 363, 377, 379–380, 382–387, 436, 441–442, 444–445, 446n, 448–449
Wilkes, John, 190
Wilkinson, James, 445n
Wilkinson, John, 446, 447n
Williams, Eric, 12–15, 18, 26–27, 117, 378, 389, 447n
Williamsburg, Va., 64
Wilson, David, 195

Wilson, Kathleen, 52

Wilson, Rachel, 410

Wilson, Thomas, 360

Woods, Joseph, 286, 411, 418, 426, 429–430

Woolman, John, 88, 90, 259, 396–397, 406, 411, 420–422

Woolridge, Rev. Thomas, 286

Worcester, 445

Worcester, Mass., 107–108

Workhouses (England), 44, 79

Wray, Sir Cecil, 422, 431

Wynne, John Huddleston, 209

Wyvill, Rev. Christopher, 183–184, 186–187, 190, 202, 408, 431, 445, 448

Yarmouth, 448

Yorke, James, 194, 196

Yorkshire, 157, 184, 190, 377, 382, 411, 420, 428, 431, 448

Yorkshire Association, 445

Yorktown, Va., 204, 301

Young, Alfred F., 108

Young, Arthur, 220, 275

Zong (slave ship), 284, 426